A
POLITICAL
ECONOMY
OF THE
MIDDLE EAST

UPDATED 2013 EDITION

A POLITICAL ECONOMY OF THE MIDDLE EAST

THIRD EDITION

Alan Richards

UNIVERSITY OF CALIFORNIA, SANTA CRUZ

John Waterbury

UNIVERSITY OF BEIRUT

NYU ABU DHABI

Melani Cammett

BROWN UNIVERSITY

Ishac Diwan

HARVARD UNIVERSITY

WESTVIEW
PRESS

A Member of the Perseus Books Group

Westview Press was founded in 1975 in Boulder, Colorado, by notable publisher and intellectual Fred Praeger. Westview Press continues to publish scholarly titles and high-quality undergraduate- and graduate-level textbooks in core social science disciplines. With books developed, written, and edited with the needs of serious nonfiction readers, professors, and students in mind, Westview Press honors its long history of publishing books that matter.

Find us on the World Wide Web at www.westviewpress.com.

Every effort has been made to secure required permissions for all text, images, maps, and other art reprinted in this volume.

Westview Press books are available at special discounts for bulk purchases in the United States by corporations, institutions, and other organizations. For more information, please contact the Special Markets Department at the Perseus Books Group, 2300 Chestnut Street, Suite 200, Philadelphia, PA 19103, or call (800) 810-4145, ext. 5000, or e-mail special.markets @perseusbooks.com.

The Library of Congress has catalogued the Third Edition as follows:

Library of Congress Cataloging-in-Publication Data
Richards, Alan, 1946–
    A political economy of the Middle East / Alan Richards, John Waterbury. — 3rd ed.
        p.   cm.
    Includes bibliographical references and index.
    ISBN-13: 978-0-8133-4348-8 (alk. paper) ISBN-10: 0-8133-4348-8 (alk. paper)
    1. Middle East—Economic conditions—1979– 2. Middle East—Economic policy.
3. Working class—Middle East. 4. Middle East—Politics and government—1979–
I. Waterbury, John. II. Title.
HC415.15.R53 2007
338.956—dc22
                                                        2006037317

ISBN 978-0-8133-4928-2 (updated 2013 edition paperback)
ISBN 978-0-8133-4929-9 (updated 2013 edition e-book)

10 9 8 7 6 5 4 3 2 1

CONTENTS

ILLUSTRATIONS

FIGURES

PREFACE TO THE THIRD EDITION

The first edition of this book was published sixteen years ago, and the second appeared in 1996. During the interim, much has changed, not least the authors themselves. John Waterbury has been President of the American University in Beirut since 1998. Serving the vital and influential community of students, faculty, staff, and alumni of that venerable institution is, to say the least, a full-time job. Accordingly, John did not have the time to participate in preparing this third edition. Readers therefore please note: *Any differences between this and previous editions are my responsibility alone!* Urged on by the publishers and by some younger colleagues (you know who you are!), for better or for worse, I agreed to undertake the task of preparing a third edition.

Since the second edition appeared, not only the region but also Americans' perceptions of and involvement in the region have undergone considerable change. The trauma of September 11, 2001, spawned a huge public debate, much of it sadly ill informed, about the region and America's role in it. The events of that day came as a particularly rude shock after a decade of American triumphalism following the demise of the Soviet Union. The responses have not always been wise. As of this writing, the American military adventure in Iraq has lasted longer than any American war in the past one hundred years.

As this edition goes to press, there is growing public uneasiness with the muscular, largely military approaches of the United States to the region since 9/11. We believe that the public is beginning to grasp a lesson of this book (which they have certainly not read), namely, that the problems of the region are deep, structural, and entrenched. They do not, therefore, readily lend themselves to any simple "solution," whether emanating from inside the Beltway or from dissident Muslim preachers. This edition, like previous editions, is intended to provide readers with an understanding of the complexity and the depth of the region's long-term developmental problems.

In the introductory chapter we note how two "great games" have long been played in the region. The first game is the "game of nations" or international relations; the second—the subject of this book—is the political economy of development. These games have always been interrelated, as we noted in previous editions. However, since 9/11 their interconnection has become increasingly visible. For example, the president of the United States proclaimed a "Greater Middle East Initiative," ostensibly to stimulate the economies of the region, since it was increasingly understood that rising unemployment and stagnant economies did little to foster the legitimacy of existing regimes. American officials, pundits, and analysts have also made much of the "democracy deficit" of the region and have, at least rhetorically, advocated "democratization" as a "solution" to the region's many problems.

While these two games are intertwined, they are linked in ways that are often obscured in many discussions of them. The interaction of the forces of demography, health, education, urbanization, economic policymaking, natural resource scarcity, and political legitimacy is an extremely intricate—and sometimes highly lethal—dance. It is far too easy—and increasingly dangerous—for outsiders to imagine that, instead of this complex minuet, the region has embarked on a simple, short jog down a clearly lit path. It is unhelpful, to say the very least, to assume that all we have to do is remove a few miscreants and provide better lighting, and then everyone will naturally run straight down the road we have helped to pave. Modernization theory—the view that all societies will inevitably wind up the same as they go through the processes of economic development and structural change—is, regrettably, very much alive in American political discourse.[1] We hope that readers of this book will understand how delusional such a perspective continues to be.

There are factors of continuity, as well as differences, within the trends in the political economy of development in the Middle East, which we observed in earlier editions. The rise of the largest, best-educated, and most urbanized generation of young people in the region's history, while visible earlier, has become increasingly evident. This phenomenon is documented in Chapters 4 and 5. In Chapter 4 we shall see that the "demographic transition" is now well advanced in many countries in the region; indeed, one country (Iran) experienced one of the fastest transitions in the historical record. Yet in other countries, particularly those of the Arabian Peninsula and some West Asian Arab countries, fertility remains stubbornly high. Even here, however, there are signs of improvement, as the percentage of young women receiving a basic education continues to increase.

Even where fertility has fallen, however, it has done so only recently and from high levels. Consequently, the labor force continues to grow very rapidly in most countries. This growth will slow, but only gradually. The result is a tidal wave of young people, better educated (Chapter 5) and more urbanized (Chapter 10) than ever before, who are increasingly frustrated. Their discontent is not limited to economic matters. Like young people everywhere, they are deeply concerned with questions of authenticity and fairness and are disillusioned by their government's failures on these counts. Moreover, they are very concerned about the way outside forces have intervened in the region. This interaction of demographic and economic problems with issues of political legitimacy and authenticity is one of the most important ways the two great games are intertwined in today's Middle East.

A recurring theme of this edition, as with previous editions, is the constant interaction of politics and economics. In Chapter 5 we shall see that health has greatly improved in most countries—and that the exceptions (Iraq, Palestine, and Sudan) have straightforward political explanations. In Chapter 6 we shall see how food security for most Middle Easterners continues to be quite respectable—with the ghoulish, politically generated exception of famines in Sudan. We shall see in Chapters 7 and 8 how state-led, inward-looking development created new problems for economic progress, and we shall also see in Chapter 9 how attempts to shift the balance between state and market have always been politically driven and have often been politically blocked. States have been agile in making only those changes that protect the incumbents' powers.

Another element of continuity with previous editions is the inescapable role of natural resource endowments. The abundance of oil and the scarcity of water remain critical features of the region. The water constraint binds ever tighter, and although all states grapple seriously with this problem (they have no choice), the problems remain severe (see Chapter 6). These challenges will not go away.

This edition documents the many changes in demography, education, labor markets, urbanization, water security and agriculture, and international labor migration in the region during the past ten years. The current edition differs from previous editions in three additional ways. First, the international economic environment is markedly different from what it was in 1996. Middle Eastern political economy remains tightly tied to oil prices. At the time of our second edition, oil prices had been extraordinarily low for more than ten years (and would go lower still)—a situation that put huge pressure on all governments in the region. Since the early 2000s, however, the price of oil has risen to levels not seen since the oil crisis of the early 1970s. If falling oil prices induced the necessity to "renegotiate the social contract," that necessity has been, at least temporarily, removed for many countries. However, we believe that the demands for more accountable and legitimate governance have at least as much to do with rising education and urbanization as with low oil prices. It is clear that the rise of oil prices over the past decade, and the subsequent increase in government revenues, have done little to encourage movement away from authoritarian governance.

Second, our approach to the issue of the shifting balance of state and market is more nuanced than the one adopted in the second edition. When we revised this book in the mid-1990s, we shared the current enthusiasm for "economic reform," or what came to be called the "Washington Consensus." As with so many grand schemes to improve the human condition, however, this approach, while making important contributions, proved not to be the panacea anticipated by many of its advocates (including us, ten years ago). To be sure, the turn toward the market was, and is, necessary, and where economic reform was implemented, there are some important achievements to its credit. Yet nowhere has it ignited the kind of economic growth necessary to dramatically raise living standards or to significantly reduce the numbers of unemployed youth. The extensive revision of Chapter 9 reflects our current views on the mixed record of the "Washington Consensus."

Third, our views on the economic impacts of Islamism, the subject of Chapter 14, have shifted somewhat since the second edition. In this new edition, we have treated the phenomenon as a vast, diverse social movement, with many conflicting participants. It is essential for readers to understand this diversity, since it is highly likely that Islamism will continue to play a vital role in the region's future. It is not, of course, the only political force in the region. But increasingly, many people look to this movement as they attempt to make sense out of the bewildering, disorienting interaction of the two great games being played out all around them.

The third edition, then, documents the process of the political economy of development in this vital, sadly violent region. The problems facing the region's political economies are difficult, and history has been unkind. Yet the hopeful signs of demographic transition and rising education may still make it possible for the peoples of the region to fashion a better future. This can only happen, however, if outsiders refrain from imposing, whether from greed, anger, or ignorance, ill-informed "solutions" for the complicated problems inherent in the struggle for economic development and political legitimacy.

In preparing this edition, I have incurred many debts. The greatest is to my coauthor. John and I jointly planned and wrote and rewrote the first two editions. Although I drafted the revisions for this edition, the book rightly also bears his name, since we developed the fundamental perspective, and much of the analysis, together. I will always be grateful to John for his deep insights, his extensive knowledge, and his unwavering friendship.

The preparation of the third edition occurred while I was on sabbatical leave from my home institution, the University of California, Santa Cruz. I am grateful to the Department of Environmental Studies, the Division of Social Sciences, and the Office of the Academic Vice-Chancellor for making this leave possible. Research funding was provided by the Faculty Senate of UCSC, in a grant held jointly with Paul Lubeck. I am very grateful to Elaine Yu, my research assistant, for her cheerful, patient, and highly competent preparation of all of the graphs and tables. One could not ask for a better assistant. I would also like to thank my editors at Westview Press, Karl Yambert, Kay Mariea, and Jennifer Swearingen, for their exceptional competence, thoughtfulness, and courtesy.

Finally, during the past ten years I have received a great deal of support—sometimes intellectual, sometimes personal, and often both—from Carolyn Atkinson, Edmund Burke III, Kris Eriksen, Bob Faulkener, Isebill V. Gruhn, Michael Hudson, Kenneth Kletzer, Paul Lubeck, Steven Simon, Nirvikar Singh, and Gordon Wheeler. Without the help of each and all, this edition would never have been prepared. And, of course, none of them is in any way responsible for what I have written.

Alan Richards
Santa Cruz, California
September 15, 2006

NOTE

1. For some skeptical observations on this phenomenon, see Richards (2003).

ACRONYMS AND ABBREVIATIONS

AAAID	Arab Authority for Agricultural Investment and Development
AMIO	Arab Military Industrialization Organization
ANM	Arab National Movement
ASU	Arab Socialist Union
CBR	crude birthrate
CIA	Central Intelligence Agency
CNRA	National Council of the Algerian Revolution
CPA	Coalition Provisional Authority
DC	developed country
DISK	Confederation of Progressive Trade Unions
DOP	Declaration of Principles
FAO	Food and Agriculture Organization
FATAH	Palestine Liberation Movement
FDI	foreign direct investment
FIS	Islamic Salvation Front
FLN	National Liberation Front
GATT	General Agreement on Tariffs and Trade
GCC	Cooperative Council for the Arab States of the Gulf
GDI	gross domestic investment
GDP	gross domestic product
GNP	gross national product
HAMAS	Islamic Resistance Movement
ICOR	incremental capital-to-output ratio
ICP	Iraqi Communist party
ILO	International Labour Organisation
IMF	International Monetary Fund
IMR	infant mortality rate
ISI	import-substituting industrialization
LDC	less-developed country
LEB	life expectancy at birth

MAPAI	Israel Labor party
MENA	Middle East and North Africa
MVA	manufacturing value added
NATO	North Atlantic Treaty Organization
NER	net enrollment ratio
NIC	newly industrializing country
NIF	National Islamic Front
NLF	National Liberation Front
OECD	Organization for Economic Cooperation and Development
OPEC	Organization of Petroleum Exporting Countries
ORT	oral rehydration therapy
ÖYAK	Armed Forces Mutual Assistance Fund
PA	Palestinian Authority
PDRY	People's Democratic Republic of Yemen
PKK	Kurdish Workers' party
PLO	Palestine Liberation Organization
PPP	purchasing power parity
PRC	People's Republic of China
RCC	Revolutionary Command Council (Iraq, Egypt)
RCD	Constitutional Democratic Rally
RPP	Republican People's party
SAVAK	Iranian Security and Intelligence Organization
SNS	National Steel Corporation
SPLA	Southern People's Liberation Army
SSU	Sudanese Socialist Union
TFR	total fertility rate
UAE	United Arab Emirates
UAR	United Arab Republic
UGTA	General Confederation of Algerian Workers
UGTT	General Confederation of Tunisian Workers
UK	United Kingdom
UNESCO	United Nations Economic, Scientific, and Cultural Organization
UNICEF	United Nations International Children's Emergency Fund
USAID	United States Agency for International Development
VAT	value-added tax
WHO	World Health Organization
WTO	World Trade Organization
YAR	Yemen Arab Republic
YSP	Yemen Socialist party

A

POLITICAL
ECONOMY
OF THE
MIDDLE EAST

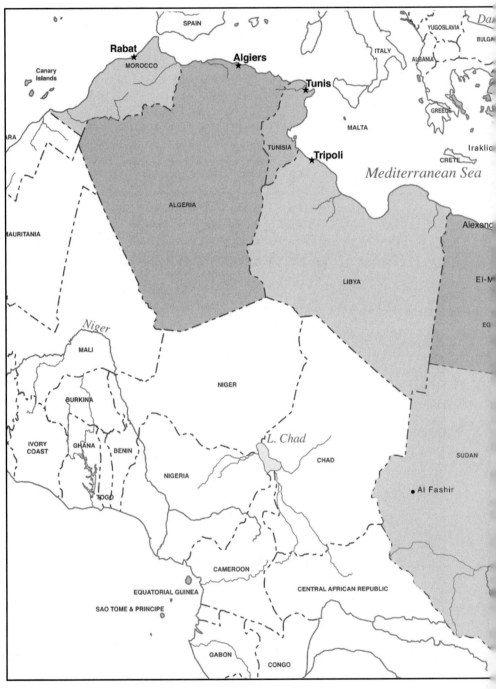

Map 0.1   The Middle East and North Africa

1

INTRODUCTION

Two great games are being played out in the Middle East today. One, upon which this book is focused, is a quiet game that seldom makes headlines. It is the game of peoples and governments, states and societies, sometimes in cooperation but more often at odds, trying to advance the prosperity and overall development of the region's nations. The other is the more conventional great game in which regional and superpower politics intersect (see Brown 1984; Walt 1987). It has been the unhappy fate of the Middle East to be the stage for an extraordinary amount of conflict, much of it generated within the region itself and the rest provoked from without. In the twentieth century alone, it was a major theater in two world wars and witnessed a war for liberation in Turkey and seven years of colonial war in Algeria. There were four wars between Israel and several of its Arab neighbors, prolonged civil wars in Lebanon and the Sudan, major long-term insurrections in Iraq and in the former Spanish Sahara, prolonged violence between Israelis and Palestinians, and until the fall of 1988, one of the two longest conventional wars of this century, between Iraq and Iran (the other being that between Japan and China, 1937–1945).

Since the first edition of this book, Iraq has invaded Kuwait and then been deprived of its prize by an international force led by the United States. Since 1992 Turkey has been conducting a costly campaign, mostly on its own territory but sometimes in neighboring northern Iraq, to snuff out a Kurdish insurrection. In the summer of 1994 southern and northern Yemen, nominally united since 1991, fought a brief but bloody civil war in which the north defeated the south. In Algeria near–civil war has developed since 1991 between the central government and militant Islamic groups. The second Palestinian *intifada* erupted in 2000, militants of al-Qaeda attacked the United States on September 11, 2001, the United States invaded Iraq in 2003, and Israel and Hizbollah fought a six-week war in the summer of 2006. At the time of this writing, 140,000 US troops remain in Iraq.

Against this backdrop of continued military tension were two fragile breakthroughs to less belligerent behavior: the end of the Lebanese civil war in 1989 and the establishment of peaceful relations between Israel, on the one hand, and the Palestine Liberation Organization and the Kingdom of Jordan, on the other, in 1993 and 1994. Although the Palestinians and Israelis have returned to fighting each other, so far both the Jordanian peace with Israel and the internal peace in Lebanon have held.

The Middle East throughout history has been center stage in world politics. It has been endlessly fought over, coveted as strategic real estate on the world's major trade routes, and occasionally used as the launchpad for homegrown expansionist powers, the latest of which was the Ottoman Empire. The Middle East will not be left alone; that is its curse and its blessing. Geopolitical significance draws resources and special treatment from outside powers, but it also draws interference, meddling, and occasionally invasion. Notwithstanding, much of our argument is premised on the assumption that the game of development, no less painful and destructive in some ways than the game of conflict, is of equal if not greater importance. But the two are closely interrelated, as conflict obviously influences the course of development and vice versa.

History has made clear, for instance, that regional conflict, even single events, can set in motion processes that destroy resources and disrupt societies, thereby irreversibly altering the political economies of large populations. One need think only of the assassination of the Archduke Franz Ferdinand in Sarajevo, which triggered the events leading to World War I, to realize what extraordinary consequences small incidents may have. The June War of 1967 in the Middle East could have been avoided—in fact, it took some colossal bungling on the part of all parties to launch it. Once launched, however, it changed not only the military and political landscape of the region but its economic landscape as well. Much the same could be said of the long war between Iraq and Iran. It is likely that future historians will say something similar about the US "war of choice" in Iraq, as well.

That said, the sheer scale of military conflict in the region cannot be passed off as a series of unfortunate accidents. The Middle East, more than any other developing area, was crucial turf in the playing out of the cold war and superpower rivalry. Lying on top of two-thirds of the world's known petroleum reserves and astride the main sea and overland links between Asia and the Mediterranean, it was an area in which no local conflict could be conducted without great-power involvement, if not direct then through local proxies. In addition, preparation for war has been continuous. In Chapter 13 we look at the economic costs of mobilization for and the actual conduct of war and internal conflict; it is harder to assess the social and political costs. We do know that two or three generations in several Middle Eastern countries have known little but military rule, preparation for war, and all too frequently, the reality of conflict.

In the midst of these tensions and conflicts, rapidly growing populations must be fed, educated, and employed, water conserved, agricultural productivity increased, industrialization promoted, universities founded and expanded, technology acquired, armed forces trained and equipped, and some semblance of political order maintained. These are the issues with which we are concerned, and we address them through the lenses of political economy. What we have in mind is the formulation of public policies that determine the allocation of resources within societies and their political consequences. Public policy is about choice, alternatives, and opportunity costs. Sometimes small groups of leaders make public policy choices and then impose them on their societies. Sometimes choices reflect the aspirations of major sectors of society, and sometimes they are made through the society's elected representatives. However they are made, choices always produce relative losses and gains for various sectors of society. Normally we expect those who benefit to try to consolidate their advantages and privileges and those who have fared poorly to try to alter the status quo. Contending groups have various means at their disposal, some legal and some illegal, to try to influence public authorities and public policy in their favor. And as we shall show repeatedly, those authorities—the people who make up the governments and staff the upper echelons of the bureaucracies and public enterprises—frequently constitute an autonomous set of actors and interests in their own right.

Middle Eastern societies range from the very poor, such as Yemen and the Sudan, to the very rich, such as Kuwait and Saudi Arabia. The highest generalized standards of living are probably to be found in Israel. Similarly, in political terms these societies run the gamut from authoritarian rule by cliques and juntas to the qualified democracies of Israel,[1] Turkey, Palestine, and, until the outbreak of civil war in 1975, Lebanon. No simple generalizations can be made about the economic resources available to Middle Eastern nations or about the permissible channels through which Middle Easterners may seek to influence the allocation of those resources. What can be said is that there is a constant dialectic between state actors and various segments of their societies and that over the past century the dialectic has yielded dynamic, constantly changing equilibria. Like the unicorn, the status quo in the Middle East is a figment of fertile imaginations. Nonetheless, as we shall see, several military authoritarian regimes in the region have fought stubbornly to contain the consequences of socioeconomic change.

In many respects our endeavor in these pages is unique, but it has many forerunners and sources of inspiration. We have tried to write an integrated, analytic text covering all of the contemporary Middle East. We believe that we were the first to have tried to do this in the political-economy mode, although Samir Amin's *The Arab Economy Today* (1982) might be seen as a cursory and polemical antecedent. Galal Amin's *The Modernization of Poverty* (1980) is richer and analytically more satisfying. Generally one encounters anthologies of country case studies, often descriptive and not necessarily related to any set of analytic themes.

There have been some notable attempts at synthetic analysis, although, with a few exceptions, none has adopted a political-economic approach. Halpern's *The Politics of Social Change in the Middle East and North Africa* (1963) is a landmark work and, although dated, still of great value. Hudson's *Arab Politics* (1977) is also highly recommended, as is Bill and Springborg's *Politics in the Middle East* (1994). Limited to the Maghreb are Moore's now-dated *Politics in North Africa* (1970) and Entelis's *Comparative Politics of North Africa* (1980). In other disciplines there have been illustrious forerunners: in sociology, for example, Berger's *The Arab World To-day* (1964) and Lerner's *The Passing of Traditional Society* (1959). The study of North Africa by Hermassi (1972) is one of the rare contemporary contributions to sociological synthesis. Two economic historians have unquestionably been a source of inspiration for us in that their writings have been explicitly in the political-economy vein: Issawi, for his *Economic History of the Middle East and North Africa* (1982) and his pioneering article "Economic and Social Foundations of Democracy in the Middle East" (1956), and Owen, for *The Middle East in the World Economy* (1981). Most recently, Henry and Springborg's *Globalization and the Politics of Development in the Middle East* (2001), and Owen and Pamuk's *A History of Middle East Economies in the 20th Century* (1998) are notable contributions.

Many writers have used political economy, implicitly or explicitly, in single-country studies. We have utilized them extensively throughout this work, as our citations attest. Our bibliography is, of course, only very partial. Work on political economy of the region has exploded since our first edition, and we have cited only very selectively from this now-vast literature. We could not, and do not, attempt to be exhaustive.

There is much else that we do not attempt to do in this text, and some analytic approaches that we leave aside are admittedly important. We shall not, for instance, dwell much on psychological variables in explaining political and economic outcomes. We do not deny their importance, and there is a significant literature now that examines psychological factors affecting Middle Eastern leaders and elites: see, inter alia, Brown and Itzkowitz, *Psychological Dimensions of Near Eastern Studies* (1977), Volkan and Itzkowitz, *The Immortal Atatürk* (1984), and Zonis, *Majestic Failure* (1991).

Political culture is another important tool in understanding the Middle East but, again, one that we shall largely pass over. Much has been written about the cultural attributes, political predispositions, and styles of governance in the Middle East. We hear of the quest for martyrdom among Shi'ite Muslims as explaining in part the way in which the Iranian revolution unfolded and the course of the war with Iraq. Israel's "Masada Complex" is said to determine the country's outlook toward its adversaries. The docile, wily peasant society of Egypt has been credited with that country's style of government since the pharaohs, and Morocco's tribal past has been invoked to explain contemporary elite behavior (Waterbury 1970).

The enormous journalistic and scholarly concern lavished in recent years on political Islam and contemporary Islamism in general frequently takes the form of political-culture analysis. Various writers have tried to discern the values and ideals that inspire those Muslims who seek the political kingdom and to describe the socioeconomic contexts that purportedly give rise to the movements. We shall have a great deal more to say about these movements and their professed ideals in Chapters 11, 12, and above all, 14, and we shall save reference to the relevant studies until then.

In general, we view political-culture analysis as potentially a more powerful tool than the psychological analysis of leaders, and we shall refer to political-cultural variables with some frequency. Still, how much they can explain is seldom clear. Let us hypothetically compare Egypt and Iran in terms of tax delinquency. We could hypothesize in political-cultural terms that those in Iran who failed to pay their taxes during the time of the shah did so with a relatively clear conscience, because to Shiʻites awaiting the return of the true Imam all secular authorities are in some way interlopers and usurpers and hence without legitimacy. In Egypt, by contrast, the tax dodger may be seen as playing an age-old game of manipulating or evading a large, tentacular state whose legitimacy, however, is not at stake. But whatever the cultural explanation of the phenomenon, the end result is the same: tax evasion and decreased government revenues. More important, the means by which to extract more taxes may not vary much from one culture to another. Even in those rare instances when we can assess the independent effect of culture on politics and economic life, we must remember that cultures change rapidly too, as the patterns of employment, residence, and lifestyle themselves change.

In sum, our approach is to focus on major problems in the social and economic transformation of the Middle East, not on specific countries. All the societies of the region face similar problems in extracting and investing resources, building an industrial sector while modernizing agriculture, and absorbing an ever-larger proportion of a growing population into cities, all the while trying to maintain political order and to build a credible military establishment. This set of problems confronts all developing countries. What differs is the human and material resources available to the twenty-three countries in the region, and those differences determine in an important way the strategies of resource allocation, the process of class formation, and the political process in each.

We are convinced that in general the process of economic and social change in the Middle East and North Africa (MENA) is not qualitatively different from that in most of the less-developed countries (LDCs).[2] We hasten to add that the differences in levels of overall development, including industrialization, and in standards of living and welfare are as great among the LDCs (compare Brazil, for example, with Rwanda or Nepal) as between the developing and the advanced industrial nations. As we shall see, the variance among Middle Eastern nations is also very great (see especially Chapter 3). Thus we hope that our detailed examination of Middle Eastern experience will contribute to a more general understanding of the development process.

At the same time there are facets of the development process in the Middle East, flowing from its long history of intense and generally adversarial interaction with Europe, that do set this region apart. We try to be attentive to these distinguishing traits and to signal to the reader where and when we think they make a qualitative difference in the processes under scrutiny.

In Chapter 2 we set forth the premises of our analysis, which centers on three vertices: strategies of economic transformation, the state agencies and actors that seek to implement them, and the social actors such as interest groups that react to and are shaped by them. Each of the three vertices entails questions about the nature of the state, the emergence of economic interests, and the effects of various development strategies—questions that should be asked in any developing country. We do not pretend to have definitive answers to any of them, but we do have some strongly held views and, we think, solid evidence to back them.

NOTES

1. Israeli democracy is the real thing, but only for the country's Jewish citizens. Non-Jews, although enjoying a range of political rights, are second-class citizens.

2. LDC means low- and middle-income countries, as defined by the World Bank.

2

THE FRAMEWORK
OF THE STUDY

Many of the major problems and questions facing the Middle East today can and should be approached in much the same way as one would approach the problems of any set of LDCs. Accordingly, we shall begin by presenting a broad-brush model of LDC political economy.

Outcomes in LDC political economy can best be conceptualized as the product of three variables: (1) economic growth and structural transformation, (2) state structure and policy, and (3) social actors, whether groups or individuals. We shall start with fairly conventional definitions of each of these concepts, discussing major conceptual difficulties, disputes, and so forth, surrounding each as we proceed.

Economic growth means simply the increase over time in total output in the economy. Since the concept is often also associated with some idea of increasing welfare for the population, per capita growth is usually also implied. Such growth is almost always quite uneven, however. Some sectors grow faster than others, some groups' wealth and power may increase faster than those of other groups, and in some extreme cases the absolute standard of living of some (usually poor) individuals and groups may actually decline in some phases of the process. Although the ubiquity or necessity of these outcomes is much disputed, several other features of unevenness do appear to be universals: the decline of the percentage of both national output and employment accounted for by the agricultural sector and the increasing proportion of the population that is urban rather than rural. The process of unbalanced sectoral growth just characterized is called *structural transformation*. By *state structure and policy* we mean the organization of the monopoly of coercive means within society, the interventions into the economy that such a monopoly makes possible, and the institutions through which intervention is carried out. Finally, by *social actors* we mean any and all interests, groups, and classes that interact with the state, seek to shape its policies, and are affected by the state's growth strategies.

Each of these definitions can be questioned, of course. As noted, economic growth may not be associated with increasing welfare for some groups and/or inequality among social groups may increase. Measured growth may seriously overstate social progress, when, for example, environmental destruction or the loss of natural capital is not included in national accounts.[1] Similarly, there is little agreement on the role of the state in the development process—on its freedom of choice of policy with respect to powerful domestic classes and international actors such as the International Monetary Fund (IMF) or the World Bank. And finally, what drives groups—material interests, shared values, or shared blood—is at the heart of a debate in the social sciences that ranges far beyond the scope of this book.

We do not suffer from the delusion that we can settle such debates or persuade all potential critics. We believe that each of the major variables is vital for an understanding of outcomes in the political economy of the region, as we hope to show through the concrete analysis of specific development problems in subsequent chapters. The proof of the pudding will certainly be in the eating. Before proceeding to a more detailed discussion of each of our three variables in the context of the Middle East, it is worth emphasizing that they are interdependent. Each one influences and shapes the others; each is therefore both cause and effect, both starting point and outcome. Our model is one of reciprocal causation (Figure 2.1).

We do not imply any rank ordering of the arrows of Figure 2.1; this is a fully simultaneous model. The meaning of the interconnections may be illustrated as follows:

1. Economic growth and structural transformation have unintended outcomes to which state actors must respond. For example, if the pattern of industrialization is highly capital-intensive, the state may need to respond to a growing employment problem.
2. Although there is much debate on the precise effect of specific policies, few deny that state structure and fiscal, monetary, and trade policy affect the rate and form of economic growth.
3. Social actors mold state policy. Interest and pressure groups and, most broadly, proprietary classes seek to protect and promote their own interests through the state. In some cases, the influence of a particular social actor may be so strong that the state becomes its "instrument."

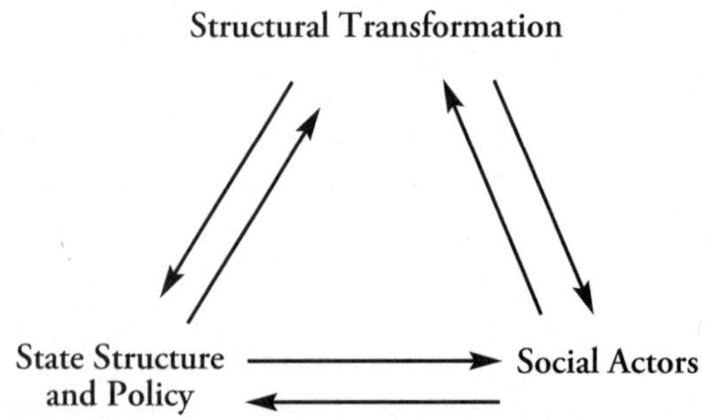

FIGURE 2.1   The three main axes of Middle Eastern political economy

4. The state shapes, even creates, social actors, including classes. If, for example, classes are defined primarily with respect to property rights and if property rights always require enforcement, then it is difficult to see how the concepts of "state" and "class" could *not* be closely linked. In the context of LDCs, the impact of the state on class is especially striking, as the state redistributes property through nationalizations, land reforms, and privatizations.

5. Economic growth and structural transformation shape social actors. A "manufacturing bourgeoisie" emerges only as the result of the growth of industry; the more rapidly industry develops, the stronger that bourgeoisie becomes. High rates of unemployment among educated youth contribute to the rise of militant Islamist groups. That unemployment is the result in turn of the slow growth of the nonagricultural sector combined with rapid growth of the educational system.

6. Finally, social actors affect the rate and form of economic growth not only indirectly, through their impact on state policy, but also directly. For example, an initial concentration of landownership will probably have favored a capital-intensive pattern of agricultural growth, with consequences for employment, income distribution, and the growth of different industrial sectors. Similarly, the concentration of rural assets may retard the emergence of a rural domestic market. A highly concentrated distribution of urban income may favor the rapid growth of certain sectors (e.g., consumer durables) rather than others.

We now turn to a more detailed discussion of each vertex of our triangle and of the interactions among these variables.

ECONOMIC GROWTH AND STRUCTURAL TRANSFORMATION

Economic growth is usually measured by gross domestic product (GDP) in a unit of common currency, usually dollars, in order to facilitate international comparisons. GDP is obtained by weighing all outputs by their prices and adding them up. Since output and income are closely related concepts, the measure also serves as a kind of summary statistic for the level of income in the country. When expressed in per capita terms, the GDP is often employed as a crude indicator of average social welfare.

Several criticisms have been made of this concept. First, as already noted, measurement errors, particularly for natural capital, may be serious. A measure of GDP is constructed using prices. If negative externalities are not priced, it follows that measured GDP overestimates social welfare. In effect, countries count depleting capital as income—obviously a flawed perspective. This problem is likely to be particularly acute for those countries that sell oil. Most of this revenue is not income that can be sustained over time. Stauffer (1984) estimated that the "reproducible" component of GDP of Saudi Arabia may be as little as one-quarter to one-half of reported GDP. Some, often most, of GDP in the Gulf is not "income" but "liquidation of capital."

Second, research suggests that increasing GDP (or increasing personal incomes, for that matter) has little impact on how well-off people actually *feel* (see, e.g., Easterlin 1995; Layard 2005). Third, GDP per capita offers no evidence on distribution. Therefore one can use increases in GDP as an indicator of increasing social welfare only with great caution.

Measurement problems go beyond negative environmental externalities. For example, measured GDP explicitly excludes nonmarketed output; this is a problem especially for the evaluation of changes in the agricultural sector over time. A shift from home production to market production could result in a measured increase in GDP when total output actually remained unchanged. Further, the exclusion of nonmarketed output from the calculation systematically neglects household production; much of the contribution of women to production thus escapes notice. A variant of this problem is that the value of production and services in the "informal sector" goes unmeasured or is at best crudely estimated. As we shall see in subsequent chapters, the informal sector plays an important but poorly understood role in Middle Eastern economies.

The use of official exchange rates as the common denominator for international GDP comparisons introduces further distortions. To say that the average annual income in Egypt is US$1,000 evokes the image of an American buying only US$1,000 worth of goods in a year. In fact, however, an Egyptian with the equivalent of this dollar sum, when converted at the official exchange rate, would be able to buy more goods and services than the American. This is because the price of nontradable goods (e.g., housing and haircuts) in relation to that of tradable goods (e.g., wheat, cars, textiles) is typically much lower in LDCs than in developed countries (DCs). Using official exchange rates to compare incomes across countries ignores this difference (see Box 2.1). Even if Egyptians spent the same percentage of their income on nontradable goods as Americans (which is unlikely, given the relative prices), the Egyptians' purchasing power relative to the Americans' would be understated by using official exchange rates to compare them (Kravis, Heston, and Summers 1978). Figure 2.2 shows the disparity between the two measures for some selected MENA countries.

Despite these problems and issues, the GDP, employed with caution, offers us the most comprehensive available set of statistics on national income. The above problems will be taken here as cautionary notes about the concept rather than devastating criticisms, if only because national governments often behave as if increasing (measured) national income is a central policy (and political) goal. However flawed the measure, governments—and international agencies—seek to promote the growth of GDP through policy choices.

Economic growth invariably involves unevenness across sectors, or structural transformation. Despite the wide variation in the patterns of economic growth, in virtually all countries rising per capita income is accompanied by a decline in agriculture's share of output and employment and a corresponding increase in the share of industry and services. Structural transformation, so defined, is one of the very few "universals" of modern economic history.

◉ BOX 2.1

Purchasing Power Parity

To say that the average annual income in Egypt is US$1,310 evokes the image of an American buying only US$1,310 worth of goods in a year. In fact, however, an Egyptian with the equivalent of this dollar sum, when converted at the official exchange rate, would be able to buy more goods and services than would an American with that sum of money. This is because the price of nontradable goods (e.g., housing and haircuts) in relation to that of tradable goods (e.g., wheat, cars, textiles) is typically much lower in LDCs than in DCs. As an economy grows, productivity in tradable goods production (agriculture and industry) increases much faster than it does for nontradable goods: It is much easier to raise the productivity of auto workers than of barbers. Competitive pressures in labor markets (combined with the fact that goods are far more mobile internationally than is labor) will raise the wages of workers (and therefore, of costs) in nontradable goods production, following the rising wages in traded goods production. But since productivity doesn't change much in nontradable goods, relative costs rise. Hence the conclusion: The price of nontradable goods relative to tradable goods is higher in rich countries than in poor ones.

Using official exchange rates to compare incomes across countries ignores this difference. Even if Egyptians spent the same percentage of their income on nontradable goods (which is unlikely, given their relative prices), Egyptians' purchasing power relative to that of Americans would be understated if official exchange rates are used to compare them (Kravis, Heston, and Summers, 1978). Figure 2.2 shows the disparity between the two measures for selected MENA countries. The average Egyptian has the US purchasing power equivalent of approximately US$4,120—not US$1,310 (World Bank 2006b).

There are numerous interactions among sectors as development proceeds. Since labor productivity and therefore incomes are much higher in industry than in agriculture, the transfer of population to industry raises national income. Furthermore, the rate of technological change that raises income per person is typically faster in industry. Consequently, many have thought of industry as the leading sector of development, a sort of engine that pulls the rest of the train behind it. Although there is truth to this picture, neglect of the agricultural sector can be disastrous. The agricultural sector provides not only labor but also food, raw materials for processing, exports, needed foreign exchange, a domestic market for local industry, and an investable surplus that may be used to construct industrial facilities. As we shall see, Middle Eastern states, like many LDCs, have neglected or mismanaged the linkages between agriculture and industry. Bottlenecks such as inadequate food supplies, stagnant exports, and feeble domestic markets have sometimes undermined economic growth and structural transformation.

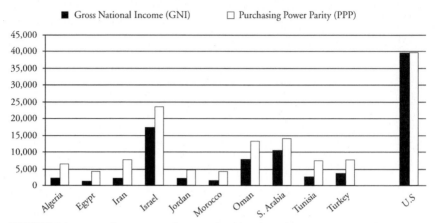

FIGURE 2.2   Ratio of gross national income (GNI) and purchasing power parity (PPP) measures of per capita income, 2004

The concept of "services" in the national accounts is something of a residual category. It contains activities as diverse as government service and street peddling. Moreover, the mix within the service sector also changes over time, with the proportion of self-employed, typically very poor service-sector workers declining as national income rises beyond a certain level. The increase in the proportion of the population employed in services may be as much an indicator of economic weakness as of strength, as large numbers of unskilled rural migrants arrive in the cities and engage in a host of small-scale activities that are carried out at low technological levels and generate paltry incomes. In most cases, however, it seems clear that these people believe that they have improved their lot by migrating, and the available evidence suggests that they know what they are talking about. After all, productivity, technology, and incomes for some agricultural workers may be and often are even lower than those obtainable in the urban informal sector (see Chapter 10).

Economic growth and structural transformation typically spawn a variety of distortions and unintended outcomes. Such distortions are both the consequence and the cause of state economic policies. The first distortion is a final cautionary note on the definition of economic growth and its links to welfare. It is clear that "economic growth" as measured by changes in per capita GDP is not the same as the usual notion of "economic development." The latter concept recognizes that improvement in living standards includes the meeting of the basic needs (e.g., food, housing, safe drinking water, and education) of all members of a society. It is equally clear that there is only a loose correlation between improvement in the satisfaction of basic needs and increase in GDP. Some countries with relatively high per capita incomes have quite poor records on meeting basic needs (e.g., Brazil), whereas some with quite low per capita incomes appear to have gone very far toward doing so (e.g., Sri Lanka and the People's Republic of China [PRC]).

There is a particular connection between economic development and the development of skills, or "human-capital formation." Indeed, by some accounts (e.g., T. W. Schultz 1981) growth is inconceivable without the improvement of human skills; in this view, education and other types of skill formation are the core of the development process. Technological change, which lies at the core of the process of economic growth, is impossible without an increasingly skilled population. In addition, the very unevenness of economic growth and structural transformation creates numerous disequilibria. Schultz hypothesized that the more educated and trained the population, the more rapidly it can respond to such imbalances and therefore the more quickly they are eliminated.

A second blockage or distortion to the process of economic growth and structural transformation is the problem of foreign exchange. For a variety of reasons, some Middle Eastern governments (for example, the Sudan, where growth has collapsed, and Tunisia, Morocco, and Turkey in the late 1970s and early 1980s) found their growth process interrupted by the inadequacy of foreign exchange. Turkey's growth in the late 1970s was likewise slowed by the steadily increasing demand for imports at the same time as export revenues lagged. Both external factors (falling terms of trade) and internal policies that encourage imports and discourage exports (overvalued exchange rates, the need to import machinery for industries producing industrial goods for local consumers) created these problems.

Such difficulties are endemic in LDCs and are especially associated with import-substituting industrialization (ISI). Although many Middle Eastern countries have been spared this squeeze, largely because of oil revenues, their regional multipliers (such as investment), and especially, workers' remittances, the experience with such revenues shows that ample foreign exchange is not a panacea for the problems of economic growth and structural transformation. Indeed, the influx of large amounts of foreign exchange can itself cause problems.

The sudden influx of foreign currency can lead to a phenomenon known as the "Dutch Disease," so called because of the experience of the Dutch economy with the large influx of North Sea gas revenues in the 1970s. Government spending of oil revenues induces labor and capital to shift from tradable goods (industry and agriculture) to nontradable goods (services). There are two proposed causal sequences. A monetary version holds that the spending of oil revenues stimulates a rate of inflation that is higher than that of the major (typically Western) trading partners of the oil-exporting country. Since LDC nominal exchange rates are usually fixed, the differential inflation leads to overvaluation of the real exchange rate. Since tradable goods' prices may be denominated in Organization for Economic Cooperation and Development (OECD) currencies (say, the dollar) while nontradable-goods prices are, of course, in local currency, such revaluation of the real exchange rate is the same thing as an increase in the relative price of nontradable goods relative to tradable goods.

An alternative version arrives at this same conclusion by a nonmonetary ("real-economy") route. In that version, the spending of government revenue increases demand for both tradable and nontradable goods. For most small countries the supply of tradable goods is perfectly elastic; that of nontradable goods is not. Therefore, the

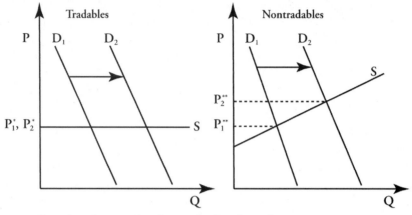

P = price; Q = quantity; S = supply; D = demand

FIGURE 2.3 Changes in the relative price of tradable and nontradable goods. (Assume that both sectors face the same shift in the demand function. The price of tradable goods remains the same; the price of nontradable goods rises, and their relative price [P*/P**] falls.)

increased spending will bid up the price of nontradable goods more than that of tradable goods (see Figure 2.3). This effect will be compounded if government spending is concentrated in nontradables, such as services and construction, as happened in the oil-exporting countries during the 1970s. Once again, the prices of nontradable goods relative to tradable goods will increase. The advantage of this latter formulation is that it allows for the fact that some so-called nontradables actually do move in international trade. There are international construction firms, financial and insurance services have international markets, foreign teachers may be hired, and so forth. The only question becomes differential supply elasticities, which can in principle be determined empirically rather than simply assumed.

 Whatever the causes, these relative-price changes reallocate capital and labor and shift resources out of the production of tradable goods into nontradable-goods production (see Figure 2.4). This allegedly fosters stagnation of the agricultural and manufacturing sectors while government and the building industry boom. International competition holds down the prices of, say, food and manufactures, whereas wages and costs in domestic agriculture and industry rise, catching local producers in a profit squeeze. The Dutch Disease contributes to the rural exodus, as farmworkers abandon the countryside in search of construction jobs in the cities. The increase in wage levels thus combines with the overvalued real exchange rate to diminish international competitiveness in agriculture and industry.

 There is evidence for such effects in the Middle East and elsewhere, most notably in agriculture. As with any growth-rate comparison, one can obtain quite different results for slightly different time periods. For example, according to the World Bank, Tunisian agriculture grew at a 4.1% average annual rate from 1970 to

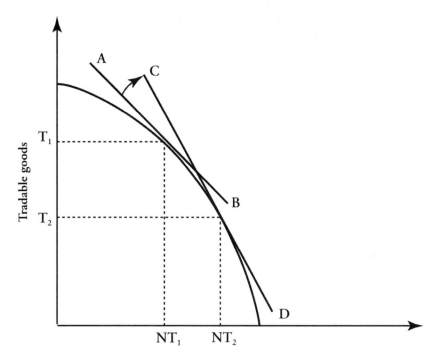

FIGURE 2.4   Reallocation of resources in response to a shift in the relative price of tradable and nontradable goods. (The shift in relative prices is shown by the change in the price line from AB to CD. Resulting reallocations of labor and capital reduce the equilibrium output of tradables $[T_2 < T_1]$ and increase that of nontradables $[NT_2 < NT_1]$).

1981 but at only 1.6% from 1973 to 1983. For some oil exporters such as Algeria, growth rates of manufacturing and agriculture were greater during the 1973–1983 period than they had been during the previous "cheap oil" decade. The reason for the discrepancy between this evidence and the predictions of the theory was that Middle Eastern and other oil-exporting governments often intervened directly to counteract these relative-price shifts, usually by subsidizing their tradable-goods sector. Such subsidies, of course, create problems of their own, and no country has fully met the challenges posed by rural emigration. In addition, both the seriousness of the disease and the cure have varied considerably from one country to another. The case of the Dutch Disease illustrates the argument that state policy both shapes development and responds to the unintended outcomes of that same process.

The inflow of oil revenues also has important direct political consequences. Oil revenues are rents. Economic rent is the difference between the market price of a good or a factor of production and its opportunity cost (the price needed to produce the good or to keep the factor of production in its current use) (see Box 2.2). For example, oil rents in the Persian Gulf are the difference between the market

⊌ BOX 2.2 _____

The Concept of Economic Rent

Economists define rent as the difference between the market price of a good or factor of production and its opportunity cost. Owners of certain assets or providers of certain services enjoy strategic positions in markets that allow them to set prices well above the opportunity cost for what they are providing. The revenue stream that is generated is not directly related to greater efficiency in production or to new investment. When oil prices were quadrupled by the Organization of Petroleum Exporting Countries in 1973 (see Chapter 3), the new market price reflected neither increases in the cost of production nor new investment. Rather, consumers of petroleum had to accept the new price, and only with the passage of considerable time could they reduce consumption through improved efficiency in energy use. In the interim, the oil-exporting states of the MENA region reaped enormous rent streams.

These rents are referred to as "external," and analysts of the Middle East have attributed a host of ills to them. Access to rents has allowed several states to avoid improving the efficiency of production and has hurt particularly those sectors producing tradable goods. In addition, rents have allowed governments to avoid heavily taxing their own citizenries, thereby breaking that vital, often adversarial link between governments and the people they tax. Out of such links governmental accountability may flow; in their absence governments may ignore their citizens.

External rents are not confined to petroleum revenues. Several Middle Eastern nations had continuous access to "strategic rents" throughout the cold war era. Countries enjoying peculiar geostrategic value in the confrontation between the two superpowers could count on financial flows and aid designed quite openly to buy their allegiance to one side or the other. Israel has been by far the greatest regional beneficiary of strategic rents: By some accounts, US assistance to Israel averaged $14,630 per Israeli over the period 1949–2004 (*Washington Report on Middle Eastern Affairs* 2006). Starting from low levels in 1959, assistance climbed to roughly $3 billion per year during the twenty years from 1984 to 2004. In the latter year, US aid was approximately $638 per Israeli, according to US sources (US Embassy, Tel Aviv 2004). The nearest competitor for US aid was Jordan, with $285 per Jordanian. Egypt and the Palestinians lagged far behind Israel in per capita terms: $30 and $34, respectively. The noneconomic rationale behind these aid transfers can be seen in the relative per capita GDPs for that (or any other) year: Israel, US$PPP 19,700; Jordan: US$PPP 4,300; Egypt: US$PPP 3,900.

continues

◑ BOX 2.2 *continued*

Not all economic rents are external. The notion of "rent-seeking behavior" refers primarily to the search for strategic privilege in domestic markets. Such privilege is usually bestowed by public authorities through the issuance of import licenses, targeted tariff protection, franchises, and the like. When the privileged are protected from competition in specific markets, revenues and profits are generated without changes in productive efficiency or new investment (beyond the cost of acquiring the privilege).

price (as of this writing, near US$60 per barrel) and the cost of producing oil there (about US$1.50). Furthermore, these rents are collected directly by governments, increasing their freedom of maneuver. Oil rents are politically centralizing. However, as the revenues are spent, new domestic actors emerge (as contractors, agents, recipients of subsidies) who, in turn, begin to limit the freedom of maneuver of the state. This is a very typical pattern; state autonomy may rise in a particular conjuncture but then typically will decline with its exercise over time.

A further effect of oil rents is that they permit the evasion of hard development choices. This is not a problem if the rents are very large or are assumed to be very stable. For many middle-income oil exporters, neither condition holds. Consider the case of Egypt in the early 1980s: With annual oil receipts of some US$2.8 billion, along with ample foreign-exchange revenues from workers' remittances (about US$3 billion) and from other "locational rents" (tourism, the Suez Canal, and US aid), the country could avoid a thorough reform of both its highly distorted pricing system and its structurally imbalanced labor market. By the time the rents declined and the day of reckoning arrived, the problems and their potential solutions were all the more painful.

Rents may also retard the expansion of the domestic supply of food. The Middle East is the least food-self-sufficient area in the world. Demand for food rose by 4–5% per year during the 1970s, driven by rapidly rising per capita incomes and by population growth rates that were surprisingly high given national incomes. Supply was constrained by nature and by political economy. Scarce water resources, urban bias, unequal land-tenure systems, and the Dutch Disease all contributed to the relatively sluggish supply response. In the 1980s and 1990s, growth in food demand slowed as incomes fell and supply increased modestly due to improved policies. The range of agricultural outcomes in the region was extremely wide, however, extending from the Sudanese famine of 1984 to Turkish net grain exports (see Chapter 6).

Such agricultural problems impede economic development and create problems for policymakers. Food and agriculture imports accounted for nearly one-third of all imports in Algeria, Egypt, and Yemen from 1993 to 1999 (Lofgren and Richards 2003). This is perhaps acceptable, provided that the states in question can offset these imports with exports. The difficulties of agricultural transformation, such as the rural exodus toward already bulging cities and the provision of adequate food supplies, are among the most pressing of the disequilibria of economic growth and structural transformation facing the region today.

The pattern of industrial growth has exacerbated the employment problems fostered by rural neglect. Partly because of a desire to have the most modern technology available and partly because of distorted price signals, much of the industry installed in the Middle East during the past generation has been capital-intensive. Consequently, the amount of investment required to create a job has been very high. Because of managerial inefficiencies and foreign-exchange bottlenecks, these same industrial facilities have been plagued by idle capacity, driving up the amount of investment needed to add to output. Only a few Middle Eastern countries have internationally competitive industries.

Finally, the state itself has often become a drain on resources in the Middle East. This is not to say that the state should not (still less, could not) intervene in the development process. In certain conjunctures, however, the state can inhibit the very process that at least officially it seeks to promote. Not only do its interventions often generate misleading price signals for private actors (e.g., undervaluing foreign exchange and local capital), but its bloated bureaucracies and inefficient state-owned enterprises often devour resources. State borrowing to finance its own activities may crowd out private investors from credit markets. One could include military spending and the maintenance of large, lethal arsenals and standing armies among the burdens that the state itself creates for the growth process (see Chapter 13).

In summary, the course of economic growth and structural change is far from smooth. Extensive state intervention, numerous bottlenecks, and serious macro- and microeconomic problems are the norm. Many of these problems have their origins in state policy; each generates a policy response. It is important to remember, however, that these distortions and problems have rarely been the result of obvious error or stupidity. Hindsight is always 20/20, while future outcomes and unintended consequences are always opaque. Many of the price and other distortions generated by state policy originated in states' attempts to mobilize savings. Agriculture had to be taxed because, for countries like Egypt in the 1950s, there was no alternative source of investable funds. Industry tended to be capital-intensive because planners believed this was necessary to create a modern industrial core. Growth and modernization of production were to take precedence over employment generation and agricultural development, because growth itself was expected to automatically provide the latter two. Rapid industrial development under state auspices was also held to be essential to national security. State-led growth was designed to weaken or destroy internal and external enemies. States intervened to accelerate the process of economic growth and to forge a powerful modern nation. Their leaders held certain images of the future that explicitly included industrialization, but the reality often turned out to be different from the image.

Perhaps no state in the Middle East had formulated a more detailed image of its future than Algeria. By 1969, seven years after independence and a bloody colonial war, Algeria launched a four-year plan that was intended to be the first of several. It was premised on a "big-push" strategy of heavy industrialization entirely within the state sector. The crucial element in the strategy was the country's hydrocarbon riches: petroleum and natural gas. It was expected that exports of these resources would generate foreign exchange to pay for imported technology, capital goods, and turnkey industries. More important, they were to be the source of energy and basic feedstock for large industrial undertakings in petrochemicals and basic metals.

These industries were in turn to provide a wide range of intermediate and finished goods: fertilizers, butane gas, plastic sheeting and sacking, irrigation pipes, tractors, motors, and consumer durables. It was assumed that the rural sector, under socialist management in the most favored areas, would become the principal consumer of these products, but little attention was paid to issues of agricultural productivity. It was also assumed that with the importation of state-of-the-art technology (for instance, gas liquefaction plants), many of these industries would be able to compete in international markets.

In terms of structural transformation, Algeria's technocrats saw the agrarian sector primarily as a customer for the industrial sector, one whose workforce would continue to dwindle and whose per capita productivity would rise. The regime was prepared during the big-push phase to tolerate high rates of urban unemployment and high levels of worker migration to France. Eventually, rising incomes in agriculture and in the new industrial sector would generate substantial demand for goods and services, which would create the jobs necessary to absorb the unemployed. President Houari Boumedienne (1965–1978) saw no reason to worry about Algeria's 3.5% annual population growth rate because he expected that the economic growth projected by his plan would yield the prosperity necessary to lower fertility.

The whole strategy came to be known as "industrializing industries," a label affixed to it by its major foreign architect, G. Destanne de Bernis (1971) of the University of Grenoble. It was an integrated plan, and therefore, when one of its parts failed to conform to the overall strategy, the whole process quickly collapsed. Mismanagement in the socialist agrarian sector and production declines throughout the agricultural sector meant that the latter could not become a reliable customer for industry. The new industries soon faced problems of idle capacity, compounded by the sophistication of their imported technology and inadequate management skills. Except for some petroleum products, seeking external markets was not a feasible alternative. Unemployment and underemployment mounted while the rural exodus continued. The population continued to grow as broad-based prosperity remained a distant goal. Increasingly large amounts of foreign exchange had to be used to import food and sustain urban standards of living.

By 1976 it had become clear that the big push was in trouble, and after Boumedienne's death in 1978 Algeria's new president, Chadli Benjadid, moved to break up the large state industrial sector into smaller, decentralized units, stimulate the agricultural sector through more favorable prices, and encourage the long-maligned private sector to play a more active role in the country's development (Lawless 1984). In the 1980s Algeria's earnings from petroleum exports fell from US$11 billion to US$4 billion. Not only was any further big-push development out of the question, but the decline in rents made even downsizing the state extremely difficult. By the end of the decade Algeria was in economic crisis and political turmoil, and during the 1990s perhaps 100,000 Algerians were killed in a merciless civil war.

It is instructive to compare Algeria's experience with that of another oil-rich country, Iraq, two decades earlier. In 1950 Iraq was still a monarchy, nominally independent but closely allied to its former imperial master, the United Kingdom. In that year royalties paid the Iraqi government on the production and sale of oil increased by 30%, and by 1958 the royalties had grown nearly sixfold to over US$200 million. The government, not unwisely, wanted to use these revenues for long-term development purposes. Toward this end, an autonomous Development Board was established, and 70% of oil royalties were earmarked for it. The board had the authority and the finances to set Iraq's growth course (Penrose and Penrose 1978, 167–177).

Unlike Algeria, Iraq aimed its big push at agriculture. The Development Board began large hydraulic projects to master floods in the Tigris-Euphrates system, store water, irrigate new lands, improve drainage, and cope with soil salinity. Whereas Algeria's slogan was "Sow oil to reap industry," Iraq's was "Sow oil to reap agriculture," and that sector was to be the engine of long-term growth. The flaws in this far-sighted strategy were that it neglected immediate problems of agricultural production, had no particular industrialization program, and devoted no resources to social infrastructure (such as housing and health). The hydraulic projects were not likely to contribute to the economy for years, if not decades. In the meantime, peasants continued to pour into Baghdad and other cities as floods, soil salinity, and grossly inequitable land distribution impeded increased production. In the cities, neither the urban job market nor the network of social services was adequate to provide a decent standard of living to the hundreds of thousands of Iraqis crowded into slums and shantytowns. When elements of the Iraqi armed forces moved to overthrow the monarchy on July 14, 1958, their advancing tank columns were accompanied by masses of denizens of the shantytowns who wanted to assist in bringing down the regime. With its demise came also that of the Development Board's strategy. The military and its Ba'ath party successors elaborated an entirely new image of the future not unlike that of Algeria.

STATE STRUCTURE AND DEVELOPMENT POLICY

The interaction of state policy and the process of economic growth and structural transformation is not merely one of images of the future. Most states of the region have had visions of where they would like to go—how they hoped their societies would appear in the future. The problem, of course, has been getting there. What strategy would be employed, and who would implement which parts of it? We shall now examine these questions of strategies and agencies.

Without prejudging whether economic-development strategies are "choices" or "sequences" or whether they are politically imposed from within (e.g., by domestic proprietary classes) or from without (e.g., by international financial agencies), we can identify five major routes from predominantly rural, agricultural, political economies to urban, industrial ones. These are the paths of agro-exports, mineral exports, import-substituting industrialization, manufactured exports, and agricultural-development–led industrialization. Let us examine these in turn.

Economic-Development Strategies

Agro-export-led growth.   The usual justification for the agro-export strategy is as follows: At the beginning of the process of structural transformation, most people are by definition rural and agricultural. If there are underexploited land and/or labor resources, these could be used to produce more crops for sale, but because of the poverty of the local population and (perhaps) the relatively small number of people, the domestic market is quite limited. Exports provide the exit from this impasse. The incomes of the farmers may rise, and if some of the profits from such activities are reinvested in increasing productivity and expanding the productive base of the economy (e.g., by investing in industry), a process of self-sustaining growth may be launched (Lewis 1954; Myint 1959). Further, the process of industrialization requires imports; in the long run, such imports can be financed only by exports. Since such countries may have little to sell except agricultural commodities, developing such exports then provides the foreign exchange needed for structural transformation. Finally, the country may have a strong international comparative advantage in the production of a particular crop, such as cotton in the Nile Valley or wine grapes in Algeria.

However, for better or for worse, reliance on agro-exports is commonly associated with colonialism. Historically, of course, the two were closely linked all over the world. The Middle East was no exception; cotton cultivation for export to Europe was expanded under colonial rule in Egypt and the Sudan, while wine production was introduced and flourished in the settler areas of North Africa. A division of labor between metropole and colony was an integral part of colonial ideology. The agro-export strategy faces several problems besides its historical associations, among them declining terms of trade for agricultural-export products, the favoring of certain classes, and excessive taxation.

Critics of agro-export-led growth strategies have long maintained that there is a long-run necessary tendency for a unit of agro-exports to buy progressively fewer manufactured products. Although one might reject the more extreme forms of this proposition, it is nevertheless clear that countries have experienced uncomfortably long periods of declining terms of trade (e.g., the Sudan, 1978–1985). Third, price fluctuations cause problems in their own right, independently of longer-run trends. If commodity-export prices fluctuate greatly from year to year, so also will export revenues. Since the point of any agro-export-led growth strategy is to acquire funds for industrialization and since industrial planning often involves fairly long lead times, such fluctuations can seriously disrupt industrialization efforts.

A second problem with this strategy is that (as with any strategy) certain domestic classes are more favored than others. In particular, many critics of the agro-export approach argue that it strengthens powerful urban commodity-trading interests, which may block further development. If such classes' power derives from the unchallenged economic dominance of their sector, they may especially resent any attempt to impose tariffs on imported domestic goods or taxes to finance infrastructure for industry.

It is not clear from the historical record of the Middle East that agro-exporters failed to invest, eschewed industrial projects, or generally blocked the rise of "infant industry." The Egyptian case is particularly instructive. Wealthy indigenous Egyptian cotton producers often invested in the agricultural sector and provided the bulk of the capital for the initial industrial endeavors of the Bank Misr in the 1920s (Davis 1983; Tignor 1984). Their loyalty to the nation also seems never to have been seriously in doubt. But it is true that such groups ultimately failed to solve the many pressing domestic political, economic, and social problems facing the country and could not rid the country of the British imperial presence. Their demise as agents of development also spelled the demise of the agro-export-led strategy.

A third problem that often arises with agro-exports is the temptation of the government to tax the sector excessively. This problem is the reverse of the previous one. Whereas the argument against compradors and oligarchs is based on the political *power* of these classes, the problem of excessive taxation is a result of the political *weakness* of export-crop producers. This situation usually arises if the producers are small peasants whose number, poverty, and geographical dispersion render collective action difficult. Governments are then often tempted to place the burden of growth on such classes, usually through establishing government control over marketing, input supply, or both. Such an approach is usually self-defeating, however; small peasants shift land, labor, and other inputs out of the controlled-export crops into other uncontrolled ones or resort to smuggling.

A final problem with this strategy is that it assumes an adequate natural resource base. In MENA, as we shall see in Chapter 6, the water constraint bites ever tighter on the agricultural production potential of all countries. We shall also see that the abuse of natural resources, often induced by misguided policy, is equally rampant.

Mineral-export-led growth.   The second principal strategy is also based on the export of natural resources: mineral-export-led growth. In the Middle East, petroleum and phosphates are the major exports of this type. Jordan and, above all, Morocco have substantial phosphate reserves and large exports. Moroccan phosphate exports are the largest in the world, and reserves (including those of the Western Sahara) are 40% of the world's total. Petroleum, of course, is by far the most valuable and significant natural resource in the region.

One should distinguish between those oil and mineral exporters that have other resources, for example, substantial populations and considerable agricultural potential, and those whose economies are entirely dominated by mineral exports. The first group includes Algeria, Morocco, Tunisia, Iraq, and Iran, while the second set consists of Libya and the Gulf States.[2] Saudi Arabia is a unique case because of the size of its petroleum reserves. The officially stated goals of the mineral-based export strategy are quite similar to those of agro-exporters: to acquire revenue from mineral exports to create an industrial base for sustained development after the natural resource is exhausted. This strategy is distinguished from the agro-export-led strategy by the very different pattern of international price developments (for oil but not for phosphates) and by the exhaustibility of the exported natural resource. By using the receipts from a depleting asset, a future without oil can be built.

This is a perfectly reasonable approach for countries that have significant nonpetroleum resources, but it is much more difficult to see what economic future is in store for Libya and the Gulf States after their oil runs out. Perhaps sufficient financial assets can be accumulated, which can then serve as a reliable source of income. Before the Iraqi invasion of 1990, Kuwait reached this "pure-rentier-state" stage, with income from foreign investments exceeding that from petroleum exports. But such rentier activity leaves a nation very much at the mercy of international political developments; financial assets are fairly easy to seize or impound. Kuwait had to spend them during the Iraqi occupation for military, diplomatic, and political purposes related to regaining its independence. But the absence of arable land, water, and nonoil mineral resources and the presence of a small, poorly educated population suggest that the future without oil may be bleak.

The Saudis, for example, have perhaps one-fifth of the world's petroleum reserves. These reserves can be expected to last 50 to 250 years, depending on the rate of production. The Saudi strategy of oil-based development has had three major components. First, funds have been used to expand infrastructure, leading to one of the most massive construction booms in economic history. Despite numerous bottlenecks (inevitable given the low level of infrastructure and the size of the projects), roads, schools, hospitals, shopping centers, offices, and other buildings have mushroomed throughout the kingdom. Second, surplus funds—funds that could not be spent immediately—were placed in Western financial institutions. The Saudis thereby gained the benefit of those institutions' expertise in investment. Finally, the Saudis have invested in petroleum-based industry. They have selected industries for expansion that are highly capital- and energy-intensive and/or use oil or gas as a feedstock. The principal investments have been in petrochemical complexes, fertilizer plants, aluminum smelting, and steel production, using natural gas in a direct reduction process to convert imported iron ore.

None of these industrial schemes would be viable without oil; they are in no sense, then, "creating a future without oil." Instead, they are increasing the percentage that remains in Saudi Arabia of the value added in the final output of petroleum- or energy-intensive industries. Saudi petrochemicals are now so highly competitive internationally that there have been protectionist moves against them in Western Europe and the United States. Despite such problems, the strategy of stretching out the life of its already massive reserves of petroleum makes good sense for Saudi Arabia. It is not really a viable strategy for other oil exporters, none of which enjoys reserves on the Saudi scale.

Any mineral-export-led growth strategy faces two major problems. First, most countries are likely to have only one significant mineral for export. Consequently, their export revenues are highly dependent on price developments for that product or products. This subjects their economies to the problems and difficulties of a sudden fall—or a sudden rise—in the price of their export. Second, the existence of large oil revenues combines with political structures and imperatives to create cradle-to-the-grave welfare systems. Although potential human capital is the only non-oil resource that many of these countries have, the incentives to develop it are limited. Why should a Saudi become an engineer if he can more easily become a joint director of a company whose head must always be Saudi? Why should a woman pursue higher education if there will be only a very few interesting job opportunities open for her? Although these problems may be overcome with time and although the ease of life for the poorer classes of Saudi society may be readily exaggerated, the presence of large oil rents poses problems for the accumulation of human capital.

The situation of these oil exporters is in many ways unique. The combination of massive reserves, small populations, and few additional resources makes their development strategies and prospects *sui generis.* Oil exporters of the first group, however, are in a rather different situation. Only Iraq was a capital-surplus nation before its invasion of Iran. Countries such as Iran, Algeria, and Iraq faced a problem rather similar to that of Egypt after its period of agro-export-led growth: how best to foster the rise of industry. All of these countries adopted an approach of import-substituting industrialization and because of their petroleum rents have been able to sustain it longer than countries that do not export oil.

Import-substituting industrialization.   Import-substituting industrialization (ISI) is one of the LDCs' most tested development strategies. Its logic is compelling. It is designed to move economies traditionally dependent on the export of primary commodities and raw materials to an industrial footing. The new industries are expected both to produce goods that were previously imported (everything from textiles and shoes to fertilizers and refined sugar) *and* process domestic raw materials (e.g., cotton, minerals, sugarcane, petroleum). The result would be economic diversification and reduced dependency on volatile external markets for primary products and on high-priced imports.

Through ISI, it was hoped, developing countries could escape the agrarian trap into which imperialist powers or, more anonymously, the international division of labor had thrust them. The place to begin was with known domestic markets. As the process gathered steam and raised revenues for the new workers and managers as well as for the producers of agricultural commodities destined for processing, new markets would develop, and infant industries would achieve economies of scale that would make them profitable and competitive. Eventually, the first industries would produce backward linkages, stimulating new enterprises in capital goods, basic metals, machine tools, and the like. In Egypt in the 1960–1965 period, when this strategy was pursued with vigor, it was envisaged that the textile sector, using Egyptian cotton and replacing foreign imports, would "link back" to the setting up of an industry to manufacture spinning and weaving machinery, itself utilizing steel from the new iron-and-steel complex.

Before these linkages could be firmly established and economies of scale achieved, the new industries would have to be protected from foreign competition by high tariff walls. Moreover, given the narrowness of domestic markets, any industry might enjoy, de facto or de jure, a monopoly in its particular sector. Thus, although seen as a temporary phenomenon, ISI implied and frequently meant monopolistic production and marketing at costs higher than for similar imports. It also frequently meant lower-quality goods than those that could be imported.

Turkey pioneered among Middle Eastern states in pursuing an ISI strategy. Atatürk's republic, founded at the end of World War I amid the debris of the Ottoman Empire, was the first fully independent country in the region, and its leader was determined to transform it into an industrial and "Western" nation. During the 1930s, in the absence of a formulated strategy and without any socialist justification, the Turkish state began to launch industries in textiles, cement, and basic metals. With the impact of the Great Depression, Turkey in 1933 launched its first five-year industrial plan and, with some advice from Soviet planners, entered a phase of concerted state-led growth. Next door in Iran, Reza Khan, the founder of the Pahlavi dynasty, was moving in a similar direction, and throughout the Arab world young men who would lead their countries in the 1950s observed Turkey's experiment closely.

With Algeria's independence in 1962, all major states in the Middle East had won formal sovereignty (the one exception was the former Aden Protectorate, which became the People's Democratic Republic of Yemen [PDRY] in 1969). With rare exceptions, these states pursued, to varying degrees and with different ideological underpinnings, ISI strategies. These made good sense for the larger, more differentiated economies in the region, those with important domestic markets that could sustain large industrial units. They made less sense for the small, undiversified economies of the not-yet-rich oil-exporting countries and for some without oil, such as Lebanon and Jordan. We should note, however, that one large country, the Sudan, only briefly toyed with an ISI strategy, while three large oil-exporting countries, Algeria, Iraq, and Iran, pursued it resolutely.

The most determined efforts to follow in Turkey's footsteps were undertaken by Egypt, Iran, Tunisia, Algeria, Syria, and Iraq. Israel followed the policy mainly with respect to military industries, but given its small population and economic isolation within the Arab world, it could not afford a broad-based ISI strategy. ISI projects tended to fall within the following categories:

1. Consumer durables destined for established middle- and upper-income markets
2. Textiles, shoes, and other apparel for mass markets
3. Soft drinks and tobacco products for mass markets
4. Processing of local agricultural produce: canning, sugar refining, spinning and weaving, manufacturing of beer and wine, etc.
5. Processing local raw materials: petroleum to fertilizers and plastics, iron ore to iron and steel

ISI strategies led several states to ignore what neoclassical economists saw as their comparative advantage in world trade: the export of raw materials and unprocessed agricultural produce. But the states' object was precisely to promote economic diversification by building new skills within the workforce, to capture for national purposes the value added in processing that had heretofore accrued to the advanced industrial nations, and to reduce the states' dependency upon unstable world markets for primary produce. ISI has experienced widespread setbacks in the Middle East and elsewhere, but that does not mean that it was conceptually wrong at its inception.

The setbacks in the ISI strategy stemmed primarily from the degree of protection granted to the infant industries and the proportion of public resources devoted to them at the expense of the agricultural sector. The agricultural sector was taxed through various devices to provide an investable surplus for the new industrial undertakings, while the foreign exchange earned from agricultural exports went to pay for the technologies, capital goods, and raw materials required by the industrial sector. The price paid for these income transfers was frequently slow or nonexistent agricultural growth. This in turn meant, as we have seen in the Algerian case, that the large rural populations could not generate the demand to keep the new industries operating at full capacity. Consequently, idle capacity and production costs rose, but because the industries were protected against cheaper imports by high tariffs and enjoyed sectoral monopolies in domestic markets, they had no incentive to keep costs down. The industries were in general capital-intensive and under the best of circumstances not providers of large numbers of jobs. When operating below capacity, they could either lay off workers (a rare occurrence) or increase operating costs further by carrying redundant labor. In no way could they meet the challenge of providing jobs for rural workers abandoning a depressed agricultural sector for life and livelihood in the cities.

The net result in many instances was high-cost production destined either for upper-income luxury markets (such as automobiles and refrigerators) or for mass markets in which retail prices were subsidized by the government (everything from fertilizers to sugar). The new industries could not, because of their high costs, export their products and earn the foreign exchange needed to pay for imported raw materials and equipment. Thus they contributed to the growing balance-of-payments crises that plagued several ISI experiments. Clearly this was a greater problem for the oil-poor states, such as Turkey, Egypt, Syria, and Tunisia, than for the oil-rich nations, such as Iran, Iraq, and Algeria.

In order to lower the price of goods imported for the new industries, most governments maintained overvalued exchange rates for their currencies. These, in combination with foreign-exchange-rationing systems that favored the new industries, put no pressure upon those industries to reduce the import content of their operations. By contrast, traditional exporters in the agricultural sector in some instances lost their competitive edge in foreign markets because the artificially high exchange rate dampened demand for their commodities.

The need for the government to subsidize the price at which the products of the new industries were sold to consumers, be they other industrial users or buyers at the retail level, contributed significantly to the mounting public deficits and thereby to increasing rates of domestic inflation. Faced with sluggish agricultural performance, industries operating at a loss, large domestic deficits, and growing balance-of-payments difficulties, Middle Eastern governments turned to borrowing

abroad to fill these gaps, incurring large foreign debts and heavy servicing requirements (payments of interest and principal).

Not all Middle Eastern countries adopted this strategy, but for many that did,
the 1970s brought a far-reaching reappraisal of what they had undertaken. For some,
the moment of truth was brought about by the huge increase in their petroleum-
import bill after 1973; for countries with abundant oil (for example, Algeria after
1976), the issue seemed to be more one of overheating and structural inefficiencies. The collapse of oil prices in the mid-1980s sounded the death knell of ISI in
the region.

Growth led by manufactured exports. For Western creditors of heavily indebted
Middle Eastern economies, a way out seemed to lie in dramatically increasing manufactured exports to the markets of the OECD countries. South Korea, Taiwan, Singapore, India, and Brazil, among others, had succeeded in this to varying degrees,
earning themselves the epithet of "newly industrializing countries" (NICs). What
recommends this strategy is that it addresses two of the main problems arising from
ISI. First, it earns the country foreign exchange without sacrificing the goal of industrialization. Second, if it is to have any chance of success, it requires the reduction of
production costs so that the exporting industries can compete abroad, and therefore
the problems of idle capacity, operating losses, and redundant labor have to be overcome. With world markets as their target, economies of scale can be achieved even
for countries with relatively small domestic markets (Hong Kong, Singapore, Hon-
duras, and Costa Rica demonstrate the possibilities).

There are daunting domestic challenges to this strategy. "Bad habits" that may
have developed during the ISI phase may be dealt with only at high political cost.
Some analysts, such as Lipton (1977) and Bates (1981), have suggested the existence
in LDCs of an urban or at least nonagrarian alliance consisting of industrial management and capitalists in protected industries, the organized industrial workforce, civil
servants, and virtually all urban consumers. All have become accustomed to protection of inefficient management, redundant labor, and consumer and input subsidies.
None of this protection can be allowed to endure if export-led growth is to gain momentum. Moreover, devaluation may have a particularly sharp impact on urban consumers, who will see the price of many imported items skyrocket.

A government contemplating this strategy must think carefully of the constituencies it will alienate, some of which are part of the state apparatus itself. The owners and managers of import-substituting industries may try to sabotage the new
experiment, and they will find tacit allies among the workers who risk being laid off
as enterprises streamline or who may face relative reductions in salary. All urban
constituents may see a sharp rise in the cost of living. It is important to remember
that the negative effects of the new strategy will be felt immediately, whereas the
economic payoffs may be years in coming. No politician likes that sort of bargain.

Despite the risks, some Middle Eastern countries have moved in this direction.
Two of the earliest experiments took place in Morocco and Tunisia, both of which
negotiated preferential trade agreements with the European Union in the late

1960s. Tunisia was moving away from a period of concerted ISI under state auspices, while Morocco was seeking to diversify its exports beyond its traditional combination of phosphates and citrus. Both hoped to attract light industry from Europe in ready-made apparel, electronics, consumer-durable assembly, and so forth, or to stimulate their own private sectors to move into similar fields. They accelerated these efforts after the mid-1980s (Chapter 9).

For more than three decades Turkey, already a member of the North Atlantic Treaty Organization (NATO), has aspired to full membership in what is now the European Union (EU). Since the early 1970s it has been trying to restructure its economy (after the experiment in ISI launched by Atatürk) so as to be able to compete in European markets. The process took on added urgency in the late 1970s as Turkey, without petroleum deposits, absorbed the full impact of rising international prices for fossil fuels at the same time that European labor markets were closing themselves off to migrant Turkish workers. Balance-of-payments crises, growing external debt, mounting domestic deficits, and inflation produced a situation of political instability and eventual military intervention in 1980. Since then a return to civilian rule has been accompanied by a concerted and partially successful export drive for Turkish manufactures and construction services.

Israel's economy has always been dependent on aid and trade. Like Tunisia and Morocco, and well before them, it negotiated a preferential trade agreement with the European Economic Community (EEC), the forerunner of the EU, and it has had great success in marketing avocados, citrus, and vegetables in Europe. Its major manufactured export has traditionally been finished industrial diamonds. In the past decade, however, diamonds have been eclipsed by manufactured metal products and high-tech electronics. Equally important is Israel's major role in the international arms trade, supporting the scale and sophistication of its own armaments industry by developing foreign markets for its weaponry. Despite its relative success in all export sectors, Israel found itself in the early 1980s facing huge domestic deficits, high labor costs that limited the areas in which Israel could be competitive internationally, the largest per capita external debt in the world, and a domestic inflation rate in 1985 second only to Bolivia's. Since 1985, however, Israel has simultaneously pursued economic reforms at home and export promotion abroad. By 1995 it had earned from London's *Economist* the epithet of "tiger," normally reserved for the export dynamos of East Asia.

Growth led by agricultural development. A final strategy that has received emphasis among political economists is growth led by agricultural development (e.g., Adelman 1984; Mellor 1976). The strategy is especially aimed at very poor countries with most of their population still in agriculture, without vast mineral resources, and with little prospect of penetrating foreign markets for manufactured goods. It is particularly designed to minimize any conflict between growth and equity in development. This strategy draws on the "basic-needs" approach popular with international agencies during the 1970s, which focused on providing adequate nutrition, health, and education to all people, but it places more stress on sustaining human-capital investments by raising productivity and establishing realistic price signals for achieving growth-with-equity. Although no Middle Eastern countries have adopted this strategy, if austerity and sluggish international markets persist, poorer countries like Yemen and Sudan could do worse than to try to implement it.

The strategy relies heavily on the linkages between the growth of small-farm agriculture and the labor market. Empirical evidence suggests that agriculture is the most labor-intensive of any industry; increasing output per unit of land also raises the demand for agricultural laborers, usually the poorest people in any country. Furthermore, farmers spend a high proportion of their increased incomes on labor-intensive manufactured goods such as housing, furniture, and bicycles. Consequently, agricultural productivity growth, which augments farmers' incomes, raises the demand for industrial labor. Increases in agricultural output can be obtained at a relatively low cost in imported goods (unlike, say, automobile manufacturing, where all of the parts may be imported, as was true in Iran under the shah). Finally, activities that improve agricultural infrastructure (roads, irrigation and drainage systems) are also typically very labor-intensive. This strategy takes advantage of the agricultural production function and farmers' tastes to create "virtuous circles" of increased food production, improved health, steadily growing labor absorption, and relatively equitably rising incomes.

The choice of strategies.   Countries in the region will probably continue to combine several of the elements of these strategies. For example, ISI and manufactured-export-led growth strategies are not mutually exclusive. It is in fact likely that most of the more developed countries will try to combine elements of both, just as poorer countries may combine agricultural-development-led growth with agro-exports or some modest import substitution. We may find two sectors side by side—one following the ISI pattern in such industries as metal refining, automobile assembly, and fertilizer production and the other oriented toward external markets in finished textiles, electronic appliances, and instruments. Turkey in the 1980s was pursuing an export-led strategy without totally renouncing its heritage from the years 1930 to 1970 of protected, domestically oriented industries. Other countries have exhibited elements of three strategies: primary exports, ISI, and manufactured exports. Oil exporters such as Iran are prime examples, while Egypt and Tunisia represent countries that have continued traditional exports (cotton, olive oil, and in the 1970s petroleum), maintained an important ISI sector, and sought to promote manufactured exports with variable success.

Although strategies may be selected simultaneously, it may often be the case that strategies were adopted in a sequential pattern. Put simply, ISI may have been adopted as *the* strategy but produced a host of unintended and undesirable consequences, at which point the country shifted to an export-led strategy. There is ample evidence of such sequential shifts in the Middle East; Turkey, Egypt, Israel, Morocco, and Tunisia have all proceeded in similar fashion. Whether strategies are adopted sequentially or simultaneously, the state continues to play a preponderant role in shaping the experiment through control of credit, foreign exchange, tax policy, and investment budgets. Stimulating the private sector or honoring the market does not mean abdicating to either. The prominent role of the state in the Korean "miracle" (and still more in China) is instructive in this respect.

A final caveat on strategy choice is in order here: The choice is never uncon-strained. Some specific set of state actors makes the choice, and the choice is bounded by a host of factors, some of which are more obvious than others. There are resource constraints: Israel cannot export oil or any other raw material on a signifi-cant scale, but it does have a highly skilled workforce. The Sudan can export cotton, but it does not have a highly skilled workforce. Saudi Arabia can export oil and im-port a highly skilled workforce. ISI, as noted, is ill suited to economies with small markets, and in most instances, it does not make sense to establish industries to pro-cess resources one does not have.

The choice is also constrained by the relative gains and losses that will be incurred by domestic interests, classes, and ideological factions—this indeed is the primary fo-cus of this book. The choice will be further influenced by the country's regional and international allies, any of which may have its own image of the future and some levers with which to promote it. And the choice will be shaped by international mar-kets and financial flows. The Sudan invested heavily in refining sugar destined for ex-port on the eve of the collapse of the world sugar market. Countries whose external debt is denominated in US dollars found themselves in the early and mid-1980s sad-dled with huge unanticipated servicing requirements due to the surge in US interest rates and the constant revaluing of the dollar against all other currencies.

Finally, the state cannot implement all elements of a strategy. It must use agencies external to itself, perhaps the local private sector or the capitalist farming sector or multinational corporations. Since the late 1980s few countries have not succumbed to the pressures of the international donor community to open their economies and reduce protection of domestic markets. Most countries in the region have adhered to the General Agreement on Tariffs and Trade (GATT) and to the rules and guidelines of the Uruguay Round of trade negotiations. Bahrain, Egypt, Israel, Jordan, Mo-rocco, Oman, Qatar, Saudi Arabia, Turkey, Tunisia, and the United Arab Emirates (UAE) have joined the World Trade Organization (WTO), the successor to GATT. Under the new rules of the trading game, it will be increasingly difficult to combine protected, ISI sectors with policies designed to promote exports and to open the economy to untaxed imports.

Instruments and Intermediaries

There are instruments and intermediaries that the state chooses, more or less will-ingly, to implement its strategy, and there are those that impose themselves, more or less, upon the state. What the state does voluntarily or is forced to do is determined to some extent by its professed ideology. But one must hasten to add that the pro-fessed ideals of the political regime are, as often as not, honored in the breach.

Until the 1980s, most Middle Eastern states advocated some form of socialism, however vague the content of the label and however insincere the regime's commit-ment to it. Even Egypt and Tunisia, as they moved in the 1970s toward greater reliance on the market, the private sector, and profits as incentives, still spoke of themselves as socialist states. The dominant philosophy in Israel until the advent of the Likud government under Menachem Begin in 1977 was a kind of Zionist hybrid of Fabian socialism. The Sudan, the Yemen Arab Republic (YAR), Syria, Iraq, Libya, and Algeria all have laid claim to socialism. One has the impression that their socialism, like that of Tunisia and Egypt, has consisted mainly in a large public-sector and extensive welfare programs. On that score, monarchical Morocco, the Islamic Republic of Iran (as well as the Pahlavi dynasty before it), Turkey, Israel, and all the conservative princedoms of the Gulf and the Kingdom of Saudi Arabia could lay equal claim to socialism. But they do not. Morocco vaunts its political and economic liberalism, while Turkey today speaks mainly of the latter. Still we find the self-proclaimed liberals maintaining large state sectors and interfering in all aspects of market transactions. Similarly, socialist regimes tolerate and sometimes aid and abet private-sector actors in trade, small-scale manufacturing, construction, and farming. By any measure the largest and most dominant state sectors in the Middle East lie in the small oil-exporting countries, where the petroleum deposits, the producing and refining companies, and all the proceeds of oil sales are under the control of the state.

Throughout the Middle East since the 1970s, Islam has come to play an increasingly important role in shaping ideology and sometimes policy. For the moment we note only that Islam reinforces nationalist suspicions of virtually all outside agencies and nations. The question for Muslims, especially Muslim thinkers, is not one of socialism versus capitalism or public versus private property but rather one of the inherent dangers in dealing with any non-Muslim power. Such dealings can never be neutral or benign but are necessarily conflictual. One may choose among lesser Satans, but the ideal is to make no choice at all.

Many scholars of developing countries have argued that their governments really have no sovereign choice of strategies—that these are determined by core capitalist countries, and the nominal differences among strategies are superficial. The international division of labor in this view is not the product of the working of the forces of supply and demand within world markets but the result of the pressure on international capital flows that are in turn determined by the dominant capitalist economies in the world system. This understanding of the dynamics of international capital flows and markets is common to the proponents of dependency and world-systems analysis, and it presumes that the major impulses toward various strategies come from advanced economies and that the range of choice is, by and large, strictly bounded. It is not difficult, for example, to explain the collapse of the socialist economies of Eastern Europe and the Soviet Union in these terms. The core capitalist countries have powerful instruments at their disposal with which to impose their models of proper economic development: multinational corporations, multinational donor and financial institutions such as the IMF and the World Bank, and major private banks that hold much of the aggregate debt of the LDCs and control of huge flows of funds through a myriad of capital markets that have sprung up throughout the developing world.

As will become clear in several places in this book, we are not comfortable with this line of analysis, particularly with regard to its tendency to deny the possibility of a significant area of sovereign choice for developing countries. The Middle East certainly displays a wide range of experiments and strategies, and although they are constrained by external forces and institutions (one wonders how it could be otherwise under any set of international political circumstances), they are not wholly determined by them. ISI as a strategy, for example, was advocated by Latin American economists as a way of breaking or attenuating the dependency of Latin American economies upon the advanced economies of Europe and North America. It was adopted elsewhere, in Turkey for example, in that spirit. One could argue that its widespread difficulties show that core interests successfully sabotaged it, but one would have expected that, given the alleged power of these interests, they would have seen to it that the strategy was never adopted in the first place.

There is no question that when crises in the external accounts of LDCs become manifest in failure to service private external debt and balance-of-payments deficits, the range of choice available to developing nations narrows significantly. The movement of "portfolio" money through emerging markets is increasingly influenced by levels of domestic savings and the current-account balance. When domestic savings are low, investment high, and the current-account balance in deficit, portfolio money heads elsewhere at literally the speed of light, as Mexico discovered in the winter of 1995. Such crises, however, may be exacerbated but are seldom caused by the functioning of international markets, financial institutions, or multinational corporations. More often than not, the culprits are lagging agricultural production, inefficient industrial production systems, and costly, oversized public bureaucracies. However, once the crises become manifest, the agencies of the core gain significant leverage over policy and strategy choice in LDCs. In essence, new lines of credit and the rescheduling of existing debt and new infusions of foreign direct investment are traded against structural reforms in the economy of the developing country. Since the mid-1970s, scores of developing countries have been driven toward far-reaching and painful structural adjustment programs designed in consultation with the IMF, the World Bank, and Western aid agencies, and the countries in the Middle East have been no exception (see Chapter 9). And, as we shall see, the luster of "free-market strategies" is somewhat tarnished after the experience of the past fifteen years, despite its continued advocacy by the United States and international agencies.

One general observation can be made at this juncture, as a much fuller treatment is provided in future chapters. ISI strategies have typically relied upon publicly owned enterprises mainly because the initial investments have usually been very large and beyond the capacity of local entrepreneurial groups, if there are any. In contrast, as countries move toward export-led growth, there is often an attempt by public authorities to mobilize the private sector to play a significant role in these programs. The foreign donor and creditor community frequently pushes the authorities in this direction, but there may also be an independently formulated expectation that the private sector can adjust more rapidly than the public to the challenge of reducing costs, improving quality, and seeking out customers abroad for the country's products. Ideology is then left to catch up with the new reality.

Whether or not they are called upon to play an active part in the implementation of strategies, certain interests, strata of the population, and classes will benefit, while others will be penalized, depending on the strategy or policies selected. It is generally the case that the rural sector does not benefit from ISI strategies because the state usually turns the domestic terms of trade against it. In an export-led strategy, it is likely that capitalist farmers, and not the peasantry as a whole, will benefit from export incentives. If one looks at urban constituencies affected by ISI, organized labor in the new industries, managerial strata charged with implementing state-financed projects, and middle- and upper-income consumers are generally the major beneficiaries. Large-scale industrialists in the private sector may suffer when state banking institutions and government investment programs favor public-sector enterprise. In contrast, small-scale industrialists may benefit from subcontracting on public-sector projects, especially in the construction sector. The move toward a manufactured-export–led strategy will likely have an adverse effect on the real incomes of workers, as wages are usually allowed to lag behind inflation. Moreover, if the strategy is accompanied by devaluation, a shift in the domestic terms of trade in favor of agriculture, and some reduction in consumer subsidies, all citizens in the nonfarm sector, and especially those on fixed incomes, will experience a sharp rise in the cost of living.

Common to both Marxist and liberal schools of analysis is the assumption that forces essentially external to the state are able to control and guide it, using the state to promote or defend their interests. This is an "instrumentalist" view of the state, one that looks, in the liberal tradition, to parties, unions, and interest groups as capturing the state through elections and lobbying or, in the Marxian tradition, to a dominant class controlling the basic means of production as being able to use the state to perpetuate its dominance.

We question the premises of both liberal and Marxist understandings. First, the process of structural transformation and the nearly universal shift toward the preponderance of the nonagrarian, urban sector in economic and social terms produces new social actors and economic interests and undermines the old, irrespective of differing production systems, ideologies, or state formations. Second, at a less macroeconomic level, a given development strategy may set in motion a process that virtually creates new social actors. This process should be seen as an unintended by-product of the strategy choice, not as conclusive evidence that the state was acting in the interests of a class or economic pressure group that had not yet taken shape. The increasing strength of the Turkish private industrial bourgeoisie emerging out of the decades of statist, ISI-oriented politics is a case in point.

Third, in the Middle East, as in most LDCs, class alignments and interest group formation are fluid. Traditional class and economic interests have lost influence. For instance, landowning groups have been undermined by land reforms, but new and as yet unorganized commercial farming interests have begun to take shape. Nowhere have peasantries developed class cohesion. To the extent that capitalist bourgeoisies existed in the first half of this century, they were frequently made up of foreigners of one sort or another and preferred trade to manufacturing. Because industrialization has come very late to the region, the proletariat is weak. That leaves a relatively powerful state apparatus, with its legions of civil servants and managers, a relatively powerful military establishment, and a numerically important but organizationally weak stratum of craftspeople, service people, small-scale manufacturers, and myriad petty tradespeople. For the most part, these social actors are not sufficiently coherent or well defined to manipulate the state. Like any other collectivity, they may find it difficult to act collectively: The "free-rider" problem is often serious.[3] It is our contention that the Middle Eastern state, as often as not, is best seen as the instrument of the upper echelons of its own personnel and that it is in their interests to ensure that the state continues to control as much of the economic resources of the society as possible.

Departing from that premise, we go one step further. Given its relative power and relative autonomy, the state may be the creator of interests and social actors. That is, the somewhat disembodied politico-military power of the state has been used to allocate resources in the process of structural transformation in such a way that new interests are called forth and establish their own claims on resources. The policy levers at the disposal of the Middle Eastern state to act in this manner are formidable. It may own and manage the major productive assets in the economy, own and derive revenue from all mineral resources, act as the single largest employer in the economy, control if not own the major banking institutions, regulate and tax economic activities of all kinds, set basic education policy, control prices, and exercise, in Max Weber's terms, the legitimate monopoly of coercive force. Crucial struggles, then, have occurred not so much between the state and the forces in civil society that seek to control the state as within the ranks of the state elites themselves.

How the state as interest-producer works out in practice will be developed throughout this book, but a few examples of what we have in mind are in order here. Agrarian reforms in the Middle East and the implementation of new production strategies in the agricultural sector have frequently resulted in the elimination of large landowners as a major political force and the expansion of the ranks of small- and middle-sized landowners, a stratum of which is allowed disproportionate access to rural credit and control over rural institutions such as cooperatives and village councils. This stratum is then in a position to take full advantage of unregulated markets for agricultural produce or to lead the way in export drives.

The groups the state favors need not be of a kind. We should expect a great deal of inconsistency in the doling out of incentives, for the state is not a monolith in its dealings with civil society. For example, in the Sudan, the state and the economy as a whole long depended on the performance of the Gezira Scheme, in which tenants on state land grow cotton for export. The Sudanese state has traditionally sought to extract savings and foreign exchange from this scheme, and in the constant bargaining that goes on between the state and the tenant cultivators the latter have become a powerful interest group in Sudanese society. At the same time the Sudanese government has encouraged through easy credit and forfeitary land-leasing arrangements the emergence of a sizable group of private commercial farmers undertaking mechanized cultivation of sorghum destined mainly for export. Thus it simultaneously promotes policies to help it extract resources from a huge state farm and fosters a process of "primitive accumulation" among a growing stratum of capitalist tractor farmers, a stratum that thirty years ago scarcely existed.

Consider one final example. Turkey hopes one day to join the European Union, and to this end it has been lowering tariff walls and trade barriers in the face of more efficient European producers. The policies of Turkey in the 1980s, formulated by the then–prime minister, Turgut Özal, were designed to favor the country's large industrial and construction firms through tax incentives and credit policy. These policies in turn have led to the consolidation of a native capitalist industrial bourgeoisie for the first time in any Middle Eastern society.

SOCIAL ACTORS

The final vertex of our theoretical triangle consists of social actors. There is nothing neat or tidy about this category. Indeed, as we have emphasized, fluidity of class, economic interest groups, and all other interests in contemporary Middle Eastern society is a given. What needs to be stressed, however, is that, in contrast to the somewhat state-centric thrust of the discussion thus far, social actors are not inert or passive in the face of state initiatives. Societal interests and social actors penetrate the state and colonize parts of it. They form alliances with key state actors and enter into explicit or implicit coalitions with public officials, including the head of state. On occasion, they defy or resist the state through the sabotage of policies or through open resistance.

Our inclination is always, as a "first cut," to search for the material or economic incentives that shape group and individual action. Our generalizations apply best to the actions of economic interest groups (for example, the union of secondary school teachers) or of class actors (for example, private industrialists or public-sector managers). In a fundamental sense the allocation and protection of property rights by the state is the starting point for understanding interest-group and class formation. The property "regime" established by law and maintained by force at any point in time will be defended by the beneficiaries and contested by those who feel excluded.

Since the mid-1970s the array of social actors interacting with and confronting the Middle Eastern state has become far more complex than it was at the end of World War II. The middle classes—those owning "real" and intellectual (i.e., specialized educational training) capital—have grown prodigiously. Economic specialization has spawned new interests, and the creation of new wealth has slowly given those interests the ability to further their objectives. Whereas thirty years ago most social actors were "policy-takers" in the face of autonomous states that they could not significantly influence, much less hold to account, by the 1990s a process of bargaining between the state and social actors had become common. If democratic practice is to take root in the Middle East, it will be as the result of the *formalization* of this bargaining process.

That said, we recognize that not all groups are defined by economic interests alone. The literature on Middle Eastern civil society (see Kazemi and Norton 1995; Salamé 1994) grapples with the nature of group identity. Are Islamic political movements driven primarily by religious values and fervor or by less edifying struggles for power and resources? Are ethnic groups and movements explained best by near-mystical notions of blood, ancestry, and historical injustice, or are they mainly seeking recognized claims to national resources? Are both Islamists and ethnic movements crassly manipulated by politicians who see in religion or blood powerful implements for mobilizing a following? Are Islamist movements best seen as an attempt to forge a culturally authentic vision of modernity? Undoubtedly power hunger, material betterment, group fear, creative political vision, and true piety all play their part. It is up to the analyst to decide what motivations predominate when. We will try our best in the coming chapters to do just that, but in each instance we will test first material explanations.

STRUCTURAL TRANSFORMATION
AND INTEREST FORMATION

Europe's structural transformation over a number of centuries from an agrarian to an industrial-urban base has shaped our general understanding of the process but has not provided a model that will be faithfully replicated in developing countries. The latter may skip some stages by importing technology or may telescope others. Developing countries will cope with population growth rates that Europe never confronted. So, too, the process of class formation in the Middle East and elsewhere has varied considerably from that of Europe. What, schematically, are the major differences between the Middle Eastern and the European experiences in the interaction of class, state, and structural transformation?

The first set of distinctions revolves around the legal institutions of private property so prominent in European history but relatively absent in Middle Eastern. In the Middle East, India, and China, Marx saw evidence for what he called "the Asiatic mode of production." The elements he saw as crucial to this mode shifted over time in his analysis (see Anderson 1980, 484–485; Islamoğlu and Keyder 1977, 395), but there were some constants that we believe do define a regime peculiar to the Middle East and South Asia. The basic elements were (1) an absence, in the juridical sense, of private property in land, and (2) a state that extracted tribute, through appointed intermediaries, from undifferentiated villages that combined agriculture and handicrafts and that displayed few organic linkages among themselves. Nomads and tribes competed with the state for the surplus that sedentary populations could produce. The Middle Eastern state retained the right (but not always the ability) to dispose of landed property as its rulers saw fit. What it granted were temporary rights to appropriate the produce of the land, that is, usufruct rights. In contrast to European ones, these rights were not permanent and sanctified by law but temporary privileges bestowed upon clients by the ruler—the caliph or sultan and his governors in far-flung regions of the Islamic empires.

Many historians have observed that the state's eminent domain often gave way in practice to what amounted to hereditary access to state-granted land or to the right to collect tribute in the state's name. But the arrival on the scene of a powerful sultan would, and not infrequently did, lead to the revocation of those quasi-hereditary privileges. Likewise, local notables could, in the face of a weak or financially constrained sultan, assert "stable" claims to privilege. The law was indifferent to the outcome of these power struggles; it only endorsed the right of the state to dispose of the public domain as its rulers saw fit.

Between the sultan and his government and the tribute-paying villagers and tribes lay a more or less thick stratum of tax-farmers, tribute gatherers, and rural notables. Some were military figures, such as the Ottoman *sipahis,* charged with raising tribute and troops for the sultan in exchange for fief-like estates known as timars. Others were tax-farmers pure and simple, granted the right to tax a certain population to whatever extent possible in return for turning over to the sultan a predetermined amount.

As the Middle East, from the seventeenth century on, was drawn into international trade dominated by the newly industrializing nations of Europe, and Islamic states everywhere (the Ottoman Empire, Persia, Moghul India, Morocco) dealt with military inferiority vis-à-vis the Europeans, important changes occurred in the relation of these states to their tribute-paying subjects. The need to raise revenues to pay for an enlarged and modernized military establishment pushed the sultans toward conversion of timar land into hereditary private land, while tax-farmers *(multazims)* gained heritable and salable rights to their territories. After a time, local notables began to profit from a lucrative agricultural-export trade with Europe and were allowed to establish commercial estates *(çiftliks)* that were tantamount to privately owned commercial farms.

The question of state revenues is crucial in grasping one of the profound differences between European and Middle Eastern patterns of economic change. For the most part, state revenues were drawn from the agrarian sector in the form of taxes in kind or in cash on land, animals, and huts. As much as 80% of state revenues may have been so derived, and as much as 15% of total agricultural production may have been absorbed in tribute (Issawi 1982, 68–69; Owen 1981, 106; Katouzian 1981). These proportions of course varied enormously in time and in place and should be taken only as orders of magnitude. The remaining 20% of state revenues came from taxes on overland trade, excise duties, state monopolies, and taxes on markets and guilds.

The paradox here is that public authorities seldom paid much attention to improving agricultural conditions so as to maximize production and, derivatively, state revenues. The one *partial* exception may have been the highly productive irrigated agrarian sector of Egypt, where the state on occasion had to concern itself with flood-control projects and the maintenance of the irrigation infrastructure. But even there, the state was mostly concerned with organizing its tribute gatherers and capturing within its net a peasantry that had nowhere to hide.

Even had the state been in all epochs more benevolent in its approach to its rural populations, there is reason to doubt that the kinds of locally inspired technological breakthroughs in agriculture that occurred in Europe would have been replicated in the Middle East. The reasons involve the ecology of the region and the existence of large nomadic populations. When we consider the vast extent of the Middle East or even its subregions, its rugged terrain characterized by mountain ranges interspersed with large desert expanses, and the prevailing aridity throughout, we can say that it would have been surprising had the Middle East duplicated European agricultural progress. Take only Saudi Arabia with its 2.2 million square kilometers, or about four-fifths of the Arabian Peninsula. This surface, the equivalent of most of Western

Europe including the Iberian Peninsula and Italy, is mainly desert. Whereas European governments dealt with compact areas and generally favorable rain and soil conditions, Middle Eastern states faced staggering distances and hostile terrain that defied centralization, the habits of regular administrative practice, and the consistent maintenance of law and order.

The very ecology of the region produced a social phenomenon, the nomads, that had no counterpart in Western Europe. The nomads in the Middle East, even into the twentieth century, constituted at least 10% of the total population in most areas. Their turf was the "coastal" zones where the few well-watered areas of sedentary agriculture gave way to the desert proper. It was in these zones that they grazed their animals and pitched their tents. Their self-image was one of warriors, freemen who had only scorn for peasants enslaved to the land. Like the state, they often preyed on the very populations from which they needed tribute. Not until the twentieth century would distance be conquered, nomads subdued, and the control of the government extended on a permanent basis over all the territories of sedentary population.

What, then, of the cities and trade as a source of revenue? Urban centers have for millennia been critical features in the political and economic landscape of the Middle East. We think first of the ancient cities of Jerusalem, Damascus, Antioch, and Carthage, but in the Muslim Middle Ages major cities stretched from Spain in the west to India in the east: Fez, Cordoba, Tunis, Cairo, Aleppo, Istanbul, Izmir, Tabriz, Tehran, and Baghdad were in size and diversity the rival of anything in Europe. These cities thrived on the long-distance trade linking Europe to the Far East and, to a lesser extent, to Africa. Muslim states were themselves centered in these cities and were able to tax in various ways the commerce passing through them and the crafts and services that were stimulated by overland trade. The cities were the centers as well of Muslim learning and culture.

To some extent, commerce, urban life in general, and high culture were divorced from the sedentary hinterlands of the cities (Amin 1980, 21). But whereas the state might find in the cities and caravan routes a source of income independent of the fluctuating fortunes of agriculture, its approach to urban business was hardly more benign. Writing of Moghul India, Barrington Moore observed (1967, 322): "In general, the attitude of the political authorities . . . toward the merchant seems to have been closer to that of the spider toward the fly than that of the cow herd toward his cow that was widespread in Europe at the same time. Not even Akbar, the most enlightened of the Moguls, had a Colbert."

By the eighteenth century the Ottoman and other sultanic states in the region faced a momentous fiscal crisis resulting from four factors: (1) the diversion of some overland trade to the new sea routes to the Far East; (2) overextension of the administrative capacity of the empire at the expense of settled agriculture; (3) the quest for new revenues in order to undertake military modernization that resulted in the assignation of land and tax-farming rights of a quasi-hereditary nature; and (4) the consolidation of a rural notability engaged in commercial agriculture for export. The privatization of the state's domain that we usually associate with direct colonial rule was well under way before European powers carved up the Middle East.

If we then look at the class "products" of this historical process, we find a relatively undifferentiated peasantry whose surplus was coveted by both the state and the armed nomadic tribes, urban merchants engaged in both overland and internal trade, urban artisans who produced for upper-income urban consumers as well as for peasants and tribesmen, and the legal experts of Islam, the *ulema* (plural of *'ālim,* "one who knows"). The *ulema,* along with the soldiers and the bureaucrats of the state, constituted class actors of a sort, but actors who did not necessarily own or directly control property or means of production. Rather, in the name of the state and of Islam, they exercised the authority and, frequently, the naked power to dispose of property and productive means.

DEFENSIVE MODERNIZATION AND COLONIAL TRANSFORMATION

There is no denying that the mid- and late nineteenth century is a watershed in state and class formation in the Middle East. Although processes of monetization, commercialization, and privatization may be discerned prior to that period, they accelerated markedly thereafter as the increasingly mature industrial societies of Europe contended for geopolitical and economic advantage in the Middle East.

The military threat posed by those societies, as well as by czarist Russia, had been clear for some time, and Ottoman sultans and their governors had begun to transform their military establishments along European lines. Large standing armies, modern industries for manufacturing artillery pieces and firearms, and road and railroad construction to facilitate the movement of troops and goods all required expenditures by the state on an unprecedented scale. The search for revenue led Middle Eastern states into new domestic taxation devices and into external debt to European banks.

By midcentury a so-called reform program (the Tanzimat) was under way throughout the Ottoman Empire and was echoed in Qajar Iran and in Morocco (the *nizam al-jadid,* or new order). The general tendency was to develop the legal infrastructure of private property; the European creditors of the empire argued that stable title to land and wealth would increase productive activity and hence the sultan's tax base. In Egypt the *khedive,* or Ottoman governor, granted private title to land to anyone who paid five years of agricultural tax in advance. In addition, the collection of taxes in cash became the norm, forcing cultivators into commercial agriculture in order to acquit their obligations. The process was not at all smooth; the Ottoman bey of Tunis in 1857 introduced a head tax in cash (the *majba*), which led to a rural revolt in 1864. The tax, which had produced 50% of the beylical state's revenues, was rescinded, and Tunis then borrowed its way into an unmanageable external debt (Anderson 1986).

The development efforts of the Middle Eastern state thus had as a direct consequence the promotion, if not the creation, of new propertied interests. The growth of a rural notability through trade and tax-farming was visible everywhere. As land became alienable, it could serve as collateral against loans. This change brought investment into agriculture and began, in parts of the Ottoman Empire, to attract foreign capital to export agriculture. Middlemen proliferated: private moneylenders, real estate banks, buyers and brokers for export crops. Frequently the middlemen were foreigners or from religious minorities that were not subject to Islamic strictures on interest: hence the prominence of Greeks, Armenians, Jews, and Coptic Christians. Increasingly, they linked the new squirearchy of commercial agriculture to foreign markets. The squirearchy itself was mainly indigenous, but we should remember that in Algeria, after the French conquest of 1830, Europeans owned the best lands and dominated the export of wine to France.

Again, in the effort to stabilize rural revenue sources, the state encouraged tribal and nomadic chieftains to settle by granting them title to what had been quasi-communal lands, while state officials, high-ranking military figures, members of the ruling family or dynasty (such as the Qajar aristocracy in Iran or the dynasty of Muhammed 'Ali in Egypt), and even "aristocratic" urban families such as those of the city of Hama in Syria established private title to what became veritable latifundia (Iraq, Iran, parts of Syria, and eastern Anatolia were particularly affected).

Similar processes were at work in the cities. The public bureaucratic function increased in importance, as did the bureaucrats themselves; the military establishment became more elaborate; and a new merchant bourgeoisie, overlapping substantially with the agents of commercial agriculture and just as frequently foreign, took root (see Figure 2.5). The point we wish to stress in all this—one that informs all of our analysis—is that the state authorities can initiate broad-gauged policies in fairly unfettered fashion. Moreover, in the pursuit of specific goals, those authorities will stimulate processes of economic change whose consequences in the creation of new economic actors and class strata are as momentous as they are unanticipated.

In the late nineteenth and early twentieth centuries, Islamic states collapsed in the face of European imperialism. All of the Middle East except Turkey, Iran, and the Arabian Peninsula fell under European rule. The colonial states that were implanted were truly autonomous from the societies they governed. With modern military technology (aircraft, among other things) and administrative practices, they completed the subjugation of territories and peoples that the sultans had begun. Private property, the cash economy, and the tax collector advanced together. The colonial state added two new and vital elements: public education for a limited number of natives and the promotion of a professional civil service. The norms underlying these elements, norms that we now call Weberian, were those of achieved status, that is, position won on the basis of training and competency regardless of factors of birth, blood, or income. Even though Turkey and Iran escaped direct European control, their leaders attempted, more successfully in Turkey than in Iran, to apply these standards to their own bureaucracies.

The colonial state was in general expected by the metropole to be financially self-sufficient. A modern civil service was necessary to manage roads, railroads, ports, and power, to run the mail and telegraph services, to identify and tax the population, to staff all echelons of local administration, and to assume all the intermediate positions between the colonial authorities and the population for which mastery of the colonial and the native languages was essential. By the 1930s one finds a new protoclass asserting itself. It was educated, white-collar, and salaried. Its status was dependent

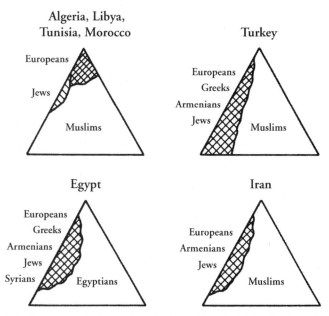

FIGURE 2.5 European and minority shares in the wealth of the Middle East before World War II. *Source:* Charles Issawi, *An Economic History of the Middle East and North Africa,* New York, Columbia University Press, 1983, p. 9. Copyright © 1982 Janina Issau; used by permission.

not on its ownership of private property—of which it might possess very little—but on its professional attainment. It was bourgeois in aspirations and lifestyle. It was in embryo what Halpern (1963) was later to call "the new middle class."

The major achievement of the colonial state in interest formation consisted in consolidating the position of landowners and in midwifing the birth of the new middle class. The postcolonial state in the Middle East has gone much further than either the Islamic or the colonial state in redrafting the class map of the region. Few postcolonial states had, to begin with, or maintained for long, strong links to wealthy classes in their societies. Syria and Iraq up to 1958, Lebanon, and Morocco were the only major exceptions. The more autonomous states—Turkey, Iran, Egypt, Algeria, and Syria, and Iraq after 1958—engaged in far-reaching class engineering. The latifundists mentioned earlier were undermined by agrarian reform, and the merchant bourgeoisie was hemmed in by state regulations, price controls, public trade monopolies, and nationalizations. Foreign and minoritarian commercial groups faced systematic discrimination.

By contrast, varying combinations of agrarian reform and ISI bolstered the ranks of small landowners, left small-scale capitalist farmers at the top of the rural hierarchy, and led to rapid growth in the new middle class through mass education and bureaucratic expansion. Meanwhile, the creation and absorption into the public sector of important productive, commercial, and banking assets spawned a new managerial state bourgeoisie.

Two or three decades of state-led growth had brought to a halt or significantly slowed the process of privatization that had begun in the early nineteenth century. But the regional oil shocks of the 1970s, coupled with the inefficiencies of state-led ISI, opened up the possibility of a new era of privatization in the 1980s. ISI had tremendous spin-off effects in subcontracting to existing private sectors that weathered the hostile socialist or simply anticapitalist (as in Pahlavi Iran) programs of the state managers. Drawing on state business and credit from public banks and sheltered behind tariff walls put up to protect the public sector, these private sectors found themselves positioned to respond to a growing mood among public authorities that efficiency would have to take precedence over redistribution if their national economies were to survive. Thus, we are witnessing the gradual reduction of the autonomy of the state and its recapture by economic interests that the state had itself created.

Turkey serves as bellwether for the region in this process. It is one generation in advance over all its neighbors in the Middle East, having begun in economic policy and state building in the 1920s what most other countries would not attempt before the 1950s. It now contains a powerful and highly differentiated entrepreneurial bourgeoisie with a well-organized industrial segment. This bourgeoisie developed virtually ex nihilo after 1920. The war for national liberation led by Kemal Atatürk resulted in the mass repatriation to Greece of the most experienced entrepreneurs that Anatolia and Istanbul could offer. During forty years of state-led growth, the infant indigenous bourgeoisie acquired skills and capital and may now be ready, if the international economy remains hospitable, to consolidate Turkey in the ranks of the NICs and to make the Turkish state responsive to its needs.

CONCLUSION

The three variables that undergird our analysis—economic growth patterns, state structures and policies, and social actors—will be treated sequentially in the following chapters. One should not lose sight of the fact that they interact simultaneously and that the sequence in which we approach them implies neither an order of importance nor a line of causality. The next four chapters (3–6) do, however, lay out a broad contextual framework for understanding the rapid social and economic change that has characterized the region over the past one hundred years. They are a necessary starting point for a full consideration of state and class. We begin with a fuller presentation of our understanding of economic growth and structural change.

NOTES

1. Such omissions can make a major difference. Dasgupta (2001b) shows how, with even a modest accounting for wasting natural assets, growth rates become negative in most Asian countries for the period 1980–2000.

2. The Gulf States include Saudi Arabia, Kuwait, Bahrain, Qatar, Oman, and the United Arab Emirates.

3. The free-rider problem arises when an actor cannot be excluded from the benefits of collective action. Consequently, he or she may shirk or fail to participate—and still reap the benefits; he or she gets a "free ride" on the efforts of others. See the classic treatment by Olson (1965) and the more nuanced analysis of Axelrod (1984) or Ostrom (1990).

3

ECONOMIC GROWTH AND STRUCTURAL CHANGE

The political economy of the Middle East is dominated by three simple facts: little rain, much oil, and increasingly many (and therefore young) people. Most of the Middle East lies in the arid zone of the Eastern Hemisphere, a zone that stretches from Morocco to Mongolia. Much of the region receives less than twenty inches of rain per year, an amount that makes unirrigated agriculture extremely risky. Precipitation is also highly variable not only from year to year but also seasonally. Most of the region experiences distinct wet and dry periods. Even within the rainy season, precipitation is often quite irregular. Annual precipitation figures are often deceptive, since much rain may fall in a short space of time. For example, during 1985–1986, rainfall in Tunisia was 150% above normal in March, but little rain fell during the crucial planting months of October to December. With the exception of some highland (e.g., Yemen) and coastal (e.g., the Caspian Sea region of Iran) areas, the Middle East lacks the relatively heavy and reliable rainfall of the Asian monsoons, and long, devastating droughts have occurred throughout the region's history.

Only irrigated lands could support a dense population in preindustrial times. Such areas were sharply limited: the Nile Valley of Egypt, parts of the Tigris-Euphrates Valley, and other, more localized areas. All of these irrigation systems underwent extensive changes in their long histories, expanding with stability and peace, contracting with upheaval, war, and mismanagement. Irrigation networks have faced important ecological constraints, such as increasing salinity (Hodgson 1974, 389–391), and have also created international political problems, since most of the major rivers of the region cross national boundaries. The difficult agro-ecology has contributed to the large and growing gap between consumption and domestic production of food in the region, a gap that drives much of the political economy of agriculture (see Chapter 6).

MENA covers about 11–12% of the world's land area[1] (an area about one-third larger than the United States) and contains roughly 7% of the world's population. Its overall population density is about 32 persons per square kilometer, roughly the same as the United States. The region is much less densely populated than India (369 per square kilometer) or China (140 per square kilometer) but more densely populated than Latin America (27 per square kilometer) (CIA 2006).

The density figure for MENA masks a stark reality, however. Because of the region's aridity, only about 7% of the area is cultivated. There are approximately 452 Middle Easterners for every square kilometer of arable land. The most striking case is Egypt. The country's area is roughly 1 million square kilometers, an area about the size of France and Spain combined, but nearly the entire population of roughly 80 million (2006) lives in the approximately 38,850 square kilometers of the Nile River Valley and its delta. The resulting population density of about 2,060 persons per square kilometer is comparable to that of Java and parts of India and China.

The total population of the countries in the MENA region is approximately 443 million (2004), or roughly 8% of the population of developing countries. However, there are more than two Middle Easterners for every five citizens of all of the industrialized market economies. Middle Easterners are more numerous than US citizens and only slightly less numerous than the population of the European Union (457 million). Because of the ecological features of the region, no country supports the huge populations of monsoon Asia. The region contains three countries (Turkey, Iran, and Egypt) with populations exceeding 65 million (comparable to Italy, France, or the UK), but it also contains eleven countries with populations less than 10 million (the population of greater New York City) and four more (Morocco, Iraq, Saudi Arabia, and Yemen) with populations less than 36 million, the population of California (Table 3.1).

There are now more than four times as many Middle Easterners and North Africans as there were in the late 1950s. The region's population is growing at about 2.2% per year, which means that it will double in about thirty-two years. Within just three generations (of twenty years each) the region's population will have increased *twelvefold*. The current number of Cairo residents (approaching 15 million) exceeds the total population of Egypt in 1919 (12–13 million). Of major world regions, only the population of sub-Saharan Africa is growing more rapidly. The rate of growth is now higher than it was in the early 1950s (although it is falling—see Chapter 4). Because of this rapid rate of population growth, most people in the region are under twenty years old.

A large and growing percentage of these people live in cities. Although different countries use different criteria for defining a "city," which makes cross-country comparisons notoriously unreliable, at least 60% of the inhabitants of MENA live in urban areas, with, again, wide variations among countries. Cities were always central to the preindustrial and precolonial social formations in the region. This importance has steadily increased; the region now has more than sixteen cities with more than 1 million inhabitants (see Chapter 10).

The region also displays great diversity in per capita income (see Figure 3.1). Indeed, it has more variation in per capita income than any other major region, as it includes wealthy countries such as Israel and the UAE as well as extremely poor countries like the Sudan and Yemen. This diversity has had important political implications.

TABLE 3.1   Population, GDP per Capita, 2004, and Average Annual GDP per Capita Growth
Rate, 1992–2004

	2004 Population, (millions)	GDP per Capita	
		2004 (constant 2000 US$)	1992–2004 Growth Rate (annual %)
Algeria	32.4	1982	1.1
Bahrain	0.7	13852	2.5
Egypt	72.6	1615	2.5
Iran	67.0	1885	2.5
Iraq	–	–	–
Israel	6.8	17788	1.5
Jordan	5.4	1940	2.2
Kuwait	2.5	17674	–0.8*
Lebanon	3.5	5606	2.3
Libya	5.7	7397	1.5*
Morocco	29.8	1349	1.2
Oman	2.5	8961	1.9
Qatar	0.8	–	–
Saudi Arabia	24.0	8974	–0.2
Sudan	35.5	434	3.4
Syria	18.6	1115	1.6
Tunisia	9.9	2336	3.3
Turkey	71.7	3197	2.2
UAE	4.3	22173	–0.8
WBG	3.5	–	–6.4*
Yemen	20.3	534	1.5
United States	293.7	36655	2.1

*Comments on GDP per Capita Growth Rate: Kuwait 1996–2004; Libya 1999–2004; West Bank
and Gaza 1995–2004.
SOURCE: WDI Online 2006

THE NATURAL RESOURCE BASE

The region is not particularly rich in nonhydrocarbon mineral resources. A wide
variety of minerals are exploited,[2] but with the exception of Algeria (mercury) and
Morocco (phosphate rock), no country's output amounts to even 5% of world production. Most minerals are found in the mountainous areas of North Africa, Turkey,
and Iran. Morocco and the Western Sahara hold over two-thirds of the world's phosphate deposits; Morocco is the third-largest producer, after the United States and the
former Soviet Union. Algeria is the region's leading iron-ore producer (ranking only

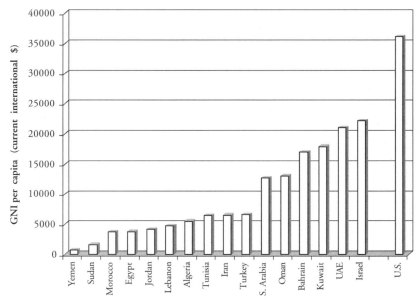

FIGURE 3.1 GNI per capita, selected MENA countries, 2002
SOURCE: World Development Indicators Online, 2006

twentieth in the world), and Turkish production is about 20% less than Algerian. Only Turkey has significant coal deposits. The 1980s saw considerable exploration efforts and significant new finds. For example, Libya, Egypt, Saudi Arabia, and Algeria all discovered new iron-ore deposits, and Saudi Arabia discovered gold and coal. Many of these new deposits were found in remote and isolated areas, which raises the cost of exploiting them (Blake, Dewdney, and Mitchell 1987).

All of this is in marked contrast to the region's hydrocarbon resources. The region has about two-thirds of the world's oil. The usual measure of available oil is "reserves," classified as "proved," "probable," "possible," or "speculative." In 2004 the region held nearly 70% of the world's proved reserves (see Table 3.2), nearly all of which was in the Persian Gulf (OPEC 2005). Over half (about 57%) of all oil reserves are in the Gulf, while Saudi Arabia alone has about one-quarter of all the oil on the planet; its reserves are more than twelve times those of the United States. Discovery apparently exceeded production for the first twenty years of OPEC dominance (which began in 1973), despite the rapid exploitation of those reserves. For example, Saudi discoveries from 1972 to 1992 exceeded the cumulative production of those heady years by some 230% (OPEC 1993). However, there have been very few additions to reserves since then; Saudi reserves in 2004 (264.4 billion barrels) were apparently only slightly higher than in 1993 (261.4 billion barrels).

We say "apparently" because the data on "proved reserves" must be treated with caution. The concept is defined as "reserves recoverable with present technology

TABLE 3.2   Oil Reserves, 1980 and 2004

	Reserves (Millions of Barrels)		% of World Reserves	
	1980	2004	1980	2004
North America	36610.5	26191.0	5.7	2.3
United States	29805.0	21891.0	4.6	1.9
Latin America	74032.5	118952.2	11.4	10.4
Eastern Europe	65800.0	91467.5	10.2	8
Western Europe	22761.0	17391.6	3.5	1.5
MENA	394320.0	793311.6	69.9	69.3
Asia and Pacific	33305.0	39229.7	5.1	3.4
World	647887.2	1144013.1		

SOURCE: OPEC Annual Statistical Bulletin; Online: http://www.opec.org/library/Annual%20
Statistical%20Bulletin/interactive/2004/FileZ/Main.htm

and prices" (*Oil and Gas Journal,* December 28, 1988). Higher oil prices could, in theory, mean higher oil reserves for three reasons: (1) higher prices should induce further exploration and discovery of new fields; (2) higher prices should stimulate improvements in the technology of recovery from existing fields; and (3) for existing wells, with existing technology, higher prices should make some additional oil recoverable. Because oil prices have such a large rent element, the last argument is not particularly apposite, particularly for MENA. The first point will apply only if sovereign states encourage such exploration and development; some observers think that the Gulf countries did little of this during the 1990s, when, as we shall see, oil prices were quite low. Although there have been dramatic improvements in oil recovery technology, these also seem relatively independent of output price changes.

A more serious problem with the concept of proved reserves is that some countries have been quite secretive about the numbers they release. In 1987 four OPEC countries (Venezuela, the UAE, Iran, and Iraq) released data that showed that total world proved reserves had increased by roughly 27%. The new estimate may have been credible for Venezuela, where extensive surveys of the Orinoco basin revealed very large amounts of heavy oil. The increases in Iran (90%) and Iraq (112%) were very startling, however. Could these two countries, then locked in a desperate military struggle, really have devoted the resources to exploration that would have led to such finds? If they had known that they had such oil before the war began (1980), why did they wait until 1987 to announce it to the world? A leading trade publication, *Oil and Gas Journal,* rather gingerly pointed out that these numbers might reflect a belief on the part of the issuing governments that oil production quotas within the Organization of Petroleum Exporting Countries (OPEC) would be allocated on the basis of "proved reserves" (December 27, 1987, 33–34). Some observers (e.g., Campbell and Laherere, 1998) believe that some countries, such as Saudi Arabia, report "total discovered" reserves, instead of "remaining reserves," for similar political reasons. Given these political realities, one should use considerable caution when interpreting data on petroleum reserves.

Nevertheless, the geographical concentration of petroleum deposits in the Middle East is indisputable. Several other geological facts are relevant to the political economy of oil. First, much of the world's proved reserves come from thirty-three "supergiant" fields (reserves estimated at greater than 5 billion barrels); of these, twenty-eight are in the Middle East, including nine of the ten largest fields. The largest, the Ghawar field in Saudi Arabia, contains an estimated 60 billion barrels of oil, more than twice the reserves of the *entire* United States, which amount to about 21.9 billion barrels (OPEC 2004). Oil reserves are concentrated within the region. Four countries (Saudi Arabia, Iraq, Iran, and Kuwait) have about 75% of the region's oil reserves and about 55% of all the oil in the world.

The size of these reserves implies that events in the region will always be critical to the international oil market. It is common (although of dubious interest) to point out how long countries' reserves will last at current production rates. The data for 2005 in Figure 3.2 are significant for showing the "time horizons" of national governments, a feature that is important for understanding various regional governments' differences over pricing strategies within OPEC. Other things being equal, countries whose oil will last a long time have little interest in large price increases, since these will induce more conservation and discovery of new sources of supply. The numbers are only illustrative, however. Production varies, estimates of reserves change, and patterns of resource use shift dramatically if consumers are given enough time (say, ten to twenty years) to adjust. The differences among countries are dramatic: Kuwait and the UAE can go on exploiting oil for a century, whereas Algeria's official reserves will last for about a generation at the current (2006) rate of production.

More important from an economic point of view, Gulf oil is the cheapest oil in the world to produce. The estimated current cost of production of a barrel of Saudi, Kuwaiti, Iraqi, or Iranian Gulf oil is about US$1.50 per barrel. By comparison, non-OPEC production costs are typically around US$6 per barrel. which is also the range of production costs for most other regions of the world (ExxonMobil 2005). These low production costs are the key to the massive transfer of economic rents to the oil states, rents that fueled economic expansion and change throughout the region.

There is currently a raging debate about whether world oil production will (or has already) reach its maximum. This "peak oil" debate pits pessimists (who are usually geologists) against optimists, who are often economists. All agree, of course, that oil is a depletable natural resource. All agree that at some point in time, oil production will peak. But there is no agreement about the imminence of that date. "Peak oil" advocates, such as Campbell and Laherere (1998), argue that the "Hubbert's Peak" hypothesis of M. King Hubbert, who in 1956 correctly predicted the coming decline of US oil production, applies to the world as a whole. They argue that (1) most of major oil fields have already been discovered; (2) discoveries peaked in the 1960s and have declined every decade since then; and (3) although technology has increased recovery rates, there are physical limits to how high these rates can

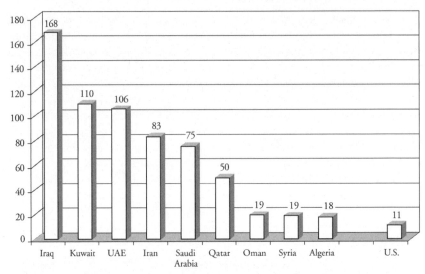

FIGURE 3.2   Approximate years of remaining oil production, 2005
SOURCE: Calculated from EIA World Proven Crude Oil Reserves data for 2007 and EIA World Crude Oil Production data for 2006 at http://www.eia.doe.gov

go. Saudi officials admitted in 2004 at a conference in Houston that the Ghawar oil field, the largest ever discovered, was more than half depleted (Roberts 2004). The optimists, such as the doyen of petroleum economists, Maurice Adelman of M.I.T., argue that every previous prediction of oil depletion has been proved false. They stress the economic (and in some cases, political) barriers to investment in exploration, discovery, and recovery during the period of very low oil prices in the 1990s and argue that today's higher prices will stimulate a supply response.

Only time will settle this dispute. It is also important to note that the consequences of the world's increasing use of fossil fuels, with its attendant impacts on global climate change, will likely shape the demand for—and therefore the price of—oil in the near future. Of course, such changes will occur only if the policies of major oil-consuming countries change to accommodate these serious climatological realities. At this writing, there is little evidence that such changes are underway, particularly in the United States. Many scientists think that the negative consequences of such negligent behavior will dwarf the "peak oil" controversy (IPCC 2002). For good or ill, however, oil from the Middle East will continue to be central to the world's energy economy for several decades to come.

OIL SUPPLY, DEMAND, AND ECONOMIC RENTS

Economic rents from oil production in the Middle East are huge.[3] If the opportunity cost of producing a barrel of Saudi Arabian light crude oil is approximately

US$1.50 and the price of that barrel on international markets is approximately US$60.00 a barrel, the economic rent is US$58.50. Even in December 1998, when real oil prices were at their post-1973 nadir of US$10.81 per barrel, over four-fifths of the price was economic rent. Oil revenues of the Gulf States overwhelmingly consist of rent on a depletable natural resource.

The minimum price is given by the cost of production, but what determines the maximum price? In theory, the "price ceiling" is determined by the cost of production of the closest available substitute, often called the "backstop technology." Because crude oil has so many different uses, this price ceiling varies with the crude oil's intended use. These price ceilings decline with time and are themselves partly a function of price. We would expect that if the price of crude oil approaches the rent ceiling and if entrepreneurs believe that this price will persist, there will be more research and development into alternative technologies. Such activity should lower the cost of these technologies, pushing down the rent ceiling. By the mid-1990s, a common estimate of the rent ceiling was about US$25 per barrel (World Bank 1995a). Events since 1998 have shown the weaknesses of such estimates.

Of course, the *actual* price of crude oil is determined by supply and demand. The course of these prices is shown in Figure 3.3. Small libraries have been written on why prices rose and fell; we will sketch only the main elements of an explanation.[4]

Demand-side forces played a crucial role both in pushing prices to unprecedented heights in the 1970s, in dragging them down and keeping them low in the late 1980s and the 1990s, and then pushing them up again since 1998. In the 1950s and 1960s, the relative price of oil was both low and declining; the major industrialized countries increasingly switched from energy sources such as coal to oil. In 1950, oil accounted for 40% of US energy use, 14% of Western Europe's, and 5% of Japan's; by 1973, those shares (of a vastly larger total) had risen to 47%, 60%, and 76%, respectively (Stobaugh and Yergin 1979). For both Western Europe and Japan, such a switch increased dependence on imports, especially imports from the Middle East. For the Japanese, with no oil and little coal, there was (and is) little alternative to such imports. Even today, about 50% of Japanese energy comes from oil, all of which is imported and over 85% of which comes from the Middle East. Western European dependence on Middle Eastern oil also increased during the 1950s and 1960s as conservative governments sought greater independence from striking coal miners and as social democrats tried to improve environmental quality. All were drawn to the lower direct cost of oil.

The US dependence on oil imports increased steadily. Domestic oil producers persuaded the US government to restrict imports of (much cheaper) foreign oil in 1958. Until the mid-1960s, the United States retained considerable surplus capacity, which made the country (and its friends) considerably less vulnerable to threats of embargoes or to sudden price shocks. This was an unintended outcome of the system to protect domestic producers—the so-called pro-rationing system, whereby state agencies regulated and reduced oil production. In the late 1960s and early 1970s, however, the growth of demand for energy outpaced the expansion of domestic energy supplies. Price controls inhibited the development of natural gas, and

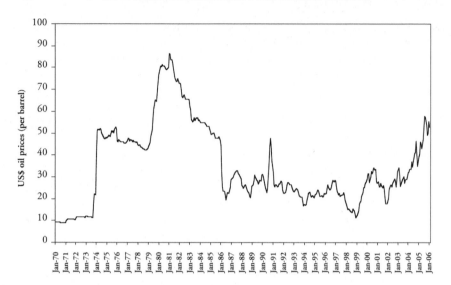

FIGURE 3.3   Crude oil prices, 1970–2006 (2004 $US per barrel)
SOURCE: Energy Information Administration (EIA), 2005, http://www.eia.doe.gov

little new oil that was competitive at current prices was discovered. By 1973 the United States had no spare capacity; indeed, domestic oil production fell at a rate of 3% per year from 1970 to 1973 (Schneider 1983, 195). Oil imports, including Middle Eastern oil, supplied a steadily increasing percentage of US energy needs, reaching 38% by 1974.

~On the supply side, there were two interrelated dynamics; cash and control (Rustow and Mugno 1976). "Cash" refers to producing countries' attempts to get a higher percentage of the oil rents; the contest for "control" was between the nation-states and the oil companies. One might say that the history of the oil business has been that of repeated attempts to create a cartel followed by the erosion and demise of that cartel. The eight major international oil companies[5] had managed by 1953 to control 95% of non-US noncommunist reserves, 90% of production, 75% of refining capacity, and 74% of product sales (Blair 1976). Interrelations among these companies were extensive, long-term (e.g., twenty-year) supply contracts, with joint ventures being the most prominent mechanisms. Perhaps the high-water mark of the oil company cartel's control of world oil came in 1953, when the cartel countered Mohammed Mossadegh's nationalization of British Petroleum's (BP's) Iranian oil facilities by simply refusing to refine or market Iranian oil. When Mossadegh was overthrown and the Pahlavi shah reinstated, another joint venture was established in which nearly all of the major oil companies were represented.

Even with the low prices of the 1950s and 1960s, costs of production were so low and demand was growing so steadily that there were numerous incentives for "independent," or smaller, oil companies to enter the market and attempt to wrest a piece of it away from the "majors." Such developments were actively encouraged by governments of some European countries, especially Italy. Some Middle Eastern countries—most important, Libya under King Idris—had the wisdom to cede oil concessions to a wide variety of oil companies, especially independents. This had major consequences for developments in the early 1970s.

In one of the ironies so typical of the region, the crushing Israeli defeat of Arab armies in 1967 set the stage for the explosion of oil prices that triggered the flood of rent into the region. The war closed the Suez Canal, requiring Gulf crude to be transported around the Cape of Good Hope, a journey that both raised the cost and provoked a tanker shortage. Western European nations increased their reliance on cheaper oil from west of Suez and from Libya in particular.[6] Libyan oil also had a lower sulfur content and was therefore favored on environmental grounds. The new government of Mu'ammar Qaddhafi (who took power in 1969) immediately de-manded an increase in the "posted price" of oil.[7] Although the larger oil companies refused, the independent oil companies were more vulnerable to pressure. Libya prevailed through a classic divide-and-rule policy. Its success prompted the Gulf producers to follow suit, and nominal oil prices began to rise.[8]

The October War of 1973 completed the shift of both cash and control from consumers and companies to producing governments. The decision of the Nixon ad-ministration first to resupply the Israelis (October 13) and then to give them US$2.2 billion of military assistance (October 19) prompted the Saudi embargo of the United States and the Netherlands on October 20. Oil companies cushioned the im-pact of this embargo on those two countries by reallocating world supply. However, the embargo created an atmosphere of panic buying on the spot (or open) market; the shah of Iran in particular took the opportunity to hold an auction in order to see what price his oil might fetch. The answer was between US$9.00 and US$17.34 per barrel (Schneider 1983, 236), while the Rotterdam spot price hit US$26.00 per bar-rel (Danielson 1982, 172).

The final price that OPEC agreed to charge customers on the "marker crude"[9] was US$11.65, a price negotiated between the "price doves," led by Saudi Arabia, and the "price hawks," led by Iran. This was to be expected, given the huge gap be-tween the cost of production and the rent ceiling, on the one hand, and the very low short-run elasticity of demand for oil, on the other. With nearly all excess capacity inside the OPEC countries and with few short-run alternatives, consuming countries had little choice in the short run but to pay whatever price OPEC demanded.

The resulting transfer of resources was massive.[10] The dramatically higher pay-ments for oil contributed to the phenomenon of "stagflation" (recession combined with inflation) in the developed world. Inflation, in turn, slowly eroded the real gains of 1974, while recession weakened demand; real oil prices in 1978 were slightly be-low those of 1974. Europe and Japan responded to the change not only by passing on prices to their consumers but also by increasing tax rates on oil and by fostering the development of alternative energy supplies (e.g., North Sea oil and gas and nu-clear power). However, the world's largest consumer, the United States, dithered. US imports of OPEC oil continued to grow from 38% of total consumption in 1974 to 47% in 1979. OPEC's market share dropped only slightly, from about 66% of non-communist oil production in 1974 to about 62% in 1978. The stage was set for the second oil shock of 1979.

Political events again opened the next act in the oil-price drama. The Iranian revolution removed about 2 million barrels a day from production; although the Saudis at first tried to make up the shortfall, they had already been producing close to capacity in an attempt to restrain further price increases, which they (reasonably) believed were not in their medium- and long-term economic interest. However, the conclusion of the Camp David Accords, with their neglect of the Palestinian issue, angered the Saudis considerably. In response, they actually *reduced* production in the immediate aftermath of Camp David, setting the stage for another round of panic buying on the spot market (Quandt 1981). The resulting record-breaking market price helped the OPEC hawks to carry the day, and the OPEC reference price leapt first to US$17.26 in 1979 and then to US$28.67 in 1980.

The resulting price hike was lower in proportional terms than that of 1973–1974 but considerably greater in absolute dollar value. The increase in revenues was prodigious.[11] Governments launched even more massive development projects than before. Never had so much been paid by so many to so few; never before in human history had such an enormous amount of wealth been transferred in such a short amount of time to governments with such (typically) small populations.[12] As we shall see, however, the wealth was shared widely, albeit indirectly, in the Middle East and North Africa through labor migration (Chapter 15).

But booms do not last forever. Although it was not immediately apparent, OPEC overreached itself in 1979–1981. For some uses, petroleum prices now exceeded the rent ceiling. Conserving energy became very profitable, especially once the United States decontrolled petroleum prices. OPEC soon fell afoul of both the "external" and the "internal" cartel problem. The external problem refers to the simple fact that if prices are very high, consumers and producers have incentives to change their behavior. The demand for oil is a derived demand; we want oil not for its own sake but because we want to move around, heat our homes, light our lamps, and so forth. With high oil prices, consumers had every incentive to find ways of using less oil to accomplish these ends and also (during the recession of the early 1980s) to make do with less transportation, heating, and electricity. In short, conservation was greatly stimulated. By the late 1980s, the industrial countries were using less than 70% as much oil per unit of output as they had been in 1973 (see Figure 3.4). Non-OPEC producers compounded the external cartel problem. Such producers had strong incentives, often reinforced by consuming governments, to seek, find, and exploit new sources of petroleum and alternative energy sources. Alaskan, North Sea, and Mexican oil became especially important new sources of oil, and OPEC's market share of world oil production fell from 48.8% in 1979 to 28.7% in 1985 (OPEC 1993; see also Figure 3.5).

These developments aggravated the internal cartel problem—that is, it was in the interests of cartel members to cheat on production quotas. Actually, OPEC

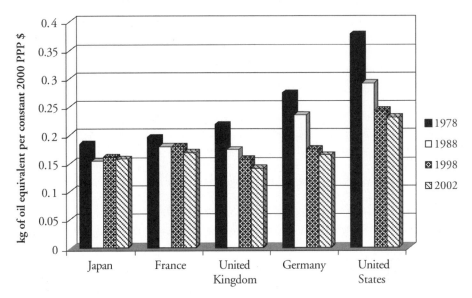

FIGURE 3.4   Energy use per PPP GDP (kg of oil equivalent per 2000 PPP $), 1978–2002
SOURCE: World Development Indicators Online, 2006

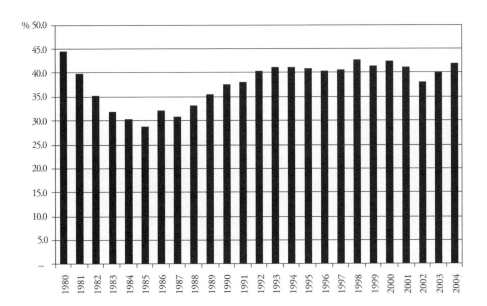

FIGURE 3.5   OPEC share of crude oil production, 1980–2004
SOURCE: OPEC 2004 Annual Statistical Bulletin

lacked formal production quotas until 1982, and quotas have often been openly ignored (e.g., by Iraq before 1991 and by Iran). In practice, just as OPEC was the "residual supplier" to the world market, Saudi Arabia was the "residual supplier" within OPEC. Only the Saudis could play this role: They could vary their production from a low of just above 2 million barrels per day (2.2 in August 1985) to a high of nearly 10 million barrels per day. (By way of comparison, their *low* figure exceeds the current production figure of any other Middle Eastern producer.) The Saudis had long demanded that other oil producers agree to production quotas and had consistently argued that the post-1979 prices were too high. They remonstrated vainly in OPEC councils: Quota agreements, first established in March 1982, were violated almost as soon as they were drafted. The Saudis saw their own market share steadily erode from 21% in 1980 to 8.5% in 1985 (*Oil and Gas Journal,* December 27, 1987). With the decline in market share, Saudi government revenues declined, yet it had made extensive commitments to development expenditures and projects. Saudi spending began to exceed revenues in 1983.

The Saudis' patience was finally exhausted. In July and August 1986 they opened the taps, producing about 6 million barrels per day; in late August they were producing at a rate of about 7 million barrels per day (*Oil and Gas Journal,* December 30, 1986, 65). Prices collapsed, falling to under US$10 in late summer of 1986. By this action, the Saudis sent messages to fellow OPEC members ("Quit cheating! We can take losses better than you can!"), to non-OPEC producers ("Let's make a deal; your production costs are much higher than ours"), and to investors in conservation technology ("We can push the price down and drive you out of business!").[13] Only the last message seems to have been heard. Although OPEC tried to fix production quotas, enforcement mechanisms were weak and cheating remained rife. Britain refused to cooperate with OPEC, and prices rebounded to around US$18 per barrel and hovered there until the end of the 1980s.

The Iraqi invasion of Kuwait further weakened OPEC and strengthened the hands of both OECD consumers and Saudi producers. Although there was sufficient excess capacity to roughly match the increase in lost production from occupied Kuwait and embargoed Iraq, prices doubled in two months as fear gripped oil markets. The rapid defeat of Iraqi forces in Operation Desert Storm and the increase in production from elsewhere (especially Saudi Arabia) swiftly brought prices back to their prewar levels. In the early 1990s prices continued to hover around US$18 per barrel in nominal terms. A key impact of the Gulf War of 1991 was the final demise of even the pretense of Saudi Arabia acting as a "swing producer." From that time forward, the Saudis have sought to maximize their revenue by producing close to capacity, taking full advantage of the absence of Iraq from oil markets.

As Figure 3.3 shows, oil prices reached their post-1973 nadir in 1998 (US$10.81 in December) and have shot up since then. The forces explaining these changes can be divided into underlying structural forces and the power of traders' expectations. Structurally, on the demand side, the apparently insatiable thirst for oil from the developing countries of Asia has steadily shifted the demand function for oil. As the Chinese and Indian economies have boomed, oil consumption has grown in tandem. Chinese oil consumption rose from some 2 million barrels per day in 1990 to more than 7 million barrels per day in 2006. Indian consumption roughly doubled during the same period. In the United States, low oil prices, combined with the lack of government policies supporting conservation, spurred demand for ever larger, more fuel-intensive cars, particularly the notorious gas-guzzling SUVs. Because US energy production had stagnated during the 1990s, imports supplied a steadily growing percentage of consumption. On the supply side, the alarm prompted in the region by the extremely low prices of the late 1990s prompted the two largest Gulf producers, Saudi Arabia and Iran, to settle their differences and coordinate their oil policies. OPEC cut production by 1.5 million barrels per day, or about 5.4%, from 1998 to 1999. OPEC discipline continued through 2002. Such coordination was naturally greatly assisted by the steadily growing demand from Asia and elsewhere.

The surge in oil prices after 2002 very likely has a different explanation, however. One must always remember that the price of oil is an asset price. Because oil can be stored (in the ground or in warehouses), its price, like the price of real estate, depends on market agents' forecasts about the future. This insight has been fundamental to the economic analysis of oil ever since the seminal work of Harold Hotelling (1931). For oil, political violence, actual or feared, drives expectations. The dramatic increase in the price of oil since 2003, while partially explained by the underlying structural forces sketched in the preceding paragraph, was also driven by the perception of growing instability in the Gulf, thanks to the US invasion and occupation of Iraq and the crisis between the United States and Iran over Iran's nuclear development. Real oil prices in the spring of 2006 exceeded those immediately following the first oil shock of 1973.

Have we, then, gone "back to the future"? No one knows. Blindfolded chimpanzees throwing darts at random number tables have done about as well as economists in forecasting future oil prices. All that can be said with certainty is that the demand for oil is likely to continue to rise, that the Gulf continues to have the world's largest reserves and the lowest production costs, and that political crises driven by the social and economic forces described in this book seem likely to persist for some time. Consequently, few doubt that Middle Eastern producers, and especially Saudi Arabia, will continue to play a major role in determining the future path of oil prices.

PATTERNS OF ECONOMIC GROWTH

Growth and structural change proceeded briskly in the region for thirty years after 1950 and then stagnated through the early 1990s. During the past fifteen years, growth has resumed in some countries, particularly after the rise of oil prices after 1998 (see Table 3.1). In assessing the numbers in the following tables and figures, several things should be kept in mind. First, the data are often merely the best guesses of informed observers; for some of the least developed and poorest countries they are of very poor quality. For all countries, data should be taken as indicating orders of magnitude rather than precise "truth." Second, many countries of the region have started the process of economic growth from a very low base; in some cases (Yemen, Oman) that process began little more than a generation ago.

The range of income in the region is, as we have seen, extremely wide. Indeed, no major area of the world shows a higher variance in per capita incomes across nation-states (see Figure 3.1). The region boasts high-income countries—Bahrain, Israel, Kuwait, and the UAE—whose inhabitants enjoy a material standard of living like that in the developed countries. Israeli per capita GNP exceeds that of Greece, Portugal, and the Republic of Korea, and unlike the high-income oil exporters, the country possesses a diversified economic and industrial structure and levels of health and literacy that rival those in southern Europe. At the same time, the average Sudanese lives in poverty as extreme as that in sub-Saharan Africa, and millions of Egyptians and Moroccans live very close to subsistence (Chapter 10). The diversity of experience with economic growth and structural change is just as wide. At one extreme, MENA contains not only industrialized and developed Israel but also Turkey, formerly the heartland of one of history's greatest empires and a pioneer in industrialization outside of Europe and Japan. Manufacturing accounts for 13% of all output in Turkey (see Table 3.3), nearly the same as in the United States. In contrast, the region also contains Oman, whose former sultan kept the country hermetically sealed in medieval poverty until his son deposed him in 1970. Some less-colorful distinctions are found in the rates of growth and structural transformation; the size, efficiency, and diversity of industrial production; the trend in agricultural production; and the composition of international trade.

Overall growth rates of GDP for 1960 to 2003 are shown in Table 3.4. Unsurprisingly, given the impact of the oil boom, the per capita output in the region grew more rapidly than the average for LDCs. From 1990 to 2003, some countries (Egypt, Jordan, Oman, Syria, and Tunisia) grew faster than 4% per year, slightly more than doubling per capita incomes during the past two decades. Only Israel, the Sudan, and Morocco have grown more slowly than the average for countries of their income group, while growth in Turkey has been roughly equal to the group average.

The collapse of the oil boom and persistent policy failures made the period 1985–1995 much grimmer (see Chapters 8 and 9). During this period output per person declined, but there were significant differences among countries (see Figure 3.6). Viewing the 1990s as a whole, GDP growth was 4.0% for resource-poor, labor-abundant countries (Egypt, Jordan, Morocco, and Tunisia), 1.2% for resource-rich, labor-abundant countries (Algeria, Iran, Syria, and Yemen), and 3.5% for the wealthy oil exporters of the Gulf Cooperative Council (GCC) (World Bank 2005a).[14] Although population growth rates fell in most countries during the decade (see Chapter 4), the average for all countries was approximately 2.2%—and considerably higher in some countries. In no country was the rate of growth of output sufficient to keep up with the growth in the labor force—which was estimated to be between 5% and 7%—much less to significantly raise real wages. Even today, real wages and labor productivity in many countries are not markedly different from what they were in 1970. Significant poverty (Chapter 10), joblessness (Chapter 5), and social unrest are direct results of such sluggish growth.

TABLE 3.3 Structure of Production: Sectoral Shares of GDP (% of GDP), 1990 and 2003

	Agriculture		Industry		Manufacturing		Services	
	1990	2003	1990	2003	1990	2003	1990	2003
Algeria	11	10	48	19	..	10	16	56
Egypt	19	16	29	34	18	19	52	50
Iran	24	11	29	41	12	13	48	48
Jordan	8	2	28	26	15	16	64	72
Morocco	18	17	32	30	18	17	50	54
Oman	3	–	58	–	4	–	39	–
Saudi Arabia	6	5	49	55	9	10	45	40
Sudan	–	39	–	18	–	9	-	43
Syria	28	23	24	29	20	25	48	48
Tunisia	16	12	30	28	17	18	54	60
Turkey	18	13	30	22	20	13	52	65
UAE	2	–	64	–	8	–	35	–
Yemen	24	15	27	40	9	5	49	45
United States	2	2	28	23	19	15	70	75

SOURCE: World Bank Indicators 2005

TABLE 3.4 Growth of GDP, 1960–2003

	1960–1970	1970–1980	1980–1990	1990–2003
Algeria	4.3	4.6	2.7	2.4
Egypt, Arab Rep.	4.3	9.5	5.4	4.5
Iran, Islamic Rep.	11.3	–	1.7	3.7
Iraq	6.1	12.1	–6.8	–
Israel	8.1	4.8	3.5	4.3
Jordan	?	?	2.5	4.6
Kuwait	5.7	2.5	1.3	2.9
Lebanon	?	?	..	4.6
Libya	24.4	2.2	–7	..
Morocco	4.4	5.6	4.2	2.7
Oman	19.5	6.2	8.4	4.3
Saudi Arabia	–	10.1	–1.3	2.1
Sudan	0.7	5.6	2.3	5.7
Syrian Arab Republic	4.6	9.9	1.5	4.3
Tunisia	4.7	6.8	3.3	4.6
Turkey	6	5.9	5.3	3.1
UAE	–	–	–2.1	4.2
Yemen	–	–	–	5.8

SOURCE: World Bank Development Indicators 2005

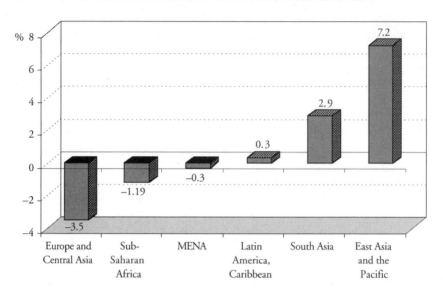

FIGURE 3.6   Average annual per capita GNP growth rates, 1985–1995
SOURCE: World Bank

Growth was also uneven across sectors (see Table 3.5); this is the essence of structural transformation. The share of agriculture has declined in all countries (Table 3.3). Two groups of countries saw rapid rates of growth of manufacturing: oil exporters such as Algeria, Libya, Saudi Arabia, and the UAE, all of which started in 1965 with very little industry; and countries with a longer industrial history such as Turkey, Iran, and Egypt. Tunisia, which also had little industry at independence and which exports very modest amounts of oil, also registered a high rate of growth of manufacturing output. As usual, the residual category of "services" accounts for one-third to over one-half of output. The percentage share of "industry" in national product for most countries is either the same as or slightly below what we would expect on the basis of their per capita incomes. Although Iran and Saudi Arabia have a much higher percentage of output from industry than the average for upper-middle-income countries, this is deceptive because "industry" includes the petroleum sector. The same is true for low-income Yemen.

A better picture of industrialization levels (and, as argued in Chapter 2, "sustainable" structural change) is given by the percentage of output that comes from manufacturing or by the size and growth of manufacturing value added (MVA) (see Table 3.6). Total MVA in the region is slightly larger than that of Mexico, and about three-fourths of that produced by Korea's 23 million people. It is instructive to compare MVA for the top three MENA countries (Turkey, Egypt, and Iran) with that of Italy. Italy's MVA is some 7.5 times that of Turkey, 12 times that of Egypt, and nearly 17 times that of Iran. These three MENA countries, plus Saudi Arabia, account for more

TABLE 3.5   Sectoral Rates of Growth, 1980–2003

	Agriculture		Industry		Manufacturing		Services	
	1980–1990	1990–2003	1980–1990	1990–2003	1980–1990	1990–2003	1980–1990	1990–2003
Algeria	4.1	3.9	2.6	2.2	4.1	−1.7	3	2.6
Egypt	2.7	3.2	3.3	4.5	..	6.5	7.8	4.6
Iran	4.5	3.3	3.3	−0.7	4.5	5.8	−1	7.5
Jordan	6.8	−2	1.7	4.9	0.5	5.6	2.3	4.7
Kuwait	14.7	–	1	–	2.3	–	2.1	–
Lebanon	–	1.7	–	−0.4	–	-1.7	–	2.7
Morocco	6.7	0.9	3	3.3	4.1	2.9	4.2	3
Oman	7.9	–	10.3	–	20.6	–	5.9	–
Saudi Arabia	12.5	1.6	−3.8	1.7	6.2	5.3	0.6	2.5
Sudan	1.8	9.1	1.6	6.2	4.8	2.1	4.5	3.2
Syria	−0.6	4.2	6.6	8.1	–	8.9	1.6	2.8
Tunisia	2.8	2	3.1	4.6	3.7	5.3	3.5	5.3
Turkey	1.2	1	7.7	3	7.9	3.8	4.5	3.3
UAE	9.6	–	−4.2	–	3.1	–	3.6	–
Yemen	–	5.6	–	6	–	2.7	–	5.7

SOURCE: World Bank Development Indicators 2005

TABLE 3.6   Shares of Manufacturing Value Added, 1990 and 2001

	Food, Beverages and Tobacco		Clothing and Textiles		Machinery		Chemicals		Other	
	1990	2001	1990	2001	1990	2001	1990	2001	1990	2001
Algeria	13	–	17	–	–	–	–	–	70	–
Egypt	19	–	16	–	9	–	14	–	43	–
Iran	12	10	20	6	20	23	8	19	40	43
Iraq	20	–	16	–	4	–	11	–	49	–
Israel	14	10	9	5	32	33	9	2	37	51
Jordan	28	30	7	7	4	5	15	18	47	41
Kuwait	4	7	3	4	2	4	3	2	88	83
Morocco	22	36	17	17	8	8	12	13	41	27
Oman	–	9	–	2	–	3	–	3	–	84
Syria	35	27	29	24	–	–	–	–	36	49
Tunisia	19	16	20	34	5	10	4	9	52	31
Turkey	16	3	15	1	16	–	10	–	43	96

SOURCE: World Bank Development Indicators 2005

than 70% of the region's manufacturing value added. Manufacturing in MENA is geographically concentrated.

During the oil-boom years, growth rates of MVA were respectable but not spectacular; the region boasted no such star performers as the Republic of Korea (16.8% per year, 1965–1985) or Brazil (11.4% per year) (World Bank 1987). Tunisia's industrial growth was approximately the same as Spain's, while growth rates in Algeria, Egypt, and Saudi Arabia exceeded those of the PRC (7.0%). The contrast with the years of the oil bust is striking: Only in Morocco did the growth of MVA accelerate after 1985, and in the two major oil producers with significant industry, Algeria and Saudi Arabia, MVA declined.

As we shall see (Chapters 7–9), industrial growth has been hampered by numerous political and economic problems; the search for their solution is a key to the political economy of the more industrialized countries of the area. Some progress was made during the 1990s and early 2000s, although the record is mixed. Growth of MVA accelerated in Egypt, Iran, Jordan, and Saudi Arabia but fell in Morocco, Tunisia, and Turkey (see Figure 3.7). For the main four manufacturers (Turkey, Egypt, Iran, and Saudi Arabia), however, growth equaled or exceeded 5% per year, quite a respectable performance.

The pattern of distribution of MVA holds few surprises. Many countries' industries process agricultural outputs or produce textiles. Because of the labor-intensity and relatively well-established technology of such industries, most countries concentrate on them initially. The more industrialized countries have gone far beyond this

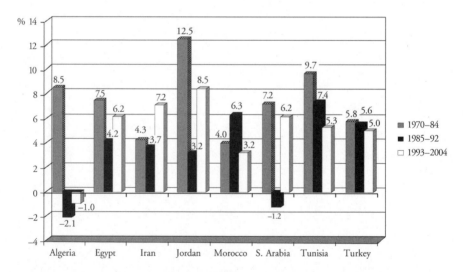

FIGURE 3.7   Growth of manufacturing value added, 1970–2004
SOURCE: For years 1970–1992, World Bank (1994g, 172). For years 1993–2004, World Development Indicators Online, 2006

TABLE 3.7 Sectoral Distribution of the Labor Force, Selected Countries, early 2000s

	Agriculture	*Industry*	*Services*
Algeria	14%	23.4%	62.6%
Egypt	32	17	51
Iran	23	34	43
Israel	2.6	31.7	65.7
Jordan	5.0	12.5	82.5
Libya	17	23	59
Morocco	40	15	45
Qatar	0.2	80.1	19.7
Saudi Arabia	12	25	63
Sudan	80	7	13
Syria	30	27	43
Turkey	35.9	22.8	41.2
U.A.E.	7	15	78
Yemen	48.5	15.1	36.4

SOURCE: Iran: UN, 2003; Yemen: IMF, 2002; All others: CIA Factbook, 2006

stage, producing significant quantities of machinery, chemicals, and a host of other products. The most industrially diversified countries are Israel and Turkey; the drive to create a competitive manufacturing sector in Turkey is examined in Chapter 7.

Trends in the distribution of the labor force are shown in Table 3.7. A number of features stand out. First, the percentage of the labor force in agriculture declined considerably in all countries (except Kuwait) over the long run. Whereas in 1950 between one-half and two-thirds of the workforce was in agriculture, that sector's share of total employment had fallen to one-third or less by the end of the 1980s in many countries. By the early 2000s, more than one-third of the labor force worked in agriculture only in Morocco, Sudan, Turkey, and Yemen. The different rates of decline of the farm labor force across countries has multiple causes. Countries with very weak natural resource bases (especially, lack of water) unsurprisingly have little employment in agriculture today. The rapid fall in agricultural employment in Saudi Arabia is a result of policy: The country continued to subsidize farm production into the 1990s, despite its economic and environmental irrationality (see Chapter 6). These policies, however, were changed during that decade. In some countries, policies were more favorable to the agricultural sector than those adopted elsewhere. The decline of the share of the agricultural labor force decelerated beginning in 1980 in many countries.[15] The explanations here vary widely but certainly include the impact of negative per capita growth.

Although industry now often employs between one-fifth and one-third of the labor force in many MENA countries, often well over half of these workers are in small establishments employing fewer than twenty people. The growth in "service" employment is often in the so-called informal sector, inhabited by firms with very low capitalization, selling in easily entered markets, and offering low-paying, insecure jobs. The rate and pattern of industrial growth have failed to provide enough decent jobs for all members of the rapidly growing labor force. This gap between labor-force growth and job creation is one of the central issues facing policymakers throughout the region (see Chapters 4 and 5).

The problem of insufficient job creation is not the result of too little investment. In general, MENA countries have invested as high a proportion of national output as other LDCs (see Chapter 8). The Algerian case is instructive here: After Algeria relentlessly invested over one-third of its output for a generation (one of the highest investment rates in history), in the mid-1980s nearly one in five workers was unemployed. Rather, the difficulty was with the efficiency of investment. For Algeria, for example, generating an additional dollar of output required twice as much investment during the 1970s as was the case in the labor-intensive, rapidly growing South Korean economy. Many economists believe that the culprit for the relative inefficiency of investment in the region can be found in government policies (see Chapters 8 and 9).

Few of the countries of the region that do not export oil escaped the typical LDC problem of a balance-of-trade deficit during the 1970s (see Table 3.8). Development economists usually argue that such deficits are perfectly appropriate for a developing country *as long as exports grow commensurately*. In theory, capital *should* flow from capital-abundant developed countries to capital-scarce LDCs. However, if exports fail to grow, then the trade gap becomes a debt trap. Although debt did accumulate in some countries, exports grew faster than imports in many countries during the past decade.

A number of countries in MENA face significant debt burdens. One critical debt ratio, the present value of debt as a percentage of exports, is shown in Figure 3.8. As a rule of thumb, any country with a ratio over 200% is said to suffer from "debt overhang"—a level of indebtedness that deters private investors from risking their capital. During the early 1990s, Algeria, Morocco, Syria, Turkey, and Yemen had important debt overhang difficulties, while the problem in the Sudan seemed quite unmanageable. However, debt declined in all countries in the region during the latter part of the decade, except in Syria and Turkey. Lebanon is particularly afflicted now, as post–civil war construction was financed by borrowing—and it now needs to completely rebuild the infrastructure destroyed by Israeli bombing during the conflict of summer 2006.

Finally, the commodity composition of trade is shown in Tables 3.9 and 3.10. Of course, petroleum exports dominate the trade (and entire economies) of many countries in the region. As discussed in Chapter 2, the region has three countries that export mainly manufactured goods: Turkey, Israel, and Tunisia. Countries such as Egypt, Yemen, and Jordan relied heavily on the export of human labor (international labor migration) for foreign exchange until the Gulf War of 1991, which thoroughly disrupted these flows. A notable feature of the commodity composition

TABLE 3.8   Growth of Exports and Imports, 1970–2004

| | Imports (current US$ Millions) | Imports (current US$ Millions) | Growth rates (%) | | | | | |
| | | | Exports | | | Imports | | |
	2004	2004	1970–1980	1980–1992	1992–2004	1970–1980	1980–1992	1992–2004
Algeria	34,067	21,808	−0.5	4.3	3.8	12.1	−5.1	2.9
Bahrain	9,077	7,069	–	–	–	–	–	–
Egypt	22,518	22,810	−2.6	3.1	5.5	7.8	−1.2	3.4
Iran	52,021	49,033	−6.8	14.5	2.4	11	8.6	−3.6
Israel	51,485	67,600	10.0	6.0	*7.5	3.5	5.1	*4.9
Jordan	5,479	9,182	19.3	6.1	4.8	15.3	−0.2	7.2
Kuwait	33,543	18,510	–	–	*0.6	–	–	*3.5
Lebanon	4,646	9,014	–	–	10.2	–	–	3.8
Morocco	16,568	19,669	3.9	5.5	5.2	6.6	4.4	4.6
Oman	13,836	10,379	−2.1	8.6	7.2	40.9	0	8.1
Saudi Arabia	131,920	62,350	5.7	−2.4	2.0	35.9	−6.2	3.5
Sudan	3,799	4,470	−3.5	0.2	*24.0	−0.6	−4.8	*9.2
Syria	8,430	8,059	7	19.4	8.2	12.4	4.6	6.5
Tunisia	12,573	13,498	7.5	6.4	4.9	12.5	3.1	4.5
Turkey	87,456	105,004	4.3	9	11.9	5.7	9.6	12.6
UAE	85,770	68,031	–	–	*7.7	–	–	*9.5
WBG	–	–	–	–	*−6.6	–	–	*−3.6
Yemen	3,246	4,327	–	–	16.1	–	–	6.9

*Comments on time-span. For 1992–2004 Export and Import growth rates: Israel 1996–2004; Kuwait 1996–2003; Saudi Arabia 1998–2003; Sudan 1994–2004; UAE 1994–2003/04; WBG 1995–2003.
SOURCES: 1970–1992 growth rates World Bank (1994g, 186–187); 1992–2004 WDI Online 2006.

of imports is the high percentage of food imports in countries such as Egypt, Morocco, and Algeria. Imports of fuel for countries without oil and imports of capital goods (machinery) for the more industrialized countries are also evident.

CONCLUSION

It is possible to discern certain patterns in the midst of all the diversity of detail in the region. We offer a taxonomy of national economic growth and structural change patterns, dividing the countries into five groups on the basis of past performance and what we believe are potentially viable strategies. Needless to say, performance within any of these groups often varies considerably.

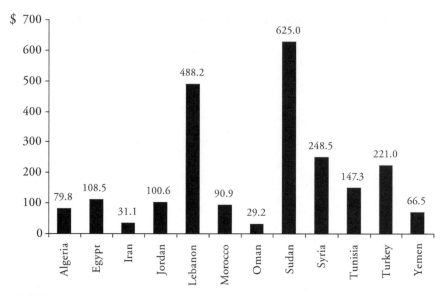

FIGURE 3.8   Debt as a percentage of exports of goods and services, 2004
SOURCE: World Development Indicators Online, 2006

TABLE 3.9   Structure of Merchandise Exports, 1990 and 2003

	Food		Agriculture Raw Materials		Fuels		Ores and metals		Manufactures	
	1990	2003	1990	2003	1990	2003	1990	2003	1990	2003
Algeria	0	0	0	0	96	97	0	0	3	2
Egypt	10	9	10	7	29	44	9	2	42	31
Israel	8	5	3	1	1	0	2	1	87	93
Jordan	11	15	0	0	0	0	38	16	51	69
Lebanon	..	19	..	2	..	0	..	10	..	68
Libya	0	..	0	..	94	..	0	..	5	..
Morocco	26	21	3	2	4	1	15	7	52	69
Oman	1	5	0	0	92	80	1	1	5	14
Saudi Arabia	1	1	0	0	92	89	0	0	7	10
Sudan	61	18	38	6	..	72	0	0	1	3
Syria	14	14	4	3	45	71	1	1	36	11
Tunisia	11	8	1	1	17	9	2	1	69	81
Turkey	22	10	3	1	2	2	4	2	68	84
UAE	8	1	1	0	5	92	39	4	46	4
Yemen	75	..	10	..	8	..	7	..	1	..

SOURCE: World Development Indicators 2005 (World Bank)

TABLE 3.10 Structure of Merchandise Imports (% of total), 1990 and 2003

	Food		Agriculture Raw Materials		Fuels		Ores and metals		Manufactures	
	1990	*2003*	*1990*	*2003*	*1990*	*2003*	*1990*	*2003*	*1990*	*2003*
Algeria	24	22	5	2	1	1	2	1	68	73
Egypt	32	25	7	5	3	5	2	2	56	49
Iran	..	11	..	2	..	6	..	2	..	79
Israel	8	6	2	1	9	11	3	2	77	80
Jordan	26	18	2	2	18	17	1	2	51	60
Kuwait	17	15	1	1	1	1	2	2	79	75
Lebanon	..	18	..	2	..	16	..	2	..	62
Libya	23	..	2	..	0	..	1	..	74	..
Morocco	10	11	6	3	17	16	6	3	61	67
Oman	19	17	1	1	4	3	1	5	69	71
Saudi Arabia	15	16	1	1	0	0	3	3	81	79
Sudan	13	19	1	1	20	5	0	1	66	74
Syria	31	19	2	4	3	4	1	3	62	70
Tunisia	11	9	4	3	9	7	4	3	72	78
Turkey	8	4	4	4	21	13	5	6	61	68
UAE	14	11	1	1	3	1	4	2	77	86
Yemen	27	..	1	..	40	..	1	..	31	..

SOURCE: World Development Indicators 2005 (World Bank)

The coupon clippers: Libya, Kuwait, Oman, the UAE, Bahrain, and Qatar. These states have abundant oil and little of anything else, including people. They have been and will continue to be almost entirely dependent upon oil and any money earned from overseas investments. (Some—Bahrain and the UAE—have been able to play an entrepôt role, as "offshore" banks, free-trade zones, and reshipment centers.)

The oil industrializers: Iraq, Iran, Algeria, and Saudi Arabia. These countries enjoy substantial oil exports and revenues as well as large enough populations and/or other resources to make industrialization a real option. They should really be divided into two subgroups. The first three share the main features of large oil exports, a substantial population, other natural resources, and a chance to create industrial and agricultural sectors that will be sustainable over the long run. Tragically, all three suffer from such serious political disabilities that development has stalled in Algeria and collapsed in Iraq. Its massive oil reserves place Saudi Arabia, the world's largest rentier state, in a class by itself. Although it lacks the other resources of the first three countries, its current and future petroleum resources and access to capital are so enormous that it, too, can contemplate specializing in capital- and energy-intensive industry. Saudi Arabia has its share of economic problems, but its massive oil reserves provide it with a unique cushion.

The watchmakers: Israel, Jordan, Tunisia, and Syria.   These four small countries have limited natural resources and must therefore concentrate on investing in human capital and on exporting skill-intensive manufactures. All have made major efforts to educate their people (see Chapter 5); manufactured goods now account for 93% of Israeli, 69% of Jordanian, and 81% of Tunisian exports. Although Syria lags behind on both counts, we believe that this path is the most logical one for the country to follow over the long haul. The same would be true for any future Palestinian state.

The NICs: Turkey, Egypt, and Morocco.   These countries either have little or no oil (Turkey and Morocco) or lack enough to provide the basis for any long-run growth strategy (Egypt). In regional terms they have relatively large populations, relatively good agricultural land or potential, and long experience with industrial production. Turkey is clearly a full-fledged NIC, more similar to countries such as Mexico than to many countries of the region. The current regime has opted for a growth strategy led by manufactured exports. Students of the Egyptian economy have been saying for decades that the country had no choice but to industrialize; they are still right. The country must continue to improve its already very productive agriculture, but 932,400 square kilometers alone cannot support 79 million people (2006). The country has the largest skilled labor force and pool of technical talent in the Arab world. Moroccan industry, spurred by direct foreign investment and a favorable policy environment, has shown the most rapid rate of growth of any country in the region. Despite serious ecological problems (frequent droughts), its agricultural potential remains impressive. Continued industrialization, linked to agricultural development, could increase both the welfare of its people and its stature as an NIC.

The agro-poor: the Sudan and Yemen.   These are the poorest countries of the region and ones for which a growth strategy led by agricultural development seems to offer the only hope. The Sudan has great agricultural potential but also enormous political, social, ecological, and infrastructural problems. Until the discovery of oil, its growth performance was the worst in the region. Like the Alpine regions of Europe during that continent's industrialization, Yemen has remained agricultural while increasingly depending on emigration and remittances. The Gulf War and its aftermath have been catastrophic for Yemen, removing its main source of foreign exchange and employment. In a worst-case scenario, both countries could come to resemble "pirate states" like Afghanistan, with little public order, warlordism, endemic violence, and economic specialization in the trade in illegal drugs and arms. Although oil revenues have shored up these weak states, the prospects remain grim.

This taxonomy is meant to be only suggestive; its boundaries are porous. For example, Egypt and Tunisia are partly oil industrializers. Unless important new discoveries are made soon, dwindling Algerian oil reserves will turn that country into an NIC—or a chaotic mess—in a generation. Syria and Egypt collect rents on their strategic locations, and Morocco shares some features with the agro-poor (as well as a flourishing drug trade based in the Rif). Like any taxonomy, the aim of this one is to help organize our thoughts. We should also note that this economic taxonomy does not correspond to our political taxonomy (see Chapter 11).

One might object that all this is simply "closet modernization theory": the argument that all of the world will reenact the history of Europe and its overseas offspring (United States, Canada, Australia). We certainly *do* believe that the process of economic growth includes structural change; the data given above amply demonstrate the declining weight of agriculture in the economies of the region and the increase in a *kind* of industry in most cases. This process was, of course, also true of the now-developed countries. If this be modernization theory, make the most of it!

We emphatically do *not* believe, however, that the process of economic growth is smooth. It is uneven over time, over space, and over people; there are losers, and some of the winners do rather better than others. Until the revival of oil prices, retrogression and decline, rather than growth and development, characterized many countries' performance. Furthermore, as we argued in Chapter 2, we believe that the process of economic growth and structural change is replete with unintended outcomes. And we do not believe that all (or even any) of the MENA countries can or will "look like" the industrialized West or Japan economically. It is implicitly understood in the chapters that follow that economic growth in the region has many crucial differences from that found in the history of any now-developed country, if for no other reason than that rents have played such a critical role in regional growth. Still less do we think that Middle Eastern and North African countries will resemble the West politically or (most absurd of all) culturally. We simply argue that the course of politics cannot be understood without an understanding of the process of economic growth and structural change, a process that has a logic of its own.

Finally, we must add one more cautionary note. "Development" of the usual kind may have become impossible for the world as a whole. Ecological constraints must be taken seriously. Global climate change is clearly real; we may have already unleashed forces whose long-term effects are frightening to contemplate. Increased heat and aridity would undermine *any* development strategy in the Middle East and North Africa. If the droughts of the recent past become more frequent, the region (and the world) will face a human and ecological disaster. Understanding how such tragedies might occur and what might be done to prevent them will surely require first an understanding of the interaction of economic growth, state policies, and social actors. Even if the worst environmental nightmares are avoided, the continued pressure of population on scarce resources poses serious problems for the region. The political economy of population growth is the topic of the next chapter.

NOTES

1. Excluding Antarctica.

2. The more significant mineral resources are antimony, chromite, copper, iron ore, lead, lignite coal, manganese, mercury, phosphate rock, and silver.

3. Recall from Chapter 2 that "economic rent" is the difference between price and the opportunity cost of production, that is, the amount of resources required to keep a factor (or factors) of production in its current use.

4. For more details see, inter alia, Cremer and Salehi-Isfahani (1991), Heal and Chichilnisky (1991), Yergin (1991), and Roberts (2004).

5. The so-called Seven Sisters—British Petroleum (BP), Texaco, Exxon, Royal Dutch Shell, Mobil, Standard Oil of California (Chevron), and Gulf Oil—plus the state-owned Compagnie Française de Petrol (CFP).

6. Nigerian oil shipments were disrupted by the civil war that broke out in 1967.

7. The "posted price" was the price on which the companies agreed to pay royalties to the countries, as opposed to the market price, which could fluctuate.

8. *Real* oil prices were roughly constant from 1970 to 1974; most of the nominal increases simply kept pace with the accelerating inflation in the industrialized countries.

9. "Marker crude" at the time was Saudi Arabian light crude oil. The price of other oils was determined by various markups or discounts from the price of Saudi Arabian light.

10. The combined oil import bill of the United States, Germany, France, Japan, and Italy rose from $23.8 billion to $67.6 billion from 1973 to 1974.

11. OPEC revenues increased by over $82 billion from 1978 to 1981 (Petroleum Finance Company).

12. The only competitor would be the Spanish plundering of the Americas of precious metals in the sixteenth century.

13. Political considerations also influenced the Saudi decision to open the taps. The Saudis sought to deny revenue to the Iranians, who were advancing in the Fao peninsula of Iraq at that time. Some reports assert that William Casey, the director of the CIA, asked the Saudis to slash prices to deny revenue to the Soviets. When economic and political interests coincide, it is impossible to determine their relative weights.

14. The Gulf Cooperative Council, which was created in 1981, is a regional organization that includes Bahrain, Kuwait, Oman, Qatar, Saudi Arabia, and the United Arab Emirates.

15. For both Jordan and the UAE, the slow pace of change in the 1980s and 1990s merely says that the transformation was already largely complete.

4

THE IMPACT OF DEMOGRAPHIC CHANGE

For good or ill, every year the population of the Middle East and North Africa continues to grow rapidly. Despite dramatic recent drops in fertility in many MENA countries, only sub-Saharan Africa has a higher rate of population growth than the Middle East and North Africa. Before 1985, population growth accelerated, as falling death rates outpaced (relatively modest) declines in fertility. During the past two decades, however, much of the region has undergone a "demographic transition": Population growth rates fell from 3.4% in 1985 to 2.7% in 1992 to 2.2% in 2003 (World Bank 2004c). Sharp declines in fertility drove this change, and there are reasons to expect further drops. Nevertheless, populations will continue to expand, both because fertility remains well above replacement levels in many countries and because past population growth ensures that there are many women who will soon enter their childbearing years—an additional 30 million of them during the next twenty years. Population forecasting is fraught with difficulties, but even optimistic demographers (e.g., Courbage 1999) project the regional population to be 562 million by 2025, while others (e.g., UN 2000) place it at 639 million (see Figure 4.1). By comparison, the regional population in the 1950s was about 100 million and currently numbers approximately 443 million (2004).

Such numbers may be viewed as catastrophic or problematical, or alternatively, as an occasion for rejoicing. The old debates on the political economy of population, first incarnated as "Malthus versus Marx," have lost none of their vigor. While neo-Malthusians believe that rapid population growth dooms any attempt at development to failure (e.g., Ehrlich 1968), many Marxists reverse this causality, maintaining that poverty and underdevelopment cause rapid population growth (e.g., Mamdani 1972). Finally, neo-Panglossians such as Simon (1982) argued that population growth is an unalloyed blessing because "the mind is greater than the stomach": The more talented, energetic people there are, the better off the human race will be. For them, economies of scale, accelerating human-capital formation, and

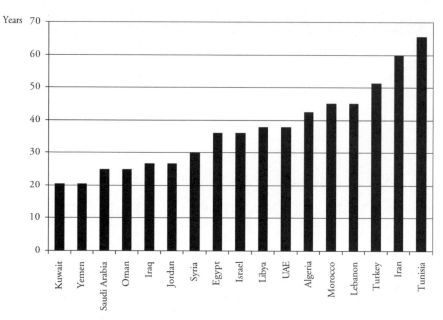

FIGURE 4.1   Doubling times of populations at 2000–2005 average growth rates
SOURCE: Calculated from UNFPA, *State of World Population 2003*

rapid technological and institutional innovation put humanity on a continual upward path of progress as its numbers steadily expand.

We reject all three of these views, agreeing with the majority of modern demographers that population growth (1) is at least partially the result of social conditions
and economic incentives (i.e., crude Malthusian "population determinism" is silly),
(2) is not *solely* determined by economic conditions (and therefore family planning
programs have an independent impact on fertility), and (3) exacerbates development
problems, particularly the ability to provide adequate education and employment for
the young. We think that rapid population growth retards the development process
and stresses the polity. Deceleration of population growth presents both opportunities (e.g., a decline in the dependency ratio leading to the so-called demographic
dividend—see below) and challenges (e.g., the increasing burden of caring for an aging population). Policymakers must confront such difficulties. To reduce fertility, for
example, they can respond both directly by promoting family planning programs
and indirectly by altering the incentives for couples to have children. However, both
sorts of instruments are often politically controversial.

COMPARATIVE DEMOGRAPHIC PATTERNS

Several demographic developments in the region stand out (see Table 4.1). In the
second half of the twentieth century, population growth accelerated for nearly forty
years. In 1950–1955, the rate of population growth, at 2.64% per year, was the

73

TABLE 4.1 Demographic Indicators, 1970–2005

	Population Growth Rate (%)				Crude birth rate[a]				Crude death rate[a]				Total fertility (per woman)			
	1970–1980	1980–1990	1990–2000	2000–2005	1970–1980	1980–1990	1990–2000	2000–2005	1970–1980	1980–1990	1990–2000	2000–2005	1970–1980	1980–1990	1990–2000	2000–2005
Algeria	3.1	3.0	1.9	1.5	47	38	25	21	14	9	6	5	7.3	5.9	3.5	2.5
Bahrain	4.6	3.5	3.1	1.6	35	32	24	19	7	4	3	3	5.6	4.4	3.1	2.5
Egypt	2.2	2.4	1.9	1.9	40	37	28	26	15	11	7	6	5.6	5.1	3.7	3.3
Iran	3.1	3.7	1.6	0.9	43	42	25	19	12	10	6	5	6.5	6.1	3.4	2.1
Iraq	3.3	2.7	3.0	2.8	44	40	39	36	10	8	10	10	7.0	6.3	5.5	4.8
Israel	2.6	1.8	3.0	2.0	27	23	22	21	7	7	6	6	3.6	3.1	2.9	2.9
Jordan	3.2	3.8	4.2	2.7	48	41	34	28	11	8	5	4	7.6	6.3	4.7	3.5
Lebanon	1.2	0.2	2.2	1.0	31	29	24	19	8	8	7	7	4.5	3.6	2.9	2.3
Libya	4.3	3.5	2.0	2.0	48	39	24	23	14	8	4	4	7.5	6.4	3.8	3.0
Morocco	2.4	2.4	1.7	1.5	43	34	26	23	14	10	7	6	6.4	4.9	3.3	2.8
Occupied Palestinian Territory	3.0	3.8	3.8	3.2	47	45	44	39	15	8	6	4	7.6	6.7	6.2	5.6
Oman	4.6	4.4	2.8	1.0	49	44	32	26	13	6	3	3	7.2	7.0	5.7	3.8
Qatar	7.2	7.1	2.6	5.9	31	27	21	19	11	4	3	3	6.4	5.1	3.7	3.0
Saudi Arabia	5.1	5.3	2.7	2.7	47	40	33	29	14	7	4	4	7.3	6.7	5.3	4.1
Sudan	3.1	2.7	2.3	1.9	46	42	37	34	18	15	12	11	6.6	6.1	5.1	4.5
Syria	3.4	3.6	2.7	2.5	47	43	32	29	10	6	4	4	7.5	6.7	4.3	3.5
Tunisia	2.3	2.4	1.5	1.1	37	32	21	17	11	7	6	5	6.0	4.5	2.7	2.0
Turkey	2.5	2.1	1.8	1.4	36	30	24	21	11	9	7	7	5.0	3.7	2.8	2.5
UAE	15.1	6.1	5.5	6.5	32	30	21	16	9	4	2	1	6.0	5.0	3.5	2.5
Yemen	2.6	3.9	4.0	3.1	55	55	46	41	23	15	11	9	8.5	8.5	7.2	6.2

a = Per 1,000 population
SOURCE: United Nations, 2005. *World Population Prospects: The 2004 Revision.* New York: United Nations (Department of Economic and Social Affairs: Population Division)

second highest of the major cultural-economic regions of the world. During 1970–1980 the growth rate rose to 2.8% and then to 3.1% for 1980–1992; by the 1980s the region's population was growing at the fastest pace in the world. However, in the late 1980s population growth reached a peak and began decelerating, falling to 2.2% during the 1990s and to about 2% today (World Bank 2004c). In the simplest terms, population growth accelerated because the birthrate declined more slowly than the death rate. Since no one advocates population control by raising the death rate, population policy analysis focuses on the birthrate.

The key population issue in the region is the relatively slow decline in fertility. Fertility has always been high in MENA. In 1950–1955, the regional crude birthrate (CBR, defined as the quotient of the number of births and the total population) was the highest in the world, 50.5 per 1,000. The CBR fell to 45 in 1970, to 34 in 1992, and to 27 in 2003. Of course, the decline in the birthrate is a worldwide phenomenon: The CBR for total world population fell from 33 in 1970 to 21 in 2003, and for LDCs, from 39 to 24. Even the CBR of sub-Saharan Africa declined: from 48 to 40 in the same time period. The decline in fertility in MENA has been large. Still, the region's CBR remains the world's second highest, above both the world and the LDC average.

A more revealing statistic for tracking population growth is the total fertility rate (TFR), which tells us roughly how many children the "average woman" will have during her lifetime.[1] By this measure, Middle Eastern women were the most fecund in the world in the early 1950s and were second only to sub-Saharan African women by the early 1980s, when Middle Eastern women were still bearing an average of six children each (National Research Council 1986). In the early 1990s the region's women were still giving birth to, on average, just under five children apiece, but today, the average woman gives birth to between three and four children; in some countries in the region, fertility among educated women has fallen to, or below, replacement levels.[2] During the past fifteen years the rate of decline in fertility in MENA has been the fastest in the world (UNICEF 2005).

There has also been a striking change in the relationship between fertility and income during the recent past. Formerly, fertility rates in the region were high in relation to incomes. In general, fertility falls with increases in per capita income. The relationship between fertility and income for several MENA countries in the early 2000s is shown in Figure 4.2. The relationship is not a simple one. Indeed, if everything else remains the same, higher incomes may lead to more children, since poor health due to low-income levels may limit a woman's ability to bear children. The inverse relationship can be thought of as the outcome of a highly complex social process in which new attitudes, new preferences, and new habits are generated. One theory of economic demography holds, in effect, that parents start to substitute "child quality" for "child quantity" as they become richer (e.g., T. W. Schultz 1981). But for both the sociological and the economic theories of fertility, increased incomes *alone* are unlikely to reduce fertility; additional socioeconomic change is required.

Up to the 1990s, MENA fertility rates exceeded what would be expected, given per capita incomes in the countries of the region, with the exceptions of Egypt, Tu-

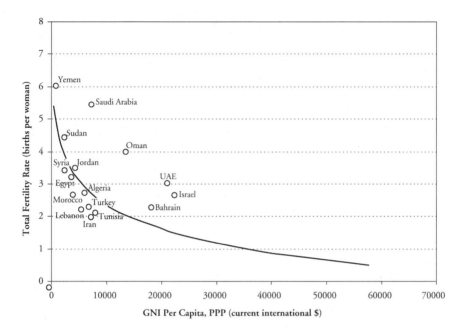

FIGURE 4.2 Per capita gross national income and total fertility rate, 2002–2003
SOURCE: World Bank, Development Indicators Online, 2006

nisia, and Turkey. The disparity was most notable for major oil-exporting countries but was not limited to them. However, the relation between income and fertility has changed profoundly in some countries over the past decade; today fertility rates in roughly half of MENA countries are now *below* what we would expect on the basis of income alone, while rates in some relatively wealthy countries remain stubbornly high (see Figure 4.2).

How can these differential fertility changes be explained? Modern demographers do not agree on the precise determinants of fertility. All concur that economic conditions play some role and that the social position of women is highly significant. In addition, all concede that high infant mortality is correlated with high fertility rates. But different analysts accord varying weights to these and to other factors. This is hardly surprising. The decision to have a child is so complex and the available data are so open to various interpretations that dogmatic positions are out of place.[3] Accordingly, we will survey some of the plausible explanations for varying fertility rates in the Middle East without offering a firm conclusion. We do believe that the social position of women and national policymaking are central to any satisfactory explanation for the varying levels of MENA fertility rates

One hypothesis is that poor health conditions raise fertility rates. Much evidence suggests that high infant mortality stimulates fertility. The logic is clear: For both economic and emotional reasons, parents are interested in *surviving* children. If many infants die, people will, on average, tend to have more children to compensate. One study found that more than one-third of the decline in fertility was "explained" (in the statistical sense) by health improvements (Dyer and Yousef 2003). Although infant mortality rates in the region are high relative to those of advanced industrial countries, they have come down very sharply in the past several decades: from 128 per thousand births in 1970 to 92 in 1980, 59 in 1990, and to 45 in 2003. MENA infant mortality is below the average for LDCs (60) and well below that for Africa (104) and South Asia (67). Studies of Iran stress the role of improved health in that country's dramatic fertility decline (Abbasi-Shavazi 2001; Roudi-Fahimi 2002; see also Box 4.1). Conundrums appear among countries in the region. For example, Turkey has a notably higher infant mortality rate than Syria (33 versus 16), yet fertility in Syria (3.3) is well above that of its northern neighbor (2.4) (UNICEF 2005).

Economic analysis provides a useful perspective on fertility. Although any couple's decision to have a child is a complex product of social norms and personal psychology, some insights can be gained if one views the decision as similar to any other economic decision, as a balancing of "costs" and "benefits," recognizing from the outset that neither of these will be exclusively monetary. This view suggests that since most people like children they will tend to have *more* of them as they become richer, just as they buy more clothes, meat, radios, and entertainment. How, then, are we to explain the observed correlation between higher incomes and lower fertility? Economic analysts of demography argue that the key is the rising *opportunity cost of having children* as family incomes rise. This rising cost has two major components: (1) the increased amount of money that parents wish to spend on each child, and (2) the higher opportunity cost of parents' time. If rising incomes do not generate enough to meet these costs, increased wealth may do little to reduce fertility.

An important component of the opportunity cost of having children is their economic activity: The earlier children can perform productive labor, the sooner their net contributions to the family budget will be positive. In most peasant societies, including those of the Middle East, children can and do perform numerous tasks, ranging from caring for younger children to harvesting cotton. In general, the more child labor is performed in agriculture, the lower the opportunity cost of having many children and therefore the higher the fertility rate. This aspect of the argument that low levels of development engender high fertility is certainly reasonable and is confirmed by evidence from the region. This relationship is much less evident in urban areas. Consequently, rapidly increasing urbanization (see Chapter 10) may facilitate fertility declines.

Similarly, children perform an important function as "pension funds"—as the providers of income and care in old age. If, as in MENA, such a burden falls on the sons and if child mortality is high, an average peasant or urban poor family will rationally want to have seven births to ensure that two sons survive to provide for them in old age. Here, too, MENA countries resemble most developing countries, and therefore the "insurance" motive for children cannot explain the relatively high fertility levels in half of the MENA countries—especially those with higher capita incomes.

A critical component of the economic analysis of fertility is the opportunity of *women's* time, since women have primary responsibility for child care everywhere in the world. If women are illiterate and if they are more or less systematically excluded from alternative employment, the opportunity cost of their time will be low. When such considerations are combined with and reinforced by social pressures on women to have many children, the result is likely to be a high fertility rate.

The socioeconomic status of women is therefore crucial to fertility. Despite important improvements, the adult literacy figures for women in the Middle East remain low in international comparative perspective (see Table 4.2). There is much evidence that higher education is correlated with lower fertility (see Figures 4.3 and 4.5). Educated women both want to have fewer children and are more likely to use birth control to achieve their desired family size. However, anomalies remain: Within all countries, more educated women have fewer children than their less educated counterparts. But the variation across countries is large; for example, illiterate Moroccans have fewer children, on average, than university-educated Palestinians

TABLE 4.2   Adult Literacy Rates, 2003

	Male	*Female*	*Total*	*Females as % of males*
Algeria	76	57	67	75
Egypt	67	44	56	66
Iran	83	69	76	83
Iraq	55	23	39	42
Israel	97	93	95	96
Jordan	95	84	90	88
Kuwait	84	80	82	95
Lebanon	92	80	86	87
Libya	91	68	80	75
Morocco	62	36	49	58
Oman	80	62	71	78
Saudi Arabia	83	67	75	81
Sudan	69	46	58	67
Syria	88	60	74	68
Tunisia	81	61	71	75
Turkey	93	77	85	83
UAE	75	79	77	105
Yemen	68	25	47	37

Source: UNICEF

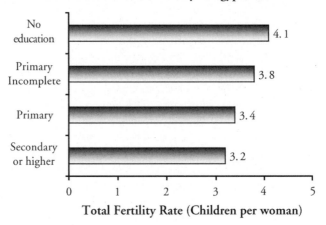

FIGURE 4.3   Fertility and education level in Egypt, 2000
SOURCE: ORC Marco, country final reports. Demographic and Health Surveys, at www.measuredhs.org

(see Figure 4.5). And as Figure 4.4 shows, fertility rates of illiterate Moroccan women have also declined over time.

Women's employment also lowers fertility, provided that it is outside of the home. Although many Middle Eastern rural women do participate extensively in crop and livestock production, such work is typically integrated with child care and thus creates little pressure to reduce fertility. Egyptian surveys showed that women who worked for cash outside of the home had an average of 3.2 births, compared with 4.9 for women who did not (USAID 1992). Women's participation in work that is more directly competitive with child rearing is, with a few exceptions, relatively low in the region; the female labor-force participation rate increased from roughly 25% in 1980 to 32% in 2000 (World Bank 2004c, 65). Despite these improvements, women's participation in the labor force remains the lowest in the world.

These considerations pose the question of how "culture" affects fertility and, in particular, what role Islam plays in promoting population growth. It should be obvious that the answer to the broadly stated question "Does culture affect fertility?" must be "Of course!" The social norms regulating the sexual division of labor and, indeed, all aspects of relations between the sexes powerfully shape individual actions. Specifying the precise ways in which culture influences reproductive behavior is extremely difficult, but we can offer a few general points. It is important to remember that most MENA countries have been until very recently largely peasant or herder societies. There are *no* peasant societies in which women are treated equally with men; everywhere the norm has been women's "social marginalization and economic centrality" (Meillassoux 1981). The importance of family life, the social and

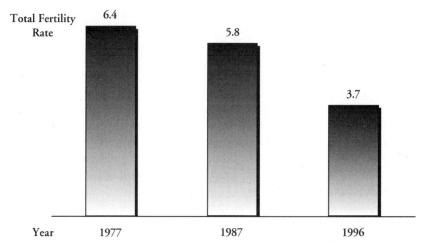

FIGURE 4.4 Changes in fertility of illiterate Moroccan women, 1977–1996
SOURCE: Courbage 1999

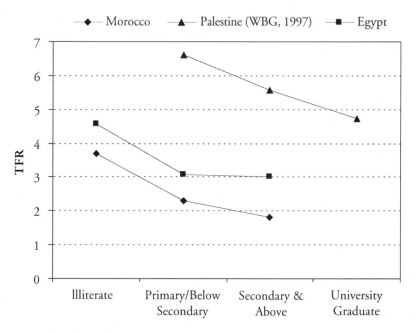

FIGURE 4.5 Total fertility rate and education level, Morocco, Palestine, and Egypt, 1996–1997
SOURCE: Courbage 1999

economic pressures to bear sons, and the strict control of women's sexuality are found in most peasant societies, whether Muslim or non-Muslim. Therefore, at least part of the subordination of women (and consequent high fertility rates) may be due to their position as peasants rather than as Muslims.

But this can hardly be the whole story. After all, China remains overwhelmingly a peasant society, yet its fertility rate has plummeted over the past several decades. Furthermore, to an outsider, Muslim societies seem especially socially restrictive for women. There are stringent practices of female seclusion and segregation of the sexes. Islamic law defines women as juridical minors; men can easily divorce women, whereas the reverse is not true; the father, not the mother, typically gets custody of the children. Some Muslim women try to have large families as a kind of "insurance policy" against divorce: A man might be more reluctant to divorce the mother of six than the mother of an only daughter.

— International evidence suggests a positive correlation between Islam and fertility. Albania (a majority Muslim country) has the highest fertility rate in Europe; Muslims in Malaysia have higher fertility than other religious groups in Malaysia. In Israel, Muslim women's TFR in 2000 was 4.5, whereas the rate for Christians was 2.35 and that for Jews was 2.53 (Courbage 1999). In India, Sri Lanka, and elsewhere, adherence to Islam has been shown to have an independent and positive impact on fertility (Mishra 2004). Not all studies find such a correlation, however; in Cameroon and the Central African Republic, Muslim fertility was not higher than adherents of other religions (Wasao 2001).

One must avoid essentialism here. Islam is a living religion. There is much debate in the Muslim world over personal-status questions. Many Muslim scholars believe that many of the practices that Westerners label "Islamic" are in fact corruptions of Islam, derived from other sources such as 'urf, or customary law. They are horrified by practices such as female genital cutting (also widely practiced in non-Muslim Africa and more rarely in West Asia) and regularly denounce them. This debate is critical; only internal change that is consistent with people's beliefs has any chance of affecting such deeply personal issues as the regulation of family life. When we say that "Islam" promotes the subordinate status of women and thus high fertility, we mean "Islam as currently practiced by (many) Muslims." Inconveniently for essentialists, the most rapid fall in fertility in world history occurred in the Islamic Republic of Iran! (See Box 4.1.)

More generally, all cultures are flexible; they can accommodate wide-ranging changes in economic, political, and social life. For example, one might summarize the above discussion by saying that Islam places great stress on family life and considers that women's primary place is in the home. But, then, of how many cultures could one say otherwise? Few would try to argue that family life is marginal in Chinese culture, yet fertility rates in China declined precipitously in the past several decades. Before the 1950s, the status of women in Chinese society was lower than in the poorest Muslim society: A married Chinese woman could own no property distinct from her husband's, divorce was even easier for men than in Muslim societies, and women were essentially the property of their husbands. Yet governments as diverse as that of the PRC, Taiwan, and Singapore have all succeeded in educating women, raising their legal status, and dramatically lowering fertility rates. "Culture" is not immutable.

The question is not whether "culture" or "belief systems" affect behavior but whether they would continue to produce high fertility *even after* substantial changes elsewhere in social and economic life. For example, it is clear that early marriage contributes to higher fertility. Few children are born outside of marriage in the Middle East; if couples are formed early in life, fertility will be higher. Demographic historians have shown that postponing the age of marriage was the principal mechanism for limiting fertility in preindustrial Europe and Japan (Mosk 1983; Wrigley and Schofield 1981; World Bank 1984). Early marriage is common in Islamic countries and receives social sanction and reinforcement. In the early 1980s about one young woman out of three was married before her nineteenth birthday (Lapham 1983). However, the median age at first marriage has risen in every Arab country since then. One study found that changes in nuptuality (marital status) were the key force lowering fertility in Tunisia, Morocco, and Algeria (Rashad and Khadr 2002). Significant changes in this area also occurred in Jordan and Syria. Contraceptive prevalence has also risen in all countries reporting data (except Iraq). At least one-half of married women in Algeria, Bahrain, Egypt, Iran, Israel, Jordan, Lebanon, Morocco, Tunisia, and Turkey use contraception (UNICEF 2005).

State policy can have a dramatic impact on fertility rates. A wide range of policies exist in the region, both those that affect desired family size (sometimes called "indirect" policies), such as health and education programs, and those that affect the number of children a couple actually has (birth control). Policies in MENA have eschewed coercion and have only lightly relied on disincentives (e.g., higher taxes for larger families). The main family planning policy approach (when there has been one at all) has been to subsidize birth control technology and to disseminate information through government health networks and the media.

Some countries—Turkey and Tunisia—have followed a consistent policy of promoting family planning since 1965. The Tunisian government has pushed for universal female schooling, raised the legal marriage age, made divorce more difficult, and ensured that birth control technology is widely available. The percentage of teenage women who were married fell from 42% in 1956 to only 6% in 1975. Fertility rates fell from over 7 at independence to 3.8 in 1992 to 2.0 in 2003—the last being the lowest in the region (see Table 4.1) and below replacement level. Reforms of family law were part of Atatürk's broader developmental vision for Turkey (see Chapters 2 and 7). After 1965 the Turkish government promoted family planning with subsidies and propaganda, support that has continued without significant interruption.

Other countries have displayed on-again, off-again family planning policies. Both Egypt and Iran fall into this category. Egypt launched a family planning program in 1965 that focused on the supply of birth control technology. However, the program languished under Sadat. The slogan of the time was "Development is the best contraceptive," and the focus was (in theory but not in practice) on, among other things, better health and increased female school enrollment. Gilbar (1992) argues that this shift was political—that Sadat tried to use the Muslim Brotherhood and other Islamists against the pro-Soviet left (see Chapter 14) and accordingly yielded to the Islamists' pronatalist views. Mubarak's government reversed this position, however, and with considerable donor assistance, launched a sustained program of family planning that began to show results in the early 1990s. Iranian policy reversals have been still more dramatic (see Box 4.1).

Most countries in the region now have some kind of family planning program (see Table 4.3). Yemen, which adopted a program in 1991, has, along with Turkey, Egypt, and Iran, set fertility targets for its program. Only countries whose leaders feel beleaguered—by war (Iran in the 1980s; Iraq under Saddam Hussein) or by the weight of numbers of unfriendly neighbors (Israel, Kuwait)—have explicitly pronatalist policies.

Apart from politically motivated pronatalism, neglect of family planning policy has several determinants. First and probably most important, the benefits of reduced population growth accrue in the future. Here, as elsewhere, myopia characterizes most government policy. Second, some governments believe that rapid population growth is not a problem; these pronatalist countries want more people. To evaluate this position one must consider the economic consequences of population growth and the politics of ethnic differences in population growth (see below). Third, many believe that changing economic conditions will reduce population growth, so the problem will take care of itself. This argument, however, ignores the considerable evidence that the availability of family planning exerts an independent negative pressure on fertility rates.

Perhaps the critical point here is not whether governments can affect fertility (they can) but, rather, how hard they have to try—what it costs them politically. We should also ask what the role of religion is in such costs. The legal age of marriage is

TABLE 4.3   Policy on Fertility Level, 2004

Policy on access to contraceptives	Raise fertility	Maintain fertility	Lower fertility	No Intervention
Direct Support	n.a.	Bahrain, Iran, Jordan, Lebanon, Yemen	Algeria, Egypt, Morocco, Tunisia, Qatar	Djibouti, Iraq, Syria
Indirect Support	n.a.	n.a.	n.a.	Kuwait
No Support	Saudi Arabia	Oman	n.a.	Libya, UAE

n.a. Not applicable
SOURCE: United Nations, World Bank

◌ BOX 4.1

The Fertility Revolution in Iran

Iranian family planning has undergone two sharp reversals. In 1965 the shah instituted a family planning policy that, like most such programs at the time, stressed the "supply side": the availability of contraception. The program collapsed after the Islamic Revolution, since the new regime associated it with both the shah and the West, which had helped to finance it. Notwithstanding the fact that the Ayatollah Khomeini issued a *fatwa* permitting contraception and family planning, social traditionalism and the war with Iraq combined to produce a pronatalist policy. The minimum age for marriage was reduced, the High Council for Coordination of Family Planning was disbanded, contraceptives became harder to get, and the government provided large families with special housing and food subsidies. These policies contributed to the reversal of fertility decline. The TFR rose from 6.5 in 1976 to 7.0 in 1986 (Omran and Roudi 1993). The rate of natural increase rose from 2.9% between 1966–1967 and 1976–1977 to 3.9% between 1976–1977 and 1986–1987; the total fertility rate in 1994 was 6.2 (Bulatao and Richardson 1994).

The census of 1986 served as a "wake-up call" for planners, and the end of the war with Iraq in 1988 provided them with their opportunity. Fertility had already begun to fall, but only slightly, and it remained unacceptably high. The government completely reversed course, establishing a Population Committee in the Ministry of Health and Medical Education. The committee set a goal of reducing the TFR to 4.0. Contraceptives were reintroduced into the primary health care system, which covered Iran's vast rural areas as well as the cities, a crucial factor according to most analyses (Abbasi-Shavazi 2001; Roudi-Fahimi 2002). In 1990 the government legalized female sterilization, and both male and female sterilization were offered without charge (for any man or woman with three or more children). Seminars and the media have been, and are, extensively used to promote family planning. In May 1993 the *majlis* (Iranian parliament) passed a law requiring the withdrawal of some subsidies from families that had a fourth or higher-order child after May 1994.

The results of these policies, combined with increasing female literacy and (probably) economic hardship, have been dramatic. The country's total fertility rate fell to 2.8 by 1996, and today it is between 2.0 and 2.1—below replacement level! Rural fertility fell exceptionally swiftly: from 8.1 in 1976 to 2.4 in 2000 (Roudi-Fahimi 2002). Whereas some 37% of married couples practiced contraception in 1976, 74% did so by 2000. Fertility fell in every province and among all ethnicities. Iran's fertility decline has been one of the fastest in history. Policy matters—greatly.

still only fifteen in countries such as Kuwait and Yemen. Raising it prompts opposition from Islamic revivalists, as in the mass demonstrations against King Muhammad VI's plan to increase the legal age of marriage for girls in Morocco to eighteen. It is probably not accidental that Moroccan television did not begin showing family planning information until 1982, when economic crisis left little choice. But the politics here are complex: In Morocco, the king prevailed, and the legal age of marriage changed from fifteen to eighteen in January 2004. Meanwhile, the first change in the Turkish Family Code since 1926, raising the legal age of marriage and increasing women's rights in marriage and divorce, occurred under the moderate Islamist government of Recep Tayyip Erdoğan. In Turkey, the desire to join the European Union trumped any patriarchal ideology in the political project of his Justice and Development party. Each government, and each political party, maps its own strategy. Such stories strongly suggest that high fertility levels are the result of political, not cultural, problems in the Middle East.

THE ECONOMIC CONSEQUENCES
OF DEMOGRAPHIC CHANGE

How does demographic change affect economic development? A few analysts believe that population growth is a good thing. Members of this minority can point out that in the Middle East, for example, the standard of living and life prospects of the roughly 60 million Egyptians alive today far exceed those of their 10 million grandparents in 1900. They also note that some of the development problems of the Sudan are the result of a highly dispersed population. One could accept such arguments without necessarily swallowing the more-is-better line whole, but one does need to specify just how high fertility and rapid population growth will affect national economies.

Pressure on Educational Systems

A critical feature of the demography of Middle Eastern countries is the large proportion of the total population that is young. A comparison of age pyramids for a few countries in the region with that of the United States is instructive (see Figure 4.6). Nearly half of Middle Easterners are younger than twenty years old, and young populations are by nature rapidly growing populations, as their reproductive years lie ahead them. It is worth noting, however, that the age pyramid for the Middle East in the nineteenth century, before rapid population growth began, would have looked quite similar. This is because declines in mortality, which drive increases in population growth, affect the survival of not only the young but also the old; the relative percentage of young people does not shift much when the death rate falls. By contrast, a sharp drop in the fertility rate quickly reduces the proportion of young people in the population, and this proportion is further reduced by continued improvements in health that prolong old age. However, the *scale* of the problem today is entirely different; it is the absolute number of young people now,

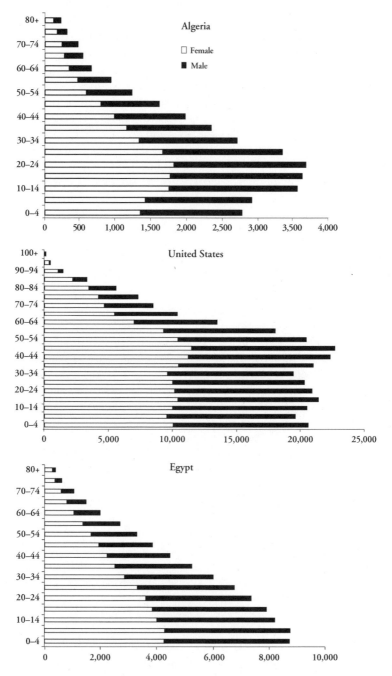

FIGURE 4.6 Distribution of midyear population by age and sex in Algeria, the United States, and Egypt, 2006
SOURCE: US Census Bureau, International Database

rather than their proportion to the rest of the population, that makes the critically important difference.

There is near consensus among demographers that rapid population growth leads to a reduction in the amount of money spent per pupil (see the discussion in National Research Council 1986). This usually takes the form of reduced teacher salaries and high pupil-teacher ratios. As we shall see in the next chapter, most countries try very hard to fund education adequately. A country committed to educating its children will find it more difficult to offer primary education to all if their numbers are growing rapidly. For example, although the total number of Algerian children enrolled in primary school nearly quadrupled from 1962 to 1978, there were still more than 1 million school-age children not in school in 1978 (Bennoune 1988). Similarly, although education absorbs over one-fifth of the Yemeni government budget, nearly half of girls are still not in school (Republic of Yemen 2004). During the next twenty years, the number of young Palestinians requiring education will rise by about 50%; in Yemen it will rise by 45% (Courbage 1999). Rapid population growth swamps even the most determined attempts to diffuse basic education.

Rapid Increase in the Number of Job Seekers

The problems that a burgeoning number of young people create for society are not limited to educational difficulties. The impact on the job market is equally profound. Indeed, the rapid increase in the number of job seekers may be *the* key challenge facing the region's political economy. Everywhere in the region, the labor force is growing much more quickly than the demand for labor. The numbers are startling. The growth rate of the labor force steadily accelerated every decade from the 1960s through the 1990s (see Figure 4.7). Despite the recent deceleration (which tracks the deceleration in population growth, with a lag), the rate of growth will remain the highest in the world through at least 2020. The total numbers of new job seekers have risen steadily: 47 million for the four decades from 1950 to 1990; 32 million during the decade of 1990s; 42 million from 2000 to 2010; and 39 million from 2010 to 2020 (World Bank 2004c). A simple way to put this is that MENA economies must create jobs *roughly four times as fast as the US economy* just to maintain current (high) levels of unemployment. The challenge is daunting.

Two forces drive labor force growth: (declining) population growth rates and (rising) female labor force participation rates. Since past population growth rates have changed differentially, the future rates of growth of the labor force vary considerably across countries. In some cases, for example, Yemen and Palestine, growth is accelerating; in others, for example, Tunisia, it is decelerating; in still others, for example, Morocco, it has stayed roughly the same. Iran now faces a surge in labor supply. When these rates (whether rapidly accelerating or slightly declining) are applied to expanding bases, we have a *demographic momentum* that ensures large future total additions to the labor force.

Some analysts (Fargues 1994; Courbage 1999) use the deceleration in past fertility to predict the year when additions to the labor force will be just matched by

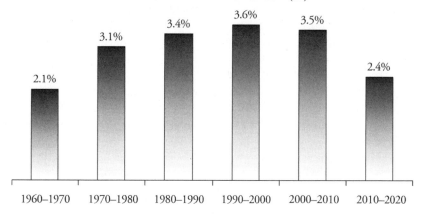

FIGURE 4.7   MENA labor force growth rate
SOURCE: World Bank 2004

those reaching retirement age (defined as sixty to sixty-five). The predicted year is 2015 in Tunisia, 2020 in Morocco and Algeria, 2025 in Egypt, and even farther in the future in Syria. These analysts note that the number of new job seekers entering the labor market every year will range from an increase of 40% of the 1990 level in Tunisia to an increase of 125% in Syria. The general conclusion that the Maghreb is in considerably better shape than the countries farther east seems valid, but even the best performer, Tunisia, faces a demographically driven tidal wave of young job seekers for at least the next ten years.

The number of job seekers will not be driven by demographic forces alone. Precisely the same social force that brings down fertility rates (and thereby reduces, with a fifteen-to-twenty-year lag, demographic pressure on the labor market) also increases the number of women looking for work. Better-educated women tend to want fewer children and a job outside the home. Increasingly, growth in the labor force will be driven by this social (rather than purely demographic) force. Fargues suggests that a critical determinant of women's labor force participation in the region is the *gap* between a husband's and a wife's education: "It is the husband, and not the children, who keeps the woman out of the labor market" (1994, 169). When measured by enrollment ratios, men's education in the region is about a generation ahead of women's. Given the rapid increase in female enrollment ratios during the past two decades, the current younger generation has a smaller gap than older-age cohorts. Accordingly, Fargues argues, men will be less likely to try to keep their wives out of the labor market. Rising female labor force participation will increasingly displace demography as the engine of labor force growth in MENA.

It is perhaps not coincidental that the Islamists seem so obsessed with the position of women (see also Chapter 14). Part of their appeal is precisely the "send them back to the kitchen" rhetoric that often becomes prominent in many societies when unemployment rises. There is often a gap in the educational level of young men and their (prospective) wives. The combination of rising unemployment among urban males, men who are not only young and relatively well educated but also unmarried (in Morocco, 80% of the unemployed in the largest cities are unmarried), and rising female labor force participation creates intense psychological pressure.

Even if the number of jobs created can match the number of jobs sought, the result will be simply some combination of stable unemployment and stagnant real wages (see Chapter 5). A rapidly expanding labor force compels the diversion of investment to providing jobs with a given amount of capital per worker. Since increasing the amount of capital per worker is typically necessary to raise worker productivity and therefore incomes, rapid population increase slows the growth of per capita incomes, if all other factors remain unchanged. Rapid population growth means that money must be spent just to create jobs, rather than to improve those that already exist or to create more productive ones. It is particularly difficult to create the entry-level jobs that the young labor force requires, especially when skilled older workers are so scarce. The problem is particularly acute in states without oil resources: Where funds for investment remain scarce, rapid population growth slows the pace of growth and development.[4]

Other Development Problems

Rapid population growth exacerbates other development problems as well. Investable funds are diverted not merely from "capital deepening" but from any form of job creation to social-overhead investment (e.g., housing, water and sewage systems). Some investment may be necessary simply to repair the damage caused by population growth, such as the rehabilitation of ecologically degraded areas. Rapid population increase contributes to the very rapid growth of cities, which are expanding at roughly twice the rate of the overall population in the region. Such rapid urban population growth not only diverts investment funds but also strains the administrative capacities of governments and generates political problems. Rapid population growth contributes to a soaring demand for food in the region and increases pressure on already-scarce water supplies (see Chapter 6). Finally, by increasing the supply of labor relative to capital and by raising the ratio of unskilled to skilled labor, rapid population growth probably worsens the distribution of income.

Population growth is neither an exogenous force nor a monocause of development problems. It is merely one (albeit important) variable in the ensemble of relationships in the political economy. But the rapid growth of population does slow economic development in the region, and it also poses political problems.

A "Demographic Dividend"?

Just as accelerating population growth poses serious development problems, the recent deceleration in population growth may offer an important economic opportunity. The encouraging recent declines in fertility may lead to a rapid decrease in the "dependency ratio" (the number of people under fifteen and over sixty-five divided by the working-age population). There is some evidence that this is already happening (Williamson and Yousef 2002). When this happened elsewhere, as in East Asia in the 1970s and 1980s, dramatic increases in national savings rates ensued. The logic is straightforward: People save during their working lives, whereas children and the retired do not (or save at a much lower rate). Williamson and Yousef assert that the demographic change causes the increase in the savings rate (based on their life-cycle savings model). They are quick to note, however, that whether the increased savings find their way into productive and job-creating investment depends on other factors, including governance. That is, politics will determine whether this demographic dividend pays off or whether it becomes yet another sad "might-have-been" in regional history.

THE POLITICS OF YOUNG POPULATIONS

In countries with moderate or low population growth rates, political leadership is generally drawn from an age pool that contains a significant proportion, if not the majority, of the population. In North America, Western and Eastern Europe, the former Soviet Union, and Japan, not only are most citizens legal adults (about 70% of the US population is twenty years old or older), but the populations as a whole are aging. There is in these countries a much more profound sharing of experience between leaders and their major constituencies than is to be found in societies experiencing rapid population growth. Political generations are often depicted as having been shaped by national crises. For example, Churchill, Roosevelt, Truman, Stalin, and de Gaulle all spoke for a generation that shared the trauma of the world Depression and World War II. In 1980 there were 57 million Americans, or 26% of the population of the United States, who were born before 1925, grew up during the Depression, and were at least teenagers during World War II. That experience provided them and their elected leaders a common language and a set of symbols that were drawn from their own lives.

The situation in the Middle East, as in many developing areas, is radically different. When we note that in 2000 two-thirds of the Algerian population was under thirty years old, we can see startling political implications. First, only one-half of the population are adults in the legal sense, entitled to vote and stand for election. Also, more than 70% of all living Algerians were born after independence in 1962. They had no direct experience of the French colonial presence or of the seven years of war and devastation that preceded independence. By contrast, *all* of Algeria's presidents since 1962—Ahmad Ben Bella (1962–1965), Houari Boumedienne (1965–1978), Chadli Benjadid (1979–1991), Mohammed Boudiaf (January–June 1992), 'Ali Kafi (1992–1994), Liamine Zéroual (1994–1999), and Abdelaziz Bouteflika (1999–)— have been of the generation shaped by the revolutionary war. Their legitimacy, such as it is, stems directly from their role in the struggle against France, but for most Algerians that struggle is history, not a living memory or a shared experience.

Equally striking is the phenomenon of the Ayatollah Khomeini of Iran. Born at the turn of the century, he lived through the demise of the Qajar dynasty, the constitutional struggles of the 1920s, the consolidation of the autocratic regime of Reza Shah, the postwar confrontation between Reza Shah's son and the nationalist prime minister, Mohammed Mossadegh, and finally, the shah's launching of the White Revolution in 1963. It was Khomeini's virulent opposition to various changes wrought by that revolution that forced him into an exile that ended in 1979 with the deposition of the shah and Khomeini's triumphant return to an Islamic and republican Iran.

The majority of Iranians have been born since Khomeini went into exile. They did not live through the effervescence and occasional violence of the shah's White Revolution, which consisted of a series of measures involving land reform, female suffrage, the right of non-Muslims to stand as candidates, and the creation of a literacy corps. They did not hear or witness Khomeini's denunciations of some of these measures or his opposition to the special legal status granted to US personnel at that time. Even rarer are Iranians old enough to have participated in the events of 1953, when Prime Minister Mossadegh nationalized British oil interests and drove the young shah, Mohammed Reza Pahlavi, into brief exile.

One could go on with examples of the enormous disparities in age and experience of leaders and followers in the Middle East: Habib Bourguiba, born in 1903 and president of Tunisia from 1956 to 1987, and the septuagenarians that led Lebanon for years (Camille Chamoun, Suleiman Frangieh, Kemal Jumblatt, Pierre Jamayyel) are cases in point. Although Muqtada al-Sadr (born in 1973) has recently risen to prominence in Iraq, by most accounts the septuagenarian Ayatollah Sistani (born in 1930) remains Iraq's most politically influential single person. Only in the past decade has a new generation of leaders finally emerged in Jordan, Morocco, Palestine, and Syria.

There may yet be enough deference paid to age in the Middle East that the youthful majorities of the region will not reject or confront their relatively aged leaders. Khomeini's prestige among Iranians appeared undiminished at least until the cease-fire with Iraq in the summer of 1988, and hundreds of thousands of young Iranians died in the name of an anti-Iraqi crusade that he insisted on pursuing. There is evidence, however, that Islamic movements have been successful in mobilizing young people hitherto kept on the fringes of political systems that claim to represent them (see especially Chapters 12 and 14).

THE POLITICS OF DIFFERENTIAL FERTILITY

In defining the rights and obligations of citizens, the constitutions of most Middle Eastern states are blind to their ethnic or religious origins. Nonetheless, in a de facto sense, the relative weights of religious and ethnic communities are important in the political calculus of each state's leadership. There is an unstated expectation that the flows of public patronage will reflect communal weights. If the pattern of income distribution, particularly the locus of poverty, corresponds closely to ethnic or religious boundaries, then a potentially explosive situation may develop. The violent assertion of Shi'ite demands in Lebanon is a dramatic example.

The only way to know the population of various ethnic communities is through the national census. Censuses are carried out under the control of the national authority and can be manipulated to reflect its interests. In Turkey, where since the 1920s there have been repeated assertions of Kurdish separatism in Eastern Anatolia, the national census provides no head count of the ethnic Kurds. In Iraq, where ethnicity (Kurd/Arab) cuts across religious sect (Sunni/Shi'i Muslim), regimes before 2003 were dominated by Sunni Arabs. Periodically there was talk of autonomy for regions in which Kurds predominate, but to delimit these regions requires a census. While negotiating over conducting a census, the regime of Saddam Hussein resettled Arabs in Kurdish areas and Kurds, who are Sunni Muslims, in Shi'ite areas in order to achieve a desired census outcome. (Under the American occupation, these trends have been reversing, often violently.) In Egypt the problem is one of adjusting census results. The Coptic Christian minority there has always protested that it has been undercounted by some 50% in Egypt's national census.

The problem of ethnic and sectarian head counting is most acute in Lebanon and Israel. The system of political representation in Lebanon, cobbled together by the French after World War I, was founded on sectarian communities. Representatives in parliament competed for seats that were allocated in proportion to the numerical strength of each religious group in the population. The basic ratio consisted of six Christian seats in parliament for every five Muslim seats. After 1989, when fourteen years of civil war finally came to an end, the ratio was adjusted to five to five.

The original formula resulted from Lebanon's last official census in 1932. At that time the total population was 793,000. The Maronite Christians alone constituted 29% of the population, while Greek Orthodox, Armenians, Greek Catholics, and others gave the Christians a narrow but absolute majority of the population. The second-largest religious group was the Sunni Muslims, with 21% of the population. The Shi'ites were, in 1932, 18% of the population.

It was clear to everyone that the natural rate of increase of the Muslim populations was more rapid than that of the Christians. Moreover, the rate of long-term migration outside of Lebanon was higher among Christians than among Muslims. There was little doubt that a post–World War II census would show that the Christians had become a minority in Lebanon. Following the logic of the confessional system of apportionment, they would have lost the presidency and the majority of the seats in parliament. The result: No official census has been taken in Lebanon since 1932. In the past few decades there have been several informal attempts to measure the Lebanese population. They all show that the Shi'ites have become the single largest religious group in Lebanon. Neither the Christians nor the Sunni Muslims wish to concede this fact officially.

Estimates of the Lebanese population distribution have varied widely. Consider Table 4.4. The two sets of data for 1983 reveal a discrepancy of more than 1 million people. Only Arnon Soffer (1986), source of one of the two sets of data for 1983, explained the derivation of his figures, which assume 80,000 dead in the civil war

TABLE 4.4   Lebanon's Estimated Population by Sect, 1932 and 1983

	1932		1983		1983	
	Population	*%*	*Population*	*%*	*Population*	*%*
Total Christians	410,246	51.7	1,525,000	42.6	965,000	36.6
Maronites	226,378	28.6	900,000	25.0	580,000	21.0
Greek Orthodox	76,522	9.6	250,000	7.0	185,000	6.8
Creek Catholic	45,999	5.8	150,000	4.2	115,000	4.2
Armenians	31,156	4.0	175,000	4.9	70,000	2.6
Others[a]	30,191	3.8	50,000	1.4	40,000	1.5
Total Muslims and Druze	383,180	48.3	2,050,000	57.6	1,435,000	60.2
Sunnis	175,925	22.2	750,000	21.0	600,000	25.0
Shit'ites	154,208	19.4	1,100,000	31.0	665,000	27.5
Druze	53,047	6.7	200,000	5.6	180,000	7.7
Total	793,426	100.0	3,575,000	100.0	2,400,000	100.0

[a]Includes Jews.
SOURCES: First and last columns from Soffer (1986, 199); middle column from Minority Rights (1983), as cited in *Middle East*, March 1986, 41

(more recent estimates put the death toll close to 150,000) and the emigration of 400,000 Lebanese, half of whom were Maronite Christians. He also put the foreign population of Lebanon at 220,000 Palestinians and 80,000 others. The Shi'ites are the poorest of all the religious sects. They are concentrated in the impoverished southern agricultural area bordering Israel, with large pockets of relatively poor migrants in Sidon and Beirut. Their resentment over years of neglect took violent form during the civil war of 1975–1989, when the Shi'ites sought to win economic and political rewards commensurate with their numbers.

In Israel, questions of ethnic and religious numbers are equally sensitive, and as in Lebanon, communal boundaries correspond to differential socioeconomic status. However, in Israel censuses have been taken regularly, and the resulting data alarm the Israeli establishment. The question is not as simple as how many Jews and non-Jews live in Israel. The Jews themselves are divided between the Ashkenazim, of East European origin, and the Sephardim (or more accurately the Oriental Jews), of Middle Eastern and Spanish origin. Israel's political establishment has been dominated since independence by the Ashkenazim. As a group they are highly educated and relatively wealthy, and they tend to have small families. The Oriental Jews, by contrast, occupy lower socioeconomic positions in Israeli society and are seen as more traditional. Birthrates among the Oriental Jews are higher than among the Ashkenazim, and the former and their Israeli-born offspring have become a majority of the Jewish population. They have yet to inherit the political kingdom.

Far more crucial is the question of Israeli-Arab birthrates. Over the period 1950–2000, the Israeli-Arab community grew at the extraordinary rate of more than 4% per annum, or from 160,000 to 1,345,500 in 2004, out of a total population of 6.9 million. Non-Jews thus represented just under one-fifth (19.5%) of the total population. Even with significant in-migration from abroad, the Israeli Jewish population over the same period grew by only 2.6% per annum during the second half of the twentieth century. Jewish rates of natural increase and of immigration declined over time, although the influx of Soviet Jews after 1989 marginally reversed that trend.

Since the June War of 1967, Israel has occupied the West Bank, formerly under Jordanian control, and Gaza, formerly under Egyptian control, and has annexed East Jerusalem and the Golan Heights. In 2003 there were some 1.2 million Palestinians in Gaza and 2.4 million in the West Bank and East Jerusalem. Israel's dilemma is twofold. First, if present trends continue, Israeli citizens of Arab origin will come to constitute nearly 20% of the population. A minority of that size, if not fully reconciled to the Israeli state, could severely test its democratic system. Second, if Israel decides, for security or religious reasons, to annex the West Bank and Gaza, that would raise the proportion of non-Jews in Israel to around one-half (see Figure 4.8). On political grounds alone, few Jewish Israelis are prepared to accept that. In a more profound sense it would constitute the abandonment of the Zionist quest for a Jewish state. There are three alternatives: (1) expel the Palestinian populations from the West Bank; (2) concede sovereignty over the West Bank and Gaza to some sort of Palestinian entity through negotiations; or (3) unilaterally withdraw from selected areas. In 1993, after years of *intifada*, Israel and the Palestine Liberation Organization signed the Declaration of Principles that seemed to cast the die in favor of the second alternative. The trauma during the years 2002–2007 has led to Israeli implementation of the third approach beginning in 2005.

Although the problem has been seemingly less acute, Kuwait, the UAE, Qatar, and Saudi Arabia face politically perilous demographic situations. Like Israel, they domicile large numbers of residents without citizenship. For the most part these are migrant workers and professionals from the oil-poor countries of the region, as well as from India, Pakistan, and points farther east. In Kuwait there was also a substantial community of Palestinian refugees before 1991. In these countries, not only is most of the workforce foreign, but nearly half the resident population may also be foreign (see Chapter 15). Moreover, because they are worker-migrants, they are adults and preponderantly male. Illustrative sex-age charts for countries sending labor to the Gulf (Yemen) and those receiving labor (Qatar) appear in Figure 4.9. Although the economic life of these countries is dependent upon these workers, they have been excluded from political life. To date they have not exploited their strategic economic position to express political demands, but the possibility that they might do so is sufficiently alarming that all the host states are actively pursuing policies to diminish their numbers (see Chapter 15).

Nearly every country in the Middle East is to some extent affected by the issues of counting various minorities and the different rates at which their numbers grow. In policy terms the ideal of the homogeneous nation-state in which every citizen is equal to every other is something of a myth. In that sense, the national census

2005

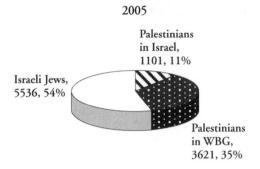

2020

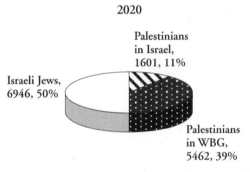

FIGURE 4.8   Share of Israeli Jews and Palestinian Arabs in Israel and in West Bank/Gaza, 2005 and 2020
SOURCE: Courbage 1999

becomes the instrument both for determining relative weights and for granting or denying formal recognition to specific minorities.

RAPID POPULATION GROWTH AND THE WOULD-BE MIDDLE CLASS

More than forty years ago Manfred Halpern (1963, 62–66) wrote of the new middle class and the would-be middle class in the Middle East and North Africa. He had in mind those educated Middle Easterners who had moved into the white-collar ranks of the civil service and the professions as well as the educated Middle Easterners who aspired to those ranks but could find no room in them. Part of the danger that Halpern foresaw was the formation of a kind of intellectual proletariat made up of upwardly mobile but frustrated young men. It must be stressed that it is only recently that educated Middle Eastern women have entered the job market in appreciable numbers.

Over the past three decades, the structural problem that Halpern sketched has become far more acute. Today there are roughly 135 million Middle Easterners between

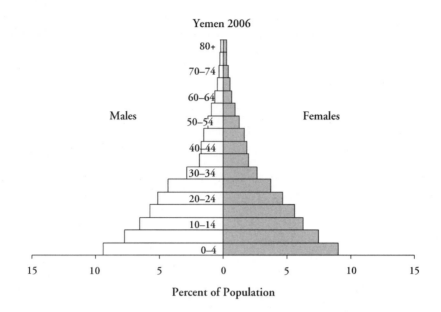

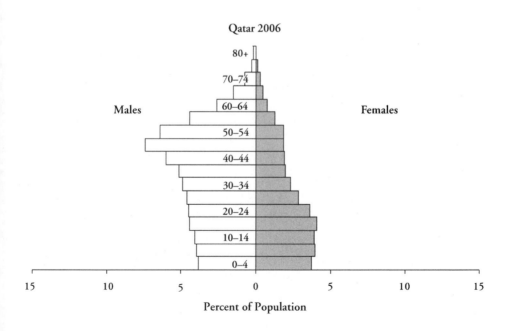

FIGURE 4.9   Age and sex profiles of Yemen and Qatar, 2006
SOURCE: Calculated from US Census Bureau, International Database

the ages of fifteen and thirty out of a total population of over 440 million. Most of the males among them have some education. Until the 1950s a high-school diploma would have qualified the recipient for a comfortable if unglamorous white-collar job, a decent standard of living, and a modicum of prestige. That is no longer the case. The young Middle Easterners recruited into the civil service and professions during the 1960s are only now beginning to retire. They have enjoyed rapid promotion, and some have risen to the top of their administrative hierarchies. Yet behind them are new, even larger cohorts of men and women with equal aspirations and sometimes better professional credentials. They are being offered make-work jobs, if offered a job at all, salaries that lag behind inflation, and low social status. Their numbers are growing and will continue to grow for at least a generation. It is hard to see how and where they can be productively absorbed into the workforce. Because they are literate and politically aware, denying them material security is potentially dangerous.

It is reasonably clear that this age group contributes significantly to various kinds of radical movements, from the street fighters of Baghdad to the Islamic militants of Cairo, Gaza, and Tunis. One would be wrong, however, to attribute common political attitudes to an entire age cohort. Its members are just as likely to be worker-migrants to the Gulf States or to be following conventional career paths in the bureaucracy or service sector as they are to be political activists. Yet the opportunities for them to achieve their aspirations will narrow as their numbers increase. They have not been, nor are they likely to become, passive in the face of this situation.

Middle Eastern regimes have experimented with an array of policies to contain the menace, from the creation of redundant civil service jobs to the encouragement of migration abroad. Until the rate at which jobs can be created comes into equilibrium with the rate at which this generation grows, these young people will constitute an important source of political instability in the Middle East. The region is not unique in this respect; much the same analysis could be applied to India or Mexico or a host of other developing countries. In the Middle East, however, the problem is more acute because, as we have seen, the growth of the region's labor force is greater than elsewhere.

CONCLUSION

The approaches to population growth and control in developing countries have taken some peculiar twists. In the 1950s and 1960s the United States and other developed nations urged the LDCs to adopt national programs of family planning and population control. Many in the developing world saw these urgings as racist in nature—as white fear of the rising tide of blacks, browns, and yellows. Moreover, it was an era of grandiose development plans and optimism in the Third World. High rates of economic growth suggested that ever-larger numbers of people would be provided for and employed. It was assumed that larger cohorts of the young could be educated and trained so as to contribute to the growth effort rather than be a drain upon it. A striking example of this outlook is provided by President Houari Boumedienne, who in one speech (June 19, 1969) squelched a campaign for family planning that had been quietly building in Algeria. Inaugurating a huge steel works at Annaba, he said (as quoted in Waterbury 1973, 18):

> Our goal . . . over the next twenty years is to assure that our people, who will number 25 million souls, will have a standard of living which will be among the highest of the modern peoples of the world of tomorrow. I take this opportunity to say—concerning what is called "galloping demography"—that we are not partisans of false solutions such as the limitation of births. We believe that that is the same as suppressing difficulties instead of searching for adequate solutions. . . . We believe that the real solution to this problem resides in development, even if that demands greater efforts.

Few leaders in the Middle East today would be prepared to make such a statement. Indeed, despite the admonitions of Muslim leaders who tend to see the strength of Islam as lying in numbers, secular leaders have come to see the need to lower birthrates. As we have seen, even the Islamic Republic of Iran has dramatically reversed ground on its pronatalist policies and since the early 1990s has been actively pursuing policies of fertility control.

There do seem to be "carrying capacities" in various economic systems, and although they may be elastic, they are not infinitely so. To contribute to economic growth, each Middle Easterner needs good health, education, and some vocational or professional skills, but numbers have often overwhelmed the capacities of economies and administrations to provide these goods. In the next chapter we examine the record of the Middle East in this regard.

NOTES

1. That is, "the total fertility rate represents the number of children that would be born per woman, assuming that she lives to the end of her childbearing years and bears children at each age in accord with prevailing age-specific fertility rates" (World Bank 1984, 282).

2. The replacement level TFR is generally assumed to be 2.1.

3. A recent sophisticated statistical analysis found that 38% of the variance of regional TFRs was "unexplained" (Dyer and Yousef 2003, cited in World Bank 2004c, 51).

4. This conclusion would be invalidated only if more rapid population growth either increased the domestic savings rate or stimulated additional capital inflows from abroad. Little evidence supports either conjecture.

5

HUMAN CAPITAL

Health, Education, and Labor Markets

Whatever one's views of population growth, few dispute the necessity of ameliorating health conditions and educating people as widely as possible—of investing in human capital. Two sturdy conceptual pillars undergird this consensus, so unusual in social science. First, all agree that good health and universal literacy are ends in themselves. A society that fails to educate its children and to eradicate preventable disease may be justifiably accused of neglecting the general welfare. Second, analysts believe that healthier and better-educated people are more productive. There are important "virtuous circles" among education, health, fertility decline, and labor productivity. Neoclassical economists point to high rates of return on investments in human capital, while Marxists stress the need for socialist regimes to liberate the productive potential of the masses. It is rare in the field of development studies to find such substantively similar conclusions emanating from such radically different perspectives. Human capital issues are particularly important for the countries of the Middle East and North Africa because, with the obvious exception of oil, the region is relatively poor in natural resources. Therefore, many argue that development of human resources should lie at the center of national development plans.

Although performance varies widely by country, in general, the region made dramatic progress during the past generation. The average child born today in MENA can expect to live twenty-five years longer than could one born in 1970 (World Bank 2002). Despite the persistence of pockets of neglect, nearly four out of five children are now in primary school. Although adult illiteracy, especially among women, remains widespread, the "gender gap" in school enrollments is narrowing everywhere. The status of women's education is critical; considerable evidence suggests that basic education for women dramatically improves the health of their children. For the first time in history, more than four of five boys and seven of ten girls can read and write.

Such positive changes provide a welcome contrast to the sea of other, more somber news about the region's political economy.

Despite these gains, the education that Middle Easterners receive often fails to provide them with the skills and training that modern industrial and commercial life requires. When the demand for skills and the supply of skills are poorly matched, the labor market experiences constant disequilibria and unemployment is high. The relationship is reciprocal: misconceived labor-market policies send socially ineffi-cient signals to privately rational individuals and families; when an academic degree opens access to potential lifetime employment, people demand more (and a differ-ent kind of) higher education than society needs. Once such policies are in place, they consume scarce resources, leaving less for the more socially productive tasks of universal literacy. The expansion of education, coupled with rapid population growth, has created a potent political force: secondary- and university-level students who often cannot find jobs consistent with their skills and aspirations.

In the second edition of this book we wrote:

> We have a glass half-empty/glass half-full situation: Current levels of health and education are unimpressive when compared with per capita incomes or with other regions, but change during the past generation has often been quite rapid. Starting from extremely low levels of health and literacy, many Middle Eastern nations have made dramatic advances during the past quarter century. They still have much unfinished business, but the achievements are undeniable.

Today, the glass is no longer half empty—but it is not yet entirely full. Most countries in the region continue to make important progress; however, there are still significant national, regional, gender, and social class gaps in access to the basic human rights of health and education. In addition, labor markets function inade-quately, and unemployment plagues individuals, families, and entire nations. De-spite real progress, the "ultimate resource" of human beings continues to be wasted far more than the region can afford.

HEALTH CONDITIONS

Although most countries have significantly improved their citizens' health condi-tions, these conditions still fall short of aspirations. "Good health" is obviously a multidimensional phenomenon, and therefore measuring it is difficult. Two assess-ments are widely used as indicators of health conditions: life expectancy at birth (LEB) and the infant mortality rate (IMR). LEB may be the single most robust indi-cator of national health conditions. Based on age-specific mortality rates, it tells us how long, on average, a newly born child can expect to live. It summarizes health, nutritional, and other welfare factors in a single, easily understood number. LEB fig-ures for the region are shown in Table 5.1. IMR is a second key indicator of the over-all state of health of a country (see Table 5.1 and Figure 5.1). Avoidable infant deaths

TABLE 5.1   Basic Health Indicators: Life Expectancy and Infant Mortality Rates, 1970–2005

	Life Expectancy at Birth				Infant Mortality Rate			
	1970–1980	1980–1990	1990–2000	2000–2005	1970–1980	1980–1990	1990–2000	2000–2005
Algeria	56	64	69	71	119	74	51	37
Bahrain	64	70	72	74	98	88	80	76
Egypt	53	59	66	70	130	94	56	37
Iran	56	61	67	70	108	79	48	34
Iraq	59	64	59	59	77	54	84	94
Israel	72	75	78	80	20	13	8	5
Jordan	59	65	69	71	74	47	31	23
Kuwait	68	73	76	77	37	21	13	10
Lebanon	67	67	70	72	43	39	29	22
Libya	55	64	71	73	93	44	26	19
Morocco	54	61	67	70	116	82	52	38
Occupied Palestinian Territory	59	66	70	72	74	43	26	21
Oman	55	65	72	74	97	48	22	16
Qatar	64	68	71	73	52	27	16	12
Saudi Arabia	56	65	70	72	92	50	29	23
Sudan	46	51	54	56	125	103	85	72
Syria	59	66	70	73	74	45	27	18
Tunisia	58	65	71	73	104	57	31	22
Turkey	58	62	67	69	127	82	50	42
U.A.E.	64	70	75	78	48	28	14	9
Yemen	42	51	57	60	170	116	86	69
Sweden	75	77	79	80	9	7	5	3
More Developed Regions*	72	74	74	76	20	14	9	8

*More developed regions comprise Europe, Northern America, Australia/New Zealand, and Japan.
SOURCE: United Nations, 2005. *World Population Prospects: The 2004 Revision.* New York: United Nations (Department of Economic and Social Affairs: Population Division)

are not only especially poignant but also symptomatic of wider health problems such as malnutrition, polluted water, and poor infant feeding practices. As we saw in Chapter 4, high infant mortality fosters high fertility and rapid population growth. From a demographic perspective as well as from a simple humanitarian one, understanding the causes of and remedies for high infant mortality is critical.

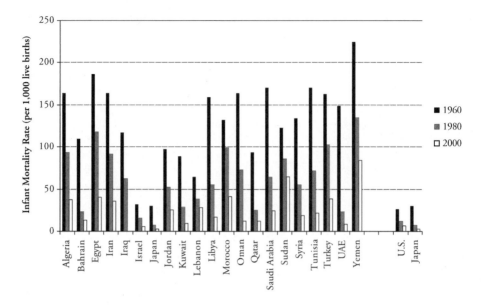

FIGURE 5.1 Infant mortality rates, 1960, 1980, 2000
SOURCE: World Development Indicators Online, 2006

Health Levels and Rates of Change

Our evaluation of Middle Eastern health performance will vary depending on whether we compare it with conditions in other LDCs or with those of more-developed countries. Furthermore, a focus on health *levels* will yield different conclusions than an analysis of *rates of change* in those levels. In regard to the first perspective, infant mortality in the region (44 per 1,000) is below both world (54) and LDC (59) averages. Within LDCs, the infant mortality rate of MENA is lower than those of sub-Saharan Africa and South Asia but higher than those prevailing in East Asia and Latin America (see Figure 5.2). As with all LDCs, health conditions in MENA are far worse than those in industrialized countries; for example, nearly nine times as many infants die in MENA as in more-developed countries (UNICEF 2005).

The national numbers in Table 5.1 conceal considerable regional and social class variation. Throughout the region, rural infant and child (under five years old) mortality rates routinely exceed those of urban areas (UNDP and Arab Fund for Economic and Social Development 2002) (see Figure 5.3). Consider the Egyptian case: In 2003, the Egyptian infant mortality rate ranged from 58 in rural Upper Egypt to 26 in urban governorates (UNDP 2004b, 28). Class position has an even greater impact than urban/rural residence: Babies born to poor Egyptian parents are nearly 3.5 times as likely to die before their first birthday than the children of rich Egyptians (el Saharty

102

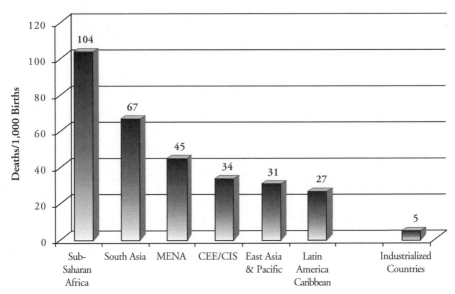

FIGURE 5.2   Infant mortality rates of major world regions, 2003
SOURCE: UNICEF Online, 2005

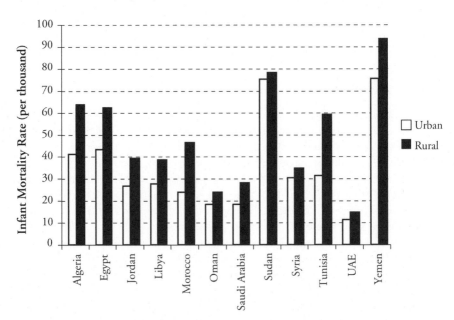

FIGURE 5.3   Infant mortality rates, urban versus rural, for selected countries
NOTE: Algeria, 1992; Egypt, 2000; Jordan, 1997; Libya, 1995; Morocco, 1997; Oman, 1995; Saudi Arabia, 1996; Sudan, 1993; Tunisia, 1994; United Arab Emirates (UAE), 1995; Yemen, 1997.
SOURCE: Human Development Indicators (AHDR 2002, 145)

et al. 2005).[1] There is evidence that the gap between the rich and the poor widened in Egypt from the late 1980s to the late 1990s (Minujin and Delamonica 2003). Nearly one-third of children in Khartoum squatter settlements die before their fifth birthday, a child mortality rate more than three times the Sudanese average (Eltayib 2003). In the Middle East, as elsewhere, the poor watch more of their children die than do the rich.[2]

There are two grim exceptions to the improvement in MENA human development indicators over the past several decades: the children in Iraq and the victims of famine in Sudan. Iraq presents a unique—and historically unprecedented—case. Fifteen years of war and economic sanctions have dramatically reversed earlier progress (see Box 5.1). (The Sudanese case is discussed in Chapter 6.)

Gender differentials in LEB are less striking in the region than in other LDCs (particularly in South Asia). Life expectancy for women exceeds that for men by 2.5 to 3.5 years. (In countries of high human development, however, the differential can be as high as 11 years [UNDP and AFESD 2002].) Maternal mortality remains tragically high. Although a mother in MENA is far less likely to die in childbirth than one in sub-Saharan Africa or South Asia, she is far more likely to die than women in East Asia or Latin America, and *forty times* more likely to die than a mother in an industrialized country (see Figure 5.4).

Nevertheless, infant mortality today is much lower—and therefore LEB is much higher—than it was even twenty years ago. Of course, LEB also varies widely by country, ranging from 59–60 years for a Yemeni or Iraqi baby to 77 for a Kuwaiti child to 80 years for an Israeli one (see Table 5.1). Since the fall in IMR and the associated increase in LEB has been a worldwide phenomenon, we need a comparative perspective. We know that medical advances potentially affect all nations; for any given income level, IMR falls and LEB rises over time. However, the MENA region has done relatively well in improving health as measured by IMR and LEB in comparison with other regions of the world. Most notably, *the decline in its infant mortality rates from 1980 to 2000 was the fastest of any region in the world* (Cornia and Menchini 2001).

Unlike the situation a decade ago, Middle Eastern health conditions are no longer much worse than would be predicted on the basis of incomes. Nonetheless, although LEB is somewhat better than would be predicted on the basis of income, IMR remains, in several cases, worse than would be expected (see Figure 5.5). We know that economic growth improves health. Carcinogenic industry notwithstanding, there is a clear positive correlation between LEB and per capita income; for a set of over one hundred countries, 45% of the variance in LEB (the dependent variable) can be attributed to variation in per capita income (Cornia and Menchini 2001).

Although no other single variable plays so important a role in explanations of cross-country differences in LEB, over half of the variance remains to be explained. The recent experience of countries such as China and Sri Lanka shows that increased income is not a necessary condition for improving health; for both of these countries LEB is comparable to that of advanced industrial countries, even though the World Bank considers them LDCs. Conversely, a highly inegalitarian pattern of economic growth may reduce infant mortality only very slowly.

◔ BOX 5.1 _____

Iraqi Child Mortality, 1991–2006

Before Saddam Hussein's invasion of Kuwait in 1990, and even during his brutal war with Iran, Iraqi progress on health indicators was, on average, better than elsewhere in MENA. Infant mortality fell from 117 in 1960 to 90 in 1970 to 63 in 1980 and to 40 in 1990. In 1992 the IMR for MENA was 58. But the Gulf War of 1991, the sanctions regime of 1990–2003, and the Anglo-American invasion and occupation from 2003 on dramatically transformed the health situation of the country.

The six weeks of Allied air attacks of 1991 destroyed more Iraqi economic infrastructure than did the entire eight years of war with Iran (Tripp 2000). In particular, power facilities and water-pumping stations were devastated. In the spring of 1991, the UN Security Council continued the sanctions regime created in the run-up to the Gulf War in order to force Saddam Hussein to dismantle his nuclear, biological, and chemical weapons programs. By most accounts, this was the most thorough sanctions program in history. Food and medicines were theoretically exempt from the embargo. However, constant conflict between the Iraqi government and the UN Security Council, led by the United States, created shortages of both. Additionally, prohibitions on the imports of so-called dual-use items (e.g., many chemicals, spare parts for power, water, and sanitation systems) crippled attempts to repair infrastructure.

Although sanctions may well have achieved their political goal—the denial of weapons of mass destruction to Saddam's regime (Lopez and Cortwright 2004)—the cost, in terms of human lives, was appallingly high. During the 1990s, a highly charged political debate over sanctions emerged. By now the outlines of the situation are clear: Beginning in mid-1991, hundreds of thousands of Iraqi children died who would not otherwise have perished. A number of different studies (not all of which agreed with each other) showed that child mortality in Iraq during the 1990s was very much higher than what one would anticipate without the sanctions regime (see, e.g., Ascherio et al. 1992; Garfield 1999; UNICEF 1999; and for a review of UN studies, see Rowat 2000).

After an FAO mission to Iraq in 1995, two team members published a letter in the British medical journal *The Lancet,* asserting that "excess deaths"[3] of children in Iraq from 1990 to 1995 were about 567,000 (Zaidi and Smith-Fawzi 1995). This number—usually rounded off to 500,000—was widely disseminated by critics of the sanctions regime, not least by the Iraqi government. A 1999 study by Richard Garfield of Columbia University

continues

● BOX 5.1 *continued*

Medical School surveyed different data and estimated excess deaths at roughly half that figure, or approximately 227,000. UNICEF then conducted a child and maternal mortality survey in 1999 and estimated excess deaths for the years 1991–1998 at about 500,000 (UNICEF 1999). Then, in 2002, Garfield revised his estimate of excess deaths, based on all of the research conducted up to that time. He calculated that between 343,900 and 529,000 excess deaths of children under age five occurred from August 1991 to June 2002 (Global Policy Forum 2002). Professor Garfield described the unusual nature of this health crisis in his 1999 study: "Sustained increases in young child mortality are extremely rare in this century. Such a large increase as that found here (227,000) is almost unknown in the public health literature . . . Living conditions in Iraq . . . represent a loss of several decades of progress in reducing mortality" (Garfield 1999, 45).

The proximate causes of child death were diarrhea and respiratory illness. Contaminated water, inadequate breast-feeding, and the absence of supplies in the curative medical system killed many. The isolation and austerity of the 1990s strongly impacted the educational system. Elsewhere in MENA, the younger the age group, the higher the literacy rate. But this is not the case in Iraq; the literacy rate for 15–24-year-olds (those who grew up in the 1990s) is *lower* than for 25–34-year-olds (71% versus 75%) (UNDP and Iraq Ministry of Planning and Development Cooperation 2005, 32). Mortality was highest in the southern, largely Shi'ite-inhabited provinces (the poorest and least-educated region), in rural areas, and among the poor and uneducated (Garfield 1999). A vicious cycle of ignorance, child death, high fertility—and more child deaths—was instigated. Whereas multiple, mutually reinforcing forces drove down child mortality elsewhere in the region, in Iraq, these same forces were, essentially, reversed.

The Anglo-American invasion and occupation of Iraq ended the sanctions regime. The debate then shifted to total excess deaths (i.e., including adults) after March 2003. A study published in *The Lancet* using cluster sample survey methodology estimated the most probable number of excess deaths since the invasion to be 98,000, most of which were due to violence (Roberts et al. 2004). In the spring and summer of 2004, the Norwegian Statistical Agency and the Iraqi government carried out a sample survey by which they estimated the total number of violent deaths at 18,000–29,000 (UNDP 2005).[4] Between May and July 2006, researchers from Johns Hopkins University and Iraqi colleagues again deployed the standard epidemiological methodology of a cluster sample survey to estimate excess deaths since the invasion in April 2003 (Burnam et al. 2006). They estimated that

continues

◉ BOX 5.1 *continued* _____

"as of July 2006, there have been 654,965 (392,979–942,636) excess Iraqi deaths as a consequence of the war," the vast majority (over 600,000) of which were violent deaths, most commonly due to gunfire.[5] Child malnutrition, which had fallen to 4% in 2002 (UNICEF 2005), climbed to 7.7%. That is, roughly 400,000 Iraqi children suffered from chronic diarrhea and dangerous protein deficiencies. The country's water and sewage systems remained in disarray; the Norwegian survey observed standing sewage in the streets in front of 39% of houses (Garfield 2005; Vick 2004). Meanwhile, many doctors have fled the country, fearful of being kidnapped for ransom or killed (Steele 2006).[6]

Debate still rages on the allocation of responsibility for this macabre escalation of child mortality.[7] Here we simply note that whether one blames Saddam Hussein, the US government, the UN Security Council, or all of the above, the Iraqi experience during the past fifteen years constitutes a grisly counterpoint to the health progress that has characterized the rest of MENA during the same time period. However the blame is apportioned, the identity of the victims is clear: the children of Iraq.

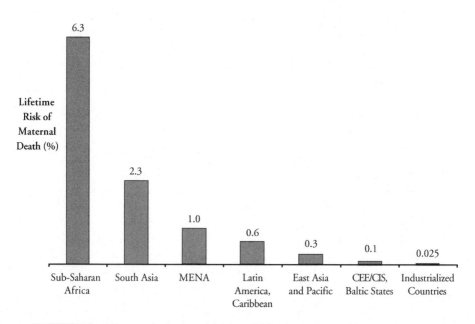

FIGURE 5.4   Lifetime risk of maternal death in childbirth in major world regions, 2003
Source: UNICEF 2005

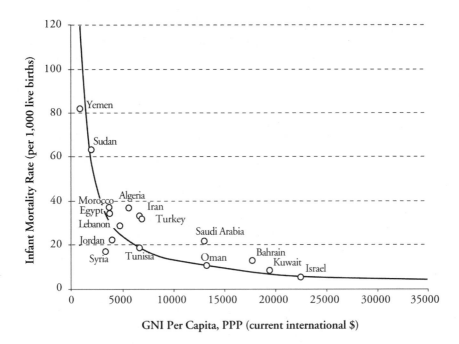

FIGURE 5.5   Infant mortality as a function of GNI, 2006
SOURCE: World Development Indicators 2006

Explanations for Health Performance

Total spending on health provides only a very partial explanation for health improvements. For example, on average, countries of the MENA region devoted a higher percentage of GDP to health during the 1990s than East Asia, yet they had significantly poorer health conditions (World Bank 2002). The key problem is how the money is spent. One approach to this problem is to ask what diseases kill young children (the "proximate" causes of death) and why they contract these diseases or are not swiftly cured (the "underlying" causes). A great deal is known about both of these. The tragedy of high infant mortality rates is that most children in the Third World die from diseases that can be prevented, often at very low cost. A large (although declining) percentage of infant deaths are due to diarrhea.[8] Other major child killers are diphtheria, whooping cough, tetanus, measles, tuberculosis, and malaria. With the partial exception of malaria, these diseases can be prevented with proven methods at relatively low cost.

During the 1980s, UNICEF and other international health organizations advocated a package of simple practices that could sharply reduce infant mortality: growth monitoring, oral rehydration therapy, breast-feeding, and immunization. Growth monitoring refers to the use of simple weight-for-age and weight-for-height charts in infant and early child care to identify children who are malnourished and therefore susceptible to disease. Although we can all recognize a starving person, most of us cannot discern less advanced malnutrition without special training. Many mothers of malnourished children *do not know* that their children are suffering from this condition until they become sick, when it may be too late to do much about it. But if the children are brought into clinics for regular checkups, they can be weighed and their growth progress monitored using these simple charts, which act as "early warning devices" for malnutrition and disease. Oral rehydration therapy (ORT) employs a simple mixture of sugar, salt, and water that when ingested enables the body to retain the fluids whose loss is the cause of death in fatal cases of diarrhea. The cost of such packets is less than US$0.05 apiece, and the mixing requires only a cup and a spoon. This is one of the most important and promising innovations in infant health care in decades. Breast-feeding is essential for child welfare in the early months of infancy not only because human milk is the best "formula" for humans, but also because the many antibodies in human milk provide crucial protection for the otherwise highly vulnerable infant. (After about six months a diet of human milk alone is inadequate and must be supplemented with other foods.) Finally, immunization is strongly recommended to prevent the ravages of the major infant and child killers listed above.

Middle Eastern countries have had a mixed experience with such practices. The problem with growth charts is that their use usually requires mothers to visit clinics. There are typically too few of these in most countries of the region, and the staff is too poorly paid to avoid significant delays and long waiting times. Consequently, many (especially poorer) residents use them only as a last resort, when the child is already sick and perhaps beyond simple treatment (US Institute of Medicine 1979). In addition, in many countries such clinics are more abundant in urban areas than in rural areas, and too often the "treatment of patients by doctors is depersonalized and haughty" (US Institute of Medicine 1979, 76). Regional variation is wide: Even thirty years ago in Tunisia it was only in areas of extremely dispersed population that access to some kind of health care was a problem (H. Nelson 1979, 104). Yet even today, in the countries with the highest infant mortality rates, rural outpatient clinics remain scarce. In Yemen, for example, less than one-fourth of the rural population has access to a clinic (USAID 2003).

The large majority of MENA families now have access to ORT packets, although, as usual, Yemen and the Sudan lag far behind. Egyptian experience is illuminating. During the 1980s, mothers' knowledge of ORT increased from 12% to 98%, and the utilization of the packets by mothers rose from 27% to 68%. Fewer than one in ten Egyptians lacks access to ORT packets. In 1980, dehydration from diarrhea killed over 100,000 Egyptian children every year; today fewer than one-third that number die of the same cause. However, UNICEF reports that fewer than one in three children suffering from diarrhea receive ORT treatment in Morocco, Algeria, Jordan, the Sudan, and Turkey (UNICEF 2001).

Although most Middle Eastern women breast-feed their children, use of substitute infant formulas is widespread in Yemen, for example. One study found that

Yemeni children fed with (often dirty) plastic nipples and bottles were *eight times* as likely to die as breast-fed Yemeni infants (UNICEF 1986). By contrast, breast-feeding until the age of six months appears to be nearly universal in Egypt (US Institute of Medicine 1979). However, only in Iran and Egypt (as in Bangladesh, China, India, and Indonesia) are more than 40% of infants exclusively breast-fed (WHO's recommended practice) (UNICEF 2006).

There has been a regional revolution in child immunization during the past quarter-century. In 1980 most children in most countries failed to complete the three shots of the DPT (diphtheria, pertussis, tetanus) series. During the 1980s the percentage immunized rose dramatically in all countries; the change in Yemen (from 1% to 84%) may have been the most striking, but others performed impressively, as well. Progress continued, albeit at a somewhat slower pace, for the next fifteen years. Only Algeria, Iraq, Turkey, and Yemen faltered during the 1990s (UNICEF 2006). Significantly, immunization among the poor improved dramatically in some regions; for example, in the six years from 1992 to 1998, the percentage of immunized children in rural Upper Egypt, the poorest region of the country, rose from just over 50% to 90% (UNDP 2002, Annex, 109).

Three other measures are essential for reducing infant mortality: the so-called three F's of family spacing, food supplements, and female education. There is a strong correlation between infant health and the length of time between births. Too little time between births weakens the mother, thereby threatening her own health and that of her children. The region has the highest prevalence of short birth intervals in the world (Aoyama 2001, 42). The consequences are grim: In both Egypt and Yemen, the IMR for births occurring less than 24 months after the birth of a sibling is more than twice as high as the IMR for births occurring two to three years after the birth of a sibling (Aoyama 2001). Short interbirth intervals are clearly the result of the failure to practice contraception, since, in contrast to practice in many sub-Saharan African societies, prolonged sexual abstinence after the birth of a child is not common in the region.

Food supplements are designed to break the synergies between malnutrition and disease. Not only does malnutrition reduce resistance, but disease can also engender malnutrition by impeding the body's ability to absorb or properly utilize ingested nutrients. Compared with other Third World regions, Middle Eastern countries have done well here. UNICEF estimates that only 9% of the people of the region receive "insufficient calories for an active working life" (i.e., less than 90% of the caloric intake recommended by the Food and Agriculture Organization/World Health Organization [FAO/WHO]), as compared with 7% in Latin America, 17% in East Asia and the Pacific, 31% in sub-Saharan Africa, and 47% in South Asia (see Figure 5.6). Nonetheless, child malnutrition ("stunting") afflicts 18% of the region's children.[9]

The prevalence of malnutrition varies significantly among nations in the region. The percentage of the population that is undernourished exceeds 30% in Yemen and 20% in the Sudan (Lofgren and Richards 2003). More than half (53%) of Yemeni children suffer from stunting, similar to the percentages in Afghanistan and

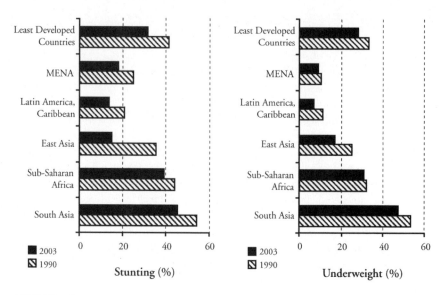

FIGURE 5.6   Malnutrition in major world regions, 1990 and 2003
SOURCE: UNICEF

Ethiopia (UNICEF 2001), while 23% of Iraqi children suffer from chronic malnutrition (UNDP 2004a). Throughout the region, rural areas with scarce arable land appear to be worse off than urban areas, where extensive food subsidy systems prevail.

Significant class biases also exist. Typically, the lack of purchasing power, rather than a failure of national (much less global) food supplies, causes hunger everywhere (Sen 1981a; World Bank 1986b). Three times as many poor Egyptian children are severely undernourished as rich children (el Saharty et al. 2005, 18). And as elsewhere within disadvantaged groups, the members suffering most severely from malnutrition are children and pregnant and lactating women. This is where food supplements could have a dramatic impact in reducing infant mortality rates. However, few Middle Eastern governments have supplementary feeding programs, although most have sharply reduced malnutrition through extensive, untargeted, and costly consumer food subsidy systems.

The last F, female education, may be *the* key to health conditions in the region. John Caldwell (1986) surveyed ninety-nine countries and found that the best predictor of both infant mortality rate and life expectancy at birth was the 1960 female primary enrollment rate. He argued that nations with "exceptionally good" performances (China, Sri Lanka, the Indian state of Kerala, and Costa Rica) had relatively high degrees of "female autonomy" and that nine of the eleven worst performers were Middle Eastern, Muslim countries. Since in all Third World countries women have primary responsibility for child care, it is essential that they be sufficiently well educated and accustomed to taking initiatives on their children's behalf. They must recognize early warning signs (such as a child's failure to grow properly), understand disease origins and prevention, and be ready and able to act immediately to seek remedies. All such behavior, of course, presupposes female literacy. Caldwell argued that this kind of basic education is only a necessary, not a sufficient, condition for such autonomy. If a woman is educated but is not in the habit of venturing out of her home unaccompanied, child health will still suffer.

Much evidence supports this reasoning. A 10% increase in girls' primary school enrollment has been shown to decrease infant mortality by 4.1 deaths per 1,000 live births, while a 10% rise in secondary enrollment decreases infant mortality by another 5.6 deaths per 1,000 live births (Aoyama 2001). In Egypt in 2000, the child mortality rate for women with no education was 89, while the rate for mothers who had completed primary education was 55, and the rate for those with at least a secondary education was 38 (Roudi-Fahimi and Moghadam 2003).

For assessing current health, the key statistic is literacy among women aged 15 to 24 ("youth literacy"). Since today's Middle Eastern mother is typically young, such a number is a proxy for basic health knowledge. Over 70% of young (ages 15–24) Arab and Iranian women are literate, while nearly all (95%) young female Turks can read and write. This is a profound, albeit quiet, social revolution; as recently as twenty-five years ago, when we first began thinking about writing this book, for example, less than two out of five young Iranian women were literate. Even the poorest countries have made important, rapid progress: Only one in four young Yemeni women were literate fifteen years ago, compared with one in two today (UNESCO 2005). Millions of children's lives have been saved as a result.

In recent years, some prominent scholars (e.g., Lewis 2002), attempting to explain the political strife in the region, have asked, "What went wrong?" in the Middle East. With respect to the education of young women and its positive impact on health conditions, the evident answer is, "Less than you think!" Neither culture (still less religion) nor type of political system seems to be a critical factor in explaining improving health conditions. The recent increase in female enrollment in primary school and the decline in infant mortality have been rapid under regimes espousing a socialist ideology (the People's Democratic Republic of Yemen [PDRY], Iraq, Libya, and Syria) and under more conservative governments (Tunisia, Turkey, and Pahlavi Iran). With the exception of the former PDRY, none of these regimes was/is officially non-Muslim, while the Islamic Republic of Iran now has enrolled all girls in primary school. Indeed, the performance of that Islamist-governed country in both education and health is one of the best in the region. There is little doubt that most regimes dominated by male Muslims (i.e., all regimes in MENA except Israel and, to some extent, Lebanon) have rapidly expanded the enrollment of girls in school and the education of young women. This progress has had critical, positive impacts on both health and fertility (see Chapter 4). In the first edition of this book we wrote, "It is plausible to predict that the decline in infant mortality rates in the region will accelerate as the schoolgirls of the 1980s become the mothers of the 1990s and 2000s" (112). This is exactly what has happened.

EDUCATIONAL SYSTEMS

As with health conditions, how we assess Middle Eastern progress in education depends very much upon whether we look at the current situation or at the speed of change. On the one hand, present levels of literacy[10] in the Middle East are low; on the other hand, most nations have expanded educational opportunities rapidly during the past generation. Educational levels vary considerably by country, region, gender, and social class. The education of women has also advanced markedly in recent years—from a very low starting point. Finally, the rapid *quantitative* expansion of school systems, particularly when combined with fiscal austerity (see Chapter 9), has generated serious *qualitative* deficiencies in education.

Literacy Rates

In international comparative perspective, MENA rates of adult literacy remain unjustifiably low (see Table 5.2). Only in Israel, Jordan, and Palestine can more than 90% of adults read and write. More than 80% of adults are literate in Bahrain, Kuwait, Lebanon, Libya, Qatar, and Turkey; more than 70% are literate in Iran, Oman, Saudi Arabia, Syria, Tunisia, and the UAE. Literacy stands between one-half and two-thirds in Algeria, Egypt, and Sudan. Just over half of adults are literate in Morocco and Yemen. Some 65 million Arab adults are illiterate, nearly two-thirds of them women (UNDP and Arab Fund for Economic and Social Development 2002).

Female illiteracy remains a glaring deficiency. In only seven countries of the region can a majority of adult women read and write; by contrast, in Southeast Asia and Latin America, only in Cambodia, Guatemala, and Haiti are more than 50% of women illiterate. Egyptian female literacy is about equal to that in India and lower than that in Rwanda. Even in rich countries like Saudi Arabia, more than one in four adult women are illiterate.

As elsewhere in the LDCs, both male and female illiteracy in the Middle East is concentrated in rural areas and among the poor. In Yemen, for example, urban literacy in 1996 was 66%, while it was only 36% in rural areas (al-Amri et al. 2003). Although about 70% of urban Egyptian adults are literate, fewer than two-fifths of their country cousins can read and write. Nearly 70% of rural Moroccans are illiterate. Finally, even in countries that have devoted large resources to primary education, population growth has assured that there are now more illiterate people than there were a generation ago.

These statistics are sobering. A comparative perspective affords only partial comfort. As before, three types of comparison seem apposite: with other regions, with respect to per capita incomes, and with the recent past. If adult literacy is our standard, the Middle East is relatively backward. Regional adult literacy, now 68%, somewhat exceeds that of sub-Saharan Africa (62%). The figure for Arab states (64%) is only slightly better. Only South Asia (59%) has a poorer level of literacy performance than MENA, while nine of ten adults in Latin America and East Asia are literate. Adult literacy rates in the region are also below what we would predict

TABLE 5.2   Adult Illiteracy, 1980–2003

	1980	*1985*	*1990*	*1995*	*2000*	*2003*
Algeria	63.4	55.1	47.1	39.7	33.3	30.1
Bahrain	28.8	23.3	17.9	14.8	12.5	10.9
Egypt	60.7	56.8	52.9	48.9	44.7	42.3
Iran	50.3	44.1	36.8	30.0	24.0	20.9
Iraq	68.4	66.3	64.3	62.5	60.7	59.6
Israel	13.9	11.2	8.6	6.7	5.2	4.4
Jordan	30.8	24.4	18.5	13.5	10.2	8.7
Kuwait	32.2	27.9	23.3	21.0	18.1	16.5
Lebanon	27.6	23.7	19.7	16.7	14.0	12.6
Libya	47.3	39.2	31.9	25.5	20.1	17.5
Morocco	71.4	66.5	61.3	56.1	51.2	48.3
Oman	63.8	54.5	45.3	36.3	28.3	24.2
Qatar	30.2	25.6	23.0	20.8	18.8	17.5
Saudi Arabia	49.1	40.8	33.8	28.8	23.8	21.3
Sudan	65.8	60.3	54.2	48.5	42.3	39.0
Syria	46.7	40.6	35.2	30.1	25.6	23.1
Tunisia	55.1	47.4	40.9	35.3	29.0	25.8
Turkey	31.6	26.1	22.1	18.2	15.0	13.5
UAE	34.6	31.2	29.0	26.6	23.8	22.2
Yemen	80.0	74.1	67.3	59.9	53.6	49.7

SOURCE: UN Common Database (UNESCO estimates) Globalis Online

on the basis of per capita incomes alone (see Figure 5.7). These human-capital deficiencies place the region at a serious disadvantage in competing in international markets with countries from Eastern Europe, the former Soviet Union, Southeast Asia, and Latin America.

However, a historical perspective partially mitigates this grim picture. One must remember that Middle Eastern countries launched their educational efforts from an extremely low base. The anciens régimes of the region did essentially nothing to educate most of their people. In some cases, education of the rural poor was actively discouraged, as on the estates of wealthy Egyptians under the Farouk monarchy (Richards 1982; Adams 1986). Arab and Berber children in North Africa were either entirely excluded from education or channeled into segregated schools under French colonial rule.[11] These countries faced severe difficulties in expanding their educational facilities after independence. There was a mass exodus of teachers, nearly all of whom were Europeans: In Algeria, 27,000 of 30,000 teachers left in 1962; only one-fifth of the 20,000 new Algerian teachers were qualified (Bennoune 1988, 220). Many countries have come a long way since colonial days, when two-thirds to three-quarters of the people of the region were illiterate. By way of comparison, when

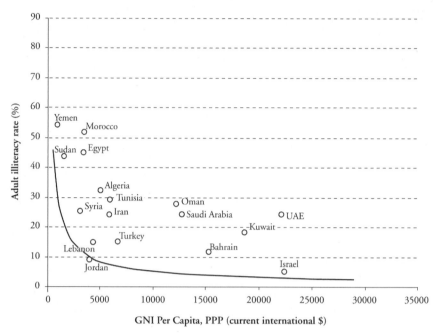

FIGURE 5.7   Adult illiteracy as a function of GNI, 2000
SOURCE: For adult illiteracy, UNESCO Online, 2002. For GNI, World Development Indicators Online, 2006

South Korea shifted its development strategy to export-led growth in the early 1960s, over 70% of the population could already read and write.

Historical legacies alone do not explain persistently high adult illiteracy. With the exception of Iraq, Algeria, and the former PDRY, Middle Eastern countries have largely ignored the problem of illiterate adults, choosing instead to concentrate resources on educating children. Here the record is considerably more encouraging, although some countries of the region still have much unfinished business (see Table 5.3). As with health conditions, the "movie" (change over time) is better than the "still photograph" (levels of achievement in global comparative perspective).

Consider primary school enrollments. The second international Millennium Development Goal for 2015 is to "achieve universal primary education." One benchmark for achieving this goal is a net enrollment ratio (NER) of 95% or better.[12] At least five countries (Algeria, Bahrain, Israel, Syria, and Tunisia) have achieved this goal, according to UNESCO data.[13] Many countries are close and will very likely meet the goal (see Table 5.4). The most rapid progress has been in Oman, which went from essentially no schooling (3% enrollment) to nearly three of four children in school within a single generation.

In 1960 the large majority of Middle Eastern girls never saw the inside of a schoolroom. Today, nearly four of five girls attend primary school: According to

TABLE 5.3   Gross Primary School Enrollments, 1970, 1991, 2002

	1970		1991		2002	
	Total	*Female*	*Total*	*Female*	*Total*	*Female*
Algeria	76	58	95	88	109	104
Egypt	72	57	101	93	97	95
Iran	72	52	112	105	92	90
Iraq	-	-	-	-	110	100
Israel	96	95	95	96	112	112
Jordan	-	-	97	68	99	99
Kuwait	-	-	-	-	94	94
Lebanon	-	-	-	-	103	102
Morocco	52	-	66	54	110	104
Oman	3	1	100	96	81	80
Saudi Arabia	45	29	77	72	67	65
Sudan	38	29	50	43	60	56
Syria	78	59	109	103	115	112
Tunisia	100	-	117	110	111	109
Turkey	110	94	110	110	91	88
UAE	93	71	115	114	97	95
West Bank and Gaza	-	-	-	-	99	99
Yemen	22	7	76	37	83	68

NOTE: Figures include re-enrollments and thus may exceed 100%
SOURCE: UNICEF (1986, 120-121); World Bank (1994g, 216-217); World Bank Indicators 2005

UNESCO, the current NER for the region is 78%. Today, roughly 90% of girls, or more, are enrolled in primary school in Algeria, Bahrain, Egypt, Israel, Iraq, Jordan, Lebanon, Morocco, Qatar, Syria, Tunisia, and the West Bank and Gaza (see Table 5.4). Gross enrollment figures suggest that more than one of five girls remain out of school only in Oman, Saudi Arabia, the Sudan, and Yemen (see Table 5.3).

A majority of the most dramatic change in primary enrollments occurred from 1970 to 1990. In the latter year, the net enrollment ratios for Arab boys was 82% and 67% for girls. By 2002/2003, the rates were 85% for boys and 78% for girls (UNESCO). For both Iran and Turkey, UNESCO data suggest lower NERs for 2002/2003 than in 1990/1991! (It is worth noting that the United States had the same experience; the US NER fell from 97 to 92 during the same time period.) For the Arab countries, the good news is that the gender gap in enrollment is narrowing (see Figure 5.8). The more difficult news is that, as so often, reaching children in remote areas is extremely difficult. As with long-distance running, so with providing universal primary education: The last few miles of the long race are not easy.

In contrast to the total number of illiterate persons, the total number of children not in school has declined in most countries since 1960. Illiteracy is increasingly a

TABLE 5.4   Primary School Net Enrollment Ratio (NER), Arab Countries, 2002

	NER
Algeria	94.9
Bahrain	89.9
Egypt	91.4
Iraq	90.5
Jordan	92.0
Kuwait	83.4
Lebanon	90.6
Morocco	89.6
Oman	71.9
West Bank and Gaza	90.9
Qatar	94.5
Saudi Arabia	54.4
Syria	97.9
Tunisia	97.3
UAE	83.1
Yemen	71.8

SOURCES: UNESCO Institute for Statistics; EFA Global Monitoring Report 2006, statistical annex

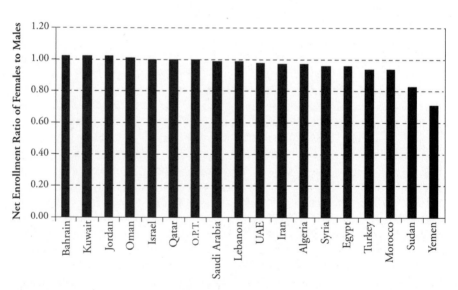

FIGURE 5.8   The gender gap in primary school enrollment, 2002/2003
NOTE: O.P.T. = Occupied Palestinian Territories
SOURCE: Human Development Report Online, 2005

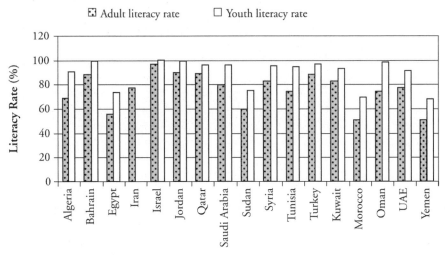

⊡ Adult literacy rate   □ Youth literacy rate

FIGURE 5.9   Youth literacy versus adult literacy, 2000–2004
SOURCE: UNESCO Institute for Statistics Online, 2005

phenomenon of older people (see Figure 5.9). More than 90% of 15-to-24-year-olds can read in every country reporting data except Egypt (73%), Morocco (70%), and Yemen (68%).[14] The largest generation in the history of the region is also the first to be educated. As they now come of age, their current political experiences may shape their attitudes for the rest of their lives. The political implications of this situation may profoundly shape the future history of the region (see Chapter 14).

Educational-Allocation Decisions and Their Effects

MENA countries have made strenuous efforts to improve education. Most governments allocate a relatively high percentage of expenditure to education; shares range from a low of 8.3% in Saudi Arabia (1998/1999) to a high of 32.8% in Yemen. During the austerity of the 1980s, however, real spending slowed and in some cases declined. In Egypt, for example, educational spending had only just regained 1980 levels by 1990, and although educational spending's share of the government budget rose from 10.2% in 1990/1991 to about 17% in 1998/1999, real government educational spending actually fell in the first half of the decade (UNDP/INP 2003). This was a regional pattern: Arab country per capita educational expenditure fell during the second half of the 1980s. Arab countries continue to spend more per pupil than other LDCs, but this advantage has been narrowing since 1985. Meanwhile, the (large) gap between Arab countries and the industrialized ones doubled from 1985 to 1995 (UNDP/Arab Fund 2002).

This picture is further darkened when we consider how the money is spent. Gender, class, and to a decreasing extent in some countries, rural/urban biases remain in many countries' educational-allocation decisions. As everywhere in the world, there are class biases in educational expenditures and enrollment profiles. In Morocco, children from upper-income families are twice as likely to be enrolled as children from low-income families. Rural enrollment rates are still lower than urban rates in the large, relatively poor countries of Egypt, Morocco, and Yemen. The gap has narrowed but has not yet disappeared. For example, in the late 1970s, while over 90% of urban Egyptian children were in school, only 70% of rural delta children and 60% of rural Upper Egyptian children were enrolled (Nyrop 1982). By 2000, however, the gap for boys had all but vanished for boys (88% rural versus 89% urban boys).[15] For girls, the rural/urban gap in enrollment remained strong: 92% of urban girls versus 75% of rural girls (El Zanaty and Way 2001). Similar gaps in the rural/urban rates of school enrollment for girls occur in Yemen (Watkins 2001).

Promoting rural education is challenging. The children of widely dispersed rural families are often far from any school. Countries that insist on separate schools for girls and boys multiply the costs of schooling, and it is especially difficult to attract women teachers to rural areas. At the same time, many rural families see no point in educating all of their children. It is quite common in the region for rural families to make sacrifices to educate at least one son. One study of Turkey found that the highest rates of return to investment in education were obtained by the sons of farmers attending primary school (Özgediz 1980), while observers of rural Egypt often note that peasant families will try to educate at least one son through high school in the hope that he will obtain a secure government job. Educating all children, and especially all daughters, is expensive and has low priority. Children can and do contribute to peasant family budgets at young ages by tending animals, helping with processing, harvesting cotton, weaving rugs, and so forth. And peasant attitudes toward women's status die hard; Upper Egyptian peasants asserted to one researcher in the 1980s that sending girls to school was "shameful" (Adams 1986, 142). Such attitudes are, however, slowly changing, as the steady increase in school enrollments, and the steady decline in youth illiteracy, attest.

Throughout the region, primary education receives the same amount of funding, or less, than secondary education, despite the much higher primary enrollments (UNESCO 2002). University education, which is far more expensive to fund than other levels of education, gobbles up anywhere from 69% (Libya) to 16% (Morocco) of all educational spending (UNESCO 2002). Such allocations are extremely difficult to justify economically; much evidence suggests that if educational spending is (properly) treated as an investment, the social rate of return[16] is highest to investment in lower grades. The most recent calculations have confirmed what has long been known: The social returns are highest from investment in primary education (Psacharopoulos and Patrinos 2002). However, private returns increase with investment in higher education (see Figure 5.10). Politics, not economics, dictates the bias in favor of secondary and, especially, higher education.

The politics of this all-too-common distortion in the allocation of human-capital spending is not hard to understand. First, there is some complementarity between diffusing primary education and widening more advanced educational opportunities.

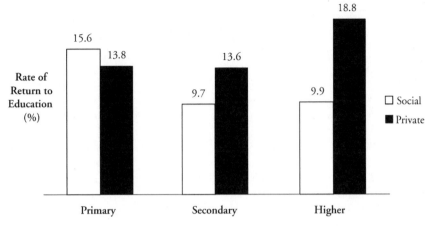

FIGURE 5.10   Private and social rates of return to different educational levels, 2002
SOURCE: Psacharopoulos and Patrinos 2002

Someone has to teach the children, and a growing, industrializing economy needs more advanced skills as well as basic literacy and numeracy. This need is especially acute in countries that inherited little skilled labor from colonial regimes and that are eager to defend their independence. Given the "national project" of Arab Socialist, Atatürkist, and other early developmentalist regimes in the region, it is hardly surprising that they have vigorously promoted the development of university training.

Second, the urban middle classes have had a disproportionate influence on policy. Planners themselves typically come from such backgrounds, and regimes have sought to open up more room at the top, through greater access to higher education, as a mechanism of income redistribution. And since the private rate of return due to investment in higher education remains very high, middle-class families press for space in the universities. Regimes wishing to mollify this social group have responded by rapidly expanding secondary and higher education. Vested interests, created by past state policies (by history), may be the main blockage to more socially rational and equitable allocation of educational resources (see Box 5.2).

Other commonly voiced complaints about Middle Eastern education are that its quality is very low, that dropout rates are high, and that too few students master technical subjects, especially math and science. However, these choices are individually rational; Middle Eastern students, like their counterparts in the West, select careers with an eye on the job market. Thus although agricultural studies retain their traditionally low status in the country, many students enroll in them because of expanding placement opportunities. If students are not developing the proper skills, it is because the society and, especially, the state are not sending them the correct signals.

One way to employ the swollen numbers of secondary and university graduates in countries with low adult literacy rates would be to launch adult-literacy campaigns. However, few states in the region have initiated such a program. In most cases, the

◗ BOX 5.2

The Misallocation of Educational Resources in Egypt

Egypt provides perhaps the most striking case of class bias in education. Fifty years after Nasser's revolution, 44% of adult Egyptians cannot read and write, while the country boasts 21 public and 12 private universities. Nearly one-third (31.5% in 1999) of educational spending is allocated to universities, which enroll perhaps 6% of students at all levels. (In East Asia, universities receive about 15% of total educational spending.) The current proportion, although high, is lower than the 37% of educational funding universities received at the beginning of the 1990s (UNDP/INP 2000).

How did this happen? Between 1952/1953 and 1976/1977 the number of secondary school students in Egypt rose from 181,789 to 796,411, or at a rate of 14% per annum. Primary school enrollments rose at exactly half that rate, and university enrollments rose at an extraordinary 32% per annum. Higher education enrollments doubled in only four years (1971–1976) and then increased another 50% by 1984 (to over 600,000). In fiscal 1984/1985 higher education consumed nearly 38% of all spending on education. Meanwhile, nearly one-quarter of girls were not enrolled in primary school. The proportion of science students declined from 55% in 1971 to 25% in the mid-1980s, and at all levels the quality of education was dominated by rote memorization.

These trends were unintended consequences of the worthy goal of democratizing education, a process that had started even before the military seized power in 1952. The main nationalist party, the Wafd, controlled the government and parliament in 1950 and, in what Kerr termed "a demagogic bid" (1965, 176), not only opened the secondary schools to anyone who completed primary school but also made instruction tuition-free. After the abolition of the monarchy and the establishment of the Egyptian republic, the Free Officers continued these policies. In 1957 an unusually tame Egyptian parliament rose up against an attempt to restrict admission of secondary school graduates to the university and imposed a policy of tuition-free admission to universities for any Egyptian in possession of a secondary school diploma. The fatal sequence was thus established: All primary school graduates could go to secondary school, all secondary school graduates could go to university, and all university graduates were entitled to a government job.

Much of the demand for secondary and higher education was a demand for the credential necessary for a government job. Over half of university graduates and more than half of secondary school graduates sought jobs in the public sector (Fergany 1991). From 1976 to 1986, 90% of new jobs for Egyptians came either from the government or from emigration abroad (Handoussa 1989).

continues

● BOX 5.2 *continued*

The government made university education especially attractive by heavily subsidizing students and by guaranteeing government jobs to all graduates, thereby greatly increasing the private returns to university education. It is privately rational for a family to sacrifice to get a member through the university; the graduate can then join the job queue for government employment (effectively lifetime), which can easily be combined with a second job and provides a kind of "income insurance." The educational system thus interacts with labor-market policies to misdirect social spending and to generate unemployment (since graduates tend to wait for government jobs). Even ignoring the fact that many of these graduates acquired only marginally useful skills, the country's development would have been better served by shifting resources away from more advanced education toward primary schooling.

During the past fifteen years there have been some important policy shifts. These have mainly involved large increases in total educational spending (up 90% in real terms during the 1990s) and a shift of investment spending away from higher education toward secondary and primary. Primary enrollment is nearly universal now (see text), and in the late 1980s, university enrollments actually declined by about 100,000. Enrollment growth resumed in the early 1990s, with enrollments in 1995 approaching those in 1985 (roughly 850,000) (World Bank 2000). By the end of the decade, enrollments totaled some 1.2 million (Said 2001). This expansion occurred even though the government's job guarantee was in practice being ignored. Basically, the jobs of those already employed in the government have been preserved by a tacit suspension of the job guarantee to the young (World Bank 2004c). Vested interests and political calculations have kept the law on the books, however. A study found that the private rate of return on education for males was 8.3% for primary education (contrast this with 39% in Asia), 31.7% for secondary education, and a whopping 62% for higher education (UNDP/INP 2000, 80). Misguided educational policies can have profound, long-lasting effects.

explanation seems to be that the government fears the political impact of such campaigns; the young people who would go to the slums and villages to teach may hold political views that are inconsistent with government interests. Governments might plausibly fear fostering contact between Islamist students and the large number of illiterate adults, many of whom might be sympathetic to the political messages that are usually imparted along with literacy in such campaigns. Only if a regime feels politically secure and confidant that it can control and shape the content of the materials used in literacy campaigns will such efforts occur. The fact that the Egyptian regime launched such a program in the 1990s testifies to the thoroughness of that government's control of society.

Increasing class size has not been a significant problem in Middle Eastern primary education. There is little evidence that learning or later performance is linked to class size (Colclough 1982). Class sizes vary from 12 to 15 in rich countries like Bahrain, Israel, Qatar, Saudi Arabia, and the UAE, to 29 to 30 in the poorest countries (Sudan and Yemen) (UNESCO 2000). Clearly, something other than class size affects educational achievement, as average class size in the Republic of Korea, whose students regularly shine in international comparative testing, is rather large at 31.

More important than class size are pedagogical methods, teacher quality, and morale. Far too often, education in the region mimics traditional *madrasas* (Islamic schools, where boys memorize parts of the Qur'an), with their emphasis on rote learning, rather than stressing problem solving, writing skills, or creativity. Few teachers, especially in poorer areas, have access to any materials but simple textbooks and paper; even these may be in short supply. Teachers in the Middle East do not enjoy markedly high social status, and rural posts are too often assigned to those with the worst academic performance. Teachers receive low pay, as do all civil servants. The upper end of the Egyptian teachers' salary scale exceeds the national poverty line by only 10% (UNDP/INP 2005).

Much of the money spent on education goes to teachers' and administrators' salaries; very little is left over to spend on books, equipment, or other educational materials. Educational quality has been crushed between constricting budgets and exploding enrollments. In Egypt, for example, salaries consumed 64% of primary and secondary spending in 1982/1983 and 71% in 1998/1999 (UNDP/INP 2005). These fiscal realities play a large role in the rote-memorization approach to learning from kindergarten to university throughout the region.

Given the working conditions in the poorer countries, it is hardly surprising that many teachers seek employment in the oil states. Egyptian schoolteachers can make at least *ten times* their domestic salaries in Saudi Arabia; small wonder that tens of thousands of them are working abroad, while many thousands more seek to leave. Indeed, one of the difficulties with maintaining, much less advancing, the educational systems of countries such as the Sudan and Yemen has been the departure of the small number of trained teachers to the Gulf States. Yemeni and Sudanese teachers in the Gulf, however, suffered the same fate as their fellow nationals during the Gulf crisis of 1990—expulsion (see Chapter 15).

Although a more extensive discussion of the consequences of international migration is offered in Chapter 15, a few points on the impact of migration on the educational systems of both sending and receiving countries are in order. First, given the extremely low levels of adult literacy in most of the major oil-exporting countries at the onset of the oil boom, rapid expansion of their primary enrollments required large-scale importation of teachers. Second, such teachers had to be fluent in Arabic, and therefore Egyptians as well as Jordanians and Palestinians were prominently represented. Third, such teachers usually dramatically improved their private welfare. Fourth, there is little evidence that such emigration outflows exceeded the recruitment and training of new teachers; as noted above, pupil-teacher ratios continued to fall during the 1970s in Egypt, Jordan, and other major suppliers of teachers. Fifth, although this implies that the export of teachers had few negative consequences in countries with high enrollment ratios, the same argument is much weaker in Egypt and the Sudan. After all, the favorable pupil-teacher ratios were achieved in part by slow growth of the numerator—by sluggish improvement in the (low) percentage of Egyptian and Sudanese children in school. The Gulf crisis opened up new opportunities for Egyptian and Syrian teachers, thanks to the expulsion of Palestinians, Jordanians, and Yemenis.

Secondary Education, Social Mobility, and Politics

Prior to direct European control and the consolidation of large bureaucratic state systems, literacy in the Middle East was a skill limited to a relative few and, among Muslims, one valued more for providing access to the sacred text of the Qur'an than for its contribution to everyday life. As the range of government activities grew, so did the need for literate, white-collar staff: clerks, accountants, and (although not many) managers. After World War I, nationalist movements throughout the Middle East put mass education at the top of their list of demands. Their concerns were twofold. First, nationalist leaders believed that Europe's strength in large measure stemmed from its educational systems and educated citizenries. As long as Middle Eastern societies were deprived of such systems and citizens, the societies would remain backward and subjugated. Second, these same leaders decried the elitism inherent in the new school systems promoted by colonial powers in the Middle East. Secondary education was limited to a narrow stratum of the population, often the offspring of the indigenous well-to-do, whom the colonial authorities wished to keep on their side. The object of the systems was to produce the clerks necessary to staff the colonial administration itself and the banks and businesses that sustained the economic links between the colony and the metropole. Only a handful of Middle Easterners ever received a university education. With the exception of Cairo University, universities in Istanbul and Ankara set up by the independent Turkish republic, and the American University of Beirut, there were no universities in the region. The very fortunate could go to the United Kingdom, France, Germany, or even the United States for advanced studies. In Algeria on the eve of the revolutionary war in 1954, out of a native population of 10 million only 7,000 were in secondary school, and only 600 had gone on to university-level studies. Although the elitism of the Algerian situation was more pronounced than elsewhere, it was a difference in degree, not in kind.

Thus the colonial authorities could and did use the educational system as an instrument to bestow favors on select groups and to produce the staff that would work in the trenches of the colonial administration. The nationalist leaders who criticized the elitism and manipulativeness of these policies knew whereof they spoke. Overwhelmingly they were among the elite and not infrequently cogs in the colonial administrations' wheels.

In the interwar years a number of ideas became rooted in the popular mind, among them the belief that education and literacy are rights of all citizens rather than privileges. Once independence was achieved, nationalist leaders were held to this notion. In addition, the link between secondary education and stable, respectable white-collar employment was firmly established. All, from peasants and tradespeople to craftspeople and manual laborers, saw their children's education as the key to moving upward in society and also as a hedge against the day when they would be too old or infirm to work.

The new states of the Middle East kept their promises in various ways. There was the temptation to yield to popular (i.e., middle-class) pressure and open the gates of secondary and university education nearly as wide as those of primary education. In most cases the financial costs of such a policy appeared prohibitive. Typically, per student outlays in secondary school are two to three times higher than in primary school, and university outlays may be ten times higher. The demands for and costs of teacher training for secondary education are also commensurately higher. Alongside these concerns was the realization that the economy needed skilled craftspeople, technicians, and low-level supervisory personnel as much as or more than it needed civil servants. Secondary education has nevertheless become much more widespread in the past twenty years (see Table 5.5). The increasing flood of secondary school students into the labor market constitutes a critical challenge facing economic policymakers and political strategists (see below and Chapter 15).

Those with the lowest secondary enrollment ratios in general are also the poorest, the Sudan and Yemen. The richest economies tend to have higher ratios, but Jordan and, especially Egypt, appear to be exceptional performers in comparison with their per capita incomes. Despite this apparently excellent performance, only Iraq before the Anglo-American invasion (91%) and Israel (89%) have had net secondary enrollment ratios that compared with those in advanced industrial countries.[17] However, Palestine, Qatar, and Jordan are not too far behind. The same bleak and politically ominous scenario as that sketched above for Egypt (see Box 5.2) is characteristic of a number of other states, especially those that followed programs of state-centered socialism (Syria, Iraq, Tunisia, and Algeria, in particular). Moreover, as in the case of rapid population growth itself, the "problem" is one posed for the society and economy as a whole. For any individual, the private returns to any education are very high; to be frustrated in one's career aspirations is better than to be denied those aspirations in the first place.

The costly effort throughout the region to expand secondary and university education has to some extent backfired because it has proved impossible to maintain exacting standards of instruction at the same time. In poorer countries like Morocco, schools, whether urban or rural, are primitive—drafty and cold in the winter, ovenlike in the spring. They are run-down because of inadequate budgets for maintenance; there may be no or very little artificial lighting, broken windows, missing blackboards, primitive and insalubrious plumbing, and classrooms crowded with benches and desks looking like relics from a war zone.[18] The din has to be heard to be believed. The students who suffer through this are often ill-clothed and ill-fed and must return to homes where there is no place to study and perhaps little understanding among the older generation of what modern education is all about.

TABLE 3.3 Secondary School Net Enrollment Ratios, 1990/1991 and 2002/2003

	1990/91				2002/03			
	Total	Male	Female	note:	Total	Male	Female	note:
Algeria	54	60	48		67	65	69	
Egypt	-	-	-		78	80	76	2000/01
Iraq	-	-	-		91	98	83	2000/01
Israel	87	86	87	1998/99	89	89	89	
Jordan	78	76	81		80	79	81	
Kuwait	88	87	89	1998/99	79	78	81	2000/01
Morocco	-	-	-		36	38	33	
Oman	-	-	-		69	69	70	
Palestine	-	-	-		84	80	85	
Qatar	70	68	72		82	80	85	
Saudi Arabia	31	34	28		53	54	52	
Syria	43	49	37		43	44	41	
Tunisia	-	-	-		64	61	68	
Turkey	-	-	-		-	-	-	
UAE	58	53	64		71	70	72	
Yemen	-	-	-		33	46	19	1998/99

SOURCE: UNESCO

Under such circumstances, morale is very low among both the students and the teachers. For the latter, pay is low, student-teacher ratios high, and support equipment nonexistent. That teachers resort to rote learning punctuated by long periods of chanting and calisthenics in what passes for the schoolyard is hardly surprising. Nor is their absenteeism. Young male teachers, thrust as bachelors into village schools, face long periods of sexual and social frustration. The teaching profession, like the diplomas it produces, has lost much of its prestige. Normal schools attract the least capable university students. It is a miracle that the system functions at all.

In this situation, privileged classes have reproduced themselves in part through their ability to put their children through an educational process that gives them career advantages and excludes most of their compatriots of a similar age. Thus, despite the professed ideal of the region's governments to develop and maintain an educational system that is free and open to all, a number of practices have developed that have maintained its class bias.

One avenue is offered through private schools, although it is safe to say that nowhere in the Middle East is there a truly elite system of private secondary schools such as one finds in the United States, the United Kingdom, or even India. At one time Victoria College in Alexandria or Robert College in Istanbul played such a role, but that is no longer the case. Christian missionary schools in the past were occasionally sought out because of high-quality education and foreign-language training, but their day, in societies that are preponderantly Muslim, has passed. The Christian minority of Lebanon has always maintained good private educational institutions, and even the civil war failed to disrupt them. We are currently witnessing a resurgence of private Muslim education, especially at the primary level. Its aim is, however, to safeguard Muslim values and practices rather than to promote the interests of a privileged class.

A second prop for the protection of privilege comes through the acquisition of foreign languages, especially English. Whether one points toward a career in industry, foreign trade, or banking and finance, mastering English, German, or French may be requisite to rising to the top. This brings us to the consequences—perhaps unintended, perhaps not—of Arabization, or Persianization, or Turkishization. Having all one's young citizens learn the national language is a logical and laudable policy, a strong foundation for democratization and cultural revitalization. But those who learn only Arabic, Turkish, or Persian will be able to rise only so far in the civil service, in professions such as medicine or engineering, or in modern industry and finance. Some critics have seen in the efforts to Arabize curricula and texts a plot on the part of the privileged to keep control of the commanding heights, for their children can afford secondary schools with quality instruction in foreign languages and are likely to do their university studies abroad or in disciplines that require foreign-language competency.

This question is most relevant for the Maghreb, formerly French North Africa. There indigenous civil service and professional elites were educated almost exclusively in French. Even after independence, French continued to be the official language of the government and the military. Such a situation was seen as absurd, as the local populations were very largely Arabic-speaking and thus unable to share the discourse of those who governed them. The governments of Tunisia, Algeria, and Morocco began to Arabize primary and secondary school curricula and then university curricula while slowly promoting Arabic as the main language of government. In theory, a North African today, monolingual in Arabic, has an equal chance with one who knows more than one language to achieve any position in society. In practice, it is probably still the case that entry into the technocratic and intellectual elites requires a mastery of French or English. The offspring of incumbent elites are the most likely to have that competency.

In many Middle Eastern societies the public school system may be the only one available to the well-off. Facilities and teaching quality are supposed to be uniform throughout the system. Everywhere it is the central government that finances school budgets, so the local tax base is not relevant to school quality. Still, schools in urban areas are better equipped and better staffed than in the rural world, and schools in wealthier districts tend to have lower student-teacher ratios and an atmosphere more conducive to learning. These kinds of variations in what are supposed to be systems of uniform quality are common throughout the world. One may add to them the fact that although the public system is free to all eligible children, the well-off can afford books, pens, and pencils, decent clothing, and decent food and housing for their offspring, giving them a range of material advantages over the poor.

Going well beyond these types of class bias is the phenomenon of tutorials. Most of our evidence is drawn from Egypt, but the logic of the phenomenon is so compelling that we feel that it must manifest itself elsewhere as well. In Egypt, students sit for a general exam at the end of the secondary cycle. The scores obtained on the exam determine the university faculties to which they will gain admission. Engineering and medicine require the highest scores and are, indeed, the most sought-after faculties. In short, high scores on the secondary school exam determine access to the faculties that will produce the next generation of elites.

Enter the underpaid teacher and the anxious middle-class parent. The teacher wants to supplement his or her meager income, and the parent wants to give his or her child a leg up. The result is fee-based tutorials to prepare for the exams. Depending on the subject matter and the number of students in the tutorial, the fees can be very high, sometimes more than a low-income Egyptian may earn in a year. An Egyptian teacher can earn ten times as much from tutoring as from his or her government salary; anxious Egyptian families spend about 7 billion Egyptian pounds (LE) on these services (UNDP/INP 2005, 84). Thus, an informal parallel educational system, based on fees, has grown into existence—a system that favors the rich and penalizes the poor. The parallel system helps ensure that the children of the well-to-do accede in disproportionate numbers to those professional disciplines that will be most highly rewarded in terms of income and prestige.

Having stressed educational strategies that reflect class bias, we must even more strongly emphasize that the mass educational systems set up in most Middle Eastern countries have been catalysts for real social mobility. The evidence for this assertion is fragmentary; systematic studies of the socioeconomic background of secondary- and university-level students have not been carried out. We do not know how profound the democratization process has been in higher education. All indications, however, point in the same direction, to wit, that the children of the lower-middle-income strata, the petty bourgeoisie of craftsmen and service providers, the clerks, the teachers, and the agrarian smallholders, have seized the educational opportunities offered to them and moved well beyond their parents in status and wealth. The phenomenon was first observed in the 1930s, when in various countries admission to institutes of higher education and, most important, to officer's candidate schools was determined by competitive examination. Hardworking, ambitious, intelligent offspring of the lower-middle class outperformed all others and entered educational and professional domains that had been reserved to the upper classes. Gamal ʿAbd al-Nasser, the son of a rural functionary, and a number of others who overthrew the Egyptian monarchy in 1952 entered the military academy between 1936 and 1938 and attained the rank of colonel in the postwar years. A similar process got under way in Syria a few years later and yielded Hafiz al-Assad and other officers of rural, lower-middle-class background.

With independence, the process accelerated. One of the most striking examples is that of Damascus University, where in 1968 half the student body was of rural origin and only 65% of the students had fathers with university education (Hinnebusch 1979, 28–29). Rapidly expanding public bureaucracies, educational systems, state enterprises, and military establishments provided a growing job market for these young people. They also became functionaries in some of the more coherently organized political parties, such as the Republican People's party in Turkey, the Ba'ath party of Syria and Iraq, and the Neo-Destour (New Constitution) party of Tunisia (now known as the Constitutional Democratic Rally [RCD]).

By contrast, it would appear that the offspring of peasants, salaried workers, and common laborers—that is, the majority of the low-income strata—have not gained access to secondary and university education in numbers that come near to being proportional to their weight in society.

In recent years in many parts of the Middle East, there have been reassessments of mass-educational policies and sometimes timid, camouflaged attempts to slow the rate of increase in secondary school enrollments and to restrict admission to universities. Such attempts are usually accompanied by efforts to orient primary school students and those who fail general secondary school exams toward vocational-training institutes. Such institutes have been regarded as dead-ends, and students and parents alike have gone to great lengths to avoid them.

All governments of the region have for years stressed the need for vocational and technical training for their youth. Egypt's goal in 1985 was to provide primary and preparatory education to all children and then orient 60% of secondary students toward vocational and technical training. The remaining 40% would follow the traditional secondary school curriculum, with admission to university as the final target. Egypt is a long way from achieving this distribution, as are all other states in the area. Again, if we take Egypt as representative, we find that most of the vocational students are being trained in commerce, probably simple accountancy, and relatively few in industry and skilled trades. As in many developing countries, there is still a marked preference for white-collar, desk-bound employment. Even when herded into vocational education, Middle Eastern students opt for potentially white-collar skills in accountancy rather than certifying themselves as electricians, mechanics, or plumbers.

These attitudes may be changing, however. The great construction boom of the 1970s in the Gulf States created a heavy demand for masons, carpenters, electricians, and the like. Wages for these trades rose rapidly not only in the oil-rich countries importing labor but in the sending countries as well. Within a few years, plumbers or mechanics in Egypt could earn far more than a university-educated civil servant. Moreover, in addition to the oil boom, a technological transformation of the region was taking place. In the cities, high-rise buildings entail elevators, which in turn require maintenance. Air-conditioning in places of work and private homes also requires maintenance, and so do tractors and diesel pumps in the countryside. In short, a booming market for skilled repair persons emerged, whose relative wages do not seem to have changed with the oil bust. Substantial incomes can still be earned in these fields, but that realization is slow in dawning on a populace obsessed with the respectability of university education and white-collar jobs.

It is not at all clear that a bigger public effort to promote vocational training would remove these bottlenecks. Too often, it appears, vocational training is mired in routine. There is little interaction with the markets for which the students are presumably being trained. The same skills are taught in the same way year after year without regard to changing needs and changing technologies. The result is students who may have to be retrained by their employers. In fact, it may make good sense for public authorities to help likely employers to design their own on-the-job training. For many trades this takes place anyway through the traditional system of master and apprentice. If one looks in any auto mechanic's workshop or notices who is carrying the plumber's tool bag, one is likely to see a boy learning the trade. Whether he also goes to school is irrelevant. He may be paid little more than subsistence, but working side-by-side with the master, he will become familiar with a range of real-life situations—such as dismantling five different kinds of automobile engines—that the vocational trainee will not face. Such private, on-the-job training is almost everywhere superior to public or "official" training. Given the structure of labor markets (see below), it is unsurprising that publicly funded vocational training has largely failed.

The secondary and vocational school environment provides a special political chemistry. The main actors, students and teachers, have particular characteristics. The teachers are themselves young and most often male. They are of course educated but may well have aspired to a loftier or more remunerative career than teaching. As mentioned earlier, they may have too few resources and too many students to carry out their job effectively. Often they are politically aware, if not active, and today they—and their students—constitute fertile recruiting ground for Islamist movements.[19] In the Arab countries they may be monolingual in Arabic and resent the fact that this precludes their ascent to elite status. In sum, secondary school teachers are seldom content with their lot or with the system for which they work.

The same can be said for many secondary school students. Although they may have survived the screening process after primary school, access to university-level studies will be available to, at most, a quarter of them. And for those in vocational schools, that possibility does not exist at all. We have, then, physically mature adolescents, often from low-income backgrounds, a cut above those with only a primary school education and with ambitions to match. They are also politically aware and at a point in their lives when high-risk political action may appeal to their sense of adventure or at least relieve their frustration. In their teachers they may find mentors not much older than themselves who can focus their actions.

Finally there is the school itself, a physical locale that brings the actors together on a day-to-day basis. As is the case for the mosque or the church, it is very difficult for the authorities to control political activities among people who congregate in a perfectly legal manner. When there are disturbances in schools, they are highly visible and noisy and spill out to disrupt life in entire city neighborhoods or small rural towns. The issues that trigger protests, the violence that may ensue, the reprisals, arrests, and police beatings immediately resonate through a much broader stratum of the population—parents, siblings, and other relatives, who all have a stake in the secondary student's education. A student protest over poor food in the canteen or increased fees may rapidly activate many people with a more extensive list of grievances (see Chapters 10 and 14).

These patterns are neither very new nor unique to the Middle East. Some of the region's better-known political leaders came out of the teaching corps or received their political baptism as secondary school students. Probably the single most important Muslim political leader of the first half of the twentieth century was the Egyptian Hassan al-Banna, monolingual in Arabic and a primary school teacher, who founded the Muslim Brotherhood in 1929. Of a very different political persuasion were Michel Aflaq and Salah Bitar, the Syrian secondary school teachers who founded the Ba'ath party that continues to rule in Syria. Several of the nationalist movements in the Middle East, such as the RCD party of Tunisia, the Istiqlal of Morocco, the National Liberation Front (FLN) of Algeria, the Wafd of Egypt, and the Ba'ath, relied to some extent on schoolteachers and students to develop the local infrastructure of their organizations. Whether we consider the adolescent Gamal 'Abd al-Nasser experimenting with the Young Egypt party (Misr al-Fatat) in the 1930s or the lycée student Ait Ahmad Hocine, who was a militant in the Algerian People's party (PPA) and later one of the six historic chiefs of the Algerian revolution, we see a pattern of the political awakening and active political involvement of secondary school students from the 1930s on.

Leaders of the independent countries of the region are acutely aware of the strategic importance of both students and teachers at this level. Habib Bourguiba of Tunisia was able to harness them to his Neo-Destour party but lost some of them to his more militant rival in that party, Salah Ben Yussef. The shah of Iran, after 1963, tried to mobilize students and teachers in literacy campaigns in the countryside, while Houari Boumedienne, president of socialist Algeria, put them to work in 1972 on a survey of landholdings prior to an agrarian reform (Leca 1975). Kemal Atatürk and his successor, Ismet Inönü, saw secondary school teachers as the vehicles for promoting the secular values of the Turkish republic. Village institutes were created to train rural youth to be teachers and to carry the message of republicanism, secularism, and statism to the traditional rural populations. People's houses, functioning as local cultural centers, were set up to propagate the new credo to people outside the school system. In Egypt, during its most pronounced socialist phase in the mid-1960s, the single party, the Arab Socialist Union, relied on local schoolteachers, veterinarians, co-op officials, and other white-collar functionaries to break the influence of local landowning groups (Harik 1974, 81–100).

These efforts at co-optation often ring hollow among the targeted groups. Part of the reason stems from the yawning gap in age between the political elites relative to the students they are trying to control (see Chapter 4). The co-opters lack credibility. In addition, as we argue throughout this book, the period of austerity from the mid-1980s to roughly 2000 has made access to jobs something of a lottery in which the majority of students draw losing tickets.

Islamic movements have exploited this situation to their advantage. They have always viewed the educational system as a crucial battleground, control of which may yield control of the hearts and minds of students. In some ways political Islamic groups seek political power not for its own sake, but rather because it would provide them control—so they believe—over the cultural and educational institutions and the mass media. To the young, they offer leadership that is closer to them in age and spirit than the aging leadership of the status quo and values that stress probity, the separation of the sexes, and religious faith. They move along three tracks: (1) the assault, direct or indirect, on the bastions of political power, (2) the infiltration of the public education system, and (3) the establishment of private schools under their direct control. During Algeria's civil war, the struggle was violent and waged extra-legally by the Islamic Salvation Front (FIS). In Turkey, the Welfare party waged its struggle at the ballot box, a struggle continued by the Justice and Development party. The Muslim Brotherhood has used the same strategy in Egypt. In Palestine, the Islamic Resistance Movement (HAMAS) does both. The goals of all of these movements vis-à-vis youth and the educational system are roughly the same.

The Universities

Prior to the twentieth century, the Middle East had no modern public universities. There were a few higher institutes of Islamic studies such as the Qarawiyin in Fez, Morocco, and Egypt's prestigious al-Azhar. The first university on the Western model in the region was the American University of Beirut, which was private and established as part of the Protestant Mission in Lebanon. By 1925 Cairo University had been chartered as a fully public institution, and national universities were started in Turkey and Iran. The Hebrew University was founded in Jerusalem, in Mandate Palestine, in 1925. These aside, there were no universities in the region until the 1950s and 1960s.

With full independence throughout the region, there was an explosion in the establishment of universities and in the number of students attending them. Algeria, which had no universities in 1962, now has twenty-four. In 1994, there were only two universities in Yemen (Aden and San'a). Today, however, there are fifteen, including eight private institutions, with 111 faculties and some 130,000 students. Tehran University was founded in Iran in 1934, and by the mid-1970s another eight universities had been established, with total enrollments of around 60,000. Ten years later, enrollments had more than doubled (to over 145,000). Today there are more than 1.5 million students attending more than fifty public universities and more than two hundred private institutions. By the end of the 1980s, Turkey had an equivalent number enrolled in universities. In the region as a whole, the proportion of 18-to-23-year-olds attending institutes of higher learning grew from 4% in 1960 to 10% in 1980 to 15% in 1993 to 20% in 2006. In addition, tens of thousands of Middle Easterners pursued university educations abroad.

The institutional expansion within the region necessarily sacrificed educational standards. For many years the growing economies and governments of the Middle East could absorb all the graduates the universities produced almost regardless of the quality of their preparation. By the late 1970s, however, administrations were clogged with fairly young civil servants, expansion of public-sector enterprises had slowed, and except in the Gulf, the construction booms of the 1960s and 1970s were over. The formation of a "dangerous" class of the educated unemployed had begun.

Universities and institutes of higher learning exhibit a greater degree of class bias than secondary schools. There has undoubtedly been a certain measure of democratization, as we saw with respect to the University of Damascus, with members of the lower-middle class in particular bettering their position through access to a more open educational system. Still, findings from a survey of university applicants carried out in Turkey in the mid-1970s may be applicable throughout the region (Özgediz 1980, 507). Only 30% of all applicants were from rural areas, while 47% were from the three major cities, Istanbul, Ankara, and Izmir. The success rate in passing entrance exams was three times higher for applicants from upper-income strata than for those from lower-income groups.

The first universities were all located in major cities. Cairo alone has three major public universities and well over 200,000 students. No regime likes to see that kind of concentration of potentially volatile, young, educated people in one place. In recent years there has been a general move throughout the Middle East to establish provincial campuses. This policy serves several purposes. It demonstrates to more remote regions the government's concern to make higher education directly available to their populations. It helps satisfy the relentless demand from all sectors of the population for university education. And it eases the concentration of students in economic and political capitals, where their agitation is highly visible and disruptive. The strategy does not always work. For over twenty-five years the University of Assiut in Upper Egypt has been a hotbed of clashes among Islamic student groups, other students, university authorities, and the local police. Many of the provincial universities dispense a thoroughly mediocre education. Even more than the older universities, provincial universities are understaffed, underfinanced, underequipped, and overpopulated. In most instances they are monuments to political expediency.

Middle Eastern universities are preeminently and self-consciously political. Various elements within them claim to speak for the nation's intelligentsia as well as for the generation that will furnish the nation's leaders. By its very organization the university, in its research and instruction, touches upon all the issues that are of great moment to the nation as a whole. All the political currents of the nation will be manifested within the university. There is a constant battle within its walls for control over the institution, and particularly in the authoritarian systems that typify the region, the conduct of that battle is seen as a bellwether for the entire polity.

Student elections of one kind or another may be more hotly contested and less easily controlled than other elections in a given society. In the absence of other indicators of shifts in public opinion or in the relative weights of political forces, such elections are closely scrutinized. Every regime will have its tame student association or union to enter the fray. In single-party regimes, such as those of the Ba'ath in Syria, the RCD in Tunisia, or the FLN in Algeria, the student union will be directly affiliated with the party. So, too, will associations of professors and administrators. In this way the university is supposed to remain a place of learning, subordinate to the regime, but it seldom works out that way in practice. Although student or faculty activists may be a minority of the university population, they are ubiquitous, visible, and highly motivated.

The Middle Eastern university is enveloped in contradictory symbols and practices. Its origins are Western, and most countries of the region at least honor the fiction of the physical and intellectual inviolability of the university. However, the sanctity of academic freedom, as well as the campus itself, is frequently violated. In many countries the university is called upon to "serve the revolution" or contribute to the development of the nation, slogans that mean in fact that it should remain subservient to regime goals, if not politically inert. When university organizations or movements criticize the government precisely for betraying the revolution (e.g., Algeria in 1966 after Boumedienne seized power from Ben Bella), thwarting the development of the country (Iran throughout the 1970s and Turkey in 1978–1979), or capitulating to its enemies (Egypt in 1971–1972 and in all the years since the 1979 Camp David Accords), then the spokespersons for those organizations are denounced as agents of foreign powers. The Moroccan monarchy on occasion has simply drafted troublemakers into the armed forces.

The freedom of teaching and research is highly circumscribed. There may be subjects that cannot be researched and questions that cannot be asked. Classes will typically have their share of police informers. Some regimes have resorted to strong-arm tactics, with party-affiliated toughs enforcing the proper line, breaking up unauthorized meetings, and intimidating student leaders. Israeli authorities have since 1967 engaged in a running battle with Palestinian students and faculty at Bir Zeit University and al-Najah University on the West Bank. Still, the spirit of the university as an institution with a peculiar responsibility to the fate of the nation is kept alive, and university students are often prepared to take great risks in making their views known. The best among them will in all likelihood be the nation's future leaders. In fact student militancy has often been the stepping-stone to high official position, as incumbent leaders identify their challengers and set about co-opting them. It is for all these reasons that in national power struggles contenders may see capturing the university to be as strategically important as capturing the armed forces.

LABOR MARKETS

As the "human-capital" metaphor suggests, better health and education make people more productive. But such enhancements can materialize only if labor markets can match these healthier, better-trained individuals with jobs that utilize their skills. If no jobs or the wrong kinds of jobs are created, some combination of unemployment or lower real wages will follow. Educational systems and labor markets are closely linked; if markets send distorted signals, privately rational choices will spawn socially inefficient outcomes.

Labor-market structures and dynamics in MENA are problematic. Too few jobs are created, and for decades many government policies have stimulated the acquisition of formal credentials rather than of marketable skills. We saw in Chapter 4 that the region's labor force is growing at the most rapid rate in the world. Unfortunately, the demand for labor has not been keeping up, and the structure of labor markets—primarily, the preponderance of government employment and intrusive regulation of (larger) private employers—further impedes job creation.

The employment problem may be the most politically volatile economic issue now facing the region. Despite data deficiencies, several generalizations can be made: Current levels of unemployment are high, and the problem will probably get worse in the near to medium run. Unemployment affects primarily young, semi-educated people, whose anger fuels political unrest. Unemployed youth provide fertile ground for Islamist radicalism throughout the region (see Chapter 14).

Unemployment

By all accounts, unemployment plagues the region. According to the International Labour Organisation (ILO), unemployment is higher in MENA than in other regions of the world (see Table 5.6).[20] The World Bank asserts that only sub-Saharan Africa has higher rates. Over the past decade, the number of unemployed in MENA has grown (ILO 2006); the total number of unemployed now exceeds 20 million (World Bank 2004c). Some estimates of national unemployment rates are shown in Table 5.7. It is evident that estimates vary widely, depending on the source. Two factors underlie these differences: data quality issues and, more important, differences in definitions.

Data on unemployment comes from surveys. Although countries try to conform to international definitions, the frequency and coverage of surveys is far from uniform. "Unemployed" means "without a job, and looking for work." Because high unemployment discourages workers from looking for jobs, measured unemployment can be a serious understatement of the problem. For example, one study of Egypt found that relaxing the definition increased unemployment rates by more than 50% for women (El-Kogali 2002). Finally, governments and international agencies have their own agenda. Unemployment data, whether in the United States or the Middle East, can be used as political weapons, and political actors are not shy about wielding them. All data must be treated with great caution.

TABLE 5.6   Unemployment Rates in Major World Regions, 2005

Region	Unemployment Rate
MENA	**13.2%**
Sub-Saharan Africa	9.7%
Latin America	7.7%
Central Europe and CIS	9.7%
("Commonwealth Independent States": i.e. former USSR)	
East Asia	3.8%
SE Asia	6.1%
"Developed Countries"	6.7%

SOURCES: ILO, Global Employment Trends Brief, January 2006

TABLE 5.7 Unemployment Rates in Selected MENA Countries

	Unemployment Rates	*Comments:*
Algeria	22.5	2005
Bahrain	15	1998
Egypt	10	2005
Iran	11.2	2004
Iraq	25–20	2005
Israel	8.9	2005
Jordan	15	official; unofficial rate is ~30%, 2004
Kuwait	2.2	2004
Libya	30	2004
Morocco	10.5	2005
Oman	15	2004
Qatar	2.7	2001
Saudi Arabia	13	male only; local bank estimates as high as 25%, 2004
Sudan	18.7	2002
Syria	20	2002
Tunisia	13.5	2005
Turkey	10	?, 2005
UAE	2.4	2001
WBG[a]	19.9	2005
Yemen	35	2003

[a]West Bank and Gaza
SOURCE: CIA World Factbook

Nevertheless, the outlines of the situation are clear. First, unemployment is often greater in cities than in the countryside; second, unemployment is mainly an affliction of the young; third, educated workers are more likely to be unemployed than uneducated ones (although this depends, to some extent, on the definition of "educated"); and fourth, unemployment rates for women exceed those for men. As usual, there is country variation in all of these general features.

In most countries, unemployment is higher in the cities than in the countryside. In Morocco, measured open unemployment rates are roughly four times higher in cities than in rural areas, 20% compared with 5% (USAID 2002; Achy 2002). Turkish urban unemployment is more than twice that of rural areas, and similar patterns are found in Jordan. More than 70% of those unemployed in Iran in the early 1990s lived in cities (Amuzegar 1993, 66).

However, this picture is changing in some countries. Although the overall urban unemployment rate continues to exceed the rural rate in Egypt, the gap narrowed during the 1990s: from an urban rate three times higher than the rural rate to one only about 40% higher. The male rural unemployment rate actually exceeded the urban rate; all of the difference was due to high female unemployment in urban areas (El-Kogali 2002; Assaad et al. 2000). In Iran, youth unemployment for rural males was slightly higher than for urban young men. As in Egypt, higher urban female unemployment accounted for the difference (UN 2003).

Rural labor markets tend to be more flexible than urban markets. Agriculture and informal rural labor-market outcomes are best explained with supply-and-demand models such as wage flexibility. The best-documented case is Egypt. A study of the 1970s and 1980s found that an essentially neoclassical model best explained the large changes in Egyptian farm labor markets during and after the oil boom of the 1970s (Richards 1994). Both supply and demand were inelastic with respect to the wage, and real wages were (and remain) very flexible, rising and then falling sharply with international oil prices. Supply shifts explain these real-wage changes. These in turn are primarily the outcome of international labor migration. All of this is entirely compatible with a flexible wage model.

Measured open unemployment in agriculture is very low. Of course, there exists significant seasonal unemployment, which is a factor in rural poverty. Agricultural workers often also work in services, construction, handicrafts, and/or small-scale manufacturing (see, e.g., Radwan and Lee 1986 on Egypt), in part as a means of offsetting the inherent seasonality of agricultural work. Particularly in densely populated Egypt, "rural" has long ceased to be the equivalent of "agricultural." As we shall see, part of the reason for the declining rural-urban differential in Egypt's unemployment is the increased "informalization" of the Egyptian urban economy.

Rural-to-urban migration plays a role in increasing pressure on urban labor markets in many countries. The rural population is growing much less rapidly than the urban population, despite the (generally) higher fertility rates in the countryside (see Chapter 10). Everywhere in the world, young, increasingly educated young people seek to leave rural areas. In a sense, unemployment is "exported to the cities," where it has significantly different political consequences from what would be expected if it were found mainly in rural areas. Many sociological studies (e.g., Ibrahim 1994; Roy 1994) have found that the most likely members of Islamist groups are recent immigrants from the countryside who have some education.

Most of the unemployed are young. Although this is a universal phenomenon, it is particularly salient in MENA, which has the highest rate of youth unemployment (25%) in the world (Kabbani and Kothari 2005). More than half of the region's unemployed are younger than twenty-five years old; the percentage of youth contributing to the total unemployed is highest in Syria, where it approaches 75%. In Morocco, where urban unemployment is about 20%, youth unemployment stands at 36% (USAID 2002). Egyptian unemployment rates for young men (15–24) are some *seven times* higher than for men over thirty (El-Kogali 2002). In Iran, youth unemployment rates exceed rates for those over thirty by a factor of four (about 20% compared with less than 5%) (UN 2003). Unemployment is particularly severe for youth with intermediate levels of education. Among university graduates, rates of unemployment vary considerably among countries. In Egypt, the rate of unemployment among university graduates is approximately half that of those with

TABLE 5.8 Unemployment Rates in MENA Countries, by Gender and Education Level

		None			Primary			Secondary			Tertiary			All		
Country	Year	T	M	F	T	M	F	T	M	F	T	M	F	T	M	F
Algeria	1995	9.6	–	–	30.9	–	–	30.9	–	–	68.4	–	–	27.9	26	38.4
Egypt	1998	4.1	3.6	6.6	5.7	4.7	18.2	22.4	12.9	42.1	9.7	6.5	17	11.4	6.9	26.9
Morocco	1999	9.4	9.7	8.9	26.3	24.9	31.1	32.4	30.4	37.3	37.6	31.8	48.2	15.6	15.7	15.4
Oman	1996	5.6	5.6	5.6	13.4	12.2	29.6	24.8	13.5	79.4	2.8	2.3	5	10.8	8.7	28.6
Tunisia	1997	10.2	–	–	20.8	–	–	15.4	–	–	6.4	–	–	15.7	15.4	16.7

NOTE: T = total; M = male; F = female; - = not available
SOURCE: World Bank 2004c

only a secondary education (see Table 5.8), but this is not the case in Algeria, Morocco, and Jordan (Bourdarbat 2005; Nabli and Keller 2002; World Bank 2004c). The World Bank goes so far as to say that "unemployment [in the region] is essentially a labor market insertion problem for youth" (World Bank 2004c, 90).

Some explanations for youth unemployment in OECD countries stress the lower "commitment" of the young to the job market. Working-age children of heads of households are more likely to be unemployed than heads of households (World Bank 2004c). Unencumbered by wives or children to support and sheltered and fed by their own families, youths can more easily spend some time looking for jobs, switch jobs, and so on. In short, they are better equipped for the job search than older workers; they can afford to wait. Many young people are particularly eager to get a government job, with its (historically) higher wages and better benefits. This phenomenon has been observed, for example, in Egypt, Jordan, Morocco, and Saudi Arabia.

Several implications follow from the observed relationship between education and unemployment. First, the evidence is consistent with the general notion that the unemployed wait for jobs. Educated people are likely to conduct longer job searches than illiterate workers because they can reasonably hope to find a good job, whereas the illiterate know that they have almost no such chance and must take the first job available. Second, a basic determinant of unemployment is the relative rates of growth of the number of "qualified" (school-leavers), on the one hand, and the number of jobs created in the modern sector, on the other. Third, the very high rates of unemployment among secondary school-leavers suggest that "a little knowledge is a dangerous thing." These young people have received enough education to have altered their expectations and aspirations but not enough to compete effectively for the (very scarce) good jobs in the formal sector. In the Maghreb, this situation particularly afflicts those who have received their instruction in Arabic rather than French. The large numbers of students and the absence of reading materials in Arabic on modern subjects ill equips Arabic-trained graduates to compete for scarce modern-sector jobs.

As noted above, women's unemployment exceeds that of men (see Table 5.8). In MENA countries, as elsewhere, women may have a lower commitment to the labor market, entering and leaving to accommodate family needs (entering for income and leaving for child rearing), but this is very unlikely to be the whole story. As women become more educated, they also increase their labor force participation—they look for jobs. However, if it is difficult for educated men to take jobs "beneath their status," this problem is still more acute for women in the region. Female unemployment, even more than that for men, may then partly be attributed to rising education. Although severe economic pressures may ultimately push women to enter the informal sector, they typically wait as long as they can for a government job. Young women and their families need reassurance that they will be safe in the workplace and that others will perceive their employment as "respectable." For many women, this means either working directly with male family members (e.g., in a small family-owned shop) or working in a large, modern office. Public-sector jobs offer respectability and regular, relatively short hours—working conditions that are particularly attractive to women. They also offer better benefits. Families will support daughters, sisters, and wives rather than have them take inappropriate jobs. Because of the increasing feminization of public-sector jobs, women are differentially and adversely affected by slower job creation in that sector (Moghadem 2001). Economic austerity, with its cuts in government budgets (see Chapter 9), has imposed a particularly high price on educated women.

This picture of unemployment among women, the educated, and the young seems broadly consistent with Gunnar Myrdal's hypothesis, based on observations in India, that "unemployment is a bourgeois luxury"—something that only those with some means, however modest, can afford. Nonetheless, unemployment among illiterate Moroccans was some 10% during the 1990s (World Bank 2004c), and Palestinian unemployment after 2001 has afflicted the educated and the underprivileged alike. And low unemployment among illiterate Egyptians (just under 5%) hardly ensures them an acceptable standard of living; they simply take "jobs" that pay extremely low real wages. They may be employed, but they are also very poor (see Chapter 10).

Labor-Market Structures

We can divide urban labor markets into three major sectors: public, private formal, and private informal. The public sector is in turn composed of bureaucracies and state-owned enterprises. Public employment is very secure: It is almost impossible in many cases to lose one's job. On average for the region, public-sector wages are approximately 25% above those in the private sector—the highest differential in the world (Schiavo-Campo et al. 2003). Until recently, the public sector provided the first jobs for the growing masses of educated and semi-educated young men. Although this remains true for nationals in the Gulf countries, elsewhere (e.g., in Egypt, Morocco, Yemen), most new jobs (60% in 1998) are now created in the private informal sector (World Bank 2004c).

The private formal sector varies greatly in size but is typically the smallest of the three sectors. There are several definitions, but usually a minimum of ten to fifty workers is required to classify an enterprise as belonging to this sector. Additionally, workers in it are assumed to have some job security, although less than in the public sector, and their employers pay payroll and social protection taxes. Workers in the private formal sector often receive higher wages than their counterparts in the public sector. In some countries (e.g., Turkey, Tunisia) many may belong to trade union organizations. Some analysts (e.g., Harberger 1971) treat this and the public sector as "protected" sectors, as they offer wages above market-clearing levels, a situation that naturally creates queues of workers seeking these jobs.

Most importantly, there is the private informal sector. The definitions of this sector vary considerably in the literature. Sometimes the term is used as a euphemism for "slum dwellers" or "poor people." Most commonly, the sector is defined as including all self-employed persons plus those employed in firms with fewer than ten workers; sometimes the unskilled, casual laborers employed by larger firms are added. In Algeria, Egypt, Morocco, Tunisia, and Syria, the self-employed account for at least half of the sector's workers (World Bank 2004c). Examples include small-scale manufacturing and handicraft workers; itinerant and jobbing artisans, like carpenters and masons; providers of personal services (servants, porters, watchmen); as well as car washers, street hawkers and vendors, garbage collectors, etc. (Abdel-Fadil 1983). A defining feature everywhere is that informal "firms" are unregistered and untaxed. Typically, there are few or no barriers to entry in the informal sector. Capital per worker is very low, and incomes fluctuate considerably both seasonally and annually. The sector usually employs a higher proportion of women, children, and young adults than other sectors.

How large is the informal sector? Because the activity is unregistered, much uncertainty surrounds the answer. Most estimates are that the sector accounts for anywhere from one-fifth to one-third of national output, and for a low of about two-fifths of nonagricultural employment (Syria) to a high of 55% in Egypt (ILO 2006; World Bank 2004c). Notably, in many other Third World countries, the sector's share in nonfarm employment is even higher (e.g., Brazil, 60%; Kenya, 72%; Indonesia, 83%) (ILO 2002). The share of this sector in employment has grown under the impact of economic reform in Algeria, Egypt, and Morocco. The change in Egypt has been especially striking; although the sector created only about one in five jobs for new workers in 1970, by 1998 it was creating six in ten new jobs (World Bank 2004c).

Most MENA countries experience a kind of "labor-market dualism," with two radically different labor-market mechanisms. On the one hand, we find an essentially neoclassical labor-market mechanism (albeit with some imperfect information properties; see Assaad 1997) in the informal sector (and agriculture), with flexible wages and low unemployment but (often) low wages and high levels of poverty. These markets are relatively "efficient": they match supply and demand. Unfortunately, these "efficient markets" are mainly for poorer, less-educated workers. Needless to say, these are not the jobs that young, relatively well-educated men and women want, but, increasingly, these are the only jobs they can find. On the other hand, government employees work in "administered" labor markets, where job slots and wages are determined by bureaucratic criteria, not supply and demand. Such labor-allocation mechanisms dominate the public sectors and are highly inflexible.

A plausible story, based on the Egyptian case, goes like this: Young people seek to obtain jobs in the public sector, despite their declining real wage, because such jobs (1) are very secure (it is almost impossible to fire a bureaucrat), (2) are respectable (which is important for "marriage-market" considerations for both men and women), and (3) permit considerable moonlighting. At middle levels, such jobs may also have some value because they make it possible to collect rents (bribes, in plain English) and/or to become a member of a vertically organized network of patronage. The jobs also provide pensions. In order to obtain a government job, graduates must place themselves on a government list. However, a person's name is removed (in theory) from the list if he or she obtains another job. To remain on the list, one must either be unemployed or work surreptitiously. Families bear the costs of their sons and daughters waiting because of the valuable benefits. Similar patterns have been observed in Algeria (Chemingui and Ayadi 2003) and Morocco (Bourdarbat 2005). Jordanian labor markets combine high unemployment of the educated with immigration for unskilled work; there is strong evidence that young Jordanians will not take low-paying unskilled (or in some cases, semi-skilled) manual jobs. Jordanian analysts often stress the role of a job as a status indicator—especially relevant for marriage concerns and other social factors. The result is high unemployment, combined with large numbers of (often Egyptian) immigrant workers.

The public-sector wage mechanisms are similar in all cases. The differences (such as they are) across countries seem to be mainly explained by differences in the share of the public sector in total employment. The public sector looms large in nonagricultural employment. Its share ranges from a high of 70% in Egypt to a low of 20% in Morocco (Gardner 2003). In the Gulf, the public sector employs over half of all nationals in Kuwait, Oman, Qatar, and the UAE, over 40% in Saudi Arabia, and one-third in Bahrain (Fasano and Goyal 2004).

The inflexibility of the public segment of the labor market contributes to the problem of youth unemployment, with its potentially explosive political consequences. There is also often an anti-employment bias in laws regulating private employment. In some countries it is very difficult for private employers to fire workers, particularly after they have been employed for more than six months to a year. The result is that firms either substitute capital for labor or evade regulations by avoiding expansion beyond a small size. Such government policies impede some of the more productive segments of the informal sector from becoming an "engine of growth," as small business can often be.

None of this is intended to suggest that labor-market structures and institutions alone are responsible for sluggish job creation. Clearly, given the growth of the labor force documented in Chapter 4, only rapid economic growth could create the necessary jobs. Table 5.7 shows one estimate of the gap between the supply of labor (growth of the labor force) and demand (approximated by the rate of economic growth necessary to keep up with the growth of the labor force in the 1990s). Egypt, Iran, and Tunisia "ran fast enough to stand still"; their economies grew just fast enough to keep their unemployment rates roughly the same and to prevent real wages from falling further. The others did still worse. Other sources give only a slightly different picture: According to the ILO, the regional unemployment rate fell from 14.3% in 1995 to 13.2% in 2005, an improvement largely attributed to the recovery of oil prices in the last five years (ILO 2006). Of course, the absolute numbers of the jobless rose. Every year since 1996, an additional 500,000 people in the region have been added to the ranks of the unemployed (ILO 2006).

CONCLUSION

Nearly all Middle Eastern governments have promised their citizens health, education, and jobs. Until this century, jobs were not much of a problem for an overwhelmingly agricultural population, which was also ignorant and often sick. Progress in both domains has been rapid and real, but starting from such low bases has meant that many Middle Easterners—infants who die young or adults who remain illiterate—still suffer from the twin scourges. The progress registered is not commensurate, by international standards, with the average levels of income and per capita GDPs of these countries. Moreover, the rapid increase in population in the region makes the effort to catch up extremely costly. Past population growth means that during the next quarter-century the number of people below the age of fifteen will double. At the same time, government budgets remain constrained, especially in those countries without sizable oil resources (see Chapter 9). It is remarkable, under these circumstances, that so much has nevertheless been achieved. Nearly all children are in school in most countries; infant mortality, while still tragically high, has plummeted. Starting from so far behind, governments of the region have made heroic efforts—yet the health and educational outcomes still fall well short of the aspirations of its people.

The existing educational system has left the current generation of school-leavers between two stools: On the one hand, their aspirations have been raised, making them reluctant to take manual, low-status jobs; on the other hand, the overcrowded, underfunded, rote-memorization educational system provides them with few of the skills needed for modern-sector employment. Few students develop the "ability to respond to disequilibria" that Theodore Schultz felt was the essence of human capital. The quality problem must be addressed even as the quantitative demands remain very heavy.

Some countries may soon have a respite. The rate in increase of new school entrants is decelerating in all countries whose fertility rates have fallen markedly; the emerging "demographic dividend" (see Chapter 4) may already be visible in education budgets.[21] There is now, in many countries, slightly more scope for devoting funds to enhancing the quality of education. Here, however, there is still a very long road ahead; the region lost ground relative to other countries during the past decade. Higher oil prices may help some countries. All will need to continue reallocating limited resources toward more socially efficient uses. The region must improve both the quantity and the quality of education if it is to stimulate the necessary economic growth. Providing the human rights of basic health and education and enhancing labor productivity continue to challenge the political economies of the region.

NOTES

1. Rich and poor are defined, respectively, as the bottom and the top quintile of the income distribution.

2. For a sobering analysis of this phenomenon worldwide, see Farmer 2003.

3. The term "excess deaths" is defined as the difference between observed mortality and the prewar, presanctions level of mortality, or what is presumed to have been the pre-1990 trend. Since child mortality fell dramatically in the region during the 1990s, the second assumption seems the more reasonable standard of comparison.

4. Their number excluded deaths from "criminal murder." In the absence of political authority whose legitimacy is widely recognized, it is not at all clear what this phrase might mean.

5. The figures in parentheses denote, respectively, the lower and upper bounds of the 95% confidence interval.

6. These conditions have not improved at the time of writing (March 2006).

7. For a dispassionate narrative of the moves and countermoves of the various players, see Tripp (2000), pp. 259–264.

8. Diarrhea kills by dehydrating and "starving" its victims, whose bodies cannot absorb the nutrients in their food.

9. Stunting is defined as "the proportion of under-fives falling below minus 2 and minus 3 standard deviations from the median height-for-age of the reference population" (UNICEF 2001).

10. Unless otherwise stated, "literacy" means adult literacy in this chapter.

11. Segregation in Algerian schools formally ended in 1948, but the system remained strongly biased in favor of *colon* children until independence.

12. "Net enrollment ratio" is defined as the number of children of a certain age group in school divided by the total number of that age group. The other commonly used measure, "gross enrollment ratio," divides the total number of children in school (whatever their age) by the total number of children of the age group. The latter number, typically higher, would include, for example, thirteen-year-olds still in the sixth grade in the numerator, whereas the net enrollment ratio would not.

13. There is some dispute about Saudi enrollment figures. A recent report (United Nations 2002) asserts, "Primary school enrolment (sic) ratio registered 96.1% in year 2000, resulting from a male enrolment (sic) of 97.3% and 94.8% rate for females" (p. 15). It appears that this figure refers to the gross enrollment rate. The World Bank gives a less sanguine picture, however. Using the same indicator, the World Bank reported that in 2002, the overall gross primary enrollment rate was 67%, 69% for boys and 67% for girls.

14. Sudan does not report such data. It is unclear what such data would mean, given the violent conditions plaguing large regions of the country outside of the Nile Valley.

15. Defined as 10–14 years of age.

16. The social rate of return on an investment is the internal rate of return, calculated using international prices (as opposed to distorted domestic prices) and taking into account externalities. A crucial—and dubious—assumption of these studies is that wages accurately reflect productivity.

17. For example, in 2002/2003 the ratio in the United States was 88%, in Japan 100%, in Germany 88%, and in South Korea 87%.

18. In Yemen, nearly half of primary schools have neither electricity nor water; over 40% have no toilets (Al-Amri et al. 2003).

19. Police actions provide evidence for this phenomenon: In November 2005, the Egyptian education minister removed "a large number of teachers with Islamist tendencies" from their posts (*Gulf News,* November 23, 2005).

20. The numbers in Table 5.6 are among the lowest figures in circulation; they are very conservative.

21. By the same logic, countries with persistently high fertility (e.g., Palestine, Yemen) will have to keep "running faster in order to stand still."

6

WATER AND
FOOD SECURITY

The Middle East cannot grow enough food to feed itself. Escalating demand and constrained supply response have made it the least food-self-sufficient region in the world. The emergence of this "food gap" does *not* mean that agricultural supply has stagnated. Although this has happened in some cases, the more common experience has been that both public and private responses to the food deficit have failed to restore food self-sufficiency. This, however, is not necessarily a bad thing. Indeed, food self-sufficiency is physically impossible and economically undesirable for the region. It is also politically (nearly) irresistible.

The water constraint dooms dreams of self-sufficiency in the region, and the situation grows more serious daily. Renewable water resources per capita fell from 3,500 cubic meters in 1960 to 1,250 cubic meters today. Population growth ensures that these numbers will fall further in coming decades; the World Bank projects that there will be only 667 cubic meters per person by 2025, compared with a worldwide average of 4,780 cubic meters per person in that year (World Bank 1994f). Eleven countries' (plus Gaza's) water use already exceeds 100% of renewable water supplies; water quality problems plague another ten (see Table 6.1). Forty-five million people lack access to safe drinking water, and 85 million people lack access to proper sanitation (World Bank 2001b).

The demand for water rises thanks to population growth, rapid urbanization, and expanding irrigation. The recent resumption of income growth in some countries will also increase water demand.[1] Water used by households and industry has a much higher economic value than water used in agriculture, which is overwhelmingly the largest water user in the region (see Figure 6.1 and Table 6.2). As water's scarcity increases, agriculture will have to get by with less. For example, Israel and Jordan will have little choice but to save water by cutting back on irrigated agriculture, increasingly using recycled waste water for farming, and also making investments in expensive technologies such as desalination—as they have begun to do. Although there is scope for greater efficiency in irrigation, there is

TABLE 6.1   Severity of Water Quantity and Quality Problems

	Water Quantity *Problems*[a]	
Water Quality Problems	*Low*	*High*
High	Algeria, Egypt, Iran, Iraq, Lebanon, Morocco, Syria, Tunisia	Gaza, Jordan
Low		Bahrain, Israel, Kuwait, Libya, Oman, Qatar, Saudi Arabia, UAE, Yemen

[a]*Low:* water use <100% of renewable supplies; *high:* water use >100% of renewable supplies
SOURCE: World Bank 1995b

simply not enough water in the region to permit anything remotely approaching food self-sufficiency.

Food self-sufficiency is, however, a very different concept from food security, which is an insurance concept. Ensuring food security means guaranteeing that consumers are reasonably certain of being able to eat properly. The concept may be analyzed at various levels; for example, global, regional, national, or household. In this chapter we focus largely on the regional and national levels, leaving the household level (mainly an issue of income purchasing power or poverty) to Chapter 10. A very simple, if grim, illustration of the difference between food security and food self-sufficiency is to note that in 1984, the Sudanese "self-sufficiency ratio"[2] was 85%; in that same year, several million people perished from famine. Self-sufficiency does not equal food security.

Nevertheless, policymakers all too often conflate food security with food self-sufficiency, and the resulting policies are transforming agricultural production and relations between both rural and urban citizens and their states throughout the region. By now the necessity to import "virtual water"[3] is quietly recognized by many policymakers. The region now imports a volume of food whose water content exceeds the

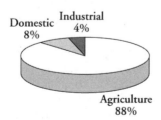

FIGURE 6.1   Sectoral water use in MENA, 2000
SOURCE: FAO Online, 2005

TABLE 6.2   Renewable Water Resources, 2001

	Withdrawals		Usage		
	m^3/N	As % of natural recharge	Agriculture (%)	Domestic (%)	Industrial (%)
Algeria	443	39	52	34	14
Bahrain	175	270	57	39	1
Egypt	830	127	82	7	11
Iran	1,900	59	92	6	2
Iraq	3,111	80	92	3	5
Israel	265	108	54	39	7
Jordan	169	151	75	22	3
Kuwait	10	3,098	60	37	2
Lebanon	1,219	33	67	27	6
Libya	109	801	84	13	3
Morocco	936	43	89	2	10
Oman	364	181	93	5	2
Qatar	91	626	74	23	3
Saudi Arabia	111	955	90	9	1
Syria	1,541	55	90	8	2
Tunisia	577	54	86	13	1
Turkey	3,344	17	73	16	12
UAE	56	1,614	67	24	9
Yemen	206	123	92	7	1

SOURCE: World Resource Institute: Earthtrends (WB UNEP, UNDP, USAID, SIDA, Neth Ministry of Foreign Affairs, WRI)

annual flow of the Nile River (Allan 1999; FAO 2003). The inevitability of reliance on food imports is much more widely recognized today than it was a decade ago.

Still, the political siren song of self-sufficiency remains very strong. Although outside economists may view water as an economic good, local policymakers more commonly view it as a social good that is vital to the livelihood of a large proportion of the population. Further, current water users—particularly, well-to-do farmers—often constitute a politically potent lobby (Allan and Olmsted 2003; Richards 2002). Recent international political experience has also been unhelpful: Iranian, Iraqi, Libyan, and Syrian policymakers have firsthand experience of the dangers that politically induced embargoes can pose to food security.

At the end of the day, any nation can obtain its food in only three (not mutually exclusive) ways: by producing it (national production), by buying it (imports), or by being given it (food aid). The first two are overwhelmingly the most important for all but the very poorest (usually disaster or conflict-wracked) countries. Any country is likely to use both domestic production and imports in meeting food security goals. For MENA counties, each faces significant constraints, and each poses political, economic, and social challenges. We turn now to a brief sketch of how the balance of national production and imports have changed since 1970.

THE FOOD GAP

A sketch of the stylized facts of food security at the national level must distinguish between two different periods: the oil boom of the 1970s, when the "food gap" exploded; and the more austere 1980s and 1990s, when policymakers implemented a variety of strategies to narrow this gap.

The Exploding Food Gap of the 1970s

During the 1970s, rapidly increasing populations and oil rents fueled per capita income growth, sharply raising the demand for food. Income growth was not limited to oil exporters; thanks to large-scale labor migration to the oil-exporting countries, poorer countries also benefited (see Chapter 15). Demand growth has three determinants: population increase, per capita income advance, and the income elasticity of demand.[4] During the 1970s, MENA population growth rates were among the highest in the world. Such population growth rates in themselves posed a challenge to food producers, but the very rapid growth of incomes during the 1970s compounded the task. For five countries, per capita GDP grew more than 5% per year, with incomes doubling in fifteen years. With the major, tragic exception of the Sudan, per capita incomes advanced swiftly in the region during the oil-boom years.

The impact of this income growth upon food demand depended, of course, on the specific foodstuff. Demand for cereals for direct food consumption (as opposed to use as livestock feed) grew at approximately 3.7% per year from 1966 to 1980; although this was mainly due to burgeoning population, increasing incomes accounted for roughly 25% of this growth. Demand for cereals for livestock feed grew more rapidly still (4.8% per year); about one-fourth of all cereals consumed in the region is eaten by animals (Paulino 1986, 26). Income growth particularly stimulated the growth of consumption of meat, fruits, and vegetables. In the Middle East as everywhere, when people get richer they eat more of everything, but they especially consume more meat, dairy, fruits, and vegetables.

Domestic supply response was sluggish in the 1970s because of the Dutch Disease—policies that excessively taxed and limited investment in the agricultural sector (see Chapter 3). Cereal production was especially weak, caught between rising labor costs, marginal rainfall, and government-imposed price disincentives. By contrast, the production of higher-value crops such as fruits, vegetables, and livestock did much better. Almost everywhere, the food gap could be plugged with imports; abundant foreign exchange and improving terms of trade permitted a dramatic increase in food (and especially cereal) imports.[5]

The levels of dependency on food imports of the 1970s alarmed policymakers. The risk of a politically motivated food embargo became something of an obsession with many government planners. The power of the "food weapon" may have been overrated; after all, only a multilateral embargo could be effective. Bilateral embargoes (e.g., by the United States) would simply open lucrative markets for European Union or Australian wheat, a fact not lost on the US farm lobby. But threats of embargoes raised concerns and political fears—which are entirely understandable, given the region's history. Heavy reliance on food imports, particularly for basic foodstuffs like wheat, entails political risks, and threats of embargoes raised the perceived political risk of relying on imports for food security. Egyptian policymakers were acutely aware of this risk; by the mid-1980s, Egypt was purchasing nearly 50% of its wheat and wheat flour, *the* staple food in the country, from the United States.[6] Such dependence, even on friendly countries, makes policymakers nervous. And of course, no country in the world—least of all the United States or the European Union—relies exclusively on comparative advantage and market forces in its food system.

Unsurprisingly, therefore, state reactions to the imbalance between domestic supply and domestic demand for food were not limited to increasing imports. From the economic point of view, states could either focus on diversifying their exports (thereby increasing the stability of their foreign-exchange earnings) or launch programs to increase the proportion of domestic supplies to total consumption, or both. Increasingly, the water constraint will force most countries of the region to increase their reliance on the former approach. In the 1970s, however, few were prepared to undertake the kind of economic policy reforms that such an export-oriented food security strategy would have required.

Partially Redressing the Balance: 1980–2005

During the 1980s, income growth in the region collapsed as a whole and turned negative for many countries. Consequently, population expansion became the sole source of additional demand for food. The deceleration in demand provided a temporary respite for harried agricultural planners, who succeeded in formulating and implementing significant policy shifts.

Policymakers viewed dramatically escalating food imports with alarm. They considered such reliance on foreign supplies to pose unacceptable economic and political risks. Partly in response to these fears, they shifted their agricultural policies. In the early 1980s subsidies of inputs usually either continued or increased (although this had begun to change by the end of the decade), while taxation of output through price policies typically eased. Governments often began to allocate a larger share of investment to agriculture, and many urban entrepreneurs entered the production of horticultural crops, poultry, and livestock. By now, the latter constitute a significant "farm lobby" in most countries, a fact of considerable relevance for water policy (see below).

In part because of these policy shifts, most countries' agricultural sectors managed at least to keep up with population growth during the 1980s and 1990s. FAO data on the growth of food production, both aggregate and per capita, for the 1980s and for the period 1990–2003 are shown in Figures 6.2 and 6.3.[7] During the 1980s, twelve countries' output kept up with population growth (sometimes just barely), while in five others output lagged behind. In the 1990s, output growth decelerated in ten countries, but accelerated in seven others, including the largest Arab country, Egypt. For the region as a whole, the trend in per capita food production was (just) positive for each decade: The population-weighted average grew at an annual rate of 0.5–0.7% (Lofgren and Richards 2003). Perhaps the safest conclusion to draw from

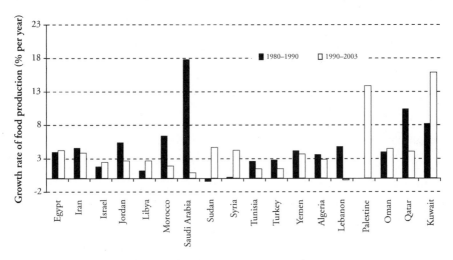

FIGURE 6.2   Growth of total food production, 1980–1990 and 1990–2003
SOURCE: World Development Indicators Online, 2006

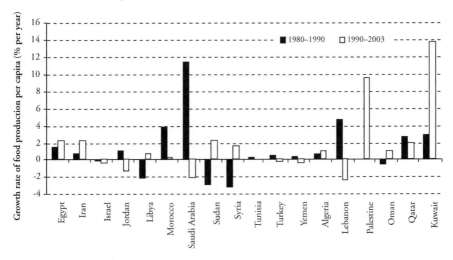

FIGURE 6.3   Growth of per capita food production, 1980–1990 and 1990–2003
SOURCE: World Development Indicators Online, 2006

these disparate studies is that food self-sufficiency at least did not deteriorate during the 1980s. This is a markedly different experience from that of the oil-boom years.

The picture, however, varies considerably not only by country but also by food-stuff. For example, while Egypt's wheat production boomed in the late 1990s in response to price policy shifts, maize imports (mainly used for animal feed) soared. And even though Egypt has one of the strongest agricultural sectors in the region (essentially all agriculture is irrigated), it saw substantial increases in both the quantity and value of food imports. In countries where more farmers rely on (erratic) rainfall, the picture was more varied. For example, Iran became 80% self-sufficient in wheat in the mid-1990s, only to endure subsequent repeated, severe droughts that reduced this figure to 44% in 2000 (UN 2003).

Output gains required using additional inputs. The arable area continued to increase in those countries that experienced the strongest agricultural growth, and irrigated land expanded nearly everywhere (see Figure 6.4). Fertilizer use increased but at a diminishing rate (see Figure 6.5). Mechanization, especially tractorization, continued throughout the region (Figure 6.6). The farm labor force either continued to grow or resumed growing after an oil-boom-induced decline in most countries. The boom of the 1970s drew labor out of agriculture; in Algeria, Iraq, Jordan, Libya, Syria, and Tunisia, the adult male farm labor force actually declined during the 1970s. However, the 1980s largely reversed this Dutch Disease phenomenon in all but Iraq, Jordan, and Libya (see Table 6.3). In short, agriculture in MENA used more land, more water, more fertilizer, more machines, and more labor—all just to keep up with population growth.

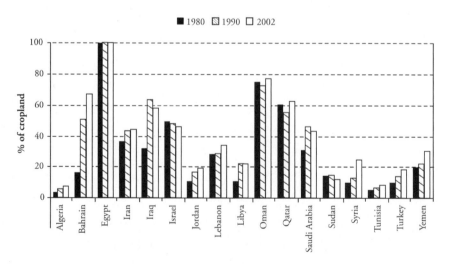

FIGURE 6.4   Percentage of cultivated land under irrigation, 1980–2002
SOURCE: World Development Indicators Online, 2006

There is some evidence of deceleration in both output growth and input usage in the 1990s. Again, country experience is highly varied. In ten countries, the rate of growth of food production decelerated in the 1990s compared with the previous decade, but it accelerated in seven others (see Figure 6.2). Input use seems less ambiguous: In the Near East, for example, the rate of growth of tractor usage fell from

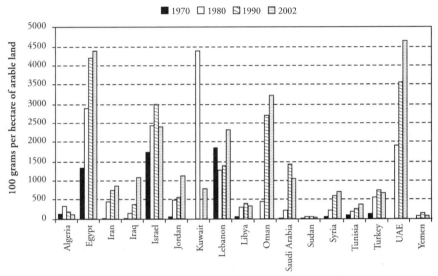

FIGURE 6.5   Fertilizer use, 1970–2002
SOURCE: World Development Indicators Online, 2006

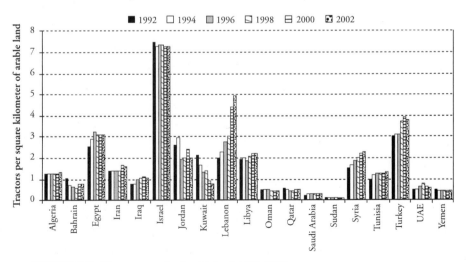

FIGURE 6.6   Tractors per unit of arable land, 1992–2002
SOURCE: World Development Indicators, 2006

TABLE 6.3   Agricultural Labor Force, 1961–2002

	1961	1970	1980	1990	2002
Main oil-exporting countries					
Algeria	2310	1955	1744	1824	2660
Iran	4186	4312	4636	5405	6374
Iraq	1237	1408	1001	712	626
Oman	99	102	167	256	358
Saudi Arabia	832	1019	1232	1031	680
Subtotal	8664	8796	8780	9228	10698
Main non-oil-exporting countries					
Egypt	6651	7588	8481	7577	8475
Israel	110	103	86	73	68
Jordan*	126	148	94	123	192
Kuwait	2	4	9	11	14
Lebanon	197	132	108	62	43
Morocco	3124	3306	3903	4073	4274
Sudan	3840	4271	5177	6526	7740
Syria	894	1068	981	1178	1563
Tunisia	838	755	855	798	958
Turkey	11130	11565	11472	12994	14697
Yemen	1494	1605	1783	2132	2921
Subtotal	28406	30545	32949	35547	40945
Total	37070	39341	41729	44775	51643

*refers to the East Bank only
SOURCE: FAO Online 2004

5.5% in the 1980s to 2.6% in the 1990s, while fertilizer growth slowed from 4.9% per year in the 1980s to 1.4% in the 1990s (FAOSTAT 2005). Similar decelerations occurred in the Maghreb. Of course, continued output growth with decelerating input use is a positive sign.

The Fading Mirage of Food Self-Sufficiency

The welcome resumption of modest income growth since the early 2000s will intensify the challenge of the growing demand for food. However, given the increasing scarcity of water, food self-sufficiency will be increasingly out of reach. Happily, however, food self-sufficiency is unnecessary to achieve food security. The common conflation of food security with self-reliance tacitly assumes that domestic production is a less risky mode of satisfying domestic demand than dependence upon international trade. To be sure, international trade poses risks, both economic (price fluctuations) and political (US-led embargoes and sanctions). Yet relying on national production is also risky. In much of the Middle East, agriculture is ineluctably a gamble on the rains. About 75% of the arable land in the region is classified as "semi-arid," receiving an average of less than 400 mm of rain a year. Cereal production remains highly variable in the region, as weather shocks disrupt staple food production. Only Egypt, with its entirely irrigated agriculture, is relatively safe from the effects of repeated weather shocks, but even this venerable food production system suffered from repeated low Nile floods (due to drought in Ethiopia) in the late 1980s. Elsewhere in the region the situation is far worse. In Syria, for example, food production falls below the average by more than 5% *every third year*. As a result of these shortfalls, planners in the Maghreb must find supplementary foreign exchange to buy "unusual" amounts of food four years out of ten.

The devastating droughts in the Maghreb and the Sudan underscore the climatic threat. In Morocco, production of wheat fell by nearly 40% from 1976 to 1977, while in the Sudan, millet and sorghum output fell by 38% and 58%, respectively, in 1982 and 1983, and continued to fall the following year (FAOSTAT). The social, economic, and political impacts were severe: Some 4 to 5 million northern Sudanese were forced from their homes, moving either into the Nile Valley or farther south to less severely affected areas. The wrenching population movements, combined with various power struggles among ethnic factions in the region, led to the politically driven mass killings of today's Darfur (see Box 6.1).

Serious drought returned to the Maghreb in the 1990s and early 2000s. In the 1995 drought, Moroccan cereal production fell to 1.8 million metric tons from 9.6 the previous year (Hazell et al. 2003). The drought of 2005 was the worst in six decades. Nor has the Mashreq been spared. The drought in 1999/2000 reduced Syrian sheep flocks (a crucial source of livelihood for the poor) by up to 80% (IFAD 2001). Still more ominously, there is increasing disquiet that global warming may be exacerbating and intensifying droughts (Hazell et al. 2003). In short, all agricultural sectors in the region outside of Egypt must contend with meager, variable rainfall. Relying on domestic production is an extremely risky strategy for ensuring food security in MENA.

Fundamentally, arid zones like MENA cannot escape geography; water is and will become increasingly scarce in the region. Thanks to the water requirements for photosynthesis, there will be serious barriers to the achievement of self-sufficiency in food or agriculture anywhere outside of Turkey or (potentially) the Sudan. We have seen that agriculture uses about 85% of the region's water. Water problems are especially acute in the Mashreq and the Arabian Peninsula, where unsustainable rates of usage are increasingly common. Increasing pollution of water is also a growing problem. The region uses 63% of its renewable water supplies, compared with 9% globally (FAO, ACQUASTAT). By 2025, per capita water availability for all purposes could be as low as 700 cubic meters. Food self-sufficiency is an expensive, wasteful, and ultimately doomed food security strategy.

◡ BOX 6.1 _____

Food Insecurity and Ethnic Cleansing: Darfur, Sudan

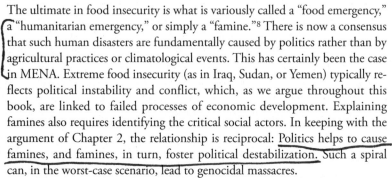

The ultimate in food insecurity is what is variously called a "food emergency," a "humanitarian emergency," or simply a "famine."[8] There is now a consensus that such human disasters are fundamentally caused by politics rather than by agricultural practices or climatological events. This has certainly been the case in MENA. Extreme food insecurity (as in Iraq, Sudan, or Yemen) typically reflects political instability and conflict, which, as we argue throughout this book, are linked to failed processes of economic development. Explaining famines also requires identifying the critical social actors. In keeping with the argument of Chapter 2, the relationship is reciprocal: Politics helps to cause famines, and famines, in turn, foster political destabilization. Such a spiral can, in the worst-case scenario, lead to genocidal massacres.

The current horrors of Darfur provide such a scenario. This vast (150,000 square miles), remote (Darfur's capital, El Fasher, is a dusty road trip of more than 600 miles from Khartoum) northwestern province of Sudan was neglected by the British administration (starting in 1916) and by successive independent Sudanese governments in Khartoum. The experience of Darfur supports the perspective that extreme food emergencies are fundamentally political.

Most analysts begin their analysis of the current crisis with the severe drought and famine of 1984. Tellingly, this was called *maja'a al-gutala,* "famine that kills"—as opposed to the quotidian dearth that normally plagues this extremely poor region. Many authorities assert that more people died of disease than outright starvation (Devereux 1993), although, given the interactions of nutrition and disease resistance, it is likely that food deprivation contributed to the estimated 95,000 deaths (out of a population of approximately 3.1 million) (Prunier 2005).

From the perspective of explaining today's violence, perhaps the most important aspect of the events of 1984 was the further destabilization of the symbiotic, partly conflictual, yet also partly cooperative relationship between social groups relying mainly on livestock herding and those relying mostly on farming. Older mechanisms of conflict resolution came under great stress thanks to drought, population growth, and the bankruptcy and incompetence of local government nominally beholden to national authorities in Khartoum. As a leading student of the phenomenon notes:

> A succession of local conflicts erupted . . . the pastoral groups were pitted against the farmers in what had become a bitter struggle for dimin-

continues

ishing resources. The government couldn't intervene effectively, so people armed themselves . . . There was an attempt at a reconciliation conference in 1989, but its recommendations were never implemented. (de Waal 2004a)

Transnational forces likewise stirred the pot. An ongoing civil war in neighboring Chad spilled over into Darfur, flooding the area both with Kalashnikov rifles and other modern weapons, and, perhaps even more lethally, with an imported, racist ideology of "Arab" supremacy (Prunier 2005; ICG 2004a; de Waal 2004a). (The definition of the concept "Arab," particularly in the Sudan, has a long and highly complex history—see Prunier 2005 for an extended discussion.) Further, the Islamist regime in Khartoum, which came to power in 1989, as well as the Libyan government, armed many Darfuri "Arabs" and used them as *murahiliin,* or irregular forces, to fight the Southern People's Liberation Army (SPLA) in southern Sudan and to terrorize southern civilians. An interplay of war between the SPLA and the Khartoum government, in-fighting among various Islamist politicians, and escalating violence among increasingly polarized, heavily armed Darfuri ethnic groups continued through the 1990s.

Ironically, it was the approach of peace between the SPLA and the Khartoum government, combined with a revolt in Darfur, that launched the current round of horrors. Threatened by rebellion from Muslim Darfuris, particularly suspecting their ties with out-of-power Islamist politician and former President Hassan al-Turabi (see Chapter 14), the Khartoum government armed and abetted the *janjaweed* ("evil horsemen"), militias based in the nomadic "Arab" population. These then embarked on a horrifying campaign of ethnic cleansing against "Africans," mainly agricultural speakers of Fur, Tunjur, and Masalit, as well as Zaghawa-speaking pastoralists. This campaign, labeled "counter-insurgency on the cheap" (de Waal 2004a), has killed hundreds of thousands of Sudanese civilians. Mortality estimates as of April 2006 ranged up to 400,000 (see, e.g., www.darfurgenocide.org). In addition to outright murder and rape, *janjaweed* depradations made foraging for "famine foods" or edible wild plants, which saved many lives in the 1984 famine, much too dangerous. Violent political insecurity thus produced food insecurity. The modern history of Darfur is "a deeply sad story about the struggles of resilient people, poor even by Sudanese standards, who have been pitted against each other by a forbidding environment, a long history of political neglect, and a ruthless national government" (de Waal 2004b).

Fortunately, food security can be achieved through trade. Export-oriented production is necessary to buy the food to save the water, as well as to provide the jobs needed for the rapidly growing labor force (see Chapter 5). Middle Eastern political economies will have to emulate other economically successful but agricultural-resource-poor nations to achieve food security in the years ahead. Unfortunately, the spectacle of harsh US-led sanctions against Iraq, as well as US trade sanctions against Iran and Libya until 2005, raises the perceived risk of the trade option for food security. Opposition politicians are quick to argue that self-sufficiency is possible and fault the government for "selling out to foreigners" and "failing to protect the nation."[9] Implementing credible economic reforms faces formidable political obstacles (see Chapter 9), but because of policy and, still more, physical constraints on increased food production, countries of the region will increasingly have to export in order to eat.

POLICY CONSTRAINTS TO OUTPUT GROWTH

We can (loosely) divide the policy constraints on food production into two parts: (1) skewed access to land and other "property-rights" problems, and (2) limited incentives for farmers. Farm output growth is also constrained by investment problems; these will be taken up as part of the discussion of the key physical constraint, limited water supplies.

Land Tenure

Although there is significant diversity across countries of the region, we propose five generalizations concerning land tenure and property rights: (1) pre-reform land tenure more nearly resembled the bimodal pattern of Latin America than the small peasant systems of East Asia; (2) the state has been exceptionally active in shaping patterns of land tenure; (3) land reforms implemented roughly between 1953 and 1975 reduced but did not eliminate the inequalities inherited from the past; (4) the state has had mixed success in substituting itself for the expropriated landlords as marketing agent, crop selector, and so forth; and (5) states have recently retreated from land reforms and especially from public-sector agriculture, a retreat that is part of a wider trend toward increased reliance on the private sector. States have created social actors through land reforms and other policies with regard to property; the actors so created now often constitute an important force-shaping policy—a farm lobby.

During the nineteenth and early twentieth centuries, large landholdings emerged in many MENA countries. Relations between the state and local social groups and expanding markets for crops provided opportunities for private aggrandizement. States typically resisted this process; rulers tried to remove intermediaries between themselves and the tax-paying peasantry. The success or failure of such policies depended on local, regional, and international political forces.

The intrusion of European colonialism always fostered bimodalism.[10] The pattern was most striking in the Maghreb, where agrarian changes resembled those of Latin

● BOX 6.2

The Variety of Agricultural Performance

The aggregate data on agricultural performance conceal significant differences among countries and among crops. Agricultural performance was only weakly linked to overall economic growth during the 1970s; countries with high over-all GDP growth rates have included agricultural success stories, such as Syria in the 1970s, and relative failures, such as Morocco. The two extremes may be Turkey, intermittently the sole cereal exporter of the region, and the Sudan, which experienced famine in 1983/1984, in 1987/1989, and in the early 1990s. In the 1980s, two of the best performers were Jordan and Morocco, while Syrian agriculture stagnated. Saudi agriculture was in a class by itself, but its extraordinary growth was fueled by massive subsidies (depending on the year, domestic wheat prices were 600 to 1,000% above world prices) and un-sustainable exploitation of fossil water. The 1990s saw similar diversity, as Egyptian growth accelerated while Moroccan and Syrian agriculture were dev-astated by repeated droughts. As in the previous decade, some high growth rates were the results of water mining, as in Yemen, or because of recovery from previous natural and political disruptions, as in the Sudan.

The rate of growth of production of various crops has also varied widely. In general, in the Middle East as in Latin America, output of "luxury" foods such as fruits, vegetables, poultry, and livestock products has increased more rapidly than that of cereals. Much of this increase is simply the result of the higher income elasticity of demand for horticultural and livestock products. Until very recently, price and credit policies also contributed to these trends. Such developments do little to reduce the food gap. They may actually in-crease it; for example, increasing poultry production stimulates feed imports.

America: Foreign conquerors seized the best agricultural land for themselves, relegat-ing the indigenous inhabitants to marginal areas for subsistence farming, to wage la-bor on the European modern farms, or, commonly, to both (see Box 6.3). "Indirect" colonial rule generated a similar result in Iraq and Egypt. Charles Issawi has aptly summarized the pre-reform land-tenure systems: "large estates, accounting for a quar-ter to four-fifths of privately owned land and in the main tilled by sharecroppers; a huge number of very small peasant proprietors, often with highly fragmented hold-ings; short and precarious leases; high rents . . . large debts, rising land values; and a growing landless proletariat earning very low wages" (Issawi 1982, 138).

Land reform swept through the region in the quarter-century after World War II. Echoing David Ricardo, critics charged that wealthy landlords were economic drones, failing to invest their profits and rents domestically. Although modern historians reject

◑ BOX 6.3 _____

Colonialism and Land Tenure

In Algeria between 1830 and 1880, *colons* and the French state seized nearly 900,000 hectares of land in Algeria; by 1962, 30% of the cultivated area was owned by *colons,* of which some 80% was held in large farms consisting of more than 100 hectares (Smith 1975). By 1914 nearly 20% of the arable land in Tunisia was in European hands, and over half of it belonged to only sixteen extremely wealthy absentee owners. By 1953 Europeans held nearly 1 million hectares in Morocco, concentrated in the fertile, well-watered plains of the west and north. The Italian Fascists seized some 500,000 hectares of land in Cyrenaica (Libya). The dispossessed indigenous population was forced onto more marginal lands, while the European farms enjoyed privileged access to government loans and other favors (Abun-Nasr 1971; Nouschi 1970). Population growth shortened fallows, extended cultivation into ever more marginal land, and reduced the amount of land available to each peasant family even as large estates continued to expand (van der Kloet 1975).

The British in Iraq shored up the sheykhs and aghas as counterweights to (nationalist) urban groups and to the king (Batatu 1978, 78–100; Dann 1969, 4). By confirming the registration of formerly tribal land in the names of sheykhs, the British, and later the independent Iraqi government, placed vast amounts of cultivated land in a few hands. By 1953, 1.7% of landowners held 63% of the land, while nearly two-thirds of the population held less than 5% of the land. Over three-fourths of the rural population was landless (al-Khafaji 1983, chap. 7).

In Egypt, Muhammed 'Ali had initially attempted to eliminate all intermediaries between the state and the peasants. When internal economic difficulties and British pressure forced him to decentralize, he granted land to court favorites, military officers, and the like. These actions created a class of large, typically absentee landlords known as "pashas." By 1900 large (over 50 feddan) farms (1 feddan = 0.42 hectares = 1.03 acres) covered 40% of the cultivated area of the country (Baer 1962; Owen 1986; Richards 1982).

this portrait (Davis 1983; Tignor 1984), there is little doubt that the land-tenure systems fostered huge social inequities and impeded human-capital formation. The real impetus behind land reform was political. Reformers expropriated enemies: Nasserists dispossessed the family and friends of King Farouk; Syrian Ba'athists (often 'Alawi or Druze) took away the lands of urban (typically Sunni) merchant absentee landlords; the Algerian FLN seized the farms of fleeing *pied noir* colonists; Iraqi nationalists and communists dispossessed the sheykhs who had often supported the deposed Hashemite monarchy. Even the shah of Iran, shortly after he was reinstalled by the

United States in 1953, agreed to launch a land reform, mainly because he believed that this would weaken his opponents, such as friends of Mossadegh (himself a landowner) or the Shi'i *ulema* (Hooglund 1982; Katouzian 1981). Large landlords have ceased to exist as a political force in any country that has had a significant agrarian reform.[11]

The contributions of land reform to equity and economic growth were mixed. The Egyptian agrarian reform, which became the model for other Arab regimes, affected only 12% of the land area. Landless workers were excluded, since only tenants were believed to have the necessary agricultural experience. This pattern was repeated in Algeria, where the permanent workers seized the estates of the departed *colons*. When the land seizures were institutionalized under *autogestion* (self-management), temporary and seasonal laborers received nothing (Zghal 1977). Subsequent reforms of the 1970s affected some 30% of the rural population (Tuma 1978).

The administration of land reforms often created serious production problems. Governments sometimes removed large landowners, who often had also supplied credit and seed to tenants, without replacing them with anyone else. This was a function of continual political upheaval, as in both Iraq and Syria during the 1960s, and of the lack of sufficient cadres, a problem that was more serious in Iraq than in Syria and that had become less acute by the late 1970s (Springborg 1981).

Most land-reform beneficiaries were obliged to join government-sponsored service cooperatives. Peasants farmed their own lands as private property, but input supply, marketing, and often crop choices were regulated by the cooperatives. The cooperative system, pioneered in Egypt, also appeared in Tunisia, Algeria, Syria, Iraq, and the former PDRY. Such cooperatives became the principal instrument for channeling resources out of agriculture toward industrial projects. Land reform was the handmaiden of state-led industrialization strategies. Some scholars (e.g., Hansen 1992) have argued that the disappearance of the large owners in Egypt removed a powerful lobby on behalf of all farmers, leaving the farm sector exposed to the significant taxation increases that such growth strategies entailed (Hansen 1991). However, few countries succeeded in mobilizing the agricultural surplus for industrial investment through land reforms and cooperatives. Land reforms also failed to create a wide domestic market.

The limited scope of land reform, the use of state-supported cooperatives to distribute and subsidize inputs, and the lingering legacy of the colonial era often combined to generate a "new class" of rural rich, the more prosperous sections of the peasantry. Large landlords had been eliminated, while official cadres relied on the wealthy peasants for information and for social activities. Such farmers dominated their areas and ensured that government policies and cooperatives favored or at least did not threaten their own interests (Adams 1986). Nevertheless, reforms throughout the region greatly reduced the gross inequities in land tenure that were inherited from the pre–World War II era.

Over the past decade, the trend has been toward much greater reliance on private farming and on market incentives in agriculture. Throughout the region, the extensive experience with large-scale state farms has been disappointing. Whether in

Tunisia in the 1960s, in Iraq and Syria in the 1970s, or in newly reclaimed lands in Egypt, wholly public-sector farms have been abandoned. In Algeria, 2,000 "self-managed" farms were subdivided into 6,000 smaller and more specialized units, while "other land is being leased to state farm workers or coop members who want to farm privately" (USDA 1987, 23). Privately owned large farms have fared little better; in Pahlavi Iran the large "farm corporations" set up by the shah not only disrupted rural society but also failed to outproduce medium-sized peasant holdings by any of several measures (Moghadem 1982).

The turn toward the private sector and a greater role for market forces has sometimes stimulated rural social conflict. In Egypt, for example, Law 96, passed in 1992, loosened Nasser-era restrictions on farm size and on tenancy contracts. In particular, the law has made it easier to raise rents and to dismiss tenants. Under the old laws, the former owners retained de jure ownership—but because tenants could not be removed, they held a de facto property right to the land. Law 96 abolished that de facto right. As usually happens when property rights are redistributed, violence surged. An Egyptian NGO, the Land Committee of Human Rights, reported "at least 107 deaths and 565 injuries" in conflicts over Law 96 in 1998–1999 alone (LCHR 1999; see also Bush 2002). In a pattern that any student of rural politics in Latin America or India will recognize, landowners use police and private security guards to drive unwanted tenants off the land, often with considerable brutality, while human rights activists protest, petition, and sue in court.

Despite such upticks in rural social conflict, as the food security problem loomed ever larger, governments from Algeria to Iraq turned to the private sector to solve their domestic agricultural supply problems. For such a strategy to succeed, however, incentives had to be provided. The results here are mixed.

Price Signals

Heavy taxation slowed agricultural growth in MENA. The mechanisms chosen to transfer resources out of the farming sector distorted farmers' incentives and misallocated scarce resources. Two types of price policies were particularly problematic: (1) direct or sectoral taxation, in which government marketing agencies enjoying monopsony power offered farmers prices well below those prevailing on world markets, and (2) the indirect or macroeconomic taxation implicit in an overvalued real foreign-exchange rate. Both types of taxation originated in import-substituting industrialization programs; the choice of such a development strategy thus implies bias against agriculture (Little, Scitovsky, and Scott 1970; Johnston and Kilby 1975; Timmer, Falcon, and Pearson 1983). Both of these forms of taxation were used extensively; both had the predictable effect of slowing production growth. Consequently, as food security fears increased, such taxation mechanisms were gradually reformed in some countries.

The first mode of taxation typically relied heavily on government-marketing monopolies. These were extensively used by national governments throughout the heyday of ISI economic development strategies and were closely linked to the land reform/"cooperative" systems described above. Indeed, such "cooperatives" are best understood as taxation devices rather than cooperatives in the American or European sense. In the Sudanese Gezira Scheme, for example, the Sudanese government's cotton-marketing monopoly permitted the government to pay farmers below the international price and pocket the difference.[12] Until the early 1990s, Egypt followed a similar system for cotton, sugar, and rice, as well as imposing extensive quantity and area controls for other crops. Algeria, Morocco, and Tunisia did the same; the Algerian government's interventions were the most extensive, but even supposedly "liberal" Tunisia fixed the producers' prices for eight of the major farm outputs.[13]

Sectoral price policies engendered inefficiencies and may have retarded output growth. It is widely agreed that farmers are highly responsive to price signals *among* crops. Because some crops are more heavily taxed than others, farmers reallocate land, labor, and purchased inputs toward less-taxed, more-profitable crops. The resulting distortions can be extensive. For example, Egyptian farmers fled from cotton and rice into horticultural crops and from wheat into clover, whereas Sudanese farmers in the Gezira switched their land and labor away from heavily taxed cotton toward sorghum, peanuts, and wheat. In Algeria, value added in (taxed) cereals stagnated between 1974 and 1986; during this same period, value added in vegetables grew at 7.4% per year and that of fresh fruit at 4.3% (World Bank 1987; *FAO Production Yearbook*, various years).

Such static resource misallocations mattered. In Egypt the value of the allocative distortions amounted to some 7% of total GDP and fully 30% of agricultural GDP (Dethier 1989; Hansen 1991). In the Sudan the incentive bias against cotton reduced the average yield of that crop by roughly 50% between 1974 and 1980/1981 (World Bank 1985). Since cotton is that country's largest export, farmers' responses to such policies exacerbated the country's severe balance-of-payments problem. In the early 1980s some 15% of the value of Moroccan agricultural GDP was transferred out of the sector (Tuluy and Salinger 1991). There is little doubt that the resource reallocations brought about by distorted price signals had important efficiency consequences.

Overvalued exchange rates also blunted farmers' incentives. Such overvaluation creates excess demand for foreign exchange, which is then usually rationed by (often complex) government regulations. These policies lower the value of exports and raise the value of imports, while also increasing the prices of nontraded domestic goods relative to products that are traded internationally. The first effect hurts producers of export crops (e.g., cotton, rice, vegetables) and those of the major import-competing crop, cereals. Furthermore, government rationing of scarce foreign exchange usually favors industrial and military users; farmers are often last in line, finding that they must pay higher prices for inputs or consumer goods if, indeed, they can get them at all. The increase in the relative price of nontradables to tradables also hurts farmers, because a large portion of the sector's costs is nontradable inputs such as land and labor, while its outputs are, of course, tradables. All of these effects reduce farmers' incomes.

In Egypt, for example, exchange-rate overvaluation increased the taxation of agriculture by 50–200%, depending on the year, between 1970 and 1985 (Dethier 1991). The overvalued Turkish lira more than compensated for the sectoral subsidies that politically active Turkish farmers were able to obtain during those fifteen years.[14] A similar phenomenon occurred in the Islamic Republic of Iran, which also combined sectoral subsidies (input credits, price supports) with a seriously overvalued real exchange rate.

As usual, the variation in countries' experience with both direct and indirect agricultural taxation is wide. Although foreign-exchange largesse is supposed to be detrimental to agriculture in models of the Dutch Disease, countries with surplus capital often found ways to offset such problems. Their hefty oil rents eliminated the need to transfer resources from agriculture to other sectors, their demand for food was growing the most rapidly of all the countries in the region, and their food security fears were acute. In response, major oil-exporting governments lavishly subsidized their farmers. The most extreme case of this is the experience of Saudi Arabia (see Box 6.4).

As food security fears mounted, more and more countries began to reform their price policies. Already in the 1970s, four countries (Jordan, Morocco, Libya, and Saudi Arabia) actually subsidized their wheat producers even when taking exchange-rate overvaluation into account. Moroccan cereal farmers came to enjoy increasing protection (i.e., subsidies) during the 1980s; the ratio of Moroccan to international prices (calculated at market-exchange rates) rose from 140% in 1984 to 180% by the end of the decade (Tyner 1993). The Syrian government paid wheat farmers about 30% more than the international price in the early and middle 1980s; maize farmers received over twice the international price, while sugar beet, sugarcane, and cotton farmers also received prices above international levels (World Bank 1986a). Syrian wheat farmers continue to receive prices above international levels (World Bank 2001c). Some countries' farmers may enjoy "natural protection" due to transportation barriers; for example, farmers in the YAR in 1982 received cereal prices that were, on average, 360% above those prevailing on international markets (World Bank 1986a).

By the late 1990s, many countries had moved toward greater reliance on market forces. In Egypt, Morocco, and Tunisia, governments reduced levels of protection, permitted private traders greater leeway, and reduced input subsidies. Shifts in macroeconomic management were also implemented in order to reduce the real exchange-rate overvaluation. Adherence to WTO agreements and bilateral agreements with the EU reduced rates of protection in agriculture (e.g., in Tunisia and Morocco). Although these results may have improved efficiency, some studies suggest that the efficiency gains were small relative to the redistribution effects (Chemingui and Thaber 2001).

Further, the impact of price distortions on aggregate farm output (and on sectoral growth) is less clear than their impact on the cropping pattern. As Binswanger (1989) has pointed out, the basic argument for inelasticity of aggregate farm output was made over forty years ago (by Johnson 1950): Aggregate sectoral output can in-

◑ BOX 6.4

Sowing Oil Rents in Saudi Arabia

Saudi Arabia paid farmers from five to six times the international price of wheat during the early 1980s while simultaneously subsidizing inputs; the effective rate of protection (the combined impact of protected output prices and subsidized inputs) may have reached 1,500% in the late 1980s (Wilson and Graham 1994). Saudi government loans to farmers rose from under US$5 million in 1971 to over US$1 billion in 1983; from 1980 to 1985 the Saudi government spent some US$20 billion on agriculture, mostly in the form of subsidies (*Economist,* April 6, 1985, 80–83). The results were spectacular for the key food security crop: Wheat output rose from less than 3,300 tons in 1978 to over 3.9 million tons in 1992—at an estimated cost of $2.12 billion in subsidies. The kingdom became the world's sixth-largest wheat exporter. Libya, Kuwait, and the UAE also offer generous farm incentives. These policies are, to put it mildly, dubious both economically and ecologically, but food security concerns and the vested interests of subsidy recipients (often well-placed ruling-family members) swept these concerns aside.

Reality sunk in during the early 1990s, however. In 1992, wheat consumed one-third of all irrigation water used in the kingdom. In 1993, the government cut the wheat area eligible for price supports to 25% of previous levels. Thanks to this change in policy, the amount of water pumped from nonrenewable aquifers fell by nearly half (46%) (Abderrahman 2001). The area planted in wheat continued to fall in the 1990s, but some 624,000 hectares were still planted in wheat in 2002 (World Bank 2003). Policy shifted—but the problem of groundwater overdraft, though slowed, remains.

crease only if more resources (land, labor, and capital) are utilized or if there is technological change. Binswanger reviewed a series of econometric studies of aggregate supply response from around the world; although there were the usual methodological debates and conundrums, the conclusion was clear: Aggregate supply elasticities are very low in the short run, usually below 0.2 and often below 0.1. Several studies of Egyptian agriculture indicate that the responsiveness of the entire sector to shifts in its terms of trade is rather low (see, e.g., Alderman and von Braun 1984).

As usual, however, the longer the time period, the greater the response: Price distortions may inhibit technological change and/or bias its direction in socially undesirable ways (Valdes 1989). Even if *elasticities* are low, a large *output response* could occur; for example, if prices rise 100%, then output could rise by 10–20%—a result that regional policymakers would certainly welcome (Braverman 1989). The most sensible conclusion is probably that price reform is a necessary but not sufficient condition for agricultural growth. In some cases, complementary price policy shifts and technological innovations have led to dramatic output gains, as the Egyptian example shows (see Box 6.5). The available evidence strongly suggests, however, that technological and physical constraints are likely to be at least as important as price policies over the medium and long run. The deceleration of output growth in the 1990s, the decade when the price reforms typically became effective, is con-

○ BOX 6.5 _____

Egyptian Price Policies

The Egyptian government used its monopolies over domestic marketing (implemented through the cooperative system) and over international trade to pay farmers prices below international levels. In the 1970s, regulations and controls affected cotton, wheat, rice, sugarcane, beans, and winter onions. All of these crops were taxed. Livestock products, in contrast, were protected because of consumers' preferences by explicit tariffs and the complex bureaucratic hurdles placed before importers until 1987. Horticultural crops (fruits and vegetables) were entirely unregulated.

As a result of these policies, and despite area controls, cotton yields stagnated, and the area planted in wheat declined in favor of *birsim* or Egyptian clover. Farmers had ample incentives to divert variable inputs (labor, fertilizer) away from (heavily taxed) crops like cotton and wheat. Finally, foreign-exchange scarcity in the mid-1980s led to the restriction of nonwheat agricultural imports, which increased the degree of protection of crops that competed with cotton (Dethier 1991). Egyptian price policies not only robbed the country of the foreign exchange that it could have obtained through exporting cotton (in which the country has a strong comparative advantage) but also exacerbated the food gap by retarding wheat production.

Egypt began dismantling these policies in the late 1980s and accelerated the process after the Gulf War. By 1995 only cotton and sugarcane retained controls. Particularly dramatic was the case of wheat. The combination of the release of a new variety along with decontrol of the wheat market was highly effective: Wheat production tripled, the area planted in wheat doubled, and yields rose by 50% from 1986 to 1998 (Kherallah et al. 2003). The increase was partly due to the adoption of high-yielding varieties—whose adoption had been retarded by the earlier policies, which made wheat straw nearly as profitable as wheat grain. Since high-yielding varieties produce less straw, the shift in the relative price of straw and grain in favor of the latter was not independent of price policies. Although there is a debate about the accuracy of national wheat data,[15] it seems very likely that wheat production responded well to price policy shifts. Total food production more than doubled from 1980 to 2000—yet roughly one-third of Egyptian cereal consumption is still imported (WRI).

sistent with this view. However, a case may be made that the price policy changes were necessary to prevent further deceleration, as the natural resource constraints, above all of water, began to bind ever more tightly. The changes in price policies implemented in the past twenty years were likely necessary, but not sufficient, to promote food security at the national level.

WATER AND THE IMPERATIVE OF A 11:62 *21 Feb*
NEW FOOD SECURITY STRATEGY

Five key water problems face most nations of the region in the coming decades. (1) Water is becoming increasingly scarce, whether measured by some simple indicator such as supplies per capita or by more sophisticated projections of water demand. (2) Water quantity problems are exacerbated by water quality problems, which become increasingly serious as nations seek to solve water quantity problems through reuse of water. Technologies exist to do this safely, but they require considerable funds and careful management. Neither of the latter is abundant. (3) From an economic perspective, the burden of adjustment to increasingly scarce water must fall on the agricultural sector, because the economic value of water is much lower in farming than for domestic or industrial use. Politically, however, such a shift is very difficult; past government programs to reclaim or redistribute land and increase domestic agricultural production have created powerful interest groups that will oppose reallocation of scarce supplies away from their farms. (4) Government water management systems suffer from lack of funds and are geared to a situation of relatively abundant water. (5) Most water resources in the region are rivers and aquifers that cross international frontiers. There is a sharp clash between economic/engineering logic, which would favor managing a river basin as a unit, and political considerations, marked by fear and distrust of one's neighbors.

Highly desired+ scarce, quality problems,

Water Quantity

Since water supplies throughout the region are essentially fixed (with a few exceptions), as population grows the total amount of water per capita must decline. But such information is not sufficient to answer the question of whether there will be enough water, since much depends on how the water is used. Of the various empirical measures of water scarcity, one of the most popular is that developed by Malin Falkenmark, who estimated that a country was "water-stressed" if it had less than 1,000 cubic meters per person per year of available water supplies (Falkenmark 1989). The calculation includes an allocation for agriculture as well as estimates for domestic and industrial use. An alternative measure has been created by Hillel Shuval, who takes the current estimate for municipal and industrial use in Israel (about 100 cubic meters per person per year) and adds an additional 25 cubic meters for gardening and miscellaneous to arrive at what he calls the "minimum water right" of 125 cubic meters per person per year (Shuval, personal communication). A comparison of these rough indicators with the estimates of available resources in 2025 illustrates the dimensions of the emerging challenge.

Discussions of water quantities often refer to "water needs." Since water is necessary for life, there is some amount of water that is a basic need or a human right, but that amount is very small in relation to most uses of water. In the United States, for example, water for drinking and cooking accounts for only 1.5% of residential use (Gibbons 1986). And as Figure 6.1 and Table 6.2 show, most of the water in the region, as in most countries, is used not by households directly but by farmers.

In consequence, water economists typically split the demand for water into two parts: a small amount treated as a "merit good," a basic need to which everyone is entitled, and the rest of water use, better viewed not as a "need" but as a "demand." Water for large domestic use (e.g., watering lawns) or for industry and agriculture is to be treated as a commodity like any other: as a good the demand for which depends on its price, people's incomes, and the prices of substitutes and complements. The key concept then becomes the economic value of water (see Box 6.6).

Considering water *demands* instead of water *needs* complicates the simple picture of population growth pressing against fixed supplies. First the bad news: Water is like food—people demand more of it as their incomes rise. From this perspective, the water situation is, if anything, even more serious.

Fortunately, the demand approach also offers good news: The demand for water, although price-inelastic, is by no means completely unresponsive to price. A World Bank review estimated that the price elasticity of domestic water demand averaged –0.45 (cited in World Bank 1994d); a modeling exercise for Egyptian agriculture estimated the price elasticity of demand for irrigation water at –0.37 (Hazell et al. 1994). Everywhere in the region, water use is heavily subsidized. In many countries, not even the costs of operations and maintenance of water systems are recovered. In none are the capital costs recovered from users; only in Syria are farmers charged any portion of the capital cost of water supply (World Bank 2001c). The marginal cost of water for most surface irrigation users in the region is effectively zero, since water-use charges are typically a fixed charge, which varies only by the area planted, not by water used.[16] Mechanisms to raise the private cost of water to users may well be critical to the management of increasing scarcity. But creating such mechanisms, particularly equitable mechanisms, faces formidable institutional, managerial, technological, and political challenges.

A particularly acute problem in the region (as in the world) is overpumping of groundwater. Groundwater provides vital irrigation to farmers, because the reliability of private pumps greatly exceeds the reliability of surface-flow systems, particularly for farmers at the "tail-end" of canal networks. Being able to water crops at critical moments in their growing season has a dramatic impact on crop yields (Shah et al. 2000). But everywhere in the world, overcoming groundwater overuse is a serious problem, and MENA countries are no exception. In Syria, for example, under the stimulus of food self-sufficiency goals, the area irrigated with groundwater more than doubled from 1988 to 1998. Today, 60% of irrigated farmland uses groundwater, all of which has been privately developed. However, nearly 50% of the wells are illegal; severe overpumping and pollution problems have been the inevitable result (World Bank 2001c). The problems in Yemen are still more serious;

◑ BOX 6.6

The Economic Value of Water

Like any commodity, water must be scarce to have an economic value. If water is scarce, the "shadow price" of water is the amount by which one additional unit of water (say, 1 cubic meter) will increase our utility. Put differently, we should be willing to pay a price for water that is just equal to its contribution to our goals. For domestic uses, water economists treat the household as the final consumer. Under some reasonable assumption (e.g., that expenditures on water are a small percentage of total expenditures), price, willingness to pay, and marginal utility are all the same. For drinking water, surveys in the Cairo slum of Embaba showed that consumers were willing to pay up to £E4.00 per cubic meter (more than US$1.17 per cubic meter at mid-1995 exchange rates), which was more than the cost of producing water by desalination.

Willingness to pay for water on the part of industrial and agricultural users is determined by the marginal value product of water. Water is an input into industrial and agricultural production processes. Farmers are willing to pay a price for water that is just equal to the marginal physical product of water (e.g., the amount of additional cotton made possible by one more cubic meter of water) times the price of that output. Industrial values are lower than domestic users' willingness to pay but higher than that for farmers. For example, the marginal value product of water in Egyptian sugarcane production may be as low as £E0.1 (World Bank 1993a). This means that (1) agriculture is the "residual user" of water, and within agriculture, the residual users are those producing crops with low marginal value products (a cubic meter of water used for tomatoes in Egypt produces about £E0.8—eight times more value than water used for sugarcane), and (2) price policy reforms that raise crop prices also necessarily raise the demand for water. Farm price liberalization without reform of the water system exacerbates water shortages.

indeed, by some accounts, the problem there is the worst in the world (see Box 6.7). Unsustainable groundwater use plagues the entire region and poses an increasingly serious challenge to policymakers.   11:13 ≈ 15 minutes w/ notes

Water Quality

One approach to dwindling per capita water supplies is to recycle water. Water analysts distinguish between water *use* and water *consumption*. For example, water used by a household is all the water that it takes from taps and pipes, but water consumed

☉ BOX 6.7 _____

The Political Economy of Groundwater Overuse in Yemen

Yemen may offer the most serious case of groundwater overuse in the world. The area irrigated by wells rose from 37,000 hectares in 1970 to 368,000 in 1996. Government policy strongly encouraged this development. Until 1995, diesel fuel, which is used to power the irrigation pumps, was priced at around $0.02 per liter, while international prices ranged from $0.15 to $0.20 per liter. Agricultural borrowers also enjoyed generous interest subsidies, paying 9–11% compared to market rates of 50–60%. Consequently, water was priced at $0.04 per cubic meter, although the marginal costs of extraction were actually three to five times higher. The government also protected the domestic fruit and vegetable market and did nothing to restrict the boom in *qat*, a mild narcotic, whose cultivation consumes about 30% of all irrigation water in the country (Ward 2000). Unsurprisingly, experts describe the groundwater situation in the country as a "basket case." Extraction now exceeds recharge by 400%, and "Yemen is probably the only country where groundwater extraction exceeds recharge for the country as a whole" (Shah et al. 2000, 1). Water tables have fallen dramatically, as wells have been deepened two to four times in the Sa'adah basin (Liechtenthaeler and Turton 1999).

The respectable growth of Yemeni agriculture during the past decade (5% per year) is clearly unsustainable. This has serious negative implications for Yemen's welfare, since roughly 75 percent of the labor force works in agriculture. During the past decade, the Yemeni government, faced with a large balance-of-payments crisis in the wake of the expulsion of Yemenis from the Gulf during and after the Gulf War, has embarked on a process of economic reform, including reforms that should enhance water conservation. The path, however, has been rocky.

In the Sa'adah basin of North Yemen, communal systems of land use prevailed until the mid-1970s. Escalating conflict between herders and farmers over the use of run-off water was adjudicated by religious scholars; a decision in 1976 (unanimously accepted by all tribes) induced many tribes to privatize their land. Subsequently, merchants and other tribesmen of comparative wealth were able to capture most of the groundwater by investing in pumps (Liechtenthaeler and Turton 1999). The Yemeni government raised the price of diesel fuel from $0.02 per liter in 1996 to $0.10 per liter in 1996, to $0.16 per liter in 2000.

The changes were implemented in order to cope with Yemen's post–Gulf War economic crisis. When hundreds of thousands of Yemeni workers were expelled from Saudi Arabia and other Gulf states in 1990–1991, the resulting

continues

◡ BOX 6.7 *continued*

precipitous fall in remittances exposed deep structural weaknesses in the Yemeni economy. After the civil war that ultimately reunited the country, the government embarked in 1995 on a stabilization and structural adjustment policy. Increases in diesel fuel prices, as well as the end of credit subsidies and the lifting of import bans on fruits and vegetables, were intended to provide significant incentives for greater water conservation and more efficient agricultural use of water (Ward 2000).

The Yemeni case indicates that such changes are likely to exact a political price, however. In 1993 the public rejected the government's first proposal to raise diesel fuel prices. In 1995 the government's tripling of prices sparked riots in which twenty people were killed (Ward 2000). Similar government actions triggered further riots in 1996 and especially in 1998, after which Islamic activists emerged as the opposition leaders to the government, and denunciations of "foreign interference" in the economy became more widespread. The protests were not specifically focused on water issues. Rather, they concentrated on the related increases in fuel and food prices as well as governmental corruption and the lack of transparency of the entire process (*Yemen Observer,* January 10, 1999). The turmoil continues. When the cabinet removed diesel fuel subsidies in 2005, and prices rose from 17 to 45 rials per liter, riots broke out all over the country, and at least twenty-five people were killed (Al Jazeerah, July 21, 2005).

by the household is only that fraction (typically about 50%) that does not then flow back into the system as waste water. In crop production, *use* is the water applied to the fields; *consumption* is the water lost to the system through evapotranspiration, that is, water lost to the process of plant transpiration and water lost through evaporation. The rest may return to the river or seep into aquifers, where it can often be tapped as groundwater. The realities of water reuse temper optimism that enhanced irrigation efficiency can alleviate the water constraint in the region (see Box 6.8).

To the extent that water can be reused, water supplies can be augmented so that more users can be accommodated. However, using water reduces its quality, even if consumption is low. This is most obvious in industry, where the ratio of consumption to use is often very low (e.g., 1:6), but the quality of the water pouring out of a factory is very different from the quality of the water that flows into it. The same is true on farms: Repeatedly used irrigation water increases in salinity, for example. Some crops (e.g., rice) are more salt-tolerant than others, but there are always limits on recycling. Increased concentrations of heavy metals and toxic organic substances pose still more serious challenges. These problems are exacerbated by outmoded treatment plants, poor managerial practices, and inadequate and/or underenforced

● BOX 6.8 _____

Irrigation Efficiency and Water Demand

One might reasonably expect that a significantly larger quantity of food could be produced with a given volume of water by increasing irrigation efficiency. Certainly there are gains from adopting water-efficient irrigation technology. The best experience is that of Israel, where crop yields per unit of land have doubled while water use has fallen by 50%. Whether more efficient irrigation reduces the demand for water is less certain, however.

One must be cautious here. Excess irrigation water must go somewhere; usually it flows back into a river or into an aquifer. In either case, there is often scope for reuse of the water. However, in such a closed system, enhanced irrigation efficiency may lead to the degradation of the quality of existing water supplies. The effect of reuse on water quality is not well understood at this time. Perhaps the safest conclusion is that improved irrigation efficiency, though desirable, is no panacea for increasing water scarcity. The percentage of water used in agriculture (and therefore the total amount of water) will necessarily decline as municipal and industrial demands grow. The main role of irrigation efficiency may be to ensure that food production does not decline with reduced water use. Technologies such as drip irrigation are thus not an answer to regional food security problems.

pollution-control regulations. For example, until 1999, Syria had *no* wastewater recycling facilities (World Bank 2001c). Most of Lebanon's sewage is dumped into the Mediterranean. Heavy fertilizer use in Tunisia has led to the eutrophication of some reservoirs. Many countries have serious water-quality problems (see Table 6.1).

It may be possible to safely increase the reuse of water in most MENA countries but only if treatment technologies and, especially, institutions and management systems improve dramatically. Recycling of water and greater water-use efficiency can certainly reduce pressure on supplies, but doing so will require significant changes in behavior and incentives at all levels of the water system.

The Implications of Agriculture Being the Residual User

As water demand increases, some users will not be able to obtain all the water they want—or formerly obtained. A simple thought experiment illustrates the situation. Suppose that, at a zero price, all consumers can have all the water they want (as was the case in countries such as Egypt until recently). Now suppose that, as rising population and incomes push up demand, demand exceeds supply at a zero price. Assume further that water is priced. As the price rises, uses whose economic value is less than price will be terminated. For example, if the only source is desalinated water, at an average cost of $0.55–0.80 per cubic meter,[17] only domestic users will buy water. At such a price there will be no agriculture at all; even for high-value crops in a highly productive farm system like Egypt's, the marginal value product of water is less than US$0.30. This situation, in which increasing water scarcity forces irrigated farming to make do with less and less water, is becoming increasingly apparent in very water-scarce countries such as Israel, Jordan, and the West Bank and Gaza. Forecasts in Israel, for example, suggest that agriculture will have to rely almost exclusively on recycled wastewater in the not-too-distant future. Economic logic strongly suggests that agriculture, as the marginal user, will bear the brunt of increasingly limited water supplies. The implications for food security strategies are obvious: Food security cannot be achieved through domestic production alone.

As is so often the case, however, the political calculus yields a very different answer. The region's states have sponsored irrigation expansion for decades, in some cases (Egypt) for over 150 years. The interests that have been created, including national bureaucracies and prosperous farmers, are formidable indeed. Farmers can invoke nationalism as a defense for subsidized water: In Israel, irrigated farming is closely connected to the Zionist dream of "making the desert bloom"; in Jordan, the Jordan Valley Authority aims to strengthen Jordanian farmers along the border with the West Bank and Gaza; in Egypt, plans to funnel water from the Nile to the Sinai desert through the El Salaam canal seem motivated by political desires to populate the Sinai with Egyptians (lest, it is said in private, Israel reassert claims to the area).

States have invested in irrigation, hoping to reduce national food dependency. The problem of food security is visible today; the problems of increasing water shortages are only now becoming acute. Once again, the lethal politics of the region have encouraged planning that favors the short run over the future, but in this arid region, nature's revenge is often cruelly swift.

Irrigation has also provided the state with an opportunity to extend its authority in the countryside and to pursue its "vision" of development. The Egyptian government insists on pursuing land reclamation and concomitant irrigation expansion to the fringes of the Nile Valley, although most studies show that the returns to water in such uses are very low. The Moroccan government has used irrigation development partly as a kind of substitute for land reform and partly as a mechanism for bestowing benefits on the rural notables who constitute such an important source of political support (Leveau 1985; Swearingen 1987). Morocco continues to be firmly committed to irrigation expansion (see Box 6.9). Throughout the region, according to the World Commission on Dams, the single busiest decade for commissioning dams in the region was the 1990s.[18]

The result of past irrigation expansion is that powerful vested interests block adoption of better management strategies for coping with scarcity. Farmers oppose the imposition of operations and maintenance charges, often claiming (with some justice) that the quality of service is so poor that they should not have to pay for it. But changes in water policy are possible, as the Israeli case demonstrates. The drought of 1986 forced the Israeli Water Commissioner to cut water to farmers, but the lobby's strength overturned this decision. When the country suffered three

◓ BOX 6.9 _____

Irrigation in Morocco

The commitment of the Moroccan government to irrigation has deep roots. Older Moroccans can remember the implications of complete dependence on rain-fed farming in a climate so prone to drought. A drought that began in 1935 and lasted for more than two years in southern Morocco deprived several hundred thousand Moroccans of food. The rural exodus was so massive that roadblocks were established and the population was diverted to camps. Half a million people became entirely dependent on government food distribution. The experience led to the creation of the first major irrigation perimeter in which land was allocated to Moroccans rather than to French *colons*. There was worse to come: In 1945 Morocco was hit by the most severe drought of the twentieth century. For eight months there was no rain whatsoever. Half of Morocco's livestock perished; a massive relief operation was undertaken to distribute grain brought in from the United States, Canada, and Argentina. Distribution weaknesses meant that relief stations could distribute only 6–9 kilograms per person per month; since an average person needed about 15 kilograms per month, widespread starvation ensued.

With this historical background, it is hardly surprising that the government of Morocco is so committed to the development and extension of irrigated agriculture. Irrigation development has another attractive feature: It allows the government to reward its friends and to strengthen its support among leaders in rural communities. Ever since 1961 its rural development programs have sought, successfully for the most part, to strengthen rural elites, who have long been among the key supporters of the monarchy (Leveau 1985). In the mid-1980s 9,000 to 9,500 large landowners owned some 2.2 million hectares, or nearly 30% of the country's farmland (Swearingen 1987, 187). They continue to constitute a critical constituency for the palace, as do the much larger number of smaller farmers who know perfectly well that their relative wealth is in large measure the result of public investment.

Public investment in large dams and infrastructure has been the key. According to Swearingen (1987), from 1912 to 1956 (the French Protectorate period), fourteen dams were constructed. In the first ten years of independence (1957–1967), three dams were built. In 1968 the government proclaimed a "politique des barrages," designed with the assistance of the World Bank, and by 1991, fourteen more dams had been completed. The goal, originally proclaimed by the French Protectorate, was to bring the total area under irrigation to 1 million hectares. Although this goal has been achieved, current plans call for continued dam construction. The Al Wahda Dam on the Ouergha River in the Sebou basin, completed in 1996, is the second-largest dam in Africa, smaller only than the Aswan High Dam in Egypt. Fifty-one additional dams are planned for the coming thirty years.

consecutive additional drought years, the cuts were re-imposed in 1991, and the agricultural sector's water allocation was slashed a whopping 65%. Although much of the water was restored after the drought ended, the sector nevertheless wound up with 25% less water than it had in 1986. Part of the explanation was the shift in economic (and political) clout in Israel, thanks to the country's rapid transformation into an industrial and skill-intensive services economy.[19] Yet farmers did not lose all of their subsidies: In return for acceding to the (eminently efficient) policy establishing agriculture as the "residual user" of water in the event of a drought, farmers were granted a price of $0.20–0.25 per cubic meter for irrigation water, far lower than the real cost of delivery, which was $0.65 (Allan and Karshenas 1996). Water conservation measures came to Israel thanks to drought, development, and a deal.[20]

Farmers strongly oppose water charges. This is understandable. Water has had a zero price, but as it has become more scarce, its value has been capitalized into the value of land. Farmers reasonably view the imposition of water fees as an expropriation; they feel that they have already paid for the water. The pricing of water also raises religious (and therefore political) objections in Muslim countries. For these reasons, some analysts recommend granting farmers tradable water rights. Such a system would give the rents of water to farmers rather than to the government and simultaneously create incentives for water conservation (Rosegrant and Binswanger 1994). The concept is intriguing, but so far no country in the region has implemented this approach.

Financial and Managerial Constraints

The financial challenge of providing water is daunting. The World Bank estimates that even when the GCC countries are excluded, the region will have to invest more than $40 billion in various water projects over the next ten years. In the GCC countries, Israel, and North Africa, considerable sums are being invested in desalination plants. Enthusiasm for dam construction remains high (World Commission on Dams 2000). A recent study for private investors that focused on urban and wastewater investment alone (that is, it excluded irrigation investment) estimated that some 430 projects, with a combined value of more than $126 billion, are planned in the region during the next decade (Global Water Intelligence UK, 2004). To make matters still worse, many smaller dams in the region are increasingly threatened by siltation of reservoirs, and canal maintenance often lags behind need (FAO 2003).

Financing will mostly come from either international donors or national governments. The strain that this places on national budgets is not helped by the fact that all countries heavily subsidize water use, particularly water for agriculture. Water charges rarely cover operations and maintenance costs, much less the opportunity cost of water in alternative uses. Only in Syria do water charges even begin to capture some of the investment costs needed to provide additional water (World Bank 2001c).[21]

The managerial constraints are no less severe than the financial constraints. The current system of centralized public-sector management of water systems breaks the link between suppliers' incentives and users' needs. Privatization of municipal water systems could greatly improve not only access to capital but also managerial efficiency and responsiveness to users' needs. Yet privatizing water supply systems has often led to significantly increased costs for drinking water, and therefore, to jeopardizing the meeting of basic needs for the poor. Water bureaucracies in the region suffer from the many ills of public-sector management (see Chapter 8). Poor pay and performance and haphazard ministerial coordination (in most countries, a number of ministries have responsibility for different aspects of water systems) are among the most serious.

As water becomes increasingly scarce, governments will have little choice but to devise mechanisms for choosing which consumers do *not* get all the water they want. Whether this is done by administrative diktat, by differential taxing of land planted in water-using crops, by volumetric pricing of water, or by tradable water rights, *some* mechanism for rationing scarce water resources will have to be found. The course of these changes will be central to the region's political economy in the decades ahead.

International Hydropolitics

However serious the domestic political impediments to the management of scarcity, they pale beside the international political complications. Many countries in MENA depend for much of their water supply on sources that are either outside of their boundaries (rivers) or shared with other countries (aquifers). The major international rivers in the region are the Nile, the Jordan, and the Tigris-Euphrates. Internationally shared aquifers include the Eastern Erg (Algeria and Tunisia), Nubian Sandstone (Egypt, Sudan, and Libya), the Saq Formation/Disi aquifer (Jordan and Saudi Arabia), the Ras al-'Ain aquifer (Turkey and Syria), and the Yarkon-Tanimim and coastal aquifers (Israel and the West Bank and Gaza).

Sharing water resources with one's neighbors can lead to severe problems in water quality and quantity. We have seen how water is used and reused. Water can be diverted or polluted by upstream states, leaving downstreamers with either less water or poorer-quality water or both. International law is generally unhelpful, and in any case, only two of the rivers are governed by even limited agreements (the Nile Agreement of 1959, signed by Egypt and the Sudan, and the Israeli-Jordanian Peace Agreement of 1994, which contains a water protocol). Beyond accords to share flow data, there are no agreements governing the other international water resources.

Needless to say, in the volatile political environment of MENA, the sharing of water resources holds the potential for international conflict. From an engineering and economic perspective, water basins and aquifers are best managed as units. However, political leaders are very reluctant to entrust their water supplies to other nations. It does not help that upstream and downstream states often have serious political differences over other issues (e.g., Turkey, Syria, and Iraq; Israel and Jordan; Israel and Syria; Jordan and Syria; Israel and the West Bank and Gaza). Even Egypt and the Sudan, which have normally enjoyed reasonably cordial relations, have confronted the specter of conflict over water: As accusations and counter-accusations flew between Cairo and Khartoum in the wake of the assassination attempt on President Hosni Mubarak, Sudan threatened to "cut off Egypt's water." The fact that the Sudanese lack the engineering capacity to do such a thing did little to dampen hysteria in the Cairo press. Water conflicts are potentially serious throughout the region.

Two important points need to be emphasized: First, the increasing pressure on surface water and aquifers among the sovereign nations of the region has introduced into foreign policies and interstate bargaining a range of issues that have traditionally been seen as domestic and none of the business of one's neighbors. For example, the on-field efficiency of water use in a given agricultural sector may be scrutinized by neighbors who contest the status quo or the "real" needs for water of a state with which they share a river or aquifer. Even the selection of crops with different crop-water needs may appear on the international bargaining agenda.

Second, the reluctance of sovereign states to put their claims to water at risk by integrating storage and delivery infrastructure across international boundaries may stymie any future attempts to create regional water markets. The only way in which quantities of water could be transferred among riparians in an international basin is through dams, reservoirs, pumping stations, irrigation grids, and pipelines running across boundaries. Narrow concerns for national and food security may prevent such integration even at the cost of suboptimal solutions such as overexploitation of limited national water resources or investment in costly desalination technologies (see Box 6.10).

☉ BOX 6.10 ————————————————————————

Was the Aswan High Dam Worth It?

Egypt's agriculture had been dependent on the Nile flood for millennia, but the country's irrigation system underwent a fundamental transformation in the nineteenth century with the transition to year-round irrigation, a transformation that concluded in the 1960s with the completion of the Aswan High Dam. There are certain inescapable facts about Egyptian irrigation development. (1) Summer irrigation made possible the production of cotton on a substantial scale and was thus an important part of that country's integration into the international economy during the nineteenth century. (2) Year-round, dependable irrigation makes it possible for Egyptian yields to be among the highest in the world; for example, the Aswan High Dam allowed maize (until very recently the main rural foodstuff) yields to increase by over 70%. (3) The expansion of irrigation not only redistributed land, especially in the nineteenth century, but also increased the role of the state in the countryside. (4) Political forces have determined the pattern and timing of irrigation investment, with the result that the technological externalities that often accompany irrigation development were ignored and neglected (Waterbury 1979; Richards 1982).

continues

☙ **BOX 6.10** *continued*

The debate on the merits of the high dam at Aswan has raged for at least thirty years. Although its problems were and are serious, the achievements of the dam are too often overlooked. First, there is no doubt that some form of "over-year storage" for Nile water was absolutely necessary to provide increased irrigation water to keep up with the country's expanding demand for food. Egypt's food security problem would have been much worse much earlier without the dam. When the annual Nile flood was unusually low in 1972, the country's agriculture suffered relatively little—thanks to the dam. The devastating droughts that ravaged Ethiopia and Sudan in the early 1980s would have severely affected Egypt also had it not been for the dam. Even with the dam, disaster has been narrowly averted; the level of Lake Nasser was only 147 meters in August 1988 (at 145 meters, the turbines of the dam would have had to be shut down). Second, there was really no alternative to the dam; all other technically feasible approaches faced insuperable political obstacles. It is hardly surprising, given the need and given the alternatives, that the Aswan High Dam was constructed.

The technological externalities were severe, however. Some of these were unique to the dam: problems of shoreline erosion (because all silt was trapped behind the dam), decline in fish catches in lakes and in the Mediterranean, scouring of the Nile banks, and high evaporation losses of the water stored in Lake Nasser. However, the most serious problems were really not qualitatively different from problems that had repeatedly plagued the extension of year-round (i.e., summer) irrigation in Egypt for more than half a century: inadequate drainage and disease. The incidence of schistosomiasis and ancylostomiasis in Egypt is very ancient but was certainly exacerbated by earlier (khedivial and British) irrigation works just as it was by the Aswan High Dam. From the point of view of agricultural production, however, the main problem with irrigation expansion both was and is the neglect of drainage. The ecological consequences of such neglect are straightforward: All water contains soluble salts and minerals, and even if farmers use water with maximum efficiency, inadequate drainage will permit these salts to accumulate, dramatically lowering soil fertility. By the late 1970s, this problem afflicted some two-thirds of Egypt's cropland. Massive investments funded by the World Bank have since largely overcome it.

CONCLUSION

The future of the region lies in nonagricultural development. There is simply not enough water available for countries to become self-sufficient in food, even if they were willing to bear the (considerable) costs of such an economically inefficient strategy. They will increasingly have to export in order to eat, to reform and revamp their water allocation mechanisms, and to find new, often unpalatable ways of cooperating with their neighbors. Nonetheless, some of these exports may well be high-value agricultural products for niche markets (as argued, e.g., by Devlin 2003). Such shifts, in turn, will require a rather dramatic change in the role of the state in the economy. We devote the next three chapters to this central issue.

NOTES

1. According to the World Bank, for LDCs as a whole, the average income elasticity of water demand is approximately 0.30.

2. The self-sufficiency ratio is the percentage of total food consumption that is produced locally.

3. "Virtual water" is the water contained in food. Food imports are, among other things, imports of water. Professor J. A. Allan of the University of London coined the phrase and has analyzed its ramifications in many publications (e.g., Allan 2001).

4. The formula is $D^* = N^*(y^*)e$, where D^* is the rate of growth of demand, N^* is the population growth rate, y^* is the rate of growth of per capita incomes, and e is the income elasticity of demand, or the percentage change in quantity demanded for every 1% change in income. Urbanization, which changes people's food habits, is another force in shifting demand patterns.

5. In 1970 a barrel of oil would buy roughly one bushel of wheat; by 1980 the same barrel would purchase six bushels, and even in May 1986 a barrel of US$14 oil would buy over three bushels. At the post-1973 nadir of oil prices in December 1998, a barrel would still buy 2.7 bushels. By early 2006, a barrel would buy *over 15 bushels* of wheat.

6. Such concerns finally led the government to raise wheat prices to farmers, with dramatic results (see Box 6.4).

7. As usual, there are questions about the accuracy of all data. Different sources often conflict; for example, FAO and World Bank data often differ from data from the Arab Organization for Agricultural Development. Studies in Egypt have shown significant differences between data from national sources and data extrapolated from sample interviews with farmers (Kherallah et al. 2003).

8. See de Waal (1989); Prunier (2005); Devereux (1993); and the seminal work of Sen (1981a).

9. As argued by a Muslim Brotherhood delegate in Jordan's parliament in February 1994.

10. Bimodalism refers to a land-tenure system that combines a small number of owners holding very large estates with a large number of owners holding very small farms.

11. The shah's land reform provoked Ruhollah Khomeini to attack the policies so vociferously that he was forced into exile in Iraq, thus beginning the long saga that culminated in the revolution of 1978–1979.

12. The list of disincentives to Sudanese cotton production in the late 1970s was formidable: an overvalued exchange rate, explicit taxes on cotton, allocating the input costs of *all* crops in the Gezira Scheme to cotton, and long (sometimes up to two-year) delays in payments. Many of these problems were ameliorated in the early 1980s.

13. In the early 1980s price controls applied to cereals, olives, wine grapes, sugar beets, milk, dates, beef, and poultry; prices for pulses, lamb, forage crops, fish, and most vegetables and fruits were uncontrolled (Cleaver 1982, 36).

14. Sectoral policies (e.g., price supports) transferred *into* agriculture a nominal sum equal to 1.3% of GDP, but when the impact of exchange-rate overvaluation is included, 3.8% of GDP was transferred *out of* agriculture between 1961 and 1985 (Hansen 1991).

15. Tim Mitchell has argued that much of the increase in wheat production may be a statistical artifact. He asserts that many peasants simply concealed their wheat production from the authorities under the compulsory quota system; when this was abolished, they were more forthcoming about their production (Mitchell 2002).

Since measured wheat production tripled, such a practice can explain the entire increase in measured wheat production only if one assumes that *fellahin* were hiding two bushels for every one they admitted to producing.

16. However, this is not true for all users. Urbanites who buy drinking water from water vendors typically pay the full cost of water provision, while farmers who pump groundwater pay both the capital and the operation and maintenance costs of such services—unless fuel is subsidized. The current situation, in which some users pay the full costs while others pay nearly nothing, is both inefficient and inequitable.

17. Desalination costs have fallen considerably recently, from around $1.00 per cubic meter to as low as $0.53 per cubic meter in a new Israeli plant.

18. World Commission on Dams, Africa/Middle East, at http://www.dams.org/kbase/consultations/afrme/dam_stats_eng.htm.

19. By 1997, agriculture accounted for only 2% of Israel's GDP, compared with 17% for industry, and 81% for services (CIA, World Factbook, 2000).

20. However, after a subsequent drought in 1991–1992, water use in agriculture rose again. The drought ended dramatically, with very heavy rains, and Israel sought to increase its water use to strengthen its bargaining position with the Palestinians. Israeli water use rose throughout the negotiation period (1992–1999) (Allan and Olmsted 2003).

21. That is, only Syria charges farmers the long-run marginal cost of water—the cost of supplying an additional unit of water, which water economists regard as the efficient price. In Syria, the World Bank estimates that perhaps 40% of the capital costs are covered by charges to farmers.

7

THE EMERGENCE
OF THE PUBLIC SECTOR

Our concern in this chapter is to document and analyze the prodigious growth in the economic functions of the Middle Eastern state. Despite nearly two decades of economic crisis and adjustment, the relative shares in the economy of the Middle East's public sectors have not diminished. There is little that is unusual about the region in this respect. What is striking, however, is the relative lack of variation in the degree and scope of state intervention across countries that otherwise differ greatly.

Middle Eastern states are big; they employ large numbers of people as civil servants, laborers, and managers—sometimes, as in the case of Egypt, as much as half of the nonagricultural workforce. These states monopolize resources; they control large investment budgets, strategic parts of the banking system, virtually all subsoil minerals, and the nation's basic infrastructure in roads, railroads, power, and ports. Whether size and resources translate into strength is a question to be examined on a case-by-case basis. Certainly the potential for strong states is there, especially when resources are coupled with control over, or control by, the military. There is, unsurprisingly, abundant contrary evidence that size spawns red tape and administrative paralysis, that resources are diverted into corruption and patronage, and that authoritarian leaders cannot push administrative agencies at a speed and in the directions that they would like.

Though attenuated after years of economic stagnation and crisis, the legitimacy of an interventionist state has long been widely accepted in the Middle East. This does not mean that most Middle Easterners accept the legitimacy of the particular state under which they live—that frequently is not the case. Rather, it has been conceded in the abstract that the state and its leaders have a right and an obligation to set a course for society and to use public resources to pursue that course. Two principles flowing out of the Western liberal tradition are given short shrift. One is that state authorities, to the extent possible, should confine themselves to the maintenance of law and order, regulation (but not too much) of economic life, provision of basic social-welfare benefits (health and education), and defense of the borders. The

Middle Eastern state has taken on functions vastly more complex than these, and its citizenry—including the powerful Islamist opposition—has endorsed the effort. The other is that the emphasis is on the ends of state intervention, and checks and balances are seen not as preventing abuse of power but as impeding the state's progress toward its goals. Therefore, to some extent, there has been an acceptance of a high concentration of power—economic, administrative, and military. It can be argued that in Muslim society political authority is legitimate only insofar as it promotes the interests of the community of believers, the *umma*. This yields an organic image of society, a living community whose "health" the state must maintain.

Religious and cultural antecedents notwithstanding, it is our conviction that it is more the politics of decolonization and development than cultural norms that account for the interventionist, organic state in the Middle East. The caretaker states of the colonial era, concerned with law, order, and taxation, logically evoked their opposites; states that impinge upon all aspects of their citizens' lives. Moreover, the postcolonial state has seen as its duty the reparation of all the economic damage resulting from colonial policies. It has had to mobilize human and material resources on an unprecedented scale. The goal has been to overcome "backwardness" and build a prosperous, educated citizenry, a diversified economy, and national power. These tasks and goals are culture-blind. Hence we find basic similarities in the goal orientation and interventionism of states in societies as widely varied in cultural origins as Indonesia, India, Burma, Ghana, and Tanzania.

THE STATE AS ARCHITECT OF STRUCTURAL TRANSFORMATION

It is not only outside observers but also the leaders of Middle Eastern states themselves who see their tasks in terms of "engineering," architecture, blueprints, and the like. They are designing new societies, and the state is that collection of agencies that will enable them to build what they have designed. Ideologies vary, but not the perceived need for state intervention.[1] And no state in the region has been able to forgo the exercise of elaborating a national plan.

The point of departure for the state was backwardness—a condition, it is alleged, imposed on the region by imperial powers. Its three major components were (1) an economy mired in the production of cheap agricultural commodities requiring an unskilled workforce, (2) the perpetuation of this system of production by denying education and the acquisition of modern skills to all but a privileged few, and (3) the forcible integration of this backward agrarian economy into an international division of labor. To remedy backwardness required a supreme effort, a kind of military campaign on three fronts. Only the state could coordinate the campaign and mobilize the inherently scarce resources needed to carry it out. So, along with the engineers and architects there have been the inevitable Bonapartes, and as Tunisia's Habib Bourguiba demonstrated, they did not all wear a marshal's uniform.

The area had an inadequately educated, poor population and an agricultural system characterized by small pockets of high productivity in a landscape of low yields and by the inefficient use of scarce capital. However ironic it may seem in retrospect, the leaders of the state saw the need for intervention in order to avoid wasting scarce resources. The comprehensive and rational planning effort anticipated required an inventory of available resources, a strategy for their development and utilization over time and in light of the profound structural changes that would take place in the economy and society as the plan unfolded, and the construction of the economic levers needed to implement the plan.

Throughout the region it was assumed that the private sector could not be relied upon to undertake this kind of resource mobilization and planning. The least critical saw the private sector as too weak financially, too close to a commercial and trading rather than an industrial past, and too concerned with short-term profit to be the agent of structural transformation. More severe critics emphasized the greed and exploitativeness of the private sector, its links to interests in the metropole, and its tendency to export capital rather than reinvest profit. Private sectors might be tolerated, but nowhere, save in Lebanon, did they enjoy legitimacy. Reliance on private entrepreneurs and on the law of supply and demand to allocate scarce resources would be wasteful, it was believed, and would not extricate the economy from its trap.

As important as efficiency for the state leaders was equity. Gross inequalities in the distribution of assets in Middle Eastern societies, not to mention absolute poverty for large segments of the population, were associated with the colonial system of exploitation. A more equitable distribution of assets within society became a universal goal throughout the area, again regardless of ideology. Some states pursued redistribution with greater conviction than others, but all espoused it as an ideal. The Great Depression, leading to absolute declines in the standard of living of rural populations, and the privations caused by World War II sensitized Middle Eastern elites to these equity issues. It was again assumed that the private sector could do little to alleviate them and, if left to its own devices, would probably aggravate them.

The Middle Eastern state took upon itself the challenge of moving the economy onto an industrial footing, shifting population to the urban areas, educating and training its youth wherever they lived, raising agricultural productivity to feed the nonagricultural population, redistributing wealth, building a credible military force, and doing battle with international trade and financial regimes that held it in thrall. These were goals widely held if poorly understood by the citizens at large. There were no impediments, then, to the expansion and affirmation of the interventionist state.

ATATÜRK AND THE TURKISH PARADIGM

The Republic of Turkey has been an example, if not a model, for many of the other states in the Middle East. Because it achieved real independence in 1923 after successful military action against European forces (Italian, French, and Greek) that were bent on dismembering all that remained of the Ottoman Empire, Turkey showed what could be done to thwart imperialism. It possessed an inspiring leader, Mustapha Kemal Atatürk, "father of the Turks," who built a secular, republican, nationalist system in Anatolia. His sweeping reforms, from the abolition of the caliphate to the introduction of the Latin alphabet, have been too well studied to require treatment here (see, inter alia, Lewis 1961). For our purposes it is important that by the late 1930s Turkey was endowed with a credible military structure, the beginnings of a diversified industrial sector, and a rapidly expanding educational system.

Atatürk's contemporaries, including Reza Khan of Iran, who was to found the Pahlavi dynasty, looked on with varying degrees of admiration.[2] So, too, did Arab nationalist politicians, such as Habib Bourguiba of Tunisia, who would lead their countries to independence. There were also students and young army officers in the turbulent 1930s who learned from the Turkish experience lessons that they would come to apply in the 1940s, 1950s, and 1960s. An Iraqi officer who later participated in the Golden Square conspiracy to oust the British from Iraq attended Atatürk's funeral and wrote: "I saw signs of progress which amazed me . . . a social revolution in education and economics, and in cultural and spiritual affairs. I saw the pride of the Turks in their fatherland, pride in their nationalism, their self-reliance and their independence" (Salah al-Din Sabbagh, quoted in Hemphill 1979, 104).

In April 1931 Atatürk issued a manifesto containing six principles that were to be embodied in the 1937 Constitution of the Republic. He declared that the society and the Republican People's party (RPP) that he headed would be republican, nationalist, populist, secular, etatist, and revolutionary. The principles of etatism (a term meaning "statism" taken from the French and retaining a strong Bonapartist flavor), populism, and revolution are our main concern here. The first provided legitimation for a strongly interventionist state. Populism meant that the masses were the object of political and economic policy and that distributive issues were at the top of the policy agenda. The revolution lay in Turkey's rejection of empire along with the sultanate and caliphate, its militant republicanism, and its confrontation with the imperial powers of Europe. Within a few years of the enunciation of these principles, Turkey embarked upon an economic experiment that was to be emulated in several countries following World War II: "Turkey became first among the backward countries to conduct an experiment in planned development with its first five year plan in 1934" (Hershlag 1968, 74). It also built a large public-enterprise sector and pursued a policy of import-substituting industrialization under the auspices of the state.

Turkey's trajectory toward this experiment was erratic, and there is no question that the world depression forced it to revise profoundly the strategy that had prevailed in the 1920s. It is important to review these antecedents. First, Turkey was in a shambles after World War I. The empire itself had been destroyed, and the Arab portions had fallen under French or British control. The basically agricultural economy had been badly damaged, especially in the fighting against the Italians, French, and Greeks. Then, after the signing of the Treaty of Lausanne in 1923 between Turkey and the major war victors, an enormous exchange of population took place. By 1926 perhaps 1.3 million Greeks had left Anatolia, taking with them vital skills in commerce and trades. In their place came 400,000 Turks, mainly peasants from Thrace, whom the rural areas could absorb only with difficulty.

Turkey inherited the Ottoman debts, which were finally settled at the end of the decade. It was fortunate that no reparations were imposed upon it as a successor to the empire that had fought on the side of Germany in that war. The fact that Turkey had signed a treaty of friendship with the USSR in 1921 may have militated against vindictive policies on the part of the allies. The Lausanne Treaty did impose restrictions on Turkey's ability to place tariffs on imports from Europe and hence to protect its own nascent industries. Nonetheless, Atatürk was determined from the outset to promote Turkey's industrialization and to liberate its economy from dependence on the West.

In contrast to what was to transpire after 1931, the republic's strategy was to rely on private-sector initiative and to avoid taxing the peasantry in order to finance industrial growth. The Organic Statute of 1924 declared private property and free enterprise to be the basic principles of the state. Its credo, not always honored, was that "the task of the state begins where the activity of private initiative ends." With the founding of the İç (Business) Bank in 1924 to finance private enterprise, the state showed its willingness to foster the growth of an indigenous capitalist class (F. Ahmad 1981; Boratav 1981).

Again in contrast to what came later, the new republic implemented policies that were relatively favorable to the rural world. In 1924 the *'ushr* tax, or tithe, was abolished. This tax had generated as much as 29% of government revenue. Its abolition was of particular benefit to smallholders and poor peasants. In its place the government introduced a land and unutilized-property tax that fell most heavily on wealthy landlords. Throughout the 1920s agricultural prices were allowed to rise. Although agricultural production was at an abnormally low ebb following the war, it grew by an impressive 58% between 1923 and 1932, while cereals alone increased by 100%. At the same time urban consumers had to pay high prices for commodities controlled by government monopolies: tobacco, salt, sugar, matches, alcohol, gasoline. In many ways this was the inverse of the urban bias that was to develop in the 1930s and 1940s, when factory smokestacks were referred to derisively as "Atatürk's Minarets."

After 1929, with the onset of the world depression, agricultural prices collapsed. No nonagricultural private sector had yet emerged that could pick up the slack in the economy, even supposing that world economic conditions would have allowed such a development. As soon as the tariff restrictions of the Lausanne Treaty had expired in 1929 and before the onset of the depression, Turkey introduced higher tariff barriers to protect local industry. As the world crisis affected the Turkish economy, there was not enough time to see whether the private sector would respond to the protective measures.

When, on April 20, 1931, Atatürk launched the etatist experiment, he said, "We desire to have the Government take an active interest, especially in the economic field, and to operate as far as possible in matters that lend themselves to the safeguarding of vital and general interests, or, in short, that the Government ensure the welfare of the nation and the prosperity of the state" (Hershlag 1968, 69).

In May 1932 Turkey negotiated a historic interest-free twenty-year loan from the Soviet Union for the equivalent of US$8 million. This may have been the first loan of its kind to a developing country, and no other such loan was made by the USSR for the next twenty-five years. It was to be used to buy Soviet equipment for two sugar refineries and a textile mill at Kayseri. Repayment was to be made in Turkish exports to the USSR. The Soviets set up a special trade agency, Turkstroj, to implement the loan agreement, and in 1935 it negotiated with the Sümer Bank created by Turkey especially to manage the project financing of its First Five-Year Plan. A pattern of economic assistance was thus established that was repeated in Egypt, Algeria, Syria, Iraq, Iran, and Morocco in the 1950s, 1960s, and 1970s.

In the year following the loan Turkey drew up the five-year plan, and its implementation began in 1934. Atatürk, like nearly every head of state we consider in these pages, headed a coalition of interests and ideological perspectives within his government and party. Left-of-center figures who had been offstage during the 1920s were given much more prominence during the etatist era. There was much more talk now of the "Kemalist Revolution," and the private-sector strategy of the earlier years was abandoned. Rather than the state being the handmaiden of a growing private sector, it was now to seize the "commanding heights" of the economy and bend the private sector to its will. In this new atmosphere the state technocracy and party ideologues could denigrate the private sector and talk of the necessity of state intervention. The left-of-center voices found a forum in the journal *Kadro* (cadre, or party organizer). The secretary general of the RPP, Recep Peker, was known to be an advocate of forced-pace change "to tear away from a social structure the backward, the bad, the unjust and harmful, and replace them with the progressive, the good, the just, and the useful elements" (cited in Karpat 1959, 72). Finally, the prime minister, Ismet Inönü, a man who saw etatism primarily in terms of the political and administrative obligations of the state, was to some extent eclipsed by Celal Bayar, who saw the need for much more aggressive economic intervention on the part of the state. Bayar came out of the İç Bank and became minister of economy in 1932 and then prime minister, replacing Inönü, in 1937.[3]

The five-year plan was a blueprint for ISI, emphasizing local processing of Turkey's primary commodities and minerals. A major part of the program lay in developing the textile industry, utilizing Turkish cotton, and selling to a large domestic market. This kind of thrust is often associated with the so-called easy phase of ISI. Other industries of a similar nature are food processing, sugar refining, and simple assembly. But Turkey went somewhat farther, launching projects in basic chemicals—superphosphates, chlorine, caustic soda—as well as in cement, iron, paper and cellulose, artificial silk, and hemp.

Even prior to the First Five-Year Plan, the Turkish state owned several enterprises; there were processing plants associated with the tobacco monopoly, beet sugar refineries, a shoe factory, wool mills, and a cotton-weaving plant. It had taken over power generation and the railroads from foreign interests. The plan added some twenty new enterprises to the public patrimony. A State Office for Industry was set up in 1932 and by 1936 was empowered to inspect the accounts of private-sector industries and to enforce price and wage controls. The Central Bank had been established in 1930 as the bank of issue. In 1933 the Sümer Bank was created and absorbed the Bank for

Industry and Mines. Sümer Bank provided financial management and supervision to state-owned enterprises, planned new projects, and invested in others coming under the plan. By 1939 Sümer Bank's holdings accounted for 100% of production in artificial silk, paper, cardboard, iron, and superphosphates, 90% of shoes, 80% of steel and lubricants, 70% of coke, 62% of leather, 60% of wool, and 55% of cement (Hershlag 1968, 92). The Iç Bank went well beyond private-sector financing to invest in a number of joint ventures. The Eti Bank was set up in 1935 to finance mineral exploration, extraction, and marketing. In this way the state in the 1930s had the financial leverage to orient all economic actors in accordance with plan priorities.

Work on drafting the Second Five-Year Plan was started in 1936, and the plan itself was formally adopted by the Grand National Assembly in September 1938, just before Atatürk's death. Over a hundred new enterprises were planned. The first efforts at "industrial deepening" were projected. The Zonguldak-Karabük region was slated to become a pole of heavy industrial growth, built around coal, steel, and cement and serviced by its own Black Sea port. A major effort was to be made in power generation, basic chemicals, engineering, and marine transport. Part of the plan was to disperse industry in order to benefit backward areas, especially Eastern Anatolia, as well as for strategic reasons.

Some of the seemingly inevitable side effects of this sort of big-push strategy began to make themselves felt during the 1930s. The government ran a growing deficit due in large part to an outsized bureaucracy. The civil service, not including the military or part-time personnel, reached 127,000 in 1938 and 184,000 in 1945 (Karpat 1959, 129). About 35% of the budget went into their salaries. The size of the civil service was due not so much to the overproduction of university graduates that characterized most of the Middle East by the 1960s as to the absorption of the personnel of the Ottoman bureaucracy set up to administer an empire. The deficit of the government stood at TL13.8 million in 1930/1931 and TL125 million in 1939/1940. Over the same decade Turkey was obliged to borrow abroad, from the Soviet Union, Germany, and the United Kingdom. Still, in contrast to other countries in the region in the 1960s and 1970s, Turkey was able to finance most of its investment out of its own resources. The level of investment was modest by postwar standards; the government was investing annually about 5% of national income, with another 5% coming from the private sector.

World War II interrupted the Second Five-Year Plan, and a period of severe privation ensued. Import substitution continued out of necessity as Mediterranean shipping was disrupted during the hostilities. A major shift in the political domain after the war, leading to a two-party system and the victory of the Democrat party, which had come to oppose etatism, ushered in a liberal economic phase during the 1950s. Only after a military takeover in 1960 did Turkey return to etatism. By that time it had been joined by another half-dozen states in the region.

REPLICATING THE PARADIGM

It would be an exaggeration to say that other states in the Middle East slavishly imitated the Turkish experience. In fact, state-led ISI spread throughout the developing world in the years after 1945 and, as a strategy, had a logic independent of any single country's efforts. We shall see that among Middle Eastern states, the tremendous growth in publicly owned assets and the development strategies associated with them had varying sources of inspiration, some external and some internal.

We are distinguishing here between public-sector enterprise and other governmental agencies that employ the bulk of the civil servants. Generally, public-sector enterprises have their own statutes, personnel policies, and salary and wage scales. They are companies in the legal sense that they make and sell products or deliver services for a fee. They enter the national marketplace directly and usually with great impact.

If we look at the developing world as a whole around 1980, we find impressive statistics on the weight of public sectors in their economies. On average the output of public-sector enterprise, exclusive of financial institutions (banks, social security and pension funds, insurance companies), accounted for 8.6% of GDP; these enterprises on average employed 47% of the manufacturing workforce in the organized sector, utilized 27% of all manufacturing investment, and, on average, ran deficits equivalent to 5.5% of GDP (World Bank estimates). State-owned manufacturing enterprises frequently accounted for 25–50% of value added in manufacturing. Some Middle Eastern states, especially Egypt, Algeria, and Syria, were well above these averages: Egyptian state-owned enterprises accounted for around 60% of value added in manufacturing and Syrian ones for 55%. The output of Algeria's and Egypt's state-owned enterprises reached 13% of GDP, while Syria's was close to 11%. Turkey's state-owned enterprises were, in 1980, producing about 8% of GDP and accounted for 25% of value added in manufacturing.[4]

The question of publicly owned assets is important in two ways. First, the assets are always the instruments of a given state's development strategy. In that sense, they shape production, absorb and allocate scarce resources, and orient patterns of consumption. This may help or hinder the development of private-sector activity. They are always instruments of political preemption and control. Second, when we speak of publicly owned assets, we are obviously dealing with a fundamental aspect of property relations and hence of class. What the state owns private individuals or firms do not. In theory, public ownership is ownership by the "people." The state acts as custodian, manager, and fiduciary on behalf of citizen-owners. The latter monitor the state through their representatives in parliament or the party or on the boards of directors of public enterprises. But this is almost everywhere a fiction. The state builds public enterprise to pursue ends that it alone defines.

The last statement, however, raises some crucial questions. The state cannot be taken as a homogeneous bloc. It always contains diverse interests and factions that prevail at different times and in different combinations. Furthermore, crude indicators of ownership and economic weight such as those presented in the preceding paragraph tell us little of intent or direction. The states in the Middle East with the weightiest public sectors are found among the frequently conservative oil exporters. Moreover, in Turkey in the 1950s, despite the professed liberalism of the Democrat regime, the public sector actually grew. More important, public enterprises may implicitly or explicitly be put, in part, at the service of the private sector (Turkey in the 1920s) or be designed to marginalize the private sector over time (Egypt after 1961). The weight of the public sector in the two cases may not differ much, but direction and intent are quite different.

The final question is whether the managers of public assets, those "atop the commanding heights" or "in control of the major means of production," come to constitute a dominant class that seeks to reproduce itself and to exclude others from the assets it controls. We advance some tentative answers to all these questions in the remainder of this chapter.

Arab Socialism and State Enterprise

One set of Arab states adopted the Turkish paradigm and went well beyond it. These states' strategies were explicitly socialist and populist, hostile to the indigenous private sector and to foreign capital, and aimed at far-reaching redistribution of wealth within their societies. The strategy has not always been sustained and on occasion has been officially abandoned (e.g., Egypt after 1974, Tunisia after 1969, the Sudan after 1972). The principal experiences we have in mind are those of Egypt (1957 to 1974), Algeria (1962 to 1989), Syria (1963 to the present), Iraq (1963 to 2003), Tunisia (1962 to 1969), the Sudan (1969 to 1972), and Libya (1969 to the present). What all these have in common is a blueprint for the radical transformation of their societies and economies. In these states the campaign for growth, equity, and national economic sovereignty was no mere metaphor. Indeed, Habib Bourguiba of Tunisia likened his country's quest for development to a *jihad* and said that Tunisians should be dispensed of the obligation to fast during the month of Ramadan just as if they were warriors.

A number of basic assumptions underlay these experiments. The first of these was that profit and loss should not be the primary criteria for assessing public-sector performance. Rather, the creation of jobs, the provision of cheap goods of first necessity, the introduction of new economic activity to remote or poor regions, and the achievement of self-sufficiency in goods of a strategic or military nature would be more appropriate tests of success. Second, it was assumed that the operation of supply and demand was inferior to planning and the application of administered prices. In market situations, goods of first necessity (food and clothing) are often the objects of speculation, and because demand for them is relatively inelastic, prices may rise precipitously. The state had to set prices so that such goods were always within reach of the poorer strata. Similarly, the price of inputs and credits supplied to priority industries should not reflect their scarcity value.

The large-scale private sector was seen as untrustworthy. Most of the regimes under consideration nationalized it or sharply curtailed its activities. The private enterprise that remained was subjected to state licensing and price and wage controls and had to compete with the public sector for scarce credit and foreign exchange.

Foreign investment was viewed with suspicion. Entire sectors of the economy, such as basic metals, chemicals, and minerals, were reserved exclusively for public-sector enterprise; neither foreign nor domestic private capital was allowed in these sectors. The favored form of collaboration with foreign capital was through turnkey projects and management contracts in which foreign investors acquired no equity in the host country. Socialist Algeria, in the 1970s, was able to do billions of dollars' worth of business with the United States, France, Japan, and other countries through such formulas.

The setting up of closed sectors for public-sector enterprise underscores another assumption: that there is nothing inherently inefficient about monopolies. In many instances state-owned enterprises enjoyed monopolies in entire lines of production or were the sole purchasers (monopsonists) of certain inputs (raw cotton or sugar beets). Egypt, after 1961, took matters further, putting the entire banking, insurance, and foreign-trade sectors under public ownership. The supply of investable funds and the importation of vital production inputs thus became a state monopoly. For all this to work—to promote overall growth, industrialization, and a more equal distribution of income—required that the planners accurately anticipate the complex interaction of all the economic variables, that the managers pursue efficiency even while protected by tariffs and monopoly status, and that the civil servants put in an honest day's work. By and large none of those requirements were met.

Egypt.   Egypt was the first Middle Eastern country in the postwar era to adopt a strategy of radical transformation. In many ways it was far more integrated into the world economy than Turkey. It had been one of the leading exporters of raw cotton for nearly a century. The British occupation after 1881, the economic dependency on Britain that ensued, and the role of the Suez Canal in world trade made Egypt's a classic colonial economy. As in Turkey, the world depression and World War II set Egypt on the path toward ISI. It was the Egyptian private sector, partly indigenous and partly foreign, that led this effort.

In 1952 the Egyptian monarchy was overthrown by a military coup led by Colonel Gamal 'Abd al-Nasser and a group of his colleagues known as the Free Officers. From 1952 to 1956 Egypt promoted public-sector growth but, as did Turkey in the 1920s, did so either to help the private sector or to undertake projects that the private sector could not finance or manage. The old Aswan Dam was electrified to augment Egypt's power supply, and it was decided to promote a new, giant dam at Aswan to increase hydropower generation severalfold and to ensure a predictable supply of irrigation water to the agricultural sector. Work was begun on an iron-and-steel complex at Helwan and on a large fertilizer plant at Aswan.

It was not until the Suez War of November 1956 that the public sector grew at the expense of the private. Because of the participation of Britain and France, along with Israel, in a direct attack on Egypt, all assets owned by the former two in Egypt were taken over by the Egyptian government. The attack itself had been provoked by Egypt's nationalization in July 1956 of the Suez Canal Company. With the wartime sequestrations of banks, trading companies, insurance companies, utilities, and some manufacturing enterprises, the Egyptian state found itself in possession of a very substantial patrimony. It was only then that the term "socialism" was adumbrated and that left-of-center voices in Nasser's coalition gained greater prominence.

In 1957 Egypt contracted its first loan for economic assistance from the Soviet Union, followed in 1958 by a Soviet loan to help build the Aswan Dam. In 1957 Egypt began its first five-year industrial plan, with strong emphasis on state enterprise. By 1960 it considered itself ready for a five-year plan for the entire economy.

After 1956 there was some evidence of private-sector disinvestment and profit-taking and of growing suspicion between the private sector and the regime. The privately held Misr Group and Bank Misr had been essentially taken over by the state by 1960. The new Ministry of Industry was empowered to license and regulate all private industrial activity. The elaboration of the First Five-Year Plan was carried out without consulting the private sector, although the latter was called upon to mobilize about 55% of all investment over the five-year period.

The failure of the private sector to do so allegedly provoked a wave of nationalizations through the Socialist Decrees of July 1961. In one fell swoop, the Egyptian state took over most large-scale industry, all banking, insurance, and foreign trade, all utilities, marine transport, and airlines, and many hotels and department stores. The bulk of agricultural property remained in private hands, but new desert reclamation projects were owned by the state.

The First Five-Year Plan embodied a straightforward ISI strategy, combining aspects of the easy (textiles, sugar, automobile assembly, pharmaceuticals) and hard (heavy engineering, steel, chemicals, and fertilizers) phases. It generated 1 million new jobs and growth rates of 6% per annum. Yet in 1965 it ended in crisis.

The Achilles' heel of ISI, whether under public or private auspices, is the economy's ability to earn foreign exchange. For the major oil exporters that at one time or another pursued an ISI strategy (Iran, Algeria, Iraq) this was not a major problem, but for Turkey, Egypt, and Syria it certainly was. As Turkey learned in the 1930s, ISI often reduces imports of one kind—for example, finished textiles or refined sugar—only to increase imports of another kind—for example, raw materials such as coking coal for new steel plants or capital goods such as turbines and power looms. Egypt's new industries were designed to market their products in Egypt. They did not have the economies of scale and basic operating efficiency that would have allowed them to export to other markets. Thus, although they needed imports to function, they could not generate the foreign exchange to pay for them.

To finance its Second Five-Year Plan, Egypt had little choice but to try to borrow more heavily abroad. It was not very successful, and even the Soviet Union was reluctant to extend new lines of credit. At the same time, the state's large outlays on construction and social services drove up domestic demand without commensurate increases in the supply of goods, so that inflation reared its head. Finally, the fact that few state-owned enterprises were profitable and many were being padded with redundant personnel in an effort to create jobs meant that the government had to resort to deficit financing to cover their losses. In short, although rates of growth in production and the delivery of services were quite respectable, the Egyptian state nonetheless faced an external and a domestic fiscal crisis.

The Second Five-Year Plan, which, like Turkey's, would have led to industrial "deepening," had to be abandoned for want of adequate financing. Then came

Egypt's disastrous defeat in the June War of 1967 and Israel's occupation of the Sinai Peninsula. Egypt lost its oil fields there, the Suez Canal was closed to traffic, and tourism was badly disrupted. Egypt went into severe recession. Its strategy for radical structural transformation through public-sector enterprise had to be revised.

President Nasser died in September 1970, and his successor, Anwar al Sadat, cautiously pursued a policy of economic liberalization aimed at reforming and streamlining the public sector, stimulating the private sector, attracting foreign investment, and promoting exports. Public-sector enterprise was subjected to sharp criticism for its chronic inefficiency and huge operating deficits. Although Egypt continued to produce five-year plans, they had clearly lost their mystique, and the notion of socialist transformation was downplayed. Egypt's initial blueprint, the crises that developed in its implementation, and the revision of the blueprint constitute a sequence that has been repeated elsewhere in the region.

Even though heavily criticized, Egypt's public sector continued to grow throughout the 1970s. Entering the 1980s it included 391 companies employing about 1.2 million workers. The market value of its assets was about £E38 billion. In 1983/1984 its wage bill stood at £E5.7 billion (over 20% of GDP) and over the period 1975 to 1982 had grown at 19% per annum. It accounted for 22% of total value added in the economy. The return on its total investment was only 1.5% per annum. Counting public authorities that ran everything from the Suez Canal to the Aswan High Dam, along with the civil service, the public and governmental sector in the early 1980s, before the structural adjustment effort began, had 3.2 million employees—more than a third of the total workforce and over half of the nonagricultural workforce—and over £E90 billion in assets. Total public expenditures in 1980 represented 60% of GDP, total government revenues 40% of GDP, and the public deficit 20% of GDP. As one observer put it, "There are few, if any, developing countries in the world with such high proportions" (Ahmad 1984, ix).

Algeria.   Algeria is one of the few LDCs to rival Egypt in terms of the weight and extent of its public sector. To a greater degree than in Egypt, the overall size of the Algerian public sector was the result of ideology and long-term policy.

Independent Algeria emerged in 1962 out of seven years of revolutionary warfare against the French. Many of the leaders of the National Liberation Front (FLN) were committed socialists or, to a lesser extent, Marxists. The nature and intensity of their struggle made it inevitable that Algeria would confront France and the imperialist world in general. International business interests and the Algerian private sector itself were seen as likely enemies of Algeria's revolution (Leca 1975, 124). At no time did the state see its role as helpmate to the private sector as did Turkey during the 1920s or Egypt up to 1957. The National Charter of 1976 reiterated a position that had been constant since 1962:

> In Algeria, private property cannot be a source of social power. It cannot be the basis for exploitative relations between the owner and the workers. It can only function to the extent that it does not prejudice the interests of the laboring

masses, nor constitute a brake or obstacle to the inexorable evolution of our society toward socialism. . . . In the industrial domain, the intervention of the national private sector is restricted to small-scale enterprise involved in the last stage of industrial transformation, downstream of the production or the imports of the public and socialist sectors. (Benissad 1982, 29)

From 1966 to 1989 the commanding heights of the economy were reserved to the state. Collaboration with foreign firms was extensive but was carried out on a contract basis involving turnkey projects, technical assistance, and purchase of technology. Direct investment was carefully avoided. Like all states in the region, Algeria was the exclusive owner of all subsoil minerals. French companies that had developed the country's petroleum and natural gas deposits were nationalized between 1969 and 1971, giving the state exclusive control over their production, refining, and marketing. The hydrocarbon sector, after the surge in world petroleum prices in 1973, came to represent over 30% of GDP.

In many ways Algeria could not have avoided heavy state intervention even if its official ideology had not been socialist. On the eve of independence, nearly all of the French settler community in the country, nearly 1 million strong, packed up and left. This was an exodus even more devastating than that of the Greeks from Turkey in 1922–1923. The French settlers had dominated modern farming, skilled trades, the small industrial sector, and government services. The new state inherited agricultural, industrial, and residential property, and the first two were given over to "worker self-management" units. In the agricultural sector, over 2 million hectares were cultivated by about 130,000 permanent workers on 2,000 farms. The state owned the farms, but, in theory, the workers had full control over their operations. The same formula was applied to industrial units. These consisted of about 400 small-scale enterprises, only 5% of which employed more than 100 persons, with a total workforce of 15,000.

In the early years, when Ahmad Ben Bella was president, the experiment in self-management was seen as putting power in the hands of the working people and constituting a barrier to the emergence of a dominating and domineering bureaucracy and technocracy. The period 1962–1965 was one of near-romantic populism and socialism, but already one could see government agencies arrogating basic decisionmaking power in all spheres of production. The FLN, which had seen many of its militants absorbed into the civil service, could do little to defend the populist experiment, and the workers themselves soon reverted to apathetic clock punching.

The romantic period came to an end in June 1965 when the minister of defense, Houari Boumedienne, overthrew Ben Bella and ushered in an era of "rational" top-down planned development that, implicitly, saw the masses as a source more of disruption than of revolutionary support. Worker self-management was paid lip service but deprived of any effective autonomy.

Boumedienne met one significant challenge from Ben Bella's old coalition. In December 1967, Tahar Zbiri, the army chief of staff, and Abdelaziz Zerdani, the minister of labor, who was close to the General Confederation of Algerian Workers

(UGTA), tried to engineer a coup against Boumedienne. Zerdani saw the Algerian development strategy moving toward authoritarian state capitalism in which the workers would be made to pay a heavy price while their unions would be muzzled. He appealed to his old friend Zbiri, like himself a Berber from the Aurès Mountains and a former guerrilla fighter. The coup attempt failed, the conspirators fled, and Boumedienne, in close concert with his minister of industry, Abdesslam Belaid, pushed Algeria down the very path that Zbiri and Zerdani had tried to bar.

With the First Four-Year Plan, 1969–1973, Algeria launched a program built on heavy industry. Oil and natural gas were to serve two ends: First, they would be the feedstock for a modern petrochemical sector producing fertilizers and plastics; second, the earnings from their export would pay for the importation of plant and capital goods for steel manufacture and vehicle assembly. It was expected that the agricultural sector, especially the self-managed units, would be an expanding market for the new products (fertilizers, irrigation pipes, tractors). The local private sector was regarded as irrelevant to the effort, and foreign firms were seen mainly as providers of technology. The slogan was "Sow oil to reap industry."[5]

By the time Algeria initiated its Second Four-Year Plan, world petroleum prices had quadrupled. In contrast to Egypt, Algeria faced no financing problems in the mid-1970s. In that sense, its experience emphasizes some of the inherent weaknesses of state-led ISI, for by the late 1970s important elements of the strategy had been called into question. Rather than the agricultural sector's generating demand for new industrial products, there was a general decline in agricultural production, especially in the self-managed sector. Algeria became a major importer of food. Insufficient domestic demand coupled with tariff protection and monopoly position meant that public-sector industries operated below capacity and at high cost. They had little hope of exporting except to some of their East European creditors. Finally, some of the imported technologies, for example, in natural gas liquefaction, were so sophisticated that costly units were frequently shut down for technical reasons.

Near the end of his life, President Boumedienne acknowledged the shortcomings of his approach. In his "state of the nation" address of March 1977, he warned: "Management is henceforth a battle to win, just as we have won that of investment. In truth, the problem of the management of the economy, and more particularly the production and service units will constitute our major concern for the coming years" (cited in Nellis 1980, 410).

Boumedienne died on December 27, 1978. His successor, Chadli Benjadid, a former liberation army commander and a man who had supported Boumedienne in 1965, was elected president in 1979. During his tenure, which ended in 1991, Algeria's public sector was extensively overhauled (see Chapter 9). However, it still dominates the Algerian economy. In the late 1980s there were some fifty public-sector companies and twenty authorities with assets valued at over US$100 billion, employing 80% of the industrial workforce and accounting for 77% of industrial production. Add to this 260,000 civil servants and 140,000 teachers and other employees of the educational system and one has 45% of the nonagricultural workforce on the public payroll. Finally, the Algerian state in the late 1970s was able to invest the equivalent of 25–30% of GDP annually. This could not have been achieved, however, without stimulating inflation and increasing the external debt, which stood at US$23.3 billion in 1987 (World Bank data). The collapse of international petroleum prices in 1984/1985 forced Algeria to question the very premises of the strategies it had followed since the mid-1960s.

Syria and Iraq.   Beginning in 1953 Syria and Iraq fell under the domination of the same pan-Arab party, the Ba'ath, or Arab Renaissance party. Since its founding in Syria after World War II, this party has called for Arab unity and socialism and has tried to propagate its message throughout the Arab world. The major obstacle to its spread was perceived by its leaders to be Nasser's Egypt, especially when that country entered its socialist phase after 1961. Many of the policies of state intervention implemented by the Ba'ath in Syria and Iraq sprang in part from its socialist ideology, but just as important were the fears of Ba'athi leaders that Egypt's socialist transformation would dazzle the radical youth of the Arab countries.

Both Syria and Iraq, in contrast to Algeria, had substantial indigenous trading and landowning bourgeoisies and no foreign settler communities (see, inter alia, Batatu 1978 and Khoury 1983b). Prior to the Ba'aths coming to power, both countries pursued policies whereby the state helped the private sector through the development of infrastructure and banking credit. Neither country had made significant advances in industrial production, although Iraq enjoyed the revenues from a sizable oil sector.

In the 1950s, under the Iraqi monarchy, oil revenues gave the state tremendous leverage in the economy. The public Development Board annually absorbed 70% of those revenues and invested them mainly in infrastructural development. It was this policy that required deferred consumption and contributed to a situation in which elements of the Iraqi armed forces overthrew the monarchy in July 1958.

Almost immediately the new regime, led by 'Abd al-Karim Qassim, disbanded the Development Board and replaced it with a Planning Board and a Ministry of Planning. There was a major shift in investment away from infrastructure and agriculture and into industry. The Ministry of Industry was empowered to promote public-sector projects and to supervise and license private-sector activities (Penrose and Penrose 1978, 253).

The new regime, however, was not Ba'athist. Qassim was merely a nationalist army officer with leftist leanings. He tried, unsuccessfully, to balance Nasserist, communist, and Ba'athist forces within his coalition, contend with Kurdish dissidence, and implement far-reaching agrarian reform. All the contenders battled for the hearts and minds of the officers' corps, and in February 1963 a group of Ba'athi officers overthrew and killed Qassim and set up a government presided over by Colonel 'Abd al-Salam 'Arif. This new regime moved in early 1964 to nationalize all banks, along with thirty-two large industrial and commercial firms. With these moves the state's share in large manufacturing concerns rose to 62% of gross output, 46% of employment, and 55% of wages. Once more the state had captured the commanding heights, and most observers concede that Iraq acted in order to steal Egypt's thunder

(Batatu 1978, 1031; al-Khafaji 1983). It was not, however, until 1972–1975 that full nationalization of the petroleum sector took place.

The nationalization coincided with the first big increase in world petroleum prices. With the oil sector under state ownership, the state's share in GDP rose to 75% in 1978, although if the petroleum sector is excluded, the state's share was a more modest 23%. By 1977 there were some 400 public-sector enterprises, employing 80,000 workers. They absorbed over 60% of all industrial and commercial investment (Stork 1982, 36; al-Khafaji 1983, 36). Total government employment in 1977 reached 410,000, or nearly half of Iraq's organized workforce. Adding to this 250,000 members of the armed forces (a figure that rose to over a million in the 1980s), 175,000 in the Ba'ath militias, 260,000 in the police, 120,000 pensioners, and thousands of schoolteachers, we find that by 1980 one in four Iraqis was on the state payroll (Batatu 1978, 123). Saddam Hussein's public sector had a far more sinister aspect. Not only was it heavy with police and intelligence personnel but, it is estimated, it came to employ about a quarter of the workforce as part-time paid informants (al-Khalil 1989, 38).

Between 1958 and 1961, Syria had been a member, along with Egypt and North Yemen, of the United Arab Republic (UAR). In those three years, under Egyptian pressure, land-reform measures were undertaken as well as some steps toward expanding public-sector enterprise. Egypt's Socialist Decrees of July 1961 alarmed the Syrian private sector, which feared they would be applied in Syria. In league with sympathetic army officers, these elements brought off a coup d'état that took Syria out of the UAR and installed a somewhat conservative, pro-private-sector military regime in Damascus.

In March 1963, a month after the Ba'ath had come to power in Iraq, yet another military coup brought the Ba'ath to power in Syria. A year later, in May 1964, the regime took over the country's banks, and in the wake of private-sector protests in Hama, seven enterprises of "reactionary capitalists" were nationalized. Then in January 1965 the regime undertook far-reaching nationalizations. Assets worth US$50 million were taken over, and the public-sector share in industrial production rose from 25% to 75%. Again, part of the motive was to demonstrate to organized labor that Syria's socialist experiment was as radical and devoted to workers' welfare as Egypt's (in general, see Hannoyer and Seurat 1979; Chatelus 1982; Longuenesse 1985). In fact, Syria structured its public sector exactly on the Egyptian model, using general organizations to supervise production in specific sectors such as textiles, chemicals, and metals.

A more radical wing of the Ba'ath seized power in 1966, but its militancy was manifested mainly in confronting Israel and sponsoring Palestinian guerrilla attacks. This faction's image was battered in the June War of 1967, and in 1970, after an internal trial of strength, Hafiz al-Assad, the minister of defense and commander of the air force, took power. The shift to some extent resembled that from Ben Bella to Boumedienne. Hafiz al-Assad was an organization man, mistrustful of the masses and of revolutionary adventures. He relied on the large power structures of the country—the armed forces, the bureaucracy, the Ba'ath party, and the public sector, perhaps in that order—to control, preempt, and police, rather than mobilize.

Between 1970 and 1982 employment in public-sector enterprises rose from 57,000 to 119,000, or half the industrial workforce. In just two years the public-sector wage bill doubled, from 3.5% to 6% of GDP. In 1979 Syria's total workforce was about 2.1 million, of which about a third were engaged in agriculture. Combined public-sector and civil-service employment probably totaled 350,000. There may have been 230,000 Syrians in uniform and, although there is some overlap with the preceding categories, perhaps 200,000 members of the Ba'ath party (Drysdale 1982, 5–7). Some 220,000 workers, in both the public and the private sector, were unionized and under Ba'athi supervision. Again, as we have found in all the preceding experiments, the state not only owned the major means of production, but controlled through the payroll, the party, and the armed forces, the most strategically situated elements of the workforce.

This dominance in Syria and elsewhere was achieved at the expense of economic efficiency. The strategic sectors became used to their privileges and to low levels of performance. The state hesitated to alienate them by asking more of them or paying them less. This held true especially for the military; in 1981 Syrian defense outlays were 13% of GNP, placing it among ten nations worldwide to spend more than 10% of GNP on defense. Inflation and a growing external debt (according to the World Bank, it increased tenfold between 1970 and 1983 to $2.3 billion) plagued the economy, especially after the Syrian intervention in Lebanon in 1976.

Tunisia. Since its independence in 1956 and up to 1987, when General Zine al-Abdine Ben 'Ali deposed Habib Bourguiba on the grounds that he was medically unfit to govern, Tunisia maintained uninterrupted civilian rule. Nonetheless, during those same years it built an interventionist state system that resembled those of Egypt, Turkey, and Algeria. Bourguiba founded the Neo-Destour party in the 1930s; rallied the small-scale trading and commercial groups, the professionals and intelligentsia, and the trade unions; and led the coalition to power (Moore 1965).

Although the French settler community in Tunisia was smaller than that of Algeria, it nonetheless dominated the modern private sector. There was no such mass exodus of settlers as had occurred in Algeria, but the fact remained that there was no indigenous industrial bourgeoisie upon which the new state could rely to promote the country's structural transformation.

From the outset, then, much as in Turkey in the 1920s, Bourguiba built a powerful state apparatus, to some extent gutting the Neo-Destour of its best cadres, subordinating the trade unions, and using the state to mobilize capital and raw materials to stimulate private activity. In 1962 Tunisia launched its First Three-Year Plan, followed by a series of four-year plans. The state's role in resource mobilization was, until the 1970s, overwhelming (see Table 7.1).

Tunisia in the 1960s was quite literally boxed in between the Arab world's two most ostentatious socialist experiments, Algeria's to the west and Egypt's to the east. By 1964 Bourguiba had decided that it was necessary to give a more radical cast to the Tunisian strategy. In October 1964 the Neo-Destour party became the Socialist Destour party and called for the "coexistence" of the public, private, and cooperative

TABLE 7.1   Evolution of Total and Industrial Gross Fixed Capital Formation in Tunisia, 1962–1981

Gross Fixed Capital Formation	Three-Year Plan 1962–1964	Four-Year Plan 1965–1968	Four-Year Plan 1969–1972	Four-Year Plan 1973–1976	Four-Year Plan 1977–1981[a]
Total					
Public sector	74.7	70.9	59.1	53.2	64.7
Private sector	25.3	29.1	40.9	46.8	35.3
Industrial					
Public sector	84.7	86.7	60.5	43.7	63.6
Private sector	15.3	13.3	39.5	56.3	36.4

[a]Average for first three years of the plan.
SOURCE: Signoles and Ben Romdane (1983, table 4, 119)

sectors. The First Four-Year Plan, 1965–1968, was to embody a socialist transformation of the economy: Cultivators were to be grouped into agricultural cooperatives, and state enterprise would spearhead the industrialization drive. A young intellectual, Ahmed Ben Salah, active in the Neo-Destour and the unions prior to independence, was made secretary of state for planning and national economy and was the driving force behind the experiment.

Both the extent and the pace of state intervention had been dictated by Bourguiba's failing health. The Combatant Suprème, as he liked to be known, feared that the socialist experiment would be jeopardized if he were to die before it had been implemented. But Bourguiba's health was restored, and Ben Salah, by forcing the pace of cooperative formation, alienated much of the regime's petty capitalist and small landowning constituency. In 1969, Bourguiba turned on Ben Salah and put him on trial for treason. The statist experiment was overhauled, and Tunisia adopted a strategy of stimulating its private sector and promoting exports to the EEC. The shift in emphasis is shown clearly in Table 7.1 (see also Chapter 9). Still, the Tunisian state remained, until the late 1980s, a dominant force in the economy and, through its modest oil exports, had substantial revenues at its disposal. Those rents explain the rising share of the state in gross fixed capital formation after a decline in the early 1970s. In 1982 the public-enterprise sector alone employed 180,000 persons, or over 11% of the workforce.

The Sudan.   The Sudanese economy is, among the major countries of the region, the most heavily dependent on its agrarian sector. Over two-thirds of the population is rural, and some 80% of the workforce is employed in farming, animal husbandry, or fishing. Prior to independence in 1956, Sudanese industry was based on agricultural processing: cotton ginning, seed crushing for edible oil and feed cake, and soap manufacture. After a military coup d'état in 1958, the Sudanese state began an ISI strategy built around public enterprise. Once again the Egyptian example proved contagious, and as in Algeria, Egypt, Syria, and Iraq, the Soviet Union stepped in with technical assistance, planning advisers, and soft loans. The strategy was maintained during a turbulent return to civilian control between 1964 and 1969 and then was accelerated when Major Ga'afar al-Nimeiri seized power in May 1969. His coalition initially had a strong Marxist and communist faction that engineered several nationalizations of foreign banks and indigenous private firms.

In the summer of 1970 Nimeiri purged his government of its communist and Marxist members and within a year began to denationalize the assets he had just taken over. In the early 1970s the regime acted to support private-sector growth within the general ISI framework, but state enterprise remained the dominant economic force in the economy. Public companies dominated the sugar, textile, cement, food processing, and canning sectors and had a significant share of leather, edible oils, soap, and detergents. The million-hectare Gezira Scheme was owned by the state; cotton and groundnuts were grown by 100,000 tenant farm families. One of the largest state-owned farms in the world, it has for years been the backbone of Sudan's rural economy. The state also owned all mineral deposits, including some oil deposits in the south-center of the country, the Sudanese railroads, and all hydro- and thermal-power systems.

As has been the case for the other countries under consideration, the state in the Sudan was the country's principal employer. With over 400,000 people on the public payroll in 1977, exclusive of the armed forces, the state employed 8% of the entire workforce and 21% of the nonagricultural workforce (see Table 7.2).

Libya. The Jamahiria, or "mass state," of Libya represents the unacknowledged combination of romantic revolutionary and Islamic programs with a kind of cynical authoritarianism. As in all the major oil-exporting nations, the state dominates the economy by the simple fact of owning the petroleum and controlling the proceeds of its sale. That was the case under the Idrissid monarchy, and it has been the case since 1969, when the monarchy was overthrown by the then-lieutenant, now colonel, Mu'ammar Qaddhafi. He eventually elaborated a new theory of the state of the masses, the Jamahiria, in which all productive units and all workplaces were to be directly governed by popular congresses. Bureaucratic hierarchies, top-heavy party structures, and elaborate command channels were all depicted as antithetical

TABLE 7.2   Growth in Public Employment in the Sudan, 1955/1956 and 1976/1977

	1955/56	*1976/77*
Central government	31,283	119,115
Local government	80,000	157,457
Public corporations	65,125	132,144
Total	176,408	408,716

SOURCE: *Sudanow,* December 1977, 11

to true popular democratic control. Libya's experiment, on paper, was one of worker self-management with a vengeance (see Fathaly and Palmer 1980).

Beginning in 1979 Qaddhafi led an assault on private-sector interests unrivaled anywhere in the Middle East. He expropriated all private industry. In 1981 all bank deposits were seized without warning, and a program to abolish retail trade by replacing it with state-owned supermarkets was begun. By this time three-quarters of the workforce was on the public payroll (Anderson 1986). The Libyan state and regime never really relinquished effective control of production and administration to popular committees. The oil and banking sectors were kept under tight state control, as were and are the 60,000–70,000 men and women in the armed forces. Libya had multiyear development plans like other countries we have considered, and the leadership did not allow the "people" to question, much less change, any of the plans' major parameters.

"Liberal" Monarchies

It may be that socialism entails a significant public sector, but the converse is not true. The monarchies of pre-1979 Iran, Jordan, and Morocco all professed liberal economic credos in which the private sector was to be the leading force. The role of the state was, once again, that of handmaiden to the private sector. Yet if we look at statistical indicators of state activity, we see that these three countries possessed public sectors of a size and weight equal to those of the socialist countries. The experience of these monarchies highlights the general point that one should not confuse state ownership with socialism. Some "radical" regimes have waved the flag of public ownership to demonstrate their socialist bona fides, while "liberal" regimes have passed over in silence the substantial assets they control through state ownership.[6]

Iran.   Next door to Turkey in Iran a would-be Atatürk appeared on the scene following World War I. Colonel Reza Khan of the Persian Cossacks had de facto taken over the Iranian state by 1924, and it was his intention to proclaim a republic, have himself made president, and build a state system as Atatürk was doing in Turkey. The Shi'ite clergy of Iran, however, vehemently resisted the plan for a republic and persuaded Reza Khan to proclaim himself shah (emperor) in 1925 and found the Pahlavi "dynasty."

Aside from this nontrivial distinction, Reza Shah set about building a nation in the ethnically and geographically fragmented society he inherited from the Qajars. The state apparatus and the armed forces grew side-by-side, and as in Turkey, the depression pushed the Iranian state into ISI. The private sector benefited from credit provided through the state Industrial Bank as well as from high tariff walls against imports. But the state did not wait to see how the private sector would respond to these incentives, and by 1941 there were public enterprises in textiles, sugar, cement, and iron and steel. Through consumption taxes and trade monopolies, the Iranian state, over the period 1926–1940, was able to invest some US$400 million in industry and infrastructure, a very substantial sum for that era. Another

US$120 million was invested by the private sector. All this was done with very little foreign borrowing. The modest revenues from the sale of oil in those years were turned over to the military (Issawi 1978). Iran was neither populist nor revolutionary, but it was just as etatist as Turkey.

Reza Shah was sent into exile in 1941 by the Allies, who feared his collaboration with the Axis. His young son, Mohammed Reza Pahlavi, became the new shah. He did not consolidate his grip on power until his showdown in 1953 with the prime minister, Mohammed Mossadegh, a nationalist leader who brought under state ownership the British-controlled Anglo-Iranian Oil Company. After that time, Iran's economic strategy marched on three legs: petroleum exports, continued ISI, and a division of labor between the public and private sectors. State enterprise undertook the deepening process in iron and steel, copper, machine tools, aluminum, and petrochemicals, while a dynamic private sector, sometimes in joint ventures with foreign capital, moved into finished metals and special steels, synthetic fibers, paper, automobile assembly, and sugar. Iran in 1944 established a Plan and Budget Organization and launched its first national plan. In this respect it was well ahead of all countries in the region except Turkey.

This kind of division of labor was what one would have expected—it reconciled the regime's professed economic liberalism with a strong state presence in the economy. But in the 1970s a very significant shift in the division of labor occurred, one that contains lessons about the logic of public enterprise in the Middle East. With the first great surge in petroleum prices in 1973/1974, the shah's state had at its disposal a tremendous volume of rents. Neither the shah nor his advisers nor the state technocracy proposed investing these rents in private-sector growth. Rather, the new funds allowed the state to expand and consolidate in an atmosphere in which public authorities either disregarded or were actively hostile to the private sector (Razavi and Vakil 1984, 66; also Katouzian 1981, 237).

The dream of the Great Civilization had established a subjective development goal in the shah's mind. It was then necessary to refine the strategy of development. This was to be a big-push type of industrialization financed by oil revenues. Given that oil reserves were seen to have a twenty-year horizon and that the shah probably knew himself to be fatally ill, the speed with which the big push was to be implemented became very important in the shaping of expenditure patterns.[7]

Those expenditure patterns revealed a dramatic reorientation in the 1970s (see Table 7.3). In 1973 the shah prophesied that by 1980 there would be no more than 2 million people, or 300,000 farmers, left in Iran's agricultural sector (Katouzian 1981, 304). In essence, he had resurrected his father's blueprint: a powerful state and a powerful military establishment. By the end of the 1970s, government investment and consumption represented 43% of GNP. Military expenditures, which neared US$10 billion in 1978, were the equivalent of 10% of GNP. One-quarter of the nonagricultural workforce, 1.5 million people, were on the public payroll.

A few general propositions can be extracted from this example. First, regardless of the ideology of the regime, one of the major factors making for the expansion of the state's economic role is the *control* it offers the nation's leaders over resources and

TABLE 7.3   Public and Private Shares in Gross Fixed Capital Formation in Iran, 1963–1977

Gross Fixed Capital Formation	Third Development Plan 1963–1967	Fourth Development Plan 1968–1972	Fifth Development Plan 1973–1977
Public	74	146	734
Private	77	141	319

SOURCE: Razavi and Vakil (1984, 76)

people. It denies those resources and people to other contenders for power. In this sense it is doubtful that the shah ever wanted a powerful and autonomous private sector to develop in Iran. A prosperous, subordinate, parasitic private sector, yes; a true national bourgeoisie, no. When given his monopoly over Iran's external rents in the 1970s, the shah showed the real content of his liberalism.

Has the Islamic Republic of Iran reversed this pattern since 1979? The question is of more than passing interest, for Iran's Muslim state could be something of a harbinger for the rest of the region. The constitution of the Islamic republic is explicit on the role of the public sector, which is to include "all major industries, foreign trade, major mines, banking, insurance, power, dams, major irrigation systems, air, sea, land and rail road transport." Shortly after Khomeini's return to Iran, a wave of nationalizations took place in June and July 1979 involving 27 banks, insurance companies, and heavy industries, such as the Iran National Auto Works, with 12,000 workers, and the Behshahr Industrial Group, with 13,500. By the end of 1982 the National Industrial Organization controlled about 600 enterprises, with 150,000 employees. In addition, the Foundation for the Disinherited (Bonyad-e Mostaz'afin) was created to take over the assets of the Pahlavi family, the Pahlavi Foundation, and the expropriated property of the shah's entourage, including farms and apartment buildings (Bakhash 1984, 178–184).

There was, then, no rollback of the state under the Islamic republic, yet it is clear that the new regime was deeply divided on the issue of state ownership and intervention in the economy. The Guardianship Council, whose duty it is to monitor the constitutionality of legislation, in 1982 declared unconstitutional land-reform measures passed by the parliament, as well as the law giving the state a monopoly in foreign trade. At the same time, an important faction of radicals in the parliament sought to use the state to engineer a far-reaching redistribution of wealth in Iranian society. In early 1988 Khomeini's pronouncements showed that he was leaning in the direction of the more radical, statist elements. Since his death, and despite the emergence of the more pragmatic Hashemi Rafsanjani, followed by Muhammad Khatami, the same tension continues unresolved (see Chapter 9).

The Kingdom of Jordan.   The Jordanian economy is small and, since the Israeli occupation of the West Bank in 1967, severely truncated. It is dynamic and growing but highly dependent on external assistance. In 1976/1977, for example, when GNP stood at US$1.7 billion, external assistance exclusive of military aid stood at US$500 million.

The Jordanian state has controlled the economy in three ways. First, as the direct recipient of external assistance, it has been able to channel investment in the ways it sees fit. This channeling has taken the form of large-scale joint ventures with state, foreign, and local private capital in fertilizers, cement, petroleum refining, and so forth. State pension and social security funds, as well as the Housing Bank and the Industrial Development Bank, have been the conduits for substantial public finance. In 1980 the state had a significant equity stake in private firms in mining (42%), manufacturing (23%), tourism (27%), and transport (20%) and owned 90% of the shares of the Jordan Phosphate Mines Company, 100% of the Jordan Automatic Banking Company, and 99% of the Agricultural Products Manufacturing Company (Rivier 1980, 111, 206). The second lever in the hands of the state has been the phosphate sector, the country's single largest export and foreign-exchange earner. The third lever has been the defense budget, which stood at US$763 million in 1988, or 15% of GNP.

The Jordanian private sector, a large proportion of which is of Palestinian origin, has been given the lead in promoting exports of fruits, vegetables, and manufactured goods to Arab and regional markets. If it were not so internally divided between Palestinians and non-Palestinians, Jordan would have been a good candidate for an export-led growth pattern à la Hong Kong or Singapore. Its relatively well-educated and hardworking population and its no-nonsense political leadership might have been sufficient to attract foreign investment and technology. There is no way, however, given its small population and narrow resource base, that Jordan could have pursued an ISI strategy.

The Kingdom of Morocco.   Morocco and Iran up to 1979 followed similar development strategies. Morocco, like Iran, had a substantial trading bourgeoisie that was never totally eclipsed by French economic interests during the protectorate, 1912–1956. The country's economic ideology has always been liberal and pro–private sector. Yet, like the shah, King Hassan II may have been reluctant to see a national bourgeoisie with its own resource base gain an undisputed foothold in the economy. Finally, although Morocco is not an oil exporter, it has been the world's leading exporter of phosphates, and through the giant public holding company, the Cherifian Phosphates Office (OCP), it controls the most important sector of the economy.

The state's control of the economy has taken the form of direct ownership of assets (mines, railroads, dams, sugar refineries) and equity positions through public holding companies. The OCP and the Cherifian Foreign Trade Office (OCE) own assets themselves and have a controlling interest in a host of affiliated enterprises. The OCE, for example, between 1965 and 1975 helped launch twenty-five branch operations involved in citrus exports and wound up controlling about US$5 billion in assets. In addition, the state controls a number of special investment agencies such as the Caisse de Dépôt et de Gestion, which handles social security and pension funds, and the National Bank for Economic Development, which has been a favored channel for World Bank credits.

The post-1973 surge in world petroleum prices was followed closely by a large jump in world phosphate prices. The Moroccan state found itself in control of windfall rents and, just as had occurred in Iran, used them not to invest directly in the private sector but to expand the public sector. The 1973–1977 plan was revised in midcourse, with public investment targets rising from 11 billion to 29 billion dirhams (ca. US$6 billion), destined mainly for the steel, sugar, cement, and chemical sectors. The number of public-sector firms increased from 137 in 1970 to 238 in 1976 and state equity in them from 700 million to 2.2 billion dirhams (el-Midaoui 1981, 234–238; el-Malki 1982, 175). The share of the government and the public sector in total gross fixed capital formation reached 19% in 1977 (see Table 7.4). The Moroccan state employed well over 400,000 persons in the civil service and public sector. There were at least another 150,000 in the armed forces and police. At least one-quarter of the nonagricultural workforce was on the public payroll.

Since the big push in public-sector expansion in the mid-1970s, phosphate prices have tumbled, and Morocco's military involvement in the Saharan war cost the country on average US$300 million per year for a decade. The government by 1983 had been driven into large public deficits and a cumulative external debt of around US$10 billion. It was obliged to restrict its current expenditures and investment and to revert to its pre-1974 policy of stimulating the private sector and luring in foreign investment. Although the number of enterprises in which it had a majority stake increased, the share of the state in total equity of these companies declined.

TABLE 7.4   Sources of Gross Fixed Capital Formation in Morocco, 1968–1977

Gross Fixed Capital Formation	1968	1970	1972	1975	1977
In millions of current dirhams					
Government[a]	500	580	710	2,150	4,650
Public enterprises	950	1,050	950	3,400	4,530
Of which: transfers	(390)	(500)	(400)	(1,190)	(1,940)
Other sectors	740	1,360	1,520	3,310	6,170
Of which: housing	(250)	(440)	(580)	(1,130)	(2,180)
Total	2,190	2,990	3,180	8,860	15,350
In percentage of GDP					
Government[a]	3.1	3.0	3.1	5.6	9.6
Public enterprises	5.8	5.4	4.2	8.9	9.4
Of which: budget transfers	(4.2)	(2.6)	(1.7)	(3.1)	(4.0)
Other sectors	4.5	7.0	6.6	8.7	12.8
Of which: housing	(1.5)	(2.3)	(2.5)	(3.0)	(4.5)
Total	13.4	15.4	13.9	23.2	31.8

[a] Includes civilian investments only.
SOURCE: World Bank (1981, 25)

Princes and Kings of Oil

The most conservative regimes in the Middle East, the princedoms of the Gulf and the Kingdom of Saudi Arabia, are also those with the largest state sectors. They are conservative in the sense that they share nonrepublican forms of government, a concern for the protection of Islamic values, a fierce anticommunism throughout the cold war era, and dominant classes with roots in older maritime and transdesert trading communities.

Their economies were swamped by oil revenues. They combine small populations (Saudi Arabia is by far the biggest, with about 21 million inhabitants of local origin), little or no agriculture (with the exception of Saudi Arabia; see Chapter 6), no tradition of manufacturing, and a common resource, oil, that has generated tremendous rents. The share of the oil sector in the gross national products of these countries reached the following levels in 1980: Saudi Arabia, 66%; Kuwait, 51%; the UAE, 65%; Oman, 69% (World Bank data). Kuwait's lower figure merely signals that its rents had diversified and that the country had begun to draw significant revenues from its foreign investments.

With this kind of financial clout at the disposal of the state, it was inevitable that all new investment programs would fall within the state sphere. For most of the princedoms, industrialization will never be a realistic option except in the petrochemical field, where public enterprises have formed joint ventures with foreign multinational corporations (Kubursi 1984). Private-sector activity is booming and occasionally crashing, as in the Kuwaiti stock market (known as Suq al-Manakh) scandal of August 1982 (Beblawi 1984, 232–234). But such activity is confined to trading and speculative investment, while the public sector dominates the productive sectors and, of course, the civil service.

The civil administration grew prodigiously in all these countries. Kuwait's expanded from 22,000 in 1963 to 146,000, of whom 90,000 were foreigners, in 1980. Saudi Arabia's grew from 37,000 in 1962 to 232,000 in 1981, to which we should add another 81,000 part-time or nonclassified employees (Ayubi 1985; see also Islami and Kavoussi 1984; Chatelus 1982, 23). The entire native Saudi workforce in 1980 totaled 1.5 million, and there were 800,000 foreign workers in the country.[8] Ayubi saw this expansion as a function of increased educational output unaccompanied by significant industrialization. Public employment serves the purpose of political control of the educated. It also serves as window dressing: "a respectable and modern looking tool for distributing part of the oil 'loot' and for 'disbursing' largesse camouflaged in the language of 'meritocracy and national objectives'" (Ayubi 1985).

Saudi Arabia has gone farther and established a giant public-enterprise sector, with more than forty corporations in housing, storage, agriculture, and basic industries. In the plan period 1976–1980 alone, Saudi Arabia disbursed US$290 billion, which went into infrastructure, port development, and new industrial cities at Jubail and Yanbu. The 1980–1985 development plan, although less spectacularly funded, was designed to put Saudi Arabia on an industrial footing. The oil minister at the time, Ahmad Zaki Yamani, prophesied that Saudi Arabia would soon rank alongside

Argentina, Brazil, and South Korea as a semi-industrialized country (*Middle East Journal,* March 1984, 25–27). Whereas the goal was to shift some of the burden of industrialization onto the private sector, the industrialization that did take place mainly involved public-sector joint ventures with foreign capital.

Israel and Post-Atatürk Turkey

Israel, for obvious political, social, and religious reasons, is a case apart, but in the structure of its economy, the weight of the state, and some of its ideological predispositions, it has shared many features with the socialist states of the Arab world and with Turkey. This sharing is all the more striking in that before there was any Israeli state at all, the Zionist community in Palestine had well-organized party and union structures and cohesive farmer-soldier communities in the *kibbutzim.* That a powerful and somewhat autonomous state grew out of such a highly structured civil society says much about the logic and attractiveness of the interventionist state.

It was David Ben Gurion, the first Israeli prime minister, who developed the doctrine of etatism (in Hebrew, *mamlachtiut*) and subordinated to the state his own socialist labor party, the MAPAI, and its powerful trade union affiliate, the Histadrut. The Histadrut included in its membership about 70% of Jewish wage earners in Palestine. In addition, the new Israeli state asserted its control over the Zionist defense force, the Haganah, which had fought successfully to achieve and then defend Israeli independence.

What Ben Gurion did in absorbing the labor movement into the state sector, robbing the *kibbutzim* of their most dynamic leaders, and putting the MAPAI and the Israeli Defense Forces under state control is not unlike the process undertaken by another charismatic civilian, Habib Bourguiba, in Tunisia after 1956. As Ben-Dor (1983, 109) pointed out, "there was an overwhelming paradox in a man trying to use his party as a base of power from which to destroy the party-state linkage."

There were, however, a number of factors that made Israel's experiment in state building unique. First, there was the "acquisition" by the state of all the property previously owned by Arab Palestinians who had left their homes during the hostilities of 1948 (cf. Turkey in 1923 and Algeria in 1962). Second, the Jewish immigrant population of Israel doubled between 1948 and 1952, most of the newcomers were "Oriental," and the state had to undertake their economic, cultural, and social integration into what had been a predominantly Ashkenazi society. Third, Israel, like Jordan, has always been dependent on external assistance and financial flows, and it is the state that controls their disbursement. Between 1950 and 1974, for example, such assistance totaled US$19.5 billion. Finally, the state runs Israel's military-industrial complex. Defense outlays were the equivalent of 17% of GNP in 1972 and 30% in 1979, probably the highest proportion in the world at that time (in general, see Rosenfeld and Carmi 1976; Arian 1985; and Kimmerling 1983).

What had emerged in Israel by the late 1960s was a large, paternalistic welfare state with vaguely socialist objectives and extensive public ownership. In this system, "the citizen would be perceived as an object available for the activities of the state and its bureaucracy, this latter serving as [a] paternalistic body deciding what was good for the citizens and for the collectivity as a whole. By definition, the reasoning of the authorities was better than and took precedence over the individuals and groups" (Kimmerling 1983, 99).

The Israeli variant of statism was given practical effect by state-owned or state-controlled enterprise. Histadrut in the 1970s had 1.5 million members, or 80% of the employed workforce. It in turn had controlling interests in several corporations: Solel Boneh in construction; the Koor holding company, with 250 industrial, financial, and commercial firms under its control (Koor was one of the Fortune 500); Bank Hapoalim; and others. There were 200 corporations in Israel in which the government had at least 50% equity. In addition there were some 450,000 persons on the public payroll, including the professional military, teachers, and municipal employees. Arian (1985, 36) estimated that in the late 1970s about 52% of the Israeli workforce was employed by the state and Histadrut, with the remaining 48% in the private sector.

The Israeli economy paid a heavy and familiar price for *mamlachtiut*. Huge government deficits resulting from indexing wages to the cost of living, heavy defense expenditures, and various forms of subsidies produced triple-digit inflation in the mid-1980s. Despite flows of concessional aid and grants, Israel's external debt had risen to US$12.5 billion in 1980, or 62% of GNP, the highest ratio in the Middle East. After the Labor Alliance lost power to the Likud in 1976, there were important modifications in the Ben Gurion formula, and some efforts at containing government expenditures and promoting exports through devaluation were undertaken. In 1986 Israel implemented a determined inflation-reduction program, cutting government expenditures, temporarily freezing prices and wages, and increasing tax receipts.

Since Atatürk's death in 1938, Turkish development strategy has oscillated in intent, but the weight of the public sector has remained predominant. In the decade of the 1950s—the first ten years of two-party democracy—the Democrat party, led by Adnan Menderes and Celal Bayar, rejected etatism in favor of a liberal economic policy to benefit commercial farmers and the industrial bourgeoisie. Nonetheless during the 1950s eleven new state-owned enterprises were started, the initial objective of selling off some public enterprises was abandoned, and the share of public in total investment rose from 38% in 1952 to 62% in 1959 (Roos and Roos 1971, 43).

The brief military takeover in 1960 ushered in another period of national planning and state-led ISI. This thrust was modified in the Second Five-Year Plan, 1968–1972, to put a greater burden of investment on private industry. Subsequently, the RPP government under Bülent Ecevit, with the Third Five-Year Plan, 1973–1977, resurrected the statist strategy, giving new authority to the State Planning Organization and stressing intermediate and capital goods industries (Walstedt 1980, 85–87; Hale 1981, 198–200).

At the end of the 1970s, the state sector remained the economy's center of gravity. The public share in total investment had stayed fairly constant for twenty years (see Table 7.5), while public investment in the manufacturing sector had risen from 34% in 1965 to 65% in 1980 (World Bank 1982, 218). Employment in state-owned

TABLE 7.5   Public and Private Shares in Investment in Turkey, by Plan Periods, 1963–1987

Investment	1963–1967	1968–1972	1973–1977	1979–1983	1984–1987
Public	48.0	44.0	46.4	46.1	56.2
Private	52.0	56.0	53.6	53.9	43.8

SOURCES: Celasun (1983, p. 103); TÜSIAD (1988, p. 9)

enterprises had grown from 362,000 in 1970 to 646,000 in 1980, or the equivalent of 16% of the nonagricultural workforce. In the manufacturing sector alone, state-owned enterprises accounted for 32% of value added, 36% of employment, and 43% of investment.

STATE CAPITALISM, THE STATE BOURGEOISIE, AND THE PROCESS OF ACCUMULATION

There is remarkable consensus among observers of widely differing political view-points that the interventionist state in the Middle East (and elsewhere) gave rise to a state bourgeoisie that controls but does not own the major means of production and to a process of accumulation that is called state capitalism.[9]

As Fitzgerald has pointed out (1977, 70, 87) for Latin America, there are two fundamental types of state intervention and capitalist accumulation. Both aim at structural transformation of the economy. They are not mutually exclusive and, as the Turkish case has shown, may oscillate over time. The first is a process whereby the state helps nurture or strengthen a private sector. It does so, as noted in the preceding pages, in several ways. It provides roads, railroads, ports, and electrical power to stimulate economic activity in general. Through its basic industries and mines it provides raw materials (coal, oil) and semimanufactured goods (iron, aluminum, chemicals, synthetic fibers) that feed directly into private production. It provides cheap credit and protective legislation. It may take over failing private enterprises. In this process of accumulation, the state transfers surpluses on its own operations, profits if any, and external rents to the private sector and tries to absorb all major risks for that sector.

This has been the predominant process of accumulation in the Middle East, although it is important to remember that it is frequently interrupted and that within the state sector itself there are always powerful lobbies that decry the handmaiden role. It is worth repeating that the state, when it gains access to an increased volume of external rents, uses those rents to expand its own activities with little regard to the private sector, as did Iran and Morocco after 1973/1974, and Tunisia after its oil revenues shot up in 1977. Structural crises may also provoke episodes in which the state sector mobilizes resources by and for itself, as did Egypt and Syria in the 1960s. By and large, however, we see the handmaiden process at work in Turkey since 1950, in Egypt since 1974, in Tunisia since 1969, in Morocco since 1956, in Iran since 1963, and in the Sudan since 1972. Israel also fits somewhat awkwardly into this schema. Leftist critics of the Ba'athi experiments in Syria and Iraq are wont to attribute the same role to state intervention in their economies (e.g., al-Khafaji 1983; Longuenesse 1979), but our view is that in both countries there were and are dominant coalitions committed to state power and, to some extent, to a socialist vision of society such that the private sector is encouraged only insofar as it remains subordinate to the state, the party, and the plan.

The second process of accumulation is one in which the state undertakes all the resource mobilization and infrastructure development functions mentioned above but captures the surplus of its own activities, of a substantial portion of private-sector profits, and of external rents in order to finance its own expansion. Its goal is to dominate all aspects of resource allocation and to seize, once and for all, the commanding heights of the economy. When this process is under way, the slogans of "socialist transformation" or the "noncapitalist path" have generally been used to describe it.

Turkey in the 1930s flirted with this strategy. Egypt explicitly adopted it with the Socialist Decrees of 1961 and then gradually dropped it after 1974. Algeria has described itself in those terms since 1962, although after Boumedienne's death in 1978 the regime became more attentive to private-sector interests. Tunisia between 1964 and 1969 adopted and then abandoned the strategy. Whatever the critics may say, Syria has adhered to it since 1963, as did Iraq until 2003. Finally, it may be that Libya, since 1975, has gone further than any country in the region outside the Marxist regime in the former PDRY in strangling the private sector.

The term "state capitalism" calls attention to a basic dynamic in both processes: State enterprise, whether in the service of the private sector or of itself, may not involve any major revision of the relations of workers and managers to the means of production. The simple fact of public ownership does not mean that the profit motive disappears or that the workers gain control of the surplus value of their own labor. "Exploitation," the counterpart of the drive for financial profit, does not disappear. Again, critics on the left are especially inclined to see the state technocracy substituting itself for the private sector without any fundamental change in the relations of production. It is true that no regime has rejected financial efficiency and the generation of a surplus as legitimate criteria, among others, for measuring public-sector performance. There may be "exploitation" in the process in the form of surplus transfers from agricultural populations to the service and industrial sectors. The fact, however, that public-sector enterprises generally operate at a loss, display low levels of managerial performance, and carry more workers than they need must give us pause in labeling them "state capitalism."

We approach the concept of a state bourgeoisie with the same caution. There is a compelling logic to the *assumption* of a dominant state class. After all, much of this chapter has inventoried the size and strategic importance of the assets owned by the state. They do constitute the major means of production, except in the agrarian sector, where the state nonetheless has the means to orient production. It stands to reason that the professional managers of public assets could develop the attributes of a class, standing as they do in a similar position in relation to the means of production and sharing a common set of interests and goals, that is, class consciousness. The existence of such a class is all the more plausible in that conventional class actors are weak or in decline. The old landowning classes have long since been destroyed by land reform, while an industrial bourgeoisie has yet to emerge. The managers of public assets might be expected to fill this class vacuum, but the fact is that there is little evidence that they have ever done so.

This judgment is based upon an observable paradox in the identity of the state bourgeoisie. It cannot really ensure its own incumbency or its reproduction as a state class. A dominant capitalist bourgeoisie will, in the Marxist view, perpetuate its control of the means of production and pass that control on to its offspring through the juridical device of private property until the final showdown with the proletariat. But members of the state bourgeoisie have no legal title to their offices; they cannot transfer them, and the higher they are in the state hierarchy, the less likely it is that they will hold their own positions for very long. The fate of economic "czars" in the region is illustrative: Aziz Sidqi, the driving force behind Egypt's industrialization in the 1960s, disappeared from the scene in the 1970s; Algeria's minister of industry, Abdesslam Belaid, met the same fate after 1980, although he reappeared briefly after 1991. Toward the end of his regime, the shah of Iran put under house arrest some of his longtime advisers such as Prime Minister Amir Abbas Hoveida. Bourguiba tried his own acolyte, Ahmed Ben Salah, for treason.

The survival of the members of this class is dependent upon three factors: (1) their ability to move from position to position within the state hierarchy, (2) their technical competency, making them marketable in *any* milieu, and (3) their ability to build nest eggs (farms, businesses, investments, foreign bank accounts) outside the state sector. Seen in this light, the state bourgeoisie is a strange class indeed. Property is not the source of its power; it has no juridical claim to the positions that are the source of its power; and it cannot and may not even want to reproduce itself as a state class (Waterbury 1991).

At any point we can see it as a class merely by identifying those who are in formal positions of power and the resources they control. Thus Walstedt saw that in Turkey "a self-perpetuating power group was born, linking bureaucrats, labor unions, and local politicians, that was far more powerful than any private capitalist power blocks operating in Turkey" (1980, 187). Waterbury saw 200,000–300,000 members of the state bourgeoisie in Egypt (1983, 260). But where are it and its offspring going? Perhaps into a private sector that it has helped to foster? to other sectors within the state? out of the country altogether? Or, finally, perhaps back and forth across a public-private divide that for years has had little operational and, in states such as Kuwait or Saudi Arabia, very little juridical meaning?

When social scientists do not know what is happening, they invoke "transitional phases." We can do no less. Powerful interventionist states with large public sectors and the groups that dominate them grew out of, on the one hand, the need to promote the structural transformation of their "backward" economies and, on the other, a kind of class vacuum in which a temporarily dominant class emerged on the strength of its education and competency rather than its property. The process of state intervention has contributed directly to the demise of some classes (large landowners, traditional trading bourgeoisies, craftspeople) and promoted others (capitalist farmers, bureaucratic middle classes, a small-scale manufacturing bourgeoisie). The process of intervention has also resulted in deep-seated crisis in the state sector itself and in the economy in general, calling into question the feasibility of continued intervention on the same scale as in the past. We are witnessing in several Middle Eastern societies a cautious retreat of the state and hence a gradual weakening of the state bourgeoisie. In some instances this is best seen as an effort to rationalize state intervention and to make it more efficient. Algeria is a case in point. In others, such as Turkey, an assertive private entrepreneurial sector is ready to take over from the state the role of leading the development process. Falling in between are countries like Egypt and Tunisia, where economic liberalization measures have been introduced in the absence of strong, self-assured private sectors (see Chapter 9). In the mid-2000s, after twenty to twenty-five years of reform and adjustment in several economies, it is still hard to know if we are at the dawning of a new era in which the state will confine itself to regulating market economies or merely in a period of stocktaking and statist regrouping (see Chapter 9).

Whatever the answer, what has changed—and changed dramatically—over the past forty years is the confidence that leaders and led once placed in the efficacy of state intervention. That confidence is largely gone, and the positive legitimacy granted state intervention has been replaced by a kind of resignation born of habit and the lack of alternative agents of change.

NOTES

1. In this regard, the US Coalition Provisional Authority, which governed Iraq for two years, was no different: Use state power to reshape society and its institutions.

2. It is important to remember that for many Muslims Atatürk is probably the most despised leader of the twentieth century precisely because he abolished the caliphate and tried to subjugate the Islamic establishment in Turkey.

3. Atatürk died in November 1938. İnönü became president, and Bayar resigned as prime minister. The latter returned to prominence after 1950 when Turkey's first open elections brought the Democrat party, of which Bayar was a founder, to power.

4. A number of advanced industrial nations, especially Austria, Italy, France, and the United Kingdom, revealed similar proportions in the 1980s.

5. The strategy owed a great deal to the French economist G. Destanne de Bernis (1971).

6. Recall again that we are using "liberal" in an exclusively economic context in this chapter. While far from the worst offenders, no monarchy in the region could be described as "liberal" in the conventional political sense, referring to human rights or the role of civil society.

7. As noted earlier, the fear that time was running out impelled Bourguiba to delegate broad powers to Ahmed Ben Salah in Tunisia's version of the big push.

8. By 2006, foreign workers numbered approximately 5.5 million (CIA, World Factbook, 2006).

9. On the state bourgeoisie, see, for example, Amin (1980, 8), Batatu (1979, 110), DERSA (1981, 263–283), Hannoyer and Seurat (1979, 127–133), Hussein (1971, 137–186), al-Khafaji (1983, 39–44), Longuenesse (1979, 9), el-Malki (1982, 163), Nellis (1980, 417), Raffinot and Jacquemot (1977, 99), Trimberger (1978, 119), Walstedt (1980, 187), Waterbury (1983, 232–262; 1991).

8

CONTRADICTIONS
OF STATE-LED GROWTH

It is now widely acknowledged that both state intervention in the economy and the public-enterprise sectors have, by and large, malfunctioned financially and economically. Other than in petroleum and banking, public enterprises have failed to generate profits and constitute a net drain on state resources; to remain afloat they have required subsidized credit and inputs, foreign exchange at preferential rates, and constant flows of working capital and new investment. At the same time, public enterprises have not solved many of the social and economic problems they were designed to address.

In many respects, state-led growth achieved a great deal. Both absolute and per capita national output grew at respectable rates in most countries of the region even before the massive infusion of oil rents during the 1970s and early 1980s. Structural transformation, whether measured by the share of industry in output or by employment, also proceeded at rates that were not unfavorable in international comparative perspective (see Chapter 3). This performance was no mean achievement considering the rapidity of population growth, the heavy burden of defense expenditures, the limited natural resource base apart from oil, the initially low levels of literacy, and the perennial political instability of the region.

However, industry was seldom internationally competitive; because of both price and technical inefficiencies, many "infant industries" never grew up. Overvalued exchange rates and domestic-price distortions led to serious misallocations, some of which we documented earlier for agriculture and industry. Too often, the wrong price signals led state managers and private economic actors to produce the wrong things with the wrong combination of inputs. Heavy industry grew rapidly, while agriculture and light industry were relatively neglected. International comparative advantage was often ignored. For example, in two of the leading industrial nations, Egypt and Turkey, much investment took place in industries in which profitability was actually negative if international prices were used for the calculation.

Furthermore, the multiple goals of state-owned enterprises (supplying cheap inputs to other industries, providing jobs for the rapidly expanding labor force) often gave the managers of these industries little incentive to minimize costs, even with a given technology. Capacity utilization was often poor (for example, the Algerian steel plant at El Hadjar operated at only 40% of capacity in the early 1980s [Nelson 1985, 208]), leading to higher unit costs, which had to be either subsidized from the state budget or passed on in the form of higher costs to other industries. Usually the former approach was adopted.

Allocative and "X" inefficiencies[1] were not the only problems with the state-led growth strategy. The stress on heavy industry and import substitution failed to create sufficient jobs for the rapidly expanding workforce (see Chapter 5), and as we have seen in Chapter 6, the relative neglect of agriculture until the late 1970s contributed to the widening food gap. Finally, many countries continued to rely on external sources of investment capital and to accumulate large external debts. The goals of both social justice and national economic independence proved elusive.

Many countries of the region tried to invest more resources than were saved domestically. The "resource gap" (gross domestic investment [GDI] minus gross domestic savings [GDS]) was large and in percentage terms considerably larger than that for other LDCs (see Table 8.1). There was, and is, great variability in this indicator across countries and over time. Unsurprisingly, during the oil boom the oil-exporting countries typically saved more than they invested. Indeed, this phenomenon led to the creation by the World Bank of a new category of developing country, "capital-surplus oil exporters," composed, prior to the collapse of oil prices in the mid-1980s, of Saudi Arabia, Libya, Kuwait, and the UAE. Other oil exporters, principally Iran, Iraq, and Algeria, had adequate national savings to meet investment.[2] Another group of countries (Sudan, Morocco, Tunisia, Egypt, Syria, Turkey, and Israel) had resource gaps in 1985 ranging from 2 to 11% of GDP. Two other countries (the former YAR and Jordan) had massive gaps, 36% and 34% of GDP, respectively. Mainly because of heavy debt repayments, domestic savings exceeded domestic investment in all middle-income countries from 1980 to 1985.[3] In comparison with this reference group, MENA countries had very large resource gaps, filled for the most part with continued foreign borrowing and with aid from the United States, the EEC (the precursor of the EU), and the capital-surplus oil exporters of the Gulf.

There were several reasons for this resource gap, but the inefficiencies of the state-owned enterprises certainly contributed to it. For example, the "budgetary burden," or net deficit, created by these enterprises was 4% of GDP in 1978–1981 in Tunisia and 3.5% in Turkey in 1978–1980 (Floyd 1984). These deficits contributed to high rates of inflation, which, in turn, led to overvalued real exchange rates and therefore to uncompetitive exports and domestic-price distortions. The failure to develop internationally competitive industrial (and agricultural) exports, combined with rapidly expanding domestic incomes and demand, exacerbated the deficit of the balance of trade. The public sector, originally created in part to generate foreign exchange, too often simply absorbed it.

The failure of state-led growth to close the twin gaps between domestic savings and investment and between exports and imports contributed to the accumulation of large foreign debts (see Table 8.2). In most cases, there was a marked increase in

TABLE 8.1　MENA Resource Gaps, 1975, 1985, 1995, 2003

	Gross Fixed Capital Formation (% of GDP)				Gross Domestic Savings (% of GDP)				Resource Gap (% of GDP)			
	1975	1985	1995	2003	1975	1985	1995	2003	1975	1985	1995	2003
Algeria	39	32	29	24	36	31	28	45	-3	-1	-1	21
Bahrain	–	34	17	20	–	48	26	39	–	14	9	19
Egypt	25	25	16	16	12	15	12	14	-12	-11	-4	-2
Iran	28	17	21	29	34	21	21	43	6	3	0	15
Israel	29	19	25	18	-3	6	12	11	-33	-13	-13	-6
Jordan	–	19	30	21	–	-15	8	-2	–	-34	-21	-22
Kuwait	12	20	14	9	67	30	25	25	55	10	12	16
Lebanon	–	–	36	20	–	–	-18	0	–	–	-54	-20
Libya	28	–	12	–	41	–	19	–	13	–	7	–
Morocco	25	23	21	24	15	16	14	20	-10	-7	-7	-4
Oman	36	–	15	16	52	40	23	35	17	–	8	18
Saudi Arabia	17	22	19	18	69	15	29	42	51	-7	10	23
Sudan	–	11	–	18	10	3	–	14	–	-7	–	-4
Syria	27	26	27	23	14	13	20	26	-13	-13	-7	3
Tunisia	26	28	24	23	26	24	21	21	0	-4	-4	-2
Turkey	15	15	24	15	11	13	21	19	-4	-2	-3	4
UAE	31	25	28	22	76	53	36	37	45	28	7	15
WBG	–	–	35	3	–	–	-8	-37	–	–	-43	-39
Yemen	–	–	21	16	–	–	15	12	–	–	-6	-4
LDC average												
Low & middle income	24	22	24	23	23	25	25	26	-1	3	1	3
Middle income	25	22	24	23	25	26	26	27	0	4	2	4
Upper middle income	24	20	20	18	24	25	23	23	0	5	3	5

Resource Gap equals gross domestic savings minus gross fixed capital formulation.
SOURCE: World Development Indicators, Online

external indebtedness and a rise in the debt-service ratio (debt repayment as a percentage of export revenue). Although these debts were not nearly so large in absolute terms as those of Latin American debtors like Brazil (about US$125 billion) or Mexico (about US$100 billion), they were large enough to narrow the options for policymakers and to increase the influence of international lending agencies in the policy process.

Finally, just as the goals of efficiency, growth, and national independence were only partially achieved, the ideal of increasing equity also proved elusive. The employment problem clearly was not solved, and the gap between rich and poor often either widened or remained roughly constant. It appeared to many observers that those equity gains that were achieved had a high efficiency cost, as in expensive consumer-subsidy programs or in the swelling ranks of redundant public-sector employees. And as we have seen, the education and health systems seldom promoted a real equalization of human capital in the region.

Despite high levels of redundant labor in state-owned enterprises, disguised and open unemployment remains a serious problem in most Middle Eastern societies (see Chapter 5). Some redistribution of wealth has taken place through public-sector employment drives and the location of state-owned enterprises in underdeveloped areas, but the distribution of income in most Middle Eastern countries remains highly skewed (see Chapter 10). The state-owned enterprises have not—again, except for the petroleum sector—contributed to exports, while their import needs and hence claims on foreign exchange have remained high. Finally, although the prominence of agriculture in economic activity has diminished, it has been the service sector more than industry that has picked up the slack. It is not at all clear

TABLE 8.2 Total External Debt, 1994 and 2004

	External Debt (DOD, current US$millions)	
	1994	2004
Algeria	26,267	21,987
Egypt	30,675	30,292
Iran	23,502	13,622
Jordan	7,645	8,175
Lebanon	1,347	22,177
Morocco	22,100	17,672
Oman	2,657	3,872
Sudan	15,837	19,332
Syria	20,178	21,521
Tunisia	8,693	18,700
Turkey	68,605	161,595
Yemen	5,923	5,488

SOURCE: World Development Indicators 2006

that centralized planning and state enterprise have accelerated the process of structural transformation.

Despite this generally acknowledged situation and the need for reform, little has been done in the past twenty-five years. There have been efforts to stimulate the private sector, and there has been talk of "privatization," that is, selling equity in state-owned enterprises to private investors. By and large, however, the economic weight of public enterprise in the Middle East has been little diminished.

THE CONTINUED DOMINANCE OF
PUBLIC-SECTOR ENTERPRISE

State enterprise has arisen within two broad developmental frameworks. The first is an explicitly socialist and redistributive one in which equity issues take precedence over profit-and-loss criteria in assessing state activities. When reform is first called for in such systems, it is in terms of making the public sector more efficient, reducing the deficits of specific enterprises, increasing monetary incentives for workers, allowing price increases, linking budgetary support and banking credit to performance, and perhaps even reducing the personnel list. The shift here is toward state capitalism. That shift began in Egypt in 1965, when Nasser first denounced the inefficient performance of the public sector, and in Algeria sometime between 1967 and 1969. Discipline, productivity, and profitability become the watchwords of the new era, but frequently they remain slogans more than effective guides to improved performance.

The second framework is represented by the state-capitalist experiments, in which socialism is never at issue and profitability, at least in theory, always takes precedence over redistribution. Even by these criteria, however, the performance of state-owned enterprises in nonsocialist countries such as Turkey, Iran, Morocco, and Saudi Arabia has been lackluster. When the issue of reform is raised in these countries, the main elements of the proposal are to use more public resources to stimulate private-sector activity directly and to privatize public-sector assets.

In neither framework have many steps been taken toward reform and privatization. After thirty or more years of strong state intervention in the economy, powerful bureaucratic, managerial, and political interests stand in the way of any diminution of state economic activities.

It is not always possible to discern which groups, organizations, or class interests carry the most weight in promoting or defending the state's role in the economy. Organized labor is generally a staunch supporter because of relatively high wage levels and benefit packages and, above all, because of job stability and relatively light workloads. In many ways unions in the public sector constitute a labor aristocracy (for example, the unemployed in many Middle Eastern countries outnumber those in the public-sector labor force by two to one [see Chapter 5]) and defend their privileges in the name of socialism and the toiling masses. When regimes begin to promote state capitalism, the unions find themselves in a difficult position. They sense that the public sector is under fire and seek to defend it against its critics. Yet they do not want to pay the price of greater efficiency, which entails higher productivity: more output per hour of work for the same pay. They may resist the introduction of incentive systems that reward individual or group performance and insist that pay and promotion be based on nondiscriminatory and "nonexploitative" seniority systems. In other words, they may try to sap the very logic of the state-capitalist thrust. Union leaders generally know that this is a dangerous game; if public-sector performance does not improve, its critics will inevitably call for disinvestment and privatization, an even worse outcome for the unions than state capitalism.

The managers of public assets are likely to resist efforts at reform. Frequently they have formed alliances of convenience with labor that have led to low productivity and high enterprise deficits. Managers may well prefer periodic bailouts from the state to the harder option of exacting higher levels of performance from the workers and from themselves. They have generally been drawn to the public sector by its salaries and "perks," which are better than those found in the civil service and even in parts of the private sector. Although in the 1970s, when rates of inflation were high throughout the area, these salary advantages eroded, it is still the case that the work is less demanding and jobs and promotion are more secure than in the private sector. Individual managers may have good prospects for shifts into the private sector, but most public-sector managers will prefer the quasi-sinecures they have. The opportunities for side payments and moonlighting compensate for deteriorating salary levels.

Some segments of the civil service will also have a strong interest in the perpetuation of large public sectors. Whereas the autonomy of individual enterprises varies from country to country, in all instances government ministries directly oversee their activities. They draw up and supervise sectoral and enterprise budgets, review contracts, help design projects, and control personnel procedures. Thus, in the ministries of industry, agriculture, and defense, where the bulk of state enterprise is concentrated, extensive bureaucracies have developed to monitor them. The ministry of planning may plan public-sector activity, while the ministry of finance controls enterprise budgets, credit flows, and rates of corporate taxation (see, inter alia, Roos and Roos 1971, 64). Auditing agencies check the books of hundreds of public-sector firms. Any reduction in the size of the public sector could lead to a reduction in the ranks of supervisory personnel. Civil servants may therefore resist recommendations for greater operational autonomy of state enterprises in the context of state capitalism and recommendations to sell off parts of the public sector.

For some twenty years up to the early 1980s, the external donor community showed some predilection for public enterprise and direct state intervention in the economy. The degree of that predilection was not at all uniform. For example, the US Agency for International Development (USAID) has never been a strong supporter of public enterprise, although there was a time when the US government saw the Tennessee Valley Authority as a model for regional uplift that could be exported to the developing world. The attractiveness of public-sector enterprise to other donors lay in the possibility, so it seemed, of bypassing cumbersome entrenched bureaucratic agencies in order to promote specific projects (e.g., fertilizer industries) or programs (e.g., diffusion of new varieties of wheat). For bilateral donors there was also the attraction that large public-sector enterprises could become important purchasers of equipment and technology from the donor's home economy. The point is that although the donors, since the advent of Margaret Thatcher in the United Kingdom and Ronald Reagan in the United States, have become the major proponents of public-sector reform and privatization, not so long ago they supported public-sector expansion.

Parts of the private sector frequently find it in their interest to have a large public sector alongside them. Large public enterprises in basic metals, plastics and petrochemicals, and other semimanufactures such as cotton yarn may support private-sector manufacturers with a regular and cheap supply of inputs—Turkey, Algeria, and Iraq are all notable in this respect. Likewise, the public sector may prove a reliable and not very cost-conscious purchaser of private-sector goods, from automobile components to army uniforms. Several observers have concluded that the stirrings and growth of the private sector in several Middle Eastern countries, notably Turkey and Egypt, are an assertion of class interests and that they are the principal force behind the gradual abandonment of state regulation of the economy. Private interests, sustained over decades by state contracts and protection, are alleged to be sufficiently powerful to force the state into retreat or at least to put it more directly at the service of the private sector. Doubtless, some private interests will benefit from the process of liberalization that we summarize under the rubric "economic reform." We do not believe, however, that private class interests caused such policies. Moreover, it is not clear that most private interests would have a stake in the reform of the public sector. They can have the best of both worlds through an inefficient public sector that continues to feed business to the private sector, and by comparison, makes private enterprise performance look good (see Chapter 9).

The public sector and the civil service together have been an important source of state revenues and savings that will not easily be abandoned or allowed to run down. State employees represent a captive source of income tax and social security payments. Taxes and payments are simply deducted from salary and wage payments; evasion is virtually impossible. Income tax and even social security payments outside the public sector are very difficult to collect and generally represent a tiny proportion of total government revenues. For example, in 1980, 60% of Egypt's total wage bill was paid out to civil servants and public-sector employees. Social security payments represented 10% of all government revenues, income tax on salaries of government personnel another 5%, and profits tax on public-sector enterprise, returns on public assets, and public-sector self-financing another 40%. Indirect taxes (sales tax, stamp duties) and tariffs and customs, a substantial proportion of them levied on goods produced in or imported by the public sector and the government, accounted for another quarter of total revenues. External assistance represented 13% of total revenues. The remaining 7% came from corporate and income tax revenues from the nongovernmental sector and the proceeds on bond sales (Waterbury 1983, 202). The state sector in Egypt, taken in its broadest sense, was the source of most state revenues and by the mid-1990s the locus of a captive workforce of over 4 million.

It may well be that public sectors and big government tend to conserve their pre-dominance in Middle Eastern economies, seemingly regardless of the ideologies of individual regimes, because of the extraordinary power they offer political leader-ship to preempt resources from actors outside the state system, to finance state ac-tivities, and to control strategic sectors of the workforce. It does not surprise us to see leaders of self-proclaimed socialist regimes defending their public sectors, but at first blush it seems odd to see large public sectors in nominally liberal or liberalizing economic systems such as those of Egypt, Jordan, or Tunisia. However, the eco-nomic risks of inefficient public enterprise may not outweigh the political risks of giving up the leverage over resources and people that public enterprise provides.

It is the political calculus of these two kinds of costs that determines the manner in which political elites respond to the poor performance and fiscal burdens charac-teristic of public-sector enterprise. To some extent equity (in the form of redundant labor, relatively high remuneration, and low productivity) and inefficiency have been combined and paid for through deficit financing and borrowing abroad. When foreign creditors refuse to advance new lines of credit until the fiscal mess is cleared up, a painful day of reckoning can no longer be postponed.

The timing, pace, and content of reform efforts in the MENA region have varied widely across countries (see Chapter 9). Common elements with major political consequences are the efforts to restrain public expenditures, to hold in check if not reduce the size of the public-enterprise sector, to stimulate private enterprise and in-vestment, and to remove subsidies on consumer goods, agricultural and industrial inputs, and credit. In addition, there have been efforts to liberalize foreign trade, to reduce the tariff protection of domestic producers, and to stimulate the export sec-tors of the economy. Each of these moves produces winners and losers. Combining them in the reform effort will send shock waves through well-established coalitions of economic interests and beneficiaries of the status quo.

THE POLITICAL ECONOMY OF "STRUCTURAL ADJUSTMENT"

Failures arising from mismanaged ISI and public enterprise have been experienced across all the countries in the region. They were doubtless exacerbated in countries with no or very limited petroleum reserves by the increase in world petroleum prices in the 1970s. Growing import bills coupled with stagnant exports led to bur-geoning trade deficits that had to be financed by foreign borrowing, both commer-cial and multilateral. The reaction of most Middle Eastern countries to inflation in their import bill for petroleum and nonpetroleum products was to promote the ex-pansion of their economies, perhaps with the long-range hope that such expansion would lead to increased exports.

Turkey, for example, found itself in one of the region's gravest economic crises in the late 1970s. It was governed at the time by fragile and changing political coali-tions, dominated by the Republican People's party (led by Bülent Ecevit) and the Justice party (led by Süleyman Demirel). Neither of these protagonists could afford to promote economic austerity for fear of alienating a significant part of the electorate. The result, in the words of Celasun (1983, 11), was that despite the oil crisis and related external shocks, Turkey attempted to preserve its growth momentum under the Third Five-Year Plan (1973–1977) through rapid reserve decumulation and massive external borrowing. Instead of relying upon internal adjustment to promote balance-of-payments improvement, the various coalition governments pursued expansionary policies, while allowing a decline in marginal savings ratios and negative import substitution in the energy and manufacturing sectors.

Other countries replicated this scenario to some extent, although Turkey was unique in the nature of its party-competitive political system. What we see, then, is some degree of imported inflation, combined with high domestic-investment levels. The latter, unaccompanied by significant increases in domestic production, led to high domestic inflation. Governments responded to the inflation by resorting to ill-considered deficit financing in order to maintain salary levels and to cover the operating losses of public-sector enterprises. Foreign resources were used to pay for current consumption rather than to increase production. Eventually, as foreign debt snowballed, current borrowing was used to some extent to cover payments on past debt.

Without some fundamental restructuring of the basic parameters of the economy, the vicious circle described above would lead to debt default and economic collapse. It was to address the issues of restructuring the economy that the World Bank, in cooperation with the International Monetary Fund (IMF) and other multilateral lenders, developed strategies and multiyear loan programs for so-called structural adjustment. These were no longer conjunctural, designed to deal with a particular balance-of-payments crisis or short-term disturbance in economic performance, but rather aimed at the basic assumptions of development strategy. Ideally, structural adjustment could and should take place without sacrificing growth, but even then, the process necessarily entrains deflation and austerity for important segments of the population. Whether structural adjustment programs are leveraged by the World Bank and other donors or begun spontaneously out of domestic considerations (India has been notable in this latter respect), they go to the very heart of structural transformation: the balance between agricultural and nonagricultural sectors and the adjustment of policy and investment in favor of the former; the balance among public, private, and foreign enterprise; the amount of resources devoted to the public sector writ large; and the balance between the ISI sector and sectors capable of promoting exports.

The first steps toward austerity and restructuring were frequently taken in the wake of balance-of-payments crises. Typically, the affected country turned to the IMF in order to borrow in excess of its quota in the Fund. The IMF in turn disbursed these funds in "slices" (tranches) as the country took a sequence of steps to prevent a recurrence of the balance-of-payments shortfall. These first measures became part of a short-term stabilization program or standby agreement. Often the reform measures included reductions in government spending and increases in interest rates to dampen the rate of inflation and stimulate savings. Between 1956 and 1984 Egypt,

Iran, Israel, Morocco, Syria, Tunisia, and Turkey entered into a total of fourteen such agreements.

Short-term remedies often proved inadequate to address structural problems, and issues of structural adjustment to be carried out over several years became part of the agenda. In the early and mid-1980s, Turkey, Egypt, the Sudan, Tunisia, and Morocco were all wrestling with structural adjustment programs. Even countries that had experienced no severe balance-of-payments problems, such as Algeria and Iraq, had, because of problems of food security, unemployment, and poorly integrated domestic markets, spontaneously moved in the direction of structural adjustment. Although countries that undertake structural adjustment programs at the behest of their major creditors frequently complain that economic reform is being rammed down their throats heedless of potential political upheaval, the converse may also be true. The oil boom of the 1970s allowed the shah of Iran to finance large capital-intensive projects in the public sector, continue to neglect agriculture, and generate high rates of inflation in an overheated economy. His failure to use Iran's petroleum rents for structural adjustment set the economic stage for his own downfall. As Bienen and Gersovitz (1985) argued, stabilization and structural adjustment programs may be at least as likely to contribute to political stability as to undermine it.

The simple fact is that the imbalances caused by years of unsuccessful state-led ISI exacted a high political price one way or another unless the country could borrow abroad indefinitely the resources that it could not generate at home. Otherwise some sort of "biting the bullet" became unavoidable. Let us briefly review some of the typical measures that had to be undertaken.

Generally, government deficits had to be reduced to some target level—say, 4% of GDP. To do this, governments may have to implement salary and hiring freezes and slash investment budgets. Such measures go to the heart of the state's role as employer of last resort and may deny public-sector enterprise the flows of investment to which it has become accustomed. Second, devaluation of the national currency may be called for. The object here is to promote exports, and it may be the agricultural sector that can most quickly meet the foreign demand induced by the new exchange rate. However, all imports will become more expensive. Industries reliant on imported raw materials and capital equipment will see their operating costs soar; urban consumers used to cheap food imports will likewise be hit; the military will find that its penchant for fancy imported armaments is costing much more. The short-term effects of devaluation can be devastating before its long-term benefits begin to be felt.

Structural adjustment programs generally seek to stimulate national savings by raising interest rates. This in turn will tend to dampen consumption and inflation while making borrowing more expensive. The end of cheap or subsidized credit in the long run will encourage more careful project selection and a more efficient utilization of capital, but the short-term effect may be to put many firms out of business and many people out of work.

There will be measures to reduce administrative interference in pricing mechanisms and to allow supply and demand to determine price levels. Subsidies of consumer prices and inputs in the manufacturing sector may be reduced or phased out, increasing the cost of inputs and the final price of manufactured goods. Subsidies on fuel, fertilizers, and agricultural-credit rates may be ended, raising the costs of agricultural production. Thus, despite a range of anti-inflation measures (reduced government spending and credit squeezes), the cost of living, especially for urban populations, may rise dramatically.

Structural adjustment generally entails a revision in the terms of trade prevailing between the agricultural and nonagricultural sectors. Policies that have held down the producer prices of agricultural commodities that feed into local industries (sugarcane, cotton, sugar beets) or of basic food crops (wheat, rice, oil seeds) may be raised to stimulate production. Presumably if production does increase, the prices of such commodities will eventually fall, but the near-term effect may also be to raise the cost of living for urban populations and the cost of production for the manufacturing sector.

Finally, there will be an effort to streamline the public sector and to stimulate the private. Public-sector enterprises will be called upon to increase productivity, reduce costs and idle capacity, generate a financial return on their investments, and, ideally, meet their investment needs out of their own earnings rather than relying on government financing of their deficits. The effort to make the public sector more efficient will mean that redundant labor will gradually be let go, no new hiring will take place, and management will be called upon to concern itself with issues of inventory controls, waste reduction, market research, and quality control. At the same time, new sources of commercial credit to the private sector may be opened, and the public sector may find itself competing with local private or even foreign joint-venture enterprise in areas where it had previously enjoyed a monopoly position. It will be the private rather than the public sector that is targeted to lead an export drive to reduce the country's balance-of-payments problems.

To summarize: Successful structural adjustment requires at a minimum reduced government spending; a shift of investment resources from the urban to the rural sector and from the public to the private sector; a move away from a planned economy to one in which the market plays a major role in allocating resources; and, in the most general sense, a move to an economy in which equity concerns may be "temporarily" sacrificed to those of efficiency. The process is inevitably painful. Standards of living for people on fixed incomes and/or low- and middle-income urbanites may decline; privileged labor unions may find their wages and benefits eroding; educated and skilled youth may face an economy generating very little employment. Short-term economic contraction, proponents of these policies argued, was the price that must be paid to assure future sustained growth, but getting from the short to the longer term often proved politically perilous, if not fatal.

Two kinds of pitfalls must be avoided. The structural adjustment "medicine" must not be so powerful as to lock the economy into a downward spiral of contraction, business liquidation, unemployment, and slack demand. Judicious resort to government pump priming and foreign borrowing to keep the economy expanding will be called for. But the second pitfall is related directly to seeking that delicate balance between austerity and growth. The application of stabilization and structural adjustment programs may be so diluted that they achieve the worst of both worlds—a deterioration in standards of living for important segments of the population without the structural reforms that would set the stage for further growth.

There are basically three kinds of response to such pressures that national leaders may adopt. The first is outright rejection of structural reform, generally citing the deleterious consequences for equity and the likelihood of economic stagnation. In Turkey's turbulent party-competitive system in the 1970s, none of the major political leaders could afford to advocate belt tightening. A second gambit is to adopt a posture of rejection of some or all of the recommended reforms but quietly to pursue their implementation. Both Sadat and Mubarak of Egypt from 1976 on followed that tactic to some extent. The risk, of course, is charges of hypocrisy and subterfuge when and if the game is revealed (Bienen and Gersovitz 1985, 749; J. Nelson 1984, 986–991). Finally, leaders may accept the reforms but claim that they are being implemented purely out of domestic concerns and because they make sense. One might view the reforms introduced in Turkey after the military takeover in September 1980 in this light.

The major risk, however, at least as it is perceived by political leadership, is that austerity will provoke violence, especially among urban populations. Cost-of-living rioting in Middle Eastern cities has severely tested the regimes of Morocco in 1965, 1982, and 1984, Tunisia in 1978 and 1984, Egypt in 1977, Algeria in 1988, Jordan in 1989, Yemen in 2005, and the Sudan, where it may have been the catalyst to the overthrow of Nimeiri in March 1985. We have already noted the crisis into which Turkey's expansionary policies had driven the economy in the 1970s. Even before the military seized power in the midst of escalating civil violence, the civilian government, in January 1980, introduced sweeping policy changes that included sharp increases in the prices of public-sector goods, elimination of a wide range of price controls, a major currency devaluation, export incentives, favorable legislation for foreign investors, and curbs on government spending. It is moot whether this program could have been implemented with the same force had the military not intervened to put an end to civil violence as well as to open democratic life. The trade unions and universities were muzzled, and the return to civilian government in November 1983 was under the strictures imposed by Turkey's senior officers. The figures in Table 8.3 give some indication of the impact of the austerity measures in the 1980s.

In Egypt, the challenge of structural adjustment was first posed unequivocally in 1976. The country had fallen in arrears on payments on its commercial debt; the government deficit and domestic inflation were growing in lockstep, the public sector was riddled with idle capacity and large aggregate losses, and price disincentives prevented agriculture from taking up the slack. Egypt entered into a standby agreement with the IMF in the spring of 1976. Part of the reform package was to reduce the level of subsidies of several consumer goods in order to lower the deficit. In November 1976 President Sadat faced Egypt's first openly contested parliamentary elections since 1952. He put off action on subsidy reductions until January 1977. When the price increases were announced, three days of severe rioting ensued in

TABLE 8.3   Unemployment and Wages in Turkey, 1979–1983

Year	Unemployed	Wages (TL/day)	
		Gross	Net *
1979	189,467	75	41
1980	263,354	56	29
1981	341,336	52	33
1982	468,654	50	31
1983	549,081	51	32

TL = Turkish Lira
*Net of insurance payments, income tax, stamp tax, and "financial balance tax."
SOURCE: Central Bank, Republic of Turkey (1984, 110)

Alexandria, Cairo, and several other Egyptian cities. Sadat immediately revoked the price increases, and the stabilization program was shelved.

That Egypt's economy did not then founder was the result of great luck and some skillful political maneuvering. In the fall of 1977 Sadat made his historic trip to Jerusalem in search of a peace that might, among other things, enhance Egypt's image as a home for foreign investment and lighten the burden of military expenditures on the economy. In fact, the Camp David Accords of March 1979, which established formal peace between Egypt and Israel, led to Egypt's ostracism from the Arab world and a drying up of Arab aid and private investment in the Egyptian economy.

In the late 1970s, however, other processes, unplanned and unanticipated, were in train. The booming oil economies of the region needed manpower at all skill levels to implement their gargantuan development plans. By 1980 hundreds of thousands of Egyptian migrant workers were remitting to the home economy upwards of US$3 billion per year. The recovery of oil fields in the Sinai Peninsula after years of Israeli occupation coincided with a second surge in international petroleum prices. By 1980 Egyptian oil exports were earning the country US$4.5 billion per annum. The surge in oil prices also was reflected in increased transit fees in the Suez Canal. According to the IMF, these fees earned the economy nearly US$1 billion in 1981/1982. Finally, the peace between Israel and Egypt did stimulate tourism, which in 1980 generated US$700 million in revenues.

Egypt was awash in unanticipated foreign exchange, and it became increasingly dependent on foreign rents (see Figure 8.1). These external resources could have been used to cushion the impact of the structural adjustment process initiated in 1976 and aborted in 1977. Instead they were used to pay for increased consumption, mainly in the form of imports and increased consumer subsidies. They allowed Egypt to avoid structural adjustment rather than to make the process less painful. By the middle 1980s, a global oil glut was manifest, and the bottom dropped out of international oil prices. Egypt's oil earnings plummeted, the demand for Egyptian

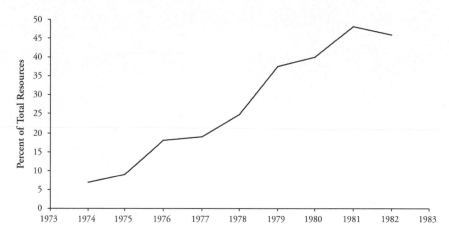

FIGURE 8.1   Share of exogenous resources in total resources in Egypt, 1974–1982
SOURCE: World Bank, 1983, 5

labor in Arab oil-exporting economies slackened and the flow of remittances began to diminish, tanker traffic through the Suez Canal tapered off, and numerous terrorist incidents in 1985 and 1986 scared away tourists. Ten years after first nibbling at the bullet, Egypt was once again faced with the entire structural adjustment package. In the early 1980s, the World Bank and other donors became increasingly alarmed at Egypt's economic prospects in light of softening petroleum prices and the lack of domestic economic reform. A 1983 World Bank report put the matter starkly:

> Egypt's public finances are extraordinary in several respects compared to those of other countries at similar income levels. The public sector's dominance in its economy requires the mobilization and expenditure of a vast amount of resources. Total public expenditures are 60% of GDP, total revenues are 40% of GDP and the public-sector deficit is 20% of GDP. There are very few, if any, developing countries in the world with such high proportions. These heighten the normal fiscal issues of the efficiency, equity and development impact of public-sector economic operations.

The reforms envisaged by the bank and others involved the following:

- Reduction of consumer subsidies, which were running at about £E4 billion per annum in the early 1980s or about 7% of GDP.
- Energy pricing and conservation: Petroleum products in Egypt were priced at about 16% of the world prices prevailing in the early 1980s; this indirect subsidy to the rest of the Egyptian economy was worth US$2.5 billion per annum.
- Exchange-rate management and trade policy (i.e., devaluation and export promotion).

- Tax reform to introduce a unified, global income tax–rate structure.
- Agricultural production policies to improve the terms of trade between the agricultural and nonagricultural sectors and to promote agricultural exports.
- Public-sector reform, giving state-owned enterprises greater financial and managerial autonomy and requiring them to sell their products/services at their real market value and to pay market wages to attract skilled labor but also to shed redundant unskilled labor. (The bank did not at this time recommend privatization or divestiture.)

These reforms were advocated at a time when bank forecasters sketched out oil-price scenarios that they thought were fairly pessimistic. They saw a decline in world prices to about US$25 per barrel but thought that price would hold, at least in nominal terms, throughout the 1980s. In fact, by 1986 the price had dropped to around US$15 per barrel. Egypt's day of reckoning seemingly could no longer be postponed.

In the mid-1980s Egypt had become one of the world's major debtor nations, with more than US$38 billion in foreign obligations (not including Soviet military debt) and annual debt service charges in excess of US$4 billion (i.e., as much as or more than earnings from the export of oil). Since the late 1970s, Egypt's military debt to the United States had grown to US$4.5 billion, and interest on that debt ran at 13% per annum. "Peace," as anyone would have predicted, did nothing to lessen the economic burden of Egypt's military preparedness. In 1986 Egypt had fallen US$1 billion in arrears in some of its foreign payments.

The Egyptian government's internal debt in the mid-1980s had reached nearly £E30 billion or about US$20 billion at the market exchange rate prevailing at that time. The budgetary deficit of the government, already at 16% of GDP in 1981/1982, increased to over 20% in the mid-1980s. An acceptable level from the point of view of the World Bank and the IMF is around 4%. The annual financing requirements of state-owned enterprises alone at that time were well in excess of £E1 billion and were met largely by overdrafts on public-sector banks and the printing of money.

President Hosni Mubarak came to power in 1981 after the assassination of President Sadat by Muslim extremists. The new president was only too aware of the depth of alienation of large segments of Egypt's youth, faced with a soaring cost of living and a shrinking domestic job market. To take on structural adjustment reforms at the very moment that external markets for Egyptian labor were beginning to contract must have seemed as politically suicidal as it was economically inevitable. He searched, successfully from a political perspective, to do enough to keep the economy afloat, but not enough to destabilize the system (see Chapter 9).

Several other Middle Eastern states have to varying degrees shared in Egypt's distress. The *Economist* (July 20, 1985) surveyed one of these states and noted the following symptoms: an inflation rate of 180–200% per annum, the highest per capita foreign debt in the world (US$6,200 per person), unemployment running at 10% of the workforce, an absolute decline in the standard of living, and an annual growth rate of GNP of about 1%. The causes of the disease were seen as lying in a defense establishment that annually absorbed 20% of GNP, a massive welfare state, subsidies of basic consumer goods, the indexing of wage increases to the cost of living, a "huge socialist bureaucracy—encompassing not only trade unions but also banking, transport, farming, insurance, education," the dampening of private initiative through public quasi-monopolies, and "irresponsibly disbursed American aid." Public-sector expenditures were at a level equivalent to 30% of GNP and the deficit in 1984 was at about 16% of GNP. The trade deficit had reached US$2.5 billion. The country surveyed by the *Economist* was Israel.

Prime Minister Shimon Peres promoted austerity measures that went much farther than any attempted in Egypt. He slashed the government budget from US$12 to US$10 billion, including outlays for housing, education, welfare, and civil service salaries. Some US$800 million in subsidy reductions were being planned. Simultaneously, the government set its sights on promoting high-tech exports as well as military hardware, the latter of which earned the country over US$1 billion in 1984.

By the early 1990s, Middle Eastern societies and LDCs as a whole had come to the end of a major historical developmental phase. State-led growth had brought about a certain amount of structural transformation, but rapid population growth and the collapse of oil prices overwhelmed the income-raising effects that such transformation was presumed to yield. The state overextended its capacity to manage and guide increasingly diversified economies. It was able to give a big push to industrialization but was unable to deal with the complexities of industrial deepening, the efficient use of labor and capital, or the need to export in highly competitive world markets. Part of the complexity and diversity that state intervention brought about lay in the creation of new social actors and interests that benefited from state policies (land-reform beneficiaries or the recipients of subsidized credit) or from state business (the whole range of subcontracting). Over time, these groups became entrenched in their economic niches, absorbing resources and saving and investing in such a manner that they developed some economic autonomy and the means to lobby effectively vis-à-vis the state. Indeed, many state functionaries joined their ranks.

Yet by 2006, what is striking is that the systems of political economy in the region remain recognizably the same. To be sure, the international donor community and international capital markets have exerted pressure for change. The United States government, in particular, has strongly advocated downsizing the public sector of the economy, expanding foreign trade, and increasing integration into the global economy. The collapse of the Soviet Union in the 1990s further discredited centrally planned economies—and supporters of the status quo in the Middle East. At the same time, globalization has become a formidable force (Henry and Springborg 2001). Structural transformation under conditions of austerity will be far more difficult politically than it was when large public outlays and ISI went hand-in-hand. The logic of "economic reform" seemed unassailable, and the international political and economic environment was ripe, so it seemed only a question of time before MENA countries would bow to internal and external pressures and embrace a new model of political economy. As we shall see in the next chapter, however, developments in the region have long had a way of defying conventional wisdom.

NOTES

1. "X-inefficiency" arises when an enterprise's total costs are not minimized because the actual output from given inputs is less than the maximum technologically possible level of output.

2. Iran and Iraq joined their poorer brethren in facing a resource gap once they embarked on their mutual slaughter, but there were no international data on this issue for these two countries during and immediately after their war (1980–1988). Unofficial estimates placed Iraq's debt at as much as US$90 billion, while Iran had entirely depleted its accumulated reserves at the end of the war (*Middle East,* July 1988).

3. In that year the difference between domestic savings and domestic investment was 4% for all middle-income countries, 21% for lower-middle-income countries, and 5% for upper-middle-income countries.

9

RE-MIXING
MARKET AND STATE

*The Uncertain Career
of the "Washington Consensus"*

By the early 1990s, most economists agreed on what needed to be done to revive growth in the countries of the Global South. This common policy perspective was called the "Washington Consensus," a term coined by John Williamson of the Peterson Institute for International Economics in Washington, DC (Williamson 1990). The Washington Consensus was a response to the accumulation of macroimbalances and other contradictions associated with state-led growth, as discussed in the previous two chapters, as well as to intellectual developments in economics and political science.[1] The remedies seemed clear: macroeconomic stability (especially, price stability and real exchange rate devaluation), greater openness to international trade, and privatization of state-owned enterprises, as well as the adoption of other measures to reduce the role of the state. By "getting the prices right" and by "getting the state out of the way," it was hoped that (private) savings would flow into productive investment, thereby producing exports and creating jobs, while also stimulating efficiency, thus enhancing international competitiveness. This would foster a virtuous circle of inflows of foreign (and domestic) direct investment, bolstering financial soundness and, in turn, creating more investment, more exports, more jobs, and more wealth.

Ten key elements of the consensus were identified (see Box 9.1). The perspective derived its name from the vigorous support it received from the US government (particularly, the US Treasury), the IMF, and the World Bank—all headquartered in Washington. Although these policies have been increasingly challenged, they remain the orthodoxy of these institutions. Indeed, under the administration of President George W. Bush, elements of the Washington Consensus even found their way into US national security doctrine. For example, the National Security Strategy of 2002 proclaims:

● BOX 9.1 ───────────────────────────────────

The Washington Consensus

The basic concept of the Washington Consensus is that markets promote growth better than states. For countries enmeshed in the fiscal imbalances generated by ISI policies and the various international shocks of the 1970s (oil price increase, rise in international interest rates, recession in OECD countries), the prescription is "stabilization" of the macroeconomy, followed by "structural adjustment," or microeconomic change, such as price liberalization and privatization. Williamson (1990) summarized the perspective as consisting of the following ten points:

1. Fiscal discipline
2. Reorientation of public expenditures
3. Tax reform
4. Interest rate liberalization
5. Unified and competitive exchange rates
6. Trade liberalization
7. Opening for direct foreign investment
8. Privatization
9. Deregulation
10. Securing property rights

As experience with the adoption of such policies grew during the 1980s and 1990s, many were disappointed in the results. One response was so common that it became known as the Post–Washington Consensus. This view continued to advocate the original ten policy changes but now recommended ten additional elements (Rodrik 2004):

11. Corporate governance
12. Anti-corruption
13. Flexible labor markets
14. Adherence to WTO disciplines
15. Adherence to international financial codes and standards
16. "Prudent" capital-account opening
17. Non-intermediate exchange rate regimes
18. Independent central bank/ inflation targeting
19. Social safety nets
20. Targeted poverty reduction

Implementing all twenty components simultaneously is essentially political suicidal, since it asks governments to offend all entrenched interests at once. Accordingly, much ink was spilled concerning the timing and sequencing of such a daunting list, but as Dani Rodrik put it, in practice, the approach was "do whatever you can, as much as you can, as quickly as you can" (Rodrik 2004, 12). He noted that there is no persuasive economic theoretical

continues

◐ BOX 9.1 *continued* _____

justification for such practice, since it falls afoul of the textbook *Theorem of the Second Best.*

Rodrik persuasively (to us) advocates a more nuanced, historically and politically grounded approach. He argues that "there are some general, first-order principles of economic policy that all successful countries have more or less adhered to." These include (1) achieving macroeconomic stability, (2) integrating into the world economy, (3) providing investors with effective protection for property rights and contract enforcement, and (4) maintaining social cohesion, solidarity, and political stability (Rodrik 2004). He has asserted that such principles can be, and have been, achieved through a wide range of institutions, governance structures, and political systems. It is this perspective that seems to us most useful for understanding the recent past in the Middle East and for projecting the future course of the region.

The lessons of history are clear: market economies, not command-and-control economies with the heavy hand of government, are the best way to promote prosperity and reduce poverty. Policies that further strengthen market incentives and market institutions are relevant for all economies—industrialized countries, emerging markets, and the developing world . . . . The concept of "free trade" arose as a moral principle . . . To promote free trade, the Unites States has developed a comprehensive strategy. (Chapter VI)

The view that the solution to the problems of the region required adopting policies outlined in the Washington Consensus has dominated thinking in the US government and the international lending agencies for several decades. These actors had many levers—ranging from aid and loans to military force—that they could use to push this vision.

Elegant theories of social engineering rarely survive protracted contact with human reality, however.[2] Just as the orthodoxy of an earlier generation, the mantra of ISI, failed to deliver on all of its promises, so too has the career of the Washington Consensus been a decidedly checkered one. Also, like the experience with ISI, the adoption of the Washington Consensus principles delivered important gains in some countries. And, just as with ISI, as more experience was gained with these policies, dissenting views and heterodox practices began to emerge.

While policy wonks snacked at the elegant buffet offered by the impeccable logical consistency of the Washington Consensus, several malodorous elephants roamed the room. Some economic historians (e.g., Chang 2002) noted that the WC policies were very different from those adopted by the now-advanced industrial countries, who had relied extensively on protectionism and state controls earlier in their histories. This critique, however, could be dismissed by arguing that although ISI might indeed be a phase of development, its historical moment had now passed.

During the decade of the 1990s, however, two more troubling pachyderms waved their trunks. First, the star performers of the past thirty years, the countries of East Asia—the "Asian Tigers"—had clearly ignored broad swaths of the Washington Consensus. Taiwan and Korea, two of the larger Tigers, had relied extensively on state intervention throughout the postwar era (Amsden 1992, 2001; Wade 1990; Fishlow et al. 1994). Second, the country whose record of sustained economic growth and poverty reduction is unmatched anywhere in the historical record, the People's Republic of China, obviously did not embrace a number of allegedly critical criteria of good policy according to the Washington Consensus. The Chinese development strategy has been justly called "market Leninism"—relying on the market, to be sure, but hardly without extensive state direction. The countries that grew the fastest had not, by any means, fully adopted the Washington Consensus.

Nor was there compelling evidence that those countries that *did* adopt such policies grew particularly rapidly. William Easterly (2001) showed that the various policy "reforms" of liberalization, marketization, and so on, which gained prominence in the 1980s, failed to significantly accelerate growth between 1980 and 2000. Indeed, he described the 1980s and 1990s as the "lost decades." In general, outside of East Asia, those decades saw slower growth than the decades of ISI, the 1950s and 1960s. Other prominent economists, such as Dani Rodrik (inter alia, 2002, 2004) and Joseph Stiglitz (e.g., 2003, 2004) have made the same general point: The Washington Consensus did not seem to lead to the kind of growth its advocates had confidently predicted, nor was it either necessary or sufficient for growth accelerations.

Worst of all, in some cases, liberalization and privatization imposed huge social costs. It is widely agreed that the way capital markets were liberalized in Southeast Asia played a significant part in the Asian financial crisis of 1996, which contributed to the demise of the Indonesian government and to a very large upsurge in poverty in that country. The Asian country that weathered the storm with the lowest social cost was heterodox Malaysia, which used capital controls extensively. Although many economists, including staunch supporters of free trade, now argue that capital market liberalization should come only at the very end of the reform process, the US Treasury and the IMF continue to press for such institutional change. The collapse of the "poster child" for financial orthodoxy, Argentina, further weakened enthusiasm for the stricter version of the Washington Consensus. Turkey also suffered acutely from problems engendered by capital-account liberalization (see discussion below).

Similarly, the spectacle of Russian privatization has been less than encouraging to many observers. Although the process has its defenders, most observers agree that privatization in the absence of a functioning judiciary simply transferred vast wealth from the state to a small cadre of insiders—a classic case of "crony capitalism." The huge upsurge in poverty has also been disquieting. As the Nobel Prize–winner Joseph Stiglitz put it, "the middle class has been devastated, a system of crony and mafia capitalism has been created" (Stiglitz 2003, 133). Although many of the WC reforms were supposed to decrease rent seeking and other forms of corruption, considerable skepticism about how much improvement has actually been made is very much in order (Öniç and Senses 2003). "Nomenklatura" privatization has often marked MENA experience as well.

In response to these and related difficulties, a revised "consensus," often dubbed the "Post–Washington Consensus," emerged. This position holds that the problem with the earlier policy was that it "did not go far enough." In the new consensus, all of the original elements remain, but additional reforms are advocated (see Box 9.1). As Rodrik has put it, "we basically keep adding things on to the policy agenda, as prevailing policies continue to disappoint" (Rodrik 2004, 11). Consensus advocates can, with some justice, argue that the envisaged reforms are a "package deal," and if critical elements are neglected, growth will suffer.[3] Advocates argue that when *all* institutions have been reformed and a truly functioning market economy has been created, *then* growth will be robust. Skeptics counter that something is fundamentally wrong with the model itself, such as the assumption of perfect information (Stiglitz 2004), and that in any case, such a perspective is politically tone deaf; that is, it is political suicide to take on all vested interests simultaneously.

The additional changes advocated by the "Post–Washington Consensus" have also become increasingly political, as deficiencies of "governance" (a technocratic word for "politics") become the focus of attention. Various pathologies—including the problems of privatization (e.g., replacing a public monopoly with a private oligopoly or cartel), the failure of tariff reductions to induce foreign direct investment, and sluggish job creation even after exchange-rate overvaluation is remedied—have often been explained by "deficiencies in the rule of law" and similar "governance" issues. Foreign donors and governments then become ever more involved in advocating internal political changes. To some observers, this is just the disinterested advocacy of socially optimal policies, such as accountable, democratic governance and the rule of law. To others, it simply describes what an already developed country would look like.[4] To still others, it smacks of Western hubris and neocolonialism.[5]

A useful perspective, particularly for understanding the complex, uncertain economic policy changes in MENA, is that offered by Dani Rodrik (2004). His basic view is that although there are some general policy principles that favor growth, these can be stated only in a very general way (see Box 9.1). How these *general* goals (e.g., protection of property rights, integration into the world economy, macroeconomic stability) are achieved in practice will be locally, institutionally, and historically specific. States need to become more accountable, market mechanisms need to function more effectively, greater involvement in the global economy is essential—but the institutional specifics of *how* these general goals can be achieved are wide indeed. There is certainly no "one-size-fits-all" solution. Institutional pluralism is to be expected and, in Rodrik's view, encouraged, since we do not know—cannot know—in advance what policies will best enhance growth in any given country at any given time. Unsurprisingly, such a realistic perspective fits the experience of MENA quite well. And that experience has certainly been wide and varied, as we show in the following section.

A SURVEY OF COUNTRY EXPERIENCES

Turkey

Just as Turkey pioneered the adoption of ISI, so too did the country lead in embracing the policy shifts of the Washington Consensus. The country has transformed its development strategy from import-substituting industrialization to export-led growth and has determinedly tried to integrate itself into the European and global economies. Exports exploded from $3 billion in 1980 to $13 billion in 1990 to $30 billion in 2003 (Keyder 2004; ERF and IM 2005). The country continued its long-term policy of increasingly tight integration with Europe by joining the European Customs Union in 1996 and becoming a candidate for accession to the European Union in 1999, on which talks began in October 2005. Wide-ranging liberalization touched most sectors of the Turkish economy; powerful entrepreneurial energies have been unleashed throughout the society (Keyder 2004). Since the early 1980s, Turkish per capita income has increased by more than half (Easterly 2006, 359).

The road to the European and global market has been far from smooth, and the results have often been mixed. Throughout the 1980s and 1990s, successive coalition governments often found it impossible to maintain budgetary austerity. The Turkish experience highlights the difficulties of consolidating economic reform in a politically fragmented parliamentary democracy. The government ran large deficits and during the 1980s compensated for the ensuing inflation by frequent small nominal devaluations. Turkey liberalized the capital account in 1989, only to fall prey during the 1990s to the mix of problems that plagued several Asian economies: fiscal indiscipline, which led to high government borrowing from the banking sector, which, when combined with capital account convertibility and lax financial regulation, induced banks to finance government debt by borrowing abroad, gambling on interest rate and exchange rate differentials. When these bets turned sour, the country was hammered by three major financial crises, in 1994, 1999, and 2001. During the 2001 crisis, GNP fell by 9.4%, and more than 1 million Turkish workers lost their jobs (ERF and IM 2005).

The growth of the last two decades of the twentieth century was not particularly impressive by historical standards. From 1980 to 1989, GDP grew at an annual rate of 4.1%, and from 1990 to 1999 at 3.9%. These rates are lower than those for the previous decades: 1950–1959, 7.1%; 1960–1969, 5.4%; and 1970–1979, 4.7% (ERF 2005). Further, growth in the 1990s was highly uneven and erratic; growth rates were negative in the crisis years of 1994 (–6%), 1999 (–6%), and 2000 (–9%). The "stop-go" pattern of growth both created, and was created by, unstable governments. More recently, however, growth has accelerated; GDP grew at an annual rate of 4.5% during 2000–2004.

Several Turkish economists have labeled the growth of the 1990s "speculative-led growth" (ERF and IM 2005; BSB 2005). Growth in the 1990s can also be justly characterized as "jobless growth." During the decade, nonfarm output rose by slightly more than 50%, whereas employment rose by less than 25% (ERF and IM 2005).

The problem was exacerbated by the crisis of 2001. During the 1990s, the unemployment rate averaged 7.6%, but it jumped to 12.3% by 2002 (ERF and IM 2005). The unemployment rate would have been still higher if "discouraged workers" had been included. The stagnant job market led to a dramatic fall in the labor-force participation rate, from 57% during the early 1990s to 48.7% in 2004. The level of real wages in the manufacturing sector in 2000 was little different from that in 1980. Real wages fell in the 1980s and then shot up from 1988 to 1994 to more than compensate for the previous losses. But the wage boom was not sustainable; wages collapsed again in the aftermath of the crisis of 1994, falling some 40% by 1996, only to recover unevenly until falling again in the crisis of 2001 (ERF and IM 2005).

In the aftermath of dramatic austerity measures adopted from 1999 to 2001, a watershed election was held in November 2002. For the first time in decades, a single party, the moderate Islamist Justice and Development party, won 34% of the popular vote and an absolute majority of parliamentary seats (367 out of 550).[6] The party had managed to forge a coalition of both winners (e.g., Anatolian export capitalists) and losers (farmers, many workers) from globalization (Öniç 2004). For uniquely Turkish reasons, it rigorously followed the austerity program of the previous government, developed with the IMF, and vigorously pursued further integration with the European Union. As we shall see, this development has greatly strengthened the Turkish political economy, although serious challenges and dangers remain.

There may have been little choice but to embrace the policies of the Washington Consensus. Turkey's economic crisis in the late 1970s was grave. It was governed by fragile and changing political coalitions dominated by the Republican People's party (led by Bülent Ecevit) and the Justice party (led by Süleyman Demirel). Neither of these protagonists could risk promoting economic austerity for fear of alienating a significant part of the electorate. Despite the shocks of the 1970s oil crisis, Turkey attempted to preserve its growth momentum through rapid reserve decumulation and massive external borrowing. Instead of relying upon internal adjustment to promote balance-of-payments improvement, the various coalition governments pursued expansionary policies, while allowing a decline in marginal savings ratios, and negative import substitution in the energy and manufacturing sectors (Celasun 1983). Social conflict soared, violence erupted throughout the country, and a military coup occurred in 1980.

The new government announced a sweeping stabilization and structural adjustment policy with devaluation of the currency, fiscal austerity moves, and trade and parastatal reform. A crawling peg was adopted for the currency, tariffs were cut, and many quantitative export restrictions were lifted. Parastatals were reformed; management obtained the authority to set prices and was required to phase out subsidies. From 1981 to 1985 exporters received tax rebates and subsidized credit while nonexporting firms faced sharper increases in the real cost of borrowing. Average tariff rates fell precipitously; the average tariff rate was 11% (the same for all goods) on manufactures and only 17% on manufactured consumer goods, the most protected sector (Öniç and Webb 1994).

Turkish manufactured exports responded very strongly to this new policy environment. Manufactures jumped from one-third of exports in 1980 to three-quarters in 1985, with continued strong performance thereafter (manufactures were 66% of total exports in 1989 and 72% in 1992). There was considerable diversification of manufacturing, both by sector and geographically (Anatolian towns doing particularly well), and the sector's efficiency rose. Turkish consumer durables became competitive in the discriminating markets of the European Union and the Gulf. During the 1990s, exports grew by 9% per year, with automobiles and nonelectrical machinery leading the way (ERF and IM 2005).

Agricultural performance was more mixed. In general, it can be said that farmers under ISI policies were subsidized by one set of policies, direct subsidies, while penalized and taxed with another, exchange-rate overvaluation (Hansen 1992). Although specialists debate the issue, the terms of trade seem to have turned against agriculture during the 1980s, despite the reforms of the exchange rate and relaxation of import restrictions. Although there were important efficiency gains, there were also substantial losses, including the loss of some 100,000 agricultural jobs. Turkish farmers, long a mainstay of center-right parties (e.g., Menderes's Democrat party and its two successors, the Justice and the True Path parties), were hurt by the way in which reform was implemented. This proved to be a serious weakness when democracy resumed.

Despite the export boom, several weaknesses plagued the political economy. Successive governments could not control the budget. The public-sector borrowing requirement rose from 4.5% of GDP in 1981–1988 to 8.6% for the 1989–1997 period (Boratav et al. 2000). It peaked at 17% in the crisis year of 1994. Inflation was reduced initially in the 1980s (to 25% in 1981–1982) but then rose again to average some 40% during the decade. Inflation rose above 150% in 1994 and then fell back to double digits in 1995; the average for the 1994–1997 period was over 90% (Boratav et al. 2000).

Persistent budgetary deficits were fueled by parastatal borrowing, export subsidies, and large public spending by municipalities and by special off-budget ministerial funds, a type of largesse that usually greatly increased just before elections. Eliminating subsidies proved very difficult—until after 2001. Rather, the subsidies were restructured and reoriented to favor exporters, especially in manufacturing, and to win popular support for otherwise unpopular programs. Under great political pressure, the government granted substantial wage rate increases to public employees in 1992 and 1993 and expanded subsidies to state-owned firms. The lack of fiscal austerity before 2001 undermined the credibility of reform and contributed significantly to the financial crises of the period.

Turkey in the 1980s and 1990s was for the most part governed by a center-right coalition in which economically strong but electorally weak (because few) business interests sought allies among losers from structural adjustment (Waterbury 1992). The parties spent large sums of public money not only to foster exports but also to compensate losers. In such a fragmented democratic polity, it proved very difficult to implement the classic structural adjustment package. Turgut Özal (prime minister, 1983–1989) forged a center-right coalition to support the initial push for market reforms, incorporating key business leaders and also, as junior partners, various Is-lamist political elements. He institutionalized this coalition in his Motherland party. However, this grouping soon splintered. It is true that the institutional structure of Turkish politics supported Özal's key role; the state bureaucracy had long been far more powerful than any set of interest groups, which tended to take direction from the state rather than vigorously press their own demands. Thus the reform effort benefited from determined, skillful leadership operating within institutions that magnified its power.

Nevertheless, key weaknesses became increasingly salient after 1988. Patronage politics and the decision to seek a military solution to the Kurdish problem fueled government spending and spawned large budgetary deficits. These, in turn, stimulated inflation. Ministerial off-budget funds proved to be, as Öniç and Webb (1994) put it, a "sorcerer's apprentice" devised by the reformers to insulate technocrats, only to have the institution swamp any attempt to control spending and restrain inflation. Kurdish policy cost Turkey some US$500 million per year in the 1990s. The budgetary drain—not to mention the human and political cost—was heavy.[7] Finally, by the early 1990s, the center-right coalition's vote became divided between the Motherland party and the True Path party. The alienation of the farmers proved particularly costly electorally. The death of Özal left a leadership vacuum that Tansu Çiller of the True Path party could not fill.

Budgetary deficits were not the sole cause of the ensuing financial crises of 1994, 1999, and 2001. The manner of their financing also played a crucial role. Critically, in 1989, the Turkish government liberalized the capital account. Banks continued to suffer so-called duty losses, as they were used by the state as an instrument of subsidization (e.g., to extend often nonperforming agricultural loans). With capital convertibility, real interest rates soared, averaging 20% during the decade (Keyder 2004). Banks shifted their portfolios, taking on ever larger amounts of government debt by buying government bonds, which they financed by entering the global capital market. They were thus exposed to the risks of both interest rate and exchange rate changes. Such risks were greatly magnified thanks to government regulatory failures; in response to the first financial crash of 1994, the government guaranteed 100% of deposits, thereby creating a severe moral hazard problem for banks. (If banks gambled on interest and exchange rate differentials and lost, they were protected, since the government would bail them out.) Bank concentration, corruption, and lack of transparent bank oversight completed the witches' brew, which erupted in the financial crashes of 1999 and 2001. The entire process led to short-term, unsustainable, highly uneven growth, as populist political patronage was financed by governments borrowing from banks that borrowed from international capital markets, a process caustically known in Turkey at the time as the "chain of happiness" (ERF and IM 2005). Such chains have a long record in economic history, forever associated with the name of Charles Ponzi. Turkey was playing a Ponzi game (a pyramid scheme) in the 1990s (Boratav et al. 2000).

Such games, of course, always end in tears. Inflation accelerated, with the wholesale price index rising at an annual rate of 43.3% in 1985–1988, 62.3% in

1989–1993, and 90.6% in 1994–1997 (Boratav et al. 2000; Keyder 2004). The state debt reached 150% of GNP by the end of the decade, while external debt was some 75% of GDP. Interest payments consumed half the government budget. The real exchange rate appreciated, the current account deficit widened, and interest rates soared. In 1999 Turkey fell victim to the contagion of the Russian crisis, as well as the impact on output and confidence of the Marmara earthquake of that year. Worried international lenders called in their short-term Turkish loans, leaving Turkish borrowers in an untenable position. The resulting crash slashed output and employment and greatly magnified already considerable public discontent with the ruling parties.

These crises led to some important economic turning points. First, an emergency IMF loan (of some $16 billion) was issued in 2000, and an austerity program was instituted. The program was initially implemented by a coalition government led by the Democratic Left party of Bülent Ecevit, whose economics minister, Kemal Derviç, was a former vice president of the World Bank. Second, the deep recession, the worst in postwar Turkish history, dramatically weakened resistance to Washington Consensus policies as well as "Euro-skepticism" in Turkey (Öniç 2004). The crash and ensuing reforms also paved the way for what appears to be, as of this writing, a significant restructuring of the Turkish political economy.

The Turkish public widely perceived the beneficiaries of the "debt-boom" years of the 1990s as a small clique of hugely rich financiers. Displays of conspicuous consumption by such interests did little to enhance their public reputation. The entire process was intimately linked to politicians, who, in turn, were viewed as being "in league with bank owners, plundering the state treasury" (Keyder 2004). As the decade continued, accelerating inflation, continued heavy rural-to-urban migration, public bickering within the political elite, and the weakness of social services opened a wedge for the Islamic Welfare party to win mayoralties in Istanbul, Ankara, and elsewhere. The party gained support among the export-oriented Anatolian manufacturers, who had long felt excluded by the statist, ISI-focused, big businessmen of Istanbul and the Aegean coast. Through a coalition government, Necmettin Erbakan, head of the Welfare party, became prime minister in 1996. In the following year, the Turkish military, alarmed by the government's embrace of Islamic reforms, forced Erbakan to step down through what some have called a "postmodern coup" (Boratav et al. 2000). The Welfare party and its successor, the Virtue party, were subsequently banned.

The opening provided by the crisis, the discrediting of the old elite, and the consensus for joining the European Union provided an opportunity, which Recep Tayyip Erdoğman seized. Formerly the very successful mayor of Istanbul, Erdoğan forged a coalition of Anatolian businessmen and dissatisfied popular classes in the Justice and Development party (AKP). Benefiting from public disgust with corruption, mismanagement, economic crisis, as well as long-standing popular resentment of the Turkish elite and the "deep state,"[8] the moderate Islamist party won a sweeping victory in the election of 2002. The AKP then maintained fiscal discipline; deficits (not counting interest payments) were slashed to the point that the government ran a surplus in

2002–2004 amounting to approximately 6.5% of GDP (ERF and IM 2005; BSB 2005). Inflation fell to 7.7% in 2005, the lowest inflation rate for a generation.

There was more good news. Growth resumed, privatization picked up, and the extensive institutional and policy changes needed for a bid for EU membership accelerated. Agricultural subsidies fell from $6 billion in 2002 to $1.5 billion in 2005. From 2001 to 2004, exports doubled, as did imports. By now tariffs are, essentially, a "nonissue" in the Turkish economy, since nearly all manufactured goods from the European Union enter without duties. Nontariff barriers remain, but the Erdocan government successfully dismantled a series of these in sectors such as telecommunications, banking, and electricity. By 2005, Turkey had adopted most of the EU regulations covering these sectors, and in that same year the country introduced a new currency, the New Turkish Lira (1 NTL = 1,000,000 units of the old currency). Foreign direct investment (FDI) of some $9.6 billion flowed into the country in 2005. These changes produced "a new sense of optimism in Turkey" (Keyder 2004, 65).

Daunting challenges remain, however. "Jobless growth" continued under the AKP. Although GDP grew at 7.5% from 2002 to 2004, employment actually fell slightly (BSB 2005). In 2004, the labor-force participation rate was stalled at some 48.7%, compared with 57% in the early 1990s. In 2005, however, approximately 1 million new jobs were created (IMF and IM 2005). Some of the improvements on both inflation and the budgetary deficit were purchased at the expense of increasing appreciation of the real exchange rate, which rose 100% from 2002 to 2004. Such appreciation is widely viewed as unsustainable (ERF and IM 2005). Although exports have boomed, the current account deficit has widened. Turkish debt remains high, at about $170 billion (about 50% of GDP evaluated at exchange rates). Although the government has maintained fiscal discipline, demands for government spending for health, education, social security, and infrastructure for less-developed regions are mounting. Accession to the European Union entails significant costs, both social and budgetary. For other countries, these have been estimated at 3% of GNP annually during the transition (ERF and IM 2005). Although the AKP government's initial record is very promising, it is worth remembering that modern Turkish history is strewn with the debris of good starts gone bad.

Furthermore, the Turkish government does not control all of the critical variables. Turkey has long followed the reform strategy of "Ulysses and the Sirens" (Elster 1979): "Tie yourself to the mast." For Turkey, the mast is closer integration with the European Union and the global economy. By entering into treaty commitments with the European Union and the World Trade Organization (WTO), Turkish policymakers "tie themselves to the mast," making it hard for them to break their commitments, thus enhancing the credibility of policy change. Such a strategy also helps to defuse popular discontent, since politicians can claim that "our hands are tied."

Unfortunately, however, the mast itself may wobble—or even snap. Europe is showing distinct signs of "enlargement fatigue," as it assimilates the new member nations of Central and Eastern Europe. Sluggish growth and employment creation has reduced public enthusiasm for further EU expansion in many Western European countries. After 9/11, the Madrid and London bombings, the Paris riots of October 2005, and a number of other incidents, Muslim/non-Muslim relations in the European Union have worsened. All of these forces, combined with the continuing issue of Cyprus,[9] are "shaking the mast" of Turkish implementation of Washington Consensus–style policies. For several decades, there has been a consensus in Turkey that the country should join the European Union; during the past year, however, this consensus has weakened, thanks to the increasing perception of European lack of enthusiasm and (in Turkish eyes) foot-dragging and double standards. The situation is not helped by increasing tensions with the United States over US policy in Iraq (since 2003) and Lebanon (in the summer of 2006). Meanwhile, the "deep state" is very restless, not least over the revival of Kurdish insurgent activity based in northern Iraq.

Turkey has gone further than any other country in MENA in the adoption of Washington Consensus–style policies and integrating itself into the global economy. It has much to show for these initiatives. At the same time, these economic reforms have not provided adequate employment creation or sustainable growth. To join the European Union, the country really has little choice but to adopt capital account convertibility. At the same time, Turkey's experience in the 1990s illustrates the dangers of capital account liberalization in the face of continued political paralysis and large fiscal deficits. If modern Turkish history is any guide, the future is likely to hold wrenching surprises as well as increasingly sophisticated responses to these surprises.

Tunisia

Tunisia offers a striking exception to the generally weak economic reform performance of Arab socialist republics. Although it has had difficulty privatizing—for the same reasons as similar regimes—its history of pragmatism in development since 1969 has paid off. Tunisian reform had four advantages. First, the effort started early, and the government has very carefully lived up to all of its commitments. Second, it worked very closely with the IMF and the World Bank in constructing and implementing reform programs; Tunisian reform has been highly orthodox. Third, the president visibly backed the decisions of the Western-trained and -oriented technocrats whom he has placed in charge of economic policymaking. The generally high level of competence of the Tunisian civil service has helped to ensure adequate implementation of reform measures. Fourth, the country's strong performance in human capital formation made it relatively more plausible to embrace a strategy of opening up to foreign competition, while redeploying capital and labor to areas of comparative advantage.

Like other countries of the region, Tunisia followed the usual inward-oriented, statist approach to economic development immediately after independence. In the early 1970s it pioneered the "opening up" *(infitah)* approach better known from Sadat's Egypt. Despite early attempts to attract foreign direct investment, the private sector remained relatively small. In 1981 state-owned enterprises still accounted for about 60% of the value of manufacturing output. The budgetary burden of state-owned enterprises increased to 4% by 1978–1981. Private investment was largely limited to consumer goods production and tourism. Even for consumer goods, the government continued to manage large firms, often trying to attract joint-venture partners.

As elsewhere, the approach before 1986 was mainly one of streamlining the existing economic strategy of state-led growth, in which the government dominated the commanding heights of the economy, supplying the intermediate goods that private industry needed. The complex of controls over prices, investments, trade, credit, and foreign exchange remained in place, as did its corollary, misallocation of resources.

Events in the 1980s made this policy unsustainable. The government tried to "grow through" external shocks such as the international recession of the early 1980s, drought, rising European protectionism, and falling oil prices. Tunisian debt continued to mount, rising from 38% of GDP in 1980 to 63% in 1986. Because of strong internal demand, an overvalued currency and deteriorating terms of trade, the current-account deficit widened from 5% of GDP in 1980 to 11% in 1985–1986. The government's budgetary deficit reached 5.2% of GDP in the five years before 1986, while the resource gap averaged 9% from 1981 to 1985.

The Muhammed Mzali government instituted some halfhearted reforms, including the change of consumer-subsidy programs that provoked the riots of January 1984. The government then retreated, but the problems became even more severe; by the summer of 1986 the country had only a few days of import cover left. At this point, the government had little choice but to turn to the IMF and accept the standby agreement that it had proudly avoided for so long. As usual, a balance-of-payments crisis was the proximate cause of policy change. In August 1986 it embarked on a new round of economic reform.

Devaluation of the currency, export promotion, reduction in import protection, liberalization of banking and prices, budgetary austerity, and privatization were, as usual, the key elements of the structural adjustment program in Tunisia. Most targets were met, and the economy's performance improved significantly. Economic growth for 1987–1992 was 4.3%, compared with 2.8% for the previous five years. Exports of manufactures grew at 15% per year, and workers' remittances rose until the Gulf War. Private savings rose, as did foreign direct investment, which increased from US$75 million in 1989–1990 to US$215 million in 1992 and US$316 million in 1993. Inflation fell to 8%, and the balance of payments improved despite the adverse shock of the Gulf War. Debt accumulation decelerated markedly in the second half of the decade, and the ratio of present value of debt to export of goods and services improved, falling from 170% in 1986 to 125% in 1991. Tunisia does not suffer from a significant debt overhang problem. In 1991–1992 it achieved a positive food trade balance for the first time in twenty years. The efficiency of investment improved: incremental capital-to-output ratio (ICOR) fell from 7.7 in 1980–1984 to 3.8 in 1988–1991. During 1993–1994 the government made the dinar convertible, adopted a unified investment code, and took some limited steps to institute a stock market.

Two general features cloud this otherwise rosy picture. First, as a small economy, Tunisia is particularly susceptible to external shocks, and second, similar to other regional political economies, deeper institutional changes have been much more gradual than shifts in macroeconomic management. An external vulnerability that Tunisia shares with other MENA countries, with the exception of Egypt, is susceptibility to drought (see Chapter 6), although there is some evidence that as the country has industrialized, its economic exposure here has declined (Rivlin 2001). Changes in economic conditions in the European Union also have a strong impact, as during the 1992–1993 recession. Nevertheless, macroeconomic management has been generally strong, with inflation held at 2–3%, budget deficits manageable, and a competitive real exchange rate maintained.[10]

Financial liberalization has proceeded more slowly. Government savings have performed relatively poorly. Financial reform has fallen behind schedule; the Central Bank is often accused of excessive regulatory intervention, with the result that a truly modern, competitive banking sector has yet to emerge. There are persistent reports of collusive behavior among bankers, especially through the Association Professionnelle des Banques. Two of the largest four banks are owned by the state; public banks hold over half of the nonperforming loans in the country. Although there have been some regulatory changes (e.g., increased discretion in lending decisions by bank management), as well as some privatization (e.g., the 2003 privatization of the Union Internationale des Banques), the state retains a dominant role. The government continues, not without reason, to regard banking and telecommunications as "strategic sectors," over which it seeks to retain control.

Privatization has also moved slowly. Although the government announced goals to privatize all holdings (except for "strategic industries") by 1996, privatization was largely limited to the cement and tourist industries. Public administration and labor codes were likewise not significantly altered. Thanks to declining tariffs on intermediate goods, effective protection rates increased in the early 1990s. Up to 1994, private investment remained sluggish, and there was little FDI outside of the energy sector (Bechri and Naccache 2003). The government did create a "one-stop shop" for foreign investors (the "Investment Promotion Agency"), and a 1994 investment code permitted foreigners to own 100% of new capital investments. However, there was a perception in some quarters that reform had "stalled" in the mid-1990s.

At this juncture, the government sought to deepen the reform process by signing an Association Agreement with the European Union in 1996. As the first southern Mediterranean country to sign such an agreement, Tunisia sent important signals to its business and labor sectors about the future. The agreement "tied Tunisia to the mast" of a free-trade agreement with the world's largest economy (the EU). Tunisian authorities could now plausibly argue that "their hands were tied" and that reform "had to go forward." The strategy worked; by 2002, 40% of imports from the European Union entered without tariffs, and the average tariff rate fell steadily to 23.2% by 2002 (Bechri and Naccache 2003).

Several additional features of the agreement promoted the reform agenda. First, the agreement's provisions were phased in gradually: Free trade would not occur for twelve years. Second, both the World Bank and the European Union provided considerable funds to support the project. Particularly attractive for Tunisian manufacturers was the EU-financed technological upgrading program, "Programme de Mise de Niveau." Food processing was the main beneficiary, but construction, textiles, and electrical parts also received subsidized loans and technical assistance to upgrade their technology. No major bankruptcies occurred, and there was relatively little dismissal of labor (Bechri and Naccache 2003). In 2005, the US Department of State estimated the cumulative FDI in Tunisia at $14.3 billion, most of which was concentrated in export-oriented manufacturing; some 235,000 jobs have reportedly been created through this foreign investment (USDS 2005). Ninety percent of Tunisian exports are labor-intensive manufactures, largely textiles, automotive parts, electrical machinery components, and "niche" processed agricultural goods (e.g., olive oil). Clearly, the trade agreement with the European Union has more firmly anchored Tunisia's reform program.

Tunisia's relative success—and continued vulnerabilities—have several different explanations. One perception is that interest group alignments contributed to Tunisia's relatively successful economic reform. By first creating "offshore" export-oriented zones, domestic import-substituting manufacturers increasingly became exporters as well. This project lasted thirty years, beginning with the creation of the first export zones in 1972. By 1987, the main Tunisian business association, UTICA, was increasingly dominated by export-oriented interests (Bechri and Naccache 2003). At the same time, the General Confederation of Tunisian Workers (UGTT) successfully lobbied the government to move slowly on privatization and trade liberalization, thereby protecting jobs.

However, Eva Bellin (2002) argues that the role of interest groups can easily be overdrawn. Entrepreneurs typically lobby the government as individuals, rather than as a collectivity. And labor received concessions because Ben Ali's technocrats understood the vital role of social peace in fostering investment and promoting tourism, and perhaps more importantly, because the regime sought a popular counterweight to the growing strength of the Islamists.

It is important to note that the Tunisian economy remains a case of "state-led growth." The government continues to direct the economy, but it uses far more sophisticated and more open methods than it did during the ISI era. Ever since independence, Tunisian governmental elites have sought to emulate the rich countries of Western Europe. They perceive the way forward as one of gradual integration with the global economy, and particularly with the European Union. They have moved fairly far along this path and have some important successes to their credit: GDP grew at an average of 5% per year from 1995 to 2004 (European Commission 2003), the country is clearly slowly integrating with the European Union, and there has been no major social disruption. Unfortunately, this last success has been achieved through the ruthless suppression of human rights. Economic liberalization has not fostered "democracy," as the Tunisian state is still very much in charge (Bellin 2002).

Despite the solid successes of Tunisian policymakers, unemployment remains quite high (see Chapter 5). Of course, one could reasonably argue that it would have been higher still without the export-led growth strategy. It is also likely that Tunisia's relatively high level of human capital formation, the fruit of policies pursued since independence, has played a critical role in the relative success of the strategy. For example, the agreement with the European Union provides for extensive retraining of labor as the country opens up. Tunisian workers are relatively better able to profit from such training than their counterparts elsewhere in the region. As with Turkey, however, how far the European Union will go in integrating Tunisia into its structures remains a very open question.

Morocco

Morocco provides a striking case of a country successfully overcoming political obstacles to reform, systematically implementing a wide array of Washington Consensus policies—and then having very little in the way of growth or employment creation to show for it. Such a perspective comes not just from dissident critics but from that citadel of development policy orthodoxy, the World Bank. In a lengthy March 2006 report, a team of researchers from the World Bank and various US and Moroccan universities summarized their conclusions thus: "Since the early 1990s, Morocco has achieved macroeconomic stability and a sound external position, while partly implementing structural reforms . . . However, growth has remained insufficient to reduce poverty and tackle unemployment in a significant way" (World Bank 2006a, 1).

Morocco initially faced imperatives and blockages to economic reform similar to those encountered by other countries in the region. In Morocco, as elsewhere, the roots of structural adjustment can be traced to the legacy of state-led import-substituting industrialization, the commodities price boom of the 1970s, and the accumulation of international indebtedness (see Chapters 7 and 8). The resource boom of the 1970s also had the usual Dutch Disease effects: The real exchange rate became increasingly overvalued, shifting incentives away from tradable-goods production. Moroccan experience paralleled that of neighboring oil countries.

Even at the height of the boom, state expansion was partly financed by foreign borrowing. Expansion continued into 1976 even as phosphate prices collapsed (falling by 47%), swelling the budget deficit to 20% of GDP (Morrison 1991). Expenditures rose with the beginning of the Saharan War, the increased cost of consumer subsidies (rising from 1% of GDP in 1973 to 6.9% in 1974) (Horton 1990), the unwillingness to cancel investment projects, and the political fear of canceling public-sector salary increases. Although some initial steps toward stabilization were taken in 1977, the Moroccan government, along with many others, hoped that the adverse price shock was temporary and tried to "grow through the recession." Accordingly, its foreign debt rose from 20% of GDP in 1975 to nearly 60% (at US$10 billion) in 1980, when service payments consumed 32.7% of exports. As the burden of debt became increasingly unmanageable, the government was forced to undertake stabilization measures. As usual, the initial impetus for stabilization came from outside: Foreign creditors refused to continue to finance budgetary deficits, forcing the country to turn to the IMF for assistance. In Morocco, as in other countries of the region, the first key agent of change was external.

Because of the high political costs of austerity, most countries of the region have found adjustment policies difficult to sustain. Here, too, the experience of Morocco initially seems similar. Beginning in 1978 it reduced public spending on investment, increased taxes, restricted civil servants' salary increases, and slowed the growth of credit to private companies. However, in 1979 it retreated, granting a 10% rise of average civil servants' salaries and a 30–40% increase in the minimum wage. It also expanded food subsidies even as the prices of imported farm products rose. A second attempt at implementing a stabilization program was aborted when an extremely sharp rise in consumer prices (50%) and the government's decision to reduce subsidies on food products led, in spring 1981, to major rioting in Casablanca. In the two years (1981–1983) following the Casablanca "bread riots," Morocco pursued an expansionist policy by borrowing more and more from abroad. Foreign public debt continued to rise, reaching US$11.8 billion (84% of GDP) in 1983 (Morrison 1991). Drought added to the difficult situation, accelerating rural-to-urban migration and increasing the need for food imports. The number of state-owned enterprises rose to 700 in 1984. By 1981–1982, the current-account deficit had risen to 12.6% of GDP (from 8% in 1980) (Morrison 1991). By the middle of 1983, currency reserves were almost exhausted, forcing the government to institute emergency measures to restrict imports. As elsewhere in the region, exogenous shocks and political blockages seriously delayed the implementation of stabilization and structural adjustment.

By 1992, however, Morocco was being held up as a textbook case of successful economic reform. The World Bank's regional director for the Middle East and North Africa summarized the achievement: "Morocco is perhaps the only country in the world which has, at the same time, created a realistic hope for a durable solution to its foreign debt problem, put in place a basic program of structural adjustment, re-established a sound balance of payments situation, instituted monetary stability and stifled inflation while carrying through economic growth at about 4% a year" (*Economist Intelligence Unit*, 1992, First Quarter). The ingredients of the new policy package were the familiar ones of nominal exchange rate devaluation, budgetary discipline, tariff reduction, real interest-rate increases, and privatization.

On the macroeconomic side, the government achieved macroeconomic stability through orthodox means: contractionary fiscal and monetary policy, and floating the dirham in 1985. Budgetary deficits, which exceeded 15% of GDP in the late 1970s, steadily fell to around 2%. Inflation was held steady at an average rate of 7.2% during the 1980s and then declined to about 3% by the late 1990s. The banking sector was liberalized, prudential regulation strengthened, and positive (although low) real interest rates were maintained.

Such achievements, however, mask some important issues. First, improved budgetary balance on the expenditure side was largely achieved by cutting government investment; personnel costs rose as a percent of GDP, reaching nearly 12% of GDP by 2000 (European Commission 2003). In that year, the government awarded substantial wage increases to public employees, in part to avert a threatened general strike (Denoeux 2001).[11] On the revenue side, tax collection was hampered by (historically speaking, very common) evasion, sluggish growth, and the reduction of customs revenues. The budget was largely balanced through the proceeds of privatization. Such revenues are, of course, not a sustainable revenue source; most agree that such windfall gains should be invested. This did not happen. As Denoeux put it, "selling the family jewels to pay for food and rent is not usually seen as proof of a healthy financial situation" (Denoeux 2001, 75). Real exchange rate management was likewise mixed. Although the real exchange rate fell by roughly 40% during the 1980s, it appreciated throughout the 1990s, gaining some 15% by 2000, when the dirham was again devalued.

Overall, most economists give Morocco relatively high marks for its macroeconomic management.[12] Many do the same for structural reforms, as well. Prices were liberalized; all prices except flour, sugar, and tobacco are market prices (World Bank 2006a). Trade reforms reduced the maximum tariff from 400% in 1983 to 44% in 1988, and the government announced a goal of a uniform 25% tariff rate. Morocco joined the WTO in 1995 and entered into free-trade agreements with the European Union (1996), among others. The government announced its intent to privatize a wide range of companies; with much fanfare, the Ministry of Economic Affairs and Privatization slated 112 state entities for privatization by the end of 1995, including 75 companies and 37 hotels (Saloman Brothers 1992).

As with macromanagement, however, a closer look at structural change reveals a spottier picture. The simple average tariff was 29.5% in 2005, and tariffs were escalatory. Consequently, the effective rate of protection was also high.[13] When nontariff barriers are included, the overall trade restrictiveness index (OTRI) is high, compared with other countries like Tunisia, China, and Turkey.[14] The World Bank concludes, "The degree of import protection leaves Morocco with one not very open economy" (World Bank 2006a, 99).

The course of privatization has likewise been far from smooth. First, the actual privatizations have fallen well short of the bold pronouncements of the early 1990s. Of the 112 companies supposed to have been sold, less than half have actually been sold. The usual suspects are involved: union resistance, government wariness, and investor reluctance (Denoeux 2001). Second, as elsewhere, many observers allege that sales were often made to the politically well connected, who thereby enhanced their market share and weakened domestic competition (Bergh 2005; Hibou 2004).

The initial results of these policy shifts were encouraging. GDP expanded at an average annual rate of 4.0% during the 1980s, with manufacturing growing slightly faster (4.1%). The export response was strong, while import growth decelerated. Exports rose from 18% of GDP in 1965 to 25% in 1990. The composition of exports also shifted markedly, with large increases in farm and factory goods. Both the balance of trade and the balance of payments improved.

But the results since the early 1990s have been disappointing. GDP growth has been sluggish, averaging roughly 2% per year from 1991 to 1998, or less than 0.5% in per capita terms. Although growth improved to 3.3% in 1998–2004, Moroccan growth has been slower than that of Egypt, Jordan, Tunisia, and Turkey (World Bank 2006a)—and far below the estimated 6% growth rate needed to create adequate jobs for the growing labor force and to reduce unemployment and poverty. Growth has also been highly uneven; the economy actually shrank in 1992, 1995, 1997 and 1999, thanks in substantial part to the baleful effect of drought, which occurred during six years of the decade. The problem is not merely ecological, however; nonagricultural growth averaged only 3% during the 1990s (Denoeux 2001).

A key failure has been the sluggish growth of exports. The problems may be divided by product type, roughly, "old" manufactured exports (textiles and leather) and the development of "new" exports (e.g., ready-made clothing). Basically, the growth of the former has stagnated due to inherited inefficiencies, increasingly severe competition from Asian countries, exchange rate overvaluation, high unit labor costs, and the end of the multi-fiber agreement in 2005, which ended any Moroccan textile trade advantages in the European Union. Meanwhile, a complex combination of market and government failures have inhibited the rapid development of newer exports. Problems include monopoly power (particularly of those closely connected to the *makhzen*),[15] rigid labor market structures, credit access difficulties for smaller enterprises, weak government support of industrial restructuring and training (in contrast to Tunisia), and high effective protection rates (World Bank 2006b; Cammett 2004; Hibou 2004; Denoeux 2001). Labor-intensive exports have, so far, failed to provide the "engine of growth" of output and jobs that Washington Consensus advocates had anticipated.

The balance of trade deteriorated from –6.0% of GDP in 1996 to –13% in 2004. This has not caused serious balance-of-payments problems, thanks to the "invisible exports" of tourism, workers' remittances—and the drug trade. Between 1995 and 2003 tourism receipts rose from 4% to 8% of GDP. Tourist income, now running at approximately $3 billion a year, is exceeded by remittances from the 2.5 million Moroccans working abroad, about $4.2 billion in 2004. Exporting labor, rather than creating local jobs, continues to be a mainstay of the Moroccan economic scene (see Chapter 15).

Of course, any numbers for the illegal drug trade are only informed guesses. Various law enforcement agencies estimate Morocco's cannabis exports at $2–3 billion annually. Morocco supplies nearly 70% of the European market; the trade produces vast fortunes, provides jobs for unemployed youth, and generates a complex web of conflict and cooperation with the Moroccan state. The main producing region, the Rif, has long had relatively hostile relations with the palace, but the relationship has also always had elements of cooperation, as well. Although the 1990s saw a large-scale offensive against the trade by the government, many observers charge that, as so often in Moroccan history, the *makhzen* was highly selective in its targets, who were chosen as much for their political leanings and activities as for their smuggling. Some charged that drug money reached into the palace itself (*Le Monde* 1996), while others believe that the government moved against drug lords only when their wealth and power became sufficiently formidable as to threaten the state (Ketterer 2001).

Morocco enjoyed a number of political advantages, which helped it to carry out so much of the Washington Consensus program. Both Hassan II and his successor, Mohammed VI, provided crucial leadership and visibly supported the key technocrats, who, moreover, enjoyed considerable longevity in their posts. Broad segments of the business and agrarian elite supported the kings' programs. In many cases, policy changes (including strategic delays) were designed to provide them with benefits, and thus ensured their support. Finally, as elsewhere, the Moroccan government "tied itself to the mast," at first through the IMF, and then especially with its association agreement with the European Union. Such a constellation of interests and state structures helps to explain the rapid macroeconomic stabilization program (for all its faults) and the relatively gradual implementation of structural changes (Mansouri et al. 2004).

This balance of political forces also helps to explain the difficulties. First, organized labor has long been a force in Morocco. Although, as elsewhere, labor unions do not (cannot) represent the vast numbers of workers employed in the informal sector, they are strong in larger enterprises and in the public sector. Keeping the social peace requires at least their acquiescence. This helps explain both budgetary difficulties (e.g., high and rising public-sector wage bills), slow privatization (which the unions have often opposed), and rigid labor-market structures (which have slowed the development of export industries). As elsewhere, the "labor aristocracy" of organized and public-sector workers have benefited, while those forced into the informal sector, unemployment, or emigration have fared less well. But few governments, faced as Morocco was in the mid-1990s by strikes, street protests, massive rural-to-urban migration, and rising opposition (typically Islamist) forces, would risk alienating such a key urban constituency as organized labor.

Organized labor is hardly the only interest group active in Morocco. Employers and industrialists play a still more important role. The more established, highly interconnected oligopolistic interests associated with the older, import-substituting industries, such as textiles, constitute a powerful political force. Some observers attribute the slow change of trade regime in Morocco to their influence. In a manner reminiscent of the Turkish experience, they met important opposition from the newer money investing in export industries such as ready-made clothing (Cammett 2004). The powerful interests in the core of the state *(makhzen)* were able to make good use of this division—as well as more traditional tools of patronage and "planned corruption" (Waterbury 1973) to maintain firm control over the entire process of economic policy change (Hibou 2004).

The continuity of governance structures in Morocco, as elsewhere in the region, is striking. For example, when the World Bank pressed for tax reform, the *makhzen* obliged in the mid-1990s. However, governance hardly became more transparent as a result. In fact, "at the heart of [the *makhzen*'s] method of exercising power was the preservation of confusion" (Hibou 2004, 205). Discretion has been maintained in many other ways; for example, the funds from some of the largest privatizations have gone into the coffers of the Hassan II Foundation, which is entirely unaccountable to the legislature or any other public body. Many observers lament the failure of economic changes to produce any significant governance change (e.g., Layachi 1999; Hibou 2004; Denoeux 2001).

Such a phenomenon is widespread.[16] One can certainly argue that "social dialogue" is more advanced in Morocco than in Tunisia or Algeria (Denoeux 2001).

The new king, Muhammad VI, is certainly forward looking, and his technocrats are undoubtedly able. They have gambled on integration with Europe, even while Europeans are becoming decidedly wary of any closer economic ties with any Muslim country, whether Morocco or Turkey.[17] The *makhzen* has "tied the country to the mast" of integration with the European Union, but it cannot control the wobbly mast.

As always, history matters. The history of the Moroccan state, its governance structures and style, its ambivalent relation with Europe—and the inheritance of some of the region's worst human capital indicators (see Chapter 5)—continue to matter at least as much as the elegant policy prescriptions of the Washington Consensus. Morocco has gone quite far toward implementing such policies. During the 1990s, however, unemployment, emigration, and poverty all increased. It is small wonder that the Moroccan state continues to preserve its discretionary powers, since it will very likely need them in the years ahead.

Egypt

On the eve of the Gulf War, the Egyptian economy was in shambles. Growth turned negative in the late 1980s; by 1990 the country had amassed international debts of nearly US$50 billion; its debt/GNP ratio of roughly 150% was arguably the highest in the world. Real wages of unskilled workers had plummeted by 40% in four years, while civil servants earned only about half of their 1973 salaries (Richards 1991). The level of open unemployment had roughly doubled during the decade. The quality of government health, transportation, and educational services had declined precipitously from already dismal levels. The situation was increasingly exploited by the Islamist opposition.

At the core of Egypt's macroeconomic crisis were three macroimbalances: gaps between domestic savings and investment, imports and exports, and government revenues and spending. The collapse of oil revenues and the mounting losses of public-sector companies undermined public savings, while private savings were deterred by negative real interest rates on Egyptian pound deposits and by great uncertainty on the part of private wealth holders as to the direction and credibility of economic policy. Investment flowed into infrastructure rather than into tradable goods production; investment was increasingly inefficient and capital intensive, creating few jobs.

By 1989 the current account deficit was 7.2% of GDP, and by 1991 it was 10.2% (World Bank 1991). Since roughly two-thirds of Egyptian imports are intermediate and capital goods, there was relatively little room for import compression. Export developments during the 1980s were dominated by the decline in the value of petroleum sales, which fell from US$2.9 billion in 1983 to US$1.36 billion in 1987. Other tradables failed to fill the gap created by the decline of oil. Cotton export volume in 1990 fell to one-third that of the early 1980s, when it had already declined by 50% in comparison with 1974. In 1987 the deficit of agricultural trade was some US$2.8 billion, about one-third of the total trade deficit. Industrial exports performed only slightly better. Invisible earnings fared better. Tourism grossed over US$2 billion per year on the eve of the Gulf crisis in 1991 and provided the only really bright spot of the economy in the late 1980s. Workers' remittances outperformed most predictions until the Gulf crisis, averaging roughly US$3.4 billion from 1982 to 1989.

Egypt, like so many middle-income countries, plugged the twin gaps by borrowing from abroad, largely from foreign governments. Although there are conflicting estimates of debt because of underreporting and multiple exchange rates during the two decades, a rough estimate would be that Egypt's foreign debt climbed from about US$2 billion in 1970 to some US$21 billion in 1980 to just under US$50 billion in early 1990 (see Amin 1995); in 1990 debt-service payments consumed over 25% of exports. The situation in the mid-1990s could fairly be characterized as one of crisis, in which foreign exchange for wheat imports was hard to locate and only last-minute help from the Gulf States narrowly averted an American aid freeze for failure to service military debt.

The twin gaps were exacerbated by the government deficit. Although its size fell somewhat at the end of the decade, the average deficit for FY 1989/1990 was 21.2% of GDP; the deficit in 1991 was 21.9% of GDP. Revenue fell with oil receipts, while spending was inelastic downward for the usual political reasons: blockage by vested interest groups that would lose sinecures and economic rents and fear of popular wrath over subsidy cuts. Some 80% of government spending consisted of subsidies, public-sector salaries, interest on the public debt, and the military. The last two were sacrosanct, forcing all adjustment on the spending side onto the first two.

As new foreign lending dried up in the latter half of the 1980s, the deficit was increasingly financed by the banking system. Inflation accordingly rose to roughly 25%, with the usual baleful results: further distortion of price signals, sharply negative real interest rates that exacerbated the savings-investment gap, and (thanks to fixed nominal rates) a steadily increasing overvaluation of the exchange rate. Such underpricing of increasingly scarce foreign exchange discouraged the production of traded goods and favored imports over exports; in short, it greatly exacerbated the trade gap.

Microeconomic distortions reinforced macroimbalances. Egyptian price distortions of the 1970s and 1980s were internationally notorious. The divergences between private and social rates of return in industry were little short of astonishing (World Bank 1983). In the second half of the 1980s, price reforms began to be implemented in agriculture, but cotton remains underpriced even today. Prices in Egypt have borne little relation to opportunity costs.

Price distortions interacted synergistically with the regulatory environment to create a producer's nightmare. One example is the increase in capital intensity. The price of labor relative to capital rose as labor emigration pushed up wages, while accelerating inflation and financial regulations created strongly negative real interest rates. Supervisory personnel, so crucial to successful labor-intensive production, was particularly scarce during the migration boom. Regulations were—and remain—voluminous, ubiquitous, opaque, and arbitrarily enforced.

The Gulf War created an entirely new situation. The government struck a bargain: In exchange for massive debt relief, the government adopted a reasonably conventional stabilization and structural adjustment package, endorsed by the IMF. The government embraced reform by leveraging strategic rent. Such a bargain was attractive both economically and politically. Economically, the reduction of up to US$20 billion of debt cut yearly interest payments by US$2 billion for the next ten years. Politically, the deal was easier to sell domestically, since the government could plausibly argue that its creditors were shouldering part of the burden of past mistakes.

Macroeconomic stabilization did quite well. Debt relief and banking reform are the keys here. The United States forgave the roughly US$7 billion of military debt. Some 15% of the debt was forgiven in May 1991 following the IMF's approval of an eighteen-month standby arrangement (later extended another six months). A further 15% was forgiven in September 1993, when the IMF concluded that the first set of reforms had been successfully implemented, and agreement was reached on an extended fund facility. The final 20% of debt was to be forgiven in July 1994, contingent on satisfactory compliance with the terms of the extended fund facility, which emphasized continued fiscal reform, trade liberalization, and reform and privatization of both financial and real goods sectors. This last step did not materialize, and the reasons are revealing.

Thanks to the banking reform package, Egyptians turned dollar holdings into Egyptian pounds, generating current account surpluses. International reserves soared, rising from US$2.68 billion in 1990 to US$10.8 billion in 1992 and to an estimated US$16–18 billion in 1994. Reserves remained at about $18 billion until the end of the decade. Price reforms in the agricultural sector also proceeded according to plan (see Chapter 6), and the government increased its real revenue by replacing indirect taxation with sales taxes.

Fiscal reform was also very successful: Government deficits were slashed, plunging from over 20% of GDP before the war to 4.7% in FY 1992/1993. By 1993/1994 the overall budgetary deficit was 2% of GDP, and it remained at that level until the late 1990s. Fiscal discipline combined with tight monetary policy to cut inflation from over 25% in 1990, to 8% in 1994, to 2.6% in 2000.

The contrast between the situation in the late 1990s and that prevailing before the Gulf War is striking. GDP growth also rose significantly, from 2% at the end of the stabilization period in 1992 and going up every year until reaching a maximum of 6.3% in 1998–1999. At first glance, Egypt looks like the poster child for the Washington Consensus.

The reality was more complex, however. First, consider the sources of growth. Although the Washington Consensus view hoped that macro-stability and deregulation would stimulate export-led growth, in fact Egyptian growth was largely driven by investment in inventories and by public investment in huge infrastructural projects, such as the New Valley and Toshka Irrigation projects (ERF 2004). Second, the growth of exports—particularly job-creating manufactured exports—was unimpressive. Indeed, by one conventional measure, the Egyptian economy's integration with the global economy *declined* during the 1990s: Exports as a percentage of GDP fell from 46.6% in 1980 to 31.2% in 1990 and to 24.6% in 2000. Merchandise exports as a percentage of GDP fell from 8.1% to 4.7% from 1990 to 2000.[18] And, as we saw in Chapter 5, job creation continued to lag behind additions to the labor force, while employment and production became increasingly "informalized." The balance of trade has remained in deficit, but the overall balance of payments was rescued during the 1990s by the old reliables of Suez Canal revenues, tourism, and workers' remittances.

Several plausible stories are offered to explain this mixed picture. On one account, the very success of the banking reform reduced pressure on the exchange rate, which, in turn, stimulated real overvaluation of the Egyptian pound. The Egyptian government long refused to devalue, despite IMF remonstrations. However, three shocks made devaluation inevitable. First, although the government had not fully liberalized the capital account, the knock-on effects of the Asian financial crisis also hit Egypt in 1997/1998. Second, the terrorist attack at Luxor in November 1997 cut tourism dramatically, and third, the price of oil reached its post-1970 nadir in December 1998. The government used up close to $4 billion of foreign exchange reserves in a vain attempt to shore up the Egyptian pound, but from 2000 through the end of 2002 successive devaluations of the pound preceded the floating of the currency in January 2003. The devaluation led to a surge in inflation, although not to previous levels, now estimated at around 6 to 7%. Yet labor-intensive manufactured exports continue to respond sluggishly, and there has been no great inflow of foreign direct investment. In fact, FDI inflows reached their peak in the pre-reform era of 1986–1990. FDI is also concentrated in petroleum and telecommunications, sectors that create few jobs directly.[19] Portfolio investment peaked in 1996/1997 but failed to recover from the negative impact of the Asian crash of that year (ERF 2004).

Several intractable structural features are often advanced as explanations for the continued difficulties of export-led growth. Two stand out: low labor skills (recall that over half of adult Egyptians are illiterate; see Table 4.2), and the pace and nature of privatization and deregulation. Privatization started slowly in 1991 with legal and regulatory changes. Beginning in early 1996, the pace accelerated, with some 25 companies privatized that year, and more than 30 the next. The process then decelerated markedly. By mid-2002 the government had finished 132 complete privatizations, together with 57 partial ones, generating over $14 billion in revenues. More than half of the 314 public enterprises had been either privatized or liquidated (UNDP 2006).

Opposition forces have charged with some justification that the process of privatization was far from transparent and that regime insiders, particularly associates of the president's son, did extremely well in the process. Whatever the truth of these accusations, the close ties between the regime and segments of Egyptian big business were hardly weakened by privatization. In many respects, the process resembles the *nomenklatura* privatizations of the former Soviet Union—insiders strongly connected to the state apparatus gathered most of the benefits. Although this may have strengthened the regime in the short run, resentment over this and other forms of corruption have continued to fuel the increasingly strong Islamist opposition led by the Muslim Brotherhood. A wave of mergers and acquisitions from 1999 to 2003 very likely further reduced domestic (and export) competitiveness. Such "crony capitalism" was not on the agenda of the Washington Consensus, but in Egypt, as elsewhere, it seems to have been the outcome of the policy changes of the 1990s.

Regulations have hardly been dismantled in Egypt. Tariff rates were reduced and consolidated, but they remain high, averaging some 20% in 2004. They remain highly dispersed and continue to display a strong ISI bias. Regulations have been reformed and streamlined—but, for example, the average sea clearance time in Egyptian ports is about ten days, compared to one day in Greece and two in the UAE (ERF 2004). Quality regulations, while essential for protecting the reputation of a country's exports, is slanted in favor of large, well-connected enterprises.

The Mubarak regime successfully utilized strategic rents to "jump-start" an economic reform process, which then proceeded at the government's own pace. Major changes in macroeconomic management, privatization, and price regulations have undoubtedly occurred, and the market mechanism is more widely utilized—and there was improved economic growth to show for it. At the same time, exports, particularly of the job-creating kind, have responded sluggishly, crony capitalism has been entrenched yet more deeply, and human capital constraints, despite important progress, remain tight. The Mubarak government skillfully utilized strategic rents to delay reforms for half a decade after the oil-price collapse of mid-1986, seized the opportunity for debt relief afforded by the Gulf War, and despite foreign pressures, reformed at its own glacial pace. This pace did not provide the needed jobs to the rapidly rising number of young job seekers, but it did satisfy foreign patrons and donors and retained the government's hold on power.

Algeria

Despite oil rents and rapid growth, Algeria could not escape the contradictions of its statist, inward-oriented development strategy (see Chapter 8). The key weaknesses of the Boumedienne strategy were excess capacity, overcentralization, unemployment, massive rural-to-urban migration, and serious neglect of agriculture. These problems elicited halfhearted reform measures that helped delegitimize the government as it imposed hardships, but failed to deliver a restructured economy.

The situation in the early 1980s was increasingly difficult. Labor productivity had actually declined in both the hydrocarbon and the nonoil public-industrial sector. The rate of worker absenteeism ranged between 10 and 20%, about one-fifth of workers left their jobs each year, and "factory discipline became extremely unsatisfactory" (Bennoune 1988, 141). The iron-and-steel complex at El Hadjar was operating at only 40% of capacity in the early 1980s, thereby forfeiting economies of scale and raising costs to all final users of its output. Two-thirds of Algerian basic food was imported, and unemployment rose to 16% in the cities. Housing was extremely scarce. The regime slowly, inexorably sowed the dragon's teeth by providing young men with incentives to move to the cities, where they found no jobs and no housing.

These problems can be traced to the strategy of concentration on heavy industry and to management problems of state-owned enterprises. The economic argument for developing heavy industry was based on linkage effects: These industries were to provide the basic materials for others that would supply the population with its needs. It is true that basic metals and energy industries have high forward linkages, but they are also very capital-intensive and create relatively few jobs. Worse, in Algeria they were run as monopolies, giving enterprise managers little reason to be efficient. Furthermore, the location of these industries in and around the major cities of Algiers, Constantine, and Oran further stimulated rural-to-urban migration, already massive because of rapid population growth and the neglect of agriculture. This exacerbated the severe problems of the cities.

Beginning in 1982, the regime of Chadli Benjadid began to tinker with this system. Initially, some 66 huge state-owned enterprises were broken up into 474 smaller companies by 1985, with more following. Successive decrees were issued that were intended to decentralize decisionmaking in state enterprises. Other changes included the reallocation of public investment away from heavy industry, incentives to attract foreign investors, and measures to revive the agricultural sector. The autonomy of management was strengthened, and capacity utilization rose from an average of 30–40% in the late 1970s to 75% in 1984. Industrial workers received bonuses linked to productivity.

The regime tried to encourage both domestic and foreign private investment. The private sector accounted for about one-fourth of manufacturing output in 1985; its activities continued to be concentrated in light-industrial products. As elsewhere in the region, private entrepreneurs existed in a symbiotic relationship with the public sector, obtaining inputs from the public sector and/or selling their output to the giant monopolies. The 1982 investment code reduced the tax rate on profits and expanded credit for industries likely to generate foreign exchange (e.g., tourism). The amount of foreign currency that such firms could legally import was doubled, and the establishment of some 660 new private firms was approved. Private foreign direct investment rose from virtually zero to US$280 million in 1984. Whereas previously nearly all contracts with foreign companies had been turnkey arrangements, for the first time foreign firms were allowed to operate facilities (in joint ventures) in the country. The two most visible were in telecommunications (Sweden's Ericsson Company) and automobiles (Italy's Fiat Corporation).

A critical force driving all of these policy changes was the country's mounting indebtedness. In 1985 the World Bank reported Algerian debt at US$15 billion, while for the same year the OECD's figure was about US$24 billion. Despite austerity programs of reducing investment spending, pruning government recurrent expenditures, and slashing imports by more than 10% in one year, the government was forced to return to international capital markets in 1987.

The restructuring of the economy under Benjadid failed to alleviate debt and failed to cope with unemployment; in 1986 about 116,000 new jobs were created, while about 173,000 new job-seekers entered the labor market. As labor-force growth accelerated, growth of output declined to 3% during the 1980s. Urbanization accelerated;

the urban population growth rate rose from 4.1% in the 1970s to 4.8% in the 1980s (Bennoune 1988). International debt continued to mount, reaching US$26.5 billion in 1991, by which time a vicious civil war was well under way. Algerian *perestroika* had failed.

Algerian reform in the 1980s was fundamentally an attempt by reform-minded technocrats grouped around Chadli Benjadid to square the circle: to overcome the Boumedienne legacy of excess capacity, low productivity, overcentralization, excessive capital-intensity, galloping urbanization, and one of the most seriously neglected agricultural sectors in the region while still maintaining state control of the economy. It was a classic case of reform as survival strategy.

Much of the impetus for Algerian reform was the mounting pressure of servicing the country's international debt. Benjadid's team argued in 1982–1983 that reform was necessary in order to avoid rescheduling the debt, but in marked contrast to its Maghreb neighbors, Algeria deliberately avoided entering into an agreement with the IMF. Its reform was "structural adjustment with a nationalist face," designed in part to avoid the perceived humiliation of "losing sovereignty" to the IMF.

This reform, decidedly "heterodox," was fundamentally flawed. The key problem was conceptual: The government eschewed implementing the centerpiece of all structural adjustment programs: devaluation of the real exchange rate. A real devaluation is also an increase in the price of tradables relative to that of nontradables and, among tradables, an increase in the price of exportables relative to that of import-competing goods. It is difficult to promote agriculture, create jobs, and foster the private sector without such a change in relative prices. However, out of the same kind of nationalist pride that so infuriated Keynes in the interwar period, the Algerian government refused to devalue the dinar. It was unwilling to cut the link between state-owned enterprises and budgetary subsidies; the "soft budget constraint" remained flaccid. Consequently, it had difficulty restraining public spending and, therefore, inflation. By maintaining fixed nominal interest rates, it produced negative real interest rates, underpricing capital.

Poor conceptualization was accompanied by poor implementation. Large sections of the ruling National Liberation Front (FLN) never accepted the need for reform. Middle- and lower-level functionaries impeded the shift to the market at every opportunity. Suspicion of market activities remained high in these quarters, and even as legal changes dictated from the top removed obstacles to private-sector activity, bureaucratic resistance blocked their realization. Although reform intensified after the riots of 1988, with agreement with the IMF in 1989 and continued changes until 1993, economic reformers increasingly had to vie with hard-liners arguing that the reforms were responsible for the rise of the Islamic Salvation Front (FIS) and the Islamist insurgency. After the assassination of Mohammed Boudiaf in June 1992, the government of Abdesslam Belaid, who had been minister of industry under Boumedienne, abandoned reform and reverted to a more traditional, FLN-style policy of favoring state enterprises. The government persisted in this approach until, in the spring of 1993, the Bank of Algeria could no longer service the country's international debt, which then forced the government to begin serious negotiations with the IMF. By then, of course, internal violence had increased considerably.

The political dynamics of economic reform doomed the process from the start. The reformers were, initially, a group around Benjadid. He found few supporters for his reformist intentions in the dominant FLN or in the armed forces. Some have argued that he used the Islamists (the FIS) as a counterweight to the FLN and some army elements in an attempt to "open a space" for his reforms (Leveau 1993). One is reminded of Sadat's (ultimately personally fatal) use of Islamists as a counterweight to pro-Soviet Nasserists in the 1970s. This political strategy had serious weaknesses. The government's legitimacy had eroded significantly both before and during the reform decade of the 1980s. As one analyst puts it, the FLN "had become valued by most Algerians by what it could deliver, not for what it stood for politically or ideologically" (Vandewalle 1992, 190). As the regime's ability to deliver faltered, its legitimacy evaporated. Further, implementing highly visible reforms that changed little reduced the constituency for reform and aroused public skepticism.

Public disillusionment in Algeria was particularly strong because the regime (1) was widely perceived as thoroughly corrupt and out of touch with the needs of ordinary Algerians, (2) never intended to make a real "break for the market," and (3) pursued flawed reform policies from 1982 until 1988. Even when sensible macroeconomic policies were finally put in place after the 1988 riots, it was too little and too late: Urban young people were far too alienated, and even at this late date the dinosaurs of the FLN and the bureaucracy continued to block the market-oriented reforms that alone had a chance of creating jobs. Finally, the politics of encouraging the Islamists as a counterweight to anti-reform elements assumed that the government would retain control of the political game, but the FIS soon became at least as strong as, and then stronger than, the reforming technocrats around the president. Events since 1992 have simplified the triangle of political forces of presidential reformers-FLN/army-Islamists by removing the first group as significant players. Such polarization formed the backdrop to the bloody civil war of the 1990s.

Le pouvoir [20] managed to retain power and weather the storm of civil war, enriching itself, while failing to address the deep contradictions of the inherited state-centric development model. In 1994, the state played the "strategic rent" card to strike an agreement on debt rescheduling with the international community, led by the IMF.[21] The rescheduling may have been worth up to $20 billion to the state (Lowi 2005). At the same time, the state acceded to the usual array of Washington Consensus policy changes.

As in Egypt, the macroeconomic performance was respectable. Inflation dropped from 39% in 1994 to less than 5% by the early 2000s. The fiscal deficit, at nearly 9% of GDP in 1993, was first cut in half and then fell to 2.5% by 1997 (Chemingui 2003). Foreign exchange reserves had been restored to more than $16 billion by 2001, and the debt service ratio fell from 86% in 1988 to 49% in 1994 to 21% in 2000 (IMF). GDP growth recovered, reaching 3.4% for 1995–2000.

Even more dramatically than in Egypt, however, the microeconomic and, especially, institutional changes were far more problematic. The difficulties are classic ones. The process of privatization has been opaque, with regime insiders benefiting greatly from the privatization of some banks, import-export companies, and construction. Still more dramatically than in Egypt or Morocco, privatization in Algeria has been a *nomenklatura* privatization. At the same time, the rents engendered by the wedge between international and domestic prices had already led to the development of a "parallel economy," composed of shady traders, marginalized youth, and corrupt public officials. A number of observers (e.g., Martinez 1998; ICG 2001; Lowi 2005) have documented how such networks fueled the violence on both sides of the civil war, as economic conflict between competing mafias merged with—and in some accounts, increasingly replaced—ideological struggle.

Although the worst violence ended in 1999—after some 150,000 Algerians had perished—with the amnesty offered by President Bouteflika, popular distrust, even hatred, of *le pouvoir* remains intense. The Berber region continues to experience anti-regime violence, now increasingly of a non-Islamist type. The common cry is against *hogra,* the contempt that the elite have long shown for ordinary Algerians. Although the Algerian regime has regained macroeconomic balance and is now considerably aided by increased oil prices, the system remains very far from that envisaged by the Washington Consensus. Unemployment remains acute, housing shortages severe, and popular alienation from the state intense. Crony capitalism and corruption, fueled by oil rents, remain firmly entrenched.[22] *Le pouvoir* appears to have weathered the storm of the 1990s, containing popular dissatisfaction through patronage, divide-and-rule tactics, and violence. Ordinary Algerians have gained little.

Iran

By some measures, the Iranian economy has declined precipitously since the revolution. At the end of the Iran-Iraq War in 1988, per capita GDP was one-half of its 1977 level. Per capita incomes did not regain their prerevolution peak until 2004 (Salehi-Isfahani 2006). A combination of revolution, war, and collapsing oil prices ensured that the 1980s would see sharp declines in output. At the same time, population growth *accelerated* during the revolution (see Box 4.1). Despite the subsequent fertility revolution in Iran, the labor force grew at over 4% per year during the 1990s. Unsurprisingly, employment creation failed to match additions to the labor force. Measured unemployment rose from 10% to 14%, and more than two-thirds of new jobs created during the 1980s and early 1990s were in the public sector.

These failures need to be weighed against the dramatic improvements in a variety of human development indicators. Private consumption fell less than half as rapidly as per capita output (23% versus 50%) during the period 1977–1988 and grew more rapidly during 1997–2004 (4.6% per year) than during the boom years of 1960–1977 (Salehi-Isfahani 2006). The poverty rate fell from 47% in 1978 to 15.5% in 2001; half of the poor are covered by various government social safety net provisions (World Bank 2001a). As documented in Chapter 5, school enrollments of girls, including rural girls, boomed, infant and child mortality rates plummeted, and gaps between rural and urban human capital indicators narrowed.

These improvements were driven by public investments in drinking water, schools, rural (and urban) health clinics, and public food subsidies (Salehi-Isfahani 2006).

As with all wars between modern nation-states, the Iran-Iraq War greatly stimulated the centralization of economic decisionmaking. The basic statist economic structures, already well advanced under the shah, were markedly enhanced. The government implemented price controls, rationing of consumer goods, a deliberately overvalued exchange rate, strict quantitative regulation of imports, and tight controls over banking. It also constructed the familiar regulatory maze for private investors, who needed to obtain numerous permits. In the wake of the revolution, some 580 companies, all of them medium- to large-scale enterprises, were nationalized.

Like most developing countries, Iran displays marked industrial dualism—a large number of very small firms coexisting with a much smaller number of medium- and large-scale enterprises. This division also nearly coincides with a private-public split; all large-scale industries and the large majority of medium-scale enterprises are run by public institutions. In 1990/1991 public enterprises accounted for 73% of industrial value added, 72% of employment, and 65% of investment (Amuzegar 1993). The revolution greatly increased direct state management of Iranian industry. Manufacturing output stagnated during the 1980s (actually declining at a rate of 0.1% per year, according to the World Bank [Amuzegar 1993]). Some industries fared far worse than this; automobile production in 1992 was only 15% of the pre-1979 level. Growth revived during the 1989–1992 period, when the manufacturing sector grew at double-digit rates. However, much of this growth was capital-intensive, and less than 10% of the new entrants to the labor force were absorbed during this period.

The poor performance of the 1980s and early 1990s had three sources: the revolution itself, the usual problems of statist, inward-oriented policies, and low oil prices. The revolution and ensuing war can be blamed for political interference in management, labor strikes, exodus of managerial skills, and electrical power shortages. Inward-oriented policies such as tariffs and a grossly overvalued exchange rate insulated firms from competition, permitting inefficiency to flourish and creating a vested interest in the continuation of these policies. Oil prices collapsed in the mid-1980s, declined until 1994, ticked up briefly until 1996, and then fell to their post-1973 nadir in 1998 (see Figure 3.3 and Chapter 3). Since more than 80% of all Iranian exports consist of oil products, world oil markets delivered heavy blows to the economy.

Iran in the last two decades of the twentieth century displayed the regional symptoms of high and rising unemployment of semi-educated young people. It also showed evidence of increasing macroeconomic imbalances. As is common in the aftermath of wars, state investment for reconstruction increased; the investment rate rose from 25% of GDP in 1986 to 35% in 1991. Imports exploded, rising by 1994 to more than thirty times their (extremely compressed) 1986 level (Central Bank of Iran). The classic "twin gaps"—between imports and exports, and saving and investment—emerged with a vengeance in the first half of the 1990s.

The government also plugged these gaps in the classic manner: with monetary expansion and external borrowing. Inflation rose to 23% in 1996, although the presence of numerous price controls insulated consumers to some degree. As usual, such controls simply shifted inflationary pressures elsewhere, creating significant opportunities for (typically illegal) arbitrage. As export revenues collapsed with oil prices, the government also increased external, mainly short-term, borrowing. External debt rose from $4 billion to $22 billion in the four years from 1990 to 1994, reaching 35% of GDP in 1994 (UN 2003). The debt-service ratio rose from 15% in 1994 to over 60% in 1998 (World Bank 2001a; IMF 2006). The Iranian macroeconomic picture was further clouded by the US embargo, tightened in 1996, which made it relatively difficult for Iran to obtain external long-term financing.

Until 1989/1990 the exchange regime was tightly controlled and very complex, with some twelve different exchange rates. Although reform in 1991 simplified the system (to three rates) and reduced controls, in 1993 the free-market price of foreign exchange was *twenty times higher* than the official rate (in 1982 it had been twice as high). The government of 'Ali Akbar Hashemi Rafsanjani (1989–1994) announced various reform plans (e.g., unification of the exchange rate, privatization, and some dismantling of price controls). However, a combination of macroeconomic events and interest group pressures forced the government to retreat. On the macroeconomic side, the debt crisis of 1993, when the economy was near to default, induced the government to increase its control of the economy. Powerful interests, especially those grouped around the *bonyad,* or "foundations,"[23] likewise opposed any sharp turn toward economic liberalism.

The Islamic Republic has always rested on a coalition of groups with disparate economic interests. The coalition has included unemployed or underemployed youth and students, urban lumpens, conservative *bazaaris* (merchants), mullahs, and segments of the professional middle class. At the time of the revolution, the opposition to the shah seems to have been as widespread as Polish opposition to communist rule. Like Solidarity, the initial coalition led by Khomeini was very broad indeed. Over time it has narrowed, but the regime still rests on an uneasy alliance of two very different sets of interests: populist lower and lower middle classes and prosperous mullahs and those with whom they do business.

One observer discerns two main groups of political actors: "radicals," a grouping of "economically dependent radical *mullahs* (of mainly poor, provincial origin) and . . . left-wing elements infiltrating the high ranks of the bureaucracy," on the one hand, and "conservatives," with "strong financial and blood ties to the *bazaar* [who] have tended to represent the interests of landlords and the urban bourgeoisie," on the other (Amuzegar 1993, 32). Members of a third group, formed since Khomeini's death, the "pragmatists," have "close affiliations with the wealthy, but . . . have mainly *managed* and handled national wealth rather than *owned* it" (32). This last group was the core of support for tilting policies toward the Washington Consensus. The private oligopolists and rent seekers of the Pahlavi regime were expropriated, only to be replaced by the "economic mullahcracy" of the *bonyads* or foundations. They are often joined by wealthy *bazaaris,* who enjoy monopoly power as holders of quotas and licenses—classic rent seekers who obstruct change.

Such a configuration of interests, particularly in a context of oil-price instability, strongly suggests that economic policy will oscillate. When oil prices fall, pressures for market-oriented change become acute. Such pressures are partly accommodated, and they are also resisted. The political resistance limits the extent of the reforms, problems reemerge, and the cycle continues. Iran certainly has followed this pattern. At the beginning, the populists seemed to have had the upper hand, and a number of their views were incorporated into the constitution. Reformers first seized the initiative in the early 1990s, then retreated with the debt crisis. They resumed their push for changes by mid-decade and, as in so many other countries of the region, achieved their main successes through macroeconomic changes, rather than through structural change. Buoyant oil prices since 1999 also made changes easier, since budget cuts were no longer necessary, subsidies could be maintained, and jobs could be created. The regime was able to adapt, adjust, and maintain its power. Reformers regained the initiative again during the government of Muhammad Khatami (1997–2005).

The governments of Rafsanjani and Khatami made important changes, without altering the basic configurations of power within the polity. By 2002, the exchange rate was unified, and the country now employs a "managed float" regime for the currency. Many formerly implicit subsidies are now explicit, making for greater transparency. Both export restrictions and tariffs on imports have been reduced. Some 60% of Iranian imports enter the country with a tariff of less than 20%—not vastly different from other countries in the region. New legislation guaranteeing the repatriation of interest and capital, designed to help stimulate foreign investment, has been passed (IMF 2006).

The upward surge of oil prices since 1999, together with these gradualist reforms, have led to significant improvements in the economy. Inflation has fallen to about 15%; the debt stock fell to 10% of GDP, and debt service now consumes only 16% of exports of goods and services. Foreign exchange reserves are at a historical high of $47.4 billion, providing more than nine months of import cover. Although fluctuating from year to year, the government budget is roughly in balance, and the country enjoys a current account surplus. For the period of 2000/2001 to 2004/2005, GDP grew at more than 5.5% per year; in 2005 it grew at 5.9%. In consequence, the unemployment rate declined to just over 10%—which is still quite high (World Bank 2001a, 2006b; IMF 2006).

At the same time, progress on social indicators continues, and the coming deceleration of the growth of the labor force in the medium term offers some consolation on the employment front. Of course, much depends on the future course of oil prices. For now, however, the prognosis here, too, is decidedly bullish, from an Iranian perspective.

Problems undoubtedly remain, however. The growth surge is almost entirely due to the increase in oil prices; productivity has shown no increase (Mojaverhosseini 2003). The US embargo has impeded investment in the petroleum sector;[24] although Iran has managed to attract some $10 billion of investment in the sector, most observers think that this is far below what is needed (IMF 2006). By spending (rather than saving), oil revenue increases, the government is stimulating the Dutch Disease, and as we would expect, there was real appreciation of the currency, estimated at nearly 12%, during

2005 (IMF 2006). Thanks to the huge surge of entrants into the job market (recall that fertility actually increased in Iran in the 1980s, leading to a surge in job-market entrants now), job creation, even during a boom, has not made a significant dent in unemployment (although it has prevented it from getting worse). Subsidies on food, medicines, and other items come to about 4% of GDP; food subsidies are entirely untargeted. Far worse is the huge implicit subsidy to energy consumption, estimated at over 15% of GDP. The price of gasoline in Iran in 2005 was $0.09 per liter ($0.34 per gallon), stimulating both horrendous air pollution in Tehran (see Chapter 10) and rampant smuggling to Pakistan, where the price is nine time higher (IMF 2006).

There has been some modest privatization; assets amounting to some 0.5% of GDP were sold on the Tehran Stock Exchange in 2000–2001, and other shares were distributed to workers. On the whole, however, the fundamental features of the political economy created by the Islamic revolution (and before) have remained very much intact. The regime has gambled, correctly as it has turned out, that more flexible macroeconomic management, external debt reduction, and other macroeconomic changes could be implemented without significant political risk. Unemployment, although high, was likewise manageable. The vast network of patronage represented by the *bonyad* ensured that regime supporters, both among the poor and the *bazaari* merchants, continued to receive benefits even during the lean years of the early to mid-1990s. Some critics of the regime expressed the hope that unemployment and discontent among young people might lead to regime change (e.g., Kanovsky 1999). But the dense web of patron-client relations of the *bonyad,* the loyalty of the war generation (Bulliet 1999), the state's firm control of the means of coercion, and the revival of oil prices ensured that such a scenario never materialized.

As this edition is written, escalating conflict between Iran and the United States over Iran's nuclear capability and the 2006 war in Lebanon clouds the horizon. As external tensions rise, the Ahmedinejad government has been able to "play the nationalist card." Even prominent dissidents rally around the flag.[25] In addition to the serious risk of escalation through miscalculation, such an environment does little to encourage any relaxation of the state's control of the political economy.

CONCLUSION

Although the problems and contradictions of state-led growth were (and are) real enough, there was—and is—no simple, much less universal, set of institutional changes that can overcome them. The problems of economic growth and structural change are intractable, complex, murky, and deeply, inescapably political. Sweeping "reform packages" were always suspect, if for no other reason than it is political folly to offend everyone at once—which is what the economic logic of the Washington Consensus often implied. Further, the benefits of reform are always uncertain, and losers may be better placed to act. As it has turned out, the benefits have often been mixed, unequally distributed, and potentially destabilizing.

It is hardly surprising, therefore, that regimes implemented economic-policy changes gradually and selectively. Regimes fear—with reason—that the full-scale embrace of the Washington Consensus entails a high risk of political destabilization. Powerful vested interests either block reforms or ensure that the specific kind of change yields disproportionate benefits to them, at the expense of other social groups. The result has been a very mixed picture, in which regimes have embraced some, often many, economic reforms. As a simple generalization, one can say that many MENA governments have markedly improved macroeconomic management but have postponed or simply balked at more complex reforms, such as privatization, regulatory reform, or development of the rule of law.

Whether due to the inherent difficulties of implementing economic policy or to the unevenness of reform, the results of economic reform have been relatively disappointing. Although in some countries economic performance in the mid-to-late 1990s was considerably better than in the previous ten years, in no country has growth been strong enough to lower unemployment or significantly raise real wages and living standards, as has happened in East Asia (see Chapter 5). Nor is there strong evidence that countries that embraced much of the Washington Consensus performed markedly better than those who eschewed many of the recommended changes.

As we saw in Chapter 8, much of the impetus for change came from the accumulation of debt and fiscal imbalances. Although these arguably had been building for some time, they became acute due to the collapse of oil prices in the mid-1980s. The decline of rents was widely noted at the time, and many analysts (including the authors of this book) thought that such a development provided an opportunity for real institutional change. Changes certainly occurred; many economies are more open to trade, most have achieved better macroeconomic management, and the private sector is more active than before. Yet it is also true that only in Turkey has sweeping institutional change occurred. Other regimes have been able to manage a "dilatory reform" process with considerable skill, and even in Turkey daunting challenges remain. The economies survived the lean years of the 1990s, and no regimes fell.[26] Regimes did enough to keep afloat, and repression did the rest.

In the second edition of this book we wrote, "The conventional wisdom in the Middle East is that its economic reform programs are the result of leaders' survival strategies." The conventional wisdom proved true, and the strategies were largely successful. Today vast rents once again pour into the region, thanks to the oil-price explosion and to renewed strategic rents (for those friendly to the United States) after 9/11. MENA government spokesmen often chided outside analysts for their lack of political realism and for underestimating the tolerance of their citizens for "muddling through." The view from 2007 is that the countries of the region were not necessarily wrong to reject calls for sweeping economic reform and that they may not have been foolish to "make haste slowly."

NOTES

1. Specifically, the so-called neoclassical resurgence in economics and the rise of rational choice theory in political science.

2. See, e.g., the discussions of this viewpoint in Scott (1998), and Gray (1998).

3. An example of this logic applied to the MENA region can be found in Dasgupta, Keller, and Srinivasan (2002).

4. "The new 'consensus' reflects what a rich country already looks like. If a developing country can acquire, say, Denmark's institutions, it is already rich and need not worry about development. The list of institutional reforms describes not what countries need to do in order to develop—the list certainly does not correspond to what today's advanced countries did during their early development—but where they are likely to end up once they develop" (Rodrik 2004, 6). This is not to say that the institutions of all rich countries are alike; the voluminous literature on corporate governance differences in the United States, the European Union, and Japan suggests otherwise.

5. The limit of this perspective may be found in the draconian neoliberal policies of the Coalition Provisional Authority instituted by the United States in Iraq from 2003 to 2005 (Looney 2004; Klein 2004). Sweeping privatization, deregulation, and downsizing of the state reached their *reductio ad absurdum,* in the increasingly Hobbesian environment of Iraq at the time. States may be sclerotic, but, as we have known since the days of Aristotle, al-Ghazali, and Hobbes, they are preferable to anarchy.

6. The discrepancy is partly explained by the Turkish rule that a party must garner at least 10% of the popular vote to receive any representation in parliament.

7. At least 1,500 villages were destroyed, and some 30,000 people lost their lives amid widespread human rights abuses by both the Kurdish rebels and the Turkish government. (Keyder 2004)

8. A Turkish phrase *(derin devlet)* covering the key players in the military, security services, courts, and other Atatürkist public institutions.

9. The Republic of Cyprus is an EU member. The Turkish Republic of Cyprus, recognized only by Turkey, is under a trade embargo by the EU. Turkey must open its borders to full trade with all EU members, including the Republic of Cyprus. Turkey argues that, while it is willing to do this, at the same time, the embargo on Turkish Cyprus should be lifted. As of this writing, this problem has yet to be resolved.

10. Tunisia deliberately maintained an undervalued real exchange rate in the late 1990s to compensate for the decline in tariff barriers under the terms of the Association Agreement with the EU (Bechri and Naccache 2003).

11. Some of the increase, however, was to improve teachers' salaries, which could be viewed as a form of investment in human capital.

12. For example, the World Bank (2006a): "Morocco has a sound macro stance" (p. 16).

13. The effective rate of protection includes the impact of tariffs on inputs, and hence costs, to domestic producers.

14. The OTRI measures "the uniform tariff that, if imposed at the border, would have the same effect on aggregate imports as the current structure of trade measures." Morocco's OTRI is 0.51, Tunisia's 0.37, China's 0.20, and Turkey's 0.12 (World Bank 2006b, 43).

15. The traditional term for the Moroccan royal state apparatus.

16. The failure of "economic reform" to produce more accountable governance in Tunisia and elsewhere is thoroughly analyzed by Eva Bellin (2002).

17. In July 2006, the EU announced that Morocco, Tunisia, Lebanon, and Israel "will be separated from European countries in the EU's European Neighborhood Policy (ENP) on the grounds that they will never be allowed to join the EU" (Watt 2006).

18. By way of comparison, during the same period, in Indonesia, another relatively large economy of the Global South, and also an oil exporter like Egypt, the corresponding figures rose from 22.4% to 40.8% for the same years. By contrast, the export share in the Moroccan, Tunisian, and Turkish economies all increased during the decade.

19. Telecommunications are a critical "network" industry, without which no country can develop viable exports.

20. "The power," or the ruling elite of army generals and crony capitalist allies.

21. When defending their abrogation of the 1991–1992 elections and asking for financial and other assistance, Algerian authorities asked members of the French government, "Would you accept that oil rent fell into the hands of the Islamists?" (Lowi 2005, 15).

22. Algeria ranks 97th of 159 countries in Transparency International's Index of Corruption for 2005, earning a composite score of 2.5 out of a possible 10.

23. The largest foundation, *Bonyad-i-Mostazafan,* "The Foundation of the Deprived," officially controls some $3.5 billion in assets (other sources cite much higher figures) and manages more than 400 companies, in sectors ranging from food processing to metals to construction materials, financial institutions, and five-star hotels. Such companies employ over 400,000 people (World Bank 2001a; Devaux 2003).

24. A US law passed in 1996 provides for US sanctions against any company investing more than $20 million in Iran.

25. For example, the formerly imprisoned journalist Akbar Ganji refused to meet with White House officials during a visit to Washington in July 2006 because he believed that such a meeting would undermine the credibility of the pro-democracy reform movement in Iran (BBC, July 25, 2006). Likewise, the Nobel Peace Prize–winner Shirin Ebadi argued that taking Iran to the Security Council over the nuclear issue weakened human rights advocates in Iran (Ebadi and Sahimi 2006).

26. Of course, the fall of the Ba'athist regime in Iraq had essentially nothing to do with the issues discussed in this chapter.

10

URBAN POLITICAL ECONOMY

The Middle East has long been dominated by its cities. Even in 1800, after several centuries of decline, perhaps 25% of the population of Greater Syria and 10% of Egyptians lived in cities of over 10,000 people (Issawi 1969, 102–103). Cities dominated their rural hinterlands and were focal points of the extensive international trade system linking Europe to Asia. Landlords and rulers alike lived in the cities, not in the countryside as did their European feudal counterparts. The medina was the center of gravity for economics, politics, religion, and intellectual life.

This historical legacy continues today. The cities of the region hold most of the industry, a large and growing percentage of the labor force, and the majority of government officials. They contain most of the modern health facilities and universities; they are the centers of drama, film, television, publishing, and intellectual life generally. Their residents enjoy higher incomes and better standards of health and education than their rural cousins. Cities also display severe economic and political problems, many of which are caused by rapid urbanization: acute housing shortages; insecure and unremunerative employment; water, power, and sewage failures; and political violence.

The overall picture of urbanization is shown in Table 10.1 and Figures 10.1, 10.2, and 10.3. The region is more urbanized than East Asia, South Asia, or sub-Saharan Africa, but less urbanized than Latin America (where over 70% of the population lives in cities). Close to 60% of the population of the region lives in cities; over half the population lives in cities in every country in the region except for Egypt, Sudan, and Yemen. Most countries are at least as urbanized as Italy; many are as urbanized as the United States (see Table 10.2).

If the term "urban" is used in the internationally accepted sense of "population aggregations above a certain size," then the region is even more urbanized than official data report. The government of Egypt, the largest Arab country and the third most populous country in the region, uses an idiosyncratic, administrative definition of "urban." According to its government, Egyptians are "urban" if they live in the governorate of Cairo or in the capital of any other governorate. By this definition,

TABLE 10.1 Urbanization Indicators

	% Urban Population			Urban Population (thousands)			Projected Urban Growth Rates	
	2000	2010	2020	2000	2010	2020	2000–2010	2010–2020
Algeria	57.1	62.6	67.5	17,311	22,323	27,301	2.5	2.0
Bahrain	92.2	94.4	95.3	590	702	803	1.7	1.3
Egypt	42.7	44.0	48.2	28,970	34,871	43,252	1.9	2.2
Iran	64.0	70.6	75.5	45,023	57,032	70,574	2.4	2.1
Iraq	67.5	67.7	70.1	15,493	20,268	25,971	2.7	2.5
Israel	91.6	93.0	93.9	5,535	6,738	7,604	2.0	1.2
Jordan	78.7	80.1	82.2	3,867	5,147	6,524	2.9	2.4
Kuwait	91.0	96.7	97.1	1,838	2,391	2,930	2.6	2.0
Lebanon	89.7	92.1	93.1	3,128	3,700	4,102	1.7	1.0
Libya	87.6	89.7	90.9	4,635	5,858	6,829	2.3	1.5
Morocco	55.5	61.7	66.7	16,571	21,796	26,583	2.7	1.9
Oman	76.0	80.8	83.9	1,928	2,841	3,982	3.9	3.4
Palestine	66.8	70.0	73.5	2,132	3,167	4,550	4.0	3.6
Qatar	92.7	94.5	95.4	524	617	694	1.6	1.2
Saudi Arabia	86.2	90.0	91.6	17,531	24,837	33,054	3.5	2.9
Sudan	36.1	45.0	51.8	11,231	17,383	23,887	4.4	3.1
Syria	51.4	55.4	60.6	8,324	11,519	15,435	3.3	2.9
Tunisia	65.5	71.3	75.2	6,198	7,576	8,909	2.0	1.6
Turkey	65.8	69.9	73.7	43,844	52,491	61,060	1.8	1.5
UAE	86.7	90.5	92.4	2,260	2,765	3,107	2.0	1.2
Yemen	24.7	28.5	34.4	4,534	7,789	13,775	5.4	5.7

SOURCE: UN Habitat 2003

TABLE 10.2 Percentage of People Living in Urban Areas, by Country, 2000

≥ 90 %	Bahrain, Israel, Kuwait, Qatar
≥ 80 %	Libya, Lebanon, Saudi Arabia, UAE
≥ 70 %	Jordan, Oman, United States
≥ 60 %	Tunisia, Iran, Iraq, Palestine, Turkey, Italy
≥ 50 %	Algeria, Morocco, Syria
< 50 %	Egypt (actually 80%), Sudan, Yemen

SOURCE: UN Habitat 2003

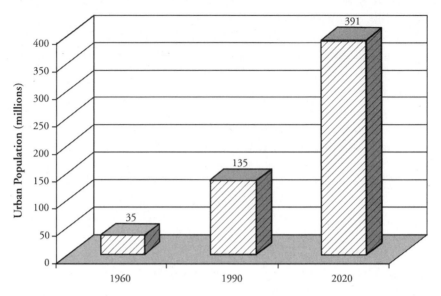

FIGURE 10.1 Urban population of MENA, actual and projected
SOURCE: World Bank 1994e

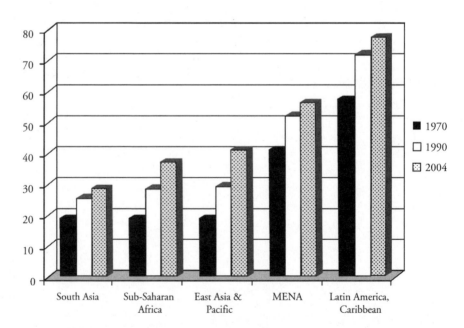

FIGURE 10.2 Urban population as a percentage of total population, 1970–2004
SOURCE: World Bank, World Development Indicators Online, 2004

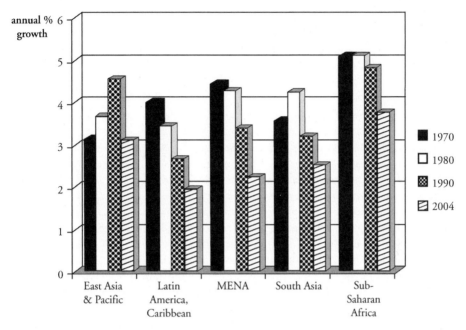

FIGURE 10.3 Urban population growth, 1970–2004
SOURCE: World Bank, World Development Indicators Online, 2004

the last national census (1996) reported that 42.6% of the population was urban. However, if "urban" means "people living in agglomerations whose population exceeds 10,000," then 66.8% of the population was "urban," and if we use the definition used in India or Yemen (agglomerations whose population exceeds 5,000), then roughly four of five Egyptians live in so-defined urban environments (Bayat and Denis 2000). Overwhelmingly, most Middle Easterners are city people.

In many cases, the urban population is concentrated in one or two very large cities. There are sixteen cities with more than 1 million inhabitants. Baghdad, with more than 5 million inhabitants, contains more than a third of all urban Iraqis and roughly 20% of the country's total population. In 1970 Beirut was home to over 60% of the urban population of Lebanon. The region's (and Africa's) largest city, Cairo, holds perhaps 15 million inhabitants,[1] making it about as large as New York City. Istanbul and Tehran are not far behind, with populations of between 11 and 12 million.

As elsewhere in the Global South, MENA cities have grown swiftly. The World Bank estimates that MENA cities grew at over 4% per year from 1980 to 2000, a rate exceeded only by sub-Saharan Africa (World Bank 2005b). As usual, the rate of growth appears the highest in the least-urbanized countries. Some observers believe that small- and medium-sized towns now show the most rapid growth

(UN-HABITAT 2004, 68). Although urban population growth is very important, in many cases, rural-to-urban migration is probably the critical component of the process—but the data are uncertain, and there is much variation across countries.

THE PROCESS OF URBANIZATION

The diverse weight of cities in populations within the region, ranging from a low of just under 25% in Yemen to over 90% in Kuwait and Israel, is broadly consistent with a simple expectation: the higher the per capita income, the higher the percentage of the population that is urban. Of course, this is not a causal statement; indeed, it is much more plausible that increased urbanization and rising per capita incomes are both the result of economic growth and, especially, of industrialization.

One of the most important aspects of urbanization in the region is its speed. The number of urban Middle Easterners has risen from 35 million (about a third of the population) in 1960 to 135 million (slightly over half) in 1990 (World Bank 1994e) to more than 250 million today (see Figure 10.1). This rapid growth has had three sources: reclassification, natural growth of the urban population, and rural-to-urban migration. In general, the higher the percentage of a nation's population that is urban, the greater the relative weight of population growth in total urban growth.

A very crude calculation would begin by assuming that rates of natural increase (fertility minus mortality rates) are the same in urban and rural areas and then approximate the rate of rural-to-urban migration (plus reclassification) as the difference between the rate of growth of cities and the overall rate of population growth. Keeping in mind the crudeness of the data and the assumptions, several generalizations can be made. Rural-to-urban migration accounts for about one-third to roughly half of the growth of cities in Iran, Morocco, Oman, the Sudan, and Tunisia. This pattern has changed over time, as argued in the previous paragraph. In the period 1965–1980, more than half of urbanization in six countries (Jordan, Lebanon, Libya, Oman, Tunisia, and the former YAR) can be explained by rural-to-urban migration; for the period 1990–2003, this was true only for the Sudan and Tunisia. The growth of the region's largest city, Cairo, is mainly due to natural increase. Indeed, population in the center of the city is falling, as soaring land prices and crowding drive less fortunate Cairenes out of the city core toward peripheral settlements (Sims 2003; Sutton and Fahmi 2001). By contrast, some 220,000 people are estimated to abandon the Moroccan countryside every year (Fadili 2000).

This methodology may underestimate the importance of rural-to-urban migration in urban growth. First of all, the assumption that the rate of population growth is the same in rural and urban areas is dubious. A priori, we would certainly expect both fertility and mortality rates to be lower in urban areas. As we have seen, much of the variance in fertility rates can be explained by income differences, and average urban incomes are typically higher than rural ones. Female literacy is higher in the cities, and infant mortality is usually lower; both suggest that urban fertility should be lower than rural. However, since mortality is also very probably lower in urban areas,[2] it is uncertain whether overall rates of natural increase are lower in the cities than in the village.

Furthermore, the high rates of natural increase in the cities are arguably them-selves linked to rural-to-urban migration. Typically, rural-to-urban migration is un-dertaken by whole families and is especially prevalent among the young. The transfer of population of childbearing age to the cities obviously raises the rate of urban natu-ral increase (Todaro 1984). A substantial portion of children born in the cities have parents who have recently arrived from the countryside. When this factor is taken into consideration, it seems clear that for most countries of the region, rural-to-urban migration remains an important explanator of the rapid growth of urban areas.

Although differences between rural and urban wages and incomes in MENA are not excessive by developing-country standards, they are substantial, usually on the order of 1.5 to 3.0. Of course, a potential migrant has to consider the risk of failing to find a job in the city—a risk usually measured by urban unemployment rates. Measuring unemployment in developing countries is difficult. Official, measured unemployment rates are often high in the region, but they are often quite low for unskilled workers (see Chapter 5). Even if we take the higher numbers at face value, however, and even if we assume that rural workers have no difficulty finding jobs in the countryside, migrating to the city is still a good investment.

It may be objected that the cost of living in rural areas is lower than in the cities. Two points should be considered here. First, such cost differentials are rarely as large as the differences in nominal wages. Although housing may be more expensive in the cities, extensive food-subsidy systems, usually confined to the cities, reduce food costs for urban dwellers to the same levels as those in rural areas or even lower. Since food usually constitutes nearly half of the total expenditure of poor persons in MENA countries, food subsidies significantly reduce rural/urban cost-of-living dif-ferences. Second, other benefits of urban life, such as better educational and health facilities, further widen the gap between real incomes in urban and rural areas.

Finally, in some cases people have left rural areas simply because they could not survive there. Some (e.g., Davis 2006) argue that this is increasingly the driving force behind the rural exodus. Much of the recent growth of North African and Su-danese cities is due to the influx of drought refugees; people whose crops or rural employment prospects were wiped out by bad weather. Such disasters may swamp growth impacts based on a Todaro model. In Morocco, for example, USAID esti-mates that urban unemployment rates are four times higher than rural rates (20% versus 5%). Government neglect of rural areas or misguided agricultural policies (see Chapter 6) have also played a major role in creating incentives for rural people to move to town.

Some of the urban influx consists of rural people fleeing political violence, as in Algeria and the Sudan. The impact of such violence is not simple, however. In Iraq, available data suggest that urban areas grew less rapidly than the population as a whole during the 1990s. If such data can be credited, then the politically induced collapse of the Iraqi urban economy may have caused some Iraqis to return to their former villages.

Two other tributaries of rural-to-urban migration flows are increased rural edu-cation and (during the oil boom) the Dutch Disease. Young men who receive some education pour out of the countryside in large numbers, often taking their families with them. One study of rural migrants to Tehran found that over two-thirds were literate, compared with overall rural literacy rates of about 20%. Over two-fifths of farmers with a primary education wanted to move to the cities (Kazemi 1980a). This is a universal phenomenon; educated people everywhere leave the farm for the cities. One of the ironies of development is that successful educational programs in rural areas swell urban populations.

HOUSING AND INFRASTRUCTURE

Probably the most visible and pressing problem facing both the increasing numbers of urban residents and their governments is the provision of adequate housing. The rapid growth of urban populations has caused demand for housing to outstrip supply, spawning shortages, overcrowding, and/or soaring rents. Governments have often allocated substantial sums to housing even while implementing regulations that hinder private housing construction. In other cases, government housing expenditures have been perceived as diversions from growth-enhancing industrial investment, and so they have been severely constrained. Public utilities have been inefficiently managed and underfunded, with their outputs heavily subsidized. The result has been poor, intermittent service and inadequate coverage. The turn toward the private sector has done little to remedy these problems.

The explosion of cities during the 1960s and 1970s created a huge housing backlog, a deficit that has yet to be erased. A few examples illustrate the magnitude of the problem. Moroccan cities have been growing by 1,000 people *every day*. Although the supply of housing units roughly doubled between 1973 and 1977, the shortfall increased from 390,000 units in 1973 to 800,000 units in 1977 (World Bank 1981). In Algeria, where public enterprises dominate the construction business, public construction of housing fell from 90,000 units in 1986 to 30,000 in 1991; during this period the annual incremental demand for housing was 200,000 units. The shortage was estimated at more than 2 million units; the average occupancy rate, about 8.5 persons per unit, was one of the highest ratios for any middle-income country (World Bank 1994a). The situation in Egypt was equally grim: A huge housing deficit (of more than 2 million units) was accumulated between 1960 and 1979. Much of the existing housing stock was (and remains) decidedly substandard; in 1982, 23% of urban households had no electricity, over one-sixth had no access to potable water, and nearly two-thirds lacked sewage hookups (Mohie el-Din 1982). Much of modern Cairo, where vast districts (Masr al-Qadima, Sayyida Zeinab, Darb al-Ahmar, Gamalia, Bulaq) became almost uniformly run-down, is substandard. More than a half-million Cairenes still live on rooftops, and well over a million live in and around the tombs of the City of the Dead. New construction lagged slightly behind new households, and therefore the gap remains vast (World Bank 1990b). Further, much of the new housing was, and remains, extremely expensive and certainly well beyond the reach of most young men seeking to start a family. At the same time, rent control forced some luxury flats overlooking the Nile to rent for the price of an off-season watermelon.

Regrettably, this picture changed little during the 1990s and the early years of the new millennium. The public sector, increasingly downsized as part of the "economic-reform" process, has built little housing, and private housing, in MENA as everywhere else, depends on income. Since incomes, particularly for the poor, either stagnated or grew only slowly, it is not surprising that the problems accumulated during earlier decades have remained unsolved. Continued rapid urban growth, as well as decreasing family size, ensured a soaring demand for housing.[3] For the poor, supply was, at best, a makeshift affair. They may reasonably be said to live in "slums."

In 2003, the United Nations published a worldwide study of "slums," defined as neighborhoods combining substandard or illegal housing, inadequate or nonexistent services such as water and sewerage services, and overcrowding (UN-HABITAT 2003). Based on these criteria, huge numbers of people in the region live in slums (see Table 10.3). The slum population of Cairo, for example, was estimated at more than 12 million in 1996 (Sims 2003). In fact, this number includes only people living in "informal settlements"; it does not include the people living in the "deteriorated urban core." In Greater Khartoum, now a city of more than 5 million people, 3.5 million live in slums (Eltayib 2003). The region's largest single slum is Sadr City

TABLE 10.3 MENA Slums

	Number of People Living in Slums (10^3)	Percent of Urban Population Living in Slums
MENA	87,433	35.8
Algeria	2,101	11.8
Bahrain	12	2.0
Egypt	11,762	39.9
Iran	20,406	44.2
Iraq	9,026	56.7
Israel	113	2.0
Jordan	623	15.7
Lebanon	1,602	50.0
Libya	1,674	35.2
Morocco	5,579	32.7
Oman	1,214	60.5
Qatar	11	2.0
Saudi Arabia	3,609	19.8
Sudan	10,107	85.7
Syria	892	1.4
Tunisia	234	3.7
Turkey	19,080	42.6
Yemen	3,110	65.1

SOURCE: UN Habitat 2003

of Baghdad, with a population of more than 1.5 million (UN-HABITAT 2003). As the Middle East and North Africa urbanizes, it is becoming a "region of slums."

Of course, not everyone lives in slums. Every city in the region has neighborhoods of well-maintained, comfortable, often elegant housing inhabited by the upper end of the social scale. In the Maghreb, upper- and middle-class Moroccans, Tunisians, and Algerians often occupied the dwellings of the (often hastily) departed French. Moroccan cities boast new residential developments, with comfortably low densities; even densely populated Cairo has its favored districts (such as Zamalek, Doqqi, and Maadi). The phenomenon of "gated communities," so familiar to urban Americans, is increasingly popular in Egypt, Turkey, and elsewhere (Dundar 2003; Bayat and Denis 2000). The hopes of the well-to-do inhabitants are often reflected in the names of these settlements, such as "Dream Land," "Utopia," or "Beverly Hills," in Greater Cairo (Bayat and Denis 2000).

The class bias of the housing problem partly reflects two facts: (1) In all countries, most housing construction is in the private sector, which, of course, responds to ability to pay; and (2) public-sector housing and other subsidy schemes for low-income housing in general have been inadequately funded or misconceived or both. In some cases, class bias has been an official element of policy; in the Moroccan plan of 1973–1977, the first goal of housing policy and spending was to meet the needs of those with the ability to pay (World Bank 1981). In Tunisia, although the large majority of units built under the 1977–1981 plan was designed to satisfy the needs of the poor, the average cost of new units was out of reach for the poorer half of the population (H. Nelson 1979, 101). The Egyptian officer corps, and other privileged social segments, have housing generously subsidized by the public purse. In the region, as elsewhere, access to capital markets, and thus to private housing, is far easier for the already relatively privileged.

Some policies intended to benefit the poor have been misguided. Two of these seem especially prominent: rent control and attempts to clean up shantytowns. Official rent control in Cairo has had the usual effects: (1) it depressed private investment in housing; (2) it led to the substitution of "key money" for rent and other ways of circumventing the rules; and (3) it discouraged people from moving, presumably either reducing the flexibility of the labor market, increasing the demand for (grossly inadequate) urban transportation, or both. In short, it engendered inefficiencies with little compensatory increase in equity (Mohie el-Din 1982).

Most of the cities of the region are surrounded by squatter settlements: neighborhoods of relatively poor urbanites, with nonexistent or insecure title to the land they occupy, living in dwellings made of very crude materials. The various national names illustrate their nature: *bidonvilles* ("tin-can cities": Morocco, Algeria), *gourbivilles* ("peasant-style mud-hut towns": Tunisia), *gecekondu* ("housing built overnight": Turkey), and *ashwaiyyat* ("haphazard" or "random" settlements: Egypt). In 1981 about one-quarter of urban Moroccans and Turks lived in such settlements; in some cities the proportion was much higher. Nearly two-thirds of the population of Ankara live in *gecekondu*, with an average of more than two persons per room. Southern Tehran, northern Cairo, Omdurman, and Casablanca have similar conditions. Many of these people are recent rural migrants. One study for Turkey estimated that 85% of the inhabitants of *gecekondu* came from the countryside (Danielson and Keleç 1980). Squatter settlements house more than 1.3 million residents of Khartoum; the city's area has expanded *48 times* since 1955 (Eltayib 2003).

Until fairly recently, states were hostile to these urban formations, which not only were unsightly but often forced urban administrations to extend already over-stretched electric, water, and sewage facilities. Governments tried to prohibit such construction and even attempted to tear down existing structures. Residents resisted these actions (in Iran and Turkey), however, and economic reforms implied greater fiscal austerity and increased reliance on the private sector; both suggested that the government should leave shantytowns alone. Many governments have now revised their policies, embracing at least some of the arguments of John Turner, who observed nearly forty years ago that shantytown residents, like anyone else, would try hard to improve their own housing if they felt secure (Turner 1969). Self-help reha-bilitation of the *bidonvilles* is now government policy in Morocco; the Turkish government tries to offer low-cost loans to cooperative housing projects in the *gecekondu*. The available evidence vindicates Turner and the new policy approach. Turkey's *gecekondu* are considerably more substantial than equivalent shantytowns in Latin America, more solidly built and usually connected to electricity (*Economist*, June 18, 1988). The *gourbiville* residents of Tunisia replace the original mud walls first with brick, then with cement block.

Other components of urban infrastructure also show serious problems. Al-though national statistics indicate that the large majority of urbanites have access to drinking water and sanitation, in fact there are numerous shortages due to poor maintenance. Solid-waste collection is adequate in the larger cities, but disposal is a serious problem. In Tetouan, Morocco, wastes were simply piled up until they caused landslides. Waste collection is woefully inadequate in the smaller- and medium-sized cities. In Yemen, over half of all urban garbage goes uncollected. We saw in Chapter 6 that water pollution is serious everywhere in the region. The Nile at Cairo, for example, has a dissolved oxygen content of approximately zero.[4]

Other environmental problems plague the region's cities. Air pollution is often very serious. Tehran, whose geography and atmospherics resemble Los Angeles (i.e., bordered by mountains and subject to ozone-layer inversions), is one of the world's most polluted cities (Madanipour 1999). The levels of lead in the air in Cairo may cause brain damage and mental retardation in small children. Cairo's children have the highest levels of lead in their blood in the world. Nor are children the only vic-tims: Nearly 10% of the residents of Greater Cairo suffer from respiratory illnesses due to air pollution (El Araby 2002). Although automobiles are the main culprit, accounting for 60–70% of emissions, growing small-scale industry (employing fifty workers or less) in the mega-city increasingly burns soft coal (lignite), which, al-though cheap, is extremely polluting.

Solutions to these problems will cost money; the World Bank estimated ten years ago that solving the problem of municipal solid-waste collection for the region as a whole would require US$4–6 billion of investment over a ten-year period (World

Bank 1995b). Solutions to water-distribution and air-quality problems will be still more expensive. Unsurprisingly, governments failed to meet the challenge and, as in so many areas, at best managed not to fall even further behind.

For all the urban problems of the region, one remains relatively minor in comparative terms: street crime. In sharp contrast to many cities in Latin America, sub-Saharan Africa, and North America, major Middle Eastern cities have very few areas that are unsafe for men to walk in at any hour. People complain, as everywhere, about crime, but there is nothing even remotely resembling the anomie and random violence of Lagos, Bogotá, or Los Angeles in Cairo, Istanbul, or Casablanca. It is a tribute to the social cohesiveness of Muslim societies that this nearly universal plague of the modern world has been relatively mild in the region. Of course, none of this applies to cities in the midst of civil wars, like Beirut during 1976–1991 or Baghdad since 2003.

POVERTY AND DISTRIBUTION OF INCOME

All MENA governments proclaim their desire to reduce poverty and to promote equity. Evaluating their progress in these areas is fraught with both conceptual and practical problems. Data on poverty and expenditure distribution is scarce and episodic; only Israel has the thorough and effective income tax collection system that generates the ample data sets used by analysts of OECD countries. For all other countries, we must rely on sample surveys. These surveys, however, have been conducted for only a few countries in the region: Algeria, Egypt, Iran, Jordan, Morocco, Tunisia, and Yemen (Iqbal 2006; Adams and Page 2003). When the World Bank describes "poverty" in "MENA," they mean this subset of countries; note that *all* of the countries of the Gulf, including the world's largest oil exporter, Saudi Arabia, are "black holes" of ignorance when it comes to poverty assessments. The limited survey data is available only to researchers working for international agencies. Unfortunately, "in no Middle Eastern or North African country does the public have unfettered access to household survey-based poverty data" (Iqbal 2006, 2).

These surveys are usually not conducted regularly, which makes assessments of progress (or its absence) over time problematic. The data also refer to *expenditures,* rather than *incomes.* Although the former are quite useful for measuring poverty, their exclusion of savings makes them a much less reliable indicator of equity. Unless otherwise stated, all data referred to in this section are expenditure rather than income data. For these reasons, all statements concerning poverty and distribution in the region should be taken with several truck-loads of salt.

The difficulties increase when we step back to ask, What does "poverty" mean? Ever since the days of classical political economy, the concepts of poverty and subsistence have been intertwined. A "poor person" is one whose consumption falls below some minimal, subsistence, level.[5] Implicitly for Smith and Ricardo, and explicitly for Marx, the notion of subsistence or poverty was a *social* idea—the acceptable standard of living varied in place and time. Perhaps the world's most prominent economic analyst of poverty, Amartya Sen, has argued (1983) that there is a sense in which "absolute poverty" is meaningful. He argues, however, that what is absolute are the "capabilities"—the capacities to lead a rewarding life—whereas the commodities that are necessary for such a life are relative.[6] Since household surveys provide information only on commodity consumption, Sen's perspective does not much affect the following discussion.

Practically speaking, there exist four broad definitions of poverty in the available data. Two of these are the World Bank's "international poverty lines" of roughly $1 PPP per day and roughly $2 PPP per day. A debate rages on the utility of these measures.[7] The World Bank claims that its dual approach was an attempt to find out how many people were "truly poor" in the world. Critics point out that the lower definition of $1 PPP fails to meet any reasonable definition of subsistence, was created in a methodologically suspect manner, and in any case, is far too low for most countries of the region. In particular, critics have pointed out that these measures do not accurately reflect the cost of some minimal subsistence basket of commodities, which has been the conceptual basis for poverty for more than two hundred years. Nevertheless, these measures have been widely used in the discourse on world poverty. Some international comparisons using this (rather dubious) metric are shown in Figure 10.4.

For some countries, two national poverty lines have been established, a so-called lower and an upper poverty line. Both begin by specifying a minimum set of food

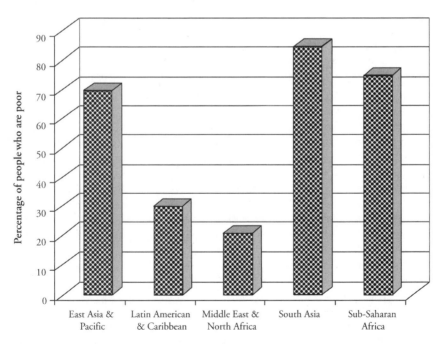

FIGURE 10.4   Incidence of poverty ($2 PPP per day standard) among developing regions, 2000
SOURCE: World Bank Global Poverty Monitoring Database

commodities deemed necessary to avoid malnutrition. Not even the most wretched human being spends all of her income on food; people will starve rather than go naked in public. In Algeria, for example, even the poorest 10% of people spent roughly one-third of their money on nonfood necessities (Belkacem 2001). Therefore, to determine the "cost of subsistence" or the "poverty line," the cost of the minimum food bundle (MFB) must be "scaled up" to include some allowance for spending on nonfood necessities. For the "lower" line, this is done by raising the MFB cost by the budget share of nonfood necessities for those people *whose total spending is equal to the cost of the MFB*. By definition, such people are not getting enough to eat: their total spending is equal to the cost of the MFB, but part of that spending is for nonfood necessities. The alternative "upper poverty line" scales up the cost of the MFB by the budget share of nonfood necessities for those people *whose food spending is equal to the cost of the MFB*. Such people are getting just enough to eat and then are buying a few other necessities. Clearly, the upper poverty line is the *only* measure that is consistent with the meaning of the word poverty in the more than two-hundred-year-old discourse on the subject in the English language.

The choice of poverty line can have dramatic implications for assessing the severity of poverty. Table 10.4 shows data for four countries, using the conventional "head count index."[8] Recently, Farrukh Iqbal of the World Bank has pointed out that only the $2 PPP line (and not the often-cited $1 PPP line) has much meaning for the countries of the region for which data exist. The data in Table 10.4 and the argument of the preceding paragraph suggest that even this benchmark is too narrow a definition of poverty in the region. Iqbal also notes that many people are very close to the poverty line, so that economic fluctuations, which have plagued the region, can have and have had major impacts on poverty (see also Chaudhry 2005). Using the lower national poverty line, Ali Abdel Gadel Ali estimated that 19% of Arabs were living in

TABLE 10.4   Poverty in MENA According to Various Standards

	Poverty Line							
	$1 PPP		"Lower" National Line		$2 PPP		"Upper" National Line	
Country	# of persons (millions)	% of population	# of persons (millions)	% of population	# of persons (millions)	% of population	# of persons (millions)	% of population
Egypt	1.70	2.60	10.70	16.70	25.90	40.40	27.00	42.00
Yemen	2.62	16.00	6.85	41.80	7.37	45.00	10.96	66.90
Algeria	0.28	1.00	6.20	22.00	4.20	15.00	9.30	33.30
Syria	0.06	0.34	2.05	11.40	1.90	10.40	5.30	30.10

SOURCES: $1 PPP, $2 PPP: World Bank
Egypt: El-Laithy et al. 2003
Algeria: Belkacem 2001
Yemen: Chemingui 2005

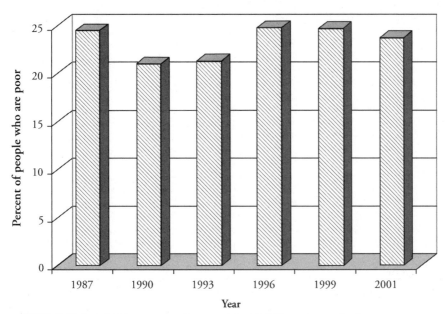

FIGURE 10.5   MENA poverty trends, 1987–2001 ($2 PPP per day standard)
SOURCE: World Bank Global and Regional Poverty Trends: *Global Economic Prospects,* 2004
(Washington, D.C.: World Bank)

(so-defined) poverty at the end of the 1990s, whereas 41% were poor when using the (more conceptually reasonable) upper poverty line (Ali 2003).

In general, poverty is concentrated among the uneducated, the socially vulnerable (e.g., widows), and in less-favored rural areas. In Egypt, for example, even when using the draconian lower poverty line, 34% of rural Upper Egyptians were poor (El Laithy et al. 2003). Private-sector workers are more likely to be poor, regardless of region, than those employed by the government. In Yemen, poverty is related to large family size, illiteracy, and employment in agriculture (Chemingui 2005). These patterns are roughly similar to those found throughout the Global South (see, e.g., IFAD 2001a).

While there is debate on the extent of poverty at any one time, there is still less clarity on trends over time. Farrukh Iqbal's recent estimate of trends, using the $2 PPP per day line, is shown in Figure 10.5. There is evidence that poverty increased during the 1990s; the World Bank estimates that 28 million more people were living on less than $2 PPP per day in 1999 than in 1990 (World Bank 2003).[9] This, of course, is consistent with the relatively sluggish economic growth (see Chapter 3) and the stagnation of real wages (see Chapter 5) that characterized the decade. An ILO study of the "working poor" found that the number of working poor with less than $2 PPP increased in the region by more than 6 million from 1994 to 2000,

TABLE 10.5   Poverty Trends in Morocco, 1984–1999

	1984/85	*1991*	*1999*
Urban %	17.3	7.6	12
Rural %	32.6	18	27.2
National %	21.26	13.1	19

SOURCES: World Bank (1993b, 4) 1984–1991; World Development Indicators Online (2006) for 1999

and by another 3.5 million by 2004 (ILO 2005). Finally, Chapter 5 presented the mixed record on nonmonetary measures of poverty, such as child mortality, malnutrition, and literacy. It is reasonable to conclude that although the problem of poverty in the region may not be as horrifyingly severe as in, say, sub-Saharan Africa, and although some progress has been made, many millions of residents of the region remain poor. It also appears that poverty reduction, which was robust during the oil-boom period of the 1970s and 1980s, has essentially stagnated (so far as we can tell) since the late 1980s.

A few comparisons over time are possible for some countries (see Tables 10.5–10.7). For Egypt, there is some evidence that poverty fell in the second half of the 1990s, although researchers worried about the impact of the "rapid decline in the construction sector since 1999 and a volatile tourism sector" on poverty in the past half-decade (El Laithy et al. 2003, 5). A study of Syria found that, regardless of measure, poverty declined between 1996–1997 and 2003–2004: from 14% to 11.4% (lower national line), or from 33% to 30% (upper national line) (El Laithy and Abu-Ismail 2005). For Tunisia, available data suggest that poverty rose slightly from 1990 to 1995 (from 16.2% to 17.1%, using the upper poverty line) and then fell by 2000 to 9.9% (Ali 2003). Poverty has likewise declined in Iran (Iqbal 2006). One study of Iran notes that many Iranians counted as poor in any one year do not remain so; mobility out of, and into, poverty is fairly common (Salehi-Isfahani 2003).

If the poverty data are opaque, the data on distribution are murkier still. Recent estimates from the World Bank are shown in Table 10.8. Data for long-term comparisons (i.e., thirty years) are available only for Egypt, Iran, and Tunisia (Iqbal

TABLE 10.6   Poverty Trends in Tunisia, 1967–1995

	1967	*1975*	*1980*	*1985*	*1990*	*1990*	*1995*
Urban %	n.a	26.5 (34)	11.8	8.4 (16)	7.3	3.5	3.6
Rural %	n.a	18.0 (43)	14.1	7.0 (31)	5.7	13.1	13.9
National %	33	22.2	12.9	7.7	6.7	7.4	7.6

SOURCES: World Bank (1993c, 50–51), reporting Tunisian government data; for numbers in parentheses, Radwan, Jamal, and Ghose (1991, 53). World Development Indicators Online (2006)

TABLE 10.7   Poverty Trends in Egypt, 1958–2000

	1958/59	1974/75	1981/82	1990/91	1996	2000
Urban %	35.0	44.0	24.0–30.0	54.5	22.5	n.a
Rural %	30.0	34.5	22.0–30.0	35.9	23.3	n.a
National %	–	–	–	–	22.9	16.7

n.a = not available
SOURCES: 1958/59 and 1774/75: Radwan (1977); 1981/82: lower estimate, World Bank (1991); higher estimate, Korayem (1987); 1990/91: Korayem (1994, 28). World Development Indicators Online (2000b) for 1996 and 2000

2006). These data suggest that in Iran and Tunisia, inequality first rose and then fell, whereas in Egypt, inequality declined (up to 1985) and then worsened somewhat thereafter (Iqbal 2006). In general, although the distribution of expenditure in the region is not as unequal as it is in Latin America, expenditures are less equally distributed in MENA than in countries such as Korea or Indonesia. Recall, however, that we have no data for the Gulf countries, where much qualitative evidence suggests that some people are very rich and some are very poor. Nor do we have any solid information on one of the poorest countries of the region, the Sudan. The truth is that we simply do not know how unequal, or how equal, the distribution of expenditure and income is when considering the region as a whole.

A final point on both poverty and distribution can be made. Some analysts (most prominently, Adams and Page 2003) have argued that the relatively low (as they measured them) levels of poverty and inequality can be explained by two factors: international migration and remittances (see Chapter 15) and government employment (see Chapter 5). As noted earlier, there are many measurement issues here.

TABLE 10.8   Distribution of Income or Consumption, 2005

	Lowest 10%	Lowest 20%	Second 20%	Third 20%	Fourth 20%	Highest 20%	Highest 10%
Algeria	2.8	7.0	11.6	16.1	22.7	42.6	26.8
Egypt	3.7	8.6	12.1	15.4	20.4	43.6	29.5
Iran	2.0	5.1	9.4	14.1	21.5	49.9	33.7
Israel	2.4	6.9	11.4	16.3	22.9	44.3	28.2
Jordan	3.3	7.6	11.4	15.5	21.1	44.4	29.8
Morocco	2.6	6.5	10.6	14.8	21.3	46.6	30.9
Tunisia	2.3	6.0	10.3	14.8	21.7	47.3	31.5
Turkey	2.3	6.1	10.6	14.9	21.8	46.7	30.7
Yemen	3.0	7.4	12.2	16.7	22.5	41.2	25.9

SOURCE: World Development Indicators Online (2006)

Nevertheless, it is also notable that the process of migration, at least during the 1970s and 1980s, did have the effect of alleviating poverty in some countries. The evidence for the "oil boom" of the past five years is less encouraging (Iqbal 2006). Government employment is likewise under great pressure (see Chapter 5). Even if we believe the data that suggest that the region's poverty and distribution problems are less severe than elsewhere (and given the data and conceptual issues noted earlier, we may well *not* believe this), the sustainability of the region's relatively benign performance is questionable.

URBAN POLITICS AND POLITICAL VIOLENCE

The region's working class, for all its geographical diversity, has a few commonalities. It is growing, and it is a composite of the urban-born and recent arrivals from the countryside, responding to the gap between urban and rural incomes. In many countries (e.g., Algeria, Tunisia, Egypt, the Sudan, Turkey, and Syria) it is segmented by sector of employment (government/private, formal/informal) and degree of job security. Many of these people are self-employed, and many wage earners work in small establishments, in which industrial relations are personalized, often even a family affair (see Chapter 5). The working class is also united by relatively low incomes, the constant problem of finding jobs (if not for fathers, then for sons), and overcrowded living conditions. Most members receive at least some consumption subsidy from the state, which both makes it possible to survive and politicizes consumption. These people have many grievances and often express their frustrations politically.

Large- and medium-sized cities in the Middle East, as elsewhere in the world, can be a stage for disruption and violence. The theatrical potential of cities evokes a level of concern on the part of governing elites that the countryside can seldom match. Relatively small groups of determined people—from spontaneous rioters to urban guerrillas—can disrupt and paralyze urban centers that sit astride national communications grids (railroads, ports, telephone systems, the international airport) and contain heavy concentrations of industry, the chief bureaucratic installations of the government, the foreign diplomatic and press corps, and the major universities.

In the 1940s and 1950s the expectation was widespread that the shantytowns of the developing world would provide an endless stream of young, poor, unskilled, uprooted males ready to answer any appeal to violence. The image that developed was one of individuals stripped of their village, family, and kin associations, thrust into a money economy in which jobs were scarce and exploitation of the unskilled common, and in which anomie predisposed the uprooted to seek a new identity in radical movements through targeted and random violence. The picture, although not wholly inaccurate, has major flaws. Shantytown populations have by and large turned out to be fairly responsible urban dwellers (J. Nelson 1979). Often they have reconstituted kin, ethnic, and religious associations in their new abodes. Generally, they have been able to find work. When city authorities have legalized access to the land on which they had been squatters, they have invested their labor and earnings in home improvement. They are upwardly mobile, and however grim the shanty slums may appear to the outsider, their inhabitants vastly prefer life there to life back in the village. For the most part, shantytowns have not been hotbeds of political agitation and violence.

At the same time, a third or more of a given city's population may live in the inner city, with its old, decaying, substandard housing, much of which may be condemned and is certainly unsafe to inhabit. These residents may be second- or third-generation migrants or trading and craftspeople of long standing in the city. Second-generation migrants may have forgotten why their parents left the village and see only the poor services offered them by the municipality—the broken sewers, crowded schools, collapsing buildings, and mounds of refuse that often make these quarters more forbidding than the shantytowns (see Wikan 1980). The solidly urban service and craftspeople may recall a bygone era when they enjoyed higher status and a higher level of income, before modern industrial production, department stores, and the like invaded their world. In short, residents of these quarters may be more violence-prone than those of the shantytowns.

Other potential actors can be found in the ranks of organized labor. Trade unions present a command structure for and sometimes a tradition of confrontation and militancy. They can respond rapidly, coherently, and on a sustained basis to unfair labor practices (plant- or industry-specific), cost-of-living issues, or ideological and political causes. Strikes among dockworkers or bus and train drivers can shut down cities and ports, and worker demonstrations of whatever nature may act as a catalyst to the involvement of other, less organized groups. But because organized labor is usually a small fraction of the entire workforce, governments are willing to make large financial settlements to buy the goodwill of union leaders. Conversely, in most Middle Eastern countries strikes are illegal, and the threat of arrest and imprisonment is not idle (as the secretary general of Tunisia's UGTT, Habib Achour, learned in 1978). Corporatist arrangements, through which the state co-opts union leadership, have been the preferred strategy for dealing with labor (see Chapter 12). Most workers in most countries, however, are not unionized.

High school and university students are viewed by municipal and national authorities with particular alarm. They have relatively little to lose—few are married or hold jobs—and are therefore willing to take big risks. Terminating their education is a real threat, often acted upon, but committed university militants may discount that threat, and many high school students may feel that their education is of little worth anyway. It is, moreover, part of student culture everywhere to take political stands, to be the nation's or the movement's conscience, to confront, be bloodied, go to jail (on Egypt, see 'Abdalla 1985). No Middle Eastern society has been spared student agitation and violence, and in some (Morocco in 1965 and 1984, the Sudan in 1964 and 1985, Turkey throughout the 1970s, Egypt in 1968 and 1977, Iran in 1978–1979) regimes have been shaken or fallen. When students go into the streets, they draw not only other students but perhaps organized labor and the slum dwellers as well.

Although they tend not to be the initiators, segments of the urban trading and merchant strata may be important actors in urban-based challenges to the authorities. The concerted clanging down of iron shop shutters in congested urban commercial

282 URBAN POLITICAL ECONOMY

districts is a time-honored and dramatic signal that even the better-off have had enough. Shopkeepers have closed down to support the war against the French in Algiers in 1958 and to oppose Israeli occupation of the West Bank, sporadically since 1967 and on a regular basis since 1987, the awarding of a monopoly in tobacco trade to foreigners in Tehran in 1896, the abandonment of Islam as the state religion in Syria in 1966, and the regime of the shah in his final months in Iran in 1978.

Finally, we should pay attention to what Marxists would call lumpen elements. All cities are full of people who in fact are rootless or, if organized, are so in ways that enjoy no respect or legitimacy: beggars, prostitutes, drug dealers, scavengers, drifters, and derelicts. Time and again, political protest draws in the lumpen elements, and organized confrontation may degenerate into random looting. Few observers in the past decade or so have failed to note the striking presence of the very young in all forms of urban violence. These are pre-adolescent or early-adolescent street urchins, kids playing hooky, runaways, orphans, and beggars. They take physical risks that even older students avoid, and they suffer casualties that the authorities generally try to cover up. They can provide tough foot soldiers for any organization that can organize them and deploy them for violent political action.

By looking at specific instances of urban violence we can better appreciate how these various elements combine (see Denoeux 1993). One of the most frequent forms of violence has been the cost-of-living riot or demonstration. The issue has become acute as various countries try to reduce their deficits through cuts in consumer subsidies, but there were instances of this form even in the 1960s. A sharp rise in the price of sugar in Morocco in 1965 triggered massive rioting in Casablanca, with scores of dead, and led to the suspension of parliament and a state of emergency that lasted for the rest of the decade. In June 1981 there was a repeat of this scenario in Casablanca, with sixty-six "officially" killed (six hundred by other accounts).

In August 1983, the Moroccan authorities reduced consumer subsidies on average by 20% and raised public-sector salaries by an equal amount. No violence occurred immediately, but in January 1984 riots broke out all over northern Morocco, as well as at Oujda and Marrakech. This time Casablanca was not a major locus of the violence. Poor political management had allowed several grievances to come together simultaneously. Secondary school students were already on strike because of an increase in the fees required to sit for the *baccalauréat* exams. In northern Morocco, where contraband trade with the two Spanish enclaves of Ceuta and Melilla helps prop up economic life, very high exit fees were imposed on Moroccan traders. Rumors, probably well founded, were rife that new subsidy cuts were in the offing. Finally, in preparation for an Islamic summit at Casablanca, a number of Moroccan cities had been stripped of their police to protect the conferees. Student strikes and demonstrations turned into cost-of-living riots, and the local forces of order in several cities were unable to contain them. Twenty-nine persons "officially" lost their lives, but some estimate the real number at around four hundred (Clément 1986).

Similar cost-of-living riots occurred in Tunis and other Tunisian cities in 1978 and 1984 (in the latter, eighty-nine were officially killed), in Egypt in 1977 (about ninety dead), and in Khartoum in 1982 and 1985 (number of dead unknown). Surely the most quixotic of these outbreaks was the one in Beirut in the summer of 1987, when Lebanese interrupted their civil war to demonstrate against the precipitous drop in the international value of the Lebanese pound. Algeria, which for nearly twenty-five years had experienced little urban violence, was rocked by cost-of-living riots in the fall of 1988, and the Kingdom of Jordan followed suit in the spring of 1989. In 2005, Yemenis in San'a, Aden, and Hodeida rioted against sharp increases in fuel prices.

National leaders are loath to admit that these riots reflect real grievances, for that would be to admit that the government cannot feed its own people. Generally, the head of state blames the riots on outside agitators—Zionism, Khomeini, Marxists, Islamists, or Qaddhafi have always been ready at hand. Nevertheless, the same heads of state typically give away the game by rescinding the measures that gave rise to the protest: Sadat, Bourguiba, and King Hassan all responded in that manner. Needless to say, with such precedents it becomes all the more difficult to reintroduce the measures, just as these precedents make it more likely that people will resort to violence in the future.

We should be cautious, however, in accepting counter-claims of pure spontaneity for cost-of-living riots. Organized political groups, from Muslim militants to Marxist radicals, are generally forewarned of impending shifts in government pricing policies and ready to incite allied groups to go into the streets. It is unlikely that their actions are decisive, but there may be more orchestration to some riots than meets the eye. In the winter of 1986, thousands of Egypt's security police, made up of young, rural, extremely underpaid but armed conscripts, rioted against an alleged plan of the government to extend their tour of duty by one year. A number of those arrested were found to have amounts of money on them equivalent to several months pay. The conclusion, never proven, was that Muslim groups had paid many of them to protest.

There have been outbreaks of violence or demonstrations driven by political issues. Perhaps the most important is the one that occurred in Cairo on January 26, 1952. In a day of rioting and arson, downtown "European" Cairo was set ablaze as denizens of the Old City (low-income, substandard housing) and of the tombs in the City of the Dead went on a rampage. These Black Saturday riots had been triggered by an assault on an Egyptian police post in the Suez Canal Zone by British troops who suspected the police of harboring terrorists. The riots introduced such a sense of interregnum and *fin de régime* that Nasser and his co-conspirators accelerated their plans to seize power and did so the following July.

Hanna Batatu recounted that in March 1959 the Iraqi Communist party (ICP) tried to pressure General 'Abd al-Karim Qassim, the Iraqi head of state, into giving the party four seats in the cabinet. At that time the party probably had no more than 2,000 members, but it was able to put *half a million* people in the streets of Baghdad. Surely very few of them were committed Marxists. Many of them may have come out of the "somber wretchedness" of the largely Shi'ite slums, and there were surely students and members of the white-collar intelligentsia (Batatu 1978, 49).

Perhaps those half-million Iraqis responding to the marching orders of the ICP were in composition similar to the millions of Iranians who demonstrated against the shah exactly twenty years later. In Iran a broad coalition of urban interests sustained direct confrontations with the Iranian police and military for most of a year. Although Ayatollah Khomeini's recorded instructions and urgings, sent from his exile in Paris, may have been the real force behind the movements, other groups, including students, bazaar merchants, organized labor, and radical political organizations, all contributed to what became an urban-based revolution.

Ashraf and Banuazizi (1985) noted the absence of participation of slum dwellers in the violence and, like Kazemi (1980b), stressed the involvement of second-generation migrants and the urban unemployed. They estimated the scope of the violence during the twelve months of 1978, a period of cyclical urban riots and mass demonstrations, as follows (1985, 22):

Number of demonstrations	2,483
Number of participants	1,600,000
Number of strikes	1,207
Number killed	3,008
Number wounded	12,184

In the last two months of 1978, demonstrators were joined by an estimated 5 million workers and employees involved in strikes, and in the first two months of 1979 virtually the entire adult population demonstrated in one fashion or another against the shah.

The final two examples we present may be harbingers of things to come. One is Turkey's urban violence during the 1970s, the patterns of which were more akin to those in Argentina, Italy, and West Germany of the same period than to anything in the Middle East—until the second *intifada* and the Iraqi resistance and sectarian conflict after 2003. The Turkish political arena underwent a kind of centrifugal process by which radical leftist, fascist, and occasionally Muslim militant groups took up arms and fought among themselves. There appears to be little doubt that fascist groups such as the Grey Wolves were the primary instigators of the troubles. They fought for control of university campuses, assassinated both one another and "marked" political leaders, and used the shantytowns as hideouts. By 1980 twenty to thirty Turks were being killed every day, and the total number of political deaths had reached five thousand.

The beginning and the end of the decade were marked by military takeover, in each instance partially justified by the need to restore law and order. It was organized labor that provided the occasion for the first intervention:

In June 1970 industrial workers in the Istanbul-Izmit area joined in a massive march to protest a new law regulating union organization and collective bargaining. The march soon erupted into a workers' riot involving over one hundred thousand demonstrators in the largest and most violent worker protest in Turkish history. Tanks and paratroopers were mobilized to quell the rioting, which had caused large-scale damage at over one hundred work sites. The organizers of the demonstration were accused both by the government and rival labor leaders of fomenting class warfare and staging a rehearsal for a proletarian revolution. Nine months later, after the government's economic austerity policies had led to an unprecedented wave of political protest that included virtually every organized sector of Turkish society and urban guerrillas had launched a Tupamaro-type campaign of bank robberies and kidnappings, the General Staff deposed the beleaguered Justice Party government in what many feared was a rehearsal for a Turkish "Eighteenth Brumaire." (Bianchi 1984, 202)

During the 1970s, labor continued to disrupt the economy, if not urban life per se. The figures in Table 10.9 show the growth in strike activity. In 1977 the 80,000 members of the Metalworkers' Union went on strike for eight months. The combination of political organizations settling accounts with arms and growing labor agitation as the two-party system polarized between the secular and increasingly left-leaning Republican People's party of Bülent Ecevit and the center-right, pro-business Justice party of Süleyman Demirel finds no equivalent anywhere in the Middle East.

Lebanon and Beirut offer the other, regrettably no longer so special, case. When civil war broke out in 1975, many assumed that it would go on only so long as it did not disrupt commerce and banking. That point was reached and passed within a few years. Anyone who stayed in Beirut, Tripoli, Sidon, or their immediate hinterlands had to be either armed or in a position to hire protection. As the fighting increased, many businesspeople and much of the intelligentsia left the country. The streets were given over to armed militias, some affiliated with older political parties, such as the Christian Phalanges (Kata'ib), with the Palestinian resistance, or with the various Shi'ite factions. It is clear that in Lebanon the young men of the slums, the squatter settlements, and the refugee camps took over the cities and staked out highly fortified enclaves. The small-scale merchants, traders, craftspeople, and service people who stayed on had to pay off the local powers, but as money came in from outside to finance the war and found its way into the pockets of the militias and their dependents, business was good.

The carnage lasted fourteen years and caused the death of an estimated 150,000 Lebanese and Palestinians. It is hard to discern any longer what causes and issues

TABLE 10.9   Strike Activity in Turkey, 1963–1980

Year	Strikes	Strikers	Days Lost
1963	8	1,514	19,739
1970	72	21,150	220,189
1977	59	15,628	1,397,124
1980	220	84,832	7,708,750

SOURCE: Margulies and Yildizoğlu (1984, 18)

drove the violence. Religion and confessional balances, greater economic equality among religious confessions, the survival or liquidation of the Palestinian refugees, and the never-ending need to avenge an avalanche of deaths were all at stake. Greed for power and habit transformed Beirut into a city where no central authority held sway and where violence was the norm and its absence a curiosity.

Tragically, a similar pattern has emerged in Iraq since 2003. The collapse of the Ba'athist regime, the sudden demise of the monopoly on violence, except that of an ill-informed occupying army, anger and opposition to the Anglo-American occupation, the influx of foreign radicals, and many bitter memories of past crimes combined to create endemic, so far unstoppable violence. As of this writing (winter 2007), although an elected Iraqi government exists, real power clearly resides with a wide variety of militias and armed gangs. It is hardly surprising that from the very beginning of this misadventure, so many Arabs everywhere looked with alarm at developments in Iraq and muttered, "*Lubnaan!*" ("Lebanon!")

The cities of Iran, Lebanon, Palestine, and Iraq seem to point toward the future. Every outbreak of urban violence in the Middle East since the Iranian revolution has had an Islamic component, and in some instances that was the only component. In late 1979 the Great Mosque at Mecca was seized by a heterogeneous group of Saudi fundamentalists and allied pilgrims from all over the Muslim world. It took weeks for Saudi security forces to flush them out. In the summer of 1987 Iranian pilgrims, under instructions from Ayatollah Khomeini, staged demonstrations at Mecca that Saudi security forces confronted with force. Over two hundred demonstrators and policemen were killed.

After President Sadat's assassination by Muslim extremists in October 1981, hundreds of those associated with the plot made their stand in large provincial cities, especially Mansura in the delta and Assiut in Upper Egypt. In the latter, pitched battles were fought and several hundred were killed. The violence there pales in comparison to the confrontation between Syria's Muslim Brotherhood and its arch enemy, the Alawite regime of Hafiz al-Assad. The Brotherhood, accused of an assassination campaign against Alawite army officers, holed up in the old Sunni city of Hama. Assad ringed the city with artillery and leveled parts of it. The death toll may have been in the tens of thousands.

In January 1980, armed bands, apparently having infiltrated from Libya, briefly seized the Tunisian mining town of Gafsa and proclaimed a set of Islamic revolutionary goals. Since then the Tunisian regime has periodically met militant Islamic groups with force. Neighboring Algeria has dealt ruthlessly with similar challenges, and its cities have been relatively free of Islamic agitation. The riots of the fall of 1988, however, were to some extent led by prominent Muslim spokesmen. In the fall of 1990, as the United States mobilized an international coalition to oust Iraqi military forces from Kuwait, both Morocco and Tunisia were rocked by urban demonstrations and riots on a very large scale. As in Algeria in 1988 and in Jordan in 1989, there was undoubtedly an element of socioeconomic protest against the harsh economic reforms the governments of all three countries were pursuing, but that protest was deeply suffused with cultural and religious protest as well.

Urban violence now is taking a predominantly religious form. Its organizers and to some extent its shock troops are drawn from a particular stratum of the urban population. They tend to be young men, and some women, from provincial cities who had come to the metropolis to pursue higher education. They tend to come from solid families rather than broken homes, and they have been raised within an Islamic value system. In confronting the big city, they are shocked by the luxury, debauchery, cosmopolitanism, and materialism that these conurbations typically display. The university campuses themselves appear to be venues of uncontrolled mixing of the sexes and centers for the propagation of debased Western mores. These young people are thus a segment of the rural lower middle class with professional aspirations and high religious ideals. They are willing and able to organize small, disciplined groups that infiltrate state agencies, the junior officers' corps, and the security forces. Alternatively, if they feel that the corrupt state monster cannot be taken from within, they withdraw into small cellular communities and, like the Prophet at Medina, prepare to take society from without (see Ibrahim 1980; Sivan 1985; al-Ansari 1986; Ayubi 1991a). And today, thanks to the Internet, they have access to each others' ideas, both ideological and military.

Such leaders and groups do draw on other sectors of urban society, and, indeed, in Lebanon the slum dwellers appear to have been the shock troops for all the contending factions, be they religious, partisan, or mercenary. These groups will also often enlist the support of militant members of the *ulema,* who lend the lay militants some doctrinal legitimacy, and they may count on support from a broad spectrum of actors from well-to-do officers in the armed forces to schoolteachers, clerks, and petty traders.

The already largely urbanized Middle East will only become more so in the near future. These urban populations have borne the brunt of the austerity measures introduced as part of structural adjustment programs. Except for the very rich, all urban dwellers have suffered, but the ones who have felt the pain most acutely have been those on fixed incomes and those with the educational qualifications for middle-class status but for whom appropriate employment has been in increasingly short supply. Managing the national economy and managing the cities are now coterminous. So far, the performance has not been altogether encouraging. In an international context of increasing foreign intervention, the future of what may become, to paraphrase Mike Davis, a "region of slums," is unlikely to be quiet.

NOTES

1. Estimates of Greater Cairo's population range from 12 million to 18 million, due to varying definitions of "Greater Cairo."

2. See Chapter 5 on rural-urban infant and child mortality figures. While mortality may generally be higher in rural areas, some observers have noted that child mortality rates for the urban poor are very high. In Khartoum, child mortality in slum areas is 300 per thousand, compared to a national rate of about 115 (Eltayib 2003). The worldwide phenomenon of high death rates among the urban poor is discussed in Davis (2006).

3. As family size shrinks, a given number of persons will need more housing. In Greater Cairo, for example, from 1960 to 1990, while the population rose 161%, the number of households rose 263% (El Araby 2002).

4. Dissolved oxygen content is a common measure of water's potential to support life and synthesize organic pollutants.

5. Consider Adam Smith: "It is but equity, besides, that they who feed, cloath and lodge the whole body of the people, should have such a share of the produce of their own labour as to be themselves tolerably well fed, cloathed, and lodged" (*The Wealth of Nations,* p. 79). Note the explicit reference to consumption of items beyond food.

6. Value pluralists such as the British political philosopher John Gray (2002) would assert that the definition of "capabilities" varies from one country, or even subculture, to another.

7. Purchasing power parity (PPP) calculations are intended to made possible international comparisons of income. "$1 PPP" implies that $1 would buy a minimum subsistence basket. Reddy and Pogge (2002) argue persuasively that the $1 PPP standard would not, in fact, make this possible in the United States. They also point out that PPP calculations are designed to correct for the large differences in purchasing power when it comes to nontraded goods. However, since traded goods (food, clothing, etc.) make up most of the purchases of the poor, the PPP data incorrectly overestimate purchasing power for the poor. They show that using a "food only" PPP calculation can result in a *doubling of* the number of people considered to be poor, compared with the World Bank's calculation. They also offer other technical critiques, such as the inappropriateness of re-scaling PPP by using consumer price indices. See Ravallion (2002) for a defense of the World Bank's methodology, and Reddy and Pogge's rejoinder to Ravallion (2002).

8. That is, the number of persons whose expenditures fall below the poverty line.

9. To underscore how sensitive estimates can be to the choice of year, the 2004 version of this paper says that "nearly 20 million" more were poor in "2001 compared with ten years previously." One wonders how 8 million persons' expenditures suddenly rose from 1999 to 2000, which were not exceptionally robust years of economic growth.

11

POLITICAL REGIMES

As Viewed by Themselves and Others

We are on treacherous ground but in good company when we try to label the political regimes of the Middle East (see, inter alia, Binder 1957; Hudson 1977). "Regime" refers not only to a type of government but also to ideology, the rules of the game, and the structuring of the polity in a given nation. "Regime change" is no mere changing of the guard or cleaning out of City Hall; it is, rather, profound structural change in all forms of political activity. Regime change may be revolutionary, as in the violent shift from a monarchical to a republican regime in France in 1789 or from Pahlavi dynastic rule to the Islamic republic (some would say "theocracy") in Iran in 1979. Regime change may, however, be relatively peaceful and incremental. Turkey moved between 1946 and 1950 from a single-party, authoritarian regime to a two-party system with openly contested elections. Egypt has been creeping hesitantly since 1971 from Nasser's single-party, authoritarian socialist regime toward a more liberal multiparty system in which private economic interests have come to play a legitimate role. Hinnebusch (1985) characterized the Nasserist regime as "authoritarian-populist" and Sadat's as "post-populist authoritarian-conservative."

There is no dearth of cumbersome labels for Middle Eastern regimes, and both their number and terminological complexity testify to the difficulties observers encounter in making coherent generalizations about the nature of these regimes. There are a number of pitfalls into which one easily stumbles. The first one is that in the Middle East, we tend, not without reason, to personalize regimes, equating or confusing them with their founders. We talk of the Nasserist, Kemalist (Atatürk), or Bourguibist systems, and doubtless for these giant figures there is a good deal of truth in equating their systems with their personae. Waterbury (1983) argued that the death of Nasser in 1970 in itself signaled the end of a regime and necessarily set the stage for a new one. But it is an abuse of the term "regime" and of empirical reality to succumb to the temptation to see all leadership changes as constituting regime changes. Constant and violent power struggles within the Ba'ath hierarchy in Syria and Iraq since the mid-1960s did not constitute regime changes. The triumph of the more managerial Hafiz al-Assad over the more populist Salah Jadid in Syria in 1970 or the eclipse of Ahmad Hassan al-Bakr in the face of Saddam Hussein in Iraq were only in-house power shifts and did not significantly alter the nature of the Ba'athi-military regimes of those two countries.

A second pitfall is taxonomic; we tend to classify regimes merely by describing what they appear to be doing at a given point in time. Rather than capturing the essence of the process of regime formation, consolidation, and decay—that is, classifying by understanding the *dynamics* of regimes—we say that regime X is "authoritarian-socialist," "radical Islamic," or "patriarchal-conservative." Now that public-sector enterprises are everywhere being compared unfavorably with those of the private sector and there is considerable talk of putting the former on the auction block, at least one scholar is using the term "authoritarian-privatizing regimes." In this way there is a tendency for each regime to become its own type, and when the regime changes a new type must be invented to describe it. All one needs to do is summarize what the new regime does in a new hyphenated label.

One must be on the lookout for a third pitfall. One way to avoid superficial and descriptive labeling is to focus on the dynamics of social and economic change within societies and how they are or are not reflected in the nature of the regime. This may enable us to see the extent to which regime change is the product of social and economic change. For instance, in 1962 there was an abrupt regime change in North Yemen. The quasi-medieval theocracy known as the imamate was overthrown through a military coup d'état and a socialist republic proclaimed. Legally, a profound change had occurred, but Yemeni society had scarcely changed at all. By contrast, one could argue that the downfall of the shah of Iran in 1979 and the proclamation of the Islamic republic came as the result of rapid and profound social change in Iran in the 1960s and 1970s. The large cohorts of literate, urban, upwardly mobile Iranians that the shah's own educational system had spewed forth could no longer be contained within the paternalistic, authoritarian, and repressive regime he had inherited from his father. Although an Islamic republic was surely not the only possible regime alternative to the shah and the shah's downfall itself was not inevitable, Iranian society was clearly ready for some profound restructuring of the polity.

We have here classified regimes in part according to how they manage publicly owned assets (Chapters 7 and 8). The three major categories are (1) regimes that use these assets to generate surplus for further state expansion at the expense of the private sector, (2) those that use assets to act as a handmaiden to private entrepreneurs, and (3) those that seek to transfer public assets to private hands. We have tried to delimit the major factors leading given regimes into one or another of these modes as well as the likely consequences of their adoption. In what follows we extend the analysis to the major policy domains of the region's regimes in order to move beyond descriptive understandings of their dynamics.

SOCIALIST REPUBLICS

Of all the regime types that have characterized the Middle East since World War II, the most prevalent has been the socialist republic. As was the case for economic-growth strategies and state intervention in the economy, the Turkish republic of the 1920s and 1930s, although never espousing socialism, was the forerunner and the model for several regional neighbors. Egypt, Syria, Iraq, North Yemen, the Sudan, Tunisia, and Algeria all replicated to some extent the Turkish model. One should also include Qaddhafi's "mass state" in Libya and the former PDRY of South Yemen. Not only are these regimes numerically dominant, but they have also demonstrated considerable longevity: Egypt, 1952–present, with a significant regime transformation beginning in 1971; Syria, 1963–present; Iraq, 1963–2003; Algeria, 1962–present, with a major constitutional change in 1989; Sudan, 1958–1964 and 1969–1985; North Yemen, 1962–1991; Tunisia, 1956–present, with a major shift in political philosophy after 1987; Libya, 1969–present; and South Yemen, 1968–1991.

Atatürk's Turkey

The interwar experience of Atatürk's Turkey set the main themes and gave them real meaning in the construction of the Turkish polity. The quest for independence and national sovereignty—the ability to stand up to the great powers—was seen as rooted in a strong industrial economy and a cohesive citizenry. Former Ottoman *subjects* had to become proud Turkish *citizens*—educated, enlightened, free of the fetters of religious obscurantism, hardworking, and patriotic. Atatürk was a practitioner of nation building—a term that was to come into vogue in the Western modernization literature long after his death.

Nationalism, etatism, republicanism, revolutionism, populism, and secularism were the watchwords of the Turkish experiment. The six-hundred-year-old Ottoman Empire and the Islamic caliphate were ended in 1923. Atatürk and his lieutenants, inspired by the writings of Ziya Gökalp, himself inspired by Emile Durkheim's *The Human Division of Labor,* sought a society in which all class conflict and parochial loyalties were subordinated to citizens' functional or occupational roles. "Solidarism"—the building of an integrated, conflict-free society—characterized an outlook that spread throughout the Middle East. Religion was to be the affair of individuals, not of the state, which would remain resolutely secular and rationalist, especially in the education it dispensed through the public school system. The political guarantor of the nation's integration was to be a single party, to mobilize the citizenry rather than to compete for power against other parties, which, in any case, were only sporadically tolerated. The Republican People's party, while the creation of the regime, became an important organization in its own right.

As we have already pointed out, the Turkish experiment put the state center-stage. This was to be an activist, interventionist state rather than a set of agencies and bureaucracies over which political factions fought for control. Together with the military, the Turkish state rose above society and sought to reshape it in the image that

Atatürk and his lieutenants thought desirable (see Trimberger 1978). This was a state with a purpose and with goals—to build a modern nation and modern Turkish citizens. The hurly-burly of electoral politics, the unfettered expression of political differences, or, worse yet, the outbreak of class conflict could, it was believed, only deflect the state from its lofty purpose.

This understanding of the proper role of the state and of the uses of public power spread throughout the Middle East in the post–World War II era and was at the heart of the socialist republican experiments. Malcolm Kerr, in a powerful essay on Arab radical notions of democracy (1963, 10–11), wrote that this radicalism was characterized by a moral preference—not just a tactical preference—for maintaining the maximum degree of unity of purpose and action at all political and social levels, by an emphasis upon the virtues of group solidarity and the evils of individual self-absorption and self-seeking, by a mistrust of competition, bargaining, and the promotion of special interests, and by a vision of strong government as a liberator rather than a danger to liberty.

Kerr noted that the Islamic reformers of the early twentieth century (principally Egypt's Muhammed 'Abduh) had arisen from the first attempts to organize the Muslim community as a "morally purposeful society" under one leader (the caliph), with a common interest in service to God, under a single law (the *shari'a*) that assured the moral and political solidarity of all members. In this conceptualization, "power is good or bad according to the righteousness of its possessor" (Kerr 1963, 10).

Atatürk tried to redefine its purpose and to strip it of its religious underpinnings, but the morally purposeful state was still the linchpin of his nation building. Many other Middle Easterners, while seeing much to admire in republican Turkey, were disturbed, indeed often shocked, by Atatürk's vehement secularism. Tunisia's Habib Bourguiba, among the Arabs, came closest to emulating Atatürk's ideas and practices, but few other Arab leaders dared try to separate national from religious identity or "church" from state.

We may note now, in anticipation of discussion to come, that the strengthening of Islamic challenges to many of the existing Middle Eastern states can be seen in large measure as stemming from the conviction that these states have failed in their mission. Some Muslim activists believe that the republican socialist mission was misconceived if not blasphemous. Atatürk, for many pious Muslims, is the villain who ended the caliphate and separated the Turkish state from serving the community of Muslim believers (the *umma*). What Islamic radicals seek to do is to put the state, once again, to its God-given purposes of promoting the unity and strength of the *umma*. There is, thus, conflict over state purposes but no conflict over the belief that power used for the right purposes should be unchecked and unbalanced. Gökalp and Durkheim lurk as unacknowledged progenitors of modern Islamism.

Nasser's Egypt and Bourguiba's Tunisia

In July 1952 a group of Egyptian officers of the rank of colonel or below seized power and ended the monarchical rule of the descendants of the old Ottoman governor in

Egypt, Muhammed 'Ali (1804–1841). A republic was soon proclaimed, and a respected senior officer, General Muhammed Naguib, was made its president. All existing political parties were abolished in 1953, and in 1954 the Muslim Brotherhood (al-Ikhwan al-Muslimun), although not legally a party, was abolished after one of its members attempted to assassinate Colonel Gamal 'Abd al-Nasser. Having swept the political arena clean, the new regime sought to build its own monopoly political organization from the top down. It was called the Liberation Rally, and its founders' programmatic priorities were largely embodied in its slogan, "Unity, Discipline, and Work." With the parties and politicians who had lived on factionalism and debilitating partisan conflict out of the way, the new leaders hoped that the populace would close ranks, put its shoulder to the wheel, and—led by the armed forces, the embodiment of the nation's will to survive—stand up to the imperialist powers.

In these early years the talk was much more of revolution than of socialism. It was only after 1956 and the acquisition of extensive economic assets taken over from the British and the French (see Chapter 7) that a socialist ideology gradually took shape. But whatever Nasser's understanding of socialism, he was always clear about the need for unity and solidarity. Egypt's second monopoly party, founded in 1957, was called the National Union. As Nasser was to say frequently thereafter, it was not a party, because parties meant partisanship, and partisanship meant dividing the body politic, and that would not be tolerated. The National Union was, rather, an assembly of the whole nation—the organizational manifestation of its unity of purpose.

After the abrupt nationalizations of 1961, the regime committed itself to socialism and the building of yet another monopoly party, the Arab Socialist Union (ASU). Nasser's goal was to use this party to extend Egyptian influence throughout the Arab world. Within Egypt it tried to organize the citizenry along functional lines. There were five broad categories—the peasants, the workers, the intellectuals and professionals, the national capitalists, and the troops—bound up in what was called the Alliance of Working Forces. One of the objectives of the socialist revolution and the Arab Socialist Union was to achieve "the melting away of class differences." As in Atatürk's Turkey, the rhetorical emphasis was on unity, cohesion, devotion to the national cause as defined by the state, and the peaceful resolution of class differences by the redistribution of national wealth through state policies. A unified Egypt would carry the socialist revolution to the rest of the Arab world, and greater Arab and socialist solidarity would protect the region from the forces of neoimperialism and from Zionism. Reality and rhetoric did not mesh very often, but we are concerned here with trying to capture the spirit of the experiment.

The origins of the Bourguibist and Destourian regime in Tunisia were far different from those of Nasserist Egypt. Habib Bourguiba, a young lawyer from Monastir in Tunisia, captured the nationalist movement of that country from an older generation of leaders and in 1934 founded a mass-based party, the Neo-Destour (New Constitution) party. The party came to mobilize organized labor, white-collar professionals, the intelligentsia, and provincial merchants and commercial farmers into a powerful coalition. The Neo-Destour helped win independence from the French in 1956, and Bourguiba served as president for thirty-one years until he was deposed in the fall of 1987.

Bourguiba had all of Atatürk's instincts; his project for Tunisia was republican (he ended the old quasi-monarchical institution of the dey), secular, populist, and, more than Atatürk's, imbued with a kind of French rationalist vision of the state that was Napoleonic in spirit. Socialism was not initially part of the project, but redistributive policies certainly were. In 1964, however, Tunisia entered a short-lived socialist era. The Neo-Destour party became the Socialist Destour, and the new minister of planning, Ahmed Ben Salah, formulated a state-led plan for the formation of agricultural cooperatives and public-sector industrialization. Egypt to the east and Algeria on Tunisia's western border were ostentatiously promoting similar socialist experiments, and Bourguiba may have felt compelled to climb on the bandwagon.

The experiment, having been implemented too rapidly, raised considerable opposition within Bourguiba's old coalition, especially among provincial merchants and capitalist farmers. In 1970 Ben Salah was dismissed and eventually jailed. The socialist experiment was ended, but all other aspects of the Bourguibist state remained. It must be stressed that Bourguibism, while similar to Atatürkism, differed in one major respect—it was resolutely nonmilitarist. Bourguiba always argued that Tunisia could never be a credible military power and that the building of a large military establishment would only consume scarce investment and perhaps thrust Tunisia into the cycles of military intervention in politics that had plagued the rest of the Middle East. Tunisia would have to use diplomatic skill rather than military power to defend its independence.

Twenty years after independence most observers saw Tunisia as one of the best-organized polities in the Arab world. Hudson (1977) compared Arab regimes in terms of three levels of political legitimacy. The first, personal legitimacy, refers to popular support and respect for leaders that does not necessarily extend to the programs and institutions they seek to develop. The second type of legitimacy is ideological, whereby citizens respect a regime's professed ideology and principles but not necessarily its leaders, who may fail to honor those principles. Finally, there is structural legitimacy, whereby citizens respect and accept the rules of the political game, the programs of the government, and the way in which goods are distributed in society. In Hudson's view, Bourguiba and the Tunisian regime enjoyed legitimacy on all three dimensions and in that sense were probably unique in the Arab world: "Tunisia may be considered as perhaps the most politically modern of the revolutionary Arab states, in terms of secularism, rationality, and institutionalized participation. Certainly it has been one of the most stable" (1977, 378).

Yet even as Hudson wrote, he noted that in 1975 the National Assembly proclaimed Bourguiba president for life. The proclamation foreshadowed a breakdown in the rationality of the regime—the reinforcement of the cult of the indispensable leader, a violation of the ideal of meritocracy and political accountability. Like Atatürk before him, the leader (the *za'im*, as such power figures are known in the Arab world) apparently did not trust the citizens created by the new rationalized political system to choose or change their leaders. For all their emphasis on national unity and purpose, the leaders of the socialist republics never leave office voluntarily. Atatürk and Nasser died in harness, and Bourguiba, in his eighties and senile, was ushered into retirement by General Zine al-Abdine Ben ʿAli, the man he had appointed minister of defense. None of these leaders could accept the full political logic of the systems they sought to build.

With age and physical decline, Bourguiba became more and more manipulable by figures in his entourage. There were, in the 1980s, occasional flashes of his old political skills, but the modernizing presidency became increasingly the focal point of intrigue and personal vendettas—as if Tunisia had tired of the French model of the state and had resurrected the Ottoman seraglio. In June 1986, at the congress of the Socialist Destour, Bourguiba simply appointed a new central committee, a body supposedly elected by party members, and dismissed the careful and unflamboyant Prime Minister Muhammed Mzali, a man who had been seen as his successor.

President Ben ʿAli changed little in the Bourguibist system except to rename the party the Democratic Constitutional Rally (RCD by its French acronym). The new order was no less corporatist than the old, only faintly more liberal, and given the man at its head, far more wedded to the military and security than Bourguiba's had ever been.

Yemen and the Sudan

Yemen and the Sudan experienced regimes in the past thirty-five years that were to some extent Nasserist in their structures and programs, but the societies onto which these regimes were imposed were and are very much different from that of Egypt or Tunisia, let alone Turkey. What was then North Yemen remains a tribal society, with backward agriculture and very little industry. It is divided between the mainly Shiʿite tribesmen, from whom the former imams were drawn, and urban Sunni Muslims, from whom the merchant class is drawn. Sunni officers seized power from the imam in 1962, proclaimed a republic, and reached out to Nasser's Egypt for support. Some Shiʿite tribes rejected the new regime and looked to Saudi Arabia to help restore the imamate. Five years of civil war ensued in which a large Egyptian expeditionary force found itself incapable of subduing the tribes in their mountainous home territories. The Egyptian expeditionary force was withdrawn at the time of the June War of 1967, and the contending Yemeni factions reached a fragile modus vivendi that preserved the republic but restored royalist leaders to positions of power. Factional struggles within the Yemeni military, backed by tribal allies, finally yielded a military regime in 1978, headed by ʿAli ʿAbdullah Salih, a Zaydi Shiʿite, who has been head of state ever since.

North Yemen's immediate neighbor to the south was the former British Protectorate of Aden, which in 1968 became the People's Democratic Republic of Yemen, an avowedly Marxist regime. Over the years it proved unable to impose Marxist secular rationality on its tribal base. The dominant Marxist elite was itself divided along tribal lines, and those divisions erupted into a bloody civil war in 1986. The victor was ʿAli Salim al-Baidh, but no sooner had he consolidated his grip on power than the PDRY's long-standing patron, the Soviet Union, drifted toward collapse and abandonment of its international commitments. Without economic or military support from the USSR, al-Baidh was obliged to save his regime by seeking unity with North Yemen. With an economy even weaker than that of the North and only 20% of the combined population of 12 million, he was in a weak bargaining position. He was nonetheless able to bargain for rough parity in an elected parliament and in government ministries. Moreover, the military establishments of the two entities were not integrated. Unity was proclaimed in May 1990.

In late April 1993, elections to the new parliament were held in the presence of international observers. Observers hailed the birth of a new democracy in this unlikely corner of the Arab world. But, as in Algeria's aborted elections of 1991, the democratic process proved destabilizing and self-destructive. South Yemen's Yemen Socialist party came in third behind two northern parties, Salih's General Congress party and the Reform party representing Islamists in alliance with the Hashid tribal confederation, both of which fiercely opposed unity with the "atheist-Marxist" forces of the South. Al-Baidh read the results in strictly regional terms; the South that he controlled could never make political inroads into the North and would inevitably be subordinated to northern interests. With Saudi support the South in effect seceded from the union. Salih refused to accept the dissolution of the union and went to war, with strong Islamist support, to prevent it in the summer of 1994. A unified Yemen was restored, the old forces of the socialist South crushed, and the experiment with democracy, for the time being, shelved. Salih, in power for sixteen years, became the head of both Yemens, unified by military force and unfettered by any democratic constraints. He remains in office today.

The Sudan, the largest country in Africa in surface area (Algeria is second), is also one of the continent's poorest. Like Yemen, it is still overwhelmingly rural and agricultural, with its 40 million inhabitants (in 2005) scattered over a territory the size of the United States east of the Mississippi. One-third of the population, living in the southern region, consists of black Nilotic and Bantu tribes who, for the most part, are neither Muslim nor Arabic-speaking, while the rest are of mixed Arab and black African stock, Sunni Muslims, many of whom speak Arabic.[1]

In 1958, only two years after independence, a military regime was established under the leadership of General Muhammed 'Abboud. Bearing some resemblance to the Nasserist regime in neighboring Egypt, it put an end to a multiparty system that had ineffectively governed the country between 1956 and 1958. It emphasized themes of national unity and solidarity and tried to deal militarily with dissidence among the southern populations. It drew up a national economic plan and promoted state industries.

The growing war in the south was the principal cause of the downfall of the 'Abboud regime in 1964. For five years, civilian parties and politicians, organized around the country's two major Muslim brotherhoods (the Ansar and the Khatmiya), sought to construct a liberal political system and to bring an end to the fighting in the south. Failing on the second count, they crippled their liberal experiment.

In May 1969 Colonel Ga'afar al-Nimeiri seized power and established a regime that was explicitly Nasserist. A few months later Mu'ammar Qaddhafi established a similar regime in Libya. Both Nimeiri and Qaddhafi looked to Nasser as a revered leader, as a source of inspiration for their own experiments, and, ultimately, as a protector who could come to their rescue if need be. Nasser died only a year after the two young officers had come to power.

Nimeiri, in his first two years, dealt with the religious power centers in the Sudan, taking on the Ansar militarily, dispersing its adherents, driving its leaders into exile, and seizing its rural properties. He then turned on Marxist supporters in his government and, in a bloody sequence of coup and countercoup in July 1970, physically eliminated several prominent Marxists and communists. As had Nasser in 1953, Nimeiri cleared the political arena, and into it he cast the Sudanese Socialist Union (SSU), yet another "alliance of working forces" derived directly from Egypt's Arab Socialist Union. Central planning was resurrected, and there was a great surge in the funding of public-sector industries. Most important, Nimeiri negotiated an end to the fighting in the south and granted local autonomy to the three southern provinces.

But Sudanese society was neither ready for republican socialism nor prepared to tolerate the authoritarian politics of young army officers. As in Yemen, traditional tribal and regional loyalties to brotherhoods and religious leaders were very much alive, and Nimeiri eventually became absorbed in elaborate games of patronage, pay-offs, and the balancing of rivals that sapped the regime of much of its socialist energy. These games were interspersed with a half-dozen attempted coups, the frequency of which may have driven Nimeiri deeper into drink (the only habit he shared with Atatürk) and corruption. Although only half Bourguiba's age, Nimeiri lost the logic of his political project and succumbed to the intrigue of his own seraglio. He probably never enjoyed much legitimacy of any sort; he was personally uncharismatic, his ideology was muddled and unconvincing, a blind imitation of Egypt's, and his political and economic structures never took root. His one achievement, ending the civil war in the south, was undone by his penchant for the strategy of divide-and-rule, which eventually alienated his own supporters among the southern populations.

In the early 1980s Nimeiri became a kind of "born-again" Muslim. He threatened to apply *shari'a* throughout the country, including the non-Muslim south. By 1983 the south, led by John Garang, was again in full revolt. In the north, Nimeiri combined a ferocious Muslim piety with a vast spoils system by which his civilian and military cronies pilfered the public purse. The Sudanese intelligentsia and uncorrupted elements of the armed forces overthrew him in March 1985. A fragile civilian regime was reestablished under the leadership of Sadiq al-Mahdi and the Ansar. He was reluctant to rescind Nimeiri's promulgation of *shari'a* in the south, and therefore the civil war raged on.

Nimeiri ruled sixteen years, exactly as long as Nasser, but at the end of the period virtually nothing of his experiment was left. The Sudan's third brush with democracy, 1986–1989, once again produced policy paralysis and an unresolved civil war. In 1989 yet another military coup, led by Lieutenant General Omar al-Bashir, brought a self-proclaimed Islamic republican regime to power. Bashir's spiritual and political guide was Hassan al-Turabi, founder of the Sudan's Muslim Brotherhood.

Oxford- and Sorbonne-educated, articulate, and sophisticated, Turabi cast himself as the dominant voice of political Islam in the Muslim world, filling the void created by the death of Khomeini.

The Islamic regime has prosecuted the war in the south with a calculating zeal unrivaled in the Sudan's recent history. What human rights organizations have identified as its deliberate use of famine as a weapon in the civil war has elicited plausible charges of genocide, charges that have been repeated more recently in Darfur in the west of the country (see Box 6.1). Within the regions that it more or less controls, the new regime established its own dominant party, the National Islamic Front (NIF). It has sought with some success to marginalize the older politico-religious parties, the Democratic Unionist party (allied with the Khatmiya) and the Umma party (allied with the Ansar). As in Iran, religious corporatism is combined with ferocious repression of tribes, non-Muslims, and intellectual dissidents. In 1999 a "soft coup" reshuffled personnel and led to the ouster of Turabi by Bashir and his allies.

The economy is marginally less state-dominated than under Nimeiri, but that is an inevitable result of the enfeeblement of the state by two decades of economic crisis and the enormous outlays on the military campaign in the south. Moreover, since the time of Nimeiri the Sudan has lost access to IMF and World Bank funds, and the Bashir government, in coming to power by overthrowing a democratically elected government, rendered any rapprochement with these and other Western sources of funds highly unlikely. By the mid-1990s only Iran and possibly Iraq could offer any assistance to the Sudan. Rapprochement with the West remains problematic in the post-9/11 era.

The result is that the Sudanese state and economy have fragmented. Public finances cannot maintain a coherent regional administration or pay schoolteachers and postmen, much less invest in infrastructure and regional development. The NIF may be able to project its Islamic message more effectively in neighboring Arab countries such as Egypt or Tunisia than in the hinterlands of the Sudan itself. However, the recent reshuffling of the government, a fragile peace in the south, and the discovery and export of oil have marginally improved the situation—outside of Darfur and other conflict zones (e.g., Beja areas in the east) (see Chapter 14).

The Radicals

Socialism in the Middle East has not been inspired by doctrinaire Marxism or sustained by coherent socialist political parties. Rather, the appending of the term "socialism" to various loosely structured political fronts has symbolized commitment to equity and distributive issues, public ownership of some means of production, the acceptance of private property, and the drive for development—the mission of the purposeful state. It has not meant indoctrination, the moral and spiritual reshaping of human beings, or the assumption that social action must be organized along class lines. It certainly has not meant the dictatorship of the proletariat or even the direct control of publicly owned enterprises by the workers themselves.

By and large, all the Middle Eastern socialist regimes except the PDRY adopted similar outlooks. What has made some more radical than others has generally been their conduct of foreign policy rather than their domestic politics. Thus in their domestic policies the regimes of Algeria, Syria, and Iraq in the 1970s and 1980s had come, de facto, to resemble those of Egypt or Tunisia, but all three were aggressively anti-imperialist, too friendly with the USSR to suit the United States, and, significantly, bogged down in foreign adventures—Algeria in the Saharan War with Morocco, Iraq in large-scale hostilities with Iran, and Syria in the Lebanese cockpit.

Algeria.   That Algeria is not more revolutionary and radical is something of a surprise. Algerian socialism and its organizational underpinning, the National Liberation Front (FLN), were shaped in eight years of brutal warfare with France between 1954 and 1962. The FLN at the time of independence was not a top-down party like the Arab Socialist or the Sudanese Socialist Union. Like the Neo-Destour, it had come out of the crucible of nationalist struggle, but in Algeria that struggle had been violent and prolonged. Some believed that once independence had been won the FLN would lead Algeria down a Marxist-Leninist path similar to Cuba's.

Organizationally and in terms of its leadership, the FLN was a heterodox coalition of all the major participants in the war for liberation. Its secular, socialist, and even Marxist image was owed to the young intellectuals who had constituted its "external team" and who had made the Algerian cause known throughout the world. Their radical views were embodied in the two fundamental documents of the revolution, the Tripoli Program of 1962 and the Charter of Algiers of 1964. Algeria's first president, Ahmad Ben Bella, was not unsympathetic to their views. In the early years of independence the radicals were able to promote worker self-management (with Yugoslav advice) on agricultural land taken over from departing Europeans and in abandoned or nationalized factories. Algeria also became a major voice in the nonaligned movement and identified strongly with Palestinians, the African National Congress of South Africa, and liberation fronts in Vietnam, Angola, and Mozambique.

But alongside the articulate and cosmopolitan radical intelligentsia were other major forces far less committed to the radical transformation of Algerian society. The guerrilla fighters were mainly mountain and steppe Berbers, fervent nationalists and pious Muslims eager for their share of the spoils of victory but by no means doctrinaire socialists. Indeed, they had always been suspicious of and hostile toward the citified and seemingly atheist intellectuals.

The guerrillas *(mujahedin)* did not have a monopoly of arms in independent Algeria. The major armed forces were large professional armies that had been trained and billeted in Tunisia and Morocco but had seen little action in the final years of the war. Their principal spokesman was Houari Boumedienne, the first minister of defense and the man who would seize power from Ahmad Ben Bella in June 1965. Boumedienne was a graduate of Egypt's major center of Islamic learning, al-Azhar. He had little sympathy for either Ben Bella's secular socialist allies or the ragtag bands of guerrillas that had borne the brunt of the fighting.

Boumedienne's seizure of power ushered in an era that was in many ways Nasserist. The new president, like Atatürk, Nasser, and Bourguiba, was obsessed with rational and orderly national development. He liked good organization and good management, and as we have seen in Chapter 7, he launched Algeria onto the path of state-led heavy industrialization. The era of romantic socialism and strident internationalism ended; the era of the planner and the technocrat began.

The FLN, while enjoying a legal monopoly within the political arena, was increasingly marginalized under Boumedienne (Leca 1975; Roberts 1984). Rather than an instrument of mass mobilization, it was to be, like the ASU in Egypt, an instrument to control Algerians while the state marshaled the nation's resources for the development effort. Real power passed to the armed forces and the bureaucracy. In the absence of a national parliament and a permanent constitution, the supreme authority in the country was the National Council of the Algerian Revolution (CNRA). Typical of the secretiveness of Boumedienne, the full membership of the CNRA was not made public. Several of the members came from the so-called Oujda Group; military associates who had been with Boumedienne in Oujda, Morocco, during the revolution and when the first units of the Army of National Liberation were being trained. Few, if any, Middle Eastern regimes had ever so divorced themselves from their mass base or so discouraged popular participation as Algeria's. Boumedienne himself was a private, dour man who never sought popular acclaim. Yet, ironically, toward the last years of his regime it could be said that Boumedienne, his statist, technocratic socialism, and his efforts to remake the Algerian economy all enjoyed considerable legitimacy.

That legitimacy was not unmitigated. In 1976 the regime organized debates in all sectors of society to formulate a new national charter. Sharp criticism of corrupt officials and heavy bureaucratic procedures poured forth. After this letting off of steam, the national charter was approved. Notably, it defined Algerian socialism as a transclass alliance. The idea of internal class struggle was played down, while that of Algeria as a "proletarian" state struggling against the forces of imperialism was emphasized (Nellis 1983, 372). With that the regime went back to business as usual until the death of Boumedienne in 1978.

He was succeeded by another member of the Oujda Group, Chadli Benjadid, who presided over a profound political and economic transformation of his country. He ruled from 1978 to January 1992, when he was deposed. Economic crisis dictated a thorough overhaul of state expenditures and macroeconomic policy that in turn opened the way to political transformation. Algeria, as a major exporter of petroleum and natural gas, was particularly hard hit by declining international prices of both commodities in the mid-1980s. As a major exporter of labor, it was simultaneously squeezed by the closing-off of European labor markets that had for two decades or more been open to Algerian migrants. Algeria had no choice but to undertake stringent austerity measures in order to bring its external accounts into some balance and to begin structural adjustment (see Chapter 9).

As in other countries in the region, the austerity measures were the proximate cause of cost-of-living riots in October 1988. These were, in Algeria, particularly bloody, resulting in thousands of deaths. The regime was shaken. As we have argued elsewhere, deep economic and political crisis, while inherently fraught with danger, offers political leaders opportunities for initiating far-reaching change. Chadli Benjadid saw that opportunity in October 1988 and seized it.

The grievances that provoked the riots went far beyond short-term material problems, signaling the delegitimization of the regime and particularly of the FLN. Benjadid took the opportunity to dissociate himself partially from the single party and, as president, to rise above it. A year before the riots he had approved a law allowing the free formation of associations in Algeria without any prior approval by public authorities. Immediately after the riots he submitted to referendum a new constitution that was given overwhelming approval. It omitted any mention of socialism and any reference to the state as guarantor of the citizens' well-being.

With the new association law and constitution in place, Benjadid moved Algeria rapidly toward its first democratic elections, first for local assemblies, then for the parliament. An Islamic opposition, the Islamic Salvation Front (FIS by its French acronym), was legalized and allowed to contest the elections. Its two principal leaders, Abbasi Madani and 'Ali Belhadj, put together a mass movement in the space of a year and in June 1990 swept the local elections, winning nearly two-thirds of the votes cast. About one-third of the electorate abstained from voting. Algeria's political establishment was shocked, but Benjadid plunged ahead with the preparations for the elections to the national assembly or parliament.

Formerly one of the most closed and least participative military authoritarian regimes in the Middle East, Algeria was on the verge of an astounding democratic transition in which an Islamic party was permitted to contest for power at the national level. The stakes were high. It was widely feared that if the FIS won the parliamentary election as it had the local elections, it would have sufficient votes to amend the constitution or do away with it altogether—in other words, that Algeria's entry into democracy might simultaneously be its exit. The Algerian senior officers' corps was particularly alarmed at the prospect of an Islamic electoral victory. It feared that the FIS would end its monopoly on political power, set the country back technologically, and turn the schools into centers of religious indoctrination. Algeria's politically active women feared being forced out of public life and employment and back into the home. Secularists feared that an FIS victory would see the imposition of *shari'a* throughout the land. The firebrand denunciations of democracy by Belhadj in particular did nothing to allay these fears.

In December 1991 the elections were held. The balloting system followed was the French one, with an initial vote for all candidates followed by a runoff between the two leading candidates in any district in which no candidate won a clear majority in the first round. The authorities believed that enough contests would be decided in the second round that, through alliances, the FLN could prevent the FIS from winning an outright majority. The calculus proved disastrously wrong, and the FIS, while winning a million fewer votes than it had in 1990, stood poised after the first round of voting to win an absolute majority in the parliament. The second round was never held, and in January 1992 the senior military moved to depose Benjadid, arrest Belhadj and Madani, and dissolve the FIS.

The military reverted to the closed, secretive style of the Boumedienne years, putting the country under the control of the High Council of State. It brought back to the presidency Mohammed Boudiaf, one of the historic leaders of the revolution

(1954–1962), who had been in exile in Morocco for many years. Boudiaf proved far too independent, and when he began to crack down on corruption in the government and military he was assassinated, on June 29, 1992. The FIS was blamed for his death, but many Algerians, including his widow, remain convinced that the military eliminated him.

Algeria then sunk into civil war. With its leadership in jail, parts of the FIS took up arms, allegedly with the help of *mujahedin* returning from years of combat in Afghanistan, where they had fought the Soviet occupying forces. Eventually a renegade armed wing known as the Armed Islamic Group broke from the FIS and fought the Algerian security forces and civilian adversaries in the cities and in the countryside with horrific savagery. Intellectuals, unveiled women, journalists, foreigners, and members of the political and military establishment were ritually slaughtered and sometimes mutilated. There is no question that the security forces resorted to the same methods and attributed the victims to the "fanatical" actions of the Armed Islamic Group and the FIS.

Returning to its closed military authoritarianism, Algeria began to lose its administrative and security grip on parts of its territory. In early 1994 the High Council of State was formally disbanded and the minister of defense, Liamine Zéroual, was made president. He pursued the initiation of a dialogue with the FIS, especially its jailed leaders, and other forces in the opposition. No observers were convinced that he had the backing of the military, and no one could imagine the compromise that might allow the violence to end. Could new elections conceivably be held with FIS participation, and, if so, according to what rules? By aborting the last round of elections, did the regime doom for the foreseeable future any possibility that the FIS could try the democratic path once again? Finally, would the Armed Islamic Group, which had little use for either the "moderates" in the FIS or for democracy, play any role but that of spoiler? Elections resumed in 1995, and in 1999, after a series of short-term leaders drawn from the military, Abdelaziz Bouteflika was elected. Effectively ended by brute force and by Bouteflika's amnesty law, the Algerian civil war drew to a close in 2002. It had claimed at least 100,000 lives.[2]

What kind of regime would have been established if the FIS or some political movement like it had come to power? As Lahouari Addi argued (1995), the FIS adopted all the populist themes of the FLN but with an Islamic twist. The Muslim people of Algeria were to be the beneficiaries of the revolution; the Muslim state needed to stamp out corruption and redistribute wealth; the economy had to be harnessed for the protection and spread of the Islamic revolution, and therefore the state had to maintain control of key economic sectors and strengthen the armed forces. An Islamic Algeria would have been expected to join other Islamic polities in resisting the economic and cultural incursions of the West and in confronting Israel militarily.

Economically, an Islamic regime's choices would have been limited. There were no wealthy Islamic benefactors to offer it significant financial support; Saudi Arabia, the only candidate for such a role, had no reason to encourage such regimes. Relations with the United States would have been testy, at best. The international financial institutions dominated by the advanced Western nations and Japan would have insisted on adherence to orthodox structural adjustment programs. An Islamic Algeria would have had difficulty attracting foreign private capital unless it followed similar guidelines. If it could not have afforded populism, redistribution, and high military outlays, it would have come to resemble the regime it replaced (or the NIF government in the Sudan), one surviving on the strength of a narrow coalition, strangling political participation, following orthodox, contractionary economic policies, and ruling by force and intimidation.[3]

Iraq and Syria. Iraq from 1963 to 2003 and Syria since 1963 have been ruled by national branches of the same party, the Ba'ath or Arab Renaissance party. Founded after World War II by two French-educated schoolteachers from Syria, Michel Aflaq (Greek Orthodox) and Salah Bitar (Sunni Muslim), it took as its mission capturing power somewhere in the Arab world and then working for Arab and socialist unity. The irony is that in the 1960s the Ba'ath contested Nasser's Arab Socialist Union for preeminence among the region's youth, and Nasserists and Ba'athists divided the Arab world between them. The enmity between Nasserists and Ba'athists took a violent turn in Iraq in 1959, but it was eclipsed by the rivalry that developed between Ba'athist Syria and Iraq after 1968. It is hard for the outsider to discern any profound doctrinal differences between the two regimes, and one suspects that older geopolitical rivalries between two states sharing the Euphrates basin may have as much to do with the enmity as anything else.

The structures of the two regimes were rather similar. Although in both countries civilians built the party (Aflaq and Bitar in Syria and the Shi'ite civil servant Fu'ad Rikabi in Iraq), they were tempted to recruit supporters among the officers' corps and seek power by means of coup d'état rather than the ballot. Unlike the Neo-Destour, which fought openly for Tunisian independence, the Ba'ath won power through stealth. Its popular base of support in both Syria and Iraq has always been narrow. In Iraq around 1980 the Ba'ath had only 25,000 full members, although there were 1.5 million "supporters" (Helms 1984, 87). Hinnebusch (1979, 21) put party membership in Syria at 100,000 in the mid-1970s. The Ba'ath has always had a Leninist predilection for a vanguard rather than a mass-based party.

The military allies of the Ba'ath tended to take it over and marginalize it, much as Boumedienne did the FLN in Algeria after 1965. In Iraq there was the Revolutionary Command Council (RCC), which grouped the major military figures of the regime and, like Algeria's CNRA, was the real locus of decisionmaking. Alongside it was the Ba'ath Regional Command (the Iraqi branch of the Ba'ath), whose membership was quite similar to that of the RCC. Finally, there was the National Command, supposedly the heart of the pan-Arab organization, of which Michel Aflaq (d. 1989), at odds with his native Syria, was the titular head. The National Command had no power at all.

The structures of the Syrian Ba'ath did not greatly differ from those of Iraq prior to 1980 and the outbreak of war with Iran. The military retained effective power but used the Ba'ath party to legitimize its preeminence. In February 1971 Hafiz al-Assad, a senior air force officer and a member of the Ba'ath since his youth, was reappointed to the presidency by a body called the People's Council. The council had itself been appointed by the Ba'ath Regional Command and included 173 Ba'athis, 40 Nasserists, and 8 communists. Assad clearly wanted to portray himself as president of *all* Syrians.

Nonetheless, the Syrian Ba'ath party remained well organized and pervasive; it was not a paper organization like the Sudanese Socialist Union. Sadowski probably had it right in this assessment (1985, 3): "Twenty-two years in power have changed the Ba'ath from a revolutionary movement into a virtual appendage of the state. But this transformation did not destroy the party's influence. Along with the army and the bureaucracy, it remains one of the foundations of the Assad regime."

Both Iraqi and Syrian politico-military elites tended to be drawn from regional and sectarian minorities. In Syria, Assad, many of his closest associates, and a number of those upon whom he trampled before and since seizing power in 1970 were drawn from the Alawite religious sect, an offshoot of Shi'ism, and from the poor hinterland of the Latakia region. As Hinnebusch noted (1979, 17), "The Ba'ath recruited from all those who were outside the system of connections, patronage or kin on which the old regime was built: the educated sons of peasants, the minorities, the rural lower middle class, the 'black sheep' from lesser branches of great families." The wearing of the Ba'athi label and the espousal of Ba'athi socialism was not enough to persuade many (mostly Sunni) Syrians that Assad's regime was other than a clan of power-hungry Shi'ites masquerading as socialists.

Still, the elder Assad reached out to Sunnis, especially in the urban business class. After the Syrian armed forces entered the Lebanese civil war in 1976, Syrian involvement in Lebanese affairs generated a lucrative flow of legal and illegal cross-border trade in which the supporters of the regime, Sunni and Shi'ite alike, claimed a share. Syria's participation in Operation Desert Storm against Iraq in 1991 won it financial support from Saudi Arabia once the Iraqi occupation of Kuwait ended. As a result, the Syrian economy grew significantly, allowing Assad to erect a fairly big tent under which to gather a broad coalition of public and private, civilian and military, and Sunni and Alawite economic interests—a coalition that continued to be maintained after Hafiz al-Assad's death in 2000 by his son Bashir.

The end of the cold war and the withering of Soviet/Russian support for its Ba'athi clients in Syria and Iraq produced different responses in the two regimes. Assad exploited Syria's crucial role in the peace process between Israel and its Arab neighbors, demonstrating that Syria's loss of a great-power patron did not deprive it of all leverage vis-à-vis the United States. Allying itself with the UN-sponsored force to drive Iraq from Kuwait was a calculated risk (not one very popular among Syrians or most other Arabs), but one that paid off handsomely. In the subsequent peace negotiations Syria was a stubborn but responsible negotiator. Assad demonstrated to the Syrians and to the region as a whole that he was still a player, courted and visited by foreign ministers and heads of state. As a consequence he could proceed with cautious economic liberalization (Heydemann 1992) while blocking any meaningful political liberalization. Despite mounting pressures on the regime of the younger Assad (the eruption of the second Palestinian *intifada* in 2000, al-Qaeda's attack of September 11, 2001, the American invasion and occupation of Iraq, and Lebanese outrage over the murder of Rafik Hariri), the Syrian regime continues essentially unchanged.

The Iraqi Ba'ath came briefly to power in the winter of 1963, on the shoulders of the military, and was moved out by a "palace" coup led by 'Abd al-Salam 'Arif, a Nasserist of sorts, who sought close relations with Egypt. An agreement with Egypt of May 1964 provided for a loose form of union between the two countries and for the setting up in Iraq of the Arab Socialist Union–Iraqi Region. Egypt had temporarily won Iraq from the Ba'ath. In terms of domestic policy, however, there was little to choose between Nasserists and Ba'athists. 'Arif's nationalization of more than thirty industrial firms in May 1964 would have fit easily into a Ba'athi program, as would all other aspects of his state-led growth (see Gotheil 1981; Penrose and Penrose 1978; Springborg 1981).

The June War of 1967, in which the Iraqi armed forces played no significant role, may have undermined whatever legitimacy the 'Arif regime still enjoyed. In July 1968 the Ba'ath came to power once again through a military coup. Iraq's new president was General Ahmad Hassan al-Bakr, but the real power of the regime lay with the prime minister, Saddam Hussein, a Ba'athi militant since his student days and a hardened veteran of the nation's internal police. Few Middle Eastern leaders have ever had as much experience with "dirty tricks" as Saddam Hussein.

Both Saddam and al-Bakr, along with several other stalwarts of the new regime, were from central Iraq, specifically the provincial town of Takrit. Iraq's new masters were bound by shared blood, their home region, and the fact that they were Arab Sunni Muslims. The Takriti clan in Iraq became the functional equivalent of the Alawite clan in Syria. There was bloodletting among Takritis, but it was minor when compared to the violence wreaked on Shi'ite Islamists, Kurdish dissidents, and any others foolish enough to challenge Saddam. When al-Bakr died in 1982, Saddam, in the midst of the war he had launched against Iran, became president. He nurtured a cult of his own personality that was unparalleled in the Middle East.

His state, like Assad's, rested on the pillars of the armed forces, the police, the bureaucracy, the party, and.his clan. Iraq's ideology had no more teeth in it than Tunisia's. Batatu dismissed the 1968 Ba'ath party constitution as formulating "a mild form of middle-class socialism." It combined acknowledgment of Islam and pan-Arabism with the ideals of social justice, the end of exploitation, the right to use private property subject to state regulation, and "a guided national economy based on the cooperation of the public and private sectors" (1978, 1084). Like the regime in Syria, the Iraqi regime redistributed income, promoted growth, spread literacy, and for a time improved the economic lot of its citizens.

Saddam Hussein gradually transformed Iraq into a police state of unparalleled proportions in the Arab world. After eliminating all real enemies inside Iraq, he had to rule by terror and the systematic seeding of suspicion and fear among all Iraqis. As noted in Chapter 7, as much as a quarter of the Iraqi workforce may have been associated with spying and intelligence gathering for the regime. Neighbors informed on neighbors, children on parents, classmates on classmates, so that civil society was atomized and rendered mute (al-Khalil 1989).

The eight years of war with Iran (1980–1988) only deepened the culture of repression and fear. They also witnessed the subordination of all economic activity to the war effort. Despite its petroleum exports, Iraq contracted approximately US$80 billion in foreign debt during the 1980s, most of it owed to Kuwait and Saudi Arabia, whom Saddam Hussein had no intention of repaying. When hostilities with Iran came to a close, he proclaimed that Iraq was liberalizing its economy, privatizing some of its public enterprises (sold to his friends), and opening the economy to foreign investment.

Saddam had expected that Kuwait and Saudi Arabia would provide much of that investment, all the while forgiving Iraqi debts. The investment did not materialize, and the issue of the debt was not resolved. It was, in part, for these reasons that he invaded Kuwait in the summer of 1990, perhaps with the intention of proceeding on to Saudi Arabia—or, at least, extorting the money he needed. One can also see the invasion as Saddam's response to the end of the cold war. His reaction to the loss of his Soviet backers was to proclaim his intention of leading an Arab crusade against Israel while he and the rest of the Arabs had the arms and technology to do so. Time, he argued, was not on the side of the Arabs in a unipolar world. No other Arab state openly shared his analysis, however, and Kuwait and Saudi Arabia seemed more concerned about recovering some of the money they had "lent" to Iraq. Meanwhile, Saddam was trying to demobilize some of the million men under arms in Iraq and absorb them into a depressed civilian economy crying out for new investment. Seizing Kuwait would, at a minimum, bring its large oil reserves, its access to the Persian Gulf, and its infrastructure under his control.

It is not our intention here to revisit Operation Desert Storm and the crisis surrounding it. Let us note simply that Iraq's infrastructure was shattered, its military capabilities greatly reduced, the Kurds placed under a kind of UN trusteeship, and the southern part of the country beaten into submission by Saddam's Republican Guard after an aborted Shi'ite insurrection. What we want to stress is that more than a decade of war transformed the Iraqi state and economy into something for which we have no ready labels. We simply do not know how the economy functioned in a country where the northern, Kurdish fifth escaped the control of the central authorities entirely and the southern, Shi'ite third was treated as enemy territory. As in the Sudan and, to a lesser extent, Algeria, there was no longer a unified national economy or an administration present and functioning in all parts of the country. Because of international sanctions imposed as a result of its occupation of Kuwait, Iraq could not market its oil. The regime lived off of contraband and billions of dollars stashed away before the invasion in foreign bank accounts. Again like the isolated regimes of the Sudan and Algeria, Saddam's regime hunkered down in the central, Sunni third of the country, playing upon Sunni Arab fears of Kurdish or Shi'ite domination were Saddam to be overthrown. For most Iraqi Sunnis, these fears were amply justified by events after 2003—fears which Ba'athists behavior did much to create by its relentless violence against Shi'ites and Kurds.[4] The roots of Iraqi civil violence and political fissiparousness, so visible after 2003, can in substantial part be traced to the Ba'athist regime of 1968–2003.

South Yemen. The Marxist experiment in South Yemen to which we have already alluded found its unlikely home in the British Protectorate of Aden. South Yemen, socially and ecologically an extension of the North Yemeni highlands, receives less rainfall and thus has only limited agricultural potential. Traditionally it survived on maritime trade. Its remote, arid valleys were populated by highly stratified tribal lineages dominated by a religious notability, the *sayyids,* putatively descended from the Prophet (Bujra 1971). The *sayyids* dominated trade and helped carry Islam to the Far East (e.g., Malaysia, Indonesia). In this peculiar society the British established one of the world's major ports, Aden, servicing the British fleet and shipping in transit to India and beyond. With the opening of the Suez Canal in the last third of the nineteenth century, the port of Aden became a vital link in Red Sea maritime traffic. It was made a crown colony, and its hinterland was put under a British protectorate.

In the port a modern workforce developed consisting of dockworkers, maintenance personnel, clerks, customs officials, suppliers, traders, bureaucrats, schoolteachers, and the like. Many were drawn from the tribal interior and, like many other Middle Eastern peoples, as individuals struck an indeterminate balance between their status in the modern world and their deeply rooted identity in blood-tribal and religious networks. Throughout the 1960s, while the rest of the Arab world consolidated its independence and while the civil war wore on in neighboring North Yemen, nationalist agitation in the port of Aden grew in strength. Abdullah al-Asnag, a labor leader, founded the People's Socialist party, which in turn was part of the National Liberation Front (NLF), to spearhead the movement. The NLF in 1968 took over the government of South Yemen from the departing British. With independence, the NLF adjusted its internal alliances. The organized labor wing and especially Asnag, its moderate leader, lost out to a group of intellectuals and a rural constituency of poor tribal peasants who had long chafed under the dominance of the *sayyid* class. Something of a Maoist scenario was enacted: Revolutionary intellectuals allied with oppressed peasants surrounded and captured the city.

The NLF was an explicitly mobilizational party seeking to activate the working class, which included women, students, and soldiers. It was also the supreme authority in the land, eclipsing the government and the Supreme People's Council as the locus of decisionmaking. The NLF can be conceived of as a vanguard party, penetrating all sectors of society through mass organizations set up along familiar functional lines: peasants, workers, soldiers, students, women. On paper there would be little to distinguish the NLF from the Ba'ath, but it would seem that its effective role in running the state and the level of indoctrination of its cadres clearly set it apart from all other Arab revolutionary parties.

From the mid-1970s on, predictable cleavages between moderate and radical wings of the NLF were exacerbated by the country's economic crisis. In the early years of the decade, the regime had backed a liberation front in Dhofar province, part of the Sultanate of Oman, in the hope of spreading and consolidating the revolution.

The front was eventually subdued, however, through a combination of Jordanian, Iranian, and Pakistani military support to the Omani sultan and the largesse of a Saudi Arabia awash in foreign exchange after the surge in international oil prices in 1973.

The PDRY was in desperate economic shape in the mid-1970s. It had lost business through the closing of the Suez Canal after the June War and also had to pay much higher prices for its petroleum imports. Saudi Arabia was willing to bail the PDRY out of its difficulties in exchange for the abandonment of the Dhofar Liberation Front and some move away from the regime's espousal of Marxism-Leninism. The chairman of the Presidential Council, Salim Robaya 'Ali, was sympathetic to the Saudi overtures, while 'Abd al-Fattah Ismail, secretary general of the NLF (renamed the Yemen Socialist party [YSP] in 1978), was opposed.

Robaya 'Ali prevailed for a time; the regime became regionally well mannered, although it hosted a large Soviet military presence and maintained close relations with the revolutionary regime in Ethiopia and the most radical factions of the PLO. But the conflict between socialist radicals and moderates had not been definitively resolved. Moreover, when it reignited, it was clear that older forms of tribal loyalty contributed to what appeared to be purely ideological or strategic disputes.

For a time, when 'Abd al-Fattah Ismail replaced Robaya 'Ali as president, the radicals appeared dominant, but in 1980 he in turn was replaced by the moderate 'Ali Nasr Muhammed, who became both president and secretary general of the YSP. Ismail went into exile in Moscow, but his supporters put increasing pressure upon the regime for his return. Curiously, the Soviet Union was not eager to have Ismail back in the PDRY, devoted Marxist though he was. The USSR cautioned 'Ali Nasr against allowing him to return, but in February 1985, yielding to internal pressure, 'Ali Nasr did so anyway. Over the next year Ismail mobilized his supporters to take over key positions in the party's politburo. It was simply a question of time before that politburo would calmly depose and dispose of 'Ali Nasr. Against this creeping coup d'état, 'Ali Nasr launched a preemptive coup in January 1986. He seemed to lack the heart to fight his opponents to the end, and as armed conflict engulfed the city of Aden he fled to his tribal homeland at Abyan and then into exile. Ismail and the hard-liners were back in power.

The end of the cold war doomed the Marxist regime in South Yemen. As we have seen it also spelled economic crisis such that unity with the North appeared to be the only way for the South to survive economically, no matter what ideological and political concessions its leaders would be forced to make. Despite the relatively good deal 'Ali Salim al-Baidh ultimately obtained in terms of the division of ministerial and governmental positions, the 1993 elections indicated that the YSP itself would remain a weak and beleaguered party in the union. Al-Baidh in essence withdrew from the union, and in the ensuing civil war the YSP and the South as a whole were crushed by the armies of 'Ali 'Abdullah Salih and his Islamist allies.

Libya.   In 1969, then-Captain Mu'ammar Qaddhafi overthrew the Libyan monarchy and proclaimed an Arab republic faithfully modeled on that of Nasserist Egypt.

Within a year Nasser had died, and Qaddhafi was left to deal with an Egypt under Sadat that was rapidly opening its economy to foreign investment and seeking rapprochement with the West. After a few quixotic attempts at full union with Egypt, Qaddhafi went his own peculiar way. In 1977 he introduced what he called the Jamahiria, or "mass state," the intent of which was to abolish all intermediaries between the people, or masses, and their leaders. There were to be no political parties or mass organizations, which would only produce new oligarchs. All agencies, enterprises, and places of work were to be run by the employees themselves, through revolutionary people's councils, and formal administrative hierarchies were to be dismantled or at least closely supervised by these councils. Simultaneously, the mass state sought to terminate wage payment for work, nationalize retail trade, and end all rents—all this in the name of the eradication of exploitation.

The blueprint was breathtaking, but its implementation has not been visible. Key bureaucracies built around the oil and banking sectors seem little affected by massism, and there is no evidence that the armed forces have been taken over by the revolutionary committees. In June 1986, after the US air strike against Libya, Qaddhafi in typical fashion unilaterally (that is, without consulting the revolutionary committee movement in whose name he spoke) resurrected the Revolutionary Command Council, including four officers who had participated in the 1969 coup d'état against King Idris.

The idea of the mass state seems vacuous when it is recalled that, like Saudi Arabia's and Kuwait's, 40% of Libya's workforce is foreign, as is 50% of its managerial and professional personnel. Foreigners cannot be members of revolutionary committees, and it is inconceivable that they are not paid wages. Libya in the final analysis is simply another rentier state with an idiosyncratic and autocratic leader who confuses theatrics with institution building. His staging is for the benefit of the Libyans, but without oil rents and worker migrants the show would end. After more than thirty years, the Libyan "model" has had no discernible appeal elsewhere.

The PLO.   A brief discussion of a possible and future Palestinian state finds its logical place here in that since 1967 the Palestine Liberation Organization and its major constituent al-Fatah followed an ideological trajectory similar to that of the radical socialist republics. In the wake of the June War of 1967 and the Israeli occupation of Gaza, the West Bank, the Golan Heights, and East Jerusalem, the PLO, led by Yasser 'Arafat, emerged as an armed movement to resist the occupation. At that time its ideology was leftist and secular and called for the "liberation" of all of Palestine, including Israel in its pre-1967 borders, and the establishment of a democratic, secular, socialist Palestine in which peoples of all faiths could reside.

Over time this vision and the organization itself were buffeted by the same forces as other regimes and movements in the region. Internally, throughout the 1970s and 1980s, the voice of political Islam grew stronger and was embodied in HAMAS (the Arabic acronym for the Islamic Resistance Movement), an organization that was initially encouraged by the Israelis as a counterweight to the PLO but soon developed a life of its own. HAMAS, which grew out of the Muslim Brotherhood, had no use for socialism or secular cohabitation in Palestine and resisted any compromise with the Israelis.

At the same time the Soviet Union became a less reliable and, because of its occupation of Afghanistan, less desirable friend of the PLO. Thus, the PLO and al-Fatah drifted ideologically toward more nationalist and proto-Islamic positions and tactically toward a more accommodationist position vis-à-vis the increasingly dominant United States and its client, Israel. In 1989, 'Arafat and the PLO accepted the existence of Israel and declared their readiness to live in peace with Israel on the basis of UN Resolution 242, calling for Israeli withdrawal from the occupied territories. It was thus an extremely misguided reversion to older rhetorical and political stances when in 1990 'Arafat and the PLO blessed Saddam Hussein's occupation of Kuwait and his blustery threats against Israel. Having sided with the loser and alienated Saudi Arabia, the PLO and 'Arafat paid dearly.

When the formal peace talks among Israel, Jordan, Syria, and the Palestinians, launched in Madrid under the joint auspices of the United States and Russia, failed to produce significant results, Israelis and Palestinians met secretly in Oslo, Norway, to iron out the details of what became the Declaration of Principles (DOP) and the historic handshake of Prime Minister Yitzhak Rabin and Chairman 'Arafat at the White House in September 1993. The DOP called for a transition period and direct negotiations toward a final settlement. During the transition Israel would initially withdraw from the town of Jericho in the West Bank and from the Gaza Strip. Further withdrawals would take place so that elections could be held in both Gaza and the West Bank.

For the past ten years, there have been two Arab democracies: in Lebanon and in Palestine. In the West Bank and Gaza, elections have been conducted regularly, voter turnout has been very high, and international observers agree that the elections have been free and fair. In some ways, this in unsurprising. The long years of the first (unarmed) *intifada* prior to 1991 and its reinforcing of Palestinian civil society, the distance of its leaders-in-exile, and the high levels of literacy and political awareness among its population have given the Palestinians of the occupied territories the sense of self and the practical experience to move beyond the tired paternalistic authoritarianism of other Arab regimes—a paternalism, be it noted, shared by Yasser 'Arafat. And, of course, 'Arafat was far more constrained by Israeli power than any other Arab autocrat. Yet he was also far more popular than many other Arab leaders. Unlike them, he was elected president of the Palestinian Authority (PA) in 1996 with a popular vote of nearly 90%—in an election monitored by many international observers.

In the January 1996 elections, the Palestine Liberation Movement (FATAH), led by 'Arafat, won approximately 30% of the popular vote. However, they won 69 of 88 legislative seats, thanks to a "winner-take-all" electoral system that favored larger parties. Yasser 'Arafat died in November 2004. The second Palestinian legislative elections were held in January 2006. In these elections, 50% of the seats were allocated to proportional lists, and another 50% to individuals in districts (as in the 1996 system). Voter turnout was 77%, and the process was intensively scrutinized by international and local observers, who agreed that the elections were fair. HAMAS won 74 of 132 seats, or some 56% of the total. As in the 1996 election, due to the electoral structure, HAMAS's share of the legislative seats was greater than its share of the popular vote, which was 44%. These nonproportional results are a consequence of electoral structure and are common throughout the world in all except strictly proportional systems.

Palestinians voted in a second presidential election in 2005. FATAH candidate Mahmoud Abbas won handily, with 62% of the vote. However, HAMAS boycotted this election. Nonetheless, voter turnout in Gaza, where HAMAS is particularly strong, was estimated at around 50%—the rough equivalent of voter turnout in American elections.

Palestinian elections, and Palestinian democracy, then, have been the real thing. However, as Samuel Huntington noted (1991), democracy solves only *one* problem—that of tyranny. Democratically elected Palestinian leaders have, so far, been unable to end the Israeli occupation, and Israeli and American officials have refused to deal with the government elected in January 2006. Poverty rates, child malnutrition, unemployment, and other ills have all skyrocketed since the beginning of the second *intifada* in late 2000.[5] These disasters cannot be laid at the door of electoral politics; there is a danger, however, that Palestinians and others may interpret them as indicating that "democracy was tried, and it failed."[6]

"LIBERAL" MONARCHIES

The kings, princes, and sheykhs of the Middle East have fostered very different polities from those of the socialist republics. The purposeful state, bent on development and military might, its citizenry tightly organized, mobilized, and above all, unified, has not characterized the monarchical systems of the region. Of course, it has not even characterized the socialist republics themselves, which, more often than not, have failed to achieve unity or development.

The distinction we wish to make is subtle and not always apparent from the written record. The shahs of Iran, father and son, were modernizers and intolerant of ethnic and sectarian cleavages in their society. As did Atatürk, they dealt with these cleavages by force. King Muhammed V and Crown Prince Hassan of Morocco likewise dealt ruthlessly with Berber dissidence in 1959. Monarchs seem as concerned with integration as republican presidents. They have also espoused the cause of economic development and have marshaled state resources and large technocracies to pursue them. All have paid lip service to an even distribution of national wealth. Most, in function of their own national resources, have sought military credibility; the last shah was obsessed by that goal.

What, then, makes the monarchs different? In our view there are two main factors. First, all claim some degree of divine right to rule. Even King Hussein of Jordan, a descendant of the Prophet, invoked his blood as a qualification to rule. The shah claimed that he spoke to God and that the Pahlavi dynasty had a divine mission to rule Iran. The king of Morocco uses the Qur'anic title Commander of the Faithful. King Fu'ad, father of Egypt's last monarch, Farouk, tried in the 1930s to lay claim to the caliphate, which had fallen victim to Atatürk's militant secularism. The point is that the monarchs do not rest their legitimacy on the expression of popular will or sovereignty. They are responsible not to the people but to God. The distinction may be somewhat artificial in that few Middle Eastern leaders, republican or monarchical, have ever enjoyed much legitimacy, but the rival sets of symbols evoke powerful emotions.

The second factor has to do with the handling of diversity and pluralism. Here the monarchical game is subtle and close to hypocritical. Monarchs speak in terms of the nation and decry the fractious elements in society that impede national unity, but they do not deny these elements legitimacy so long as they behave according to the rules of the game as the monarchy defines them. What the monarchs want is a plethora of interests, tribal, ethnic, professional, class based, and partisan, whose competition for public patronage they can arbitrate. None of these elements can be allowed to become too powerful or wealthy, and the monarch will police and repress or entice and divide factions that are becoming too entrenched. The monarch's rule is to divide, chastise, and regulate but not to humiliate or alienate important factions. The shah in the 1970s, fat with oil revenues, thought that he could violate this rule.

The rhetoric of this game is paternalistic; kings talk of themselves as fathers to their societies or, as King Hassan described himself, as a shepherd to a flock of occasionally errant sheep. They suggest that if all behaved selflessly and for the national good, all would be better off, but, alas, children will be children, and kings must settle their petty squabbles. They are thus *above* all factions and party to none, especially in that they answer to God alone.

But they must have the factions and the squabbles. It is their role of arbiter and supervisor of the distribution of patronage and state resources that makes kings relevant to the political game. They must propagate the belief that were they ever to disappear, the system would disintegrate into a chaotic war among all the petty contenders for spoils.[7] Their populations have not always believed in their indispensability, and monarchies have been overthrown with some regularity: King Farouk of Egypt in 1952, King Faisal of Iraq in 1958, the imam of Yemen in 1962, King Idris of Libya in 1969, and the shah of Iran in 1979. The first four fell to military coups that may or may not have expressed popular sentiment; only the shah was the victim of direct popular action.

The monarchy of independent Morocco emerged out of the French protectorate (1912–1956). The nationalist Independence party had used King Muhammed V as the symbol of the nationalist struggle, but with independence the king took his distance from the party, abetted its scission, from which the National Union of Popular Forces emerged in 1959, and encouraged the formation of rival parties. In other words, he deliberately increased the number of factions and political clans in the system; the better to assert his role as arbiter. Shortly after independence, Berber dissident movements in the Middle Atlas and Rif Mountains elicited a sharp military response, but at the same time Muhammed V encouraged the formation of a Berber party, the Popular Movement. (His wife, the mother of King Hassan, was a Middle Atlas Berber.)

Muhammed V died in 1961 and was succeeded by his son, Hassan II, whom he had put in direct control of the royal armed forces. Hassan never relinquished his control over the military, although he was nearly overthrown by it twice, in 1971 and in 1972. He assiduously followed the divide-and-rule tactics of his father, weakening parties, trade unions, and regional interests but never destroying them or pushing them out of the political arena. Even the Moroccan Communist party, dissolved a few years after independence, was allowed to reestablish itself legally in the mid-1970s. King Hassan put himself forward as the final protector of all interests— the parties against military intervention, the military against civilian bungling, the Berbers against the Arabs, and the Jews against the Muslims. This "balancing role" continues to be the official pose of his son and successor, Muhammad VI.

Monarchs position themselves above the contending forces in the political arena in a way that makes it easier for them than for the leaders of the socialist republics to allow contested elections and some modicum of democratic practice. The monarch can portray himself as a disinterested but authoritative arbiter of the contending interests whose sole concern is the well-being of his people. Hassan II was no exception, and since the mid-1970s, multiparty elections, neither free nor fair, have taken place on a fairly regular basis. Given an improving economy and more than thirty-five years of (relative) political tranquillity, Hassan II, while not loved by all, convinced most Moroccans that the monarchy is vital to the country's stability. Many think the same thing about his son.

Reza Khan, the founder of the Pahlavi dynasty, was, it will be recalled, inclined to follow Atatürk's path and model his state after Turkey's republic. Although he was persuaded to adopt a monarchical form of rule, much of his reign was characterized by the crushing of all regional, tribal, and ethnic dissidence and the building of a centralized state and a powerful military. Although Reza Khan built a powerful state, he left a place in its political arena for the weakened tribal leaders, for regional interests, and for the clergy. As in Morocco, as long as these groups played by the rules laid down by the shah, they could represent their interests legitimately.

The shah's son, Mohammed Reza Pahlavi, even after surviving his confrontation with the nationalist prime minister, Mohammed Mossadegh, in 1953, never managed the political game with the same forcefulness and assurance as his father. His efforts to fabricate political parties (see Chapter 12) and to exclude other parties of the Mossadegh era or before, such as the Tudeh and the National Front, merely produced a kind of vacuum that could be filled only by clandestine political groupings, either radical Islamic or radical secularist, and the notorious internal police, the Iranian Security and Intelligence Organization (SAVAK). Rather than dealing with formally constituted parties and interest groups as the king did in Morocco, the shah tried to manipulate large categories of the population—the secular intelligentsia, the clergy, the bazaar or traditional retailing bourgeoisie, a new state-dependent private entrepreneurial bourgeoisie, organized labor, and civil servants. Heady with the massive oil earnings accruing to the state treasury in the 1970s, the shah neglected many of these constituencies; he found himself in the late 1970s with only two sources of support, the armed forces and the United States, and a large source of indifference, the peasantry. All other constituencies had turned against him. He had lost his role as the accepted, indeed indispensable, arbiter of the political game.

Other monarchs also profit from cleavage and enhance their relevance to the functioning of state power by perpetuating it. King Hussein straddled the cleavage between a majoritarian, highly educated Palestinian population and a largely Bedouin minority that dominated the Jordanian armed forces and key government positions. The Bedouin looked to King Hussein to protect their privileged position and to "contain" the Palestinian intelligentsia and entrepreneurial bourgeoisie. Jordan is eloquent testimony to the fact that the cleavages that allow monarchs to survive are precisely those that can and do bring them down.

It should not be surprising, then, that it was King Hussein who took the risk of holding parliamentary elections in 1989 and 1993, the latter following the Declaration of Principles establishing peace between the Palestinians and Israelis. Both elections were free, although the electoral system used in 1993 favored individual candidates at the expense of parties, especially the Muslim Brotherhood. The Islamic vote was strong but not dominant in both elections, and many Palestinian voters abstained. Nonetheless, the elections allowed King Hussein to portray himself as above all parties and the safeguard of national integrity. His being a descendant of the Prophet helped.

His son, Abdellah II, acceded to the throne upon his father's death in 1999. Parliamentary elections were held in 2003; the Muslim Brothers (see Chapter 14) and several leftist and national parties formed an electoral alliance. The latter won no seats at all, while the Muslim Brothers won only 20 seats, the fewest in their history. They claimed widespread electoral fraud, charges that the government predictably denied. The vast majority of seats went to tribal candidates and others closely linked by patronage with the Hashemites. Abdellah appears determined to follow his father in making skillful use of the social cleavage between the Palestinian majority and East Bankers of Bedouin origin.

Similarly, the Sabah ruling family of Kuwait finds itself astride major cleavages. There is a Shi'ite minority that is sometimes seen as a fifth column for Iraqi or Iranian interests, but basically the fault line is unidimensional. Over 40% of the population is non-Kuwaiti, as is a majority of the workforce (see Chapter 15). The economy and the administration are thus dependent upon these more or less long-term worker-migrants. The Sabah family cannot claim to speak for or represent the foreign workers, but it can and does manage relations between them and the native Kuwaiti population. A large component of the nonnative workforce was once Palestinian, but because the PLO backed Iraq's occupation of Kuwait and because some Palestinians were accused of collaborating with the Iraqi forces of occupation, several hundred thousand Palestinians were expelled from Kuwait and sent primarily to Jordan.

Kuwait first introduced a parliament, in which the country's wealthy merchants were represented, in the 1930s (see Crystal 1990). However, once the Kuwaiti state and the Sabah family had control of the country's increasing petroleum rents after

World War II, the need for merchant support dwindled. The parliament, as in Jordan, led a precarious existence and was frequently dismissed by the sovereign. The rescue of Kuwait from Iraqi annexation and occupation by Operation Desert Storm came at a price; both domestic constituents and external backers pressured the Sabahs to take steps to reestablish democracy. In October 1992 elections for the National Assembly were held in which only about 70,000 male Kuwaitis of proven Kuwaiti ancestry, out of some 625,000 native Kuwaitis, were allowed to vote (Gause 1994, 188–189). Parliamentary elections were held again in 1996, 2003, and 2006. The liberalizing tendencies can be seen in two disparate facts: On the one hand, since 2003 Islamists have constituted an important voice in parliament (21 seats of 50 in 2003); on the other hand, in 2005, Kuwaiti women acquired the right to vote. After the death of Emir Shaikh Jaber al-Ahmad al-Sabah on January 15, 2006, Shaikh Sabah al-Ahmad al-Sabah became the new emir on January 25, 2006. Elections were scheduled for June 2006. With the significant exception of the disenfranchisement of long-term resident alien workers, Kuwait has a reasonable claim to be called a liberal monarchy.

The Kingdom of Saudi Arabia cannot claim similar status. It has been run since the 1920s by and largely for the sprawling royal family, descendants all of the founding patriarch, King ʿAbd alʿAziz Al Saud, and who now number in the thousands. The incorporation of commoners into the political establishment comes through co-optation, often on the basis of technical merit and competence but not as the result of electoral victories.

The Saudi monarchy does resemble the others in that it straddles social and regional cleavages within the country. These include the Shiʿite minority in the east of the country and, more important, the Najd, from which the royal family comes, and the Hijaz, which contains the holy cities of Mecca and Medina and is the home of Saudi Arabia's traditional trading and merchant families. Finally, Saudi Arabia, as the paradigmatic oil rentier state, has for decades relied upon a large pool of migrant labor, both skilled and unskilled. The bulk of the latter had traditionally come from Yemen, but because Yemen leaned toward Iraq when it occupied Kuwait the Saudis expelled some 700,000 Yemenis from the country. Since Operation Desert Storm there has been some return flow of Yemeni workers to Saudi Arabia, but there has also been an influx of Pakistanis, Indians, Filipinos, Egyptians, and others (see Gause 1994; Krimly 1993).

Despite Saudi Arabia's crucial geopolitical significance and place in US strategic thinking, the monarchy came under some pressure after Desert Storm to put on a more liberal face. It eventually did so, on August 20, 1993, when King Fahd appointed a sixty-member Consultative Council. This body was made up of nonelected representatives of prominent families, businesses, religious leaders, and the government. It was to consult and advise the sovereign but not to legislate. In this respect it conformed to the Qur'anic injunction that the leader of the *umma* should consult in the conduct of the affairs of state with those of experience, wealth, and wisdom. Even this modest nod toward liberalization must be placed against the monarchy's resort to conservative Islamic clergy to fend off the growing political Islamic challenge from within. American obsessions with al-Qaeda since 9/11 have done little to promote liberalization in the kingdom. As throughout the history of the US-Saudi relationship, in the end, concerns for stability have trumped demands for democracy.

ESTABLISHED AND WOULD-BE DEMOCRACIES

There are only three countries in the Middle East that have indulged in liberal electoral politics for sustained periods of time: Israel, Lebanon, and Turkey. The Sudan had three chances, in 1956–1958, 1964–1969, and 1986–1989, while Egypt has pursued a highly controlled liberal experiment since 1976. A number of others have conducted elections in the past ten to fifteen years. Turkey has oscillated between freewheeling electoral politics in the 1950s and 1970s and military rule in the 1960s and early 1980s. Since 1983 another and so far successful attempt has been made to revive civilian electoral politics. Only Israel since its creation in 1948 has maintained a continuous democratic regime, but that distinction must be qualified by its strict policing of the Arab populations it inherited in 1948. Over the past several years the Israelis have allowed autonomous Arab parties to function in their political arena.

Turkey failed to achieve a stable party system, and in the 1970s it suffered from a series of coalition governments with interests so diverse that no coherent economic policy could be implemented. Sound economic management fell victim to the political expediency of the Justice party, the lineal descendant of the Democrat party of the 1950s and of the Republican People's party, which became "radicalized" and more overtly socialist under the leadership of Bülent Ecevit than at any time under Atatürk. The military, as already noted, put an end to this situation, tried to put Turkey's economic affairs in order, and then, under carefully controlled circumstances, including the banning of most parties functioning before the 1980 coup, allowed new elections to be held in 1983. Turgut Özal's Motherland party won a narrow majority, and he became prime minister.

Turkey is subject to a kind of democratizing pressure, however, that no other country in the region faces. There is a shaky national consensus that Turkey should join the European Union. To do so will require not only a far-reaching restructuring of the Turkish economy but also adherence to European legal standards of liberal democracy. Rule by generals, repression of labor, and suppression of Kurdish organizations cannot be made compatible with entry into the EU.

In November 1991 the Motherland party was voted out of power and replaced by a coalition of the True Path party, the successor to the Justice party, and the Social Democratic Populist party, one of the descendants of the Republican People's party. Turkey demonstrated its ability to change party governance through the ballot box. Moreover, the True Path party went on to select Tansu Çiller as its leader and the first female prime minister of the republic. In 1994, in municipal elections, the Welfare party, a thinly disguised Islamic party (the constitution prohibits the formation of openly religious or ethnic parties), swept several cities, including Istanbul and Ankara. The party, governing in coalition, was forced from power by the military and then banned by the Turkish Constitutional Court in 1997. A successor, Virtue

Party, was likewise banned in 2001. However, supporters of right-of-center Islamist politics regrouped, and the successor Justice and Development party swept the Turkish elections held on November 3, 2002, winning 363 of the 550 seats. This moderate Islamist party, committed to joining the EU, was the first single party to be able to form a government in fifteen years.

There are three points to be made with respect to Turkish democracy. First, it appears to be here to stay and may have some demonstration effect for its regional neighbors. Second, it allows for change through the ballot box; most, but not all, Turks can find a way to be represented or identify a candidate reflecting their preferences. Third, it may show how political Islam can be accommodated within a democratic system. Whether it can survive Turkey's outright rejection by the EU (not a negligible danger), or a marked revival of Kurdish militancy stimulated by events in Iraq since 2003, remains to be seen.

Lebanese democracy after independence in 1946 fascinated Western political scientists. Here was a society that the French protectorate authorities had organized along sectarian or confessional lines. Seats in parliament were distributed in a ratio of six to five between Christians and Muslims and subdivided among the several sects in both religious communities. The 1943 National Pact, elaborated by the principal leaders of the Maronite and Sunni sects, consecrated the French arrangement. Henceforth a Maronite Christian was to be president, a Sunni prime minister, and a Shi'ite president of the Chamber of Deputies. Positions in the civil service and the armed forces were likewise distributed along confessional lines.

In a manner most theorists of modernization would find reprehensible, Lebanon had quite literally enshrined religion in politics. People ran for office or voted, won jobs or lost them, and occasionally came to blows as members of specific sects. Despite the lack of separation of "church" and state, somehow the system seemed to work. The press was free, debate open and vigorous, and elections held on a regular basis (although not without tampering), and Lebanon served as a small island of political refuge and free enterprise for the rest of the region.

Yet the fragility of the confessional balance was apparent to some early on (see especially Hudson 1968). Most obvious was the fact that confessions became more rather than less rigid as offices and spoils were distributed along confessional lines. Except at the elite level there were few crosscutting alliances, although candidates did have to seek votes outside their own confessional constituencies. The point is that the meaningful units in electoral alliances were always confessional.

Second, although population growth and migration gradually transformed the Christians into a minority (see Chapter 4), they continued to control the presidency and a majority of the deputies. Camille Chamoun, who was president up to 1958, altered the constitution so that he could succeed himself, thereby triggering a brief civil war that presaged what was to happen in 1975. Chamoun was forced from the presidency and replaced by General Fu'ad Chehab (a Maronite), who restored law and order and talked about deconfessionalizing Lebanon. He was unable to make much headway, as his talk of position through merit seemed to non-Christians to favor Christians, who enjoyed generally higher levels of education and training.

always to wed other always [handwritten marginal note]

The fruits of Lebanon's booming merchant economy were not equally shared. The oligarchs of the economy came from all sects but were dominated by the Maronite banking elite. Yet the sharing of economic interests among the very wealthy cut across confessional lines, and, some have suggested, the oligarchs saw it as to their advantage to promote confessional conflict so that class-based politics might be avoided.

Finally, after the June War of 1967 and the conflict between King Hussein and the PLO in 1970, nearly 200,000 Palestinians, many of them armed, sought refuge in Lebanon. They were not citizens and could not vote, but because they were mainly Muslim, Lebanese Christians feared that their gradual absorption into the local arena, were that to happen, would mean the loss of any semblance of balance among confessions. It was the Maronite Christian Phalange party that precipitated the civil war in 1975 in an attempt to disarm or expel the Palestinians. In the ensuing years the Lebanese state collapsed and at least four statelets (Maronite, Druze, Shi'ite, and Palestinian) emerged, the Lebanese armed forces became only one of several militias, and confessionalism became a question not merely of voter identification but of life and death.

After fourteen years of war, the Lebanese may have lost as many as 150,000 people out of their tiny population. With Saudi Arabia and Syria as intermediaries, the fighting was finally brought to a halt through a negotiated agreement known as the Ta'if Accords. These were finalized in the Saudi city of that name in 1989, and among other things, they reaffirmed the confessional nature of politics but adjusted the Christian-Muslim ratio to fifty-fifty.[8] Following the Ta'if Accords, Lebanon held parliamentary elections in 1992, which many Maronites boycotted in protest of Syria's continued presence but in which candidates loyal to Hizbollah participated and did well. The Syrian military presence in Lebanon had essentially been given an open-ended lease; the Syrians would not leave before they wanted to and certainly not before Israel closed down its security zone and Lebanese client army in the south. Although all militias were to be disarmed, Hizbollah, the dominant Shi'ite militia in the south, enjoying Iranian backing, remained fully armed. Even after the Israeli unilateral withdrawal from southern Lebanon, Hizbollah retained a military component, claiming that this was necessary due to the dispute with Israel over the Shebaa farms area.[9]

The Lebanese polity is too weak, and the region far too volatile, for Hizbollah's disarmament to be at all likely. If the Israeli Defense Forces could not force it to disarm in the summer of 2006, clearly no one—other than Hizbollah itself—can make this happen.

Unlike the situation in Turkey, it is far too soon to say that Lebanese democracy has been reestablished. It will be a generation at least before the wounds of the civil war heal. The termination of first Israeli (2000) and then Syrian (2005) military presence in the country may have set the stage for true normalcy. However, the porosity of Lebanon's confessional system will always invite outside meddling. Lebanon has managed to weather, with some difficulty, the dramatically heightened regional tensions of the past six years, but the future remains uncertain—particularly after the extremely destructive war of the summer of 2006. Lebanon is probably fated by geography and history to exhibit entrepreneurial exuberance and political fragility.

Israel's democratic system is old and vigorous but should not be taken for granted. As in Turkey, old political coalitions such as the center-left Israel Labor party (MAPAI), which dominated Israeli politics in the first two decades, have broken down and reassembled. Now the major cleavage in Israeli Jewish society is between secularists with some commitment to socialism and a strong welfare state and a conservative coalition increasingly characterized by an aggressive religious nationalism. Menachem Begin's Likud alliance, which dominated Israeli politics from the mid-1970s to the mid-1980s, has been home for Israelis favorable to private-sector growth, religious claims to the occupied territories, and repressive policies toward Israel's Arab minority. The bulk of Likud's following has come from Oriental and Sephardic Jews, who tend to be somewhat less educated than the dominant Ashkenazi elites and somewhat lower in the hierarchy of incomes. They have been joined in recent years by a half-million immigrants from the former Soviet Union who have had no experience with democracy, but their votes have gone more to the Labor party than to Likud. Although there are those in Likud and on the right in general who are passionately committed to the Zionist dream and Jewish retention of the occupied territories and who may be prepared to sacrifice democracy for their goals, there are also new business interests that see peace and regional stability as vital to their economic future.

Ultimately, the question is, as in Lebanon, whether the system can absorb a large, possibly majority non-Jewish population and still preserve the logic of one citizen, one vote. There are today some 1.3 million Arab citizens of Israel, dating from 1948, 2.4 million Palestinians in the West Bank and East Jerusalem, and another 1.2 million in Gaza. As discussed in Chapter 4, the Israeli polity faces four options. One tendency, which won the 1993 general elections, was to push forward the peace talks begun in Madrid. Although opinion polls suggest that many Israelis still support this approach, this option dissolved into political disarray with the outbreak of the second Palestinian *intifada* in 2000. A second tendency, represented by the Likud party of first Benjamin Netanyahu and then Ariel Sharon, was (until perhaps 2004) to alternatively deny the problem, stall on negotiations, and somehow hope that the problem would go away. This tendency grades into a more extreme nationalist tendency, which calls for the expulsion of the Palestinians. A fourth and, as of this writing, now governing tendency calls for unilateral Israeli drawing of the frontiers with the Palestinians in order to provide security for Israelis (it is widely believed) and to avoid the "demographic problem" of Palestinians becoming a majority of the polity.

Since the Anglo-American invasion and occupation of Iraq, a series of elections have been held, despite the chaos and violence that ensued. Developments in that sad country show, if any demonstration was needed, that elections do not solve all problems. Indeed, depending on their structure, they can easily contribute to factional difficulties. Immediately after the occupation, the Americans created the

Coalition Provisional Authority (CPA) to govern the country. The CPA appointed an Iraqi Governing Council, selected experts to write an interim constitution (the "Transitional Administrative Law"), and strictly supervised local "governing councils." The Grand Ayatollah Sistani, however, fearful that the United States would dictate the constitution-writing process, turned hundreds of thousands of his Shi'ite followers into the streets to demand elections for the Constitutional Convention. The United States, already facing violent resistance from Sunni groups, quickly agreed. Elections for these delegates were held in January 2005; the constitution itself was ratified in another election that summer, and elections for the National Assembly were held in December 2005.

The first—but not the second and third—of these elections were widely boycotted in Sunni areas. The current prime minister of Iraq, the leader of the Shi'i political party, ad-Da'wa (the Call), Nouri al-Maliki, remains quite incapable of restoring order in the country. Increasingly, the first function of government, physical protection of its supporters, falls to armed militias. The central government can perform few, if any, of the other major functions of a national government. Over 140,000 American troops remain in the country, many tens of thousands of Iraqis have been killed in intercommunal fighting, and national unity is, at best, very fragile. As of this writing, a low-level civil war now rages in Iraq, with hundreds of casualties every week. Elections do not solve underlying questions of political legitimacy. Until these issues are resolved, violent conflict in Iraq is likely to continue.

THE ISLAMIC REPUBLICS

There are two Islamic republics in the Middle East: Iran and the Sudan. We will have more to say about both in Chapter 14, and we have already touched on the Sudanese experience above. We shall focus here on Iran since the 1979 revolution that sent tremors throughout the region. The establishment of the Islamic republic under the guidance of the Ayatollah Khomeini merits the term "revolution" because it effected the complete dismantling of the shah's political regime, the remaking of Iran's foreign policy and alignments, and a cultural transformation. In the final analysis, however, it did not bring about a full social or economic revolution. Years of war had fattened a class of profiteers and speculators in scarce goods, a phenomenon common to nearly all war situations, while the regime allowed many of its own to live off sinecures in the public sector and the foundations. In some cities in the mid-1990s, when the regime tried to bulldoze shantytowns, the reaction was the same as it had been under the shah—riots and violent confrontation. In addition, the public-enterprise sector, with its center of gravity in petroleum extraction, refining, and petrochemicals, remained large. There has been little talk of privatization. Much of the property and assets taken over from the Pahlavi family and those accused of collaboration with the old regime remain grouped in state-owned foundations that spin off handsome revenues for the cronies of the new power elite.

Like the socialist republics, the Islamic republic has consistently stressed unity, combining the overriding element of being Muslim with the secondary element of being Iranian. In the months following the departure of the shah, various ethnic and linguistic groups forcefully put forward claims for greater recognition in the new polity than had ever been accorded them under the shah. As Ayatollah Khomeini and the clergy consolidated their grip on the new state, mainly through the elimination of leftists and liberal moderates such as Bani Sadr and the venerable Mehdi Bazargan, these claims were denied. Revolutionary Guards were dispatched to crush Kurdish, Turkomen, and other groups agitating for a new place in the republic. When war broke out with Iraq in September 1980, this kind of subnational agitation became at once blasphemy and high treason.

Although pluralism is officially condemned, the new regime does share one characteristic with the monarchies we have examined, and that is the denial of the principle of popular sovereignty. Sovereignty is God's alone, and although in the Islamic republic the people elect their representatives, those who rule are ultimately responsible to God rather than to the people. Rulership cannot be inherited; rather, it is the duty of the council of the foremost clerics to judge and select the best-qualified leaders to the ends of protecting the believers, applying God's law, and preserving the republic. Moreover, a Constitutional Council reviews all parliamentary legislation to ensure that it conforms with the *shari'a* and the Iranian constitution. The principle in operation here is the "trusteeship of the jurisprudents" *(vilayet al-faqih)*, whereby the elite of the clergy, on the strength of their learning, ensure that the people, in practicing Islamic democracy, do not stray from "the straight path."

The regime has been concerned with equity issues made all the more acute by eight years of war with Iraq. It has not rolled back the shah's land-reform measures, and it has invested significantly in rural infrastructure and power generation. But the majority of Iranians are urban salary or wage earners. The inflation generated by the war lowered their standards of living dramatically. Unemployment among educated male youths is still high, and a significant portion of the workforce is unemployed. The combination of unemployment and inflation means that many Iranians must survive in the informal sector, often engaging in contraband trade, drugs, and smuggling. It is no small irony that pious Islamic Iran and secular socialist Algeria have in many ways become mirror images of each other.

The Ayatollah Khomeini died in June 1989, having grudgingly blessed an end to hostilities with Iraq. The heroic, romantic phase of the Islamic Revolution had come to an end, and the mundane task of reconstruction and economic reform had begun. It fell to the new and uncharismatic president, 'Ali Akbar Rafsanjani, to take up this task. The incumbency of this cleric indicated the continuation of what Shaul Bakhash (1984) has dubbed Iran's "mullacracy." In 1997 Rafsanjani was succeeded by the liberal cleric Muhammad Khatami, who sought, vainly, to liberalize the system. He was then succeeded by the hard-line populist Mahmoud Ahmedinejad in 2005. Iranian presidents, however, do not wield the powers of American ones. The man who took on the role of the revolution's spiritual guide after the death of Khomeini, 'Ali Khamanei, is the real head of state. The mullahs control the major institutions of the state, the parliament, the Foundation for the Disinherited, and the Revolutionary Guard. Although there is some evidence that younger Iranians have begun to lose faith or interest in the Islamic regime, it is doubtful that we shall soon see a retreat of the clergy from politics. As with all right-wing governments, the Iranian one has not been shy to play the nationalist card as part of its strategy to retain power.

For someone who is male, Muslim, and loyal to the notion of an Islamic polity and reveres the memory of Ayatollah Khomeini, Iran is a vibrant, contentious, and—dare we say it?—democratic place. Iranian political cleavages are predictable and straightforward. There are so-called radicals, both clerical and lay, who want to confront the impious West, especially the United States, spread the revolution through Lebanon and the Sudan, and one day confront Israel. If Iran ever acquires a nuclear device, it will be because of these radicals. They partially overlap with social and economic radicals who want to tax the rich, punish the speculators, and redistribute wealth to the poor. They opposed the economic reforms unsuccessfully advocated by Rafsanjani. President Ahmedinejad is a good representative of this tendency.

Arrayed against them are so-called pragmatists. Some seek a more conciliatory policy toward the West in order to attract investment and promote trade. They may or may not condone the support extended by the radicals to their Shi'ite allies in Lebanon and their Sunni friends in the Sudan. They are apt to respect private property and want to encourage the private sector to invest. They are prepared to work with Western creditors, including the World Bank, to control government expenditures, reduce inflation, and deregulate the economy. Finally, there are voices, even among the clergy, who suggest that they have had their day in power, made a hash of it, and should if possible gracefully retreat to their *madrasas,* where they enjoy some comparative advantage.

In 2006 none of these tensions within the political establishment had been resolved, but the issues are being debated in a remarkably open way. The country has not fallen under the control of a religious police state. It is not ruled by the military. There are possibilities for a peaceful transition to a postmullacracy. These tendencies are unlikely to be fostered by a military confrontation with the West, when in Iran, as elsewhere, the "nationalist card" may easily trump all others.

FUTURE REGIMES: SOME SPECULATIONS

The past twenty-five years have put the state and political formations of the Middle East under enormous stress. The boom and bust of the regional petroleum economy, the tacit abandonment of any viable military option against Israel, the related rise of militant Islamic challengers to the incumbents, the rigors of economic stabilization and adjustment, and the exit of the Soviet Union as a major patron for several regimes in the system have challenged the credibility and viability of nearly every state, the failure to achieve a viable Palestinian state through a wide variety of approaches, and the American invasion of Iraq. Yet, apart from the latter case, the center has held. Regime change took place in Iran in 1979 and less obviously in the Sudan in 1989. Otherwise stasis has been the hallmark of the recent past. Only full-scale invasion by the United States led to the demise of one of the states of the Arab core.

Still, one senses a precariousness in the status quo. Regimes are aging, and a number of incumbents have passed from the scene. King Hussein, who had been in power since 1952, died in 1999. King Hassan, ruling since 1961; Yasser 'Arafat, in power since 1967; and Hafiz al-Assad, ruling since 1970, all were gone by 2005. Saddam Hussein was forcibly removed in 2003. Yet other antiquated leaders continue: Mu'ammar Qaddafi since 1969, 'Ali 'Abdullah Salih since 1978, and Hosni Mubarak since 1981—all are still governing. Even when heads of state have changed, as in Algeria, Jordan, Morocco, Palestine, Syria, and Tunisia, the political system has not. But these regimes are tired and worn. Many of the incumbents have lost any sense of national purpose, any "project" *(mashru')* with which to capture the imagination of their peoples. They offer halfhearted economic reform, which still hurts large segments of their citizenries, without offering real political opening through which grievances might be expressed. Yet civil society—the full panoply of social actors mentioned in Chapter 2—has grown in size, complexity, and voice. The Islamists have captured a significant part of it, but whether they merely reflect a high level of frustration among the citizenry as opposed to a genuine quest for an Islamic state is moot. Incumbent leaders do not want to find out which it may be, but they are increasingly finding it difficult to deny such forces their voice.

The advent of the Islamic Republic of Iran in 1979 represented the most profound regime change of the past thirty years, but it produced no domino effect whatsoever. Most incumbent regimes have dealt with their Islamic challengers by police repression of the militants, all the while cloaking their own actions in Islamic rhetoric. They have, in this manner, sought to co-opt or neutralize what might be called the moderate Islamic center. The question is whether rhetoric and some patronage will suffice to disarm all the centrist critics. King Hussein decided in 1989 that the lesser risk was to open the political system, let the center voice its grievances, and keep it within the bounds of law by offering it participation in the electoral process. Chadli Benjadid in Algeria, in 1990 and 1991, took a similar gamble but, through poor design of the voting system, lost badly. Will either of these experiments inspire other leaders in the region?

It is, perhaps, to Turkey that we should turn. Turkey's political evolution has often presaged what has transpired in the Arab world. Turkey has, in all but name, allowed an Islamist party to participate in a democratic system that has functioned impressively since 1983. The Welfare party ran several cities and had representatives in the Grand National Assembly. Today the Justice and Development party rules the country. The commitment of the party and its leader to democracy is clear; the commitment of the Turkish military to allowing any encroachment on Kemalist secularism, however unpopular among significant segments of the Turkish electorate, is more dubious.

In the mid-1990s many Western observers, including us, thought that Islamists were unlikely to win many elections. Where elections were held—the Sudan in 1986, Jordan in 1989 and 1993, Algeria in 1991, Yemen in 1993, northern Iraq in 1992, Lebanon in 1992, Pakistan in 1993, and Morocco in 1994—Islamist parties did not come close to winning outright majorities. But the past five years have been different. Clearly, we and others underestimated the appeal of Islamism to an electorate fed up with oppression, economic stagnation, corruption, and national humiliation. Islamist parties govern Turkey, Iraq, and Palestine. Were free elections ever held in Egypt, the Muslim Brotherhood would do very well. Large powerful nonmajority Islamist blocs sit in the Kuwaiti and Lebanese parliaments. Islamist parties are diverse, complicated, and vocal. They are likely to be an enduring feature of the political landscape.

This discussion has implied that if change is on the horizon, it may be toward greater democracy. Equally likely, however, are further turns in the authoritarian cycle. Ben ʿAli in Tunisia, Bashir in the Sudan, a succession of leaders in Algeria, and the American invasion of Iraq indicate that the old politics of change through violence, whether from within or without, from coup or invasion, has not passed from the scene. Leaders who come to power by this route will preserve the discredited methods of rule of their predecessors but proclaim a new mission or the relaunching of the old. They will denounce the corruption of their predecessors and their selling out to nefarious foreign forces and, if the offenders are still alive, put them on trial for treason. Then they can turn to the economic mess they will have inherited.

NOTES

1. Many Muslim Sudanese in Darfur, for example, are not native speakers of Arabic.

2. Even today, sporadic political violence continues.

3. The Algerian saga is of immense importance to the region and the world. It deserves far more analysis than we have granted it. Those who wish to delve more deeply into its crisis may consult Leveau (1993), Kapil (1990), Vergès (1993), Martinez (1998), and Kepel (2002).

4. This is not to say that Saddam's regime failed to inflict its notorious violence on many Iraqi Sunnis, as well.

5. From 2000 to 2003, the Palestinian poverty rate rose from 20% to 55%, the unemployment rate from 10% to 30%, and chronic child malnutrition in Gaza from 8.7% to 12.7% (UNDP 2006).

6. Such a response was very common in Europe during the 1930s, for example.

7. Increasingly, they, like the presidents of Arab socialist republics, pose as the sole bulwark against Islamist parties. The claim of divine right to rule is a decidedly two-edged sword.

8. Although an improvement, this distribution still almost certainly overrepresents Christians and underrepresents Muslims, particularly Shiʿites (see Chapter 4).

9. Shebaa is a small village located at the intersection of the (disputed) Lebanese, Syrian, and Israeli border. Occupied by Israel after 1967, both Syria and Lebanon claim the area.

12

SOLIDARISM
AND ITS ENEMIES

The integrated, cohesive citizenry about which Middle Eastern leaders have spilled oceans of ink and over which waves of rhetoric have crashed remains an impossible goal. The erosion of optimism and elite will that accompanied the long and dangerous wielding of power has been matched by the disillusionment and cynicism of citizens. Sensing that alienation, leaders have been driven to divide and rule rather than to unite, to contain rather than to mobilize, to repress rather than to inspire. The rhetoric of solidarism still prevails, but political practice has deviated sharply from the older goals. Some of the obstacles to the new society have lain in older forms of social and political insurance: clans, ethnic groups, tribes, and religious sects; units that, among other things, protect their members from the vagaries of powerful states and markets (see Migdal 1987). To see these forms as atavistic is to lose sight of their redefined roles in the new state systems of the contemporary Middle East.

Underlying but separated from them is the bedrock of Islam, which provides a set of standards by which political leadership is judged. When leaders who profess adherence to Islam fail in their statist enterprises, they are seen as exposing the *umma* to mortal danger. If they are unaware of their error, they must be removed and replaced by rightly guided leaders. But if they err knowingly, it is possible that they are the agents of satanic power. For many Muslims, Atatürk, Nasser, and Mohammed Reza Shah were all such agents.

There are, by contrast, obstacles to solidarism of quite a different order. Leaders nearly obsessed with control have emasculated the very political organizations they created to mobilize and integrate the masses. At the same time, in organizing strategic sectors of the working population they have created real occupational associations that have gained organizational and political skills and substantial bargaining power. Concomitantly, the disbursement of large state-investment budgets and the very real economic growth that has occurred in some Middle Eastern societies have transferred resources to white-collar workers, skilled trade unionists, capitalist farmers, and a few entrepreneurial groups that are now in a position to contest, cautiously, certain state policies. Endowed with resources and accumulated experience, they can now bargain directly with the state and its agents, and as we pointed out in Chapter 2, such bargaining may be the prelude to more formal democratic processes.

Finally, had Middle Eastern leaders been able to nurture some sort of broad ideological and programmatic consensus, it might have been possible to keep all these old and new actors within the political game. But ideologies fabricated by house ideologues or, worse yet, by bureaucrats in Ministries of Culture, Information, and National Guidance have failed to penetrate strategically placed elites, let alone the people as a whole. There is, we argue, a kind of organizational and ideological vacuum in the Middle East that several sorts of actors are trying to fill. Incumbent elites with the economic and coercive might of the state at their disposal still have the upper hand, but they may lack the conviction or confidence to use it. Secular liberals are a tiny minority, but they may have some historical momentum on their side. Today, however, they suffer from "guilt by association" with a West widely seen in the region as aggressive and intolerant of Islam. Islamists have enthusiasm and popular symbols but few answers to questions of governance and economic management (see Chapter 14). Some of them combine pragmatism with an attempt at cultural authenticity. Others remain lost in a dream world of violent utopian fantasies.

SMALL GROUPS
AND CLIENTELIST POLITICS

One trap we must avoid is seeing older forms of political organization and action as direct reenactments of their forebears. Tribe and tribal loyalty in the twenty-first–century Middle East are qualitatively different from their seventeenth- or eighteenth-century antecedents. So too are sects, ethnic groups, families, and coteries. What has changed momentously is the degree of state and market penetration into all sectors of Middle Eastern society. Just as economic subsistence is a thing of the past, so too is political isolation. Central authorities are now able to make effective claims on ever-growing proportions of societies' wealth, but they tend to do so in arbitrary and sometimes punitive ways. Markets, having captured large producing populations, do not behave predictably. And for those who play the national political game the stakes are high, with death, torture, imprisonment, exile or, at best, forced retirement as probable outcomes. Parties and formal associations have not yet provided effective means to protect members from the new order. People retreat into or invent "security groups" as much to protect themselves as to promote their interests. One may find in a small band of friends or members of one's tribe, ethnic group, home region, or religious sect a framework for mutual support, accountability, shared obligations, or plain psychological reassurance that no formal organization can offer. Putnam (1993) has termed these small-group resources "social capital."

The more people adhere to these unrecognized, loosely organized forms of political and social action, the more the formal associations and political parties lose their cohesion and viability. Leaders have so far reacted in one or both of two ways: beating the political fragments into submission and, abandoning solidarism, trying to manipulate them through state patronage. A third way, democratic pluralism, as we have seen in the previous chapter, has taken only very halting steps.

What Bill and Springborg (1994, 84–135) have called the genes of Middle East politics are congeries of small and nonexclusive units that have varying degrees of cohesion and durability. Throughout the area we find political and economic actors associating with small clusters of cronies of similar status. The members of these groups help each other along in their careers, for it is likely that at any particular time some will be doing better than others and can promote the interests of the less fortunate. People who are from the same village or region or perhaps from the same university class or who are of common descent or related through marriage may come together in such groups. Whether it is a question of Iran's *dawrehs* (circles) or Egypt's *shillas*, cronyism is an important form of political and economic insurance.

One often hears of clans in Middle Eastern politics. Sometimes we find fairly persistent coteries at the elite level, such as the Oujda Group in Algeria, but these groupings are fragile, and power struggles within them can be brutal. Despite the fact that a member of the Oujda Group, Chadli Benjadid, succeeded Boumedienne to the presidency, most of its other stalwarts have disappeared from the scene. Again, several members of Egypt's Revolutionary Command Council (RCC), which seized power in 1952, were classmates in the staff college in the late 1930s and served together in various postings and in the 1948 war with Israel. Over the years after 1952, members dropped away in disgrace, exile, or early retirement.

We hear also of the Takriti clan in Iraq and the Alawi clan in Syria. Unlike the two examples mentioned above, these clans combine cronyism with common regional and sectarian loyalties. Moreover, both Saddam Hussein and Hafiz al-Assad to some extent surrounded themselves with confidants from their own lineages. When violent change in governing elites occurred in Iraq in 2003, the new incumbents—first the Americans, and then the Shi'ite-Kurdish-dominated Iraqi government—sought to ferret out all real or suspected members of the Takriti clan. The Syrian Alawis have drawn the logical conclusion that this would also be their fate should "regime change" come to Syria. This realization makes them cling to power all the more tenaciously.

Yet another manifestation of small-group genes lies in pervasive patron-client networks. Unlike clusters of cronies, clientelistic groupings bring together people of very different status and power. The patron is the power wielder, and his clients need his protection. In turn they render him a number of services that enhance his power and hence his ability to act as their protector. The classic example in the Middle East and elsewhere is the large landowner. He monopolizes in a given locale the most precious fixed asset, land. He controls access to it, and his clients are his tenants, laborers, and sharecroppers. He protects them physically, supplies them agricultural inputs and monetary credit, assists them if they fall ill, and helps them pay for extraordinary events such as marriages and funerals. The clients in turn produce for him, supply him free labor for a host of menial tasks, vote for him if elections are an issue, and fight for him if he is attacked by outsiders. In this classic example the patron controls what are called "first-order resources"—land and money. As long as he maintains his local monopoly, his clients will have little choice but to seek his protection. Migration may be an option, but in some countries, such as Iraq in the interwar years, peasants with outstanding debts could not legally migrate. Peasants are chronically in debt. Agrarian reform has everywhere eroded the power of the classic rural patron.

Today, with the growth of large bureaucratic states that invade and regulate all aspects of one's life, the patron is more likely to be a broker. Although he may continue to control first-order resources, his real services to his clients will come through his ability to deliver public goods or to protect his clients against various forms of state action. In this sense he brokers access to state resources. He may help procure a birth certificate, a work permit, a commercial license, a passport, or any of the other vital pieces of paper that the modern state routinely requires but does not routinely deliver. He may help place a son in secondary school or the university, find a migrant a job in a public agency or factory, get the courts to drop charges for a misdemeanor, or swing a loan through the agricultural credit bank. What the patron receives in return is somewhat amorphous. In the few systems in which votes count he will surely receive votes, but his relative weight in the political system may well hinge on his ability to demonstrate the size and cohesion of his group of clients. If he is perceived as being able to "deliver" his clients, even in elections where official candidates receive 99.9% of the votes, or to keep them out of street demonstrations, strikes, or land seizures, the higher authorities will make sure that public resources sufficient to maintain his clientele are put at his disposal.

As the socialist and solidarist élan of several of the radical republics began to wane, the large, all-encompassing parties that they set up became simple conduits for the distribution of state patronage. Party cadres, rather than educating, indoctrinating, and mobilizing the populations with which they dealt, fell into the role of broker, establishing their reputations on their ability to deliver state resources to their clients. Intended to be members of the vanguard, they became ward heelers. The party thus became an instrument in the slow drift of the leadership into divide-and-rule politics; the cadres were there not to encourage the masses to do something but to reward them for doing nothing. Putting as kind a light on this as possible, some observers have referred to this arrangement as a "social pact or contract."

THE FAILURE OF PARTIES

There has been an abundance of political parties, but only a few have contested competitive elections. Seldom have they sought to represent constituents or, as organizations, challenged their own regimes. Those enjoying legal monopolies on "representing" citizens, such as Egypt's ASU or Algeria's FLN, rejected the label "party"—having no rivals, they needed no partisans. Through some mysterious chemistry from which freedom of speech, open debate, and freedom of choice were notably absent, the front or union would distill the essence of the popular will and transmit it, for policy action, to the regime's leaders. It did not take long for the citizens to recognize this hokum for what it was.

More liberal experiments fell into their own kinds of sham. Iran, Morocco, and Jordan, monarchical regimes with carefully policed multiparty systems, and Sadat's

Egypt all boasted party-competitive systems. But like several of their socialist counterparts (and, in Egypt's case, like its predecessor) the parties that were to compete for power were created from above, and the outcome of elections was more or less known in advance (al-Ansari 1986, 203). The shah of Iran habitually dabbled in the fabrication of parties. In the 1950s he established a loyal opposition party, Mardom, and a loyalist party, the Melliyun; eventually they came to be known as the "Yes" party and the "Yes Sir!" party. After 1963 the shah replaced his two creations with the Modern Iran party, run by the young technocrats who engineered the White Revolution. Then in 1975 he founded the Renaissance party and made Iran a one-party state.

We should not overlook the ground-up parties, organized in nationalist struggle or in defense of specific interests and classes. We have already discussed the Neo-Destour of Tunisia, but the Wafd party of Egypt, standard-bearer of Egyptian nationalism, is back in action again thirty years after Nasser dissolved it. Morocco's nationalist Independence party hangs on in the king's carefully controlled political arena. In some countries communist and socialist parties, often born in illegality and the objects of constant repression, have developed strong organizations and toughened cadres that compensate for their small membership. As Islamist groups increasingly capture the allegiance of the region's youth, leftist parties will find it hard to replace their aging leadership. Parties allied with the Muslim Brotherhood, established in Egypt in 1928, are significant players in Egypt, Jordan, Palestine, and elsewhere.

Against the few examples of successful party organization, a pervasive gloom envelops partisan activity in the Middle East. There are four main reasons for this. The first, outlined above, is that parties have been created from the top down and seldom strike roots in the population in whose name they claim to speak. With a stroke of a pen Sadat dissolved Egypt's ASU in 1975, and there was not the slightest murmur from the "masses" or the party's cadres. The same fate befell the Sudan's SSU in 1985, and there the "masses" were positively jubilant.

The second reason is the hesitancy of leaders to use the parties they have created to mobilize the people, to cause them to participate in national politics and share responsibility. Time and again, parties have been used to control and *de*mobilize the populace. Infiltrated by police informers, parties have become associated with the repressive apparatus of the state—in Iraq, Saddam Hussein, a "policeman," ran both the party and the government. Cadres are all too often bureaucrats who have been seconded to the party from the civil service and whose careers will ultimately be determined in their ministries.

Third, the economic strategies of many Middle Eastern states have brought forth a technocratic elite of planners, financial experts, managers, and engineers whose quest for orderly and disciplined change reinforces the party's mission as an instrument of control, especially in the workplace. Boumedienne's Algeria best represents this concept of party organization and technocratic supremacy.

Finally, where parties were alive and well prior to independence, there was a marked tendency afterward to drain them of their best cadres to staff government agencies in an ever-expanding state apparatus. Party militants became government bureaucrats, and the parties were left with no mission and very few experienced organizers. The Neo-Destour, the Ba'ath in Syria and Iraq, and Algeria's FLN have all fallen victim to this phenomenon.

THE TENETS OF SOLIDARISM

The word "corporatism," to the best of our knowledge, does not exist in any of the languages spoken in the Middle East, and despite a vast body of literature (e.g., Schmitter 1974) only Bianchi (1984) has examined a Middle Eastern political system in corporatist terms. Although the term may be foreign to the Middle East, its logic certainly is not. To oversimplify, corporatist ideologies conceive of societies as organic entities much like the human body. Societies have functioning parts that perform specific kinds of tasks. The brain (the government) and the nervous system (the party) control these parts and make sure that they work harmoniously together to achieve a desired end (once again, the teleological mission of the state and society). They *must* work harmoniously together; just as one's arms and legs cannot be at odds with one another if one is to walk, so too the functioning parts of the society must be coordinated for the body to live healthily. Occasionally diseases set in; foreign bodies (the Jews in Nazi Germany) must be purged; conflict may produce paralysis; a specific functioning part may atrophy.

The corporatist imagery comes out of European fascism. It condemns two kinds of conflict models of politics: the Marxist and the liberal. In an organic society there is no place for class conflict or any organization along class lines. Likewise, open competition among a myriad of opposed interests and parties cannot be accepted. In the corporatist model, conflict is pathological.

Thus corporatist systems structure organization and representation around the major functional groups in society—agricultural producers, industrial producers, entrepreneurs, white-collar workers, the armed forces. We have already seen how this sort of categorization has manifested itself in Egypt, Algeria, and elsewhere in the Middle East. Such functional categories cut vertically through horizontal strata of wealth and poverty; agricultural producers may range from a landless tenant to a capitalist farmer, entrepreneurs from a street vendor to a factory owner, and so forth. Corporatism prescribes representation by function and wedges people of disparate power and resources into the same functional box.

Whatever historical and cultural predispositions there may be for the twentieth-century manifestations of corporatism, we argue that those manifestations must be seen as new and culturally neutral. They emerge as a function of state building and market penetration in an age when governments cannot afford to condone wide disparities in the distribution of wealth. Resource scarcity, which is inherent in the development process and no more so than when LDCs are struggling with structural adjustment, provokes conflict. Corporatism becomes an arm of the struggle to regiment large segments of the population that are officially entitled to a fair share of the national pie but in fact are denied that share as resources are channeled away from consumption toward investment and speculation. It is rare that the relatively disenfranchised masses—peasants, workers, low-income white-collar workers—feel that they are adequately represented through corporatist structures, and they are quite literally bought off by consumer subsidies, guaranteed employment schemes, and a blind eye to moonlighting, peculation, and low productivity.

A predisposition to corporatism may emerge from the nature of military organization. No modern organization more resembles the corporatist ideal than the military. Here is a relatively large, complex organization divided into functionally specific services, in turn subdivided into functionally specific corps (e.g., engineers, logistics, supply, communications) and task-defined field units (artillery, infantry, armor). The activity of all functioning parts is minutely planned and supervised by the chiefs of staff and chiefs of operations. Although the lines of hierarchy—of subordination and command, of officers and recruits—are sharply drawn, the military ethos calls for harmony among all units and all levels of command. Insubordination entails court-martial, dishonorable discharge, and in time of hostilities, death. The military is a quintessentially purposeful organization, and all of its functioning parts must be subordinated and directed to the pursuit of specific goals. Although it is hard to advance concrete evidence, we can plausibly speculate that the prevalence of government by the military in the Middle East over the past forty years may have brought to power men who, by their training and the evolution of their military careers, were disposed to organize civil society along corporatist lines (see Box 12.1).

Corporatist organization and ideology have done battle with four major sociopolitical issues: the role of political parties, class antagonism, labor organization, and ethnic and sectarian conflict.

Corporatism and Parties

Many Middle Eastern leaders have seen partisan competition as divisive, destructive, and a potential conduit for direct foreign intervention in domestic affairs. The common pattern has been the dissolution and legal abolition of all political parties and the establishment of monopoly fronts to represent "all the people." Egypt from 1953 on, Algeria since independence in 1962, and the Sudan between 1969 and 1985 established corporatist monopolies in the ASU, the FLN, and the SSU. The Ba'ath regimes of Iraq and Syria and the Socialist Destour of Tunisia have allowed for coalitions of the dominant party with small marginal groupings such as communists, Nasserists, and liberals, but there has never been any question of these groupings being allowed to organize freely or to play anything but a subordinate role.

Corporatism and Class

Corporatist regimes sometimes deny the existence of class antagonisms, as in Atatürk's 1935 speech (see Box 12.1), or acknowledge their existence but refuse to allow any organization along class lines. This notion was at the heart of Nasser's socialism, which sought the "melting away of class differences" through a peaceful and harmonious redistribution of national wealth. There is no question that everywhere corporatism has been aimed at containing Marxists and any attempt to incite class

● BOX 12.1

Atatürk's Corporatism

In May 1935 the great innovator Atatürk set forth his conception of society in terms that were to be echoed throughout the Middle East after 1950 (quoted in Özbudun 1981, 88):

> The source of will and sovereignty is the nation. The Party considers it an important principle that this will and sovereignty be used to regulate the proper fulfillment of the mutual duties of the citizen to the state and of the state to the citizen. We consider the individuals who accept an absolute equality before the law, and who recognise no privileges for any individual, family, class, or community to be . . . populist. It is one of our main principles to consider the people of the Turkish Republic, not as composed of different classes, but as a community divided into various professions according to the requirements of the division of labour for the individual and social life of the Turkish people. The farmers, handicraftsmen, labourers and workmen, people exercising free professions, industrialists, merchants, and public servants are the main groups of work constituting the Turkish community. The aims of our Party . . . are to secure social order and solidarity instead of class conflict, and to establish harmony of interests. The benefits are to be proportionate to the aptitude, to the amount of work.

conflict, but while European corporatism was aimed directly at containing the radicalization of the industrial proletariat, that class has yet to acquire much weight in the Middle East.

Corporatism need not be a mechanism for the defense of the interests of the upper bourgeoisie; in fact it is more likely to appeal to middle- and lower-income groups. But almost never does it seek to give proportionate and effective weight to the poor majority of the adult populations of the Middle East. Nasser's distribution of 50% or more of elected seats in the ASU and the National Assembly to peasants and workers was window dressing.

Corporatism and Labor

Corporatist regimes pursue dual strategies vis-à-vis labor. One is to encourage organization and unionization. Strategically placed labor, mainly in public-sector enterprises and the transportation sector, may receive favorable wage and social-benefit packages. Such workers are co-opted by the corporatist state; their leaders are given significant roles in the "party" organization, in legislative assemblies, and sometimes in the government itself. In exchange for favorable unionwide wage-and-benefit packages, union leadership is expected to keep the rank and file in line. The second strategy is to segment the labor force, relying on the organized-labor elite to keep the economic wheels turning while looking over its shoulder at the majority of unorganized labor in the urban informal sector, in the private sector, and in the countryside—workers who would clearly love the jobs of the labor elite.

In Algeria, Boumedienne purged the unions (the peak organization, the General Confederation of Algerian Workers [UGTA]) of militant leadership in 1967 and subordinated them to his statist industrialization drive. The 1971 Charter of Socialist Management of Enterprise installed an ineffective system of worker participation in management. Every major workplace would have an elected assembly of workers, but the latter included management as well as labor. The clear goal of socialist management was to increase production, not promote proletarian democracy (DERSA 1981, 132; Nellis 1977, 549).

Labor leaders co-opted into the corporatist power structure must walk a fine line between serving the state leaders and maintaining some semblance of credibility among the rank and file. Sometimes the balancing act is impossible to maintain. In 1966 the dominant Türk-Iş labor confederation in Turkey condemned a strike in a glass works. This led to the hiving-off of a faction of Türk-Iş and the founding of the radical Confederation of Progressive Trade Unions (DISK). By 1970 DISK had 40,000 members and Türk-Iş 700,000, but DISK became an active element in the agitation of the 1970s. When the military took over in 1980, DISK was disbanded and many of its leaders were arrested.

A similar process unfolded in Tunisia. The General Confederation of Tunisian Workers (UGTT) had been a pillar of the Destourian coalition before and after independence. Whenever labor leaders appeared ready to use its organizational strength in any way that conflicted with regime goals, Bourguiba had them removed. Throughout the 1970s and the readjustment of the Tunisian economy after the Ben Salah statist experiment, the UGTT was led by Habib Achour. In 1978 cost-of-living riots broke out in several Tunisian cities. The UGTT rank and file was hit hard, yet the regime wanted Achour to condemn the violence. In order not to lose support among his following, Achour had to distance himself from the regime. As a consequence, he was jailed, but the relative autonomy of the UGTT had been asserted.

Cost-of-living riots occurred once again in January 1984, when the regime sought to reduce consumer subsidies. It could no longer rely on the relatively pampered members of the UGTT to remain aloof from the agitation. During the Sixth Five-Year Plan, 1982–1986, the regime called for a "social dialogue" and announced that the consultative Economic and Social Council would be transformed into the National Council for Social Dialogue and that in each ministry social peace commissions would be created (Baduel 1983). But corporatist discipline appeared to have broken down. After Achour was once again jailed, the UGTT called in May 1984 for a boycott of local elections and even threatened to run its own list of candidates in the 1986 legislative elections.

Corporatist discipline is always hard to maintain. Sometimes the regime will tolerate strikes and labor agitation in the private sector but forbid them in the public sector, as public enterprise is the motor of national development and, in any case, is owned by "the people." Such double standards have seldom precluded public-enterprise strikes. In 1977, only a year after the adoption of a new national charter, there were 129 strikes, involving 31,000 workers, in the Algerian public sector (DERSA 1981). Egypt experienced major strikes twice in 1968, as workers demanded that military officers responsible for the debacle of the June War of 1967 be given severe sentences by the military tribunals. In 1977 dockworkers in Alexandria sparked three days of cost-of-living riots that spread through most Egyptian cities. The prospect of privatization in 1995 triggered strikes in public-sector textile firms, especially in Kafr al-Dawar.

One of the unexpected results of corporatist experiments is to inculcate organizational skills and eventually some sort of autonomy from the state in the very functional groups the experiment was designed to control. The evolution of the Confederation of Egyptian Labor is instructive. Its autonomy was limited in the Nasserist-socialist era, when rhetoric in favor of the working man was at a high pitch. During the Sadatist era of economic liberalization, the confederation's leadership was co-opted into prominent official positions, and its leader, Sa'ad Muhammed Ahmad, was made minister of human resources, a post he held for nearly a decade. By the time of Sadat's death in 1981 "the Confederation had become the largest, wealthiest and most representative association in Egyptian society" (Bianchi 1986, 438). Under Mubarak it became an effective veto group, notably in preventing any further joint ventures between public-sector companies and foreign investors. Corporatism had thus "provided union leaders with new means for defending workers' interests and, ironically, for limiting the decisional autonomy of the authoritarian regime in critical issues" (Bianchi 1986, 434).

Increased autonomy need not entail greater radicalism. The trend in Turkey and Egypt and perhaps elsewhere is toward the development of unions and professional associations into important economic enterprises in their own right. With dues, special funds, and pension funds at their disposal, unions and associations have invested in businesses, run cooperative-housing schemes and hospitals, launched banks to mobilize their members' savings, and even participated in joint ventures with foreign capital. In this way the organizations develop a stake in the overall smooth functioning of the economic system; their members' interests are better served through the general ability of the economy to generate profits, an ability not enhanced by strikes and agitation.

The gradual distancing from close corporatist control that several Middle Eastern labor organizations have undergone has been replicated to some extent in business and professional associations (especially those of lawyers, journalists, and engineers). Corporatist organizations, like public-sector enterprise, have tended to fall into the hands of bureaucrats; clock punchers with little motivation. Just as production and profits have suffered in the parastatals, ideological commitment and indeed unity itself have suffered in corporatist fronts. The decay of corporatist structures has paralleled the erosion of the elite's confidence in its ability to change society. Rather than displacing patronage, corporatist structures have simply absorbed it. Social harmony then becomes a function of patronage carrots and the formidable stick of highly trained police.

Corporatism, Sectarianism, and Ethnicity

Ethnic and sectarian identity and conflict have vexed Middle Eastern leaders as much as they have fascinated outside observers (see Khoury and Kostiner 1990; Esman and Rabinovich 1988). We shall deal all too cursorily with the topic here. Communalism and sectarianism have been viewed in the modernization literature as anachronisms that will slowly erode in the face of economic development, literacy, and nation building (inter alia, see Lerner 1959). As any observer of the persistence of racial discrimination in the United States knows, however, issues of blood, skin color, and creed are not readily susceptible to treatment through public policy. It may in fact be easier to redistribute wealth through public policy than to wash away these parochial loyalties, prejudices, and conflicts.

The major corporatist experiments in the Middle East have to some extent foundered on the rocks of ethnic and sectarian loyalties. As early as 1926 Atatürk confronted a Kurdish rebellion with Islamic overtones in Eastern Anatolia, representing the first major challenge to the new secular, republican regime. Nasser was challenged by the Muslim Brotherhood in 1954 and 1965. Coptic Christian and Muslim confrontations became commonplace in Egypt during the Sadat era, and eventually Muslim extremists assassinated him. Bourguiba early on had to back away from his own secularizing proclivities, and today Tunisia has one of the strongest Islamist movements in the Arab world. Lebanon was nearly destroyed as a nation by sectarian strife—not just Muslims versus Christians but Shi'is versus Sunnis versus Druze versus Maronites, and so on. Today Iraq suffers the same fate, as Shi'is, Sunnis, and Kurds engage in mutual massacres, kidnappings, torture, and assassinations. Ethnic strife has plagued the Sudan throughout its history as an independent state.

The issues become murky when sect or ethnic groups overlap with relative wealth or deprivation. Lebanese Shi'is have for long been the underclass in Lebanon's economy, whereas the Maronites have formed the core of the business elite (Nasr 1985). Oriental Jews in Israel have been in a situation similar to that of the Shi'is in Lebanon. In North Yemen in the early 1960s, Shi'i tribesmen fought Sunni townsmen, and in 1986 Southern Yemeni Marxists fought among themselves along clan lines. And at least since Ottoman times, Iraqi Shi'is have been economically deprived and politically marginalized.

In certain instances a multidimensional overlap of ethnic origin, distinctive language, shared sect, geographic location, and a common economic way of life makes the ethno-sectarian issue particularly intractable. The outstanding examples in the Middle East are the Kurds and the southern Sudanese. The Kurds, perhaps 27 million strong, inhabit a mountainous homeland sprawling across the borders of Turkey, Iran, and Iraq. All three countries have suppressed attempts at Kurdish self-determination. The shah and later Ayatollah Khomeini dealt successfully but not definitively with sporadic Kurdish insurrections. In Iraq, however, Kurdish dissidence was chronic and seriously hindered Arab-dominated elites in Baghdad from consolidating their rule. After the end of the Gulf War in 1991, the northern Kurdish zone of Iraq lived under an internationally enforced no-fly zone, affording the Kurdish populations there a precarious autonomy. Their autonomy was greatly strengthened by the fall of the Ba'athist regime in 2003. The black, mainly Nilotic[1] populations of the southern Sudan make up roughly a third of the country's population and occupy a third of its land area. These people are non-Arab, speak tribal languages other than Arabic, are for the most part non-Muslim, and live as cattle raisers, fisher folk, or subsistence farmers in the vast swamps and savannas of the south. For a half-century (1955–2005) there was a chronic state of civil war in the southern Sudan, interrupted for about a decade, 1974–1983, during the Nimeiri regime. The fighting periodically led to the toppling of regimes (1964 and 1985) and crippled the economy. After 1989, the Islamic government of Bashir and Turabi prosecuted the war with great energy in the south in the name of Islam and the application of *shari'a*. A tentative and, if history is any guide, precarious settlement was reached in stages between 2002 and 2005.[2]

More often the issues are less clear-cut. Ethnic and sectarian groups may not be geographically fixed, may have considerable degrees of inequality among members, and may share important characteristics with majority populations, such as language (e.g., Shi'ite Arabs in Iraq) or religion (e.g., Muslim Berbers in North Africa). The result is a multidimensional set of actors. It is hard to know at any point what factor is driving the actors—ethnicity, region, religion, or class status. What we should bear in mind is that ethnicity and sectarianism should be seen as resources that can be drawn upon when they best suit the needs of an individual or a group. They need not be a badge that is worn constantly and with unalterable intensity (see Kasfir 1979). When communal tensions run high, when clans are settling scores, or when sectarian or ethnic witch-hunts are under way, individuals cannot shed the ethnic or sectarian labels with which they were born. In calmer circumstances, however, individuals may as easily act in terms of their occupations or their material interests. "Identity politics" is a political strategy, not an immutable force.

The Kurds and the non-Muslim populations of the southern Sudan are peoples seeking at a minimum regional autonomy, and in the case of the Kurds, national independence. These populations have at various times sought to opt out of existing systems. That desire was not shared by all Kurds or by all southern Sudanese. The leaders of the rebellion in the southern Sudan long claimed that they sought a socialist transformation *within* the nation. The signing of the new constitution in 2005 suggests that they meant what they said. Still, these two movements have little to gain from the regimes with which they have done battle; considerable autonomy remains the goal.

In contrast, most ethnic dissidence has had as its aim to opt *into* existing political systems—to use violence or its threat to extract more resources (roads, schools, clinics, industrial projects, and so forth) from the central authorities. Even though the

Turkish authorities give no recognition to their Kurdish minority, they have nonetheless invested heavily in dams, hydropower projects, and agricultural schemes in the Kurdish heartland. The Kurds of the Islamic Republic of Iran have also tried to fight for a more favored position in the newly established republic. Similarly, the Berbers of Algeria and Morocco have confronted the central authorities to enhance their position in the political establishment and to draw more resources to their home regions. Their status is highly complex. Their regions of origin are generally mountains or steppes and are generally poor. For this very reason out-migration has been heavy. Several North African cities are majority Berber in population, and hundreds of thousands of Berbers have worked in France and other European countries. Berbers are a crucial part of the North African urban proletariat. Finally, in both Algeria and Morocco many Berbers enjoy elite status, with prominent roles in the state technocracy, party leadership, and the officers' corps. The interests of North African Berbers are not homogeneous, and for that very reason there has never been a unified Berber front, much less a movement, to opt out of existing political systems (see Gellner and Micaud 1972; Roberts 1982, 1983).

When religious identity is invoked, it tends to take two forms. First, religious minorities generally adopt a defensive posture, trying to guarantee some degree of legitimacy and freedom of practice within the majority society. Some minorities have not fared well, and none worse than the Baha'is in Iran. Historically in the Middle East, the most violent repression of a religious minority was that of the Armenians in Turkey at the beginning of this century, and since 1948, when the state of Israel was founded, Jewish minorities in the Arab countries have experienced varying degrees of repression, even though the right to practice their religion has never been questioned. The second form is that taken by religious movements within the dominant Islamic majority. Here the objective is to transform existing political systems, to force them from without or to change them from within to adhere to the *shari'a* and to Islamic principles. There is no question of opting out here, only of exerting the force of the putative majority in whose name Muslim militants claim to speak (see Chapter 14).

In summary, no sectarian or ethnic group can be analyzed or understood within its own terms of reference. In every instance there will be at stake elements of the distribution of scarce resources, of making concessions that might jeopardize national unity, of reacting to minority demands in such a way as to call the regime's legitimacy into question. Just as sectarian or ethnic groups are the enemies of corporatist solidarity, so too are they often the enemies of class formation and consciousness. Sectarianism and ethnicity more often than not cut across class lines. No corporatist or class-based organization has succeeded in fully co-opting or defanging ethnic and sectarian groups. Until national political systems can provide institutions and rules of political conduct that are reliable and respected, such groups will continue to act as buffers against the arbitrary use of state power.

Let us note finally that minorities have the pesky habit of living on strategic real estate: Iraq's Kurds live in the main oil-bearing region of their country; so too, the southern Sudanese sit on that country's recently discovered oil reserves and, more important, control the headwaters of the White Nile. Central authorities almost always suspect strategically located minorities of colluding with hostile foreign powers to destroy the nation, and sometimes those authorities are right.

THE FAILURE OF IDEOLOGY

For over three decades the official ideologies spawned in the Middle East shared several common themes, all similar to, if not derived from, Atatürk's and the Turkish republic's six principles. National strength, meaning freedom from imperial control coupled with a strong economy and strong armed forces, was both a goal and a promise. Building a new citizen and a new sense of citizenship was a second ideological tenet, something that would be achieved once foreign control had been ended and domestic oppressor classes such as large landowners and compradors were eliminated. Mass literacy, public health, and a booming planned economy would take care of the physical and work needs of the population, giving each adult a new sense of dignity and self-worth. The psychic needs of the populace would be satisfied through the mass party, which would educate new generations in nationalist and civic duties. Every regime espoused the equitable distribution of the benefits of economic growth. Some called this concern "socialism" and some did not.

Curiously, all of these themes can be found in the Western modernization literature of the 1950s and 1960s. The literature of nation building could, in spirit, have been written by Atatürk or Nasser. The shah of Iran, King Hassan of Morocco, King Hussein of Jordan, and, indeed, the Saudi monarchy were as concerned with modernization and national strength as the more obvious socialist republican leaders. If one examines the rhetoric of the White Revolution launched by the shah in 1963, one finds familiar themes of destroying the feudal landowners through agrarian reform, redistributing national wealth through the sale of shares to workers in private and public industry, bringing literacy to all the people, and liberating women. Ten years later the shah added the national-military dimension, proclaiming that within a decade or so Iran would become a world military power.

Had the planned, state-dominated economies worked up to expectations, had the expansion and increasing quality of education and social services kept pace with unchecked population growth, and had Middle Eastern nations built measurably powerful military establishments (only Turkey, the Middle East's sole member of NATO, and Israel can be said to have done so), then perhaps the accompanying ideologies might have had some impact upon broad strata of Middle Eastern society. But the many performance failures, from unprofitable public enterprise to repeated military setbacks for some Arab armed forces, rendered the rhetoric hollow and ultimately a target for derision and anger. Khoury (1983a) has rightly written of regime "exhaustion," the collective playing out of a set of policy and ideological options by an entire generation of Middle Eastern leadership. The statist, socialist, and implicitly secularizing experiments of the past four or five decades have resolved few of the problems they promised to tackle. Other than in Iran, the Sudan, and perhaps Saudi Arabia, the one option that has not been tried is Islamic government, and by default, its hour may yet come.[3] Still, one must underscore the fact that nearly twenty-five years after Khoury wrote his article, the same "exhausted" regimes still cling to power.

THE ISLAMIST CHALLENGE

Many Muslim theologians and lay people believed that the dominant statist experiments after World War II were totally misguided in their attempts to define a separate and diminished religious sphere, to separate Islam from politics, to reduce the *ulema* to mere bureaucrats, to bury the *shari'a* in an avalanche of Western-inspired civil law. Nearly all political leaders could feel the repressed heat of Muslim militants; Nasser, Atatürk, and the shah, among others, broke up their organizations and put the leaders in jail. Significantly, however, nearly all republican constitutions in the Middle East state that the president must be a Muslim, and several declare that Islam is the religion of state and that all law must conform to the *shari'a*. Leaders from Nasser to Saddam Hussein have frequently invoked Muslim themes in an attempt to legitimize their rule, and few have failed to make the pilgrimage, ostentatiously, to Mecca. And we should not forget that several "secularizing" leaders, including Nasser and Boumedienne, were in fact pious Muslims who performed their religious duties regularly.

If the Islamic Republic of Iran and the republic of the Sudan are harbingers of the nature of Islamic governance and discourse, then it is reasonably clear that they have invented neither an entirely new political language nor innovative political and economic policies. In fact, as noted in the previous chapter, what they attack is *secular* solidarism, under which men, not God, make laws for men. Iranian and Sudanese leaders are just as apt as their sworn enemies to invoke an organic image of society coupled with a purposive, mission-guided state. For these leaders solidarity is inherent in the *umma,* the community of Muslim believers, who will march as one if their leaders are truly pious, devoted to God, and learned in the laws of Islam (see Box 12.2).

The current rise of Islamic militancy is partially a function of the hesitancy of incumbent elites to continue to repress and harass militant groups. It is not that these groups are so powerful but rather that the population as a whole alternates between indifference and hostility toward the elites. Although relatively few might welcome Islamic government, a far broader swath of the population shares the militants' moral indignation. Aware of this popular state of mind, elites hesitate to confront the militants for fear of isolating themselves further.

A more common and powerful explanation has to do with the current socioeconomic context. As social scientists, we have a tendency to explain a given phenomenon in terms of others. In this instance we see the strengthening of militant, and sometimes violent, Islamic groups in terms of unemployment among the educated and semi-educated, bleak career prospects, resentment of those who have done well for themselves, often through illegal means, and a quest for justice. This understanding is surely "true" to some degree, but it assumes that if economic and employment

⚲ BOX 12.2 _____

Khomeini's Solidarism

Ayatollah Khomeini, in lectures given to students of religion in Najaf, Iraq, in early 1970, envisioned the *fuqaha* (sing. *faqih*), those well instructed in Islamic law, as the future corps of governors of the *umma* (quoted in Algar 1985, 137–138):

> As for the supervision and supreme administration of the country, the dispensing of justice, and the establishment of equitable relations among the people—these are precisely the subjects that the *faqih* has to offer. For it is the *faqih* who refuses to submit to others or fall under the influence of foreigners, and who defends the rights of the nation and the freedom, independence, and territorial integrity of the Islamic homeland, even at the cost of his life. It is the *faqih* who does not deviate either to the left or to the right. . . .
>
> The entire system of government and administration, together with the necessary laws, lies ready for you. If the administration of the country calls for taxes, Islam has made the necessary provision; and if laws are needed, Islam has established them all. There is no need for you, after establishing a government, to sit down and draw up laws, or, like rulers who worship foreigners and are infatuated with the West, run after others to borrow their laws. Everything is ready and waiting. . . .
>
> Fortunately the Muslim peoples are ready to follow you and are your allies. What we are lacking are the necessary resolve and armed power, and these, too, we shall acquire, God willing. We need the staff of Moses and the resolve of Moses; we need people who are able to wield the staff of Moses and the sword of the Commander of the Faithful (peace be upon him). . . .
>
> Today we have 700 million Muslims in the world, 170 million or more of whom are Shi'is. They are all ready to follow us, but we are so lacking in resolve that we are unable to lead them. We must establish a government that will enjoy the trust of the people, one in which the people have confidence and to which they will be able to entrust their destiny.

[handwritten margin note: Advocates on behalf of no democracy]

conditions could be improved, then militant Islam would lose its constituency. It diminishes the place in Islamic identity of piety and faith. One of Morocco's best-known Islamic leaders, Abdesslam Yassin, chided a French social scientist, François Burgat, precisely for falling into this analytic error: "I find this explanation a little too easy and that it does not take into account the subjective factor. People do not come to Islam as an alternative for their social misfortunes. People come to Islam in response to a call, a call which goes very far and deep in the human soul" (Burgat 1993, 75).

There is one last sociological phenomenon that should be mentioned. Both individually and collectively, there is frequently an espousal of militancy for militancy's sake, virtually without regard for its ideological content. Individual leaders have often oscillated between political extremes—Marxists or leftist radicals in their youth and Islamic fundamentalists in their autumn years (Akram Hawrani of Syria and Ahmad Ben Bella of Algeria are examples). What may best explain these gyrations is the simple desire on the part of many politically aware Middle Easterners to do something to move their societies and to challenge the corruption and complacency of incumbent elites. In May 1959, according to Batatu (1979, 900), the Iraqi Communist party pressured the government of 'Abd al-Karim Qassim for greater representation in the cabinet. Although the party had no more than 20,000 members, it was able to put 300,000 demonstrators into the streets of Baghdad. What did these people understand by their demonstration? How much Marxism could they possibly have mastered? Can we see as their counterparts twenty years later the hundreds of thousands of Iranians who repeatedly filled the streets of Iranian cities in support of Ayatollah Khomeini? Did the latter know anything more about the doctrine of trusteeship of the jurisprudents than the former had known about the class dialectic? Probably not. What we may presume the masses saw in both movements was a tool with a cutting edge and leaders prepared to help them shape their own destinies. Much the same is likely true of many of today's Iraqi Islamist militants.

DEMOCRACY WITHOUT DEMOCRATS?

Solidarism, whether of the secular authoritarian or Islamist variety, has had difficulty dealing with electoral democracy. Both solidarisms speak constantly in the name of the people while at the same time depicting conflict as unnatural. Electoral democracy entails rule-bound competition, appeals to specific interests, and attacks on one's adversaries. It also entails a good measure of unpredictability—something that the Algerian regime learned in December 1991. Solidarism and corporatism assume harmony of interests and predictable, if not planned, outcomes in political and economic life. Solidarists want to speak in the name of the people but not to talk to them. Consequently, Middle Eastern regimes have paid lip service to popular democracy but have tried to control results through the single party, through referendums and plebiscites, and through the restrictive licensing of all political groups. There have been four sustained experiments in electoral democracy in the region: Israel, Turkey, Lebanon (from 1946 to 1975; and again since the end of the civil war), and Palestine after 1996.[4] Compared with other regions of the world, the relative absence of democratic polities is notable.

During the 1990s, it appeared that several political economic forces might change this situation. Analysts noted three interrelated factors. First, the international context had changed dramatically by the early 1990s. The collapse of oil prices forced many Middle Eastern countries to cut back public expenditures and to turn to domestic private sectors to pick up the slack in investment budgets (see Chapter 3). Simultaneously, with the collapse of the Soviet Union and the end of the cold war, the flow of strategic rents to several Middle Eastern countries dropped off sharply. Thus, and second, the military establishments and regimes of the region could no longer make the same outsized claims on national wealth that had facilitated their grip on power in earlier decades (see Chapter 13). Finally, the economic crises forced governments in the region to increase the tax burden on their own populations. The easiest targets are urban lower- and middle-class consumers and wage earners, who are assessed through value-added taxes on goods and services and income taxes at the source of income.

More recently, these forces have weakened. The rise of oil prices after 1999 replenished treasuries, enhanced growth, and lowered the need to tax the citizenry. As we saw in Chapter 9, many states found a variety of ways of coping with macroeconomic difficulties without surrendering significant power. Strategic rents and the role of the military rose again with the rise in regional tensions and war, starting with the second Palestinian *intifada,* and dramatically with 9/11 and the American adventure in Iraq. Strategic rents have been restored—to pro-American forces. At the same time, popular anger over Palestine, Iraq, and Lebanon seems mainly channeled not to democrats, but to nationalists and Islamists. Praetorian regimes[5] in the Middle East are under great stress—but they also retain important strengths, not least their continuing control of the levers of repression. Yet rising educational levels (see Chapter 5), combined with the rise of international communications (the Internet and, especially, satellite TV channels such as al-Jazeera) have contributed to a more politically aware public than ever before. This is particularly true for the youthful majority. Their sometimes contradictory demands for dignity, authenticity, and prosperity are escalating. The stresses on political systems are likely to increase, quite apart from the problems stimulated by wars and invasions.

For international actors that profess a commitment to the spread of democratic institutions throughout the region, especially the United States, there is sufficient uncertainty about the size of the "Islamic vote" to give them pause. The Algerian experience of 1991 reinforces the apprehension that democracy might yield Islamist majorities, as it has in fact done in Palestine and Iraq. As noted earlier, truly free elections in Egypt would make it impossible to ignore the views of the Muslim Brotherhood in Egyptian policymaking. A simple grasp of history suggests that democracy and nationalism are often twins, Arab and Muslim anger over the situation in Palestine, Iraq, Lebanon, and elsewhere will not be assuaged by allowing people to vote. If they are so allowed, the evidence to date suggests, unsurprisingly, that they will vote for candidates who profess to provide solutions for the problems that so enrage voters. Today we inhabit a highly contradictory world in which outsiders—foremost, the United States—advocate democracy, yet they simultaneously do little to assuage nationalist and Islamic outrage at perceived, ongoing historical humiliations. Whether the current vogue for democracy persists will be at least partly determined by how these contradictions play out.

CONCLUSION

The radical authoritarian regimes of the Middle East are ideologically exhausted but still powerful enough to repress and to cling to power. The liberal monarchies have made greater concessions to pluralism and electoral democracy, but not yet enough to permit one to say that a true democratic transition is under way. Islamists in Iran, Iraq, Palestine, Egypt, and the Sudan and their imitators elsewhere use a political rhetoric similar to that of the radical republics they so despise, adding God to the familiar themes of social solidarity and political harmony.

Up to 2001, economic change, driven by shifts in the international economy and the end of the cold war, was creating a situation in which resource-starved governments, regardless of their ideological persuasion, were turning to their citizens for taxes and, in so doing, entering into a contractual arrangement with them. It looked as if governments might be held to account, and citizens might be empowered. However, the coming of the "War on Terror" and the vertiginous rise of oil prices may have fatally undermined these forces. Yet the demands of an increasingly educated populace, watching al-Jazeera 24/7, may be impossible to deny. It may not be necessary for a generation of convinced democrats to take charge of the transition. Leaders mired in stalemated conflicts and willing to bargain with constituents whose resources they need could be enough to launch, if not sustain, a transition from solidarism to democratic pluralism.

NOTES

1. The populations of Equatoria province are, however, largely Bantu.

2. The Machakos Protocol of July 2002 created a framework for a self-determination referendum for the south; Islamic law *(shari'a)* was to remain in place in the north. A full settlement was reached with the Naivasha Comprehensive Peace Agreement, officially signed January 9, 2005, which also set the stage for the ratification of a new constitution in October 2005. As noted earlier, however, extensive violence continues to plague Darfur province.

3. Islamists also govern in Turkey and, in coalition with non-Islamist Kurdish parties, in Iraq.

4. The study of democracy in the region has exploded over the past two decades. Some early signature works include Garnham and Tessler (1995), Deegan (1994), Hudson (1994), Salamé (1994), Vatin et al. (1992). More recent contributions from Bellin (2002), Owen (2004), Carothers and Ottaway (2005), and the Arab Human Development Reports of UNDP are especially notable.

5. Samuel P. Huntington (1968, 195–198) developed the notion of praetorianism and defines it simply as the intervention of the military in politics.

13

THE MILITARY
AND THE STATE

Throughout recorded history, the Middle East has been the arena for sweeping military encounters. Enduring geopolitical struggles between the two great river systems—the Nile and the Tigris-Euphrates—date back to the pharaonic and Babylonian dynasties. As perhaps the world's most important crossroads, the area has been fought over by Greeks, Romans, Assyrians, Persians, Turks, Mongols, Crusaders, and, latterly, the imperial powers of nineteenth-century Europe. As Islam spread across this area, it was carried, so to speak, in the saddlebags of Muslim generals. Kemal Atatürk, the Gazi, or warrior, is but the most recent in a long line of military heroes of epic proportions.

THE MILITARY IN MIDDLE EAST POLITICS

History aside, the past century has been marked throughout by a high level of conflict and warfare. Since World War II, armed conflict has been carried out on a scale and with an intensity that has been rivaled only in theaters such as the Indo-Pakistani or the Indo-Chinese since the 1930s. The area has witnessed one major war for national liberation and independence in Algeria (1954–1962). Among independent states, the most salient example is the Arab-Israeli conflict, which has resulted in five major wars and several thousand deaths. Accompanying this intractable confrontation have been extraordinarily bloody civil wars in Lebanon (1976–1989), the Sudan (1959–1971 and 1983–), North Yemen (1962–1968 and 1994), and Oman (early 1970s), while the Iraqi government has sporadically fought its Kurdish minority. King Hussein of Jordan engaged armed elements of the PLO in savage battle in September 1970, and Algeria and Morocco have fought each other since 1976 in the ex-Spanish Sahara, which Morocco has claimed as its own territory but which the Polisario Liberation Front, with Algerian backing, has tried to win for itself.

The most spectacular and grisly of these conflicts has been the Iran-Iraq War, which raged from 1981 until a cease-fire in the summer of 1988. In most ways it was a conventional war, with large regular and irregular armed forces confronting each other with very high levels of firepower and means of destruction, including poison gas. Perhaps as many as a million died in what became a conflict to rival those of Korea in the 1950s and Vietnam in the 1960s. Not long after the end of formal hostilities, Iraq invaded and occupied Kuwait in the summer of 1990, and a UN force led by the United States drove Iraq from Kuwait, in Operation Desert Storm, in the winter of 1991 (see Box 13.1). In 2003 the United States and Britain invaded and occupied Iraq; although the Coalition Forces swiftly overthrew the Ba'athist regime, within a few months an insurgency, with considerable interreligious violence, began. At the time of this writing (2007) this conflict continues.

Alongside these major military confrontations, there has been a constant stream of smaller incidents: brief border skirmishes (Egypt-Libya, Morocco-Algeria), shows of force (Jordan-Syria, Syria-Iraq, Israel versus all its neighbors), and invasions of longer or shorter duration (Turkey in Cyprus, Libya in Chad, Israel and Syria in Lebanon, Iraq in Iran, and then Iran in Iraq). Since 1991 Turkey has on three occasions moved thousands of its troops into northern Iraq in an effort to eliminate the bases of Turkish Kurds organized in the guerrilla movement known as the Kurdish Workers' party (PKK).

This simple listing of military conflicts says nothing about causes and motives; they are complex and specific to each particular theater or conflict. All that it tells us is that the Middle East has had more than its share of military violence and, predictably, has devoted more of its human and material resources to defense and warfare than many other regions of the developing world.

It is also undeniable that Middle Eastern societies have experienced prolonged periods of rule by the military. Military or quasi-military government has been the rule rather than the exception. Even when, de jure, regimes are headed by civilians,

◑ BOX 13.1 _____

The Costs of War: The Example of the Gulf War of 1991

At the conclusion of Operation Desert Storm, Iraq's war with Iran and its invasion and occupation of Kuwait had incurred costs and external obligations totaling US$600 billion, nearly three times Iraq's total earnings from oil sales over the period 1931–1990 (al-Nasrawi 1995):

US$232 billion	Cost of repairing war damage
US$67 billion	Value of assets destroyed
US$97 billion	Reparation payments owed Iran
US$100 billion	Payments to UN compensation fund for victims of the occupation of Kuwait
US$100 billion	War-related Iraqi external debt

the power wielders may be military officers who have left their uniforms in the closet. Atatürk himself was the first general to follow this path and to insist that those of his officer colleagues who wished to pursue political careers do likewise. Is-met İnönü, his vice president and successor, led the way in resigning from the armed forces. Still, it is hard to see Atatürk's regime as other than quasi-military. Next door to Turkey, Reza Shah, commander of the Iranian Cossacks, founded a monarchy, but throughout his rule his regime was reliant upon the military. His son Mohammed Reza Pahlavi continued to depend on his military establishment and in fact owed his throne in 1953 to the initiative of General Fazlollah Zahedi, who, in coordination with the US Central Intelligence Agency (CIA), arrested the civil-ian prime minister and opponent of the shah, Mohammed Mossadegh.

As the Arab countries gained their independence, several fell under nearly unin-terrupted military rule. Since 1949 Syria has known only brief periods of civilian rule. Today Bashir al-Assad may wear a suit to work, but he and his fellow Alawite officers constitute the power elite of the government and of the Ba'ath party. Iraq since the toppling of the monarchy in July 1958 has had constant military rule, al-though, as we have seen, Saddam Hussein came out of the police rather than the mil-itary. Several of his closest associates from his home area of Takrit were strategically placed in the military and in the Iraqi Ba'ath party.[1] Similarly, the YAR, the PDRY, the Sudan between 1969 and 1985 and again after 1989, Algeria since 1965, and Libya since 1969 have been ruled by the military.

One should not, however, underestimate the possible significance of the "civilian-ization" of military regimes. Over time, moves that initially may be largely symbolic, such as dropping military titles and substituting mufti for uniforms, may lead to a real transfer of power and control to civilian hands. That transfer took place in dra-matic fashion in Turkey in 1950, although the military has intervened in politics in 1960, 1971, 1980, and 1997. In Egypt and Algeria over the past several decades, nonmilitary technocrats have played increasingly prominent roles in economic and social policymaking, although President Hosni Mubarak of Egypt was once a profes-sional military officer and maintains close links to the senior officers' corps. Key po-sitions in internal security and administration, national defense, and foreign affairs are still reserved for senior officers. The confrontation between the military and the FIS in Algeria has in many respects led to the remilitarization of the regime, making it the most praetorian of any in the Middle East, although the current president, Ab-delaziz Bouteflika, came from a diplomatic, rather than a military, background.

In all the major monarchies—Jordan, Morocco, Iran from 1923 until 1979, and Saudi Arabia—the king is intimately linked to the military. Members of the royal family, if not the king himself, direct the Ministry of Defense, command key units in the armed forces, and review all promotions in the officers' corps. Before becom-ing king, Hassan of Morocco was put in command of the royal armed forces, and King Hussein, whose throne was dependent upon the support of the largely Bed-ouin Jordan Legion, was always a king in uniform.

A handful of regimes have had a reputation for civilian predominance. Tunisia en-joyed uninterrupted civilian government from 1956 to 1988. The size of the military was contained, few military men played any role in the civilian administration, and there were no serious attempts at military intervention. Bourguiba single-mindedly built his coalitions among civilian forces and insulated his regime from military influence. In recent years, however, the size and cost of Tunisia's military have been growing substantially. Moreover, it was the minister of defense, General Zine al-Abdine Ben 'Ali, who deposed Bourguiba in 1988.

We have already discussed Turkey's peculiar oscillation between civilian and military rule since 1950 (see Chapters 11 and 12). The continued use of the military in an effort to eradicate the PKK has given the armed forces continued leverage in Turkish politics. If ever Turkey is to join the European Union, it will have to convince its European partners that its civilian institutions are firmly and irrevocably anchored.

There was a time when Lebanon appeared to be a solid civilian republic, but appearances were deceiving. Civil war broke out in Lebanon in the summer of 1958, at the time of the overthrow of the Iraqi monarchy. The violence provoked US military intervention. President Camille Chamoun, a civilian, was judged to have mishandled the situation and was replaced by General Fu'ad Chehab, like Chamoun, a Christian. For six years under Chehab, Lebanon was under lightly veiled military rule. Between 1964 and 1976, Lebanese presidents were civilian, but their presence did not head off the civil war that after 1975 devoured civilian institutions, the Lebanese armed forces, and the country itself. Today, however, a (fractured) civilian parliamentary system once again uneasily governs Lebanon.

Israel has apparently escaped military rule, but soon after independence Prime Minister David Ben Gurion feared a coup d'état engineered by the leaders of the outlawed Jewish terrorist organizations (principally, the Irgun, led by Menachem Begin). It is an irony of sorts that Begin went on to become prime minister himself some thirty years later through the ballot box. More important, however, is the thorough intermingling of the civilian and military spheres in Israeli politics and in the economy. Israel is a nation-in-arms. It has fought six major wars. It has faced terrorist threats of various kinds. It maintains a large defense industrial base, and many public activities are regulated by concerns of national security. The military does not have to seize power in Israel, because on most issues it is already positioned to get what it wants. Moreover, many of Israel's most visible politicians have come out of the military: Moshe Dayan, Yitzhak Rabin, Haim Bar-Lev, Ezer Weizmann, Rafael Aytan, and Ariel Sharon, to name but the most illustrious (for a contrasting view, see Gutmann and Landau 1985, 191).

In Iran, the shah's enormous repressive apparatus, built on the armed forces and the secret police (SAVAK), was neutralized by persistent street demonstrations and strikes orchestrated by both the Iranian Muslim organizations and the radical leftist groups. It would be hard to describe the Islamic Republic of Iran as civilian but equally hard to describe it as a military dictatorship. The regular military has been contained by a dominant coalition of the clergy (the mullahs) and the irregular Revolutionary Guards (Pasdaran). It is this coalition that, with Khomeini's fervent blessing, prosecuted the war with Iraq. The Islamic republic is thus a strange, if not unique, mutant of Huntington's praetorian state, led by "priests" and armed religious militants.

GOOD GUYS OR BAD GUYS?

In the 1950s and 1960s, in the literature generated under the rubric of "political development," there was a tendency to look upon military regimes in LDCs with some favor. Military officers were seen as modernizers, men with a nationalist vision, a strong sense of discipline and organization, and a commitment to the values of a meritocracy. For many observers, the military could build a nation out of the heterogeneous religious, ethnic, or linguistic particles of its society—transforming the economy, developing the infrastructure, expanding the educational system, and seeing to it that hard work and competence were rewarded with official recognition and advancement. "The army in politics cannot become an institution above the battle. It intervenes as a partisan, representing a new class with whom the majority in the country does not yet share a common consciousness" (Halpern 1963, 274). In short, the military's vision was national whereas that of its compatriots was parochial; it was organized and disciplined while the civilian population was still mired in the supposed fatalism and petty jealousies of traditional societies; it believed in performance though its countrymen trusted in fate or luck. If freewheeling democracy had to be sacrificed, temporarily, to the exigencies of building a nation and transforming an economy, that appeared an acceptable price to pay.

By the late 1960s neither the military nor its presumptive class allies were viewed with the same enthusiasm. Samuel Huntington, in his influential book *Political Order in Changing Societies* (1968), wrote with faint distaste about praetorian regimes as perhaps necessary evils to restrain popular demands for social and economic benefits that hard-pressed governments could not meet. The praetorians provided the order that would allow economic development to proceed without unmanageable unrest. The countries in the Middle East that have come closest to Huntington's model are Iran under both shahs, Turkey under Atatürk, and Algeria under Boumedienne. The experiments of Nasser in Egypt and the Ba'athi military in Syria and Iraq do not fit well because they neither really suppressed popular demands for economic benefits nor drove forward the development process to the degree that they had hoped.

In an analysis of Latin American politics in the 1960s and 1970s, Guillermo O'Donnell (1978) advanced a variant on the praetorian model that he called "bureaucratic authoritarianism." He argued that LDCs that pursue strategies of import-substituting industrialization eventually come to a point when the "easy" phase ends and a process of "deepening" must be initiated. This entails moving from the manufacture of consumer goods to the manufacture of intermediate and capital goods—sophisticated machinery, heavy engineering goods, and the full range of basic metals. It may entail cutting costs so that industries that have grown fat on captive domestic markets can compete in international markets. O'Donnell predicted that as deepening got under way a military authoritarian regime might be required to discipline the workforce and hold down wages. The military would ally itself with elements of the civilian technocracy responsible for designing and planning the deepening strategy and with foreign multinational corporations that would provide the technology and expertise.

This model, developed largely with Brazil and Argentina in mind, has been judged deficient even for Latin America (Collier 1979), and in the Middle East the only regime that has approximated it has been Turkey. In the early 1960s the Turkish military did pursue industrial deepening, but it did so behind high tariff walls and in the absence of much foreign investment. It was, however, the military intervention of 1980 that best approximated O'Donnell's model. That intervention was provoked by years of growing political violence and a profound economic crisis that called into question Turkey's long-standing ISI strategy. The generals, allied with civilian technocrats, muzzled the labor unions and the universities, cut social outlays, and pushed through an export-led growth strategy that required Turkish industry to become competitive in international markets. What was at stake was not deepening but rather export promotion.

Today it is difficult to unearth anyone who finds merit in military or quasi-military rule. The downfall of the shah, Ferdinand Marcos, Nimeiri, and the military regimes in Argentina, Brazil, Chile, and elsewhere was greeted, at least initially, as a blessing. Similarly, the collapse of the party-police states of Eastern Europe and the former USSR was seen as testimony to the failure of such regimes to provide materially or psychically for their own citizens. Whatever degree of order and discipline the military has been able to provide, it has been outweighed by the choking off of the free flow of information and ideas and the blocking of the assumption of responsibility on the part of ordinary citizens for their economic and political affairs.

Although the military clings stubbornly to power in the Middle East, its role as a transforming and dynamic institution has been discredited nearly everywhere. There is among the middle classes of the region a general sense that the military must be pushed out of politics and out of economic management. Among countries that have experienced military rule, only Turkey appears to have achieved lasting civilianization. In other countries there has been backsliding. The Sudan has reverted to military rule, Tunisia fell under it for the first time in 1988, Algeria since 1991 has deepened its praetorian character, and the Yemens were forcibly united in 1994 under the rule of a general.

THE ECONOMIC WEIGHT OF THE MILITARY

Conventional wisdom has long posited that heavy outlays on defense and warfare divert scarce resources away from directly productive investment and human-capital formation. For once, conventional wisdom may be right. A counterargument with respect to the LDCs is that large defense expenditures may act as an economic stimulus. They finance heavy industry (armaments), the acquisition of advanced technologies, the formation of skilled personnel, from truck drivers to radar operators, and the provision of employment. Defense expenditures or a large military establishment may attract foreign aid and investment and thus enhance the country's foreign-exchange position. The argument has provoked a great deal of debate (summarized in Deger 1992), and many studies have found that defense outlays bear a high opportunity cost, shifting resources from "high-growth development projects" that entail a reduction not only in public outlays but in dependent private outlays as well. Only countries flush with foreign exchange (e.g., Saudi Arabia before 1986) show any positive correlation between defense outlays and economic growth; otherwise, the two compete with each other.

What can the Middle East tell us about this argument? Unfortunately, nothing very conclusive (on Egypt and Israel, see Barnett 1992). When defense expenditures in all regional groupings in the developing world are compared, those in the Middle East come out the highest (see Figure 13.1). When oil prices were at their twentieth-century peak, Middle Eastern countries were spending US$40 billion a year on defense, with Iran and Saudi Arabia leading the way. Petroleum revenues allowed some countries to indulge in this luxury, but outlays in Egypt were about US$3 billion, and those in Syria and Morocco about US$2 billion.

One might suppose that such defense burdens would cripple most economies, at least those without significant petroleum earnings. But there is no correlation in the Middle East between defense expenditure as a proportion of GDP and rates of growth (see Table 13.1). Moreover, large outlays and relatively high growth rates come together in a few instances. We cannot conclude from this that defense expenditures contribute more than direct public or private investment to economic growth, nor can we assume a causal relation between high defense outlays and growth. We can estimate, counterfactually, the returns on alternative uses of the monies devoted to defense, but practically nowhere in the world is there any evidence that reducing defense budgets results in increased outlays for, say, social welfare or infrastructure.

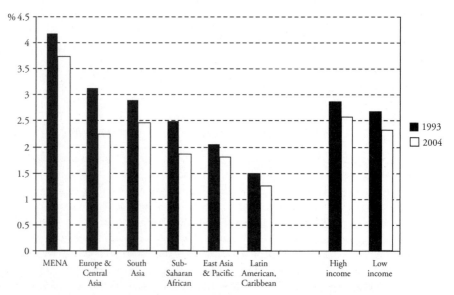

FIGURE 13.1   Military spending as a percentage of GDP, 1993–2004
SOURCE: World Development Indicators Online, 2006

TABLE 13.1 Economic Weight of Middle Eastern Military Establishments, 1993–2004

	Average GDP growth rate (annual)	Comments	% of GDP 1993–2004	Average Military Expenditure		
				Comments	% of central government expenditure	Comments
Algeria	3.0		3.39		14.85	1994–2002
Bahrain	5.1		4.55		18.36	
Egypt	4.5		3.08		12.40	1993–1997
Iran	3.9		3.52		19.74	
Iraq	6.6	1998–2004	–		–	
Israel	3.9		9.17		18.10	
Jordan	4.6		8.80		31.91	
Kuwait	6.0		9.49		22.20	1993–1999, 2001–2002
Lebanon	4.2		5.13		15.58	2000–2003
Libya	3.5		3.17	1997–2004		
Morocco	3.4		4.23		15.58	1993–1996, 1997–1999
Oman	3.8		12.68		43.71	1993–1998
Saudi Arabia	2.3		10.46		–	
Sudan	5.6		2.07	1993–2000, 2002–2003	29.18	1998–1999
Syria	3.5		6.32	1993–2003	–	
Tunisia	4.5		1.78		6.39	
Turkey	3.8		4.41		16.69	1993–1998
UAE	6.0		4.40	1993–2003	47.61	1997–1999
WBG	−2.3	1995–2003	–		–	
Yemen	5.0		6.49		27.09	1993–1999

SOURCE: World Development Indicators online, 2006

Defense outlays are laden with the symbols and sentiments of national pride and survival. People seem prepared to accept disproportionate public investment in defense. They and their leaders may find less justification in using equivalent resources to reduce adult illiteracy or to line irrigation ditches.[2] That such resources could be better spent on human welfare is undeniable; that governments are willing to make such shifts is dubious.

Similarly, big defense establishments attract foreign-resource flows because they represent important markets for arms exporters and because they are located in geopolitically strategic regions. Through the supply of arms and military expertise, great and lesser powers can buy political and strategic leverage that no other sphere of economic activity can offer. In the same vein, there is often a large concessional

TABLE 13.2   MENA Military Expenditures, 2000–2005

Rank (Out of 170 Countries listed)	Country	Military expenditures - dollar figure	Date of Information
1	U.S.	$518,100,000,000	2005 est.
10	Saudi Arabia	$18,000,000,000	2002
12	Turkey	$12,155,000,000	2003
16	Israel	$9,450,000,000	2005 est.
25	Iran	$4,300,000,000	2003 est.
35	Kuwait	$3,010,000,000	2005 est.
36	Algeria	$3,000,000,000	2005 est.
38	Egypt	$2,440,000,000	2003
39	Morocco	$2,310,000,000	2003 est.
46	UAE	$1,600,000,000	NA
48	Jordan	$1,400,000,000	2005 est.
49	Iraq	$1,340,000,000	2005 est.
51	Libya	$1,300,000,000	NA
55	Yemen	$992,200,000	2005 est.
57	Syria	$858,000,000	NA
61	Qatar	$723,000,000	NA
67	Bahrain	$627,700,000	2005 est.
71	Sudan	$587,000,000	2004
72	Lebanon	$540,600,000	2004
79	Tunisia	$356,000,000	NA
86	Oman	$252,990,000	2004

SOURCE: CIA World Factbook Online, 2006, at http://www.cia.gov/cia/publications/factbook/rankorder/2067rank.html

component in the pricing and the financing of the arms deliveries; indeed, in the Middle East, billions of dollars' worth of arms have been given away annually. As is the case with domestic military expenditures, it is unlikely that these grants would have ever materialized, at least not on the same scale, for nonmilitary development purposes.

The collapse of oil prices in the late 1980s and 1990s and its ripple effect on the region's economies had a substantial impact on the military establishments of the Middle East. From an average of 17% of GDP in 1983, military expenditures for the countries of the region fell to 4.2% in 1993. Nonetheless, relative to the

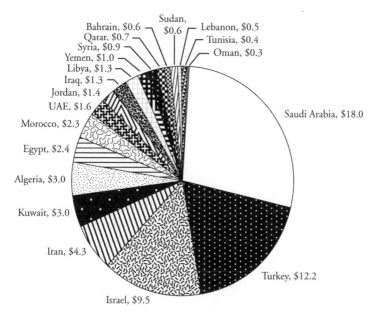

FIGURE 13.2   Distribution of MENA military expenditures (US$ billions), 2000–2005
SOURCE: CIA World Factbook Online, 2006, at http://www.cia.gov/cia/publications/
factbook/rankorder/2067rank.html

other major regions of the world, the Middle East remained the most generous in
military spending (see Figure 13.1). Note, however, that three countries—Israel,
Saudi Arabia, and Turkey—account for more than 60% of all military expenditures
in the region (see Table 13.2 and Figure 13.2). Moreover, reductions in military expenditures were not uniform across the region; they have crept up over time in Tunisia and surged in the Sudan as the government in Khartoum stepped up the
military campaign against the southern insurrectionary forces.

The beginning of peace negotiations in 1991 between Israel and its Arab adversaries raised hopes that the region might one day benefit from a large "peace dividend" (see el-Naggar and el-Erian 1993). Unfortunately, such hopes have been
dashed. First, of course, the Israeli-Palestinian conflict dramatically escalated with
the Al-Aqsa *intifada,* beginning in late 2000. Second, developments in Iraq have
greatly exacerbated regional tensions. Third, there are a number of other conflicts,
unrelated to the first two: Saudi Arabia–Yemen, Turkey-Greece, Egypt–the Sudan,
and Algeria-Morocco. These unresolved conflicts will be used by the parties to them
to justify continued high levels of expenditure and arms acquisition. They do not include ongoing or unresolved civil wars, such as those in Iraq, the Sudan, Turkey, and
Lebanon. Turkey's prime minister in 1994, Tansu Çiller, claimed that her country
was spending 5% of GDP annually in its war against the PKK. And since 2001, the

American "war on terrorism" has greatly strengthened the political voice of Middle Eastern military (and other security) officers.

The data on arms sales to Middle Eastern countries after the end of Operation Desert Storm are indicative. Over the period 1991–1993, some US$20 billion in arms were transferred to Saudi Arabia and Kuwait alone. Ten years later (2003–2004), Saudi Arabia spent over $20 billion on arms, while neighboring Iran spent over $17 billion (SIPRI 2005). Both Iran and Syria acquired missiles from North Korea and the PRC; Iran is now self-sufficient in missile production. As soon as Salih had ended the secession of South Yemen from the Yemeni union in 1994, he contracted with Moldova to purchase thirty MiG-29 fighters for US$300 million. The simple fact is that major arms suppliers such as the United States will not forgo the opportunity to mitigate balance-of-payments problems by selling arms to countries already replete with them and located in war zones. In addition, the countries of Eastern Europe and the former Soviet Union may have little else to export than surplus Soviet equipment.

The weight of the military can be measured in other ways. In several of the large Middle Eastern states there has emerged what President Dwight Eisenhower once termed a "military-industrial complex." Israel, Egypt, Turkey, and most notably, Iran, have developed extensive armaments industries that occupy a particularly important niche in their economies. For one thing, the military-industrial sector includes some of these economies' most advanced technological undertakings—research into and direct use or manufacture of strategic technologies, including supercomputers, nuclear fission, lasers, advanced telecommunications and remote sensing, telemetry, and missiles. For another, these undertakings are almost exclusively within the public sector. Although in Israel and Turkey some component manufacture is contracted out, the transfer and adaptation of high technology with obvious civilian applications is monopolized by the military establishment, and anyone who has the expertise and desire to work with such technologies becomes a servant of that monopoly. The military-industrial complex tends to invade the civilian sector of the economy, competing directly with private producers and providers of services. Finally, these growing economic domains have become important sources of foreign exchange through sales of arms. Arms exports have been crucial to Israel's balance of payments for many years, but Egypt too, partially as a result of Iraq's needs for arms, saw the value of its military exports rise from about US$1 billion in 1986 (Springborg 1987) to an estimated US$4 billion in 1988/1989, according to the US Arms Control and Disarmament Agency (1995).

Turkey's military industries employ more than 40,000 people. Many of Turkey's military contracts have been co-production deals with foreign investments in local companies averaging $300 million annually (CAAT 2002). These factories and facilities are involved in overhauling M-48 tanks, manufacturing optical equipment, and manufacturing and assembling Huey helicopters and F-1 jet fighters, submarines, patrol boats, tank guns, and missiles. Significantly, some of Turkey's large private industrial conglomerates are licensed to manufacture ground-to-air missiles, Black Hawk helicopters, heavy trucks, and armored vehicles (see Karaspan 1987; *Middle East Economic Digest,* September 7, 1985). In 1996 the military began a large-scale technological modernization program, with nearly $30 billion allocated over ten years (Hen-Tov 2004).

Egypt's defense industry is several decades old. Under Nasser it expanded from manufacture of munitions and light arms into aeronautics and even took an ill-fated leap into ballistic missiles. But real expansion occurred under Sadat, especially after 1975, when Saudi Arabia and some other Gulf States agreed to finance the Arab Military Industrialization Organization (AMIO) to produce a range of advanced weapons for the Arab countries. Egypt became the home for the AMIO, and when, as a result of the Camp David Accords, the Arab financiers pulled out of the project, it became an entirely Egyptian undertaking. Between the AMIO and the original defense industries, in 1986, the complex included some twenty-four factories, with a workforce of 70,000 to 100,000 and production worth about US$350 million per year (Stork 1987). It manufactured components for MiGs and assembled French Alpha jets, helicopters, and, at Benha Electronics, radar systems. Today there are at least fifteen production plants, making everything from small arms to tanks and rocket launchers.

During the 1970s the shah of Iran sought to make the Iranian military the dominant force in the Gulf and a rival to India in the Indian Ocean. The purchase of arms and military technology ran at more than US$4 billion per annum and led to contracts and licensing arrangements with a host of multinational suppliers: Northrop, Lockheed, Bell Helicopter, Leyland, Daimler-Benz, and others. The Islamic republic inherited this complex but had to look to other sources of supply: the PRC, the USSR, Sweden, Turkey, and the international arms market. From 1995 to 2005, Russia supplied over 70% of Iranian arms imports (SIPRI). By 2004, the country was making its own intermediate-range ballistic missile, the Shihab-3, using components that were nearly all manufactured in Iran.

Likewise, Saudi Arabia, on the strength of its petroleum revenues in the 1970s, bought entire military technologies and industries. For instance, Saudi Arabia's Peace Shield air-defense system has brought in billions of dollars in radar equipment and computers. In the two years following the end of Operation Desert Storm, Saudi Arabia imported about US$19 billion in arms and defense-related matériel, and from 1990 to 1999, the United States delivered nearly $40 billion worth of armaments to Saudi Arabia (FAS 2005).

It is Israel, however, that has gone the farthest in the development and sophistication of its military industries. Israel's technical expertise is without equal in the region. Its research-and-development facilities put it on an equal footing with the most advanced nations of the world. It is one of the world's major arms suppliers. Its scientists have provided Israel with all the requisites to assemble and deliver nuclear bombs and warheads. The country had the necessary expertise to design and manufacture a jet fighter, the Lavi, possessing all the capabilities of the US F-16C. Israel wants to be self-sufficient militarily and in all technological domains, but its own armed forces could never generate sufficient demand to sustain, economically, the range of military industries that national security would require. In 1990 its two largest armaments industries had a combined turnover of US$2.3 billion. For such industries to be viable, Israel had to seek markets abroad. The search was successful:

In 2004, according to Israeli Defense Ministry Director General Amos Yaron, Israel exported $2–3 billion worth of armaments; more than 80% of Israeli defense production was destined for export (Israel High Tech and Investment Report 2004).

Perhaps the most important aspect of the Middle East's military-industrial complexes is that they have tended to become powerful economic enclaves and, because of their strategic nature, not fully accountable to parliaments or auditors. They are in a position to harness important private-sector clients and, indeed, to invade civilian markets. They own property, productive assets, and financial institutions, and they can negotiate foreign and domestic loans and put out contracts. Frequently it is alleged that these assets and points of leverage are used by the officers' corps to line their own pockets and those of their clients.

Turkey may have pioneered in the building of a military-economic enclave. After the military coup of 1961, the Armed Forces Mutual Assistance Fund (ÖYAK) was set up. Its financial resources come from a 10% levy on the salaries of all commissioned and noncommissioned officers, and the purpose of the fund is to pay these officers pensions upon their retirement. By the mid-1970s some 80,000 officers were paying into this fund. Its assets were estimated at US$300 million by 1973, and a decade later Robert Bianchi (1984, 70) described it as "the country's largest and most diversified industrial conglomerate." At the time it had controlling interests in the Turkish Automotive Corporation, the MAT Corporation (truck and tractor manufacture), the ÖYAK Insurance Company, TÜKAS Food Canning, and a cement plant and owned 20% of Petkim (petrochemicals), 8% of Turkish Petroleum, 42% of ÖYAK-Renault (automobile assembly and manufacture), and 7% of a Goodyear subsidiary (Ayres 1983).

ÖYAK has bridged a gap between the military establishment and the private-economic sector. Since Ottoman times and even under Atatürk, the military has seen itself as an independent entity, a guardian of the nation's interests and, to some extent, a watchdog against private greed. It has always depended upon state budgetary appropriations for its needs. Now ÖYAK and other special funds are dependent on direct investments in the national economy and in joint ventures with foreign and domestic corporations. The economic interests of the officers' corps have become firmly wedded to the performance of the Turkish economy and to that of its private sector.

Egypt, especially since the advent of Field Marshal Abu Ghazala in 1981, has followed a similar path. Military industries had already claimed a portion of civilian markets for products including truck motors, telephone equipment, optical lenses, fans, and air conditioners. Annual production for civilian consumption reached about US$300 million in the early 1980s. In 1978 the National Service Projects Organization was established, and once Abu Ghazala got hold of it, its range of activities was greatly expanded. The army corps of engineers assisted civilian contractors in bridge and road construction. Armed forces communications experts implemented the refurbishing and expansion of the telephone systems of Cairo and Alexandria. Most spectacular was the armed forces' direct entry into food production, allegedly so that in time of hostilities they could ensure their own supply of food. What transpired was a capital-intensive plunge into desert reclamation, hothouse cultivation of vegetables, and commercial production of eggs and poultry. Springborg estimated the value of food produced by the military at £E488 million (roughly US$200 million) in 1986. Private producers have cautiously complained, particularly after military production drove down the price of eggs, that by using conscripts as free labor the military had an unfair advantage over the private sector. These protests may be outweighed by the ability of the military to let lucrative contracts to private firms, ensure supply or produce to designated wholesalers, and, through a network of retired officers relocated in private and joint-venture firms, maintain a far-flung system of clients and cronies. The military participates actively in two large land reclamation projects, the as-Salaam Canal and the New Valley Project.

The Syrian military has followed the same path. It was drawn into the Lebanese civil war in 1976 and wound up in effective control of eastern and northeastern Lebanon and of access to Beirut. Mildly austere socialist Syria thus met anarchic Lebanon, where freewheeling entrepreneurs still managed to thrive in the midst of the fighting. Lebanon imported a range of consumer goods that Syrians craved, and the armed forces found themselves in a position to control the movement of such goods. The result was predictable: a sprawling black market in everything from tape decks to automobiles, operated by Syrian officers, with astronomic profits distributed through several subnetworks. Even without this profiteering spawned in the Lebanese cockpit, the Syrian military controls an important economic enclave. It has been involved in public works, construction, basic industry, farm production, and the manufacture of batteries, bottled mineral water, and furniture. The largest military corporation is the Military Housing Organization (Longuenesse 1985, 18).

THE MILITARY AND NATION BUILDING

Studies of state formation in Western Europe have emphasized the crucial role of military rivalry and war (for example, Tilly 1975). It is argued that the perceived need to build powerful military forces obliged central authorities to extend their administrative grip on their societies, reduce the autonomy of the feudal estate, and extract through taxes the resources needed to pay for the military effort. Over time this process gave rise to strong, centralized states and, because war was inherent in the scheme, to protonationalism.

We may legitimately ask whether in the Middle East a singular process is under way. The answer is an equivocal no or, perhaps, not yet. Certainly war or its threat has been a constant in regional affairs since World War II, but with a few exceptions this has not notably promoted national integration and a common national identity. Perhaps our time horizon is simply too short. Moreover, because arms and what we have called strategic rents have been so readily available, and on soft terms, to Middle Eastern belligerents, the region's states have not had to develop an extractive capacity commensurate with their military burdens.

Nonetheless, there are very important exceptions to these generalizations. There is little doubt that war has been a determinant in shaping Israel's national identity.

There, the nation-in-arms is an everyday reality. The Israeli defense forces have, moreover, been used since 1948 as a primary instrument for integrating the culturally diverse Jews of the Diaspora, teaching them Hebrew, socializing them to the values of the state, and erasing differences among them through a common uniform and shared drudgery. (The only non-Jews who participate in this experience are the Druze.)

Like Israel, the Turkish republic was born and consolidated as the result of military victory, a commodity that hardly any other Middle Eastern society has enjoyed in recent centuries. It may be stating the obvious to say that, whereas defeat or perceived inferiority provokes a divisive search for culprits and traitors, military success can be claimed by all elements of a nation and serve as a symbol of national accomplishment. Thus in 1931 Atatürk could credibly claim a grandiose role for the Turkish armed forces: "the Turkish nation has . . . always looked to the military . . . as the leader of movements to achieve lofty national ideals. . . . when speaking of the army, I am speaking of the intelligentsia of the Turkish nation who are the true owners of this country. . . . The Turkish nation . . . considers its army the guardian of its ideals" (Tachau and Heper 1983, 20).

We can hardly address this issue without considering Iran and Iraq. In 1988, after these two countries had been at war for more than eight years, they reached a tenuous cease-fire. They are both societies with profound religious, linguistic, and ethnic cleavages. They contain colossal obstacles to national integration. Yet one of the astonishing elements of the combat was that each nation more or less maintained unity in the ranks. The Shi'ites and Kurds of Iraq did not defect from Iraq's war effort despite having ethnic or sectarian brethren on the other side; likewise, Iran's Kurds and Arabs did not break ranks. However, after Iraq's armed forces were crushed in Operation Desert Storm, both Iraqi Kurds and Iraqi Shi'ites rose in a failed revolt against Saddam Hussein. Clearly war did not forge an Iraqi identity that could displace those of sect or blood, as the grim sectarian fighting after the 2003 invasion further confirmed.

THE REGULAR MILITARY AND CIVILIANS-IN-ARMS

The several self-proclaimed revolutionary regimes of the Middle East have all had to confront in one way or another the issue of arming the people. In Algeria, Iran, Israel, and the PDRY, where the people were to some extent already armed when new regimes were founded, the issue was particularly sensitive. In other countries, such as Morocco and the Sudan, irregular guerrilla forces had to be absorbed into the regular military.

We can state as a general rule that the regular military views with alarm the arming of civilian militias and party paramilitary groups, not to mention the poking about in military affairs of political commissars. Regimes have come unstuck over this issue. In 1965 Ahmad Ben Bella, the president of Algeria, contemplated arming civilian groups under the auspices of the National Liberation Front. His minister of defense, Houari Boumedienne, saw this as an implicit statement that the Army of National

Liberation was incapable of defending the revolution and that Ben Bella wanted a paramilitary force loyal to him to hold Boumedienne's power in check. In June 1965 Boumedienne toppled Ben Bella, and there was no further talk of party militias.

A similar drama unfolded in Syria in the late 1960s. Salah Jadid, a senior Alawite officer and leader of the military command in the Ba'ath, sought to organize a Ba'athi militia to engage Israel in guerrilla warfare. This was clearly a major issue in driving him apart from his erstwhile ally, Hafiz al-Assad, who was minister of defense. In September 1970, in the wake of King Hussein's crushing of the PLO in Jordan, Assad had Jadid arrested and took over the presidency of the republic.

In Morocco, Algeria, and the Sudan, the regular military had to disarm and absorb into its ranks the remnants of guerrilla forces. In Morocco these came from liberation armies operating, in the two years prior to independence, in the northern mountains, the southern deserts, and some big cities, while in Algeria they came from the guerrilla armies in the interior *wilayas,* or military zones, of the FLN. In the Sudan, after the granting of autonomy to the southern provinces in 1971, the Sudanese army absorbed large numbers of freedom fighters into its ranks. One of them, Colonel John Garang, deserted in 1983 and has led a major insurrectionary movement (the Southern People's Liberation Army [SPLA]) in the south ever since. The Sudanese government has cynically manipulated *janjaweed* militias in Darfur, without necessarily being able to fully control them (see Box 6.1).

Of course, where there is no effective central government, we find armed bands and militias. In Lebanon from 1976 to 1990 and, to varying degrees, in Palestine and Iraq today, armed militias have constituted an "alternative security force." That they often act precipitously, violently, and with contempt for human rights is hardly surprising. Even when a political agreement is forged, disarming, demobilizing, and integrating such forces into the civilian economy and society is a difficult task, as the case of Lebanon since 1990 clearly illustrates.

Iran offers an example of irregular forces cohabiting uneasily with the regular military. The key actors are the Revolutionary Guards or Pasdaran, who became nationwide militia at the service of the Islamic Republican party (until that party was disbanded in late 1987). Many of the leaders came out of the radical secular leftist Mujahidin al Khalq before 1979. They were introduced to radical Shi'ite Islam through the teachings of Ali Shariati and were drawn to Ayatollah Khomeini because of his fiercely anti-imperialist and antidespotic stance. After Khomeini came to power, these militants turned on their erstwhile leftist allies, hounding them out of the country or physically eliminating them. They organized the revolutionary tribunals that meted out arbitrary justice to a host of presumed enemies of the republic. They waged war against the Kurds and were instrumental in the seizure of the US Embassy in Tehran. With time they took on the role of a security-force-cum-vigilante group in the countryside.

The regular armed forces were relatively powerless to oppose the ascendancy of the Pasdaran because the senior officers' corps had been so badly compromised in its loyalty to the shah. The armed forces were given an opportunity to refurbish their image in the war with Iraq and to some extent did so. But the Pasdaran, along with the ill-trained volunteers, or *basij,* enhanced their image in Iran through human-wave assaults on Iraqi positions and other suicidal exploits.

The Pasdaran have become a very powerful force in Iranian politics. Perhaps numbering 200,000, they are armed, control substantial financial resources through institutions such as the Foundation for the Disinherited, and espouse a common militant brand of Shi'ism. They have had powerful allies among the mullahs, such as the former prime minister Mir Hosayn Mousavi, and numerous allies in the *majlis.* By some accounts, they played a critical role in the election of President Ahmedinejad in 2005.

It is in Israel that one finds the most "comfortable" equilibrium between the professional military and armed civilians. The Israeli defense forces were born in the kibbutz movement and the irregular Haganah before independence in 1948. Although the Haganah was rapidly professionalized after 1948, it has never forgotten its civilian origins. More important, Israel's ability to mobilize its adult population quickly and its system of reserve training for all males up to an advanced age have blurred most boundaries between soldiers and civilians. Israelis board buses and sit on park benches with their weapons with the same nonchalance as a businesswoman with her attaché case. Because the military is so closely integrated into Israeli society, the nation's leaders do not fear an armed citizenry.[3]

CONCLUSION

On the whole, the prominent and long-lasting role played by the military in Middle East politics has been harmful. By and large, military regimes did not achieve the kind of structural transformation of their economies or the industrial deepening that they invariably announced as their goals. However, the heavy outlays on the military and on war preparedness that their incumbency has entailed appear to have done little to impede economic growth. The real question is whether this growth could have been more rapid in the absence of such heavy spending. It has certainly been the case that direct rule by the military has not enhanced the military performance of the region's armed forces.

The military has been the catalyst, or at least the conduit, for the introduction of advanced technologies into the region. Military industries and research-and-development facilities are often the most advanced of their nations and have a wide range of civilian applications. It is less clear, however, to what extent these technologies are merely imported as opposed to being absorbed into the scientific community. At a more mundane level, and with the major exception of Israel, the armed forces of the Middle East have not been extensively used to impart literacy and vocational training to their recruits. Because most countries maintain some form of universal conscription and most recruits may come from rural backgrounds, there is a real opportunity to build the nation's human resources during the years in which its youth is in the ranks, but that opportunity has not been widely seized.

The military has done more to build state apparatuses than to create strong economies. We noted in Chapter 12 that the very nature of military training and the functional division of the armed forces may have predisposed officers to a corporatist vision of society as a whole. Thus, together with the strengthening of the state apparatus and of the public sector, we find military rulers structuring the political arena along corporatist lines. Order has taken precedence over mobilization, organic unity over pluralism, discipline over spontaneity.

War and military rule have been the two most salient characteristics setting the Middle East apart from other regions of the world. That combination has also been the major obstacle to the emergence of more liberal political practices; it has also impeded the transition to democracy. Despite a slowly diminishing grip on national wealth, the military everywhere is deeply entrenched. The many unresolved regional conflicts will enable it to exert claims to substantial resources. The civilianization of Middle Eastern political systems will come very slowly and, in some instances, may be halted altogether by alliances of Islamist movements with military sympathizers—or by fear of the military of such Islamists.

NOTES

1. Although Iraq acquired an elected government in 2006, the presence of over 140,000 US troops suggests that military rule continues.

2. Of course, if people choose private consumption over defense outlays, social welfare will rise, even if investment and growth do not increase (and, by hypothesis, if defense spending falls, private consumption rises).

3. Palestinians, on the other hand, have much to fear from armed Israeli settlers in cities like Hebron and elsewhere.

14

IS ISLAM THE SOLUTION?

"Islam is the solution!"—the rallying cry of Islamist political parties—appears on walls in virtually every popular quarter in the Middle East and North Africa. A wide range of thinkers and political activists throughout the Muslim world increasingly frame their approaches to politics, economics, and social issues in self-consciously Islamic terms. In this chapter we investigate the impact of Islamism on the political economy of the region.

PRELIMINARIES

Problems of definition and terminology immediately confront us. Many accounts in the popular Western press refer to "Muslim fundamentalism." We find the term, and the perspective it implies, deeply misleading, since, among other things, it assumes that Islamists do not engage in interpretation *(ijtihad),* a position that is untenable.[1] Furthermore, all Muslims believe that the Qur'an is the literal "dictation" from God to the Prophet Muhammad. Exactly how to apply the whole of God's message to modern life is much debated among Muslims. The sacredness of the message itself is not. Although some careful scholars (e.g., O. Roy 1998) have used the term "neo-fundamentalist" to describe groups such as the Taliban in Afghanistan, we think that the term is better avoided.

The phrase "political Islam" is often used to describe the social phenomena covered in this chapter. This expression gained currency in Western discourse in the aftermath of the Iranian revolution. Although more apposite than "fundamentalism," the term is both too broad and too narrow for our purposes. It is too broad, because if "political" means "having religious views on social organization and governance," then Islam is inherently "political." Islam has been, from its very inception, a religion stressing people's involvement in community, society, and the polity. Islam only appeared "non-political" to Americans during the 1950s and 1960s, when Arab politics was dominated by the supporters and opponents of Arab nationalism and socialism (e.g., Nasserism and Ba'athism). Even during that era, the opponents of Arab nationalism, whether the Muslim Brotherhood or the Kingdom of Saudi Arabia, deployed an Islamic political discourse. Such opposition was often supported by other opponents of Arab nationalism, whether the United States or Israel. The term is likewise too narrow, because if "political" means "making the current acquisition of state power one's primary goal and activity," then many Islamists are not political, since they focus on spreading the faith *(da'wa),* shaping popular culture and mores, and molding popular discourse.

We choose instead to use the term "Islamism," defined as "Islamic activism" (e.g., ICG 2005). In this definition, Islamists seek to bring all elements of social, economic, and political life into *harmony with what its adherents believe* is "true Islam." Islamists criticize current social conditions as tyrannical and unjust, oppose authoritarian ruling elites, and couch their appeals and policies in religious terms (Hamzawy 2005). Minimally, they call for the application of *shari'a* (Islamic law), but they differ hugely in their interpretation of what exactly that means in the concrete circumstances of today's world.

Their tactics also diverge widely. At one end of the spectrum are those who recognize the existence of current states and boundaries and who are committed to participating in democratic political processes (e.g., the Turkish Justice and Development party). At the extreme other end are those who seek to seize power violently and who denounce both formal democracy and nation-states as illegitimate (e.g., the followers of Osama bin Laden). Still others are undecided as to what specific mix of coercion and persuasion is appropriate to pursue their goals, and there are many intermediate cases. Such differences are reminiscent of the diversity of views among European socialists in the twentieth century, when, for example, social democrats and Bolsheviks hurled anathemas at one another. As was true of socialism during that earlier time, today's Islamist tent is wide indeed.[2]

A possible typology of Islamism would first distinguish between Sunni and Shi'i Islamism.[3] Because of the existence of an organized, semi-hierarchical clergy, Shi'i Islam is less fissiparous than Sunni Islam, which lacks any such formal organization. There are, however, significant disagreements among Shi'i Islamists concerning (1) whether they accept or reject Ayatollah Khomeini's concept of the *wilayat al faqih* ("rule by the jurisprudent"), and, if they accept it, (2) *which* ayatollah they think should occupy this post.[4] These differences, however, are typically less severe than those found among Sunni Islamists.

Within Sunni Islamism, we can distinguish three broad approaches: (1) political Islamism (in a restricted sense), (2) missionary or *da'wa* activity, and (3) violent jihadism. We shall use the phrase "political Islamism" to refer to all those who (a) pursue political power in order to (b) bring society more into alignment with its adherents' understanding of Islam through (c) nonviolent means. Two prominent examples of political Islamists, as we have defined the term, are the Justice and Development party of Turkey and the Muslim Brotherhood of Egypt. They are distinguished with respect to their goals from the second group, whose focus is on diffusing their interpretation of Islam through preaching, personal example, and charitable activities. This second group includes the "New Islamists" or the *waseteyya* ("middle path") intellectuals of Egypt

(Baker 2003), who resemble the so-called Islamic modernists, like Muhammed 'Abduh of a century ago, in their creative use of *ijtihad* to develop what they view as an "Islamic" approach to social, economic, and political problems. It also includes the very different *salafiyya* movement, which stresses imitation of (what they think was) the behavior of the Prophet Muhammad and his companions. *Salafis* are very concerned with the details of living, such as how to dress, eat, sleep, and even brush one's teeth. They also have rather vague, but strongly held, views on the requirements of a true "Islamic state," which they typically find to exist nowhere.[5]

Finally, there are the violent militants. The most notorious of these, the followers of al-Qaeda and its clones, emerged as the product of two currents in militant thought: *as-salafiyya al-jihadiyya*—*salafis* who have been radicalized and have abandoned pacific missionary work to engage in political violence—and "Qutbists" or followers of the thinking of Sayyid Qutb, the Egyptian who was executed in 1966, and who applied the notion of *takfir* or "pronouncement of unbelief" to current polities in the region.[6] Qutbists believe that those who disagree with their interpretation of Islam are infidels (rather than Muslims who understand Islam differently) and that these infidels can, and should, be violently resisted and killed. Such militants often include Shi'i Muslims in the category of unbelievers and denounce participants in elections like the Muslim Brothers. The affinities of much of their thinking with radical, violent utopianism of other times and places is striking (Richards 2001).

Nearly all other Islamists sharply distinguish between the violence of *jihadi salafis* such as Osama bin Laden and the violence of the Palestinian and Lebanese Islamic resistance movements. They argue that the violence of the former is unjustified and immoral, whereas the violence of the latter is legitimate resistance to the humiliation and oppression of occupation. Some (e.g., Hizbollah or the "Party of God" of Lebanon) differentiate between al-Qaeda's attacks on the civilian target of the World Trade Center—which they denounced—and the attack on the military target of the Pentagon—which they did not criticize. A broad spectrum of Islamist factions is now visible in Iraq where there is something approaching an "Islamist civil war," pitting Shi'i Islamists (themselves divided) against *jihadi salafis* (who are allied with Ba'athists). Beyond these controversies, there is a fierce debate over the meaning of *jihad* in the Muslim world.

It is important to note that our definition and typology have inherent weaknesses. The boundary between "Muslim" and "Islamist" remains rather vague. (Is *any* Muslim trying to propagate the faith an "Islamist"?) Further, the elements of our typology are not mutually exclusive. For example, many explicitly nonviolent political movements (or political Islamists in our usage) also engage in missionary activity. Indeed, it is precisely this overlap in activity that provides the Egyptian regime's official rationale for not legalizing the Muslim Brotherhood; the government claims that they can't be both a political party and an organization devoted to the spread of religion. Circumstances also may lead political Islamists, who are nonviolent by our definition, to engage in violence when faced, for example, with the violence of others. And, as noted earlier, political Islamists, in our sense, do not necessarily renounce violence if peaceful means are blocked. In contrast to the official

US government position, we think that it is more useful to include HAMAS in Palestine and Hizbollah in Lebanon in the category of political Islamists, as we have defined it, to distinguish them from the *jihadi salafis,* with whom they are often at odds. Certainly HAMAS and Hizbollah have deployed physical force at times; however, they both participate in elections. These Palestinian and Lebanese movements more closely resemble the Irish Nationalists of Sinn Fein/IRA than the followers of al-Qaeda. Placing them in the same category as *jihadi salafis* clouds the picture more than it illuminates it.

The rest of this chapter is organized using the analytical axes of Figure 2.1: economic growth and structural transformation, state policy and governance, and social actors. From the perspective of "social actors," we examine Islamism as a social movement. We investigate the social bases of the movement and the coalitions of actors that it represents. We then turn to three modes of social activism: social welfare, electoral contestation, and political violence. From the perspective of economic growth and structural transformation, we investigate Islamists' ideas about how to cope with the many problems faced by their political economies. Like adherents of the post–Washington Consensus, Islamists agree that the key issues facing their societies are governance questions, so we turn finally to review the behavior of Islamists when they have actually wielded state power—in Iran, Turkey, and the Sudan. We begin with Islamism as a social movement.

ISLAMISM AS A SOCIAL MOVEMENT: COALITIONS OF SOCIAL ACTORS

Islamism is a "social movement": a group challenge to established authority by people sharing common purposes (Tarrow 1994). Such movements engage in campaigns, demonstrations, public meetings, electoral contestation, public announcements, pamphleteering, and any other activities that demonstrate the group's "worthiness, unity, numbers, and commitments" (Tilly 2004). As Charles Tilly argues, such movements—very much including Islamism—are *modern* phenomena. There is nothing "backward" about Islamist movements. One may deplore the goals and methods of some Islamists (e.g., *jihadi salafis*). From such disapproval, however, it hardly follows that they should be understood as "primitive" or "backward," any more than disagreement with Leninist goals and methods implies that communists were "backward."

Both international and national forces forged the context within which Islamism grew. At the global level, Islamism first appeared as a form of resistance to Western colonialism in all its forms—political, cultural, economic, and military. The classic case is the oldest Sunni Islamist movement, the Muslim Brotherhood, which arose under the leadership of Hassan al-Banna in Egypt in the 1930s (Mitchell 1969). Such opposition has always included rejection of the Zionist project, which the large majority of Islamists view as a variety of Western colonialism.

Islamists were hardly the only opponents of Western colonialism or of Zionism. Part of the strength of Islamist movements derives from the defeat of their competitors, particularly those of the secular left (Arab nationalists, communists, Ba'athists) and liberals. To some extent, the defeats of these forces were self-inflicted wounds deriving from their failures in power and their inability to create viable mass political movements. They were also undermined by external forces. The United States has long had a strategic alliance with the Kingdom of Saudi Arabia, whose state ideology is a form of *salafi* Islam known to its detractors as "Wahhabism." A core element of the relationship throughout the twentieth century was joint US-Saudi opposition to Nasserism, Ba'athism, and communism. Consequently, both governments supported Islamist movements; Saudi Arabia favored *salafi* tendencies and others allied with or friendly to its own distinctive interpretation of Islam. Cooperation between the two governments peaked during the war of the Afghan and international *mujahedin* (holy warriors) against the Soviet occupation of Afghanistan during the 1980s and was renewed in their joint effort to eject Saddam Hussein from Kuwait in 1990–1991. The role of Saudi wealth and American diplomacy, military and otherwise, in strengthening Islamism should not be underestimated (AbuKhalil 2002, 2004; Mamdani 2004).

Globalization provides a second international context for recent Islamist success. The technological revolution in computation and communication has greatly facilitated the interaction of everyone in the world, very much including Islamists. At the same time, the ideological hegemony of Western "neoliberal" ideas (e.g., the Washington Consensus [see Chapter 9] and America's increasingly muscular Wilsonianism) has prompted countermovements everywhere—as the recent upsurge of populism in Latin America attests. In the MENA region, Islamism has provided the main resistance to Western hegemony, and globalization provided Islamists with important tools for this opposition (Lubeck 1999).

Understanding the national dimension of Islamist social movements requires examining the social groups supporting such movements. What social coalitions undergird Islamism? As a rough generalization, we can say that Islamist movements often loosely join three social actors: a counter-elite composed of businessmen and professionals, a second stratum of frustrated intellectuals and unemployed or underemployed university or secondary school graduates, and a mass base of the young, semi-educated unemployed. And, increasingly, the Islamists are able to recruit from the ranks of the urban lumpen proletariat.

The relative weight of these elements in any specific Islamist coalition varies widely. Some organizations, such as the Iraqi Shi'i movement of Muqtada al-Sadr, draws most of its support from poor slum dwellers, especially in Baghdad (ICG 2006). Others, such as the Egyptian New Islamists of the Wasit party, find most of their supporters among professionals and other members of the urban middle classes (Baker 2003). The Yemeni Islamist political party, al-Islah, relies heavily on the power of various Zaydi tribes of the north, particularly the Al-Hashid confederation (ICG 2003b). In Iraq, more prosperous Shi'i tribes from around Najaf and Karbala tend to support Islamist parties such as SCIRI or Da'wa, while those from poorer, less-favored areas, such as Maysan Governorate in the south, tend to support the Sadrists (ICG 2006).[7] As with all political movements and parties, these coalitions shift, break apart, and reconfigure. Assessing the social bases of Islamism is tracking a moving target.

The appeal to the "counter-elite" of business often arises from those elements of the entrepreneurial classes who have been excluded (or feel themselves to have been excluded) from the favors bestowed by the state under ISI. Such groups have emerged in Egypt, Morocco, Turkey, and elsewhere (see Chapter 9). In Palestine, the Muslim Brothers and its offshoot, HAMAS, has "always enjoyed the support of landowners, merchants, and shopkeepers" (Abu-Amr 1994, 20). Islam explicitly sanctions a very broad range of profit-making activities, and wealth, when used for social benefit, is fully sanctioned. Where the state has been both exclusionary and aggressively secular, religiously pious businessmen form a natural component of many Islamist coalitions.

The appeal of Islamism to the young is not hard to understand. We have seen (in Chapters 4, 5, and 10) that education and exposure to the wider world have broadened their horizons, but the grim realities of the job and housing markets have dashed their hopes. Too often they cannot find jobs, especially jobs that match their expectations, and rarely can they locate suitable housing. Often they must postpone marriage, often for a long time. Because young people everywhere are trying to establish their identity, they care greatly about their relationships with others. They also care about questions of justice and fairness and find that such ethical norms are routinely violated by their own government, by Israel, and by the United States and "the West" more generally.

Increasingly, Islamism has become the region's mass movement opposing humiliation, at home and abroad. The youth of today are as attracted to nationalism as were their fathers and grandfathers. They perceive the wider community of Muslims as attacked and abused, and they identify with those who resist these attacks.

The "Afghans," or those who fought the Soviets in Afghanistan, were hugely popular during the 1990s. In the summer of 2006, pictures of Hassan Nasrallah, the leader of Hizbollah, the Lebanese Shi'i political party/movement that fought the Israelis to a standoff, were widely displayed throughout the Arab world.

The failures of the old order stimulated Islamist movements. The grandiose promises and disappointing performances of national development strategies in the region since independence have left many searching for alternatives. We will review three phases: the ISI phase, the oil-boom era, and the era of the Washington Consensus. We have seen (in Chapters 4, 7, and 8) how ISI policies increased industrial production and opened educational systems, particularly for secondary and university education. However, these policies also fostered excessive capital-intensity, which retarded job creation, generated severe balance-of-payments constraints—which slowed growth—and discriminated against agriculture—which fostered rural-to-urban migration.

The oil boom of the 1970s further blunted incentives for production of tradables through the Dutch Disease and stimulated rural-to-urban migration. It also stimulated large-scale labor emigration from poor countries to the Gulf States, the rise of new, often Islamist financial intermediaries channeling the flow of remittances back home, and the acceleration of state largesse. States trying to pursue the partial, halting liberalization known as *infitah* encouraged Islamist militants as counterweights to the socialist left. The counter-elite of Islamist businessmen and professionals was also greatly strengthened in this period.

The oil bust of the 1980s and 1990s witnessed declining resources, governmental retrenchment, and tentative, economic-reform efforts (see Chapter 9). The economic downturn and government budgetary austerity coincided with the acceleration of new entrants to the labor force, coming on top of a legacy of economic failure. Government spending cutbacks and administrative deficiencies further weakened an already tattered social safety net, and this created opportunities for Islamist movements, who moved to provide their own services. As we saw in Chapter 9, whatever our assessment of the performance of Washington Consensus policies in other economic areas, the policies failed to reduce unemployment or raise real wages by any significant measure. It seems clear that neither state-led ISI nor the Washington Consensus provide economic and social development or defend vital national interests. Unsurprisingly, Arabs, Turks, and Iranians have been examining their own traditions for the potential building material of alternative models.

In short, government policies during the past three decades have fostered a counter-elite of Islamist businessmen, dissatisfied intellectuals, frustrated educated youth, and elements of the urban poor. State economic, political, and cultural weaknesses have promoted Islamist movements by stimulating grievances and by evacuating critical spaces in the political economy. Islamist movements cannot be understood without a grasp of the uneven and sometimes stalled developmental processes that we have chronicled throughout this book.

However, as we argue in Chapter 12, the phenomenon of Islamism cannot be *reduced* to these developmental problems. Blocked careers, unemployment, rampant corruption, unavailable housing all set the context for Islamism, but they are poor predictors of exactly who will participate in such movements. Young, unemployed, frustrated men throughout the region can turn to Islamism, to drugs and crime, or to indifference, muddling through, hard work and determination, or any number of other personal coping strategies. The decision to join a social movement is a deeply personal, idiosyncratic one. Socioeconomic contexts are important for understanding these movements, but they by no means fully explain them. However, such trends, when combined with the continuing failure of Palestinians to obtain a state enjoying mass legitimacy, along with the increasing reliance by both the United States and Israel on naked military force, do much to explain the surging popularity and legitimacy of Islamism. Meanwhile, nearly any Arab or Muslim can see daily images of violence in Lebanon, Iraq, and Palestine on al-Jazeera television, while Web sites, email, and cell phones bring Islamists of all types and from all regions into close contact. The largest generation of young Muslims in history is increasingly educated, informed, frustrated—and enraged. The current historical conjuncture favors Islamist social movements.

ISLAMISM AS A SOCIAL MOVEMENT: COLLECTIVE ACTION

Islamist collective action takes many forms. The most prominent would include providing social welfare, contesting elections, and engaging in armed struggle. The mix of these activities varies widely; some Islamists engage in only one type of activity, others in all three, still others in only two. Some of the *da'wa* Islamists limit themselves to social welfare provision; al-Qaeda engages only in armed conflict. The Islamic Resistance Movement of Palestine (HAMAS) and Lebanese Hizbollah engage in all three activities, while the Egyptian Muslim Brotherhood confines itself to social welfare and electoral contestation.

Social Welfare

Social welfare provision is extremely common among all political Islamists. Islamist student *jama'at* in Egypt in the 1970s and 1980s provided their members with low-cost lecture notes and textbooks, minibus transportation for (veiled) women, and access to the study groups and tutoring services necessary to pass examinations. Islamic organizations provide day-care centers, private medical clinics and even hospitals, and schools. Consider the case of Palestine. HAMAS emerged shortly after the beginning of the first *intifada* in December 1987. The progenitor of the movement, the Palestinian branch of the Muslim Brotherhood, was particularly active in promoting charity associations, religious schools, kindergartens, libraries, and sports clubs after 1967. As is true for most Islamist movements, these activities were/are funded by *zakat* (alms), *waqf* income, and contributions from abroad.[8] With such funds, the Muslim Brotherhood also built 350 mosques in the West Bank, and 400 in Gaza from 1967 to 1987 (when the first *intifada* began). HAMAS has developed an extensive, highly respected network of charitable and service organizations. Over a quarter-million (278,000 in 2000) low-income people in the occupied territories were receiving income supplements, while in Gaza alone, nearly two-thirds of all primary and pre-primary schools were funded and staffed by HAMAS. Foreign observers agree that the organization does not demand any quid pro quo of political support from beneficiaries of such largesse. They do not need to do so; the probity, dignity, and efficiency of their staffs (widely recognized by external aid agencies in the EU, for example) create a reservoir of respect and admiration among many Palestinians (ICG 2003a). Since 2000, a cycle of rising poverty (due to conflict with Israel), increasing social need, intensified Islamist social outreach, and a wider and deeper Islamist social constituency has emerged.

The performance of Hizbollah in Lebanon is even more extensive, due in part to the group's greater financial strength and freedom of action. The party maintains a "Jihad Construction Foundation," which from 1988 to 2000 conducted some 10,500 projects to rehabilitate civil war–damaged schools, homes, shops, hospitals, clinics, and mosques. The party provided approximately 45% of the potable water needs of the largely Shi'i-inhabited southern suburbs of Beirut and maintained twenty power-generation facilities. Hizbollah also provides direct-income support to those wounded in war, as well as to the families of those whose breadwinner has been killed. An Islamic Health Unit, maintained by the party, treats some 400,000 people, deploying a budget of $5 million. From 1996 to 2001, the party's educational unit spent $14.2 million on student financial aid and scholarships. Some 23,000 students benefited (Hamzeh 2004). The organization funds and staffs orphanages and a school for children with Down syndrome (Deeb 2006).

HAMAS and Hizbollah are extreme examples of how the absence of state services provides such social movements with opportunities. In Palestine, HAMAS's efficiency and probity contrast sharply with the venality and sluggishness of the Palestinian Authority (ICG 2003a; Abu-Amr 1994). The Lebanese case is more striking still: Hamzeh notes that the Lebanese government "has almost ceased to offer social welfare services" (2004, 53). The government effectively abandoned health care in the south of the country, leaving the field to Hizbollah, while the parlous state of public education in the country likewise opens important social space for collective action by the party. The destruction of the Iraqi state by the American invasion has done the same in that country.

Less dramatic than state collapse, but working in the same direction, have been the austerity programs and social welfare spending cutbacks of structural adjustment programs in Egypt, the Maghreb, and Turkey. In Yemen, religious schools, of considerable antiquity and often now allied with Islamists, educated approximately 20% of Yemeni high school students during the 1990s (ICG 2003b). Egyptian Islamist NGOs responded quickly to provide assistance after the Cairo earthquake of 1992; their performance contrasted favorably with the sluggish response of the government (Kepel 2002).

Elections

Islamist collective action increasingly includes participating in elections. At the national level, we may observe four patterns. First, Islamist parties may contest elections, win, and then be denied the reins of government, whether by physical force or financial strangulation. The FIS in Algeria provides the first example of such a phenomenon; the Palestinian election of 2006 offers the second. The FIS won the first round in the Algerian election of 1990 and was poised to sweep the field. The ruling elite *(le pouvoir)* refused to allow it, driving the Islamists underground and provoking the civil war. Nearly three-quarters of Palestinians voted in the parliamentary elections of January 2006. HAMAS won an absolute majority of parliamentary seats (74 of 132) in an election closely monitored by external (largely EU) observers.[9] The Israeli government refused to negotiate with the party, and it withheld the customs taxes that it has collected for the Palestinian Authority since the 1992 Palestinian-Israeli agreement. The United States and European Union likewise cut off all financial aid. As in Algeria, violence escalated.

A second pattern can be seen in Egypt and elsewhere. Egyptian elections are widely derided as unfair. The government controls access to media, vetoes (and sometimes arrests) candidates, stuffs ballot boxes, and forcibly breaks up opposition demonstrations. The Muslim Brotherhood is not allowed to exist legally as a political party. Many observers believe that it would win at least a plurality of seats if allowed to openly participate in a free and fair election. Despite the sharply tilted playing field, Muslim Brotherhood candidates won 12 seats in the shady election of 2005.

Jordanian Islamists also routinely complain of electoral irregularities (e.g., BBC 2003). The Moroccan PJD (Justice and Development party) won 42 of 325 seats in 2002, in an election from which the largest Islamist party, *al-'Adl wa'l Ihsan* (Justice and Charity), was banned and its leader, Abdessalam Yassin, placed under house arrest (Entelis 2002).

Two more hopeful patterns, however, are increasingly apparent. In Lebanon, Kuwait, and Yemen, relatively fair elections have been conducted. Islamist parties have vied for seats, gained representation, and then participated in parliamentary politics. Usually, they have acted as part of the parliamentary opposition (in all three cases); in one case, Lebanon in 2005–2006, Islamist parties joined the coalition government. Such a pattern was also observable in Turkey in the 1990s, when the Welfare party governed in coalition with others. The latter case, however, reverted to the first type (although without the ensuing violence) when the Turkish state forced the party from power in 1997. In Kuwait, Islamists in coalition with other reformers won a parliamentary majority in the 2006 elections; the parliament's power relative to the emir is limited, however.

So far, there is only one case of the fourth and final pattern: an Islamist party participating in an election, winning a parliamentary majority, and then forming a government and governing the country. The single case is the Turkish Justice and Development party's victory in the election of 2002 and its governance since then. Their achievements and the challenges they face are discussed in Chapter 9. In the Bahraini elections of 2002, Islamists won 24 of 40 contested seats; since the other 40 seats are appointed by the ruler, and since the king and his ministers can block any legislation, neither the Chamber of Deputies (parliament) nor the Islamists govern.

Each of these cases shows that the forms and patterns of collective action by social movements depend upon state policy. Violence is neither inevitable nor "inherent" in Islamist social movements. Everything depends on the local context, a context profoundly shaped not only by Islamists in opposition but by non-Islamists in power—as well as the behavior of powerful extraregional actors, such as the United States.

"Armed Struggle"

The old Marxist term "armed struggle" is highly apposite to many Islamist movements, suggesting the organization of violence for revolutionary political ends by a social movement. Under conditions of occupation (Palestine, Lebanon), Islamist violence is best understood as part of the long history of anticolonial violence, a history as old as colonialism itself. Furthermore, when a party wins an election, as in Algeria, and then is denied the fruits of its victory, violence will always be an option supported by many adherents to the frustrated social movement.

Resorting to violence is a political decision, however—there is nothing inevitable about it, as the behavior of the Egyptian Muslim Brotherhood since the late 1960s suggests. The Brotherhood has a violent past—first against the British colonialists and then against the Arab nationalist regime of Nasser, which violently suppressed them.

However, the Brotherhood made a strategic decision to eschew violence, regardless of regime provocations, in the early 1970s. Indeed, it was precisely this decision that prompted various young militants to split off from the Muslim Brotherhood, engage in political violence, first in the late 1970s, episodically in the 1980s, and then launch a mini-insurrection from 1992 to 1997. The insurrection was crushed by the Egyptian state, and the Muslim Brotherhood repeatedly denounced the violence of such groups as Islamic Jihad and the *Jama'a Islamiyya.* The latter responded with vitriol; among *salafi jihadis,* the term *ikhwani* ("Muslim Brother") has become a term of abuse (ICG 2005). The defeated remnants of this Egyptian insurrection joined with Osama bin Laden's forces to become al-Qaeda, while the Muslim Brothers continue to vie for seats in elections, participate in parliament, engage in public debate, and support social welfare activities.

This is hardly to suggest that political Islamists (in our terminology) are committed democrats. They view themselves as the defenders of cultural authenticity, tradition, patriarchy, and the tenets of their religion as they understand them. Many informed Westerners would describe their gender policies as misogynistic (Rouleau 2001). They are emphatically *not* ideological liberals. The same, of course, may be said of other, non-Muslim social movements rooted in religion, including the Christian Right in the United States or Christian Democracy in Europe before World War II. All such cases strongly suggest that social and historical conditions may favor, or discourage, the political choice to substitute nonviolent political competition for armed struggle. Such comparative experiences also indicate that it is not only Islamists' actions, but also the actions of their opponents, that will determine that choice.

ISLAMIST ECONOMIC THOUGHT AND PRACTICE

The Islamist movement may be usefully understood as a broad, diverse movement demanding "cultural authenticity." It seeks to change society, and governance at all levels of the society, to conform more directly with its adherents' understanding of Islam. Since these understandings diverge, the theories and applications likewise differ. Most transnational social movements have theories, and these theories are typically diverse and varied, displaying quite different emphases, concepts, specific ideas, and particular notions—all within a broadly agreed-upon framework. Such was the case for socialism and liberalism, for example. This is certainly true for Islamism, which displays very different characteristics in, for example, Turkey, Yemen, and Iran.

Theories

There is much diversity in Islamist thinking and practice concerning economic policymaking. We will consider here only two of the many strands of thinking: a general "angle of vision," exemplified by Egyptian "New Islamists," on the one hand, and the more specific movement(s) to develop "Islamic finance," both private (Islamic bank-

ing) and public (*zakat* or alms), on the other. One perspective on the differences between these two broad approaches can be found in their understanding of Qur'anic
injunctions. The New Islamists tend to interpret the message of the Qur'an as something that must be "taken as a whole"—something whose message must be understood primarily in its ethical dimension—as opposed to those who would interpret
the Qur'anic message more literally, on a sentence-by-sentence basis. Economic thinking of the latter sort originated in the Deobandi movement of India, a defensive, liter-
alist movement akin to the *salafiyya* (Kuran 2004). By contrast, the New Islamism
derives from ex-Muslim Brothers, largely middle-class professionals and religious
scholars, who take a broader, less defensive view of Islam. Although the more literal
approach may be more visible, the broader perspective may prove to be more durable.

All Islamist economic thinking stresses the social and collective nature of human
action. The myth of Robinson Crusoe, so beloved in neoclassical economics, gets
short shrift in this tradition. Thinkers such as the very influential Egyptian religious scholar Yusuf al Qaradawy (based in Qatar) rejects such atomistic individualism, arguing that humans are restricted by belief and ethics (Baker 2003). Islamists
note that all five pillars of Islam have an inherently social dimension. While Islamists are hardly collectivists—since Islam explicitly recognizes both individual
moral responsibility and approves of private property—they place much greater
stress on ethics, particularly on a concept of justice, than is typically found in orthodox economics. Although some scholars have criticized this ethical perspective
(e.g., Kuran 2004), rejection of individualism as a basis for studying society is
hardly limited to Islamists. Indeed, even within the economics profession, giants
such as Nobel Prize–winner Amartya Sen have long been at pains to go beyond notions of simple utilitarianism.

Islamist thinkers typically view humans as "regents," as beings endowed by God
with the power to make decisions over the allocation of the earth's resources. Re-
gency confers power, but also responsibility. This ethical burden falls particularly
upon the rich, who have moral obligations toward the poor. Unlike orthodox Marxism, with its dichotomy between the "bourgeoisie" and the "proletariat" (owners
and workers), Islamist thinkers typically contrast the "arrogant" *(mustakbariin)* with
the "deprived" *(mustadha'fiin)*. Islamists, in other words, do not oppose wealth, as
such. They oppose excess, display, and neglect of the underprivileged. They judge
economic policies by their outcomes and argue that meeting the basic needs of the
poor should take precedence over other criteria. They refrain from offering views on
each and every specific policy but rather tend to stress this general ethical dimension of thinking about questions of political economy.[10] They tend to be gradualists
and pragmatists (Baker 2003).

However, a danger lurks here. Ethical critiques of existing policy, and the mobilization of political forces to act on such critiques, may well be essential for protecting
the poor. Exhortations to the rest of us to "do the right thing" can be very powerful.
But if institutions are based on the notion that humans *will* act ethically, trouble is
likely to follow. The Islamist position often seems to argue that harmony and social
order will be achieved by the promotion of individual virtue—by individuals altering

their behavior to conform with Divine Revelation. However laudable such a goal may be, it is a problematic basis for public policy formation. Since the seventeenth century, Western political thinkers have abandoned the notion that religious exhortation could be relied upon to restrain destructive human behavior. The alternative advocated by St. Augustine and Calvin—repression—merely displaces the problem to the level of the sovereign. Beginning with Machiavelli and Vico and culminating in the Scottish Enlightenment and Adam Smith, we try—whenever possible—to "make private vices into public virtues." Most notably in economics, society seeks to control the social consequences of greed by pitting greed against greed. Every businessperson would love to be a monopolist; therefore, we create rules that make this very difficult. Human viciousness is taken as a given, and so we try to design institutions, to create "rules of the game," that assume that many of us (most of the time) and all of us (some of the time) will behave selfishly, perhaps even callously. Our debates then turn on when such behavior can produce socially desirable outcomes.[11]

Such, at least, is the classical liberal theory. And yet, in a world of ever more dangerous environmental externalities (e.g., carbon emissions), an increasingly monopolized mass media, and a political system often dominated by political action committees, the harmony of the invisible hand can easily seem a utopian fantasy (Gray 1998). Many contemporary Western thinkers stress the importance of community, solidarity, "law abiding as a public good," and so on. Our own perspective would be that the danger typically lies in thinking of *any* set of social arrangements as "perfect," "ideal," or "final," whether such utopianism be Islamist, Marxist, or neoliberal. And when Islamist, Marxist, or neoliberal thinkers recognize such limitations, they may then free themselves to make valuable contributions to the complex, contradictory, constantly evolving institutional framework within which we human beings pursue our disparate goals.[12]

The history of capitalism strongly suggests that the capitalism of England, or of the United States, does not offer a blueprint that other countries must follow. For example, Japanese capitalism, Korean capitalism, and Chinese capitalism have each evolved under very different institutional frameworks. Little "convergence" is visible. Much the same is likely to be the case for Islamic capitalism. Just as Christianity and Christian democracy played an important role in the evolution of German and Italian capitalism, so is it likely that Islam and Islamism (broadly conceived) are likely to shape the evolution of capitalism in MENA. Islam will likely mold standards of public and private conduct that could strengthen both economic performance and political order and liberty.

As we have seen throughout this book, however, such standards of conduct seem often observed more in the breach than in the observance throughout the region.[13] This becomes quite clear when we examine two specific experiments with self-consciously Islamic economic institutions, *zakat* and Islamic banking. In both cases, the concept is that wealth confers social responsibility; in both cases, the hope is that institutions grounded in (an interpretation of) Islamic law will channel private funds toward socially desirable purposes, whether for basic need/social safety net provision (*zakat*) or for job-creating investment in agriculture and industry (Islamic banking). In both cases, when judged by these criteria, the results have been decidedly mixed.

Islamic Charity

Zakat or giving alms is one of the five pillars of Islam. The Qur'an, however, provides only a very broad set of guidelines. Unsurprisingly, it deals with the main sources of wealth in seventh-century Arabia—farm output, livestock, precious metals, and other minerals. Prescribed rates of giving vary (from 2.5% to 20%), and there are several exemptions and special provisions. Today, *zakat* is more widely used in Muslim countries outside of MENA than in MENA itself. In Saudi Arabia, as in Malaysia and Pakistan, *zakat* is administered by the state, levied primarily on imports into the kingdom (Kuran 2004). The Yemeni constitution of 1970 (Article 135) likewise makes the state responsible for *zakat*. Local governments in the former YAR used the notion of *zakat* in taxing migrant remittances, spending the proceeds locally on badly needed physical infrastructure. Kuran noted that even the highest *zakat* tax rate, 20%, is well below the typical marginal tax rate for upper-income brackets in most OECD countries, and therefore it seems unlikely that the effect of *zakat,* when rigorously enforced, would be very equalizing. A study of the Sudan found that *zakat* payments, often delayed for months, amounted to a lump-sum payment equivalent to the subsistence needs of perhaps three days for a family of five (Chandulal 1999). Additionally, *zakat* is often voluntary, and many people do not pay. It appears that most Yemenis do not pay *zakat* (IRIN 2006), and Yemeni businessmen have lobbied to abolish *zakat* (*Yemen Times,* January 12, 1998). Evidence of evasion has been found elsewhere (e.g., Malaysia). Many Islamists seek to recentralize *zakat* and to make it compulsory (Kuran 2004). So far, however, the system has fallen far short of making any critical contribution to meeting basic needs in the region.

Islamic Banking

Perhaps the most visible attempt to forge modern Islamic economic institutions is the phenomenon of "Islamic finance." The Qur'an forbids a practice known historically as *riba'*. Although a minority position among Islamic scholars is that this injunction prohibits only usury, the majority of scholars interpret it as forbidding fixed-interest payments. The interpretation is somewhat subtle, since all agree that Islam allows time to be priced—which is what "interest" is in orthodox economic theory.[14] Islamic scholars also assert that all financial transactions should be based on real economic activity, and certain investments (e.g., in alcohol, gambling, and armaments) are prohibited (El Qorchi 2005; Kuran 2004).

The majority view has led to the rise of a large and diverse set of financial institutions and practices. Starting essentially from zero in the early 1970s, the number of Islamic financial institutions in the world has risen to more than 300 in more than seventy-five countries. The IMF estimates that total assets of the system amount to more than $250 billion and that the system is growing at 15% per year (El Qorchi

2005). During the 1970s, oil prices exploded, and conservative actors in the Gulf sought channels for their greatly increased wealth. The Organization of the Islamic Conference established the Islamic Development Bank in 1973. The first modern private Islamic bank, the Dubai Islamic Bank, was founded in 1975. At about the same time, a series of banks was founded by a holding company, the Dar al-Maal al-Islami, controlled by Prince Muhammad al-Faisal, son of King Faisal (d. 1975). The Faisal group is active throughout the Muslim world.

Islamic banking meets a strong demand of those pious depositors who wish to ensure that their money is used in a manner congruent with their understanding of their faith. International Western banks such as Banque National du Paris, Citibank, HSBC, and UBS have opened "Islamic windows" to gain access to the funds of such depositors (Henry and Wilson 2004). In international comparative terms, however, Islamic banking remains a very small, "niche product" (El Qorchi 2005, 46).[15]

The intellectual origins of modern Islamic banking can be traced to India, with the Deobandi thinker Sayyid Abul-Ala Mawdudi (1903–1979). Other major contributions were made by the father of Egyptian *jihadi salifiyya,* Sayyid Qutb, and the Iraqi Ayatollah Muhammad Baqir al-Sadr (1931–1980; the father-in-law of Muqtada al-Sadr), who was tortured and murdered by the regime of Saddam Hussein. The underlying perspective seems to be that interest payments foster inequality and injustice. Advocates of Islamic finance argue that ideally all contracts between lender and borrower should be of the profit-and-loss-sharing type; that is, equity contracts are permitted, but debt contracts are prohibited. It is legitimate to invest money in a venture in which the investor bears part of the risk of the failure of the investment, but it is not acceptable for a lender to insist on his right to a return, regardless of the outcome of the investment. One hope of Islamist economic thinkers has been that the promotion of such profit-and-loss-sharing contracts would stimulate investment in the real economy, in a manner mimicking that of venture capital. They hoped that Islamic banking would thereby contribute to economic growth and structural transformation in their societies.

Actual practice has been rather different. Most transactions (45–67%) of Islamic banks are *murabaha* contracts, an arrangement very similar to debt contracts (Yousef 2004a).[16] The contract is a purchase and resale contract; a tangible asset is bought by the bank at the request of the borrower and then resold to the customer at a previously agreed upon marked-up price. The similarities with interest payments are striking; some *ulema* have ruled that a *murabaha* contract, to be Islamically legitimate *(halal),* must include the actual, physical delivery of the commodity to the bank. In practice, this has often not occurred; the ensuing contract is simply a form of disguised interest. These contracts are far more common than the actual "equity" contracts, called *musharika*, under which the bank and the customer co-finance a project and share the profits (or the losses) of the venture (Yousef 2004; Stiansen 2004; El Qorchi 2005; Kuran 2004)

Both Tarek Yousef (2004a) and Timur Kuran (2004) explain why debt contracts are so much more prevalent than equity contracts, even for Islamic banks, in the political economic environment of MENA. Debt dominates equity as a contract form everywhere in the world. The debt-to-equity ratio in MENA (5.0) exceeds that in the OECD (3.7) but is lower than in South Asia (7.2) or Latin America (7.6) (Yousef 2004a). Debt contracts are far less information-intensive than equity contracts. Under a debt contract, the borrower need only be convinced that the debtor has collateral; in fact, under most debt contracts, the bank retains ownership of the asset and can seize it if the borrower defaults. This is not what happens under equity contracts, where the risk is jointly shared. Such considerations underlie much of the Islamist critique of interest.

But the "principal-agent" problem is severe with equity contracts, especially in countries with fragmented markets, poor information, and highly uncertain, seriously backlogged, and sometimes arbitrary litigation systems. The prevalence of "double bookkeeping"—one set for the owner, one set for the authorities—in many places compounds the difficulties of bankers' obtaining reliable knowledge about their borrowers' activities (Kuran 2004). Both Kuran and Yousef plausibly argue that these and other institutional weaknesses in MENA impede the spread of the ideal Islamic investment contracts, those of profit-and-loss sharing (Yousef 2004a).

Even *murabaha* contracts have incentive problems. What happens if the borrower fails to meet the previously agreed upon payment schedule? In principle, this should not be a problem, since the bank has taken physical possession of the commodity being financed. In practice, this rarely occurs, and the loan is secured by a financial asset. But if the borrower defaults, the bank would have to take the borrower to court; the bank would likely prevail—but because of the prohibition of interest, it would simply receive the original (that is, not marked-up) price of the good. Such a moral hazard problem plagued Islamic banking in the Sudan, for example (Siansen 2004). As with any other set of contractual forms, Islamic contracts depend for their success on a highly developed institutional environment, one characterized by transparency, probity, and relatively swift, predictable justice systems (Yousef 2004a). The weakness of these institutional features in the region help to explain the observed phenomenon of the prevalence of contracts that mimic interest payments.

The evidence suggests that Islamic banking has not been able to become the "venture capital" system that its proponents had hoped. There is also little evidence that Islamic banking has actually increased the flow of funds to agricultural or industrial activities. It seems to have been used mainly to finance import-export trade and a variety of other, relatively short-term transactions (Kuran 2004; Henry 2004). Indeed, it may also have helped to foster capital flight from the region, as wealthy pious Muslims seek to protect their wealth by investing it where it is safest—in OECD countries (Wilson 2004).

The political consequences of Islamic banking may well be more important than the immediate economic impacts. Throughout the modern Islamic financial world, a social, economic, and (sometimes) political alliance has emerged between *shari'a* scholars and bankers. Most Islamic banks have a "*shari'a* board"—an advisory committee of *ulema* who provide rulings on the legitimacy of various practices (Kahf 2004). As with all such alliances, it is founded on mutual benefits. The board helps bankers reach potential depositors, since the *ulema*'s rulings help to persuade them that placing money in such a bank is religiously sanctioned. It provides a "competitive edge" for attracting the funds of such depositors. The scholars gain both considerably enhanced income, social respectability, and a sense of achievement—they are helping to make society "more Islamic." Based on this analysis, Islamic banks have created an alliance of businessmen, middle-class lawyers, depositors, and small entrepreneurs and in so doing have helped to consolidate part of the Islamist social coalition (Kuran 2004; Henry and Wilson 2004). By some accounts, they have had a moderating influence upon it as well (Henry 2004).

ISLAMISTS IN POWER

Policymaking rarely conforms to any theory. The requirements of coalition formation and/or maintenance typically far outweigh ideological stakes in economic policy implementation. This is especially likely to be the case when the economic policies in question cause significant hardship to many people. The key determinants of economic policymaking under Islamism are the same as anywhere else: the balance of interests, the structure of institutions, and the timing of events.

So far, there exist three cases of governing Islamism: Iran, the Sudan, and Turkey. The economic, political, social, and cultural contexts in which Islamists attained power were radically different in each case. Likewise, the international alignments of each and the international and regional conjunctures at the time each acceded to power were likewise fundamentally asymmetric. Arguably, these circumstances and these conjunctures are far more important in explaining outcomes than any putatively shared "Islamist" ideology.

We considered the cases of Iran and Turkey in Chapter 9. In Iran, a violent revolution, followed by a brutal eight-year war, consolidated statist economic institutions in one of the world's major oil exporters. In Turkey, an election brought to power a party representing Anatolian business and Islamist middle and lower classes in an environment of deep financial crisis and widespread public disgust with the governing elite. Although the mission of the Islamic Republic of Iran may be to serve as a model of Islamist governance to MENA and beyond, the Justice and Development party of Turkey has sought to weaken the hold of the Atatürkist "deep state" and to join the European Union. Once again, the breadth of the Islamist tent is clearly visible, housing both the neoliberal, pro-EU Turks and the statist, go-it-alone Iranians.

The case of the only other Islamist state in the region, the Sudan, simply confirms the point. Outcomes seem best explained by the national and international contexts in which the Islamists came to power and by the social forces that the Islamists represent. Ideology has played a vital role—in this context and for the purposes of this coalition. The Islamist regime in the Sudan has, at best, engaged in crisis management since its accession to power in 1989. At worst, it has engaged in mass murder and other grotesque violations of human dignity. The picture, in short, is hardly an inspiring one.

The Sudanese context presents a geographically vast canvas. The largest country in Africa, roughly the size of the United States east of the Mississippi, it has only 3,500 kilometers of paved roads; at least 134 languages and hundreds of dialects are spoken within the country. For nearly two hundred years, it has been marked by the domination of a Nile Riverain elite of traders and merchants, Arabic-speaking Muslims who define themselves as "Arabs." The vast western and eastern regions of the country, although overwhelmingly Muslim, have only occasionally participated directly in power, even though the anti-imperialist Mahdi uprising originated in Kordofan. Conflict between the Muslim elite in the north and the non-Muslim Southern Sudanese has been endemic. It flared into open civil war, first during 1955–1972, and again during 1983–2005. The country has been described as "one of the last multinational empires on the planet" (Prunier 2005, 105). With the exception of the vast Gezira Scheme, which grows irrigated cotton along the Nile, agriculture, the occupation of most Sudanese, depends on uncertain and fluctuating rainfall. Credit is either unavailable or available on short-term, onerous terms. Poverty, illiteracy, and low life expectancy have long been the rule. The Sudan, in short, is a huge, isolated, deeply underdeveloped, politically divided, poor African country.

However, before the 1970s, the country boasted one of the best universities in Africa, a sophisticated intellectual elite, strong trade unions (particularly among the workers on the vital railroad linking the capital, Khartoum, with Port Sudan), and a reasonably competent civil service. The dictatorship of Ga'afar al-Nimeiri (1969–1985), together with other regional developments, changed all of this during the 1970s. As in so many MENA countries during the period, Nimeiri nationalized banks and factories upon taking power. He violently repressed the Sudanese Communist party, which had briefly removed him from office in a 1971 coup. Under the impact of rising oil prices, trade and budgetary deficits ballooned, and the economy deteriorated. Nimeiri turned increasingly toward the Sudanese Muslim Brotherhood for support and imposed *shari'a* on the country in 1983. The Southern rebellion immediately reignited and widespread human rights abuses ensued, including the execution of Mahmoud Muhammad Taha, a Sufi nonviolent Islamist in 1985, after a Sudanese court had pronounced him an apostate *(takfir)* (de Waal and Abdel Salam 2004). After an interregnum of ineffectual democratic rule, led by Sadiq al-Mahdi, great grandson of the Mahdi who defeated the British in 1885, and leader of the Sufi Brotherhood–based Ansar movement, a military coup in 1989 brought the Islamist forces of the National Islamic Front, led by the charismatic intellectual Hassan al-Turabi, to power.

In sharp contrast to other Islamist movements, the 1989 coup in Sudan represented almost exclusively members of the elite; there was no popular mobilization, as in Iran, Iraq, Algeria, or Lebanon (Kepel 2002; de Waal and Abdel Salam 2004). The Islamist coalition contained three elements: Islamist intellectuals, a "new middle class," and army officers (Kepel 2002; de Waal and Abdel Salam 2004). In a quasi-Leninist manner, the intellectuals, led by Turabi, provided the vanguard of this movement. With the defeat of alternatives such as the communists or Nasserists, Islamism increasingly appealed to young, educated (or semi-educated) Muslim Sudanese in the cities. Turabi, a brilliant thinker, strategist, and tactician, ensured that a network of these young people gained positions of influence in the government bureaucracy. Under his leadership, they were then ready to implement their program once the military had seized power.

The second element of the coalition was the "new middle class." These people were distinguished both by social origins and by economic activities from the older, rural power holders, largely allied with the traditional Sufi Brotherhood political parties. The new men prospered in the export-import trade, utilizing contracts in Saudi Arabia, where huge numbers of Sudanese professionals sought employment during the oil boom. Islamic financial houses, especially the Faisal Islamic Bank of the Sudan, were Islamist strongholds, employing the movement's adherents and advancing them loans (Kepel 2002; Stiansen 2004). Such patronage helped recruit still more members from the devout lower middle classes.

The final component of the coalition was a group of army officers, led by General Omar Bashir. Although Bashir was officially the leader of the regime, until 1999 many observers felt that Turabi was actually the most powerful man in the country. The army officers, already embarked on a vicious colonial counterinsurgency campaign in the South, were offered the ideological justification of *jihad* by the Islamists. They embraced the ideology enthusiastically.

This elite coalition, brought to power through a coup d'état, ruled through intimidation and violence. They made liberal use of pronouncements of *takfir* on their Muslim opponents, driving many Sudanese intellectuals into exile. Security service "ghost houses," where regime opponents were tortured, became commonplace. The government promoted the rise of local tribal militias, such as the *muraheliin* among the Baggara in Southern Kordofan, to raid, rape, and plunder Southern communities such as the Dinka and Nuba. (This policy continued later in the very different context of Darfur, with the rise of the *janjaweed*. See Box 6.1.)

The government's economic policies were in many ways the reverse of the norm during the reform era elsewhere in MENA. We saw in Chapter 9 that, in general, macroeconomic management improved, while microeconomic changes proceeded more slowly. In Sudan, however, the latter moved fairly swiftly, as Sudan decontrolled prices, privatized some 57 companies by 2000, and slashed jobs in the public sector (Musa 2000). The economy also became increasingly open to trade by ending import and export licensing and devaluing the exchange rate. All of this was implemented under a "home-grown" structural adjustment program, without any assistance or advice from the international financial institutions. Sudan had been declared in a state of "non-cooperation" with the IMF since 1990, and the country's voting rights in the IMF were suspended in 1993. The problem was Sudan's failure to service its debt.

Until the mid-1990s, macroeconomic management was dismal. Large budgetary and balance-of-payments deficits, driven by war spending, declining terms of trade, poor rainfall, dreadful transportation networks, and increasing international isolation, were covered by printing money. The result was triple-digit inflation. Data quality do not permit any firm statement on the exact inflation rate, but by 1996, it may have reached 130% (Musa 2000). Repeated currency devaluations, in an economy dependent on imports for many necessities, also contributed to inflationary pressures.

The war economy consolidated the new middle class's power. The privatization program was of the "*nomenklatura*" variety: Formerly public enterprises became the private property of regime adherents and supporters. Islamic banks (the only kind allowed) strengthened the position of their officers and clients. In the words of two leading experts, "the hyper-inflation . . . allowed the entrenchment of a new economic elite, which had invested in consumer goods bought with hard currency and Islamic banking" (de Waal and Young 2005, 3).

Beginning in the mid-1990s, this newly entrenched elite began to shift their policies. It had been known since the early 1970s that the South contained substantial oil deposits. Indeed, many saw the war there as an "oil war" (Rone 2003). But it slowly became apparent that outright military victory over the Southern People's Liberation Army (SPLA) was impossible. At the same time, the international isolation of the country under Turabi's leadership had become intense. First, Turabi supported Saddam in 1990, leading to a cut-off of Saudi support. Second, by harboring *jihadi salafis,* such as Osama bin Laden, the government of Sudan increasingly attracted the ire of the United States. The cruise-missile bombing of an alleged chemical weapons plant in 1996 was only the most dramatic evidence of this. A number of elements in the ruling coalition, particularly among the army and the wealthier Islamist business interests, began to think that a rapprochement with the West, the Saudis, and the international community would be in their interest.

An early step in this direction was the turn toward the IMF.[17] Although Sudan remained banned from funding, the IMF did advise the government in formulating a macroeconomic stabilization plan, beginning in 1996. The plan was largely successful in bringing down inflation, which had fallen to single digits by 2002. A key to enhanced budgetary balance was the beginning of significant oil exports in 1999. In that year, for the first time, Sudan had a balance-of-trade surplus. Political changes helped open the oil tap. Beginning in 1997, the government reached peace agreements with some rebel factions, and after 2000, it began to feel its way toward a deal with the SPLA. The Bush administration encouraged this and supported the Naivasha Comprehensive Peace Agreement, signed in January 2005. This agreement strengthened the security of the oil fields and pipelines, as well as moderating some of the worst human rights abuses in the South.

Part of this transition involved a power shift at the core of the regime. Turabi was removed from power in a bloodless coup in 1999. He did not go quietly, and he retains a political presence. His attempt at mobilizing support in the West, including Darfur, against Bashir and the generals, is one of the complex forces that contributed to the destruction of Darfur. The peace in Sudan is very fragile, and in Darfur, it does not exist. Elsewhere in the country, a new elite of Islamist businessmen and military officers now benefit from oil contracts, real estate investment, and joint ventures in fields such as telecommunications (de Waal and Young 2005). By 2004, the country had a debt of some $24 billion, 90% of which was in arrears (Library of Congress 2004).

To say the very least, the recent history of the Sudan presents an unedifying picture. The fundamental Islamist notion that their rule should foster greater reliance on ethical behavior seems, in the Sudanese context, something of a sick joke. Ethnic cleansing, famine, "ghost houses," pronouncements of *takfir,* and the systematic use of rape and murder as instruments of state policy square poorly indeed with pious pronouncements. Nor has corruption, that very justifiable target of Islamists in opposition, markedly decreased; in Transparency International's 2005 ranking, the Sudan ranks *last* of all MENA countries (number 144 of 159 countries worldwide, with a score of 2.1), enjoying the same level of governance as the Democratic Republic of the Congo. Recent changes are welcome; all observers can only hope that the violence in Darfur ends, that peace with the South holds, and that the benefits of the newly discovered oil will be more widely shared. The control of inflation is certainly a necessary beginning. But the inheritances of geography and history, as well as the behavior of similar coalitions of (non-Islamist) oligopolistic businessmen and military officers, inspires no confidence. Perhaps the best that may be said is that Islamist economic management in Sudan has not been significantly worse than that under Sadiq al-Mahdi or Ga'afar al-Nimeiri. However, given all the rhetoric, the gap between hopes and realities has been huge.

CONCLUSION

Is Islam the solution? Perhaps before answering, we should ask two other questions: "Was import-substituting statism the solution?" and "Was the Washington Consensus the solution?" We have argued in Chapters 7, 8, and 9 that these latter two questions may best be answered, "Well, yes—and no!" Consider the policies of the import-substituting period. The answer is "Yes!"—since under such policies, adopted everywhere in the region, basic infrastructure was constructed, a manufacturing base was built, higher educational systems (for all their faults) emerged, and historically high rates of economic growth were achieved. The answer is also "No!"—for all of the reasons outlined in Chapters 7 and 8. The same is true for the Washington Consensus policies. The answer is "Yes!"—since in many cases, the macroeconomy was stabilized, exports increased, and greater integration into the global economy was achieved. And as we saw in Chapters 5 and 9, the answer is also "No!"—since in no country have these policies managed to create enough jobs to significantly reduce unemployment, much less to dramatically raise real wages and living standards.

We suggest that history may render a similar verdict on the Islamist experiment. This diverse social movement may make important contributions to some of the many problems of development facing the region. Suitably anchored to peaceful politics, as in Turkey, it could strengthen civil society, the rule of law, and human rights. It could provide a mechanism for upward mobility for newly educated groups, consolidate greater reliance on market mechanisms, and promote greater integration into the world, where, after all, one of five human beings is Muslim. It may also succeed, where other movements have failed, in protecting a genuine national independence.

However, Islamism seems unlikely to fulfill this promise without major ideological and political changes. To the extent that the movement finds itself in increasingly sharp conflict with Israel and the United States, development will inevitably be delayed, or even reversed, as the 2006 Israeli devastation of Lebanese infrastructure suggests. Everywhere, the movement's writings have a decidedly defensive tone. Nowhere have the problems of how to relate to non-Muslim minorities been adequately theorized or put into political practice.

Islamism, like statism and neoliberalism, is a response to concrete, complex historical conditions. It is likely to ameliorate some problems and to exacerbate others. But whatever the answer to the question that forms the title of this chapter, it seems likely that those who continue to answer "Yes!" will remain central actors in the region's immediate future.

NOTES

1. *Ijtihad* is a term from Islamic law referring to independent interpretation of the Qur'an and *hadith* (sayings of the Prophet Muhammad).

2. The literature on Islamism is huge. Key works include Kepel (2002), Ruthven (2000), O. Roy (1998), and Gerges (1999); for a very useful brief overview, see ICG (2005).

3. Our typology is drawn from the work of Baker (2003), Hamzawy (2005), and ICG (2006).

4. The followers of Muqtada al-Sadr in Iraq, for example, accept the concept of *wilayat a-faqih* but, unlike the Islamists of the Iranian government, do not think that Ayatollah Khamenei should fill that post (ICG 2006).

5. *Salafi jihadis* in Afghanistan thought that the "Islamic Emirate of Afghanistan" under the Taliban was the sole legitimate and authentic Islamic government in existence at the time.

6. Many scholars trace the origins of the concept of *takfir* to the medieval theologian Ibn Taymiyya (d. 1328) (Ruthven 2000).

7. "Porters in the *shurja* (Baghdad) souk are all Sadrists, while merchants are all Sistanists (supporters of Ayatollah Sistani)." Baghdad merchant, cited in ICG (2006), p. 19, fn 136.

8. *Waqf* income refers to the income flows derived from a piece of property, inalienably granted to charity.

9. HAMAS won 44% of the popular vote; as in Turkey, the electoral system, combined with disarray among non-Islamist political parties, produced the over-representation of Islamists in the parliament. Such over-representation of minorities is a commonplace of US politics, due to constitutional structures such as the Electoral College and the Senate (Dahl 2003).

10. Some modern utilitarians would agree. Peter Singer, for example, forcefully argues that the failure of most Americans to give at least 30% of their income to the world's poor is morally indefensible (Singer 1999).

11. Kuran (2004) makes this classical liberal critique of Islamist economic thought forcefully.

12. As Ruthven concludes in his influential study of contemporary Islam: "Freed from the rigidity which makes so much Islamist activity seem culturally sterile . . . there is a message (in Islam) addressed to the whole of humanity . . . it is a message which calls on men and women to show gratitude for the world's bounty, to use it wisely and distribute it equitably. It is a

message phrased in the language and imagery of a pastoral people who understood that survival depended upon submission to the natural laws governing their environment and upon rules of hospitality demanding an even sharing of limited resources. In a world increasingly riven by the gap between rich and poor nations, and in growing danger of environmental catastrophe, this message has an urgent relevance. It is one we ignore at our peril" (Ruthven 2000, 400–401).

13. The same, of course, may be said of Western values and conduct.

14. That is, the interest rate represents the marginal rate of substitution between present and future consumption.

15. For example, hedge funds alone had an estimated value of about $1,200 billion in 2005; the market capitalization (share price times number of shares) for global stock markets is estimated at $43,600 billion in 2006 (NY Stock Exchange).

16. There are a number of other contract forms; for more detail, see El Qorchi (2005) and Kuran (2004).

17. Another step, taken in the same year, was the expulsion of Osama bin Laden.

15

REGIONAL ECONOMIC
INTEGRATION AND
LABOR MIGRATION

Middle Eastern intellectuals have long dreamed of unity. Before the rise of secular nationalism, Muslims cherished a vision of one polity under one ruler: the Dar ul-Islam, ruled by the caliph, the Prophet's successor. Such dreams live on among some *salafi* Islamists, sometimes mixed with Arab nationalist hopes for secular unity. There have been several attempts to realize these visions politically. The best known was the formation of the United Arab Republic under Nasser, when Egypt and Syria merged for three years (1958–1961). However, Nasser's reforming military regime coexisted uneasily with a Syrian polity still dominated by wealthy merchants and landlords, and the system collapsed when Syria withdrew in September 1961. More quixotic gambits emerged from Tripoli, as Qaddhafi's Libya attempted to merge with Egypt, Sudan, Tunisia, Syria, and Morocco. These ventures have puzzled political pundits and yielded very little in the way of concrete political unification.[1]

Limited regional economic intercourse contributed to these failures. Like most LDCs, MENA countries sold their goods to, purchased their imports from, and admitted capital from the developed countries of the West, not from each other—the so-called "hub-and-spoke" system. This pattern continues today, despite some evidence of a modest increase in trade integration for some countries. Flows of labor, rather than goods or capital, remain the principal mode of regional economic integration. These flows have themselves been subject to considerable changes in recent years, but they remain critically important to the region's political economy.

A simple measure of integration is the movement of goods and factors of production across national boundaries in the region. Using exports as a measure of trade integration, a recent thorough study of the phenomenon finds that MENA trade integration changed little during the 1970s (from 6.0% of total exports in 1970 to 6.1% in 1980), rose during the 1980s (to 10.8% in 1990), but then fell modestly to 8.2% in 1998 (Miniesy et al. 2003). Using the standard "gravity model" of international trade theory, the authors of the study found that intraregional trade was lower than what would have been predicted on the basis of income levels; indeed, they argue that the creation of a regional free-trade association would more than double the percentage of intraregional trade.

Trade within subgroups of the region—Mashreq, Maghreb, and GCC—is higher. One obvious reason for the difference is lower transportation costs, but another factor is greater similarity in per capita income levels. One reason why GCC states import relatively few goods from other countries in the region is that the inhabitants of these oil states are sufficiently wealthy to be able to afford goods from anywhere in the world. They tend to buy what they regard as the best goods available, which usually do not come from neighboring countries. But such differences are not the entire story; the income levels within the Maghreb countries are also substantial, yet the proportion of intraregional trade there doubled between 1970 and 1985 (Miniesy et al. 2004).

Limited intraregional trade was not from lack of trying. Literally hundreds of bilateral trade agreements have been signed (Miniery et al. 2004). Probably the most significant agreements have been at the subregional level. The Gulf Cooperation Council (GCC), formed in 1981, and the Arab Maghreb Union, formed in 1989, are the two most important trade agreements.

However, the most significant trade treaties continue to be those negotiated with the World Trade Organization, the European Union, and to a lesser extent, the United States. Eleven countries in MENA have joined the WTO; six others are in various stages of application.[2] In addition, association agreements with the European Union are highly significant for Algeria, Morocco, and Tunisia, while the continuing national project to join the European Union remains a fundamental force in the political economy of Turkey. The same is true for investment agreements: MENA countries have signed nearly twice as many of these agreements with OECD countries than with each other (142 compared with 75). (MENA-OECD Investment Programme 2005). The "hub-and-spoke" system remains highly durable.

Integration of factor markets has gone farther. Governments have dominated the investment process in most countries, whatever the official ideology. The major oil-exporting countries spent most of their increased incomes between 1974 and 1984 on their own internal-investment projects. Most of the surplus was held in short-term liquid assets in the OECD countries, but some money was channeled toward their poorer neighbors as economic aid—both direct, bilateral assistance, and contributions to "development funds" and other multilateral agencies. Generally speaking, increasing domestic spending programs and (by the mid-1980s) plummeting real oil prices slashed such aid as a percentage of the donor's GNP. The Gulf War and the ensuing massive deficits in Saudi Arabia further reduced such assistance, but even in 1993 the Saudi government was giving away proportionally 80% more of its national income than the most generous OECD donor, Norway.[3] Such aid made up a large proportion of total investment in recipient countries between 1973 and 1987.[4] Saudi largesse continued even during the long period of low oil prices (roughly, 1986–1999). In 2003, the Saudis gave away some $2.4 billion, about 1% of their

GNI—compared with a rich country average of only 0.25% (World Development Indicators Online).

The various private, public, and mixed banks in the region engaged in lending to LDCs gave preference to other MENA countries and countries in the wider Islamic world. Lending policies have typically been conservative, concentrating on areas where managers already have some expertise, such as petroleum refining, tourism, and real estate.

Perhaps the most notable attempts to use capital as an instrument of economic integration have been the region's various development funds. The earliest of these, the Kuwait Fund for Arab Economic Development, was founded in 1961, followed by the Arab Fund for Economic and Social Development, established by the Arab League in 1968, and the Abu Dhabi Fund for Arab Economic Development, founded in 1971. These funds are run along the lines of the World Bank, extending loans for development projects ranging from railroads and fertilizer plants to sewage and water supply systems to livestock and crop production schemes.

The Arab Fund has had the most self-consciously political agenda. In addition to making development loans to specific countries, it has sought to promote the regional economy in at least three ways. First, it has invested in the Pan-Arab Communications Network, including the development of an Arab communications satellite. Second, it has promoted the development of the Arab Military Industrialization Organization to manufacture weapons for Arab armies. The international aspects of this project were terminated by the Camp David Accords, leaving Egypt to go it alone (see Chapter 13). Given its relatively large and well-developed industrial sector, much investment had concentrated on Egypt, but when Egypt was expelled from the Arab League this evaporated. Third, the Arab Fund established the Arab Authority for Agricultural Investment and Development (AAAID), allocating investments toward the Sudan in an attempt to reduce regional dependence on imported grain and sugar.

These activities did not work particularly well. Yet they had some impact, and until the Gulf War, the political commitment to their long-range goals was unshaken. For example, AAAID mounted projects in the Sudan involving mechanized farming, poultry production, sorghum and oil seeds production, vegetable farming, and dairy production. By its own account, these projects suffered from serious management problems and remained unprofitable. Public-sector managers and university experts initially oversaw operations—an unfortunate choice, since neither group had much experience in running enterprises that needed to show a profit. Plans to alter the situation were temporarily disrupted when the Sudan supported Iraq against Kuwait and Saudi Arabia in 1990–1991. However, the rupture was only temporary, and by 2005, some 88% of AAAID's loans went to companies in the Sudan (AAAID 2005).

In summary, deliberate attempts to integrate the political economies of the region at the levels of the state, trade flows, and capital and investment have shown only modest success. Far more important has been the unplanned, market-driven integration of labor markets. Indeed, labor migration on a historically unprecedented scale has been a fundamental force in transforming national political economies even as it has integrated the most remote areas of the most backward countries into the regional economy. But, as we shall see, the boom years of labor migration have passed and seem unlikely to return.

LABOR MIGRATION: AN OVERVIEW

Severe issues with the accuracy of data plague all estimates of the magnitude of migration. For labor migration, the data typically count inflows, not outflows. They usually enumerate work permits rather than persons, making no allowance for multiple entries. They also suffer from a variety of other difficulties, including, as always, the underreporting of illegal migration, which all agree is substantial. Moreover, different countries use different definitions for "visitor," "short-term migrant," and "long-term resident foreigner." The distinction between "temporary" and "permanent" migrant is contentious, as is that between "economic migrant" and "refugee." Although some of these problems bedevil EU statistics on MENA immigrant labor, they are especially severe in the data on labor migration to the major oil-exporting countries of the Persian Gulf.

Unsurprisingly, then, estimates of the magnitude of migration and refugees vary widely. For example, the number of economic migrants (the overwhelming majority of all migrants) in GCC states in 2000 has been variously estimated at between 9.5 million (ESCWA 2006) to 12.5 million (Kapiszewski 2004). The CIA estimates the number of foreign workers in Saudi Arabia in 2005 at about 5.5 million, while other sources (e.g., Kapiszewski) put the number at closer to 7 million. Some of these differences may be due to imprecise definitions; labor-force numbers are likely lower than total migrant population numbers, because, although most migrants to the GCC are single males, inevitably some dependents come to live there as well. The numbers of illegals is substantial; de Silva and Silva-Jauregui (2004) estimated the number at approximately 60,000 in Kuwait in 2006. Saudi Arabia deports some 700,000 unauthorized migrants (usually Muslim pilgrims who overstay their visas) every year. The UAE proclaimed an amnesty for illegals in January–April 2003, exempting the estimated 300,000 illegal workers from fines (*Migration News,* February 2003). All migration statistics should be treated as rough estimates.

Despite these data issues, the broad outlines of the phenomenon are clear. By global standards, MENA migration is very large. The UN estimates that the Arab Region contains 20 million migrants in total and that this number increased by 7 million from 1990 to 2005 (ESCWA 2006). This number appears to include refugees; most other sources place the figure for labor migration at about 10–12 million. Significantly, at least one-third of all migrants, and roughly two-thirds of all economic migrants are in Saudi Arabia. In addition, more than 3 million Maghrebis, and about that number of Turks, live in the European Union.

Refugee populations in the region are also considerable. The largest in terms of both numbers and political impact is the Palestinian refugee population. Some 4.3 million are registered by the United Nations Relief and Works Agency (UNRWA); another 241,000 are registered in Saudi Arabia (Baldwin-Edwards 2005). Several million Sudanese refugees live in Egypt, mainly in and near Cairo. Estimated numbers vary from a low of 15,000 (CIA 2006) to a high of 5 million (Baldwin-Edwards 2005). There are some 100,000 Sahrawis in Algeria and just under 1 million (down from over 2 million) Afghan refugees in Iran.[5]

Labor migration in MENA can be roughly divided into two "streams" and three "tiers," delineating the direction of regional migration. The two distinctly different streams are the migration flows to the European Union, on the one hand, and flows to the GCC states, on the other. The three tiers apply to the various countries receiving or sending migrant laborers: Tier 1 is made up of the major receiving countries of the European Union and the GCC states; Tier 2 consists of sending-and-receiving countries, which send workers to Tier 1 countries and receive migrants from poorer countries; Tier 3 consists of those poor, sub-Saharan African countries (e.g., Mali, Somalia) that send workers to Tier 2 countries. Countries in the second tier that contribute workers to the GCC include Egypt, Jordan, Lebanon, and Yemen; those in the second tier that send workers to the European Union include Algeria, Morocco, Tunisia, and Turkey. Regional migration has become increasingly complex over time. For example, Yemen, which sends approximately 400,000–500,000 workers to GCC countries, now hosts more than 70,000 Somali refugees. In North Africa, 63,000–80,000 African migrants pass through the Maghreb seeking entry to the European Union every year (League of Arab States 2005).

THE FIRST STREAM:
TO THE EUROPEAN UNION

The older of the two streams is the migration of Maghrebis and Turks to Western Europe. Migration from Morocco and Algeria dates back at least to World War I. However, the real boom in such migration dates to the 1960s and early 1970s, when rapid economic growth attracted large numbers of Algerians, Moroccans, and Tunisians to France and Holland (for Moroccans), as well as Turks to Germany. The Maghrebi population of France increased by about 60,000 people every year from 1968 to 1975. The flows subsequently decelerated (to about 45,000 per year in 1975–1982, and to about 30,000 per year in 1982–1990) but nevertheless remained positive. Huge wage gaps between sending and receiving countries were the fundamental drivers of migration.

During the 1990s, the total North African population of Belgium, France, and Holland—the earlier receiving countries—actually declined slightly. However, large increases in migration to other European countries, mainly of Moroccans to Italy and Spain, more than compensated for the decline in the more traditional receiving countries. Between 1985 and 1999, the number of North Africans in Spain rose from 6,000 to 214,000, of which 90% were Moroccan. While economic slowdown, combined with increasingly anti-immigrant political pressures, slowed and then marginally reversed immigration to the northern countries (Belgium, France, and Holland), economic growth, combined with proximity and extremely long and difficult-to-police coastlines, stimulated migration into Italy and Spain. The combination of high unemployment among Spanish nationals (between 15% and 25% in the 1990s) and continued Moroccan immigration suggests considerable labor-market segmentation, in which migrants fill jobs that nationals are unwilling to perform. (A similar pattern exists in the Gulf countries, which we discuss below.) Illegal migration into Spain and Italy, often by boat, has not been without risk; it is estimated that 17,000 people drowned while trying to cross the Strait of Gibraltar during 1993–2000 (League of Arab States 2005). Today, there are an estimated 1.4 million Moroccans, 1.3 million Algerians, and 436,000 Tunisians living in the European Union (de Silva and Silva-Jauregui 2004).

The phenomenon of migration boom followed by deceleration, or "maturing" of migration flows from sending to receiving countries, also occurred in Germany. The growth in the number of Turkish "guest workers" *(Gaestarbeiter)* surged along with the economic boom in (then) West Germany during the 1960s but then subsequently decelerated. In 1972, there were about 2.6 million Turks in the European Union; today there are perhaps 3.2 million. Of these, some 2.7 million live in Germany, where they face significant problems of integration. The Turkish government has estimated that in 2001, emigration had slowed to about 10,000 emigrants per year (Aslan 2005). Two further changes in Turkish immigration trends should be noted. First, during the oil-boom years, significant numbers of Turks participated in migration to Gulf countries. Second, during the past fifteen years, Turkey itself has attracted migrants, particularly Iraqis, Iranians, and Afghans seeking to obtain entry, whether legal or illegal, into the European Union. Every year, the Turkish authorities apprehend some 90,000 would-be illegal immigrants (Baldwin-Edwards 2005).

THE SECOND STREAM: TO THE GULF

As with the first stream, migration to the Gulf is driven by the huge gap in wages between sending and receiving countries. During the late 1970s an unskilled rural Egyptian could earn *thirty times* more money working at a Saudi construction site than he could on an Egyptian farm. Jordanian engineers could double or triple their incomes by going to Kuwait. Migration remains an excellent investment for workers from poorer countries. The low wages in the sending countries were caused by low productivity in agriculture and the failure of previous industrialization to absorb surplus labor. The cause of the upward spiral of wages in the oil countries was equally straightforward: The demand for labor shot up, while domestic labor supply was limited by economic, social, and political factors.

On the demand side, the explosion of oil prices in the 1970s flooded the treasuries of the oil-exporting states, which then launched ambitious development plans and investment projects. These led to huge increases in the demand for labor of all types, from construction laborers to computer programmers, from doctors to doormen. However, demography and sociopolitical factors constrained domestic labor supply. The Gulf States and Libya had (indeed, still have) small, young populations. Generally, at least 40% of the indigenous population was less than fifteen years old, and more than half were under twenty. Consequently, the economically active population and the domestic labor supply were limited. Limited female participation in the labor force further exacerbated the shortage of domestic workers in the oil-exporting states. Often, males of working age were illiterate and unskilled, and those few who were skilled were often attracted to public-sector employment, especially in the armed forces. Finally, government subsidies of food, housing, medical care, and transportation reduced the incentive for local people to take unpleasant or difficult jobs. Meeting from domestic sources the huge demand for labor that the 1970s oil boom stimulated was simply impossible. Foreigners were needed, and they came in unprecedented numbers.

This is not to say that migration in the region began with the oil boom. The modern history of migration in the region can be roughly divided into four phases. During the first phase, prior to 1974, more than 80% of immigrating workers were Arabs, mainly Egyptians, Syrians, Yemenis, and Palestinians. The major characteristics of the Gulf labor market during this period were the relatively narrow wage differentials between sending and receiving countries and the high skill level of many migrant workers. Further, Iraq and Oman, which became major labor importers during the 1980s, were net exporters of manpower.

The second phase began with the oil-price increase of 1974. During this period the absolute numbers of Arab immigrant workers rose dramatically, with immigration from poorer countries such as Egypt, the Sudan, and the Yemens being especially prominent. The number of expatriates working in the Gulf States (excluding Iraq and Iran) rose from 1.1 million in 1975, to 2.8 million in 1980 (Girgis 2002). Further oil-price increases in 1979 approximately doubled government revenues in a single year, stimulating still more ambitious development plans and projects and even more generous social-welfare programs. By 1985 the number of expatriates in the GCC countries had risen to some 4.1 million, while the number of migrant workers in Iraq, locked in the long war with Iran, had increased more than ten times, to about 750,000. The number of expatriate workers in Libya had risen from just under 50,000 in 1973 to more than 400,000 in 1980, by which time they constituted about one-third of that country's labor force (Sherbiny 1984). Despite the data issues, there is little question that the most rapid expansion of labor migration in the Gulf occurred during the 1970s oil-boom years.

In addition to the increase in the total number of workers, two other trends stand out during this period. First, the share of Arab migrant workers in the total expatriate workforce declined as Indians, Pakistanis, Sri Lankans, and other Asian workers flocked to the region. Not only was the wage gap even greater for these countries than for some of the poorer Arab countries, but Gulf States often preferred these workers. This tendency accelerated greatly after 1991 (see below). As non-Arabs, they were believed to be less likely to stay in the Gulf and were perceived as politically safer than potentially recalcitrant Egyptians, Yemenis, Lebanese, and Palestinians. Second, the growth of demand for unskilled labor slowed as major infrastructural projects were completed, while that for skilled workers to operate the completed projects accelerated. This trend has persisted up to the present.

The fall in oil revenues by the mid-1980s curtailed some development projects in the region. In turn, the demand for foreign workers decelerated in some countries, while the composition of demand continued to shift toward more skilled workers. The oil-price collapse of 1986 slashed the value of construction contracts in the region by 25% from 1986 to 1987 (*South,* September 1987, 65). However, only Iraq, fighting a major war, had actually reduced its labor imports. By contrast, the stock of workers in Saudi Arabia rose by about 1 million from 1980 to 1985. This is not surprising; the kingdom's Third Development Plan of this period allocated even more funds for development projects than had the previous one. Numbers for other countries are shown in Table 15.3. The growth of immigration decelerated in the early 1980s (growing by about 8% per year in 1980–1985) and slowed further in the "oil crunch" of the late 1980s (growth of about 3% per year in 1985–1990), but by the end of the 1980s there were 2 million more foreign workers (a total of 5.2 million, some two-thirds of the labor force) in the Gulf than there had been in 1980.

The third phase began with the Iraqi invasion of Kuwait in August 1990. Operation Desert Storm tore asunder the web of intraregional labor and remittance flows—some 2 million workers were directly affected by the crisis. An estimated 800,000 to 1 million Yemenis, 200,000 Jordanians, and 150,000 Palestinians were expelled from Saudi Arabia and the Gulf, and nearly all of the Sudanese in Saudi Arabia were expelled. In addition, some 700,000 Egyptians fled Iraq, Kuwait, and Jordan. Countries such as Jordan, the Sudan, and Yemen, as well as the PLO, which backed Iraq, paid dearly for opposing the Saudis and the Americans.

From 1990 to 1995, the number of foreign migrants in Kuwait and Saudi Arabia fell. However, the numbers in other Gulf States (Bahrain, Qatar, UAE) continued to increase, and after 1995, net immigration into Saudi Arabia and Kuwait likewise resumed (ESCWA 2006). Egyptian emigration resumed quickly, bolstered by demand in Saudi Arabia and in Libya. In 1994, there were about 2.5 million Egyptians abroad, some 25% more than in 1987. By 2005, Saudi Arabia was hosting some 1.6 million more foreign workers than in 1990 (ESCWA 2006). Although many migrants never returned to Saudi Arabia, even from hard-hit countries like Yemen, there is evidence of some resumption of labor migration; estimates of the numbers of Yemenis in Saudi Arabia range from 500,000 to 1 million (ESCWA 2006; Kapiszewski 2004). However, there is little doubt that two trends that began with the expulsions of 1990 have continued: (1) "Asianization," and (2) "nationalization" of the labor force.[6]

The fourth phase is that of the past ten years or so. During this period, migration flows to the Gulf, like those to the European Union, "matured"; that is, inflows decelerated and the composition of immigrants shifted. The decline in the proportion of Arabs is most marked in the case of Kuwait. Whereas Arab migrants made up 59% of the foreign population in Kuwait in 1989, by 2001 they constituted only 45%. By contrast, Asians constituted 67% of the total Kuwaiti labor force in 2000, up from 54% in 1989. From 1989 to 2000 the number of Asians rose by about 250,000, while the number of Arabs fell by 30,000. Of the estimated 12.5 million migrants in the GCC, more than 7 million are Asians, mainly from India (3.2 million), Pakistan (1.7 million), Bangladesh (820,000), the Philippines (730,000), and Sri Lanka (705,000). Asians have been preferred not only because of their greater political docility, but also because they are willing to accept lower wages and poorer working conditions than Arab workers.

The influx of Asians does not mean, however, that large numbers of non-national Arabs are not employed in the Gulf. Nearly 1.5 million Egyptians, 250,000 Sudanese, 480,000 Jordanians, 265,000 Syrians, and perhaps 1 million Yemenis work there today (Kapiszewski 2004). A whole range of skills are utilized, but, in general, unskilled work and domestic service in the Gulf today is largely performed by Asians, while Arabs tend to be found more in the semi-skilled and skilled tasks. For example, roughly 40% of Egyptians employed in Saudi Arabia today are scientific and technical workers; unskilled Egyptians tend to migrate to Jordan, Lebanon, and (before 2003) Iraq (Baldwin-Edwards 2005). A recent matrix of migration to the Gulf is shown in Table 15.1.

All data cited thus far refer to the stock of workers in a country at any one time. The total number of workers who have *ever* participated in work abroad is obviously much larger than the stock in any one year. Data on the turnover of workers do not exist. However, if the average length of stay abroad is two to three years, the total number of workers who had ever emigrated for employment between 1974 and 1988 would have been four to seven times larger than the stock of workers in 1974, even assuming that the stock remained constant. By even our conservative

TABLE 15.1   Foreign Workers in the Gulf States, 2002

Country of Origin	Bahrain	Kuwait	Oman	Qatar	Saudi Arabia	UAE	Total
India	100,000	295,000	300,000	100,000	1,400,000	1,000,000	3,200,000
Pakistan	50,000	100,000	70,000	70,000	1,000,000	450,000	1,740,000
Egypt		275,000	15,000	35,000	1,000,000	130,000	1,455,000
Yemen					1,000,000	35,000	1,035,000
Bangladesh		160,000	110,000		450,000	100,000	820,000
Sri Lanka		160,000		35,000	350,000	160,000	705,000
Philippines		60,000		50,000	500,000	120,000	730,000
Jordan/Palestine		50,000		50,000	270,000	110,000	480,000
Syria		95,000			170,000		265,000
Iran	45,000	80,000		20,000		40,000	145,000
Indonesia					250,000		250,000
Sudan					250,000		250,000
Kuwait					120,000		120,000
Turkey					100,000		100,000
Total	280,000	1,475,000	630,000	420,000	7,000,000	2,488,000	

SOURCE: Estimates from Baldwin-Edwards 2005

estimates, however, the stock roughly tripled during this period. A majority of the males of some countries, such as Yemen, have worked in Saudi Arabia at least once. A survey of over 1,000 rural Egyptian families found that one-third of all males had worked abroad, mainly in Iraq (Adams 1991). One estimate places the number of Egyptians who migrated at any time during 1973–1985 at 3.5 million, roughly one-third of the labor force (Fergany 1988). The socioeconomic consequences of migration are much larger and the benefits probably much more widely shared than the numbers in the tables suggest.

In all countries the vast majority of these migrants are young adult males. For example, an ILO study of Sudanese migrants found that over 90% were men and over 60% were between eighteen and thirty years old (Berar-Awad 1984). A survey in Egypt found that the average age was thirty-two (Fergany 1988). Similar patterns have been observed in the former YAR and Jordan. By contrast, the educational and occupational composition of migrants varies markedly across countries. Emigrants from the Sudan and Jordan are largely skilled. The ILO survey found that only 11% of Sudanese migrants were illiterate, compared with a national illiteracy figure of over 75%; about 63% of the migrants in the sample possessed some skills (Berar-Awad 1984). Relatively skilled workers tend to predominate among non-Arab Asian labor, although there are many low-skilled service workers (cleaners, maids). However, emigrants from the former YAR were overwhelmingly unskilled and rural; the World Bank estimated that between two-thirds and three-fourths of the half-million Yemenis abroad in 1982 were from rural areas (World Bank 1986c). Still other countries occupy an intermediate position; a 1984 survey of Egyptian migrants found that although nearly half (49%) had at least a secondary education, 31% (and 54% of rural migrants) were illiterate (al-Hanidi 1988). We have seen that skilled and unskilled Egyptian workers have increasingly gone to different countries during the past ten to fifteen years. During the past ten years, a pattern of differentiation is increasingly visible in the Gulf, with unskilled jobs going overwhelmingly to South Asians, intermediate levels to Arab migrants (and at highly variably increasing rates, to nationals), and the upper tiers reserved for nationals (and, sometimes, their expatriate European and American advisers).

THE IMPACT OF LABOR
MIGRATION ON SENDING COUNTRIES

The impact of labor migration on sending countries is much debated, and although the controversy is heated, it is often unenlightening. Poor data and conflicting values ensure that the controversy will continue. Nevertheless, some general points can be made.

The *private* benefits of emigration are evident. Presumably, if the benefits were not extensive, people would not go, particularly over decades. The fundamental force driving the private decision to migrate is the huge gap between local and foreign wages. This gap is especially large for unskilled, rural workers who obtained construction jobs, as in the Egyptian example, but it is also large for skilled and technical workers. Although immigrant workers often have to finance travel abroad, these costs are reduced by labor contractors and by various informal information systems that typically involve whole villages and urban neighborhoods. Some analysts of labor migration stress that the appropriate unit of analysis is not the individual but the household: One or two members may be selected to seek work abroad while others remain behind to tend the store or the farm, to retain government jobs, and so forth (Stark 1983). This means that migrant workers can better afford an extended job search, thus reducing the riskiness of unemployment and increasing the incentive to migrate. This household strategy has been employed by millions of Middle Eastern families, and it seems undeniable that in most cases it has improved the welfare of the emigrant's family.

However, assessing the *social* costs and benefits of labor migration is much more contentious. This debate can be decomposed into a dispute about the net social benefits of three aspects of the migration process: "people out" (emigration), "money back" (remittances), and "people back" (return migration).

Emigration, or "People Out"

Perhaps the central question in debate over emigration is its impact on employment and its role in creating labor shortages. Those who applaud the migration phenomenon argue that emigration has acted as a safety valve for the sending countries' labor markets by providing jobs for the unemployed. The critics counter that most migrants were already employed and maintain that emigration has fostered labor shortages that have impeded development.

In assessing these arguments it is important to distinguish between different types of labor. Unquestionably, migration has been very beneficial for relatively unskilled workers, thereby reducing levels of unemployment and increasing wages for the underprivileged. Although some seasonal, short-term labor bottlenecks may have been created, there is little evidence that such phenomena reduced output even at the peak of the oil/migration boom. The fall of unskilled wages and the upsurge in poverty in Egypt after 1986 and in Jordan and Yemen after 1990 dramatically illustrate the importance of emigration in a context of rapid growth of labor supply (see Chapter 4) and sluggish increases in domestic demand (see Chapters 8 and 9). One study found that, worldwide, a 10% increase in emigration reduced absolute poverty (income equivalent to less than $1 per day) by 1.9% (Adams and Page 2003). Emigration (combined with remittances) lifted 1.2 million Moroccans out of poverty in 2002 (Sorensen 2004). However, although emigration may also have helped to alleviate the chronic unemployment of university graduates, the "brain drain" made it very difficult for the public sector in poorer countries to find qualified skilled personnel. These shortages and the continual turnover of highly trained people contributed to the woes of the public sector.

Although it is true that migrants often come from the ranks of domestically employed workers, some evidence from Morocco suggests that, increasingly, unemployed people are emigrating to the European Union (de Silva and Silva-Jauregui

2004). Even if migrants are leaving jobs in their home countries for jobs abroad, their departure creates new openings for those who remain behind. From 1975 to 1985, emigration for work fueled the most dramatic growth of agricultural real wages in Egypt's modern history, with striking impacts on rural poverty. Similar ripple effects have been noted in Jordan and Morocco. Evidence of such benefits can also be seen in Tunisia and Yemen. In light of today's serious unemployment problems, the debate about economic migration causing labor shortages is revealed for what it was: the conflation of a temporary disequilibrium with a long-run structural problem.

Although emigration of adult males from rural areas of the region during the oil-boom era may have created certain short- to medium-term adjustment problems, there is little evidence that it produced labor shortages sufficient to constrain the growth of agricultural production. The same point holds for the exit of unskilled urban workers; there is simply no evidence that unskilled-labor shortages have retarded industrial growth or the building of infrastructure in the region. The emigration of unskilled labor has created far more benefits than costs for the sending countries.

This is not to say that emigration could, should, or will single-handedly solve the serious labor market problems of the region. One analysis from the World Bank (de Silva and Silva-Jauregui 2004) argues that since emigrants from Morocco to the European Union make up "only" 4.4% of the labor force, emigration does not "solve" the unemployment problem. This is obviously true. However, the unemployment rate in Morocco is close to 12%, according to the same authors. It seems likely that unemployment would be significantly higher, and wages lower, without emigration. After all, like any price, wages (the price of labor) are set at the margin. The departure of workers almost certainly contributes to ameliorating the very difficult labor-market problems of the region (consider, for example, the 8–10% of the Egyptian labor force that is working abroad).

Assessing the balance of social costs and benefits for the emigration of skilled manpower is somewhat more complicated, at least for the 1970s oil-boom era. By definition, skills cannot be reproduced overnight. Accordingly, the supply of skilled workers is relatively inelastic. As a general rule, the greater the skill, the longer the period of necessary training and therefore the greater the interval of shortages induced by emigration. However, as conventional economic theory would predict, these shortages seem to have been fairly brief, as the ever-increasing number of new labor-force entrants replaced the departed migrants. Many teachers, engineers, computer programmers, and high-level managers went to work in the Gulf States. The domestic private sector could compete with Gulf State employment much more successfully than the public sector. There is little evidence that private construction activity in Egypt, for example, had difficulties attracting and retaining highly qualified professionals such as engineers and architects. By contrast, the public educational system of that country witnessed a massive outflow of teachers. Labor migration may also adversely affect higher education; some university faculties at Cairo University (e.g., economics, statistics, commerce) had up to one-third of their regular faculty abroad during the late 1970s. By the mid-1990s, however, all such effects had been swamped by the rising tide of job seekers, and the same situation obtains today.

In summary, the impact of emigration was on balance beneficial to the economies of the sending countries. Millions of unskilled workers and their families improved their living standards; there is little reason to believe that economic growth would have been more rapid in these countries had these workers remained at home; with the exception of the emigration of the most skilled professionals, especially from the poorest countries such as the Sudan, the so-called labor shortages have been largely seasonal, short-run disequilibria. Emigration lowers unemployment, raises wages, and reduces poverty in the sending countries of the MENA region.

Remittances, or "Money Back"

Workers go abroad to earn and save money, which they hope to bring back home. They usually succeed. Some official estimates of the magnitude of remittances in selected countries of the region are shown in Table 15.2. Even after the economically devastating Gulf War started in 1990, remittances remained a crucial source of foreign exchange in the region. Indeed, remittances, estimated at some $15 billion in 2001 dwarf both foreign direct investment (about $3 billion) and official development assistance ($6 billion) for the region (Kapur 2003). For Yemen and Egypt the value of remittances exceeded that of any commodity exports. Remittances often paid for a substantial fraction of imports, especially in Egypt, Jordan, Morocco, and Yemen. On the eve of the Gulf War of 1990–1991, remittances to Egypt were the equivalent of 10% of that country's GDP, and in Yemen, remittances exceeded one-third of GDP. Lebanese remaining in their country at the end of the civil war subsisted primarily on remittances, which were the equivalent of two-thirds of Lebanon's GDP. It is important to note that although the magnitude of remittances relative to GDP has fallen in the Mashreq (largely the source of migration to the Gulf), the impact of remittances on the economies of the Maghreb (whose emigrants go primarily to the EU) has increased in relative importance. Note also that with the important exceptions of Egypt and Yemen, the total value of remittances rose between 1990 and 2004. However, some evidence points to the existence of "boom-and-bust" cycles for remittances, particularly for Egypt and Jordan (Yousef 2005).

Official figures for remittances represent only the tip of the iceberg. Much money enters labor-exporting countries through unofficial channels (Choucri 1986). For example, only about 13% of remittances to the Sudan from Saudi Arabia and Kuwait in the early 1980s came through national banks; between half and three-fourths of the total value of remittances were simply carried by hand (Berar-Awad 1984). Applying this ratio to national figures would mean that total Sudanese remittances in 1985 exceeded US$1.9 billion rather than the official US$259 million.

Although the extreme weakness of the Sudanese banking system and the gross overvaluation of the Sudanese pound in 1985 may make that country's experience unusual, a qualitatively similar phenomenon has been observed in other countries

TABLE 15.2   Remittance Flows, Selected Countries, 1990 and 2004

	Remittances (millions of US dollars)		Remittances as percentage of GDP	
	1990	2004	1990	2004
MAGHREB	**2,909**	**8,118**	**2.3**	**4.6**
Algeria	352	2,460	0.6	3.0
Libyan Arab Jamahiriy[a]	0	8	0.0	0.0
Morocco	2506	4,218	7.8	8.5
Tunisia	551	1,432	4.5	5.1
MASHREQ	**6,986**	**9,823**	**11.7**	**6.7**
Egypt	4,284	3,341	10.2	3.8
Jordan	499	2,287	12.4	21.1
Lebanon	1,818	2,700	64.7	13.5
Occupied Palestinian Territory	..	692	..	20.2
Syrian Arab Republic	385	803	3.6	3.4
Yemen[b]	1,498	1,283	3.69	9.8
GULF STATES	**39**	**40**	**0.0**	**0.0**
Oman	39	40	0.3	0.2

NOTES:
[a]Remittances include workers' remittances, compensation of employees and migrants' transfers.
[b]Yemen not included in the total for Mashreq.
SOURCE: Global Economic Prospects 2006: Economic Implications of Remittances and Mitigation, World Bank. United Nations, Department of Economic and Social Affairs, Population Division 2006

where national currencies were seriously overvalued (e.g., the former YAR, Jordan, Syria, and Egypt). Turkish remittances covered over 60% of the country's trade deficit in 1994 but then fell to some 20% in 2000—during the years of accelerating inflation, overvaluation of the currency, and financial crisis (see Chapter 9). Although Egypt's financial issues were somewhat less severe in the late 1990s, there also we have seen that the currency remained significantly overvalued. Perhaps unsurprisingly, some estimates of Egyptian unofficial remittances are more than double the official flows ($4 billion versus $1.5 billion; Kapiszewski 2004). By contrast, sound macroeconomic and financial management in Morocco ensured that most remittances moved through the banking system (de Haas 2005). Macroeconomic and financial management matters hugely for maximizing the benefits of remittances.

Critics of the effects of remittances at the macroeconomic level sometimes focus on their alleged tendency to be spent on imports rather than domestic production and their contribution to inflation. However, the two effects are mutually exclusive: If money is being spent on foreign goods, it should have no impact on domestic inflation. To the extent that domestic supply can respond to the increased demand, the result should be economic growth rather than simply inflation. Workers' remittances are hardly responsible for the constraints to expanding domestic output, which are often induced by inappropriate government policies. The way in which money enters the system could contribute to inflation. To the extent that remittances move outside of the banking system, the government's control of the money supply may be weakened, as happened in Egypt during the late 1980s.

The principal area of debate on the microeconomic effect of remittances concerns the division of the funds between consumption and investment and the types of investments that are selected. A substantial proportion of remittances is devoted to direct consumption. Additionally, perhaps one-third of Moroccan remittances, for example, enter as goods-in-kind (de Haas 2005). Some detailed surveys tend to contradict the conventional wisdom, however. For example, Adams showed that in Minya governorate in Egypt, one of the poorest areas of the country, migrants in the 1980s invested much of their earnings, particularly in housing and land (Adams 1991). Some criticize the form that such investment takes, faulting migrants for placing their savings in housing, consumer durables, dowries, and land rather than in productivity-enhancing investments such as machinery, small workshops, and improved agricultural techniques.

Remittances are indeed often spent on housing. One survey in Egypt found that more than one-fifth of remittances were so used; a similar proportion was reported in a study of Sudanese migrants' spending (Berar-Awad 1984). Parallel patterns have been found in Turkey, Tunisia, and Morocco. Other priority items of expenditure include furniture and simple household articles (some 58% in one Egyptian case study [el-Dib, Ismail, and Gad 1984]). Few who have been inside the homes of Egyptian, Yemeni, or Moroccan manual workers would question this use of remittances, especially in rural areas. Substituting a brick home for a mud hut improves the quality of life of rural people and contributes directly to meeting basic human needs. To the extent that poorly ventilated, poorly heated, or excessively hot, vermin-ridden housing is a threat to human health, the spending of remittances on better housing may be viewed as an investment in human capital. Although building on irreplaceable agricultural land constitutes an Egyptian national disaster, faulty incentives may be more reasonably blamed than migration.

Remittances are also frequently invested in land. Since the supply of land is inelastic, the increased demand pushes land prices sharply upward. Of course, not all of the rise in land prices can be attributed to remittances. Land-price increases occurred primarily in the highly inflationary environment during the decade of the 1970s oil boom. From California to Kuwait, investors move into real estate during inflationary periods.

Some remittances have found their way into productive investments, such as irrigation equipment, small workshops and factories, and transportation equipment (trucks and cars), but these investments probably constitute a relatively small proportion of the total spending of remittances. This is hardly the fault of the migrants or of emigration. Instead, we should blame national policies for reducing the profitability of investments in productivity-enhancing technologies. For example, the ambivalence of many governments of the region toward private-sector manufacturing, combined with overvalued real exchange rates and other macromanagement problems, continues to discourage the kind of industrial investment that critics of the observed pattern of remittance spending prefer.

One challenge for policymakers is to determine how to channel remittances into needed public and semipublic goods and services, especially in rural areas. It is difficult to entice private funds into irrigation works, roads, public-health facilities, and schools. One promising attempt to solve this problem is the rural development associations of the former YAR, using *zakat* to finance spending on wells, schools, and roads (Cohen et al. 1981).

One crucial aspect of remittances has been increasingly noted: its impact on human capital investment. This seems to be particularly evident for girls' education. Evidence (and simple economic theory) suggests that only when a family achieves some minimally comfortable living standard will they contemplate educating their children. Given gender biases prevalent in many rural and poor urban areas, this is likely to be particularly true for girls. Remittances that increase household incomes and consumption thereby make possible one of the most important of all investments in the region: investment in female education (see Chapters 4 and 5) (Kapur 2003).

The combination of labor migration and remittances does undermine the potential for an export-led growth strategy. To the extent that wages in the oil-producing countries contain an element of oil rent and these rents have seeped into the wage structure of the sending countries, the latter will find it difficult to compete in exporting labor-intensive products. Some critics of emigration have argued that labor exports were an alternative to the export of labor-intensive manufactured goods (Katanani 1981).

However, this was not really a choice for most countries. The political policies, institutions, and entrepreneurial skills needed for successful export of manufactured goods were nowhere in sight in the region in 1973; even today, they are often absent (see Chapter 9). Imagine how many changes the Egyptian government of the early Sadat years would have had to undertake to begin to compete in the fiercely competitive international market for textiles! The exchange-rate regime, the tariff structure, and the domestic-communications infrastructure would all have had to be altered radically. Furthermore, the manufacturers of these products in Egypt were state-owned enterprises, infamous for their rigidity and indifference to consumer tastes. By contrast, all the government of Egypt had to do to facilitate labor exports was simply get out of the way. In the short run, there was really no choice. But the instability of labor exports and the absence of the numerous dynamic linkages that characterize the growth of manufactured exports suggest that, once again, history has not been kind to the political economies of the poorer, more populous nations of the region.

Return Migration, or "People Back"

The vast majority of migrants want to return home. Neither they nor the receiving countries view labor migration as permanent resettlement. Most migrants do return home; the large majority come back at least temporarily, for major holidays and for important family events such as weddings. The impact of returning migrants ranges from labor market impacts to cultural, political, and even demographic consequences.

Consider, for example, the question of how well (or ill) national labor markets absorbed the return flow of workers in the wake of the Gulf War. Yemeni returnees constituted about 7% of the total population, 15% of the workforce of the country (Van Hear 1994). Many of those expelled in 1990 had a very difficult time re-integrating. About one-third of the returnees had been out of Yemen for so long that they no longer had any connections with local communities (Van Hear 1994). Camps sprang up, particularly on the very hot and humid Tihama plain. Even two years later, some 100,000 returnees lived in a huge camp adjacent to the city of Hodeida, with ironical names such as "Saddam Street" and "Mother of Battles District" (Whitaker 2000). Poverty and unemployment soared and remain high today (see Chapter 5). Some Yemenis clearly managed to return to the Gulf, however.

At the same time that the economic stimulus of remittances faltered, the numbers of young, first-time job seekers rose. These youths, rather than the returnees, were the ones most seriously affected by return migration. The returning migrants had often accumulated savings and had acquired or sharpened skills abroad. They were relatively well placed to compete effectively in a tightening job market or to become successfully self-employed. But this was much less likely to be true for the semi-educated youths who poured onto the job market in ever greater numbers.

The Gulf War heightened these problems. At first, returnees actually provided some economic stimulus, as they spent money on housing; this effect was particularly noticeable in Jordan. But returnees tended to settle in urban areas (although in Yemen perhaps 50% returned to villages), and there they constituted an additional drag on already overburdened labor markets, driving the unemployment rate up to 25% in Yemen and 19% in Jordan. Jordan also lost its major export markets in Iraq and the Gulf, further compounding the economic crisis there.

Egypt was more fortunate. Emigration to Libya increased considerably, and Egyptians supplanted other Arab expellees in Saudi Arabia. For Egypt the Gulf War was only a blip in its experience of emigration. It is significant, however, that the additional 500,000 workers abroad constituted roughly one year's annual addition to the labor force. It is also likely that the new emigrants and the expellees are different people; certainly there is little evidence that the illiterate, rural emigrants (two-thirds of whom were in Iraq) have found new jobs abroad. And, as noted earlier, the skill mix of Egyptians in the Gulf has shifted increasingly toward more educated and skilled workers. For Egypt, as for all the sending countries, emigration may not have collapsed, but it can no longer act as the main source of new employment.

There are two other important consequences of return migration. First, the migration during the 1970s oil boom produced a social, cultural—even political—phenomenon known in Egypt as *golfeyya*, or "Gulfization." That is, migrants to the Gulf, particularly those from poorer, less skilled, and/or more rural backgrounds tended to return from the Gulf having absorbed the more conservative social mores of that region. The diffusion of *salafi* ideas and behaviors may also have been greatly stimulated by migration to Saudi Arabia. One field study in northern Sudan found that migrants returning from Saudi Arabia had "embraced a new orthodoxy, representing a move away from local, parochial identities toward perceived conformity with a universalistic set of beliefs and practices (i.e., *as-salafiyya*)" (Bernal 1999). Such evidence suggests, once again, that the rise of Islamism is a thoroughly modern phenomenon; these Sudanese villagers associated modernity with the lifestyle found in Saudi Arabia.

A congruent impact might be found in fertility behavior. Philippe Fargues contrasts the fertility behavior of the Maghreb with that of Asian Arab countries. As we saw in Chapter 4, fertility in the latter is typically considerably above that in the former. Fargues suggests that lower fertility in the Maghreb may be in part explained by the impact of Western lifestyles, carried home by migrants returning from work in the European Union. Moreover, he found that in Egypt, the number of returnees from the Gulf as a percentage of the total population is inversely correlated with fertility across Egyptian governorates (Fargues 2005, 15). Fargues is careful not to read too much into such evidence, but it is suggestive that returned migrants shape the political economies of their countries of origin in a wide range of diverse ways.

THE IMPACT OF MIGRATION
ON RECEIVING COUNTRIES

The economic benefits of migration to the receiving countries were clearly very large. The major oil exporters simply could not have undertaken their large-scale development projects without foreign workers, who made possible the rapid physical capital formation and infrastructure construction of the oil-boom period. Saudi nonoil GDP grew at 10.5%, 13%, and 8.9% for 1970–1975, 1975–1980, and 1980–1983, respectively; in the UAE nonoil GDP expanded at 14.1% per year from 1975 to 1980. Immigration of teachers also enabled the oil countries to embark on the rapid expansion of their educational systems. As has been explained above, the enormous increase in the demand for labor that such expansion implied could not have been met from domestic supply alone. By 1980, 53% of the Saudi labor force was foreign, while 78% of Kuwait's and 89% of the UAE's workforce came from abroad. Even in Iraq, with a much larger indigenous workforce than the other states, 14% of workers were foreign in 1980 (Sherbiny 1984). By 1990, nationalist rhetoric notwithstanding, this dependence had grown. The reliance of the Gulf States on foreigners for labor has no parallel in modern economic history—even today.

The combination of such rapid economic growth with these massive influxes of foreign workers of all types had some unusual social and political consequences. To some extent, labor immigration has severed the "normal" link between economic growth and structural change, on the one hand, and class formation, on the other. Locals can and do avoid manual labor; they can continue to be merchants, soldiers, and bureaucrats. Some fear the long-run impact of the identification of hard work with foreigners—by implication, something that is less than perfect. To be sure, immigrants from poorer countries do the hard, dirty, and dangerous work in all rich countries, but only in the Gulf States do the foreign menials outnumber the indigenous leisured.

In the Gulf States, as elsewhere, large-scale immigration has created political problems, violently illustrated by the Gulf War. Immigration posed a serious political challenge to the Saudi and Kuwaiti regimes. The legitimacy problem of denying citizenship rights and benefits to fellow Arabs and Muslims and the experiences of vast differences in wealth *and* effort between citizens of receiving countries and the workers from poorer Arab countries provided much of the animus against the Gulf States that was so visible in popular demonstrations from Morocco to Pakistan during the fall of 1990. States that base their legitimacy on Arab nationalism (as in Iraq) or on Islam (as in Saudi Arabia) face contradictions when they deny other Arabs or Muslims the same treatment as nationals. However, ideological pronouncements notwithstanding, even the Iraqis (who required no visas from Arab migrants on the grounds that they were "citizens of the Arab Nation") treated their citizens differently from other Arab workers.

Large-scale influxes of foreigners made national-security agencies nervous even before the Gulf crisis, so that when it ignited it confirmed their worst fears. The disquiet in the Gulf was compounded by the volume of immigration, the political volatility of the region, and the relatively underdeveloped national-security apparatus in many Gulf States at the beginning of the 1970s when immigration soared. States handled these threats by implementing laws that required that all but a handful of immigrants be restricted to short-term contracts, by forbidding job changes unless the original employer agreed, and by requiring all workers to leave the country for a specified period once their contracts had expired. They refused to allow the families of any but the most skilled professionals into the country. They mounted particular vigilance against special security threats, such as Iranians after the Islamic revolution in Iran. The Saudis tightened security beginning in 1978 and with even more vigor after the Great Mosque incident of 1980. In particular, they sought to guarantee that *hajjis* (pilgrims) would return to their own countries and not use the pilgrimage as a means to slip into the country in search of work. Finally, the Gulf States resorted extensively to devices such as the use of turnkey construction contracts, in which the general contractor supplied the workers and guaranteed their subsequent departure.

Although the Gulf States tried to beef up enforcement by importing foreign police experts (and in some cases, foreign soldiers and policemen such as the Pakistanis in Oman and Saudi Arabia) and by investing in expanded police equipment (e.g., computers), they continued to rely primarily on more traditional, personalized enforcement mechanisms. Effectively, the employer's right to hire and fire became the

TABLE 15.3   Foreigners as a Percentage of Labor Force in the Gulf States, 1985–2003

Country	1985	1995	2000	2003
Bahrain	58	60	59	59
Kuwait	86	83	82	81
Oman	52	64	64	71
Qatar	77	82	86	86
Saudi Arabia	63	64	56	50
United Arab Emirates	91	90	90	--

SOURCE: United Nations, Department of Economic and Social Affairs, Population Division 2006

political prerogative to retain or expel a worker from the country. Not only could employers report workers to the Ministry of the Interior, but by simply dismissing them, employers ensured that they would have legally irregular status. Employers usually took workers' passports upon arrival and would not return them until the contract had expired. But all of these mechanisms proved fruitless when Iraq invaded Kuwait. Despite the fact that many Jordanians, Palestinians, Sudanese, and Yemenis had little use for Saddam, disapproved of the invasion of Kuwait, and certainly had no intention of risking their families' fortunes for Ba'athist adventurism, the sins of the few were visited on the many.

In the fifteen years since the end of the Gulf War in 1991, the Gulf States have faced another challenge: rising youth unemployment (see Chapter 5). Whenever unemployment coincides with large-scale immigration, political criticism of immigration rises. Replacing foreigners with unemployed locals is no easy matter, however. Typically, locals do not want to take the kinds of jobs that many foreigners accept. Every country in the Gulf has embarked on a "nationalization" campaign, aimed at reducing employment of immigrants and reducing national unemployment. This has been most successful in the public sector, although countries have also tried to impose restrictions on private-sector hiring, as when Saudi Arabia attempted to restrict jewelry retail trade (formerly dominated by Yemenis) to Saudis. There have been some successes here, but change is very slow. Locals prefer better paying, more secure, and more prestigious public-sector jobs; many prefer to remain unemployed, hoping for a public-sector job (Yousef 2005). Despite all the many efforts, only in Saudi Arabia has the percentage of the labor force that is foreign declined significantly—and even there, foreigners still fill one-half of all jobs (Table 15.3).

The wealthy labor-importing states remain schizophrenic about labor immigration. On the one hand, they need these workers for their economies and have become accustomed to the benefits of greater incomes and wider personal services that such migrants make possible. On the other hand, they face exceptionally severe domestic labor-market pressures—applied to profoundly segmented labor markets. The Gulf States will remain dependent on immigrant labor for some time and will continue to loathe this dependence, even as the foreign workers retain deep ambivalence of their own.

CONCLUSION

Labor migration transformed the political economy of the region. Huge numbers of urban and rural citizens of the poorer countries of the region left their homes, often for the first time, for extended stays abroad. Their departure, their remittances, and their return altered family structures, village customs, neighborhood layouts, and national economies. Labor markets have become thoroughly integrated across national boundaries. Although the Gulf War temporarily ruptured this network, the structural features underpinning labor migration (wage gaps, reluctance of Gulf nationals to take on many jobs, etc.) remained. There has been some gradual change, as labor migration flows "mature," but the Gulf States remain heavily dependent on immigrant labor, now increasingly non-Arab. It is likely that foreigners will constitute a substantial proportion of the labor force of the Gulf States for many years to come.

However, the dynamism of labor migration as a force for raising wages and living standards in the poorer rural areas of the region, so prominent during the oil boom years, is a thing of the past. Migration will almost certainly never again boom as it did in the late 1970s or even the 1980s. The evidence for this prediction comes not only from the events of the 1990s, when oil prices were low, but also for the past half-decade of much higher oil prices. The post-1999 oil-price escalation has not led to any boom in immigration. Governments have been far more prudent in their spending patterns, seeking to avoid the "Dutch Disease" impacts of the 1970s and 1980s (World Bank 2005a). Most major infrastructural projects have long since been completed; locals are increasingly educated and skilled—and also unemployed. Asians now dominate unskilled jobs, while locals compete ever more insistently with more skilled, Arab workers. Although migration and remittances continue to contribute to poverty alleviation in sending countries, these countries can no longer hope to relieve their own labor-market pressures through the "safety valve" of immigration. The boom years of migration are fading into history.

NOTES

1. Cultural integration among the Arabs has been proceeding and, arguably, accelerating thanks to rising educational levels and changes in global communications technology, for several generations. We do not attempt to analyze this complex and vitally important phenomenon here.

2. Turkey is a charter member of the WTO. Other MENA members (and date of accession) are Bahrain (1995), Egypt (1995), Jordan (2000), Kuwait (1995), Morocco (1995), Oman (2000), Qatar (1996), Saudi Arabia (2005), Tunisia (1995), and the UAE (1995). Countries in various stages of application are Algeria, Iran, Iraq, Lebanon, Libya, and Yemen.

3. In 1993, Saudi Arabian aid was 0.70% of GNP, while Norwegian aid was 0.038%. U.S. aid was 0.04% of GNP in that year (World Bank 1995a, 197).

4. Jordan, 58.2%; YAR, 27.1%; Syria, 237.8%; the Sudan, 36.2% (van den Boogaerde 1990).

5. Although not considered to be "international migrants," the number of "internally displace persons" in some countries is also substantial: Sudan, 3–5 million; Algeria, 400,000–600,000; Turkey, 350,000–1 million, and Lebanon (before 2006) 300,000 (CIA 2006). By January 2007, the United Nations estimated that some 1.7 million Iraqis were internally displaced and about 2 million had fled the country. Most of the migration occurred after 2003.

6. "Nationalization" of the labor force refers to increased reliance on locals (citizens or subjects) rather than foreigners.

16

CONCLUSION

The Political Economy of the Arab Uprisings

Since the last edition of this book was published, revolutionary movements have swept across the Middle East. The "Arab Spring" began on December 17, 2010, in Tunisia, where Mohamed Bouazizi, a vegetable seller in the central Tunisian town of Sidi Bouzid, set himself on fire to protest mistreatment by local police and government authorities. Bouazizi's act incited a wave of protests, beginning in rural areas and later spreading to urban coastal areas, which encompassed a diverse array of participants ranging from informal-sector workers, like Bouazizi himself, to unemployed graduates, workers, lawyers, and cyber-connected youth. Ultimately, these mass protests led to the ouster of Zine al-Abdine Ben 'Ali, who had ruled Tunisia in an increasingly repressive manner for over two decades. Protesters demanded justice and accountability from their government and refused to step down, even in the face of brutal repression and government promises to create new jobs and to expand civil and political liberties.

The revolutionary movement then spread to Egypt, where Hosni Mubarak, who had held power for almost thirty years, was ousted after several weeks of protests in Cairo and other cities. In Egypt, too, protesters remained steadfast in the face of a harsh crackdown, calling for Mubarak and his key henchmen to step down. In February 2011, Mubarak resigned and later faced trial for complicity in the murder of protesters. From Tunisia and Egypt, protests spread across the region to Yemen, Algeria, Libya, Syria, Jordan, Bahrain, and even Saudi Arabia. More sporadic and, in some cases, short-lived protests took place in Morocco, Iraq, Lebanon, and Palestine.

Revolutions and rebellions are complex phenomena. Likewise, the motivations for the Arab uprisings are multifaceted. Political concerns, such as outrage over dictatorial rule, repression, and restrictions on basic liberties were undoubtedly important. For many people, however, economic issues were equally if not more salient. A 2005 poll conducted by Zogby International found that expanding employment opportunities, improving the health care and educational systems, and ending corruption were the most important priorities of citizens across the region. Democracy and civic and political rights, though also cited, were ranked lower than socioeconomic concerns (Zogby International 2005). Similarly, the 2010 Arab Youth Survey found that the greatest perceived challenge and concern of Arab youth was the cost of living, followed by unemployment and then human rights. The largest *change* relative to the previous survey, which was conducted one year earlier, was the increased perception of income inequality (ASDA'A/Burson-Marsteller 2010).

More fundamentally, it is difficult to extricate the economic and political motivations for the uprisings given the evolution of Arab political economies over the past few decades. The rise of crony capitalism, which we discuss later in the chapter, underscores the ways in which politics and, more specifically, political connections have shaped economic opportunities in the region. As implied by the slogan "Bread, freedom, and social justice," which protesters chanted on Avenue Bourguiba and in Tahrir Square and elsewhere in the region, inequality of opportunity was a central concern. Thus, a political economy approach has much to contribute to interpretations of the initial motivations for the uprisings and of the dynamics of ongoing political and economic transitions.

Despite momentous political changes in the region, many insights from the third edition of this book, which was published over two years before Bouazizi set himself on fire, remain relevant. Some of the core economic and political challenges described in the book were important factors that either directly or indirectly contributed to the uprisings. Richards and Waterbury pointed to insufficient job creation, labor market pressures exacerbated by the youth bulge, the mismatch between educational systems and labor market needs, the declining quantity of water and rising dependency on food imports, the continuing decay of the public sector, the mixed record of economic liberalization, a growing housing crisis in urban areas, and the rise of political Islam across the region.

The Arab Spring also created new developments that cannot be fully appreciated without new analytical tools that were not in earlier editions of this book. With ousted leaders and struggles over the construction of new political institutions in some countries, the classification of regime types in the region must be revised. Even in countries where incumbent rulers remain entrenched, the nature of the political game has changed. Across the region, "street politics" is an increasingly important form of political expression and citizens are making more forceful and more frequent demands on their leaders. At this juncture, the context of policymaking is altered: New political regimes are emerging, and with the rise of claim-making, rulers are compelled to respond more effectively to citizen demands. Evolving political systems as well as economic developments demand new perspectives on the political economies of the region.

The Arab uprisings also highlight issues that require more in-depth analysis than prior editions of this book emphasized. In particular, the perceived increase in inequalities, discontent with public services, the political economy of cronyism, the narrowing composition of authoritarian coalitions, and succession issues in Arab republics have proven to be important developments across the Arab world.

What explains the origins and dynamics of the Arab uprisings? We believe that a political economy approach has much to offer in addressing this question. Neither purely political concerns, such as the desire of populations for democracy, nor simple economic trends can explain the decisions of protesters to call for the downfall of autocratic rulers. Rather, the interaction of political factors and real and perceived economic developments brought about the uprisings. As we argue later, narrowing authoritarian coalitions in the context of crony capitalism, the rollback of the state, and declining welfare regimes alienated formal-sector workers and tenuous middle classes. In the context of unequal life chances and rising insecurity, growing portions of Arab societies perceived that the inequality of opportunities was on the rise. Thus, neither growth rates nor absolute levels of income inequality can account for popular movements to overthrow incumbent dictators. Rather, *perceptions* of socioeconomic trends in the context of evolving political economies were at the root of mass protests.

In this epilogue, we develop these claims in more detail. First, we sketch out a picture of regional variation in the uprisings, pointing to a variety of factors that differentiate the countries of the region and help to explain their distinct trajectories thus far during this period of momentous change. The following section develops a framework for understanding the uprisings. The final part focuses on the dynamics of the transitions across the Middle East, analyzing the ways in which political and economic factors are interacting to shape the construction of new political institutions and economic reform programs.

CROSS-REGIONAL VARIATION
IN THE ARAB UPRISINGS

The outcomes of the uprisings thus far have varied across the Arab world. In some countries, such as Tunisia, Egypt, and Libya, rulers have been deposed and political actors are engaged in struggles over the creation of new institutional rules. In Yemen, regime change occurred through a more "pacted" transfer of power negotiated by elites, although mass mobilization initially precipitated the ouster of former president 'Ali 'Abdullah Salih. In February 2012, voters endorsed a deal brokered by the Gulf Cooperation Council, approving a two-year transitional presidency for Salih's vice president of eighteen years, 'Abd Rabbo Mansour Hadi.

In other countries, regimes have pushed back decisively against protesters. In Syria, the regime's harsh crackdown on initial protests sparked a bloody conflict that continues unabated as of this writing. In Bahrain, too, the ruling al-Khalifa family has harshly repressed protesters who are calling for regime change, although far less blood has been spilled than in Syria. The international community has responded in divergent ways to the crises in Syria and Bahrain. Direct intervention from neighboring Saudi Arabia and limited condemnation from the United States, which has a strategic alliance with Bahrain, have bolstered the ruling family's control. The United States and other countries have hesitated to intervene directly in Syria, in part because of Russian opposition to international involvement and in part because of stated concerns about the fragmentation of the opposition and the role of Islamist extremists in the armed opposition to the As'ad regime.

Not all uprisings in the Arab world have culminated in or even called for the dismissal of authoritarian rulers. In some countries, sustained protests were met with concessions by rulers. In Jordan, protesters by and large have not demanded an end to the monarchy but rather have issued demands for increased economic opportunities and greater freedoms under the current system. In response, King Abdullah replaced the prime minister multiple times and called early elections, although these moves have failed to appease the opposition. In Morocco, King Muhammad VI pledged to introduce greater political freedoms and held a referendum on constitutional reforms that ostensibly reduced the power of the monarch but, in practice, brought about little substantive change in the system (Benchemsi 2012). At this juncture, protests have abated in Morocco, but if the king's alleged commitment to gradual reform does not bring about significant change, they could reignite. Protests of varying scales and durations have also erupted in Algeria, Iraq, and Lebanon, compelling rulers to make some real and some rhetorical concessions. The fragmentation of political systems and exhaustion after prolonged conflicts in these countries, however, have hampered the ability of opposition movements to gain traction and bring about meaningful reform.

Opposition groups have even staged protests in the wealthy Arab Gulf monarchies. In Kuwait, which has a comparatively long history of political contestation, the parliament was dissolved and the prime minister was replaced. In general, however, protests have been more limited and short-lived across the Gulf. In most cases, incumbent rulers have taken advantage of high oil prices to quell protests through economic incentives.

Several basic economic and political factors differentiate the countries of the region, explaining some of the variation in the trajectories of the Arab uprisings. Oil wealth is the most obvious distinction among Arab countries. In the oil-rich countries with low populations, the autocratic bargain—material benefits in exchange for political quiescence—can still function owing to high oil rents. To be sure, oil is not determinative and cannot explain all politics in the Gulf, as the case of Kuwait demonstrates. At a minimum, high per capita oil wealth enables rulers to postpone serious challenges to their authority and may even prevent the emergence or spread of opposition groups in the first place.

The extent of ethnoreligious diversity and, most importantly, politicized identity-based cleavages also accounts for some variation in the dynamics of the uprisings across the Arab countries. Particularly in the Levant, notably Syria, Iraq, Lebanon, and, to a lesser degree, Jordan, ethnoreligious politics has shaped the demands of opposition groups and the course of the protests. Autocratic coalitions have historically favored some groups over others, a strategy of political control that dates back to the colonial period and continued after independence. In some of these countries, rulers incorporated minorities, who fear the tyranny of majorities. For example, in Syria, the majority Sunni population has been less privileged than Alawis and other minority groups, although Sunni elites have prospered under the As'ad family's rule as well. The Hashemite monarchy in Jordan has historically favored East Bank "Transjordanian" tribes and families, rewarding them with positions in the civil service and military that come with job security and benefits, while Jordanians of Palestinian origin tend to dominate the private sector and the informal economy.

The uprisings have undermined or destabilized core political settlements and have sometimes resulted in violence. The struggle in Syria is increasingly described in sectarian terms, with an opposition that is overwhelmingly Sunni pitted against a minority Alawi regime. The dynamics of protest in Bahrain are also depicted as sectarian: the ruling al-Khalifa family, a Sunni monarchy ruling over a majority Shi'a population, has used harsh repression to put down the largely Shi'a opposition. The uprisings have even upset the balance in comparatively stable Jordan: with economic deterioration, the monarchy's core Transjordanian constituency is increasingly disgruntled and more sympathetic to the opposition movement.

It is vital to emphasize, however, that an interpretation of political struggles based on sectarian grievances vastly oversimplifies political and economic realities in Bahrain, Syria, and other countries in the region. Ethnoreligious cleavages per se do not necessarily produce conflict (Brubaker 2006; Chandra 2012; Fearon and Laitin 1996; Lieberman and Singh 2012). Rather, identity-based differences must be politically salient in order to become a basis for political mobilization. A surefire way to activate ethnoreligious identity is to distribute resources along ostensibly identity-based lines. For example, in Iraq, most people did not prioritize their identities as Shi'a or Sunni Muslims until well into the twentieth century (Jabar 2003). Saddam Hussein's policies and, more generally, the breakdown of the state during the sanctions period and following the US invasion in 2003 were instrumental in activating religious identities in Iraq. Saddam increasingly favored Sunnis, especially those from his native town of Tikrit, and repressed the Shi'a, whose religious networks posed a threat to his rule. As a result, the Shi'a felt marginalized in Saddam's Iraq, and Shi'a political leaders have taken advantage of his overthrow to consolidate their authority. But even in Iraq, where sectarianism appears to define political life, some of the most intense conflict occurs among coreligionists. Political competition is particularly intense among different Shi'a groups and has even erupted in violence.

Finally, regime type appears to explain some differences in the nature and intensity of uprisings across the Arab world, although closer inspection may reveal this to be a spurious correlation. The record suggests that the monarchies have been less vulnerable to demands for regime change and have even witnessed less sustained opposition movements. As noted earlier, per capita oil wealth is part of the reason for the more muted nature of the uprisings in many monarchies; it cannot, however, account for the Jordanian and Moroccan cases. To explain their longevity, monarchs in Jordan and Morocco emphasize their legitimacy, an argument that is more convincing for Morocco, where the monarchy has been in place since the seventeenth century, than for Jordan, which was a colonial construction (Massad 2001). But even in Morocco, legitimacy is an unconvincing explanation, in part because it is vague and difficult to measure and in part because there was nothing inevitable about the monarchy's survival and perpetuation in the post-independence period. Rather, the structure of patronage helps to explain why monarchies have been less destabilized than republics in the Arab uprisings. In particular, monarchies have tended to establish multifaceted authoritarian coalitions, broadening their support base in society and reducing the potential demand for their overthrow (Yom and Gause 2012). Thus, rather than regime type per se, the structure of authoritarian coalitions in monarchies versus republics provides a more convincing account for the varied trajectories of uprisings in the Arab world today.[1] This is why the rising grievances among Trans-jordanians, a key part of the authoritarian coalition in Jordan, are particularly worrisome for the Hashemite monarchy.

Our emphasis on the composition of authoritarian coalitions in explaining both the durability and the breakdown of authoritarian rule points to the broader value of a political economy approach for understanding the emergence and progression of uprisings in the Arab countries. In the next section, we spell out the core elements of such an approach.

PROLONGED DISCONTENT: THE SOCIOECONOMIC FOUNDATIONS OF THE ARAB UPRISINGS

Many of the characteristics of the recent Arab uprisings are puzzling and do not fit easily within popular intellectual frames. Why did they occur at the end of 2010, when there were no apparent direct triggers such as declines in subsidies or shifts in foreign alliances, rather than in the 1990s, when the welfare state began to be rolled back? Why did the revolutions start in Tunisia and Egypt, the countries with some of the highest economic growth in the region in the preceding few years, rather than in countries such as Syria or Yemen, where economic conditions were more dire and political repression more severe? Why were they initiated by secularist middle-class youth, the supposed beneficiaries of the modernizing republics, rather than by the long-standing Islamist opposition?

In the early days of the Arab Spring, debates about the relative importance of economic versus political factors permeated journalistic and scholarly discussions about the motivations for the mass protests across the region. On the face of it, economic factors hold little explanatory value. In the preceding decade, economic growth was not low in the "revolution" countries, at about 4 to 5% of GDP per year: in 2010, growth stood at 3.1% in Tunisia, 5.1% in Egypt, 3.4% in Syria, 3.7% in Libya, 7.7% in Yemen, 3.7% in Morocco, and 2.3% in Jordan (World Bank, *World Development Indicators,* 2010). The macroeconomic situation was also relatively stable after the imbalances of the early 2000s were absorbed, with shrinking budget and current account deficits and reasonable debt levels. On the eve of the uprisings, international reserves were at comfortable levels. The unemployment rate was high in most Arab countries, between 10 and 15% of the labor force, higher than in other developing regions, but stable. Inequality as measured by GINI coefficients was lower than in other regions, with values at around 0.3 to 0.4, and was not rising fast (Belhaj and Wissa 2011).

To be sure, the 2008 global recession, coupled with the oil and food crises, did affect the region. Growth slowed down after 2008, and while it had recovered somewhat by 2010, it remained below the levels reached in 2006 to 2008. Energy subsidies increased with international prices, further eroding the ability of the state to spend on public investment and wages, while inflation rose and real wages fell.

Furthermore, rising growth rates in the 2000s were unable to reach Asian double-digit levels, which would have been needed to absorb the youth wave and the unemployed in the labor market. In cross-regional comparative perspective, youth unemployment was high in the Arab world, at around 25%, but this was not a new development and therefore cannot explain the timing of the protests. Similarly, the decline of public welfare functions and the rise of parallel networks of social welfare provision were not recent phenomena. The rollback of the state originated in the fiscal crises of the 1980s experienced across most countries in the region, particularly those with low per capita oil reserves.

In short, by 2011, on the eve of the revolts, there was no singular economic shock to point to as a candidate for igniting the uprisings. Subsidies were not being cut; unemployment, while high, was not rising; and growth rates and investment ratios were on the rise and at comfortable levels. Furthermore, as the literature on social movements argues, economic grievances at best provide incomplete explanations for mass mobilization (McAdam 1982).

Instead, as we argue later in this chapter, *discontent on the economic front interacted with a broader sociopolitical context to ignite the uprisings.* In particular, economic stagnation mixed with the *perceived* rise in inequalities and lack of "social justice," a perception that had been mounting as a result of the rollback of the state and economic liberalization characterized by cronyism. As a result, access to economic opportunities was not meritocratic or governed by a level playing field, but rather was mediated by connections to political leaders and their narrowing circles of allies. In the context of redistributive commitments by rulers to populations, which increased citizen expectations of the state in both the "populist" republics and the more conservative monarchies, the inability of government to provide for citizens and a growing sense of economic insecurity were particularly egregious. This combination of factors created a dam of accumulated grievances and rising aspirations, ready to burst. The interlinkages between economic and political grievances point to the value of a political economy perspective in understanding the Arab uprisings.

A brief application of these claims to the case of Tunisia, where the revolts began, helps to illustrate our logic. At first glance, Tunisia was the least likely country in the region to have ignited the Arab uprisings. Tunisia experienced steady growth rates in the previous decade and exceeded the regional average on a variety of social indicators, such as literacy, school enrollment, and life expectancy. Among the non-oil economies in the region, Tunisia had the most developed welfare state institutions, which helped to create a more robust middle class than was found in other Arab countries. The state also ran a variety of social assistance programs, and poverty rates were lower than in neighboring countries. In addition, until the late 1990s, business-government relations were less corrupt and capital was less concentrated than in other countries with similar industrial profiles. Politically, Tunisia also appeared to be an improbable place to set off the uprisings. The Tunisian state was notoriously repressive, leaving far less scope for civil society activism and public expression than in many other countries in the region. The ruling party had penetrated all aspects of civic and political life, a task facilitated by the country's small size. Although many Tunisians did not like Ben 'Ali, fear of unrest, as experienced in neighboring Algeria—which underwent a bloody civil war in the 1990s—seemed to reduce their appetite for regime change.

Paradoxically, Tunisia's socioeconomic achievements may be an important component of an explanation for the spread of mass mobilization against Ben 'Ali. Older generations of Tunisians had experienced genuine social mobility in their lifetimes, particularly during the first few decades after independence under Bourguiba's rule, and had developed high expectations of their state. Their children could no longer expect to advance socioeconomically, even with graduate degrees. Furthermore, the history of relatively minimal corruption in state-business relations made the concentration of economic opportunities in the hands of the Ben 'Ali and Trabelsi families all the more scandalous. In effect, under Ben 'Ali's rule, the authoritarian coalition gradually narrowed. By the time marginalized elements of society and Tunisians in neglected regions rose up against Ben 'Ali, the state's traditional sources of support—the middle classes and business interests—joined in the revolt again the ruler and his cronies (Kaboub 2012).

In the next section, we develop the elements of a more systematic account of the Arab uprisings.

Toward a Political Economy of the Arab Spring

A framework to explain the Arab uprisings should provide an account of the socioeconomic and political evolution of the Arab republics that would explain both the persistence of autocracy until 2011 and its eventual collapse and should do so in a way that is empirically verifiable. The next edition of this book will focus centrally on this challenge. Here we simply outline elements of the emerging picture. Different analysts would approach such an ambitious question in distinct ways. Some would stress contingency and agency, and undeniably, there were such elements in the particular timing of the uprisings in Tunisia and Egypt. But we contend here that there must also have been structural factors that opened up a window of opportunity from which the main protagonists in the uprisings profited.

What are the key elements of this framework? Our account begins with the rollback of the state and the decline of public services, which palpably increased insecurity among non-elite populations. With the fiscal crisis of the state and the adoption of market-oriented reforms, the social constituencies of authoritarian rulers gradually narrowed, and the class of privileged, well-connected elites who emerged profited from special access to economic opportunities. The rise of crony capitalism across the region reflected shifts in economic structures that led to the growing de facto exclusion of the middle classes from opportunities for socioeconomic advancement. Perhaps most important, cronyism and rising economic insecurity fueled perceptions of inequality and violations of norms of social justice. Later we develop each of the pieces of this story in more detail, including the rollback of the state, the shifting composition of the authoritarian coalition and the rise of crony capitalism, the perceived marginalization of the middle classes, and rising inequality. We then address the role of political Islam before, during, and after the revolts.

The Rollback of the State and Deteriorating Economic Security

In the postcolonial period, the state played an unusually important role in economies across the Arab world. In this respect, Richards and Waterbury highlight parallels between the political economies of the Middle East and the socialist economies of the former Soviet bloc.

A leading family of structural narratives on the Arab uprisings focuses on a slow transition from quasi-socialism in which the rollback of the state, which began in the mid-1980s, ultimately led to the breakdown of the social contract underlying the autocratic bargain (Karshenas and Moghadam 2006; Yousef 2004b). Such accounts cannot claim that state rollback is the proximate cause of the revolts, given the long time lag. Nonetheless, to analyze the ultimate collapse of the system we need an understanding of why and how reforms were delayed, which mechanisms were used by autocrats to remain in power, even as market forces chipped away at their authority, and which contradictions emerged in this late autocratic "equilibrium" characterized by selective repression, co-optation, and cronyism. In this section, we briefly review the empirical record of state rollback and the related decline of public welfare functions.

A look at key economic performance indicators for the Arab developing countries as a group, from 1980 to 2008, depicted in Figure 16.1, shows clearly that the rollback of the state began twenty-five years ago.

Government expenditure shot up in the 1970s on the back of rising oil wealth in the region, but fell precipitously in the 1980s, reaching 22% of GDP in the early 1990s, a low figure by international standards. At the same time, private investment did not rise significantly to make up for the shortfall.

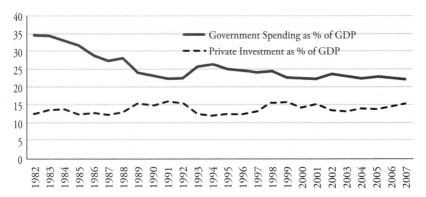

FIGURE 16.1 Government spending and private investment as a percentage of GDP for developing Arab countries, 1982–2007
SOURCE: World Bank, *World Development Indicators*, various years, averages for all developing Arab countries

Economic reforms adopted in the 1980s in the Arab world tended to hurt the poor and middle classes disproportionately. For example, subsidies to agriculture were cut deeply, which was particularly damaging to the rural poor, while lower public-sector wages and hiring freezes hurt civil servants and formal-sector workers. Given the de facto importance of government employment in post-independence welfare regimes across the region, these reforms were especially damaging to the nascent middle classes. In countries across the region, including Egypt, Jordan, Morocco, and Tunisia, protests erupted. In particular, attempts to cut subsidies on basic food items sparked "bread riots," which often compelled rulers to retract agreements with international financial institutions to reduce these expenditures.

In the post-independence period, rulers across the region, in both the "populist" republics and the "conservative" monarchies, expanded the public welfare infrastructure as part of state- and nation-building processes. In some countries, citizens had constitutional guarantees to basic health care and education. The first few decades after independence witnessed major gains in quality-of-life indicators. For example, in 1960, the infant mortality rate (IMR) was slightly higher in Arab states (154 deaths per 1,000 births) than in sub-Saharan Africa (151 per 1,000). In 2011, the IMR in the Arab world was 30 per 1,000 births and in sub-Saharan Africa it was 86. Thus, over a forty-five-year period, the Arab states maintained the highest annualized rate of IMR reduction (3.6%), three times faster than in Africa (1.2%), one-third faster than in Asia (2.7%), and slightly faster than in Latin America (3.4%). In addition, poverty rates are significantly lower in the Middle East than in other regions of the Global South.[2] Thus, in the decades after independence, Arab citizens experienced important and tangible socioeconomic gains that arguably raised their aspirations for themselves and their children.

Access to basic services and stable employment provided a sense of economic security, while human development gains enabled earlier generations in post-independence Arab countries to enjoy some social mobility. Formal-sector workers have always enjoyed far more benefits and job security than the large portion of Arab populations who work in the informal sector.[3] Formal-sector workers, however, especially civil servants and members of the security forces, were important foundations of authoritarian bargains across the region and therefore were more politically consequential for incumbent rulers. As a result, any breakdown in the public welfare infrastructure that affected employees in the public sector was bound to be politically risky.

The steady decline in public welfare institutions since the 1980s has affected all segments of the population beyond the wealthy elite, but it has been particularly damaging for the poor, who rely on government services. As Figure 16.2 shows, the Middle East stands out in cross-regional comparative perspective for its high levels of government consumption as a percentage of GDP, which broadly measures the provision of government services.

Figure 16.2 demonstrates that government consumption as a percentage of GDP in the developing countries of the Middle East exceeded that of other global regions in the 1970s but, unlike all other regions, exhibited a downward trend. In the early 1980s, it first dipped below levels in OECD countries and decreased steadily there-

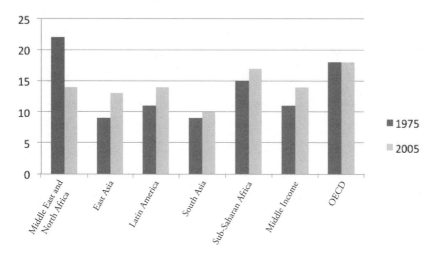

FIGURE 16.2   General government final consumption as a percentage of GDP, various global regions, 1975 and 2005
SOURCE: World Bank, *World Development Indicators,* 1975 and 2005, for all regions in the Global South, including developing countries only

after, although it still exceeded that of other developing regions except sub-Saharan Africa until the late 1990s (World Bank, *World Development Indicators,* various years).

Government spending on health and education has remained steady or even increased in the past few decades.[4] Expenditures do not, however, provide a satisfactory account of how populations actually experience their welfare regimes, since funds can be spent inefficiently or misused (Esping-Andersen 1990; Mares 2003). More systematic research is needed to track the decline of public health and educational institutions, and the fourth edition of this book will provide detail on this important issue. In particular, it is vital to know more about the quality of the services provided and about the welfare infrastructure, medical and educational personnel, absenteeism, and other difficult-to-research yet core dimensions of welfare systems.

In the absence of information on the quality of social services, the breakdown of expenditures on health offers a preliminary picture of how citizens actually experience their health systems. Out-of-pocket spending as a percentage of total spending on health care is a useful indicator of economic insecurity because it tracks the degree to which households assume the burden of health coverage, which is particularly onerous for the poor. Figure 16.3 depicts levels of out-of-pocket spending on health in selected Arab countries and compares them to the regional average and to the average for middle-income countries.

Unfortunately, it is impossible to get an accurate picture of longer-term trends given data limitations. Nonetheless, the figure shows that, even since the mid-1990s, the burden of health expenses has increasingly fallen on the shoulders of households,

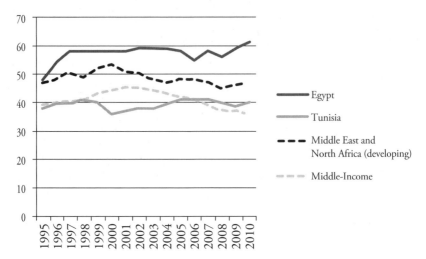

FIGURE 16.3   Out-of-pocket spending on health as a percentage of total spending on health in selected countries and regions, 1995–2010
SOURCE: WHO, *Health for All* database, various years

particularly in Egypt. In Tunisia, which is known for its relatively developed public welfare programs, out-of-pocket spending on health exhibited a gradual increase in the past decade. Although the average level of household spending on health in Middle Eastern developing economies declined slightly from a peak in 2000, it still exceeded that of middle-income countries as a whole.

As noted, the rollback of the state and declining public welfare cannot provide a proximate explanation for the Arab uprisings, but economic deterioration raises the question of why populations did not rise up against their governments when the state was no longer holding up its side of the authoritarian bargain. In the 1980s and 1990s, economic crises in other regions, such as Latin America and sub-Saharan Africa, had helped to provoke regime change during the near-synchronous "third wave" of democratization (Huntington 1991). In the Middle East, however, autocratic rulers did not open up the political space in order to reduce social pressures stemming from the decline in economic resources. To the contrary, the opposite may have happened, as suggested by Figure 16.4, which depicts the evolution of political rights between 1980 and 2010.

In 2010, the region was politically less open than in the mid-1980s, with the average score of citizen empowerment for the region falling from about 6 in 1980 to 1.2 in 2010 on a scale from 0 to 14, with 0 depicting complete dictatorship.

Although economic factors are not sufficient causes for the downfall of dictatorship (Pepinsky 2009), it is worth investigating why economic crises were associated with democratization in other regions more than in the Middle East. The literature on authoritarian durability is voluminous.[5] External support for authoritarian rule is a distinctive feature of the region and therefore a key component of any explana-

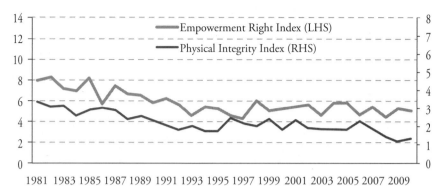

FIGURE 16.4 Repression and freedom indices, average for all Arab countries, 1981–2010
SOURCE: Cingranelli-Richards (CIRI), *Human Rights Dataset,* various years

tion for the persistence of authoritarianism in the Middle East in comparison with other regions (El Badawi and Makdisi 2007; Bellin 2004; Levitsky and Way 2010). External support provided rents in the form of aid and military support but helped to fuel the militarization of the region, which in turn facilitated state repression of opposition groups.

Repression, Co-optation, and the Authoritarian Bargain

Repression is certainly a core component of any account of authoritarian persistence. The threat of harassment, persecution, imprisonment, torture, and death is a powerful disincentive for anti-regime activism. The level of spending on security matters attests that repression had become an essential tool in the preservation of autocratic regimes in the late 1990s. Figure 16.4 depicts average levels of repression in the region as measured by the Index of Physical Integrity on a scale from 0 to 8 where 0 is maximum repression. Between 1980 and 2010, the average value of the index for the Arab countries fell from 4.5 to 2.9.

It is virtually a truism that repression is never a sufficient tool of political control, nor even the most effective. The literature on persistent authoritarianism in the Middle East has described in detail how (and in some cases why) different regimes chose to respond with distinctive mixes of co-optation and repression to maintain their control. Autocrats aimed to maximize their dwindling assets by dividing citizens into groups that benefited from cooperation while others were subject to repression and neglect. In Middle Eastern countries that lacked high per capita oil wealth, authoritarian rulers sought to strengthen their coalitions by co-opting the middle classes, which were largely composed of public-sector employees and some formal-sector workers.

Mass co-optation was achieved in large part through direct economic benefits in the form of subsidies for goods that were consumed relatively less by the poor, such as petroleum and energy. (Earlier subsidies for small-scale agriculture and for basic food items that benefited the poor had been reduced or eliminated.) A cross-regional

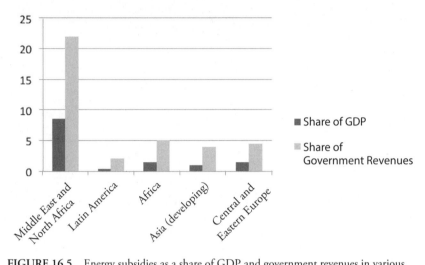

FIGURE 16.5   Energy subsidies as a share of GDP and government revenues in various regions, 2011
SOURCE: International Monetary Fund (2013)

comparison of petroleum subsidies reveals the specificity of the Middle East in this regard (see Figure 16.5).

Energy subsidies have grown over time, and by 2011 they were much higher in the Middle East and North Africa (MENA) than in any other region of the world. In absolute terms, about 50% of global energy subsidies are disbursed in the MENA region. These subsidies represent about 8.5% of regional GDP and 22% of total government revenues, which is much larger than in other developing regions; subsidies tend to be negligible in the advanced economies. Within the region, levels of subsidies vary, but twelve of the twenty countries in the region have subsidies above 5% of GDP.

About half of all subsidies in the Middle East go to petroleum products, followed by electricity. Government expenditures on these subsidies have gone up in recent years, together with energy prices. In many countries, they now represent an expense several times higher than total spending on health or on education.[6] This phenomenon is not restricted to oil exporters. For example, in 2011, energy subsidies represented 41% of government revenues in Egypt, 24% in Yemen, 22% in Jordan, and 19% in Lebanon, in contrast with "only" 10% in Kuwait, 15% in the United Arab Emirates, and 18% in Saudi Arabia. Among oil producers, Algeria and Iran had particularly large energy subsidies—27% and 50% of their respective revenues—even *after* the famous Iranian subsidy reforms.

It is well known that such subsidies are very regressive, as oil products tend to be consumed in much larger quantities by richer people. For example, a study in Egypt shows that in the case of oil petroleum subsidies, 46% of the benefits accrued to the top quintile in 2008 (Abouleinem, Al-Tathy, and Kheir-el-Din 2009). Once in place, it is almost impossible to reduce or eliminate subsidies because of the threat of political backlash by key constituents.

The large share of subsidies in the budgets of Arab governments exacerbated economic crises and furthered the decline of public services. Subsidies consumed ever-larger portions of government budgets, leaving less for investment in public services. Over time the effort to co-opt key societal groups through the extension and continuation of subsidies backfired by undermining social services and other public programs that citizens had come to expect and by limiting public investment, especially in rural and disadvantaged areas.

At the same time, fiscal regimes seem to have become more pro-rich over time. Tax rates have been relatively low, particularly in the countries with large hydrocarbon reserves. Even in the countries with low per capita natural resources, direct taxes now constitute a relatively small share of fiscal receipts. Indirect taxes, which are inherently regressive because they are applied to consumers across the board, regardless of income level (Imam and Jacobs 2007), became a more important component of tax revenue in these countries after the reforms of the 1990s.

In the mix of co-optation and repression—or carrots and sticks—changes in the former mattered more in explaining authoritarian breakdown than the latter. (Co-optation was probably more consequential for authoritarian durability too, but that is beyond the scope of this analysis.) If repression helped authoritarian regimes to endure, it cannot explain why dictatorships collapsed across the region: repression was constant, and had even been increasing since the 1990s (as seen in Figure 16.4), but rulers in multiple Arab countries were overthrown. Thus, any explanation for authoritarian breakdown must probe the evolution of co-optation. In the next section, we trace the narrowing of authoritarian social coalitions—that is, the groups that were favored in domestic political economies—and describe how this factor contributed to authoritarian breakdown.

Crony Capitalism

By the mid-1990s, the old social contract in post-independence Arab countries was already dead but had not been replaced by a new successful model. Over time alliances between autocrats and elite capital were increasingly consolidated. In this section, we describe the rise of crony capitalism, a central feature of authoritarian coalitions in the Arab countries. In the next edition of this book, the political economy of crony capitalism will be developed more fully.

The popular discontent that led to the uprisings can be traced to two main elements of economic policy: the rollback of the state and the consolidation of close relations between the state and particular elements of the business elite under economic liberalism. The central question of why the Arab region underperformed in terms of job creation, given what looked on paper to be impeccable market reforms, has been debated for years. Some have argued that the market reforms did not go far enough (Noland and Pack 2007; World Bank 2009), while others hold that economics became dominated by networks of privilege (Heydemann 2004) or even crony capitalists (Saadowski 1991) with myopic short-term interests that stifled competition, innovation, and ultimately job creation.

Conceptually, there is nothing intrinsically bad about close state-business relations. The case of South Korean *chaebols* illustrates how industrial policy can foster accumulation and the development of new sectors, even when state-business relations are characterized by cronyism (Kang 2002; Khan 2010). To the extent that they provide the right incentives to perform, close state-business relations can form the basis for dynamic capitalism. Under different circumstances and with less effective states, tight state-business relations can also become sources of undue influence, corruption, and other forms of rent-seeking that distort economic and political incentives. In the Arab world, however, particularly in the non-oil-exporting countries, crony capitalism did not appear to drive inclusive growth or development.

Popular perceptions of business elites have become quite negative in the region. Cronyism is now seen as both the key characteristic of the economic opening that started in the 1990s and accelerated in the 2000s and the source of many ills, including the job deficit, the rise in inequalities, and the perpetuation of authoritarian rule. The perceived "corruption" of the political and business elites was a key driving force of popular discontent. For example, a Pew survey reveals that in 2010 corruption was the top concern of Egyptians, with 46% listing it as their main concern even ahead of lack of democracy and poor economic conditions (Pew Research Center Report 2011). Changes in the corruption ratings of Arab countries in the Transparency International Index confirm popular perception: for example, in 2005, Egypt ranked 70th, Tunisia ranked 43rd, Libya ranked 117th, and Yemen ranked 103rd out of 158 rankings on the Corruption Perceptions Index (CPI). Perceived corruption increased markedly in the following three years. In 2008, Egypt dropped to 115th, Tunisia to 62nd, Libya to 126th, and Yemen to 141st out of 180 rankings on the CPI.

We now know that this was not just about perceptions. In both Tunisia and Egypt, the ongoing trials of leading businessmen are starting to shed light on the ways in which influence was yielded for private gain. Cronyism entailed practices such as the granting of monopoly rights to close associates of the rulers, the selling of public firms and land at reduced prices, and the manipulation of the financial markets for the benefits of a few insiders. In Tunisia, the Ben 'Ali and Trabelsi families monopolized business opportunities and even expropriated the real estate and business holdings of wealthy elites. In this relatively small country, stories of Ben 'Ali and Trabelsi were an open secret. Anonymous Samizdat tracts circulated freely, with titles such as "Les Sept Familles Qui Pillent la Tunisie" ("The Seven Families Who Are Pillaging Tunisia") appearing mysteriously in mailboxes in greater Tunis during the late 1990s and 2000s. The observations of American diplomats, revealed in cables released by Wikileaks, echoed and provided further details on the extent of corruption around the presidential palace in Tunis. Similar stories about favoritism and insiders abound in Syria, Libya, Yemen, and Algeria, where political cronies seem to control large chunks of the private sector (Alley 2010; Dillman 2000; Haddad 2012; Tlemcani 1999; Vandewalle 1998).

In Egypt, the trend accelerated in the last decade with the "businessmen" cabinet headed by Ahmad Nazif (2004–2011). Two iconic cases under investigation now illustrate the nature of privileges. The first is that of Ezz Steel, whose head has been sentenced by an Egyptian court on multiple charges of corruption. Ahmad Ezz, a very successful businessman who dominated the steel industry after 2000, is now accused of having lobbied on behalf of his firm on issues related to raising external tariffs, increasing protection in the steel sector, and relaxing anti-monopoly constraints. A prominent member of the National Democratic Party (NDP), the dominant party in the Egyptian political system, Ezz was extremely well connected. He held influential positions such as MP and chair of the Budget Committee in Parliament, which among other things oversees the work of the Competition Commission and trade policy; member of the NDP's influential Policy Committee, which was chaired by Gamal Mubarak; and NDP secretary for organizational affairs. A second example, also the focus of several current court cases, is that of Palm Hill Corporation, the second-largest real estate developer in Egypt. The main owner of Palm Hill, Ahmed El-Maghrabi, was minister of housing in the Nazif cabinet and has been accused of exploiting his ministerial position to sell the company large tracts of land in various parts of the country at exceptionally cheap prices, giving his firm a big advantage over competitors (Ahram Online 2011). In Tunisia, the case of Orange Tunisie, the local affiliate of a French telecommunications company, is widely cited. In 2009, Investec, a company held by Marwan Mabrouk and his wife, Cyrine Ben 'Ali, a daughter of the deposed dictator, won a bid for the third mobile phone network in Tunisia. (The two finalists in the call for bids were both sons-in-law of the president.) After gaining the telephone network, Mabrouk was named president of the board of Orange Tunisie and obtained interest-free bank loans from institutions linked to the state. The company is now under investigation, and the Tunisian state holds 51% of its shares (Beaugé 2011).

    The precise nature of state-business relations varied from country to country, with important ramifications for the dynamics of authoritarian stability and breakdown. For example, in the aftermath of the uprising the importance of the military in the Egyptian domestic economy became well known, albeit in imprecise terms. The important stakes of military institutions and high-ranking officers in protected industries help to explain why the Supreme Council of the Armed Forces (SCAF), a key backbone of the authoritarian regime, allowed Mubarak to fall but stymied substantive democratization in post-Mubarak Egypt (Marshall and Stacher 2012). Without an understanding of the military's role in the domestic political economy, it is impossible to understand political developments during and after the uprisings. In Tunisia, the military was far less central in the authoritarian coalition, which in part accounts for General Rachid Ammar's unwillingness to shoot protesters, a key juncture in the overthrow of Ben 'Ali. Furthermore, the elite coalition in Ben 'Ali's regime appeared to have narrowed much more than in Egypt, although this hypothesis deserves more systematic analysis. As a result, by the time mass protests erupted against the Ben 'Ali regime, many Tunisian capitalists who were not integrated into his networks of privilege accepted his downfall. In Egypt, Gamal Mubarak and his allies had gained important footholds in the Egyptian economy and profited from lucrative international deals, but this faction of the regime was counterbalanced by a strong and historically powerful protectionist bourgeoisie, which included but was not limited to the military.

The literature on contemporary Arab capitalism is still in its infancy. Some work analyzes state-business relations in the period prior to the uprisings in Egypt (Kienle 2001; Roll 2010; Sfakianakis 2004), Morocco (Cammett 2007; Catusse 2008; Henry 1996), Syria (Haddad 2012; Kienle 2002), Tunisia (Bellin 2002; Cammett 2007; Hibou 2006), and the Gulf (Chaudhry 1997; Hertog 2010; Moore 2004; Vitalis 2007), as well as the region as a whole (Heydemann 2004; Schlumberger 2007). With few, if any, direct measurements of the extent of favoritism, however, there have been no serious attempts to statistically evaluate the socioeconomic impact of cronyism.

A recent study of the Egyptian stock market around the momentous events of 2010 sheds some light on these issues. In evaluating the value of firms' political connections through an event study of stock market reaction to the revolution, Hamouda Chekir and Ishac Diwan (2012) estimate these to be about 20% of the firms' value. They also compare the past corporate performance of connected and unconnected firms. In 2002, connected firms were about the same size as the other firms on the exchange, but by 2010 their median size had increased to seven times the median of nonconnected firms, which had barely grown. Their analyses indicate that connected firms had a larger market share than their nonconnected competitors and borrowed much more than their competitors, on more favorable terms. (By 2010, the top twenty connected firms received 80% of the credit going to the largest one hundred Egyptian firms.) Importantly, they also found that the connected firms were less profitable than the nonconnected firms. At a minimum, even if favors were intended as industrial policy measures, they were not particularly successful. More likely, they were run inefficiently by regime cronies who had been appointed because they were trusted rather than skilled, in part to deny the heights of the economy to potential regime opponents. Another possibility is that they directed their profits to bankrolling the ruling party and to themselves. Indeed, well-connected businessmen became very rich and are central to the perception of a large rise in the 1% in Egypt in recent years. This arrangement then channeled capital flows to relatively inefficient sectors, reducing economic growth directly, while starving small and medium-size enterprises for credit, despite the fact that they provided a disproportionate share of new jobs (Assaad 2009). Moreover, this unfair competition may have reduced the dynamism of the economy as a whole. The key question is whether a dynamic form of capitalism was emerging or whether the economy was stuck in a low investment trap. That private investment in Egypt never went beyond 15% of GDP, with large capital flight (Kar and Curcio 2011) and in conjunction with the stagnation of unconnected firms, militates for the second interpretation.

Close state-business relations in the context of underperforming economies across the Arab world highlight a puzzle about the region: Why was cronyism bad for growth in Arab countries but not necessarily in other regions? How did it affect economic growth and development in the region and how, in turn, did this play into uprisings? To address these questions, it is essential to provide systematic data on the characteristics of the *ancien régime* and to develop a clearer sense of the impact of cronyism on economic performance and, more generally, on the legitimacy of authoritarian regimes. This suggests three main areas for research on state-business relations in the Arab world: Is there systematic evidence of favoritism? How did the connected firms operate in an economy that was ostensibly liberalized and theoretically less subject to government regulation? Are there objective ways of evaluating the impact on economic and political performance of the types of state-business relations that developed in the 2000s in the region?

More work remains to be done on Arab capitalism, but at a minimum, it is clear that cronyism is a fundamental building block in a political economy account of the uprisings. Crony capitalism arguably contributed to the revolts through at least two channels. First, as we have suggested, it may be an important factor behind economic underperformance in the region. As we argue in the next two sections, cronyism signaled the narrowing of authoritarian coalitions, squeezed out the middle classes, a key constituency of post-independence Arab regimes, and fueled perceptions of rising inequality.

The Evolution of the Authoritarian Coalition and the Role of the Middle Classes

In the initial decades after independence, Arab governments—and especially the republics—introduced policies that led to significant social change. In particular, statist economic policies coupled with welfare programs and subsidies on basic food items and fuel facilitated the rise of proto-middle classes. Public-sector workers, benefiting from job security and social benefits, were the most important component of the new middle classes. Also emerging was a professional class composed of doctors, lawyers, engineers, and others who enjoyed enhanced social status and a decent standard of living.

The middle classes appear to be a central actor of change in the Arab republics. For decades, Arab autocrats had placed a premium on retaining the mainly secular, middle-class-led parties and factions, either within the authoritarian coalition or as part of the legal opposition. For the republics in particular, secular and liberal ideologies were at the center of their Arab nationalist foundations (Browers 2009). In the 1950s, leaders such as Bourguiba and Nasser adopted an Atatürkian model of modernization in which the middle classes played a legitimizing role. Thus, for Arab autocrats, losing their middle-class anchors was tantamount to becoming naked dictatorships with no operational narrative.

There are indications that the middle classes have been hurt by the economic liberalization programs of the 1990s, and especially by their acceleration in the 2000s. Apart from the direct effects on the labor market, the interests of the middle classes have been threatened in many ways by the rollback of the state and the rise of neoliberalism.[7] In addition, low public-sector wages fueled petty corruption in areas such as health and education, generating another important source of discontent. To be sure, governments retained important policies aiding the middle classes, such as subsidies on food and fuel; given policy lock-in and the threat of political backlash from a key constituency in regime coalitions, it was difficult for governments to eliminate subsidies. As a result, the authoritarian bargain of the past decade evolved into an alliance between elite capital and elements of the middle classes that delivered economic benefits to coalition members, partly in the form of subsidies, but was less and less supportive of non-elite elements.

Further research is needed to understand more clearly the changing real and perceived socioeconomic conditions of the middle classes. Data from the World Values Survey provide a preliminary indication of shifting self-perceptions of citizens in Egypt. The survey, which asks respondents to identify the class to which they belong, provides a broad, self-assessed measure of well-being that goes well beyond income in capturing lifelong income, aspirations, and ownership of assets. A comparison of data from 2000 and 2008 indicates that the size of the middle classes has shrunk from 65 to 58% of the population in favor of the poor.[8]

Beyond its relative size, the nature of the middle classes has changed over time. Until recently, specialists did not seem to believe that the middle classes could play an active role in leading political change (for example, see Bellin 2002; Cammett 2007). With the middle classes incorporated into the system as civil servants and employees of state-owned enterprises, their influence on policy formulation and their ability to play the role of an "autonomous actor" were effectively undercut. A new, market-oriented middle class rose in the late 1990s in response to economic liberalization. The newcomers tended to be small merchants and industrialists, often in the informal sector, who benefited from the pro-market reforms, as well as the small but expanding skilled component of the formal private-sector labor market. This group has been more politically active than older elements of the private sector (Nasr 2009). For example, the new, pro-market middle class played an important role in securing the success of the Iranian revolution in 1979 and the rise of the Justice and Development party (AKP) in Turkey, and it has become a more vocal and assertive element in the Moroccan business community (Cammett 2007; Catusse 2008; Demiralp 2009; Gumuscu and Sert 2009).

A comparative analysis of opinion polls in Egypt shows that the middle class dramatically increased its support for democracy between 2000 and 2008, and that this was accompanied by a large rise in perceptions of inequality (Diwan 2013). While the youth may have mobilized more than other age groups in protests across the Arab region, these surveys do not support the claim that their views differ from those of their parents on the desirability of democracy at the present juncture.[9] To the extent that the underlying forces driving public opinion are connected to the unemployment of skilled youth, a major phenomenon for the middle classes, it seems that the parents of Egyptian middle-class youth became as unhappy as their children about the lack of job opportunities and were thus compelled to favor regime change and democracy.

Deteriorating socioeconomic conditions combined with high aspirations increased discontent among the middle classes. As a result, they gradually withdrew their support for authoritarian regimes. Dissatisfaction with the status quo, however, cannot simply be inferred from real economic conditions. Perceived conditions are more important in translating grievances into action than objective economic indicators. To understand the unraveling of authoritarian coalitions, we must comprehend how the middle classes interpreted changing socioeconomic conditions in their societies. The next section addresses this component of our framework.

Perceived Inequality

The Arab region is not distinguished by exceptionally high levels of inequality, nor has inequality risen sharply (Bibi and Nabli 2011). Thus, rising absolute levels of inequality, as measured by household expenditures surveys, do not provide satisfactory explanations for the Arab uprisings. Rather, we argue that perceptions of inequality, which are refracted through particular sociopolitical contexts and reflect developments that are hard to measure, are critical to an account of authoritarian breakdown and social protest in the Arab countries.

It is tempting to make inequality a core driver of an understanding of the Arab Spring in the context of the transition from state quasi-socialism and populism toward capitalism. The equilibrium of the last decade is commonly described as a regime of crony and unequal capitalism. This system appears to have generated socially unacceptable inequalities, directly by supporting the growth of a class of the super-rich and indirectly by its inability to create sufficient good jobs for the newly educated middle classes. Yet no direct evidence suggests that inequality has risen sharply in the recent past. Household surveys reveal that consumption inequality (as measured by Gini coefficients) has risen moderately in Egypt, from about 0.3 in the 1990s to 0.35 in the 2000s (Belhaj and Wissa 2011; Bibi and Nabli 2011). In Tunisia, inequality as measured by consumption inequality fell, from about 0.43 in the mid-1980s to 0.39 in the mid-2000s, but there are also indications of a rise in the urban-rural divide. Furthermore, levels of inequality vary across the Arab transitioning countries, with lower levels in Egypt and higher levels in Tunisia (Bibi and Nabli 2011, 31).

There are two reasons to think that these statistics describe only a limited part of reality. First, household surveys are notorious for undercounting the rich. There are many indications of a rise in the income share of the 10% richest in society, who are perceived to have benefited most from a more market-oriented economy, and of the top 1%, who have benefited most from the rampant crony capitalism of the last decade. By some estimates, the top 10% in Egypt, Morocco, Jordan, and Syria may have commanded 30 to 40% of GDP by 2010.[10]

Second, grievances are also likely to be connected to changes in the *inequality of opportunities* rather than to only the inequality of incomes per se. Over time the rollback of the state had reduced the role of the state as an employer. In Egypt, for example, only 25% of the labor force worked for the state by 2009, declining from a height of 40% of the workers. In Jordan, the private sector has generated more jobs than in the past, but these jobs generally lack social insurance and/or are based on temporary or no contracts. Furthermore, the bifurcation between the formal and informal private sectors has sharpened. Informal-sector workers tend not to transition into formal-sector jobs, and although public-sector employment has increased in recent years, workers who previously held positions in the formal private sector are far more likely than informal-sector workers to move into government jobs (Assaad 2011). Recent studies show clearly that the large waves of more educated workers[11] entering the labor market were faced with an increasingly unfair situation whereby personal connections (*wasta*) and status were more important than diplomas in getting good jobs.[12] With shrinking government employment, these new entrants had to divide themselves between the formal private sector, which did not grow in proportional terms and where wages were higher than in the public sector, and a large and growing informal sector, where wages were lower than in the public sector (Assaad 2009). Furthermore, the decline of health and education systems, key drivers of social mobility, had limited the ability of non-elites to advance (Belhaj and Wissa 2011; Salehi-Isfahani, Belhaj, and Assaad 2011). Empirical research has only recently started to focus on this type of inequality, but recent work is starting to show that unlike simple consumption-based measures, such as the Gini coefficient, measures of inequality of opportunity show a dramatic increase in recent years.

To summarize, inequality based on standard consumption-based measures does not appear to be a driver of the uprisings. There is no evidence of a sharp spike in this type of inequality in the Arab countries; levels of inequality varied across the countries that witnessed mass protests, and the region as a whole does not exhibit particularly high levels of income inequality. Recent analyses, however, indicate that inequalities of opportunity were on the rise across the non-oil-exporting countries of the region. In the context of post-independence social bargains, in which citizens experienced and came to expect real social mobility as a result of state economic and welfare policies, the inability to advance socioeconomically may have been especially frustrating. Before we bring together the full narrative of our framework, it is essential to address one additional factor—the role of political Islam—in the evolution of politics across the region both prior to and during the uprisings.

The Role of Political Islam in the Arab Uprisings

In the aftermath of the Arab uprisings, Islamists have become increasingly important if not dominant actors in Tunisia and Egypt and, to a lesser degree, in Libya and Yemen. It is widely accepted that the uprisings were not driven by Islamists, or even by increased popular support for Islamists, who were the most vocal opponents of authoritarian rulers. Rather, Islamists were the main beneficiaries of the transitional political systems that emerged after dictators were ousted.

Although Islamists did not initiate or lead the revolts, they may have played an indirect role in driving the Arab uprisings.[13] In particular, two mechanisms related to political Islam may have contributed to the defection of the middle classes from authoritarian bargains. First, since the 1990s, Islamists across the region have become less threatening because they have increasingly moderated their ideology and tactics. For example, in 2004 the Muslim Brotherhood in Egypt made a public commitment to abide by a constitutional and democratic system that called for the recognition of "the people as the source of all authority," and it endorsed the principles of the transfer of power through free elections, the freedom of belief and expression, the freedom to form political parties, and the independence of the judiciary (Shahin 2005).[14] The moderation of Islamists may have altered the calculations of socially liberal groups that had feared a takeover by Islamic parties because of their divergent views on issues such as civil rights, the separation of mosque and state, the role of women in society, and foreign policy. Even in the context of declining economic benefits, middle-class elements may have opted to support autocrats as long as Islamists championed a very different picture of civic and political life. As more moderate Islamic parties emerged, they may have garnered more support or at least tolerance among the middle classes.[15]At the same time, insurgent groups using violent tactics declined. If fear of Islamism had perpetuated authoritarian rule (Lust 2011), then declining fear of Islamism undercut support for dictators.

Second, some of the messages of Islamist parties, which emphasized corruption and the lack of social justice under authoritarian rulers, reflected and may even have amplified growing discontent among the middle classes. Indeed, the leaders and cadres of mainstream Islamist groups, such as the Muslim Brotherhood in Egypt and its branches and analogous organizations in other Arab countries, were composed of middle-class professionals who were shut out of employment and other opportunities under crony capitalist systems (Burgat 2003; Esposito 1997; Fuller 2004). Islamism does not offer a clear-cut and uniform ideology on the market. Islamic thinkers and groups disagree on the extent to which the teachings of Islam call for redistributive measures. A dominant ideological strain associated with the rise of moderate Islamist parties such as the AKP or the Muslim Brotherhood in Egypt and Al-Nahda in Tunisia, however, is congruent with middle-class redistributive goals and supportive of market-based systems.

Public opinion data indicate that support for democratization increased among the middle classes during the 2000s, including among proponents of Islamism. Opinion polls in the Arab world undertaken by the Arab Barometer reveal that rising demand for democracy is positively correlated with support for political Islam: people favor more democracy and more Islamism at the same time. A more detailed analysis using data from the World Values Survey for Egypt shows that adherents of Islamism did not support democracy as much as secularists in 2000. By 2008, the same pattern held, except that middle-class supporters of Islamism had become, like secularists, a force for democratization (Diwan 2013). This finding suggests that Islamism acts as a conservative veil for the poor only, trumping their class interests. After 2008, however, this effect did not operate among the middle classes, either because they were better educated and/or because they were more likely to be influenced by more moderate parties within the Islamist umbrella. This supports and refines Mark Tessler's (2011) argument that support for political Islam is congruent with rising support for democracy and also shows that this claim applies to the middle classes but not the poor.

Islamists were not central actors in the uprisings that toppled authoritarian rulers, but their role in society and politics may have contributed to the defection of the middle classes from authoritarian coalitions, a key step in the breakdown of authoritarian rule. First, the declining fear of political Islam that accompanied the growing moderation of Islamist groups may have compelled secularists to distance themselves from autocratic rulers. Second, the messages of the Islamist opposition may have resonated with the middle classes, who viewed corruption and cronyism as obstacles to their social advancement.

In the next section, we combine the diverse factors addressed in this section to present a framework for understanding the Arab uprisings.

An Emerging Framework

The framework that emerges from this rapid exploration connects patterns of economic development (especially a shift toward a more market-based system, the decline of public welfare functions, and the rise of crony capitalism), social change (the rise in popular aspirations and grievances), and political change (the defection of the middle classes from the authoritarian coalition). This combination of changing economic circumstances and the attendant increase in inequality of opportunities fueled a spike in perceived inequality, which helped to unravel the implicit bargain between authoritarian rulers and key constituents.

To recap, this framework includes the following key elements. First, in the mid-1980s, the rollback of the state began without a concomitant democratic opening. In this context, an elite, capitalistic class benefited from personal connections to acquire disproportionate access to lucrative opportunities. The super-elite allied with state security apparatuses, which enforced their dominance through repression (sticks) and economic co-optation (carrots) to maintain the support of the middle class. Tight state-business relations within a supposedly "liberal" economic environment and political repression did not translate into a successful industrial policy. Instead, a system of gift exchange between the state and key constituents developed; the moderate performance of this system inhibited growth and thus did not foster the creation of good jobs. Across the Arab world, countries that initially adopted distinct economic strategies and political regimes ended up with variants of the same crony capitalist systems. Divide-and-rule strategies, based on a combination of blanket subsidies and repression as well as fearmongering about political Islam, were the foundation of an increasingly fragile governing coalition.

Supported by the West, this autocratic, low equilibrium lasted for several decades. For a time, with the co-optation of the middle classes through subsidies and fear of a takeover by Islamists, and with the poor repressed and struggling to make ends meet, authoritarianism could endure. Mounting fiscal pressures, driven in large part by rising subsidies and lower tax revenues, led to deteriorating social services and lower public investment, further hurting the poor and marginalized regions and leading populations to identify increasingly with the poor rather than the middle classes. In this context, middle-class elements defected from authoritarian coalitions and evolved into champions of change, driven by the lack of opportunities for socioeconomic advancement and anger about rising perceived inequalities.

THE DIFFICULTIES AHEAD:
POLITICS AND ECONOMIC REFORM
DURING TRANSITIONS

The Arab uprisings were a defining moment, a big celebration of life and creativity, reflecting a deep love of country. The protests engaged women as well as men, the young and the old, and members of all social classes. Mass mobilization in the face of repression revealed the bravery and sense of empowerment of the protesters, while the use of communications technologies highlighted the ingenuity and creativity of the youth. These moments will be remembered with affection and will enter historical founding myths. Clearly, they mark the end of the authoritarian state, even if its vestiges remain.

Revolutions tend to be protracted and messy. Economic factors often contribute to the outbreak of revolts in the first place, but once set in motion, revolutionary political change can aggravate and create new economic problems. Political uncertainty, a common feature of transitional moments, exacerbates economic crises. New institutions can take years to establish, and the simultaneous adoption of political and economic reforms is notoriously difficult.

The Arab transitional countries are entering this new era with a triple crisis—of the state, of capitalism, and even of national identity. The transitions are playing out against the backdrop of high expectations by the poor and an educated but often unemployed or underemployed middle class. In most of these countries, the economy requires serious restructuring and the state needs a major overhaul, but the attention of political leaders is presently focused elsewhere—largely on the role of Islam in politics and society. The price to pay for past sins seems enormous and carries over not just to economic technocratic issues but also to the necessity of coalition-building and long-term institutional reform. We briefly review the nature of the political and economic challenges facing the Middle East and discuss their implications for policymaking at the present juncture.

Political Developments After the Uprisings

Even where rulers have been deposed, genuine regime change remains in doubt in the Arab world. In Egypt, Mubarak was removed from power, but elements of his authoritarian coalition remain entrenched. The army retains significant privileges, despite the forced retirement of its top leaders, such as General Mohamed Hussein Tantawi. Although a new constitution was adopted and several rounds of elections were held, the process of political reform has been contested in Egypt, with opposition groups across the ideological spectrum claiming that they were marginalized and threatening to boycott elections. The process of writing the new constitution was rushed and fraught with tensions, with an Islamist-dominated body hastily writing and approving the draft while their opponents claimed they were sidelined from the process. In Yemen, the new president's cabinet and elements of the security forces retain many loyalists of the former president. In Libya, a sharp break took place in terms of both the identities of the new political leaders and the system of rule. Mu'ammar Qaddhafi was ousted, and the members of his family and close advisers are either under arrest or indicted in absentia. Nonetheless, the outcome of the revolution remains uncertain. Government authority is tenuous, and armed militias control much of the territory.

Of all the Arab countries where the protests successfully deposed dictators, Tunisia initially made the most progress toward the establishment of a new democratic system. In October 2011, elections for a constitutional assembly were held, ushering in a coalition government dominated by the main Islamist party, Al-Nahda, in alliance with secular parties. The process of writing the constitution has been more inclusive than in Egypt, with multiple drafts subject to public debate and input from diverse civil society groups. Yet politics have become increasingly polarized, particularly across the Islamist-secularist divide. Tensions have emerged over constitutional articles on the status of women and the role of religion in the constitution. Opposition groups claim that Al-Nahda has overplayed its hand by abandoning an inclusive process of political change and allying itself with, or at least tolerating, more extremist Islamist elements, which have perpetrated acts of violence with alarming frequency. As a result, further progress on political reform and efforts to tackle Tunisia's formidable economic problems are stalled.

The electoral victories of political Islam in the Arab transitioning countries were to be expected, given that Islamist parties were more organized early in the process and appeared to have deeper grassroots support. Even in Tunisia, where Islamists were brutally suppressed and virtually wiped out under Ben 'Ali's rule, Al-Nahda managed to maintain a subterranean base of supporters and quickly reactivated and expanded its local networks after its leadership returned to the country. Yet the grab for power by Islamists was surprising. In Egypt, the Muslim Brotherhood sought and won the presidency, despite earlier commitments to moderate its control over government institutions. In Tunisia, Al-Nahda became less and less willing to compromise with secular opponents once it secured the lion's share of the vote (although not the support of the majority of Tunisia when accounting for voter turnout and the inflationary effects of electoral rules on the distribution of seats).

Efforts by Islamists to monopolize power made sense in the short term, given that political domination in this critical historical moment would enable them to mold new political institutions in their favor. Moreover, the leadership of previously banned or heavily repressed Islamist groups feared that former regime elements as well as their secular opponents would deprive them of their "rightful" victories, if given the chance. In retrospect, however, Islamist domination of the political arena was probably a mistake. In light of the deterioration of political, security, and economic outcomes and the huge obstacles to delivering tangible improvements to people's lives, Islamists may face a serious drop in popular support. Mainstream Islamists, who had developed a reputation for "moderation" in the past decade, now also face the challenge of being outbid by other, more orthodox or extremist Islamist groups. Political liberalization has facilitated the rise of "Salafists," a diverse and heterogeneous category that threatens to chip away at the bases of more moderate Islamists. In response, groups such as Al-Nahda in Tunisia and the Muslim Brotherhood in Egypt are compelled to cater to more extremist constituencies and are becoming increasingly factionalized and splintered in the process. At the same time, mainstream Islamist groups, whose constituencies were based in the middle classes under authoritarian rule, are obliged to answer to a wider swath of society. For the first time, political Islam is being put to the test.

Divisions between Islamists and secularists reflect real tensions in society. In more consolidated democracies, political institutions should be able to manage these differences, addressing distributional and ideological conflict alike. In the context of institutional flux, in which new rules of the game need to be written and adopted, it is far more difficult to handle such tensions. Without capable leaders willing to compromise across ideological divides, polarization is the inevitable result. In the Arab transitioning countries, liberal elements have been pushed to reconstitute their ranks rapidly by radicalizing and mobilizing their supporters, focusing more on winning upcoming elections and blocking Islamist initiatives than on achieving good economic performance. For their part, Islamists have viewed the resort to street politics by liberal, secular groups as a nondemocratic rejection of their legitimate electoral gains. Their heightened sense of unfairness adds to a spiral of conflict that has ratcheted up tensions, making compromise all the more difficult. Ideally, upcoming parliamentary elections will reduce the cycle of polarization as coalitions are formed to craft social and economic programs, but whether inclusive elections can take place is uncertain under present circumstances.

At the minimum, it is now clear that transitions will take longer than expected. In the meantime, paralysis has taken hold, blocking decision-making by governing bodies. Moreover, the current environment, in which protracted insecurity, food shortages, and even economic collapse are real possibilities, invites the prospect of coups and military takeovers. The formation of a new political order has proved to be the greatest challenge in the Arab transitioning countries, bedeviling efforts to address the region's serious economic challenges.

Economic Challenges After the Uprisings

The revolutions were experienced as a negative economic shock. Tourism took a hit, capital flight accelerated, exports declined, and investment collapsed in Tunisia, Egypt, and Yemen. As a result, economic growth declined sharply in 2011—it was negative in Tunisia (–2%) and Yemen (–1%) and low in Egypt (1.8%) and Bahrain (2.1%). Output collapsed in Libya, given the disruption to its oil production (–60%). Across the region, unemployment increased.

Syria has been devastated. The human toll in death and suffering is staggering. Millions have been made refugees, in their country and in neighboring countries. Economic production has taken a big hit, and the destruction of assets is already estimated in the tens of billions of dollars. The economies of Lebanon and Jordan have also been negatively affected by regional instability and the influx of refugees.

Initially, governments reacted with expansionary policies to smooth out the downturn, especially in the face of rising social demands and the high expectations generated by the uprisings. Public-sector wages, subsidies, and government investment were increased in many countries around the region. In the Gulf countries, budgets were massively expanded. For example, expenditure increased by over one-third in Saudi Arabia. In the oil-importing countries, both external accounts and budget balances deteriorated. By 2012, fiscal deficits in Morocco, Jordan, Tunisia, and Lebanon had shot up to between 6 and 7% of GDP. In Egypt, the fiscal deficit ballooned at 12% of GDP, and international reserves plummeted.

As a result of these developments, by 2012 governments in oil-importing countries had no fiscal space to continue with stimulus programs, and therefore growth remained low in 2012 (about 2 to 3%). Expansionary policies were supported mainly by domestic debt levels as aid did not rise, despite repeated promises.[16] Unlike other regions that have undergone economic and political transitions simultaneously, notably eastern Europe, no external actor has eased the transition with large-scale aid and promises of a future economic and political union. Indeed, the uprisings occurred in the context of a global economic downturn and the Eurozone crisis, which has restricted the availability of external support. As a result, in Egypt, Jordan, and Tunisia, economic indicators are presently flashing yellow, and macroeconomic crises with sharp currency depreciation and banking crises are possible in the future. IMF programs are being developed in these countries, but the "street" may not allow the passage of minimal reform programs that can contain deficits to levels that are financeable (let alone sustainable). By the beginning of 2013, it had become clear that economic recovery could not proceed until the political crises were resolved. Indeed, a downward spiral may ensue as polarized politics exacerbate economic difficulties, in turn leading to more fractious politics.

While in opposition, the Islamist movements that came to power in Egypt and Tunisia had frequently criticized the economic policies of the previous regimes and had promised to combat corruption, poverty, and inequality. In the face of the political turmoil generated by the rush to fill the power vacuum, write constitutions, and compete for elections, however, Islamists have been unable to move on any of their big promises. Their commitments to promoting social justice, reducing subsidies in order to provide more fiscal space in budgets, attacking cronyism, and eliminating waste in bloated bureaucracies have not been realized thus far.

Going Forward: Economic Reforms for the Future

The political and economic challenges facing the Arab transitioning countries are compounded by high popular expectations and problematic legacies of the past. How political challenges are addressed will largely determine the course of economic policies. Unless new surprises arise, the contours of the emerging political settlement will include fewer favors for elite capital. Yet new rulers should attempt to make peace with large capital-holders and convince them to invest in the future, as is already happening in Egypt, rather than withdraw, as happened with the socialist revolutions of the 1960s. At the same time, the interests of the poor should be balanced with those of the middle classes, which benefited disproportionately under authoritarian bargains.

Certain technical challenges will remain difficult to resolve, even if politics become less polarized. The first and most immediate challenge is economic stabilization in order to avoid an economic and financial meltdown, which would further complicate the political process. Building a package of measures that reduce expenditures, raise revenues, and command some minimum level of popular support is a tricky endeavor in the best of circumstances, and it will be very challenging in the current hyperpoliticized environment. A more stable political environment, however, also offers the possibility of initiating other important reforms over the next three to five years.

The second area of focus should be the modernization of the state and the rehabilitation of public services, especially health, education, and social protection. New governments with broad popular support should be able to redirect expenditures toward social services and away from subsidies that benefit the better-off and to make tax systems more progressive while enlarging the tax base. Improving service delivery and fighting petty corruption will require increases in public-sector wages, which will be complicated by the large size of the civil service, particularly in Egypt.

The third agenda concerns the business environment and job creation. Past experiences, and especially the failures of both socialism and state capitalism, limit policy choices for the Arab region. For example, developing an effective industrial policy that supports rising sectors of the economy with targeted subsidies, as was done in East Asia, would be an unreasonable goal in the next three to five years, given institutional weaknesses and the risks of capture by powerful interest groups. Priority issues such as improving competition, democratizing credit, and reducing the constraints faced by the informal sector do not have easy solutions.

These are complicated challenges, technically, politically, and administratively. In the end, what will make a difference is the process by which solutions adapted to the particular environments of each country are found and implemented. The greatest contribution of the "revolutions" to these challenges should be in fostering greater popular participation in the policymaking process. It is the sense of empowerment of new actors such as labor unions, employers' associations, student groups, and other civil society groups—who can cross ideological lines to represent social interests and hold their representatives accountable—that constitutes the real revolution.

NOTES

1. See Pepinsky (2009) and Slater (2010) on the importance of coalitions for authoritarian durability.

2. In 2005, the percentage of the population living on $2 per day was about 17% in the Middle East and Latin America, 39% in East Asia, 73% in sub-Saharan Africa, and 74% in South Asia. When measured by the percentage of the population living on $1.25 per day, the Middle East has by far the lowest poverty rate of all regions (World Bank, *World Development Indicators,* 2005c).

3. For example, the share of the informal sector in the economy was 44% in Morocco, 33% in Egypt, 34% in Syria, 30% in Tunisia and Lebanon, and 26% in Jordan. This is higher than the share in many developing countries, such as Indonesia and Vietnam, where the informal sector accounts for about 21% and 16% of the economy, respectively. In the United States, the informal sector accounts for about 9% of the economy (World Bank, *World Development Indicators,* 2010).

4. For example, public spending on education as a percentage of GDP has hovered around 5% since the late 1970s (World Bank, *World Development Indicators,* various years).

5. For reviews of this literature, see Posusney and Angrist (2005) and Schlumberger (2007).

6. For example, spending on energy subsidies exceeds social expenditures by two to three times in Egypt and Tunisia.

7. In Egypt, real wages in the public sector declined over time. The minimum wage, which anchors all wages, declined from 60% of per capita GDP in the early 1980s to a mere 13% in 2007 (Abdelhamid and El Baradei 2009).

8. Data from the World Values Survey also suggest that the average financial satisfaction of the poor has deteriorated, that of the middle classes remains stable, and that of the rich has risen, further bolstering a sense of rising inequality during the period (Diwan 2013).

9. In 2000, however, young people were much more likely to support democracy than their elders (Diwan 2013).

10. Between 1998 and 2006, according to household surveys, GDP rose by 60% in nominal terms, while consumption stayed essentially at the same level all along the distribution, suggesting that large parts of the increase may have accrued to the undercounted rich and that very little has trickled down to the rest of society.

11. In Egypt, average years of education had risen from two years in the 1980s to eight years by 2009 (Barro and Lee 2010; Campante and Chor 2011).

12. The plight of the main character of the novel *The Yacoubian Building*, written by the Egyptian author and dentist Alaa al-Aswany (2006), shows poignantly the frustration of well-educated youth whose families lack the social standing and relationships to enable them to realize their professional aspirations.

13. During the sustained protests in Tahrir Square that led to Mubarak's resignation, the Muslim Brotherhood and other Islamist groups (along with other non-Islamist citizen groups) helped to solve the coordination problems that constrain social mobilization by opening up mosques as meeting points and medical treatment centers.

14. Similar processes of moderation took place in Turkey and Tunisia. In Turkey, a combination of the lessons from repression, opportunism, and the growth of a friendly middle class compelled the AKP to moderate (Demiralp 2009; Mecham 2004). In Tunisia, the Al-Nahda leadership claimed in 1981, "We have no right to interpose between the people and those whom the people choose and elect" (Tamimi 2001).

15. In Egypt, state repression increased after the electoral gains of the Muslim Brotherhood in the 2005 elections. When the party emerged as a credible alternative, the ruling regime cracked down on it more forcefully (Osman 2010).

16. For example, the Deauville Partnership, an international effort launched by the G8 countries in May 2011, aimed to provide assistance for economic stabilization, job creation, good governance, and regional integration in the Arab transitioning countries.

REFERENCES

The following abbreviations are used in the references:
MEJ, *Middle East Journal*, and **IJMES**, *International Journal of Middle East Studies.*

AAAID (Arab Authority for Agricultural Investment and Development) (2005), *Annual Report, 2005,* at http://www.aaaid.org/pdf/annualreport2005/english/Report1-5.pdf.

Abbasi-Shavazi, Mohammad Jalal (2001), "The Fertility Revolution in Iran," *Population et Sociétés* 373 (November), 1–4.

_____ (2002), "Recent Changes and the Future of Fertility in Iran," New York, United Nations, Department of Economic and Social Affairs.

'Abdalla, Ahmed (1985), *The Student Movement and National Politics in Egypt,* London, Zed Books.

Abdel-Fadil, Mahmoud (1980), *The Political Economy of Nasserism,* Cambridge, Cambridge University Press.

_____ (1983), "Informal Sector Employment in Egypt," in R. Lobbon, ed., *Urban Research Strategies for Egypt,* Cairo Papers in Social Science, American University in Cairo, 6, 2 (June), 16–40.

Abdelhamid, Doha, and El Baradei, Laila, (2009), "Reforming the Pay System for Government Employees in Egypt," Working paper, Cairo, Government of Egypt, Information and Decision Support Center.

Abdel-Jaber, Tayseer (1993), "Inter-Arab Labor Movements: Problems and Prospects," in Said El-Naggar, ed., *Economic Development of the Arab Countries: Selected Issues,* Washington, D.C., International Monetary Fund, 145–162.

Abdel-Khaleq, Gouda, and Tignor, Robert, eds. (1982), *The Political Economy of Income Distribution in Egypt,* New York, Holmes and Meier.

Abdel-Malek, Anouar (1968), *Egypt: Military Society,* New York, Vintage Books.

Abderrahman, Walid A. (2001), "Water Demand Management in Saudi Arabia," in Naser I. Faruqui, Asit K. Biswas, and Murad J. Bino, eds., *Water Management in Islam,* Ottowa, IDRC/UNU Press.

Abouleinem, Soheir, Al-Tathy, Heba, and Kheir-el-Din, Hanaa (2009), *The Impact of Phasing Out the Petroleum Subsidies in Egypt,* Working Paper no. 145, Cairo, Egypt, Egyptian Center for Economic Studies.

Abu-Amr, Ziad (1994), *Islamic Fundamentalism in the West Bank and Gaza: Muslim Brotherhood and Islamic Jihad,* Bloomington, Indiana University Press.

AbuKhalil, As'ad (2002), *Bin Laden, Islam, and America's New "War on Terrorism,"* New York, Seven Stories Press.

——— (2004), *The Battle for Saudi Arabia: Royalty, Fundamentalism, and Global Power,* New York, Seven Stories Press.

Abun-Nasr, Jamil M. (1971), *A History of the Magrib,* Cambridge, Cambridge University Press.

Achy, Lahcen (2002), "Labor Market and Growth in Morocco," at http://www.gdnet.org/pdf2/gdn_library/global_research_projects/explaining_growth/Morocco_labor_markets_final.pdf.

Adams, Richard H., Jr. (1986), *Development and Social Change in Rural Egypt,* Syracuse, N.Y., Syracuse University Press.

——— (1991), *The Effects of International Remittances on Poverty, Inequality, and Development in Rural Egypt,* Washington, D.C., International Food Policy Research Institute Research Report 86.

Adams, Richard H., Jr., and Page, John (2003), "Poverty, Inequality and Growth in Selected Middle East and North African Countries, 1980–2000," *World Development* 13, 12, 2027–2048.

——— (2003), "International Migration, Remittances, and Poverty in Developing Countries," Washington, D.C., World Bank, Poverty Research Working Paper 3179, December, at http://www-wds.worldbank.org/servlet/WDSContentServer/WDSP/IB/2004/01/21/000160016_20040121175547/Rendered/PDF/wps3179.pdf.

——— (2005), "The Impact of International Migration and Remittances on Poverty," in Samuel Munzele Maimbo and Dilip Ratha, eds., *Remittances: Development Impact and Future Prospects,* Washington, D.C., World Bank, 277–306.

Addi, Lahouari (1995), *L'Algérie et la démocratie,* Paris, Editions de la Découverte.

Adelman, Irma (1984), "Beyond Export-Led Growth," *World Development* 12, 9 (September), 937–950.

Africa Watch (1990), *Denying the "Honor of Living": Sudan, a Human Rights Disaster,* New York.

Ahmad, Feroz (1981), "The Political Economy of Kemalism," in Kazancigil and Özbudun, eds., 145–164.

Ahmad, Sadiq (1984), *Public Finance in Egypt, Its Structure and Trends,* World Bank Staff Working Papers no. 639.

Ahram Online (2011), "Cairo Gated Community Palm Hills Found Illegal," Ahram Online, March 1.

Alderman, Harold (1993), "Food Preferences and Nutrition," in G. M. Craig, ed., *The Agriculture of Egypt,* Oxford, Oxford University Press, 114–127.

Alderman, Harold, and von Braun, J. (1984), *The Effects of the Egyptian Food Ration and Subsidy System on Income Distribution and Consumption,* Washington, D.C., IFPRI Research Report no. 45.

Algar, Hamid (1985), *Islam and Revolution: Imam Khomeini, Writings and Declarations,* London, KPI.

Ali, Ali Abdel Gadel (2003), "Poverty in the Arab Region: A Selective Review," background paper prepared for the IFPRI/API Collaborative Research Project on "Public Policy and Poverty Reduction in the Arab Region," www.arab-api.org/wps0402.pdf.

Allan, J. A. (1999), "A Convenient Solution," *UNESCO Courier* (January).

—— (2001), *The Middle East Water Question: Hydropolitics and the Global Economy,* London, I.B. Tauris.

Allan, J. A., and Karshenas, M. (1996), "Managing Environmental Capital: The Case of Water in Israel, Jordan, the West Bank and Gaza, 1947 to 1995," in *Water, Peace and the Middle East: Negotiating Resources in the Jordan Basin,* ed. J. A. Allan and J. H. Court, London, I. B. Taurus.

Allan, J. A., and Olmsted, Jennifer C. (2003), "Politics, Economics and (Virtual) Water: A Discursive Analysis of Water Policies in the Middle East and North Africa," in Lofgren, ed., 53–78.

Alley, April Longley (2010), "The Rules of the Game: Unpacking Patronage Politics in Yemen," *Middle East Journal,* 64, 3, 385–409.

Amin, Galal (1980), *The Modernization of Poverty: A Study of the Political Economy of Growth in Nine Arab Countries, 1945–1970,* Leiden, E. J. Brill.

—— (1995), *Egypt's Economic Predicament,* New York and Leiden, E. J. Brill.

Amin, Galal, and Taylor-Awny, Elizabeth (1985), *International Migration of Egyptian Labour: A Review of the State of the Art,* Ottawa, International Development Research Center (IDRC).

Amin, Samir (1982), *The Arab Economy Today,* London, Zed Press.

Al-Amri, Arwa, Annuzaili, Khekra, and al-Deram, Arwa (2003), *Overview of the Situation of Children, Women, and ECD in Yemen,* World Bank, Early Childhood Development Virtual University, at http://www.ecdvu.org/mena/downloads/yemenreport/yemenreport.pdf.

Amsden, Alice H. (1992), *Asia's Next Giant: South Korea and Late Industrialization,* New York and London, Oxford University Press.

—— (2001), *The Rise of "The Rest": Challenges to the West from Late-Industrializing Countries,* New York and London, Oxford University Press.

Amuzegar, Jahangir (1983), *Oil Exporters' Economic Development in an Interdependent World,* IMF Occasional Paper no. 18.

—— (1993), *Iran's Economy Under the Islamic Republic,* London and New York, I. B. Tauris.

Anderson, Lisa (1986), *The State and Social Transformation in Tunisia and Libya, 1930–1980,* Princeton, Princeton University Press.

Anderson, Perry (1980), *Lineages of the Absolutist State,* London, Verso Editions.

Annuaire statistique du Maroc (1984), Rabat, Kingdom of Morocco.

al-Ansari, Hamied (1986), *Egypt: The Stalled Society,* Albany, State University of New York Press.

Aoyama, Atsuko (2001), *Reproductive Health in the Middle East and North Africa: Well-being for All.* Washington, D.C., World Bank.

El Araby, M. (2002), "Urban Growth and Environmental Degradation: The Case of Cairo, Egypt," *Cities* 19, 6, 389–400.

Arian, Asher (1985), *Politics in Israel: The Second Generation,* Chatham, N.J., Chatham House.

Ascherio, A., et al. (1992), "Effects of the Gulf War on Infant and Child Mortality in Iraq," *New England Journal of Medicine* 327, 13, 931–936.

ASDA'A/Burson-Marsteller (2010), *Arab Youth Survey 2009/2010,* Dubai, UAE, ASDA'A/Burson-Marsteller.

Ashraf, A., and Banuazizi, A. (1985), "The State, Classes, and Modes of Mobilization in the Iranian Revolution," *State, Culture, and Society* 1, 3, 3–40.

Aslan, Mehmet (2005), "A Panorama of Turkey's Migration Regime with an Emphasis on the Prospects of Turkish Immigration to the EU on the Eve of the Membership Negotiations," at http://pdf.mutual-learning-employment.net/uploads/Module Xtender/PeerReviews/34/TR_Asian.pdf.

Assaad, Ragui (1997), "Kinship Ties, Social Networks, and Segmented Labor Markets: Evidence from the Construction Sector in Egypt," *Journal of Development Economics,* 52, 1, 1–30.

―――― (2009), "Labor Supply, Employment, and Unemployment in the Egyptian Economy, 1988–2006," in *The Egyptian Labor Market Revisited,* ed. Ragui Assaad, Cairo, Egypt, American University in Cairo.

―――― (2011), *The Structure and Evolution of Employment in Jordan,* Minneapolis and St. Paul, University of Minnesota.

Assaad, Ragui, el-Hamidi, Fatma, and Ahmed, Akhter U. (2000), *The Determinants of Employment Status in Egypt,* Washington, D.C., IFPRI Discussion Paper 88 (June).

Al Aswany, Alaa (2006), *The Yacoubian Building: A Novel,* New York, Harper Perennial.

Atlantic Richfield (1994), "The Middle East: The New Economic Reality, Oil," presentation by Anthony J. Finizza, Chief Economist, at the 1994 Southwest Asia Symposium of CENTCOM [U.S. Central Command], Tampa, Florida, May 18.

Axelrod, Robert (1984), *The Evolution of Cooperation,* New York, Basic Books.

Ayres, Ron (1983), "Arms Production as a Form of Import-Substituting Industrialization: The Turkish Case," *World Development* 11, 9, 813–823.

Ayubi, Nazih (1985), "Arab Bureaucracies: Expanding Size, Changing Roles," master's thesis, Politics Department, University of Exeter.

―――― (1989), *The Centralized State in Egypt* (in Arabic), Beirut, Center for Arab Unity Studies.

―――― (1991a), *Political Islam: Religion and Politics in the Arab World,* London and New York, Routledge.

―――― (1991b), *The State and Public Policies in Egypt Since Sadat,* Reading, UK, Ithaca Press.

Azzam, Henry (1994), "Development of Capital Markets in the Middle East," paper presented at the conference "The New Middle East: From Istanbul to Kabul . . . from Beirut to Cairo," The Brookings Institution and the US-Arab Chamber of Commerce, October 19–21.

El Badawi, Ibrahim, and Makdisi, Samir (2007), "Explaining the Democracy Deficit in the Arab World," *Quarterly Review of Economics and Finance,* 46, 813–831.

Baduel, Pierre-Robert (1983), "Le VIe plan tunisien: 1982–86," *Grand Maghreb,* March 21, 54–57.

Baer, Gabriel (1962), *A History of Landownership in Modern Egypt, 1800–1950,* London, Oxford University Press.

Baker, Raymond William (2003), *Islam Without Fear: Egypt and the New Islamists*, Cambridge, Harvard University Press.

Bakhash, Shaul (1984), *The Reign of the Ayatollahs,* New York, Basic Books.

Baldwin-Edwards, Martin (2005), *Migration in the Middle East and Mediterranean. A Regional Study Prepared for the Global Commission on International Migration,* Geneva, Global Commission on International Migration.

Barkey, Henri, ed. (1992), *The Politics of Economic Reform in the Middle East,* New York, St. Martin's Press.

Barnett, Michael (1992), *Confronting the Costs of War: Military Power, State, and Society in Egypt and Israel,* Princeton, Princeton University Press.

Barro, Robert J., and Lee, Jong-Wha Lee (2010), "A New Data Set of Educational Attainment in the World, 1950–2010," Working Paper no. 15902, Cambridge, National Bureau of Economic Research.

Batatu, Hanna (1978), *The Old Social Classes and the Revolutionary Movements of Iraq,* Princeton, Princeton University Press.

_____ (1979), "Class Analysis and Iraqi Society," *Peuples Méditerranéens* 8 (July–September), 101–116.

Bates, Robert (1981), *Markets and States in Tropical Africa,* Berkeley, University of California Press.

_____ (1990), "Macropolitical Economy in the Field of Development," in James E. Alt and Kenneth A. Shepsle, eds., *Perspectives in Positive Political Economy,* Cambridge, Cambridge University Press.

Bayat, Asef, and Denis, Eric (2000), "Who Is Afraid of *ashwaiyyat*? Urban Change and Politics in Egypt," *Environment & Urbanization* 12, 2 (October), 185–199.

BBC News (2003), "King Loyalists Win Jordan Poll," June 19, at http://news.bbc.co.uk /2/hi/middle_east/2999556.stm.

Beaugé, Florence (2011), "Orange Tunisie Passe sous la Tutelle de l'État Tunisien," *Le Monde,* March 30, 18.

Beblawi, Hazem (1984), *The Arab Gulf Economy in a Turbulent Age,* London, Croom Helm.

Bechri, Mohamed Z., and Naccache, Sonia (2003), "The Political Economy of Development Policy in Tunisia," Cairo, ERF, www.erf.org.eg/grp/GRP_Sep03/Tunisia -Pol_Econ.pdf.

Belhaj, Nadia, and Wissa, Christiane (2011), "Inequality Trends and Determinants in the Arab Region," paper presented at the conference "Inequality in the Arab Region," Economic Research Forum (ERF), Cairo, Egypt.

Belkacem, Laabas (2001), "Poverty Dynamics in Algeria," Kuwait: Arab Planning Institute, www.erf.org.eg/html/Laabas.pdf.

Bellin, Eva (2002), *Stalled Democracy: Capital, Labor, and the Paradox of State-Sponsored Development,* Ithaca and London, Cornell University Press.

_____ (2004), "The Robustness of Authoritarianism in the Middle East: Exceptionalism in Comparative Perspective," *Comparative Politics,* 36, 2, 139–157.

Benchemsi, Ahmed (2012), "Morocco: Outfoxing the Opposition," *Journal of Democracy,* 23, 1, 57–69.

Ben-Dor, Gabriel (1983), *State and Conflict in the Middle East,* New York, Praeger.

Benissad, M. E. (1982), *Economie du développement de l'Algérie,* Paris, Economica.

Bennoune, Mahfoud (1988), *The Making of Contemporary Algeria, 1830–1987,* Cambridge, Cambridge University Press.

Ben-Porath, Yoram (1972), "Fertility in Israel, an Economist's Interpretation: Differentials and Trends, 1950–1970," in Cooper and Alexander, eds., 502–541.

Berar-Awad, Azita (1984), *Employment Planning in the Sudan: An Overview of Selected Issues,* Geneva, ILO.

Berger, Morroe (1964), *The Arab World Today,* New York, Doubleday.

Bergh, Sylvia (2005), *Explaining Slow Economic Growth and Poor Social Development Indicators: The Case of Morocco*, Oxford, Oxford Council on Good Governance, Economy Analysis no. 7 (October).

Bernal, Victoria (1999), "Migration, Modernity and Islam in Rural Sudan," *Middle East Report* 211 (Summer).

Bianchi, Robert (1984), *Interest Groups and Political Development in Turkey,* Princeton, Princeton University Press.

_____ (1986), "The Corporatization of the Egyptian Labor Movement," *MEJ* 4, 3 (Summer), 429–444.

Bibi, Sami, and Nabli, Mustapha K. (2011), "Equity and Inequality in the Arab Region," Policy Research Report, Cairo, Egypt, Economic Research Forum (ERF).

Bienen, Henry S., and Gersovitz, M. (1985), "Economic Stabilization, Conditionality, and Political Stability," *International Organization* 39, 4 (Autumn), 729–754.

Bill, James A., and Springborg, Robert (1994), *Politics in the Middle East,* 4th ed., New York, Harper Collins.

Binder, Leonard (1957), "Prolegomena to the Comparative Study of Middle East Governments," *American Political Science Review* 51, 3, 651–668.

Binswanger, Hans (1989), "The Policy Response of Agriculture," *Proceedings of the World Bank Annual Conference on Development Economics,* 231–258.

Birks, J. S., and Sinclair, C. A. (1980), *International Migration and Development in the Arab Region,* Geneva, ILO.

Blair, John M. (1976), *The Control of Oil,* New York, Vintage Books.

Blake, Gerald, Dewdney, John, and Mitchell, Jonathan (1987), *The Cambridge Atlas of the Middle East and North Africa,* Cambridge, Cambridge University Press.

Bonnenfant, Paul, ed. (1982), *La péninsule arabique d'aujourd'hui,* vol. 1, Paris, Editions du CNRS.

Boratav, Korkut (1981), "Kemalist Economic Policies and Etatism," in Kazancigil and Özbudun, eds., 165–190.

Boratav, Korkut, Yeldan, A. Erinc, and Kose, Ahmet H. (2000), "Globalization, Distribution and Social Policy: Turkey, 1980–1998," New York, New School University, Center for Economic Policy Analysis, Working Paper no. 20 (February).

Bourdarbat, Brahim (2005), "Job-Search Strategies and the Unemployment of University Graduates in Morocco," paper presented at International Conference on Labor

Market Dynamics, University of Bologna, Italy (May 5–8), at http://www.iza.org /conference_files/iza_ebrd_2005/boudarbat_b1612.pdf.

Braverman, Avishay (1989), "Comment," *Proceedings of the World Bank Annual Conference on Development Economics,* 259–262.

Browers, Michaelle L. (2009), *Political Ideology in the Arab World: Accommodation and Transformation,* Cambridge, Cambridge University Press.

Brown, L. Carl (1984), *International Politics and the Middle East: Old Rules, Dangerous Games,* Princeton, Princeton University Press.

Brown, L. C., and Itzkowitz, N., eds. (1977), *Psychological Dimensions of Near Eastern Studies,* Princeton, Darwin Press.

Brubaker, Rogers (2006), *Ethnicity Without Groups,* Cambridge, Harvard University Press.

BSB (2005), "Turkey in 2005 and Beyond: Macroeconomic Policy, Patterns of Growth and Persistent Fragilities," *Bagimsiz Sosyal Bilimciler* (Independent Social Scientists Alliance), posted to Global Policy Network, June 9, at http://www.gpn.org/data /turkey/turkey-analysis.pdf.

Bujra, A. S. (1971), *The Politics of Stratification: A Study of Political Change in a South Arabian Town,* Oxford, Clarendon Press.

Bulatao, Rodolfo A., and Richardson, Gail (1994), *Fertility and Family Planning in Iran, Middle East and North Africa,* Discussion Paper Series no. 13, Washington, D.C., World Bank, November.

Bulliet, Richard (1999), "Twenty Years of Islamic Politics," *MEJ,* 53, 2 (Spring), 189–200.

Burgat, François (1993), *The Islamic Movement in North Africa,* Austin, University of Texas Press.

_____ (2003), *Face to Face with Political Islam,* London, I. B. Tauris.

Burnam, Gilbert, et al. (2006), "Mortality After the 2003 Invasion of Iraq: A Cross-sectional Cluster Sample Survery," *The Lancet,* October 11, at http://www.the |lancet.com.

Bush, Ray, ed. (2002), *Counter-revolution in Egypt's Countryside: Land and Farmers in the Era of Economic Reform,* London, Zed Books.

Business Week (2006), "The New Middle East Oil Bonanza," March 13, at http://www .businessweek.com/magazine/content/06_11/b3975001.htm.

CAAT (Campaign Against the Arms Trade) (2002), Turkey Submission, at http:// www.caat.org.uk/publications/government/turkey-submission-0102.php.

Caldwell, John C. (1986), "Routes to Low Mortality in Poor Countries," *Population and Development Review* 12, 2 (June), 171–220.

Cammett, Melani (2004), "Challenges to Networks of Privilege in Morocco: Implications for Network Analysis," in Steven Heydemann, ed., *Networks of Privilege in the Middle East: The Politics of Economic Reform Revisited,* New York, Palgrave Macmillan, 245–280.

_____ (2007), *Globalization and Business Politics in Arab North Africa: A Comparative Perspective,* Cambridge, Cambridge University Press.

Campante, Filipe R., and Chor, Davin (2011), "'The People Want the Fall of the Regime': Schooling, Political Protest, and the Economy," Faculty Research Working Paper Series, Cambridge, Harvard University, John F. Kennedy School of Government.

Campbell, Colin J., and Laherere, Jean H. (1998), "The End of Cheap Oil," *Scientific American* (March), 78–83.

CAPMAS (Central Agency for Public Mobilization and Statistics) (1989), *Report of the Sample Census of 1986* (in Arabic), Cairo, Government of Egypt.

Carothers, Thomas, and Ottaway, Marina (2005), *Uncharted Journey: Promoting Democracy in the Middle East,* Washington, D.C., Carnegie Institute for International Peace.

Catusse, Myriam (2008), *Le Temps des Entrepreneurs? Politique et Transformations du Capitalisme au Maroc,* Paris, Maisonneuve & Larose.

Celasun, Merih (1983), *Sources of Industrial Growth and Structural Change: The Case of Turkey,* Washington, D.C., World Bank Staff Working Papers no. 641.

Central Bank, Republic of Turkey (1984), *Annual Report, 1983,* Ankara.

Central Bank of Iran, *Annual Review* (various issues).

Chandra, Kanchan, ed. (2012), *Constructivist Theories of Ethnic Politics,* Oxford, Oxford University Press.

Chandulal, S. (1999), "The Sudanese Strategic Report, 1997: Some Questions to Real Progress," University of Bremen, Sudan Economy Research Group, Discussion Paper no. 30 (January).

Chang, Ha-Joon (2002), *Kicking Away the Ladder: Development Strategy in Historical Perspective,* London, Anthem Press.

Charmes, Jacques (1986), *Emploi et revenues dans le secteur non-structuré des pays du Maghreb et du Machrek,* New York, Social Science Research Council.

Chatelus, Michel (1982), "De la rente pétrolière au développement économique: Perspectives et contradictions de l'évolution économique dans la péninsule," in Bonnenfant, ed., 75–154.

_____ (1984), "Attitudes Toward Public Sector Management and Reassertion of the Private Sector in the Arab World," paper presented at the Middle East Studies Association annual meeting, San Francisco, Calif., November 28–December 1.

Chaudhry, Kiren Aziz (1997), *The Price of Wealth: International Capital Flows and the Political Economy of Late Development,* Ithaca, Cornell University Press.

_____ (2005), "New and Recurring Forms of Poverty and Inequality in the Arab World," unpublished paper, University of California, Berkeley.

Chekir, Hamouda, and Diwan, Ishac (2012), "Distressed Whales on the Nile—Egypt Capitalists in the Wake of the 2010 Revolution," Working Paper no. 250, Cambridge, Harvard University, Center for International Development.

Chemingui, Mohamed Abdelbasset (2003), "What Macroeconomics Factors Explain Algeria's Poor Economic Growth Performance?" background paper for the GDN Global Research project on Explaining Growth in Developing Countries: The Case of Algeria, at http://www.erf.org.eg/grp/GRP_Sep03/Algeria-Growth.pdf.

_____ (2005), "Harnessing Public Spending for Poverty Reduction in Yemen," Kuwait, Arab Planning Institute, at http://www.arab-api.org/w_cairo5.pdf.

Chemingui, Mohamed Abdelbasset, and Ayadi, Nassima (2003), "Understanding the Poor Human Capital Contribution to Economic Growth in Algeria," Global Development Project on Explaining Growth in Developing Countries: The Case of Algeria, at http://www.gdnet.org/pdf2/gdn_library/global_research_projects/explaining _growth/Algeria_human_capital_final.pdf.

Chemingui, Mohamed Abdelbasset, and Thaber, Chokri (2001), "Internal and External Reforms in Agricultural Policy in Tunisia and Poverty in Rural Areas," Global Development Project on Explaining Growth in Developing Countries, at http://www .gdnet.org/pdf/chemingui.pdf.

Choucri, Nazli (1986), "The Hidden Economy: A New View of Remittances in the Arab World," *World Development* 14, 6, 697–712.

CIA (Central Intelligence Agency), World Factbook Online, various years, at http:// www.cia.gov/cia/publications/factbook/index.html.

CIA (1993), *Atlas of the Middle East,* Washington, D.C., Government Printing Office.

Cinar, E. Mine, ed. (2003), *The Economics of Women and Work in the Middle East and North Africa,* Amsterdam, JAI.

Cingranelli-Richards (CIRI) (various years), *Human Rights Dataset.*

Cleaver, Kevin M. (1982), *The Agricultural Development Experience of Algeria, Morocco, and Tunisia,* Washington, D.C., World Bank Staff Working Paper no. 552.

Clément, J. F. (1986), "Les révoltes urbaines de janvier 1984 au Maroc," *Bulletin du Réseau Villes Monde Arabe* 5 (November), 3–46.

Cohen, John M., et al. (1981), "Development from Below: Local Development Associations in the Yemen Arab Republic," *World Development* 9, 11/12, 1039–1061.

Colclough, Christopher (1982), "The Impact of Primary Schooling on Economic Development: A Review of the Evidence," *World Development* 10, 2/3, 1018–1035.

Collier, David, ed. (1979), *The New Authoritarianism in Latin America,* Princeton, Princeton University Press.

Commander, Simon, and Burgess, Simon (1988), *Labor Markets in N. Africa and the Near East: A Survey of Developments Since 1970,* Aleppo, Syria, International Center for Agricultural Research in Dry Areas (ICARDA).

Confédération Démocratique du Travail (CDT)/Cofitex (1997), Fes, Morocco, Barnamig Ittifaq.

Cooper, C., and Alexander, S., eds. (1972), *The Economic Development and Population Growth in the Middle East,* New York, American Elsevier.

Cornia, Giovanni Andrea, and Menchini, Leonardo (2001), "The Pace and Distribution of Gains in Child Well-Being Over 1980–2000: Some Preliminary Results," in Giovanni Andrea Cornia, ed., *Harnessing Globalization for Children*, Florence, Italy, Innocenti Research Center, Chapter 2.

Courbage, Youssef (1999), *New Demographic Scenarios in the Mediterranean Region*, Paris, National Institute of Demographic Studies (INED).

Cremer, Jacques, and Salehi-Isfahani, Djavad (1991), *Models of the Oil Market,* London, Harwood Academic Publishers.

Crystal, Jill (1990), *Oil and Politics in the Gulf: Rulers and Merchants in Kuwait and Qatar,* New York, Cambridge University Press.

Dahl, Robert (2003), *How Democratic Is the American Constitution?* 2nd ed., New Haven, Yale University Press.

Danielson, Albert L. (1982), *The Evolution of OPEC,* New York, Harcourt Brace Jovanovich.

Danielson, Michael, and Keleç, Ruçen (1980), "Urbanization and Income Distribution in Turkey," in Özbudun and Ulusan, eds., 269–310.

_____ (1985), *The Politics of Rapid Urbanization: Government and Growth in Modern Turkey,* New York, Holmes and Meier.

Dann, Uriel (1969), *Iraq Under Qassem: A Political History, 1958–1963,* Jerusalem, Israel Universities Press.

Danziger, Sheldon H., and Weinberg, Daniel H. (1994), "The Historical Record: Trends in Family Income, Inequality, and Poverty," in Sheldon H. Danziger, Gary D. Sandefur, and Daniel H. Weinberg, eds., *Confronting Poverty: Prescriptions for Change,* Cambridge, Harvard University Press, 18–50.

Dasgupta, Dipak, Keller, Jennifer, and Srinivasan, T. G. (2002), *Reform and Elusive Growth in the Middle-East: What Has Happened in the 1990s?* Washington, D.C., World Bank, Working Paper Series no. 25, Middle East and North Africa (July).

Dasgupta, Partha (2001a), *Human Well-Being and the Natural Environment,* New York and Oxford, Oxford University Press.

_____ (2001b), "Valuing Objects and Evaluating Policies in Imperfect Economies," *Economic Journal* 111 (May), C1–C29.

Davis, Eric (1983), *Challenging Colonialism: Bank Misr and Egyptian Industrialization, 1920–1941,* Princeton, Princeton University Press.

Davis, Mike (2006), *Planet of Slums,* London and New York, Verso.

Deeb, Lara (2006), "Hizballah: A Primer," *Middle East Report,* July 31, at http://www.merip.org/mero/mero073106.html.

Deegan, Heather (1994), *The Middle East and Problems of Democracy,* Boulder, Lynne Rienner.

Deger, Saadet (1992), "Military Expenditure and Economic Development: Issues and Debates," in Geoffrey Lamb and Valeriana Kallab, eds., *Military Expenditure and Economic Development,* Washington, D.C., World Bank, 35–52.

Demiralp, Seda (2009), "The Rise of Islamic Capital and the Decline of Islamic Radicalism in Turkey," *Comparative Politics,* 41, 3, 315–335.

Denoeux, Guilain (1993), *Urban Unrest in the Middle East: A Comparative Study of Informal Networks in Egypt, Iran, and Lebanon,* Albany, State University of New York Press.

_____ (2001), "Morocco's Economic Prospects: Daunting Challenges Ahead," *Middle East Policy* 8, 2 (June), 66–87.

DERSA (1981), *L'Algérie en débat,* Paris, Maspero.

Derviş Kemal, and Robinson, Sherman (1980), "The Structure of Income Inequality in Turkey, 1950–1973," in Özbudun and Ulusan, eds., 83–122.

Destanne de Bernis, G. (1971), "Industries industrialisantes et options algériennes," *Tiers Monde* 47, 545–563.

Dethier, Jean-Jacques (1989), *Trade, Exchange Rate, and Agricultural Pricing Policies in Egypt,* Washington, D.C., World Bank.

_____ (1991), "Egypt," in Anne O. Krueger, Maurice Schiff, and Alberto Valdes, eds., *The Political Economy of Agricultural Pricing Policy,* vol. 3, *Africa and the Mediterranean,* Baltimore, Johns Hopkins University Press for the World Bank, 15–78.

Devaux, Pascal (2003), "Iran: The Future of the Rentier System in Question," *Conjoncture,* London, BNP Paribas (October).

Devereux, Stephen (1993), *Theories of Famine,* New York, Harvester-Wheatsheaf.

Devlin, Julia (2003), "From Citrus to Cellphones? Agriculture as Source of New Comparative Advantage in the Middle East and North Africa," in Lofgren, ed., 33–52.

el-Dib, M.A.M., Ismail, S. M., and Gad, Osman (1984), "Economic Motivations and Impacts of External Migration of Agricultural Workers in an Egyptian Village" (in Arabic), *Population Studies* 11, 68, 27–46.

Dillman, Bradford (2000), *State and Private Sector in Algeria: The Politics of Rent-Seeking and Failed Development,* Boulder, Westview Press.

Diwan, Ishac (2013), "Who Are the Democrats? Leading Opinions in the Wake of Egypt's 2011 Popular Uprisings," Cambridge, Harvard University, John F. Kennedy School of Government.

Diwan, Ishac, and Squire, Lyn (1993), *Economic Development and Cooperation in the Middle East and North Africa,* World Bank, Middle East and North Africa Discussion Paper Series no. 9, December.

Doumato, Eleanor Abdella, and Posusney, Marsha Pripstein, eds. (2003), *Women and Globalization in the Arab Middle East: Gender, Economy, and Society,* Boulder and London, Lynne Rienner.

Drysdale, Alasdair (1982), "The Asad Regime and Its Troubles," *MERIP Reports* 110 (November–December), 3–11.

Drysdale, Alasdair, and Blake, Gerald (1985), *The Middle East: A Political Geography,* London and New York, Oxford University Press.

Duchac, René, ed. (1973), *La formation des élites politiques maghrébines,* Paris, Librairie Générale de Droit et de Jurisprudence.

Dundar, Oslem (2003), "An Example of a Gated Community from Ankara, Turkey," paper presented at conference, Gated Communities: Building Social Division of Safer Communities, Glasgow, Scotland, September 18–19.

Dyer, Paul, and Yousef, Tarik M. (2003), "The Fertility Transition in MENA: Causes and Consequences, 1950-2000," unpublished paper, Washington, D.C., World Bank.

Easterlin, Richard (1995), "Will Raising the Incomes of All Increase the Happiness of All?" *Journal of Economic Behavior and Organization* 27, 1, 25–38.

Easterly, William (2001), "The Lost Decades: Developing Countries' Stagnation in Spite of Policy Reform, 1980–1998," *Journal of Economic Growth* 6, 1, 135–157.

_____ (2006), *The White Man's Burden: Why the West's Efforts to Aid the Rest Have Done So Much Ill and So Little Good,* New York, Penguin.

Ebadi, Shirin, and Sahimi, Muhammad (2006), "UN Sanctions Over Nuclear Program Will Inflame Iran, Set Back Democracy," Huffington Post, January 18, at http://www.huffingtonpost.com/nathan-gardels/iran-nobel-winner-says-un_b_14038.html.

Economic and Social Commission for Western Asia (1986), *Study on Impacts of Returning Migration in Selected Countries of the ECWA Region* (in Arabic), DPDI/86/14, United Nations, March.

Egypt, National Population Council (2000), *Egypt Demographic and Health Survey (DHS),* Cairo, Population Council.

Ehrlich, Paul (1968), *The Population Bomb,* New York, Ballantine.

Elster, Jon (1979), *Ulysses and the Sirens: Studies in Rationality and Irrationality*, Cambridge, Cambridge University Press.

Eltayib, Galal Eldin (2003), "The Case of Khartoum, Sudan," in *Understanding Slums: Case Studies for the 2003 Report,* UN Habitat, at http://www.ucl.ac.uk/dpu-projects /Global_Report/pdfs/khartoum.pdf.

Entelis, John P. (1980), *Comparative Politics of North Africa,* Syracuse, N.Y., Syracuse University Press.

———— (2002), "Morocco: Democracy Denied," *Le Monde Diplomatique* (October).

ERF (2004), *Egypt Country Profile: The Road Ahead for Egypt,* Cairo, Economic Research Forum (December).

ERF and IM (2005), *Turkey Country Profile: The Road Ahead for Turkey,* Cairo, Economic Research Forum and Institut de la Méditerranée.

ESCWA (2006), "International Migration in the Arab Region," United Nations Expert Group Meeting on International Migration and Development in the Arab Region: Challenges and Opportunities, ESCWA, Population Division, Department of Economic and Social Affairs, Beirut, Lebanon (15–17 May).

Esman, Milton, and Rabinovich, Itamar, eds. (1988), *Ethnicity, Pluralism, and the State in the Middle East,* Ithaca, Cornell University Press.

Esping-Andersen, Gøsta (1990), *Three Worlds of Welfare Capitalism,* Princeton, Princeton University Press.

Esposito, John L. (1997), *Political Islam: Revolution, Radicalism, or Reform?* Boulder, Colo., Lynne Rienner Publishers.

European Commission (2003), *Economic Review of EU Mediterranean Partners,* Brussels, Directorate General for Economic and Financial Affairs, EU Occasional Paper no. 2 (January).

ExxonMobil (2005), *The Outlook for Energy: A 2030 View,* New York, ExxonMobil.

Fadili, Monceyf (2000), "Mobilizing Local Partnerships in Morocco," unpublished paper, UN Center for Human Settlement (UN-Habitat).

Falkenmark, Malin (1989), *Natural Resource Limits to Population Growth: The Water Perspective,* Gland, Switzerland, International Union for the Conservation of Nature.

FAO (Food and Agriculture Organization) (various years), *Production Yearbook,* Rome.

———— (1983), "Agricultural Price Policies in the Near East: Lessons and Experience," 16th FAO Regional Conference for the Near East, Aden, PDRY, March 11–15.

———— (1986), *World-wide Estimates and Projections of the Agricultural and Non-Agricultural Population Segments, 1950–2025,* Statistical Division, Economic and Social Policy Department, Rome, FAO.

———— (2003), *Sustainable Water Resources Management for Food Security in the Near East Region,* High-level Technical Workshop, FAO and Islamic Development Bank, Jeddah, October 8–9, www.fao.org/docrep/meeting/007/ad387e/ad387e00.htm.

FAOSTAT (2005), at http://faostat.fao.org/faostat/collections?version=ext&hasbulk =0&subset=agriculture.

Fargues, Philippe (1994), "Demographic Explosion or Social Upheaval?" in Salamé, ed., 156–179.

———— (2005), "How International Migration May Have Served Global Demographic Security," Annual World Bank Conference on Development Economics, Amsterdam, The Netherlands, May 23–24.

Farmer, Paul (2003), *Pathologies of Power: Health, Human Rights, and the New War on the Poor*, Berkeley, Los Angeles, and London, University of California Press.

Fasano, Ugo, and Goyal, Rishi (2004), "Emerging Strains in GCC Labor Markets," Washington, D.C., IMF Working Paper.

Fathaly, Omar, and Palmer, Monte (1980), *Political Development and Social Change in Libya,* Lexington, Mass., Lexington Books.

Fearon, James D., and Laitin, David D. (1996), "Explaining Interethnic Cooperation," *American Political Science Review,* 90, 4, 715–735.

Federation of American Scientists (FAS) (2005), Arms Sales, Saudi Arabia, at http://www.fas.org/asmp/profiles/saudi_arabia.htm.

Fergany, Nader (1988), "Some Aspects of Return Migration in Egypt," unpublished paper, April, Cairo.

_____ (1991), "A Characterization of the Employment Problem in Egypt," in Handoussa and Porter (1991), 25–56.

Fishlow, Albert, et al. (1994), *Miracle or Design? Lessons from the East Asia Experience,* Washington, D.C., Overseas Development Council.

Fitzgerald, E.V.K. (1977), "On State Accumulation in Latin America," in E.V.K. Fitzgerald et al., eds., *The State and Economic Development in Latin America,* Cambridge, Cambridge University Press.

Floyd, Robert H. (1984), "Some Topical Issues Concerning Public Enterprises," in Floyd, Gray, and Short, eds., 1–35.

Floyd, Robert, Gray, Clive S., and Short, R. P. (1984), *Public Enterprise in Mixed Economies: Some Macroeconomic Aspects,* Washington, D.C., IMF.

Fox, Robert (1995), *Cooperation and Security in the Western Mediterranean,* Ditchley Conference Report 94/11, Oxfordshire, England, Ditchley Foundation.

Frank, Robert H. (1999), *Luxury Fever: Money and Happiness in an Era of Excess,* Princeton and Oxford, Princeton University Press.

Fried, Edward R., and Trezise, Philip H. (1993), *Oil Security: Retrospect and Prospect,* Washington, D.C., Brookings Institution.

Fuller, Graham (2004), *The Future of Political Islam,* New York, Palgrave Macmillan.

Gardner, Edward (2003), "Creating Employment in the Middle East and North Africa," Washington, D.C., IMF, at http://www.imf.org/external/pubs/ft/med/2003/eng/gardner/.

Garfield, Richard (1999), *Morbidity and Mortality Among Iraqi Children from 1990 through 1998: Assessing the Impact of the Gulf War and Economic Sanctions,* Columbia University, at http://www.casi.org.uk/info/garfield/dr-garfield.html.

_____ (2005), "On the Efficiency and Effectiveness of the Development Fund for Iraq in the Health Sector," Testimony to the Subcommittee on National Security, Emerging Threats, and International Relations," June 20.

Garnham, David, and Tessler, Mark, eds. (1995), *Democracy, War, and Peace in the Middle East,* Bloomington, Indiana University Press.

Gause, Gregory (1994), *Oil Monarchies: Domestic and Security Challenges in the Arab Gulf States,* New York, Council on Foreign Relations.

Gellner, E., and Micaud, C., eds. (1972), *Arabs and Berbers,* London, Duckworth.

Gerges, Fawaz (1999), *America and Political Islam: Clash of Civilizations or Clash of Interests?* Cambridge, Cambridge University Press.

el-Ghonemy, M. Riad (1984), *Economic Growth, Income Distribution, and Rural Poverty in the Near East,* Rome, FAO.

Gibbons, Diana C. (1986), *The Economic Value of Water,* Washington, D.C., Resources for the Future.

Gilbar, Gad (1992), "Population Growth and Family Planning in Egypt, 1985–92," *Middle East Contemporary Survey* 16, 335–348.

Girgis, Maurice (2002), "National versus Migrant Workers in the GCC: Coping With Change," in Heba Handoussa and Zafiris Tzantos, eds., *Employment Creation and Social Protection in the Middle East and North Africa*, Cairo and New York, The American University in Cairo Press, 95–120.

Global Policy Forum (2002), "Iraq Sanctions: Humanitarian Implications and Options for the Future," at http://www.globalpolicy.org/security/sanction/iraq1/2002/paper.htm.

Global Water Intelligence UK (2004), *Water Market Middle East: Exploiting a Booming Market*, London, GWI.

Glueckstern, Pinhas (n.d.), Desalination: Current Situation and Future Prospects, at http://www.biu.ac.il/Besa/waterarticle1.html.

Gotheil, Fred (1981), "Iraqi and Syrian Socialism: An Economic Appraisal," *World Development* 9, 9/10, 825–838.

Gray, John (1998), *False Dawn: The Delusions of Global Capitalism*, New York, New Press.
_____ (2002), *Two Faces of Liberalism,* Cambridge, Polity Press.

Gumuscu, Sebnem, and Sert, Deniz (2009), "The Power of the Devout Bourgeoisie: The Case of the Justice and Development Party in Turkey," *Middle Eastern Studies,* 45, 6, 953–968.

Gutmann, E., and Landau, J. (1985), "The Political Elite and National Leadership in Israel," in G. Lenczowski, ed., *Political Elites in the Middle East,* Washington, D.C., American Enterprise Institute (AEI), 163–200.

de Haas, Hein (2005), "Morocco's Migration Transition: Trends, Determinants, and Future Scenarios," *Global Migration Perspectives* 28 (April), Geneva, Global Commission on International Migration.

Haddad, Bassam (2012), *Business Networks in Syria: The Political Economy of Authoritarian Resilience,* Stanford, Stanford University Press.

Hale, William (1981), *The Political and Economic Development of Modern Turkey,* London, Croom Helm.

Halpern, Manfred (1963), *The Politics of Social Change in the Middle East and North Africa,* Princeton, Princeton University Press.

Hamzawy, Amr (2005), *The Key to Arab Reform: Moderate Islamists,* Policy Brief no. 40 (August), Washington, D.C., Carnegie Endowment for International Peace.

Hamzeh, Ahmad Nizar (2004), *In the Path of Hizbullah,* Syracuse, Syracuse University Press.

Handoussa, Heba (1989), "The Burden of Public Sector Employment and Remuneration: A Case Study of Egypt," unpublished paper, ILO, Geneva.

Handoussa, Heba, and Porter, Gillian, eds. (1991), *Employment and Structural Adjustment: Egypt in the 1990s,* Cairo, American University in Cairo Press, for the ILO.

al-Hanidi, Abdel-Latif Abdel-Muhid (1988), *Egyptians Resident Abroad (Size and Characteristics)* (in Arabic), Cairo, CAPMAS.

Hannoyer, Jean, and Seurat, Michel (1979), Etat et secteur public industriel en Syrie, Lyon, Centre des études et des recherches sur le Moyen Orient Contemporain (CERMOC), Presses Universitaires de Lyon.

Hansen, Bent (1985), *The Egyptian Labor Market: An Overview,* World Bank Discussion Paper, Report no. DRD/60.

_____ (1991), "A Macro-Economic Framework for Economic Planning in Egypt," in Handoussa and Porter, eds., 189–218.

_____ (1992), *The Political Economy of Poverty, Equity, and Growth: Egypt and Turkey,* New York, Oxford University Press.

Hansen, Bent, and Radwan, Samir (1982), *Employment Opportunities and Equity in Egypt,* Geneva, ILO.

Harberger, A. C. (1971), "On Measuring the Social Opportunity Cost of Labor," *International Labor Review,* June.

_____ (1984), "Basic Needs Versus Distributional Weights in Social Cost-Benefit Analysis," *Economic Development and Cultural Change* 32, 4, 455–477.

Harik, Ilya (1974), *The Political Mobilization of Peasants: A Study of an Egyptian Community,* Bloomington, Indiana University Press.

Harik, Ilya, and Sullivan, Denis, eds. (1992), *Privatization and Liberalization in the Middle East,* Bloomington, Indiana University Press.

Hazell, Peter, et al. (1994), "Effects of Deregulating the Agricultural Production Sector on Food Availability and Resource Use in Egypt," Washington, D.C., International Food Policy Research Institute, September.

Hazell, Peter, Oram, Peter, and Chaherli, Nabil (2003), "Managing Livestock in Drought-Prone Areas of the Middle East and North Africa: Policy Issues," in Lofgren, ed., 79–104.

Heal, Geoffrey, and Chichilnisky, Graciela (1991), *Oil and the International Economy,* Oxford, Clarendon Press.

Helms, Christina (1984), *Iraq: Eastern Flank of the Arab World,* Washington, D.C., Brookings Institution.

Hemphill, Paul (1979), "The Formation of the Iraqi Army: 1921–1923," in Kelidar, ed., 88–110.

Henry, Clement M. (1996), *The Mediterranean Debt Crescent: Money and Power in Algeria, Egypt, Morocco, Tunisia, and Turkey,* Gainesville, University Press of Florida.

_____ (2004), "Financial Performance of Islamic versus Conventional Banks," in Henry and Wilson, eds., 104–128.

Henry, Clement M., and Springborg, Robert (2001), *Globalization and the Politics of Development in the Middle East,* Cambridge, Cambridge University Press.

Henry, Clement M., and Wilson, Rodney, eds. (2004), *The Politics of Islamic Finance,* Edinburgh, Edinburgh University Press.

Hen-Tov, Elliot (2004), "The Political Economy of Turkish Military Modernization," *Middle East Review of International Affairs* 8, 4 (December), at http://meria.idc.ac.il/journal/2004/issue4/jv8no4a5.html.

Hermassi, Elbaki (1972), *Leadership and National Development in North Africa,* Berkeley, University of California Press.

Hershlag, Z. Y. (1968), *Turkey: The Challenge of Growth,* Leiden, E. J. Brill.

Hertog, Steffen (2010), *Princes, Brokers, and Bureaucrats: Oil and the State in Saudi Arabic,* Ithaca, Cornell University Press.

Heydemann, Steven (1992), "The Political Logic of Economic Rationality: Selective Stabilization in Syria," in Henri Barkey, ed., *The Politics of Economic Reform in the Middle East,* New York, St. Martin's Press, 11–39.

Heydemann, Steven, ed. (2004), *Networks of Privilege in the Middle East: The Politics of Economic Reform Revisited,* New York, Palgrave Macmillan.

Heyneman, Stephen P. (1993), "Human Development in the Middle East and North Africa," in Said el-Naggar, ed., *Economic Development of the Arab Countries: Selected Issues,* Washington, D.C., IMF, 204–226.

Hibou, Beatrice (2004), "Fiscal Trajectories in Morocco and Tunisia," in Steven Heydemann, ed., *Networks of Privilege in the Middle East: The Politics of Economic Reform Revisited,* New York, Palgrave Macmillan, 201–222.

———— (2006), *La Force de L'Obeissance: Economic Politique de la Repression en Tunisie,* Paris, Editions de la Decouverte.

Hill, Allan G. (1998), "Why Does Human Development in Arab Countries Appear Low?" *ERF Forum* 5, 1 (May), www.erf.org.eg/middle.php?file=nletter/May98-00.

Hindle, Tim (2005), "Looking to Europe: A Survey of Turkey," *The Economist,* March 19.

Hinnebusch, Raymond (1979), "Party and Peasant in Syria," *Cairo Papers in Social Science* 3, 1 (November).

———— (1985), *Egyptian Politics Under Sadat,* Cambridge, Cambridge University Press.

Hodgson, Marshall G. S. (1974), *The Venture of Islam,* 3 vols., Chicago, University of Chicago Press.

Hooglund, Eric (1982), *Land and Revolution in Iran: 1960–1980,* Austin, University of Texas Press.

Hopkins, Nicholas (1983), "Social Aspects of Mechanization," in Richards and Martin, eds., 181–198.

Horton, Brendan (1990), *Morocco: Analysis and Reform of Economic Policy,* Washington, D.C., World Bank.

Hotelling, Harold (1931), "The Economics of Exhaustible Resources," *Journal of Political Economy* 39, 2 (April), 137–175.

Hudson, Michael (1968), *The Precarious Republic: Modernization in Lebanon,* New York, Random House.

———— (1977), *Arab Politics,* New Haven, Yale University Press.

———— (1994), "Arab Regimes and Democratization: Responses to the Challenge of Political Islam," *International Spectator* 29, 4, 3–28.

Huntington, Samuel P. (1968), *Political Order in Changing Societies,* New Haven, Yale University Press.

———— (1991), *The Third Wave: Democratization in the Late 20th Century,* Norman, University of Oklahoma Press.

Hussein, 'Adil (1977), *The Bureaucratic Bourgeoisie: Between the Marxist Understanding and Marxising Slogans* (in Arabic), Beirut.

_____ (1982), *The Egyptian Economy from Independence to Dependency: 1974–1979* (in Arabic), 2 vols., Cairo, Dar al-Mustaqbal al-'Arabi.

Hussein, Mahmoud (1971), *La lutte de classes en Egypte, 1945–70,* Paris, Maspero.

Ibrahim, Ibrahim, ed. (1983), *Arab Resources,* London, Croom Helm, for the Center for Contemporary Arab Studies.

Ibrahim, Saad Eddin (1980), "Anatomy of Egypt's Militant Islamic Groups: Methodological Note and Preliminary Findings," *IJMES* 12, 4, 423–453.

_____ (1994), "Sociological Profile of Muslim Militants in Egypt," paper presented at Workshop on Egypt's Domestic Stability, National Defense University, United States Department of Defense, Ft. McNair, Washington, D.C., April 28–29.

IBRD (International Bank for Reconstruction and Development) (1983), *Arab Republic of Egypt: Issues of Trade Strategy and Investment Planning,* Washington, D.C.

ICG (International Crisis Group) (2001), *Algeria's Economy: The Vicious Circle of Oil and Violence,* Africa Report no. 36 (26 October), Brussels.

_____ (2003a), *Islamic Social Welfare Activism in the Occupied Palestinian Territories: A Legitimate Target?* Middle East Report no. 13 (2 April), Amman/Brussels.

_____ (2003b), *Yemen: Coping with Terrorism and Violence in a Fragile State,* Middle East Report no. 8 (8 January), Amman/Brussels.

_____ (2004a), *Darfur Rising: Sudan's New Crisis,* Africa Report no. 76 (25 March), Nairobi/Brussels.

_____ (2004b), *Dealing with Hamas,* Middle East Report no. 21 (26 January), Amman/Brussels.

_____ (2005), *Understanding Islamism,* Middle East/North Africa Report no. 37 (2 March), Brussels.

_____ (2006), *Iraq's Muqtada Al-Sadr: Spoiler or Stabiliser?* Middle East Report no. 55 (11 July), Amman/Brussels.

IFAD (2001a), *Rural Poverty Report, 2001,* London, Oxford University Press.

_____ (2001b), *The Syrian Arab Republic: Country Programme Evaluation Report,* Rome. IFAD, Report no. 1178-SY (August).

ILO (2002), *Women and Men in the Informal Economy: A Statistical Picture,* Geneva, ILO.

_____ (2005), "Poverty, Working Poor, and Income Distribution," *Key Indicators of the Labor Market,* 4th ed., Geneva, ILO, www.esds.ac.uk/international/support/user_guides/ilo/kilm20EN.pdf.

_____ (2006), *World Employment Report, 2004–05,* Geneva, ILO.

Imam, Patrick A., and Jacobs, Davina F. (2007), *Effect of Corruption on Tax Revenues in the Middle East,* Working Paper, Washington, D.C., International Monetary Fund.

IMF (International Monetary Fund) (various years), *International Financial Statistics,* Washington, D.C.

_____ (2013), *Energy Subsidy Reforms: Lessons and Implications,* Washington, D.C., IMF.

IPCC (Intergovernmental Panel on Climate Change) (2002), *Climate Change, 2001. Synthesis Report: Third Assessment Report of the Intergovernmental Panel on Climate Change,* ed. Robert T. Watson, Cambridge, Cambridge University Press.

Iqbal, Farrukh (2006), *Sustaining Gains in Poverty Reduction and Human Development in the Middle East and North Africa,* Washington, D.C., World Bank.

IRIN (Integrated Regional Information Networks) (2006), "Yemen: Water Awareness Campaign Launched," IRIN, UNDP, UN Office for the Coordination of Humanitarian Affairs, August 14, at http://www.irinnews.org/report.asp?ReportID=44569&SelectRegion=Iraq_Crisis&SelectCountry=YEMEN.

Islami, A. Reza, and Kavoussi, R. M. (1984), *The Political Economy of Saudi Arabia,* Near Eastern Studies no. 1, Seattle, University of Washington Press.

Islamoğlu, Huri Inan, and Keyder, Çadlar (1977), "Agenda for Ottoman History," *Review* 1, Summer, 31–55.

Israel High Tech and Investment Report (2004), "Israel Accounts for 12% of World's Military Exports," at http://www.ishitech.co.il/0904ar2.htm.

Issawi, Charles (1956), "Economic and Social Foundations of Democracy in the Middle East," *International Affairs,* January, 27–42.

———— (1969), "Economic Change and Urbanization in the Middle East," in Ira M. Lapidus, ed., *Middle Eastern Cities,* Berkeley, University of California Press, 102–121.

———— (1978), "The Iranian Economy 1925–1975: Fifty Years of Economic Development," in G. Lenczowski, ed., *Iran Under the Pahlevis,* Stanford, Calif., Hoover Institution, 129–166.

———— (1982), *An Economic History of the Middle East and North Africa,* New York, Columbia University Press.

Jabar, Faleh (2003), *The Shiite Movement in Iraq,* London, Saqi Books.

Jacobson, Jodi (1994), *Family, Gender, and Population Policy: Views from the Middle East,* New York, Population Council.

Jamal, Abbashar (1991), "Funding Fundamentalism: The Political Economy of an Islamist State," *Middle East Report,* September–October, 15–17.

Jazairy, Idriss, Alamgir, Moniuddin, and Panuccio, Theresa (1992), *The State of World Rural Poverty: An Inquiry into Its Causes and Consequences,* New York, New York University Press for the International Fund for Agricultural Development.

Johnson, D. Gale (1950), "The Nature of the Supply Function for Agricultural Products," *Journal of Farm Economics* 42, 2, 539–564.

Johnston, Bruce, and Kilby, Peter (1975), *Agriculture and Structural Transformation: Economic Strategies in Late-Developing Countries,* New York, Oxford University Press.

Kabbani, Nader, and Kothari, Ekta (2005), "Youth Employment in the MENA Region: A Situational Assessment," World Bank, Social Policy Discussion Paper No. 0534 (September), at http://siteresources.worldbank.org/SOCIALPROTECTION/Resources/SP-Discussion-papers/Labor-Market-DP/0534web.pdf.

Kaboub, Fadhel (2012), "From Neoliberalism to Social Justice: The Feasibility of Full Employment in Tunisia," *Review of Radical Political Economics,* 44, 3, 305–312.

Kahf, Monser (2004), "Islamic Banks: The Rise of a New Power Alliance of Wealth and Shari'ah Scholarship," in Henry and Wilson, eds., 17–36.

Kang, David (2002), *Crony Capitalism: Corruption and Development in South Korea and the Philippines,* Cambridge, Cambridge University Press.

Kanovsky, Eliyahu (1999), *Iran's Economic Morass: Mismanagement and Decline Under the Islamic Republic,* Washington, D.C., Washington Institute for Near East Policy.

Kapil, Arun (1990), "L'évolution du régime autoritaire en Algérie: Le 5 Octobre et les réformes politiques de 1988–89," *Annuaire de l'Afrique du Nord* 29, 499–534.

Kapiszewski, Andrzej (2004), "Arab Labour Migration to the GCC States," *Arab Migration in a Globalized World,* Geneva, International Organization for Migration, 115–133.

Kapur, Devesh (2003), "Remittances: The New Development Mantra?" Cambridge, Harvard University Center for Global Development (August 25).

Kar, Dev, and Curcio, Karly (2011), *Illicit Financial Flows from Developing Countries: 2000–2009: Update with a Focus on Asia,* Washington, D.C., Global Financial Integrity.

Karaspan, Omer (1987), "Turkey's Armaments Industries," *MERIP Reports,* January–February, 27–31.

Karpat, Kemal (1959), *Turkey's Politics,* Princeton, Princeton University Press.

Karshenas, Massoud, and Moghadam, Valentine M., eds. (2006), *Social Policy in the Middle East: Economic, Political, and Gender Dynamics,* New York, United Nations Research Institute for Social Development and Palgrave Macmillan.

Karshenas, Massoud, and Pesaran, M. Hashem (1995), "Economic Reform and Reconstruction of the Iranian Economy," *MEJ* 49, 1 (Winter), 89–111.

Kasfir, Nelson (1979), "Explaining Ethnic Political Participation," *World Politics* 31, 3, 365–388.

Katanani, Ahmad K. (1981), "Economic Alternatives to Migration," paper presented to the Conference on International Migration in the Arab World, United Nations Economic Commission for West Africa (UNECWA), Nicosia, Cyprus, May.

Katouzian, Homa (1981), *The Political Economy of Modern Iran: Despotism and Pseudo-Modernism, 1926–1979,* New York, New York University Press.

Kavalsky, Basil (1980), "Poverty and Human Development in the Middle East and North Africa," in *Poverty and the Development of Human Resources: Regional Perspectives,* World Bank Staff Working Paper no. 406.

Kazancigil, Ali, and Özbudun, Ergun, eds. (1981), *Atatürk: Founder of a Modern State,* Hamden, Conn., Archon Books.

Kazemi, Farhad (1980a), *Poverty and Revolution in Iran: The Migrant Poor, Urban Marginality, and Politics,* New York, New York University Press.

———— (1980b), "Urban Migrants and the Revolution," *Iranian Studies* 13, 257–278.

Kazemi, F., and Abrahamian, E. (1978), "The Non-Revolutionary Peasantry of Modern Iran," *Iranian Studies* 11, 259–308.

Kazemi, Farhad, and Norton, Augustus Richard, eds. (1995), *Civil Society in the Middle East,* Leiden and New York, Brill.

Keen, David (1994), *The Benefits of Famine: A Political Economy of Famine and Relief in Southwestern Sudan, 1983–1989,* Princeton, Princeton University Press.

Kelidar, Abbas, ed. (1979), *The Integration of Modern Iraq,* London, Croom Helm.

Keller, Jennifer, and Nabli, Mustapha K. (2002), "The Macroeconomics of Labor Market Outcomes in MENA over the 1990s: How Growth Has Failed to Keep Up with a Burgeoning Labor Market," World Bank, unpublished paper, June, at http://www.worldbank.org/mdf/mdf4/papers/keller-nabli.pdf.

Kelley, C., and Williamson, Jeffrey (1984), "Population Growth, Industrial Revolutions, and the Urban Transition," *Population and Development Review* 10, 3.

Kepel, Gilles (1986), *Muslim Extremism in Egypt: The Prophet and the Pharaoh,* Berkeley, University of California Press.

_____ (2002), *Jihad: The Trail of Political Islam,* Cambridge, Belknap Press.

Kerr, Malcolm (1963), "Arab Radical Notions of Democracy," *St. Anthony's Papers* no. 16.

_____ (1965), "Egypt," in James Coleman, ed., *Education and Political Development,* Princeton, Princeton University Press, 169–194.

Kerr, Malcolm, and el-Yassin, Sayed, eds. (1982), *Rich and Poor States in the Middle East,* Boulder, Westview Press/American University in Cairo.

Ketterer, James (2001), "Networks of Discontent in Northern Morocco: Drugs, Opposition and Urban Unrest," *Middle East Report* 218 (Spring).

Keyder, Caglar (1979), "The Political Economy of Turkish Democracy," *New Left Review* 115 (May–June), 3–45.

_____ (1987), *State and Class in Turkey: A Study in Capitalist Development,* London and New York, Verso.

_____ (2004), "The Turkish Bell Jar," *New Left Review* 28 (July–August), 65–84.

al-Khafaji, 'Issam (1983), *The State and the Evolution of Capitalism in Iraq: 1968–1978* (in Arabic), Cairo, Dar al-Mustaqbal al-Arabi.

al-Khalil, Samir (1989), *Republic of Fear,* New York, Pantheon Books.

Khan, Mushtaq H. (2010), *Political Settlements and the Governance of Growth-Enhancing Institutions,* London, School of Oriental and African Studies (SOAS).

Kherallah, Mylene, Minot, Nicholas, and Gruhn, Peter (2003), "Adjustment of Wheat Production to Market Reform in Egypt," in Lofgren, ed., 133–160.

Khoury, Philip (1983a), "Islamic Revival and the Crisis of the Secular State in the Arab World: An Historical Appraisal," in Ibrahim, ed., 213–236.

_____ (1983b), *Urban Notables and Arab Nationalism: The Politics of Damascus, 1860–1920,* New York, Columbia University Press.

Khoury, Philip, and Kostiner, Joseph, eds. (1990), *Tribes and State Formation in the Middle East,* Berkeley, University of California Press.

Kienle, Eberhard (2001), *A Grand Delusion: Democracy and Economic Reform in Egypt,* London, I. B. Tauris.

_____ (2002), *Contemporary Syria: Liberalization Between Cold War and Cold Peace,* London, University of London, Centre of Near and Middle Eastern Studies.

Kimmerling, Baruch (1983), *Zionism and Economy,* Cambridge, Schenkman.

Klein, Naomi (2004), "Baghdad Year Zero: Pillaging Iraq in Pursuit of a Neocon Utopia," *Harper's Magazine,* September.

El-Kogali, Safaa (2002), "For Better or Worse? The Status of Women in the Labor Market in Egypt, 1988–1998," Washington, D.C., World Bank; and Cairo, ERF, at http://www.iceg.org/NE/projects/labor/woman.pdf.

Korayem, Karima (1987), *The Impact of Economic Adjustment Policies on the Vulnerable Families and Children in Egypt,* Cairo, Third World Forum, Middle East Office.

_____ (1994), *Poverty and Income Distribution in Egypt,* Cairo, Third World Forum, Middle East Office.

Kravis, Irving, Heston, Alan, and Summers, Robert (1978), *International Comparisons of Real Product and Purchasing Power,* Baltimore, Johns Hopkins University Press.

Krimly, Rayed (1993), "The Political Economy of Rentier States: A Case Study of Saudi Arabia in the Oil Era, 1950–1990," Ph.D. diss., Department of Political Science, George Washington University.

Kubursi, Afif (1984), *Oil, Industrialization, and Development in the Arab Gulf States,* London, Croom Helm.

Kuran, Timur (1980), "Internal Migration: The Unorganized Urban Sector and Income Distribution in Turkey, 1963–1973," in Özbudun and Ulusan, eds., 349–378.

_____ (1992a), "The Economic System in Contemporary Islamic Thought," in K. S. Jomo, ed., *Islamic Economic Alternatives,* Kuala Lumpur, Iqraq, 9–47.

_____ (1992b), "Economic Justice in Contemporary Islamic Thought," in K. S. Jomo, ed., *Islamic Economic Alternatives,* Kuala Lumpur, Iqraq, 49–76.

_____ (2004), *Islam and Mammon,* Princeton, Princeton University Press.

El Laithy, Heba, and Abu-Ismail, Khalid (2005), *Poverty in Syria, 1996–2004: Diagnosis and Pro-Poor Policy Considerations,* Damascus, UNDP.

El Laithy, Heba, Lokshin, Michael, and Banerji, Arup (2003), "Poverty and Economic Growth in Egypt, 1995–2000," World Bank, Development Research Group, Policy Research Working Paper no. 3068 (June).

Land Center for Human Rights (1999), "Violence in the Egyptian Countryside: 1998–1999," www.derechos.org/human-rights/mena/lchr/violence.html.

Lapham, R. J. (1983), "Background Notes and Illustrative Tables on Populations in the Middle East," paper prepared for the Conference on Population and Political Stability in the Near East and South Asia Region, Washington, D.C., March.

Lawless, Richard (1984), "Algeria: The Contradictions of Rapid Industrialization," in R. Lawless and A. Findlay, eds., *North Africa: Contemporary Politics and Economic Development,* London, Croom Helm, 153–190.

Layachi, Azzedine (1999), "Economic Reform and Elusive Political Change in Morocco," in Yahia H. Zoubir, ed., *North Africa in Transition: State, Society, and Economic Transformation in the 1990s,* Gainesville, University Press of Florida, 43–60.

Layard, Richard (2005), *Happiness: Lessons from a New Science,* New York, Penguin Press.

Lazreg, Marnia (1976), *The Emergence of Classes in Algeria,* Boulder, Westview Press.

League of Arab States (2005), *International Migration in the Arab Region and Suggestions for Key Actions,* www.un.org/esa/opopulation/publications/thirdoord2004/P15 Arab-League.pdf.

Leca, Jean (1975), "Algerian Socialism: Nationalism, Industrialization, and State-building," in Helen Desfosses and Jacques Levesque, eds., *Socialism in the Third World,* New York, Praeger.

Le Monde (1996), "A Tanger, deux milles jeunes émeutiers ont affronté les forces de l'ordre," June 7.

Lerner, Daniel (1959), *The Passing of Traditional Society,* Glencoe, Ill., Free Press.

Lesch, Ann Mosely (1985), *Egyptian Labor Migration: Economic Trends and Government Policies,* University Field Services Institute, Report no. 38.

Leveau, Rémy (1985), *Le Fellah marocain: Défenseur du trone,* Paris, Presses de la FNSP.

_____ (1993), *Le sabre et le turban: L'avenir du Maghrib,* Paris, Editions François Bourin.

Levitsky, Steven, and Way, Lucan A. (2010), *Competitive Authoritarianism: Hybrid Regimes After the Cold War,* Cambridge, Cambridge University Press.

Lewis, Bernard (1961), *The Emergence of Modern Turkey,* Oxford, Oxford University Press.

_____ (2002), "What Went Wrong?" *Atlantic Monthly*, January, 43–45.

Lewis, W. Arthur (1954), "Economic Development with Unlimited Supplies of Labour," *Manchester School of Economic and Social Studies* 22, 139–191.

Library of Congress (2004), *Country Profile: Sudan,* at http://lcweb2.loc.gov/frd/cs/profiles/Sudan.pdf.

Lieberman, Evan S., and Singh, Prerna (2012), "Conceptualizing and Measuring Ethnic Politics: An Institutional Complement to Demographic, Behavioral, and Cognitive Approaches," *Studies in Comparative International Development,* 47, 3, 255–286.

Liechtenthaeler, G., and Turton, A. R. (1999), "Water Demand Management, Natural Resource Reconstruction and Traditional Value Systems: A Case Study from Yemen," Occasional Paper no. 14, London, Water Issues Study Group, School of Oriental and African Studies, University of London.

Lipton, Michael (1977), *Why Poor People Stay Poor: Urban Bias in World Development,* Cambridge, Harvard University Press.

Little, I.M.D., Scitovsky, Tibor, and Scott, Maurice (1970), *Industry and Trade in Some Developing Countries,* London, Oxford University Press.

Lofgren, Hans, ed. (2003), *Food, Agriculture, and Economic Policy in the Middle East and North Africa,* Amsterdam, Elsevier.

Lofgren, Hans, and Richards, Alan (2003), "Food Security, Poverty and Economic Policy in the Middle East and North Africa," in Lofgren, ed., 1–32.

Longuenesse, Elisabeth (1979), "The Class Nature of the State in Syria," *MERIP Reports* 9, 4 (May), 3–11.

_____ (1985), "Syrie, secteur public industriel," *Maghreb-Machrek* 109 (July–September), 5–24.

Looney, Robert (2004), "Neoliberalism in a Conflict State: The Viability of Economic Shock Therapy in Iraq," *Strategic Insights* 3, 6, June, at http://www.ccc.nps.navy.mil/si/2004/jun/looneyJun04.asp.

Lopez, George A., and Cortwright, David (2004), "Containing Iraq: Sanctions Worked," *Foreign Affairs* 83, 4, July–August, at http://www.foreignaffairs.org/20040701faessay83409/george-a-lopez-david-cortright/containing-iraq-sanctions-worked.html.

Lowi, Miriam R. (2005), "War-Torn or Systematically Distorted: Rebuilding the Algerian Economy," paper presented at workshop, "Rebuilding War-Torn Economies in the Middle East and North Africa," Center for Near Eastern Studies, University of California, Los Angeles, February 4–5.

Lubeck, Paul (1999), "Antimonies of Islamic Movements Under Globalization," Center for Global, Regional, and International Studies, University of California, Santa Cruz, Working Paper 99–1.

Lust, Ellen (2011), "Missing the Third Wave: Islam, Institutions, and Democracy in the Middle East," *Studies in Comparative International Development,* 46, 2, 163–190.

Madanipour, Ali (1999), "City Profile: Tehran," *Cities* 16, 1, 57–65.

el-Malki, Habib (1980), "Capitalisme d'état, Développement de la bourgeoisie et problématique de la transition—le cas du Maroc," *Revue Juridique, Politique et Économique du Maroc* 8, 207–228.

_____ (1982), *L'économie marocaine: Bilan d'une décennie, 1970–1980,* Paris, Editions du CNRS.

Mamdani, Mahmood (1972), *The Myth of Population Control: Family, Caste, and Class in an Indian Village,* New York, Monthly Review Press.

_____ (2004), *Good Muslim, Bad Muslim: America, the Cold War, and the Roots of Terror,* New York, Pantheon.

Mansouri, Brahim, et al. (2004), "The Role of Political and Institutional Factors in the Moroccan Reform Process," 11th Economic Reform Forum Conference, Beirut, December, at http://www.erf.org.eg/11conf_Lebanon/Macro/Mansouri&Riger& Ziky.pdf.

Mares, Isabela (2003), *The Politics of Social Risk: Business and Welfare State Development,* Cambridge, Cambridge University Press.

Margulies, Ronnie, and Yildizoclu, Ergin (1984), "Trade Unions and Turkey's Working Class," *MERIP Reports,* February, 15–30, 31.

Marshall, Shana, and Stacher, Joshua (2012), "Egypt's Generals and Transnational Capital," *Middle East Report,* Winter.

Martinez, Luis (1998), *The Algerian Civil War, 1990–1998,* trans. Jonathan Derrick, New York, Columbia University Press.

Massad, Joseph (2001), *Colonial Effects: The Making of National Identity in Jordan,* New York, Columbia University Press.

McAdam, Doug (1982), *Political Process and the Development of Black Insurgency, 1930–1970,* Chicago, University of Chicago Press.

McClelland, David (1963), "National Character and Economic Growth in Turkey and Iran," in Lucian Pye, ed., *Communications and Political Development,* Princeton, Princeton University Press, 152–181.

Mecham, R. Quinn (2004), "From the Ashes of Virtue, a Promise of Light: The Transformation of Political Islam in Turkey," *Third World Quarterly,* 25, 2, 339–358.

Meillassoux, Claude (1981), *Maidens, Meal, and Money,* Cambridge, Cambridge University Press.

Mellor, John (1976), *The New Economics of Growth: A Strategy for India and the Developing World,* Ithaca, Cornell University Press.

MENA-OECD Investment Programme (2005), *Inventory of International Investment Agreements Concluded by MENA Countries,* Paris, OECD.

el-Midaoui, Ahmed (1981), *Les entreprises publiques au Maroc et leur participation au développement,* Casablanca, Editions Afrique-Orient.

Migdal, Joel (1987), "Strong States, Weak States: Power and Accommodation," in M. Weiner and S. P. Huntington, eds., *Understanding Political Development,* Boston, Little, Brown, 391–436.

Migration News, University of California, Davis, at http://migration.ucdavis.edu.

Miniesy, R. S., Nugent, J. B., and Yousef, T. M. (2003), "Intra-regional Trade Integration in the Middle East: Past Performance and Future Potential," in Hassan Hakimian and Jeffrey B. Nugent, eds. *Trade Policy and Economic Integration in the Middle East and North Africa: Economic Boundaries in Flux,* London, Curzon-Routledge, 41-65.

Minority Rights Group (1983), *Lebanon: A Conflict of Minorities,* London.

Minujin, Alberto, and Delamonica, Enrique (2003), "Mind the Gap: Child Mortality Differentials by Income Group," in Giovanni Andrea Cornia, ed., *Harnessing Globalization for Children: A Report to UNICEF,* Geneva, UNICEF.

Mishra, Vinod (2004), "Muslim/Non-Muslim Differentials in Fertility and Family Planning," Honolulu, East-West Center, Population and Health Series, no. 112, January.

Mitchell, Richard P. (1969), *The Society of the Muslim Brothers,* London, Oxford University Press.

Mitchell, Timothy (2002), *Rule of Experts: Egypt, Techno-politics, Modernity,* Berkeley and Los Angeles, University of California Press.

Moghadem, Fatemah Etemad (1982), "Farm Size, Management, and Productivity: A Study of Four Iranian Villages," *Oxford Bulletin of Economics and Statistics* 44, 4 (November), 357–379.

Moghadem, Valentine (1993), *Modernizing Women: Gender and Social Change in the Middle East,* Boulder, Lynne Rienner.

_____ (2001), "Women, Work, and Economic Restructuring: A Regional Overview," in E. Mine Cinar, ed., *The Economics of Women and Work in the Middle East and North Africa,* Amsterdam, JAI, 93–116.

Mohie el-Din, Amr (1982), *Income Distribution and Basic Needs in Urban Egypt,* Cairo Papers in Social Science 5, Monograph 3, November.

Mojaverhosseini, Farshid (2003), "An Inquiry into the Sources of Growth and Stagnation in the Iranian Economy," International Center for Economic Research Working Paper 12/203 (March).

Moore, Barrington (1967), *Social Origins of Dictatorship and Democracy,* London, Allen Lane/Penguin Press.

Moore, C. H. (1965), *Tunisia Since Independence,* Berkeley, University of California Press.

_____ (1970), *Politics in North Africa,* Boston, Little, Brown.

_____ (1980), *Images of Development: Egyptian Engineers in Search of Industry,* Cambridge, MIT Press.

Moore, Pete (2004), *Doing Business in the Middle East: Politics and Economic Crisis in Jordan and Kuwait,* Cambridge, Cambridge University Press.

Morocco, Kingdom of, Ministry of Economic and Social Affairs (1992), *Niveaux de vie des ménages, 1990/91,* Rabat.

Morrison, Christian (1991), *Adjustment and Equity in Morocco,* Paris, OECD Development Centre.

Mosk, Carl (1983), *Patriarchy and Fertility: Japan and Sweden, 1880–1960,* New York, Academic Press.

Musa, E. A. (2000), *Sudan Structural Adjustment Programme: Some Implications for Labour in the Formal Sector,* Tangier, Morocco, African Training and Research Centre in Administration for Development.

Myint, Hla (1959), "The 'Classical Theory' of International Trade and the Underdeveloped Countries," *Economic Journal* 68, 2, 317–337.

Nabli, Mustapha K., and Keller, Jennifer (2002), "The Macroeconomics of Labor Market Outcomes in MENA over the 1990s: How Growth Has Failed to Keep Pace with a Burgeoning Labor Market," unpublished paper, World Bank, Washington, D.C.

el-Naggar, Said, and el-Erian, Mohamed (1993), "The Economic Implications of a Comprehensive Peace in the Middle East," in Stanley Fischer et al., eds., *The Economics of Middle East Peace,* Cambridge, MIT Press, 205–226.

Nasr, Salim (1985), "Roots of the Shi'i Movement," *MERIP Reports,* June, 10–16.

Nasr, Seyyed Vali Reza (1994), *The Vanguard of the Islamic Revolution: The Jama'at-i Islami of Pakistan,* Berkeley and Los Angeles, University of California Press.

_____ (2009), *Forces of Fortune: The Rise of the New Muslim Middle Class and What It Will Mean for Our World,* New York, Simon & Schuster.

al-Nasrawi, Abbas (1995), "Iraq's Economic Policies in a Transition Period," *Iraqi Issues* 2, 3, 1–8.

National Academy of Sciences (1982), *The Estimation of Recent Trends in Fertility and Mortality in Egypt,* Washington, D.C., National Academy Press.

National Research Council (1986), *Population Growth and Economic Development: Policy Questions,* Washington, D.C., National Academy Press.

Nattagh, Nina (1986), *Agricultural and Regional Development in Iran, 1962–1978,* Cambridgeshire, UK, Middle East and North African Studies Press.

Nellis, John (1977), "Socialist Management in Algeria," *Journal of Modern African Studies* 15, 4, 529–544.

_____ (1980), "Maladministration: Cause or Result of Underdevelopment? The Algerian Example," *Canadian Journal of African Studies* 13, 3, 407–422.

_____ (1983), "A Comparative Assessment of the Development Performances of Algeria and Tunisia," *MEJ* 37, 3, 370–393.

Nelson, Harold D., ed. (1979), *Tunisia: A Country Study,* Washington, D.C., Area Handbook Series, American University Press.

_____, ed. (1985), *Algeria: A Country Study,* Washington, D.C., Area Handbook Series, American University Press.

Nelson, Joan (1979), *Access to Power: Politics and the Urban Poor in Developing Nations,* Princeton, Princeton University Press.

_____ (1984), "The Political Economy of Stabilization Commitment, Capacity, and Public Response," *World Development* 12, 10, 983–1006.

Niblock, Tim, ed. (1982a), *Iraq: The Contemporary State,* London, Croom Helm.

_____, ed. (1982b), *State, Society, and Economy in Saudi Arabia,* London, Croom Helm.

Noland, Marcus, and Pack, Howard (2007), *The Arab Economies in a Changing World,* Washington, D.C., Peterson Institute for International Economics.

Noman, Omar (1988), *The Political Economy of Pakistan, 1947–1985,* London and New York, KPI Press.

Nomani, Farhad, and Rahnema, Ali (1994), *Islamic Economic Systems,* London, Zed Press.

Nouschi, Andre (1970), "North Africa in the Period of Colonization," *Cambridge History of Islam,* vol. 1, *The Further Islamic Lands: Islamic Society and Civilization,* Cambridge, Cambridge University Press, 299–326.

Nyrop, Richard F., ed. (1982), *Egypt: A Country Study,* Washington, D.C., Area Handbook Series, American University Press.

O'Brien, Patrick (1966), *The Revolution in Egypt's Economic System,* New York, Oxford University Press.

O'Donnell, Guillermo (1978), "Reflections on the Patterns of Change in the Bureaucratic-Authoritarian State," *Latin American Research Review* 12, 1, 3–38.

Olmsted, Jennifer (2003), "Reexamining the Fertility Puzzle in MENA," in Doumato and Posusney, eds., 73–92.

Olson, Mancur (1965), *The Logic of Collective Action: Public Goods and the Theory of Groups,* Cambridge, Harvard University Press.

Omran, Abdel R., and Roudi, Farzaneh (1993), "The Middle East Population Puzzle," *Population Bulletin* 48, 1.

Öniç, Ziya (2004), "The Political Economy of Turkey's Justice and Development Party," at http://papers.ssrn.com/sol3/papers.cfm?abstract_id=659463.

Öniç, Ziya, and Senses, Fikret (2003), "Rethinking the Emerging Post-Washington Consensus: A Critical Appraisal," Economics Research Center Working Paper in Economics 03/09, Middle East Technical University, Ankara.

Öniç, Ziya, and Webb, Steven (1994), "Turkey: Democratization and Adjustment from Above," in Stephan Haggard and Steven B. Webb, eds., *Voting for Reform: Democracy, Political Liberalization, and Economic Adjustment,* Washington, D.C., World Bank.

OPEC (1993), *Annual Statistical Bulletin,* Vienna.

———— (various years), *Annual Statistical Bulletin,* online edition, at http://www.opec .org/library/Annual%20Statistical%20Bulletin/interactive/2004/FileZ/Main.htm.

Osman, Tarek (2010), *Egypt on the Brink: From Nasser to Mubarak,* New Haven, Yale University Press.

Ostrom, Elinor (1990), *Governing the Commons: The Evolution of Institutions for Collective Action,* Cambridge, Cambridge University Press.

Owen, Roger (1981), *The Middle East in the World Economy, 1800–1914,* London and New York, Methuen.

———— (1985), *Migrant Workers in the Gulf,* Minority Rights Group Report no. 68, September.

———— (1986), "Large Landowners, Agricultural Progress, and the State in Egypt, 1800–1970: An Overview," in Alan Richards, ed., *Food, States, and Peasants: Analyses of the Agrarian Question in the Middle East,* Boulder, Westview Press, 69–96.

———— (2004), *State, Power, and Politics in the Making of the Modern Middle East,* 3rd ed., London, Routledge.

Owen, Roger, and Pamuk, Sevket (1998), *A History of the Middle East Economies in the 20th Century,* Cambridge, Mass., Harvard University Press.

Özbudun, Ergun (1981), "The Nature of the Kemalist Political Regime," in Kazancigil and Özbudun, eds., 79–102.

Özbudun, Ergun, and Ulusan, Aydin, eds. (1980), *The Political Economy of Income Distribution in Turkey,* New York, Holmes and Meier.

Özgediz, Selcuk (1980), "Education and Income Distribution in Turkey," in Özbudun and Ulusan, eds., 501–524.

Paulino, Leonardo (1986), *Food in the Third World: Past Trends and Projections to 2000,* IFPRI Research Report no. 52 (June).

Penrose, Edith, and Penrose, E. F. (1978), *Iraq: International Relations and National Development,* Boulder, Ernest Benn/Westview Press.

Pepinsky, Thomas B. (2009), *Economic Crises and the Breakdown of Authoritarian Regimes: Indonesia and Malaysia in Comparative Perspective,* Cambridge, Cambridge University Press.

Pew Research Center Report (2011), "Arab Spring Fails to Improve US Image," Washington, DC, Pew Research, Global Attitudes Project.

Piscatori, James, ed. (1983), *Islam in the Political Process,* Cambridge, Cambridge University Press.

Pissarides, Christopher A. (1993), *Labor Markets in the Middle East and North Africa,* World Bank Middle East and North Africa Discussion Paper Series no. 5 (February).

Posusney, Marsha Pripstein, and Angrist, Michele Penner (2005), *Authoritarianism in the Middle East: Regimes and Resistance,* Boulder, Lynne Rienner Publishers.

Prunier, Gerard (2005), *Darfur: The Ambiguous Genocide,* Ithaca, Cornell University Press.

Przeworski, Adam (1991), *Democracy and the Market: Political and Economic Reforms in Eastern Europe and Latin America,* New York, Cambridge University Press.

Psacharopoulos, George (1980), "Returns to Education: An Updated International Comparison," in *Education and Income,* World Bank Staff Working Paper no. 402, 75–109.

———— (1994), "Returns to Investment in Education: A Global Update," *World Development* 22, 9, 1325–1343.

Psacharopoulos, George, and Patrinos, Harry Anthony (2002), *Returns to Investment in Education: A Further Update,* Washington, D.C., World Bank, World Bank Policy Research Working Paper 2881 (September).

Putnam, Robert (1993), *Making Democracy Work: Civic Traditions in Modern Italy,* Princeton, Princeton University Press.

El Qorchi, Mohammed (2005), "Islamic Finance Gears Up," *Finance and Development* 42, 4 (December), 46–49.

Quandt, William B. (1981), *Saudi Arabia in the 1980s: Foreign Policy, Security, and Oil,* Washington, D.C., Brookings Institution.

al-Qudsi, Sulayman, Assaad, Ragui, and Shaban, Radwan (1993), "Labor Markets in the Arab Countries: A Survey," World Bank Initiative to Encourage Economic Research in the Middle East and North Africa, First Annual Conference on Development Economics, Cairo, Egypt, June 4–6.

Radwan, Samir (1977), *Agrarian Reform and Rural Poverty: Egypt, 1952–1975,* Geneva, ILO.

Radwan, Samir, Jamal, Vali, and Ghose, Ajit (1991), *Tunisia: Rural Labour and Structural Transformation,* London, Routledge.

Radwan, S., and Lee, E. (1986), *Agrarian Change in Egypt: An Anatomy of Rural Poverty,* London, Croom Helm.

Raffinot, Marc, and Jacquemot, Pierre (1977), *Le capitalisme d'état algérien,* Paris, Maspero.

Rashad, Hoda, and Khadr, Zeinab (2002), "New Challenges in the Demography of the Arab Region," in Sirageldin, ed., 37–61.

Ravallion, Martin (2002), "A Reply to Reddy and Pogge," New York, Columbia University, www.socialanalysis.org.

Raymond, A., ed. (1980), *La Syrie d'aujourd'hui,* Paris, Editions du CNRS.

Razavi, H., and Vakil, F. (1984), *The Political Environment of Economic Planning in Iran, 1971–1983,* Boulder, Westview Press.

Reddy, Sanjay G., and Pogge, Thomas W. (2002), "How Not to Count the Poor: A Reply to Ravallion," New York, Columbia University, www.socialanalysis.org.

Reich, B., and Long, D., eds. (1986), *The Government and Politics of the Middle East and North Africa,* Boulder, Westview Press.

Republic of Yemen (2004), "Poverty Reduction Strategy: First Progress Report," at http://yemen-prsp.org/site/uploads/executive_summary_002_en.pdf.

Riad, Hassan (1964), *L'Egypte nassérienne,* Paris, Editions de Minuit.

Richards, Alan (1982), *Egypt's Agricultural Development, 1800–1980: Technical and Social Change,* Boulder, Westview Press.

_____ (1987), *Routes to Low Mortality in Low-Income Countries: Comment,* University of California, Santa Cruz, Applied Economics Working Paper no. 43.

_____ (1991), "The Political Economy of Dilatory Reform: Egypt in the 1990s," *World Development* 19, 12, 1721–1730.

_____ (1992), *Higher Education in Egypt,* World Bank Education and Employment Working Papers, WPS 862 (February).

_____ (1994), "The Egyptian Farm Labor Market Revisited," *Journal of Development Economics* 43, 239–261.

_____ (1996), "Arab Food Security in the 1980s: Stylized Facts and Lessons for the Future," in Michael Hudson, ed., *The Arab World in the New Middle East: Problems of Adaptation, Integration, and Interdependence,* Washington, D.C., Center for Contemporary Arab Studies.

_____ (2001), "At War with Utopian Fanatics," *Middle East Policy* 8, 4 (December), 5–9.

_____ (2002), "Coping with Water Scarcity: The Governance Challenge," University of California, Institute for Global Cooperation and Conflict, IGCC Policy Paper 54, at http://repositories.cdlib.org/cgi/viewcontent.cgi?article=1050&context=igcc.

_____ (2003), "Modernity and Economic Development: The 'New' American Messianism," *Middle East Policy* X, 3 (Fall), 56–78.

Richards, Alan, and Martin, Philip, eds. (1983), *Migration, Mechanization, and Agricultural Labor Markets in Egypt,* Boulder and Cairo, Westview Press/American University at Cairo.

Rivier, François (1980), *Croissance industrielle dans une économie assistée: Le cas Jordanien,* Lyon, CERMOC, Presses Universitaires de Lyon.

Rivlin, Paul (2001), *Economic Policy and Performance in the Arab World,* Boulder and London, Lynne Rienner.

Rivlin, Paul, and Gal, Yitzhak (2004), *Economic and Demographic Developments in the Middle East and North Africa,* Tel Aviv, Moshe Dayan Center for Middle Eastern and African Studies.

Roberts, Hugh (1982), "The Unforeseen Development of the Kabyle Question in Contemporary Algeria," *Government and Opposition* 17, 3, 312–334.

_____ (1983), "The Economics of Berberism: The Kabyle Question in Contemporary Algeria," *Government and Opposition* 18, 2, 218–235.

_____ (1984), "The Politics of Algerian Socialism," in Lawless and Findlay, eds., 5–49.

_____ (1994), "Doctrinaire Economics and Political Opportunism in the Strategy of Algerian Islamism," in John Ruedy, ed., *Islamism and Secularism in North Africa*, New York, St. Martin's Press.

Roberts, Les, Lifta, Riyadh, Garfield, Richard, Khudhairi, Jamal, and Burnham, Gilbert (2004), "Mortality Before and After the 2003 Invasion of Iraq: Cluster Sample Survey," *The Lancet* 364 (November 20), 1857–1864.

Roberts, Paul (2004), *The End of Oil: On the Edge of a Perilous New World*, New York, Houghton Mifflin.

Rodrik, Dani (1994), "The Rush to Free Trade in the Developing World: Why So Late? Why Now? Will It Last?" in Stephan Haggard and Steven B. Webb, eds., *Voting for Reform: Democracy, Political Liberalization, and Economic Adjustment*, Washington, D.C., World Bank, 61–88.

_____ (2002), "After Neoliberalism, What?" paper presented at conference, Alternatives to Neoliberalism, Washington, D.C., May 23.

_____ (2004), "Rethinking Growth Policies in the Developing World," Luca d'Angliano Lecture in Development Economics, Turin, Italy, October 8.

Rogers, Peter, and Lyndon, Peter, eds. (1994), *Water in the Arab World: Perspectives and Prognoses*, Cambridge, Harvard University Press.

Roll, Steven (2010), "'Finance Matters!' The Influence of Financial Sector Reforms on the Development of the Entrepreneurial Elite in Egypt," *Mediterranean Politics*, 15, 349–370.

Rone, Jamera (2003), *Sudan, Oil, and Human Rights*, Washington, D.C., Human Rights Watch Prognoses; Cambridge, Harvard University Press.

Roos, Leslie, and Roos, Noralou (1971), *Managers of Modernization: Organization and Elites in Turkey (1950–1969)*, Cambridge, Harvard University Press.

Rosegrant, Mark W., and Binswanger, Hans (1994), "Markets in Tradable Water Rights: Potential for Efficiency Gains in Developing Country Water Resource Allocation," *World Development* 22, 11, 1613–1625.

Rosenfeld, H., and Carmi, S. (1976), "The Privatization of Public Means, the State Made Middle Class, and the Realization of Family Value in Israel," in J. G. Peristiany, ed., *Kinship and Modernization in Mediterranean Society*, Rome, American Universities Field Staff, 131–153.

Roudi, Farzaneh (2005), "Achieving the MDGs in the Middle East: Why Improved Reproductive Health Is Key," New York, Population Reference Bureau, http://www .prb.org/Template.cfm?Section=PRB&template=/ContentManagement/Content Display.cfm&ContentID=13075.

Roudi-Fahimi, Farzaneh (2002), *Iran's Family Planning Program: Responding to a Nation's Needs*, New York, Population Council.

_____ (2004), *Progress Toward the Millennium Development Goals in the Middle East and North Africa*, Cairo, Population Reference Bureau and Ford Foundation, at http://www.prb.org/pdf04/ProgressToMillDev.pdf.

Roudi-Fahimi, Farzaneh, and Moghadam, Valentine M. (2003), "Empowering Women, Developing Society: Female Education in the Middle East and North Africa," New York, Population Reference Bureau, at http://www.prb.org/pdf/Empowering WomeninMENA.pdf.

Rouleau, Eric (2001), "Politics in the Name of the Prophet," *Le Monde Diplomatique,* November.

Rowat, Colin (2000), "UN Agency Reports on the Humanitarian Situation in Iraq," University of Cambridge (UK), Campaign Against Sanctions on Iraq, June 9.

Roy, Olivier (1998), *The Failure of Political Islam,* Cambridge, Harvard University Press.

Roy, Sara (2000), "The Transformation of Islamic NGOs in Palestine," *Middle East Report* 214 (Spring).

Rustow, Dankwart A., and Mugno, John F. (1976), *OPEC: Success and Prospects,* New York, New York University Press.

Ruthven, Malise (2000), *Islam in the World,* 2nd ed., New York, Oxford University Press.

Saadowski, Yahya M. (1991), *Political Vegetables? Businessman and Bureaucrat in the Development of Egyptian Agriculture,* Washington, D.C., Brookings.

Sadik, Abdel-Karim, and Barghouti, Shawki (1994), "The Water Problems of the Arab World: Management of Scarce Resources," in Rogers and Lyndon, eds., 1–38.

Sadowski, Yahya (1985), "Cadres, Guns, and Money: The Eighth Regional Congress of the Syrian Ba'ath," *Middle East Report* 134 (July–August), 3–8.

———— (1993), *Scuds or Butter? The Political Economy of Arms Control in the Middle East,* Washington, D.C., Brookings Institution.

el Saharty, Sameh, Richardson, Gail, and Chase, Susan (2005), *Egypt and the Millennium Development Goals: Challenges and Opportunities,* Washington and Cairo, World Bank, www.siteresources.worldbank.org/HEALTHNUTRITIONANDPOPULATION /Resources/ 281627–1095698140167/ElSahartyEgyptMDGsFinal.pdf.

Said, Mohsen elMahdy (2001), *Higher Education in Egypt,* Cairo, Ministry of Higher Education, Egypt.

Salamé, Ghassan, ed. (1994), *Democracy Without Democrats? The Renewal of Politics in the Muslim World,* London, I. B. Tauris.

Salehi-Isfahani, Djavad (2003), "Mobility and the Dynamics of Poverty in Iran: What Can We Learn from the 1992–1995 Panel Data?" Cairo, World Bank, Economic Research Forum.

———— (2006), "Revolution and Redistribution in Iran: Changes in Poverty and Distribution 25 Years Later," at http://siteresources.worldbank.org/INTDECINEQ /Resources/1149208–1147789289867/IIIWB_Conference_Revolution& Redistribution_Iran.pdf.

Salehi-Isfahani, Djavad, Belhaj, Nadia, and Assaad, Ragui (2011), "Equality of Opportunity in Education in the Middle East and North Africa," Cairo, Egypt, Economic Research Forum (ERF).

Saloman Brothers (1992), *Morocco: An Oasis of Investment Opportunity,* New York.

Schiavo-Campo, Salvatore, de Tommaso, Giulio, and Mukherjee, Amitabha (2003), "An International Statistical Survey of Government Employment and Wages," World Bank, Policy Research Working Paper no. 1806.

Schlumberger, Oliver, ed. (2007), *Debating Arab Authoritarianism: Dynamics and Durability in Nondemocratic Regimes,* Stanford, Stanford University Press.

Schmitter, P. C. (1974), "Still the Century of Corporatism?" *Review of Politics* 36, 85–132.

Schneider, Friedrich (2005), "Shadow Economies of 145 Countries All Over the World: Estimation Results for the Period 1999–2003," Department of Economics, Johannes Kepler University of Linz, Austria, at http://www.dur.ac.uk/john.ashworth/EPCS/Papers/Schneider.pdf.

Schneider, Steven A. (1983), *The Oil Price Revolution,* Baltimore, Johns Hopkins University Press.

Schultz, T. W. (1981), *Investing in People: The Economics of Population Quality,* Berkeley, University of California Press.

Scott, James (1998), *Seeing Like a State: How Certain Schemes to Improve the Human Condition Have Failed,* New Haven, Yale University Press.

Sen, Amartya (1981a), *Poverty and Famines: An Essay on Entitlement and Deprivation,* Oxford, Oxford University Press.

_____ (1981b), "Public Action and the Quality of Life in Developing Countries," *Oxford Bulletin of Economics and Statistics* 43, 4 (November), 287–319.

_____ (1983), "Poor, Relatively Speaking," *Oxford Economic Papers* 35, 1 (July), 153–169.

Sethuramen, S. V., ed. (1981), *The Urban Informal Sector in Developing Countries: Employment, Poverty, and Environment,* Geneva, ILO.

Sfakianakis, John (2004), "The Whales of the Nile: Networks, Businessmen, and Bureaucrats During the Era of Privatization in Egypt," in *Networks of Privilege: Rethinking the Politics of Economic Reform in the Middle East,* ed. S. Heydemann, New York, Palgrave Macmillan.

Shafik, Nemat (1994a), *Learning from Doers: Lessons on Regional Integration for the Middle East,* Washington, D.C., World Bank.

_____ (1994b), "Big Spending, Small Returns: The Paradox of Human Resource Development in the Middle East," paper presented at ERF/World Bank Workshop, Cairo, December.

Shah, Tushaar, Molden, David, Sahthivadivel, R., and Seckler, David (2000), *The Global Groundwater Situation: Overview of Opportunities and Challenges,* Colombo, Sri Lanka, International Water Management Institute.

Shahin, Emad El-Din (2005), "Political Islam: Ready for Engagement?" Working Paper, Madrid, Spain, Fundación para las Relaciones Internacionales y el Diálogo Exterior (FRIDE).

Sherbiny, Naiem A. (1984), "Expatriate Labor in Arab Oil Producing Countries," *Finance and Development* 21, 4 (December), 34–37.

Shlaes, Alfred (1994), "The End of the German Miracle," *Foreign Affairs* 73, 3 (May–June), 76–93.

Shorter, Frederic C. (1985), "Demographical Measures of Inequality and Development," in F. C. Shorter and Huda Zurayk, eds., *Population Factors in Development Planning in the Middle East,* New York, Population Council.

Signoles, P., and Ben Romdane, M. (1983), "Les formes récentes de l'industrialisation tunisienne, 1979–1980," in GRESMO, *L'industrialisation du Bassin Méditerranéen,* Grenoble, Presses Universitaires de Grenoble, 109–150.

de Silva Johansson, Sara, and Silva-Jauregui, Carlos (2004), "Migration and Trade in MENA: Problems or Solutions?" World Bank, Middle East and North Africa, Working Paper Series no. 40 (October).

Simon, Julian (1982), *The Ultimate Resource,* Princeton, Princeton University Press.

Sims, David (2003), "The Case of Cairo, Egypt," Case Study for *The Challenge of Slums: Global Report on Human Settlement,* UN-HABITAT.

Singer, Peter (1999), "The Singer Solution to World Poverty," *New York Times Magazine,* September 5.

SIPRI (Stockholm International Peace Research Institute), online data source.

Sirageldin, Ismail, ed. (2002), *Human Capital: Population Economics in the Middle East,* Cairo, AUC Press.

Sivan, Emmanuel (1985), *Radical Islam: Medieval Theology and Modern Politics,* New Haven, Yale University Press.

Slater, Dan (2010), *Ordering Power: Contentious Politics and Authoritarian Leviathans in Southeast Asia,* Cambridge, Cambridge University Press.

Sluglett, Peter, and Sluglett, Marion Farouk (1984), "Modern Morocco: Political Immobilism, Economic Dependence," in R. Lawless and A. Findlay, eds., *North Africa: Contemporary Politics and Economic Development,* London, Croom Helm, 50–100.

Smith, Tony (1975), "The Political and Economic Ambitions of Algerian Land Reform, 1962–1974," *MEJ* 29, 3 (Summer), 259–278.

Soffer, Arnon (1986), "Lebanon—Where Demography Is the Core of Politics and Life," *Middle Eastern Studies* 22, 2 (April), 192–205.

Sorensen, Ninna Nyberg (2004), "Migrant Remittances as a Development Tool: The Case of Morocco," International Organization for Migration, Migration Policy Research, Working Paper no. 2 (June).

Sousa, Alya (1982), "Eradication of Illiteracy in Iraq," in Tim Niblock, ed., *Iraq: The Contemporary State,* London, Croom Helm, 100–108.

Springborg, Robert (1981), "Baathism in Practice: Agriculture, Politics, and Political Culture in Syria and Iraq," *Middle Eastern Studies* 17, 2 (April), 191–209.

_____ (1987), "The President and the Field Marshal," *MERIP Reports* 17, 4 (July–August), 4–16.

Stark, Oded (1983), "A Note on Labor Migration Functions," *Journal of Development Studies* 19, 4 (July), 539–543.

Stauffer, Thomas R. (with Lennox, Frank H.) (1984), *Accounting for "Wasting Asset": Income Measurement for Oil and Mineral-Exporting Rentier States,* Vienna, OPEC Fund for International Development, November.

Steele, Jonathan (2006), "The Iraqi Brain Drain," *The Guardian*, March 24, at http://www.guardian.co.uk/Iraq/Story/0,,1738575,00.html.

Stiansen, Endre (2004), "Interest Politics: Islamic Finance in the Sudan, 1977–2001," in Henry and Wilson, eds., 155–167.

Stiglitz, Joseph E. (2003), *Globalization and Its Discontents,* New York and London, W. W. Norton.

_____ (2004), "The Post Washington Consensus Consensus," Columbia University, Institute for Policy Dialogue Working Paper, November 4, at http://www0.gsb.columbia.edu/ipd/pub/Stiglitz_PWCC_English1.pdf.

Stobaugh, Robert, and Yergin, Daniel (1979), *Energy Future,* New York, Random House.

Stork, Joe (1982), "State Power and Economic Structure: Class Determination and State Formation in Contemporary Iraq," in Niblock, ed., 27–46.

_____ (1987), "Arms Industries of the Middle East," *MERIP Reports* 144 (January–February), 12–16.

Sutton, Keith, and Fahmi, Wael (2001), "Cairo's Urban Growth and Strategic Master Plans in the Light of Egypt's 1996 Population Census Results," *Cities* 18, 3, 135–149.

Swearingen, Will D. (1987), *Moroccan Mirages: Agrarian Dreams and Deceptions, 1912–1986,* Princeton, Princeton University Press.

Tachau, Frank, and Heper, Metin (1983), "The State, Politics, and the Military in Turkey," *Comparative Politics* 16 (October), 17–33.

Tamimi, Azzam S. (2001), *Rachid Ghannouchi: A Democrat Within Islamism,* Oxford, Oxford University Press.

Tarrow, Sidney (1994), *Power in Movement: Collective Action, Social Movements and Politics,* Cambridge, Cambridge University Press.

Tessler, Mark (2011), *Public Opinion in the Middle East: Survey Research and the Political Orientations of Ordinary Citizens,* Bloomington, Indiana University Press.

Tignor, Robert L. (1984), *State, Private Enterprise, and Economic Change in Egypt, 1918–1952,* Princeton, Princeton University Press.

Tilly, Charles, ed. (1975), *The Formation of National States in Europe,* Princeton, Princeton University Press.

Tilly, Charles (2004), *Social Movements, 1768–2004,* Boulder, Paradigm.

Timmer, C. Peter, Falcon, Walter P., and Pearson, Scott (1983), *Food Policy Analysis,* Baltimore and London, Johns Hopkins University Press.

Tlemcani, Rachid (1999), *État, Bazar, et Globalisation: L'Aventure de l'Infitah en Algérie,* Algiers, Les Editions El-Hikma.

Todaro, Michael P. (1969), "A Model of Labor Migration and Urban Unemployment in Less Developed Countries," *American Economic Review* 59, 1, 138–148.

_____ (1984), "Urbanization in Developing Nations: Trends, Prospects, and Policies," in Pradip K. Ghosh, ed., *Urban Development in the Third World,* Westport, Conn., Greenwood.

Trimberger, Ellen Kay (1978), *Revolution from Above: Military Bureaucrats and Development in Japan, Turkey, Egypt, and Peru,* New Brunswick, N.J., Transaction Books.

Tripp, Charles (2000), *A History of Iraq,* Cambridge and New York, Cambridge University Press.

Tuluy, A. Hassan, and Salinger, B. Lynn (1991), "Morocco," in Anne O. Krueger, Maurice Schiff, and Alberto Valdes, eds., *The Political Economy of Agricultural Pricing Policy,* vol. 3, *Africa and the Mediterranean,* Baltimore, Johns Hopkins University Press for the World Bank, 122–170.

Tuma, Elias (1978), "Bottlenecks and Constraints in Agrarian Reform in the Near East," background paper for the World Conference on Agrarian Reform and Rural Institutions, FAO, Rome.

_____ (1987), *Economic and Political Change in the Middle East,* Palo Alto, Calif., Pacific Books.

Turner, John C. (1969), "Uncontrolled Urban Settlement: Problems and Policies," in Gerald Breese, ed., *The City in Newly Developing Countries,* Englewood Cliffs, N.J., Prentice-Hall, 507–534.

TÜSIAD (Turkish Businessmen and Manufacturers' Association) (1988), *The Turkish Economy, '88,* Istanbul.

Tyner, Wallace (1993), "Agricultural Sector Analysis and Adjustment: Recent Experiences in North Africa and the Baltics," lecture at USAID, sponsored by Agricultural Policy Analysis Project-II, Washington, D.C., May 19.

UN (United Nations) (1991), *United Nations Demographic Yearbook,* New York, United Nations.

_____ (1992), *World Population Prospects: The 1992 Revision,* New York, United Nations.

_____ (2000), *World Population Prospects: The 2000 Revision,* New York, United Nations.

_____ (2002), *Millennium Development Goals: Report on the Kingdom of Saudi Arabia,* Riyadh, United Nations.

_____ (2003), *United Nations Common Country Assessment for the Islamic Republic of Iran,* Tehran, United Nations (August 11).

UNDP (United Nations Development Programme) (1994), *Human Development Report, 1994,* New York, Oxford University Press.

_____ (2002), *Reporting on Millennium Development Goals at the Country Level: Egypt,* Cairo, UNDP, at http://www.undp.org.eg/rc/mdg.pdf.

_____ (2004a), *Iraq Living Conditions Survey, 2004,* New York, UNDP.

_____ (2004b), *Millenium Development Goals: Second Country Report, Egypt, 2004,* Cairo, UNDP and Egyptian Ministry of Planning.

_____ (2005), *Iraq Living Conditions Survey,* Baghdad, UNDP.

_____ (2006), *Programme on Governance in the Arab Region (POGAR),* at http://www.pogar.org/.

UNDP and Arab Fund for Economic and Social Development (2002), *Arab Human Development Report, 2002,* New York, UNDP.

UNDP and ARE Ministry of Planning (2004), *Millennium Development Goals: Second Country Report,* Cairo, UNDP and Ministry of Planning, at http://www.undp.org.eg/MDGs/MDGREnglish.pdf.

UNDP and Institute of National Planning, Egypt (2000), *Egypt Human Development Report, 1998–1999,* Cairo, UNDP and INP.

_____ (2003), *Egypt Human Development Report, 2002–2003,* Cairo, UNDP and INP.

_____ (2005), *Egypt Human Development Report, 2004,* Cairo, UNDP and INP.

UNDP and Iraq Ministry of Planning and Development Cooperation (2005), *Iraq Living Conditions Survey, 2004,* vol. 3, *Socio-economic Atlas of Iraq,* Baghdad, Ministry of Planning and Development Cooperation.

UNESCO (various years), Institute of Statistics, at http://www.uis.unesco.org/ev.php?URL_ID=5187&URL_DO=DO_TOPIC&URL_SECTION=201.

UNESCO (various years), *Statistical Yearbook,* Paris.

UN-HABITAT (2003), *The Challenge of Slums: Global Report on Human Settlements, 2003,* London, Earthscan.

_____ (2004), *The State of the World's Cities 2004/2005: Globalization and Urban Culture,* London, UN-HABITAT and Earthscan.

UNICEF (1986), *The State of the World's Children, 1984,* New York, Oxford University Press.

_____ (1999), *Child and Maternal Mortality Survey, 1999: Preliminary Report,* New York, at http://www.fas.org/news/iraq/1999/08/990812-unicef.htm.

_____ (2001), *Progress Since the World Summit for Children: A Statistical Review,* at http://www.unicef.org/publications/files/pub_wethechildren_stats_en.pdf.

_____ (2005), "Monitoring the Situation of Women and Children: Fertility and Contraceptive Use," UNICEF World Summit for Children, at http://www.childinfo.org/eddb/fertility/index.htm#progress.

_____ (2006), "Global Database on Breastfeeding Indicators," at http://www.childinfo.org/areas/breastfeeding/countrydata.php.

USAID (US Agency for International Development) (1983), *Tunisia: The Wheat Development Program,* PN-AAL–022, October.

_____ (1986), *Morocco Country Development Strategy Statement,* Rabat.

_____ (1992), "Country Program Strategy, FY 1992–1996: Population," unpublished report, Cairo, May.

_____ (2002), *USAID/Morocco Annual Report FY 2002,* Washington, D.C.

_____ (2003), *Interim Strategic Plan for Assistance to the Republic of Yemen, 4/2003–4/2006,* San'a, US Embassy.

US Arms Control and Disarmament Agency (1995), *World Military Expenditures and Arms Transfers,* Washington, D.C.

USDA (US Department of Agriculture) (1987), *Middle East and North Africa: Situation and Outlook Report,* Washington, D.C., Economic Research Service.

USDS (US Department of State) (2005), "Investment Climate Statement: Tunisia," at http://www.state.gov/e/eb/ifd/2005/43042.htm.

US Embassy, Tel Aviv (2004), "U.S. Assistance to Israel," telaviv.usembassy.gov/publish/mission/amb/3AmChamSpeech.ppt.

US Institute of Medicine (1979), "Health in Egypt: Recommendations for U.S. Assistance," prepared for USAID, Washington, D.C., January.

Valdes, Alberton (1989), "Comment on 'The Policy Response of Agriculture' by Binswanger," *Proceedings of the World Bank Annual Conference on Development Economics,* 263–268.

van den Boogaerde, Pierre (1990), *The Composition and Distribution of Financial Assistance from Arab Countries and Arab Regional Institutions,* IMF Middle East Department Working Paper WP/90/67 (July).

van der Kloet, Hendrik (1975), *Inégalités dans les milieux ruraux: Possibilités et problèmes de la modernisation agricole au Maroc,* Geneva, United Nations Research on International Social Development (UNRISD).

Vandewalle, Dirk (1992), "Breaking with Socialism in Algeria," in Harik and Sullivan, eds., 189–200.

_____ (1998), *Libya Since Independence: Oil and State-Building,* Ithaca, Cornell University Press.

Van Hear, N. (1994), "The Socio-Economic Impact of the Involuntary Mass Return to Yemen in 1990," *Journal of Refugee Studies* 7, 1, 18–38.

Vatin, Jean-Claude, et al. (1992), *Démocratie et démocratisations dans le monde arabe,* Cairo, CEDEJ.

Vergès, Meriem (1993), "La casbah d'Alger: Chronique de survie dans un quartier en sursis," in Gilles Kepel, ed., *Exils et royaumes,* Paris, Presses de la FNSP, 69–88.

Vick, Karl (2004), "Children Pay Cost of Iraq's Chaos: Malnutrition Nearly Double What It Was Before Invasion," *Washington Post,* November 21, A1.

Vitalis, Robert (2007), *America's Kingdom: Mythmaking on the Saudi Oil Frontier,* Stanford, Calif., Stanford University Press.

Volkan, V. D., and Itzkowitz, N. (1984), *The Immortal Atatürk,* Chicago, University of Chicago Press.

de Waal, Alexander (1989), *Famine that Kills: Darfur, Sudan, 1984–85,* Oxford, Clarendon Press.

_____ (2004a), "Counter-Insurgency on the Cheap," *London Review of Books* 26, 15 (August 5), at http://www.lrb.co.uk/v26/n15/waal01_.html.

_____ (2004b), "Tragedy in Darfur," *Boston Review,* October/November, at http://www.bostonreview.net/BR29.5/dewaal.html.

de Waal, Alex, and Abel Salam, A. H. (2004), "Islamism, State Power, and Jihad in Sudan," in Alex de Waal, ed., *Islamism and Its Enemies in the Horn of Africa,* Bloomington and Indianapolis, University of Indiana Press, 71–113.

de Waal, Alex, and Young, Helen (2005), *Steps Towards the Stabilization of Governance and Livelihoods in Northern Sudan,* Washington, D.C., USAID.

Wade, Robert (1990), *Governing the Market: Economic Theory and the Role of Government in East Asian Industrialization,* Princeton, Princeton University Press.

Walstedt, Bertil (1980), *State Manufacturing Enterprise in a Mixed Economy: The Turkish Case,* Baltimore and London, World Bank/Johns Hopkins University Press.

Walt, Stephen M. (1987), *The Origins of Alliances,* Ithaca, N.Y., Cornell University Press.

Ward, Christopher (2000), "The Political Economy of Irrigation Water Pricing in Yemen," in Ariel Dinar, ed., *The Political Economy of Water Pricing Reform,* Washington, D.C., World Bank.

Ward, R. E., and Rustow, D., eds. (1964), *Political Modernization in Japan and Turkey,* Princeton, Princeton University Press.

Warde, Ibrahim (2004), "Islamic Finance and Islamic Politics Before and After 11 September 2001," in Henry and Wilson, eds., 37–62.

Wasao, Samson W. (2001), "A Comparative Analysis of the Socio-economic Correlates of Fertility in Cameroon and the Central African Republic," Workshop on Prospects for Fertility Decline in High Fertility Countries, United Nations, Dept. of Economic and Social Affairs, Population Division, New York, July 9–11, at http://www.un.org/esa/population/publications/prospectsdecline/wasao.pdf.

Washington Report on Middle Eastern Affairs (2006), "U.S. Financial Aid to Israel: Figures, Facts, and Impact," at http://www.wrmea.com/html/us_aid_to_israel.htm.

Waterbury, John (1970), *The Commander of the Faithful: The Moroccan Political Elite, a Study in Segmented Politics,* New York, Columbia University Press.

_____ (1973), *Land, Man, and Development in Algeria,* pt. 2, *Population, Employment, and Emigration,* American University Field Services Reports, North Africa Series, 17, 2.

_____ (1978), *Egypt: Burdens of the Past, Options for the Future,* Bloomington, Indiana University Press.

_____ (1979), *Hydropolitics of the Nile Valley,* Syracuse, N.Y., Syracuse University Press.

_____ (1983), *The Egypt of Nasser and Sadat: The Political Economy of Two Regimes,* Princeton, Princeton University Press.

_____ (1991), "Twilight of the State Bourgeoisie?" *IJMES* 23, 1–17.

_____ (1992), "Export-Led Growth and the Center-Right Coalition in Turkey," *Comparative Politics* 24, 2.

Watkins, Kevin (2001), *Oxfam Education Report,* London, Oxfam.

Watt, Nicholas (2006), "EU to Downgrade Relations with Middle Eastern Partners," *The Guardian,* July 17.

Whitaker, Brian (2000), "The International Dimension," *Al Bab-Arab Gateway,* at http://www.al-bab.com/yemen/pol/bwint.htm.

Wikan, Unni (1980), *Life Among the Poor in Cairo,* London, Tavistock.

Williamson, Jeffrey G., and Yousef, Tarik M. (2002), "Demographic Transitions and Economic Performance in the Middle East and North Africa," in Sirageldin, ed., 16–36.

Williamson, John, ed. (1990), *Latin American Adjustment: How Much Has Happened?* Washington, D.C., Institute for International Economics.

Wilson, Peter W., and Graham, Douglas F. (1994), *Saudi Arabia: The Coming Storm,* New York, M. E. Sharpe.

Wilson, Rodney (2004), "Capital Flight Through Islamic Managed Funds," in Henry and Wilson, eds., 129-152.

World Bank, World Development Indicators (WDI) Online, various years, at http://publications.worldbank.org/ecommerce/catalog/product?item_id=631625.

World Bank (1979), *Yemen Arab Republic: Development of a Traditional Economy,* Washington, D.C.

_____ (1981), *Morocco: Economic and Social Development Report,* Washington, D.C.

_____ (1982), *Turkey: Industrialization and Trade Strategy,* Washington, D.C.

_____ (1983), *Arab Republic of Egypt: Issues of Trade Strategy and Investment Planning,* Washington, D.C.

_____ (1984), *World Development Report,* New York, Oxford University Press.

_____ (1985), *Sudan: Prospects for Rehabilitation of the Sudanese Economy,* report no. 5496-SU, October 7.

_____ (1986a), *Jordan: Issues of Employment and Labor Market Imbalances,* report no. 5117-JO, May.

_____ (1986b), *Poverty and Hunger,* Washington, D.C.

_____ (1986c), *YAR: Agricultural Strategy Paper,* report no. 5574 YAR, May.

_____ (1987), *World Development Report,* New York, Oxford University Press.

_____ (1990a), *Egypt: Country Economic Memorandum,* Washington, D.C.

_____ (1990b), *Poverty Alleviation and Adjustment in Egypt,* Washington, D.C.

_____ (1990c), *Sudan: Reversing the Economic Decline,* Washington, D.C.

_____ (1990d), *World Development Report, 1990: Poverty,* New York, Oxford University Press for the World Bank.

_____ (1991), *Structural Adjustment Loan Document: Egypt,* Washington, D.C.

_____ (1993a), *Arab Republic of Egypt: An Agricultural Strategy for the 1990s,* Washington, D.C.

_____ (1993b), *Kingdom of Morocco: Poverty, Adjustment, and Growth,* Washington, D.C.

_____ (1993c), *Republic of Tunisia: The Social Protection System,* report no. 11376-TUN.

_____ (1993d), *The East Asian Miracle: Economic Growth and Public Policy,* New York, Oxford University Press.

_____ (1994a), *The Democratic and Popular Republic of Algeria: Country Economic Memorandum, the Transition to a Market Economy,* Washington, D.C.

_____ (1994b), *Hashemite Kingdom of Jordan: Poverty Assessment,* vol. 1, *Main Report,* Washington, D.C., October 28.

_____ (1994c), *Islamic Republic of Iran: Country Economic Memorandum,* report no. 13029 IRN, June 8.

_____ (1994d), *Kingdom of Morocco: Water Sector Review,* Washington, D.C.

_____ (1994e), *A Population Perspective on Development: The Middle East and North Africa,* Washington, D.C.

_____ (1994f), *A Strategy for Managing Water in the Middle East and North Africa,* Washington, D.C.

_____ (1994g), *World Development Report, 1994,* Washington, D.C.

_____ (1995a), *Claiming the Promise: A Long-Term Prospective Study for the Middle East and North Africa,* Washington, D.C.

_____ (1995b), *Middle East and North Africa Environmental Strategy: Towards Sustainable Development,* Washington, D.C.

_____ (1995c), *Will Arab Workers Prosper or Be Left Out in the 21st Century?* Washington, D.C.

_____ (1995d), *World Development Report, 1995,* New York, Oxford University Press.

_____ (1995e), *World Tables,* Baltimore, Johns Hopkins University Press.

_____ (2000), *Higher Education in Developing Countries: Peril and Promise,* Washington, D.C.

_____ (2001a), "Memorandum of the President of the IBRD to the Executive Directors on an Interim Assistance Strategy for the Islamic Republic of Iran," report no. 22050 IRN, Washington, D.C.

_____ (2001b), *Middle East and North Africa Region, Environment Strategy Update, 2001–2005,* Washington, D.C.

_____ (2001c), *Syrian Arab Republic: Irrigation Sector Report,* report no. 22602-SYR, Washington, D.C.

_____ (2002), *Reducing Vulnerability and Increasing Opportunity: Social Protection in the Middle East and North Africa,* Washington, D.C.

_____ (2003), *Middle East and North Africa Region Strategy Paper,* Washington, D.C.

_____ (2004a), *Gender and Development in the Middle East and North Africa: Women and the Public Sphere,* MENA Development Report, at http://www-wds.worldbank

.org/servlet/WDSContentServer/WDSP/IB/2004/03/09/000090341_20040309152
953/Rendered/PDF/281150PAPER0Gender010Development0in0MNA.pdf.

_____ (2004b), *Middle East and North Africa Region Strategy Paper,* at http://
lnweb18.worldbank.org/mna/mena.nsf/0/B154D5429A9154A085256C6A0066
2360?OpenDocument.

_____ (2004c), *Unlocking the Employment Potential in the Middle East and North
Africa: Toward a New Social Contract,* Washington, D.C.

_____ (2005a), *Middle East and North Africa Region: Economic Developments and
Prospects, 2005: Oil Booms and Revenue Management,* Washington, D.C.

_____ (2005b), "Sector Brief: Urban Development in MENA," Washington, D.C.

_____ (2005c), *World Development Indicators,* at http://data.worldbank.org/data-catalog
/world-development-indicators.

_____ (2006a), *Kingdom of Morocco: Country Economic Memorandum: Fostering Higher
Growth and Employment with Productive Diversification and Competitiveness,* Social
and Economic Development Group, Middle East and North Africa Region, report
no. 32948-MOR, Washington, D.C.

_____ (2006b), *Middle East and North Africa: Economic Developments and Prospects
2006,* Middle East and North Africa Region, Office of the Chief Economist,
Washington, D.C.

_____ (2009), *From Privilege to Competition: Unlocking Private-Led Growth in the
Middle East and North Africa,* Washington, D.C., World Bank.

_____ (2010), *World Development Indicators,* at http://data.worldbank.org/data-catalog
/world-development-indicators.

World Commission on Dams (2000), *Dams and Development: A New Framework for
Decision-Making,* London, Earthscan.

World Resources Institute, Earthtrends, online database, at http://www.earthtrends
.wri.org/.

Wrigley, E., and Schofield, R. (1981), *The Population History of England, 1541–1871: A
Reconstruction,* Cambridge, Harvard University Press.

Yergin, Daniel (1991), *The Prize: The Epic Quest for Oil, Money, and Power,* New York,
Simon and Schuster.

Yom, Sean L., and Gause, F. Gregory, III (2012), "Resilient Royals: How Arab Monarchies Hang On," *Journal of Democracy,* 23, 4, 74–88.

Yousef, Tarik M. (2004a), "The *Murabaha* Syndrome in Islamic Finance: Laws, Institutions, and Politics," in Henry and Wilson, eds., 63–80.

_____ (2004b), "Development, Growth, and Policy Reform in the Middle East and
North Africa Since 1950," *Journal of Economic Perspectives,* 18, 3, 91–116.

_____ (2005), "The Changing Role of Labor Migration in Arab Economic Integration," paper for policy seminar, Arab Economic Integration: Challenges and
Prospects, Abu Dhabi, UAE, February 23–24.

Zaidi, Sarah, and Smith-Fawzi, Mary C. (1995), "Health of Baghdadí Children," *The
Lancet* 346, December 2, p. 1485.

El Zanaty, Fatma, and Way, Ann (2001), *Egypt Demographic and Health Survey, 2000,*
Ministry of Health and Population, Egypt, and National Population Council,
Calverton, Md.

Zghal, Abdelkader (1977), "Pourquoi la réforme agraire ne mobilise-t-elle pas les paysans, Maghrebins?" in Bruno Etiènne, ed., *Problèmes Agraires au Maghreb,* Paris, Editions du CNRS, 295–312.

Zogby International (2005), *Attitudes of Arabs: An In-Depth Look at Social and Political Concerns of Arabs,* Washington, D.C., Arab American Institute.

Zonis, Marvin (1991), *Majestic Failure: The Fall of the Shah,* Chicago, University of Chicago Press.

INDEX

Democracy 341-43

336-337 Cleavages